American Politics

SECOND EDITION

American Politics
Core Argument / Current Controversy

Edited by

Peter J. Woolley
Fairleigh Dickinson University

Albert R. Papa
Fairleigh Dickinson University

Prentice
Hall

UPPER SADDLE RIVER, NEW JERSEY 07458

Library of Congress Cataloging-in-Publication Data
American politics: core argument/current controversy / edited by Peter J. Woolley,
Albert R. Papa.—2nd ed.
   p. cm.
  Includes bibliographical references
  ISBN 0-13-087919-3
  1. United States—Politics and government. I. Woolley, Peter J. [date]. II. Papa, Albert R.
JK21.A4636 2002
  320.973—dc21   00-140047

VP, Editorial Director: *Laura Pearson*
Senior Acquisitions Editor: *Heather Shelstad*
Assistant Editor: *Brian Prybella*
Editorial Assistant: *Jessica Drew*
Editorial/Production Supervision: *Joanne Riker*
Prepress and Manufacturing Buyer: *Benjamin D. Smith*
Director of Marketing: *Beth Gillett Mejia*
Cover Photo: *S.M. Wakefield*
Cover Art Director: *Jayne Conte*
Cover Designer: *Bruce Kenselaar*

This book was set in 10/11 New Baskerville by East End Publishing Services, Inc.,
and was printed and bound by Hamilton Printing Company. The cover was
printed by Phoenix Color Corp.

Acknowledgments appear on pages xvii–xii, which constitute a continuation
of the copyright page.

 © 2002, 1998 by Pearson Education, Inc.
Upper Saddle River, New Jersey 07458

Printed in the United States of America

10 9 8 7 6 5 4 3 2 1

ISBN 0-13-087919-3

Prentice-Hall International (UK) Limited, *London*
Prentice-Hall of Australia Pty. Limited, *Sydney*
Prentice-Hall Canada Inc., *Toronto*
Prentice-Hall Hispanoamericana, S.A., *Mexico*
Prentice-Hall of India Private Limited, *New Delhi*
Prentice-Hall of Japan, Inc., *Tokyo*
Pearson Education Asia Pte. Ltd., *Singapore*
Editora Prentice-Hall do Brasil, Ltda., *Rio de Janeiro*

To Billy and Christopher

    and to Max and Mary

And to our students—

    past,

        present,

            and future,

may they be graced with courage,
conviction, and analytical ability

Contents

2 Political Culture and Ideology: The Air We Breathe   35

3 The Constitution and Its Framers   52

4 The Tensions of Federalism   86

PART TWO
THE PROCESSES OF DEMOCRACY

5 **Public Opinion and the Media: Prologue to a Democratic Farce?** 107

6 **Parties and Elections: The Crisis of Electoral Politics** 131

PART THREE
GOVERNMENTAL INSTITUTIONS

Preface

The rationale for this volume is twofold. The first is to expose students to some of the important arguments of politics that impinge on the great experiment in American government. Every chapter contains recent essays, excerpts, and speeches, but students should see that every current controversy has an ancestry of decades, if not centuries. We hope students will learn, first, to identify the great questions of public affairs in America and next to become familiar with some of the people and arguments that have over many decades or centuries addressed the persistent questions of public affairs.

Our second rationale is to provoke a discussion of American politics in the way that politics has, at root, been discussed for millennia. This discussion goes beyond merely describing the laws, the Constitution, the processes—that is, the facts. With these readings, the inquiry of students might be directed toward the proper arrangement of facts in order to test a theory of American politics, as well as to discuss the "ought" that Aristotle says is the true aim of politics. We like to frame our own introductory courses around the question, *which theory of American government best describes politics as it is?* (See Chapter 1.) Or *which theory best describes how politics ought to be?* Or *which theory has the best explanatory power?* Or *which has the best predictive power?*

Another rationale follows the first two: Instructors who wish not to evangelize in the classroom can structure their course around the *competing theories* of American politics, allowing students to evaluate the utility of those theories and to confront their own felt notions of political society.

The text presents several competing theories: *pluralism, elite theory,* and that perennial American favorite that we call *civics book democracy*. In subsequent chapters, the readings address the usual subtopics of American government but include competing viewpoints and evaluations. Thus, by studying an American government textbook, a student becomes aware of the basic details of American government and politics. But by using this volume of core readings as a supplement, the student also learns how to arrange facts, what the core arguments of public affairs are, what the strengths and weaknesses of various theories of American politics are, and how to apply those theories to current problems. At the end of a semester, the student should have the tools and practice to be an intelligent evaluator of American political dialogue.

We have done our best to excerpt, condense, or digest the pieces so that they can be read as easily as possible in a country where the language of common discourse changes rapidly—and where many students have been exposed to only the most watered down and oftentimes third-hand summaries of great controversies.

Each chapter includes several articles drawn from historical documents, as well as important scholarly works. These are the core arguments. Each chapter ends with two or more articles that address a current political topic. Judicial rulings and other primary documents are contained in the appendixes.

Each excerpt is preceded by an introductory paragraph that contains biographical information about the author and alerts the reader to the subject and perspective of the text. The reader then sets out on a journey with a road map that should help to identify important landmarks along the way and point to the ultimate destination: the author's conclusion.

We have discovered that our students prefer to be introduced to and acquainted with the writings of famous historical figures more than with relatively obscure or notorious journalists. And they equally prefer to draw their own conclusions on current controversies once armed with several good arguments. We hope this volume of collected readings will inform, educate, and arm students, whether they be political science majors, engineers, or auditors, for (and against) political debate throughout their lives.

Acknowledgments

The preponderance of credit for this volume is due to the many authors, quick and dead, whose work fills these pages. Credit is also due to numberless students whose scholarly interest and ability have compelled us to persevere in our chosen profession and, equally, to persevere in the production of this volume.

We are grateful for the essential assistance of the many faculty and staff members at Fairleigh Dickinson University. Colleagues such as Professors Kathryn Douglas, Morris Rothblatt, Bruce Larson, and Bruce Peabody, as well as Christian Breil, are sensibly encouraging and have contributed to shaping and editing these pages. We are also grateful to have a competent and pleasant staff who are persistent through many difficulties: the superlative Grethe Zarnitz and the delightful and industrious students Derya Kazak and Melissa Brand.

We also thank Prentice Hall's reviewers for their suggestions and comments: James J. Lopach, University of Montana; Fred Slocum, Minnesota State University, Mankata; Susan Lynn Roberts, Davidson College; Charles Noble, California State University, Long Beach; and Matthew H. Bosworth, Winona State University.

We are grateful most of all to our families for their support and encouragement, for rearranging their schedules to accommodate us, and for putting up with our peculiar habits.

Finally, Professor Woolley thanks Professor Papa for persevering through trying personal circumstances. As this second edition appears, we are still speaking to one another. We shall see if this holds true for a third edition.

pjw

I want to add my thanks to the people at Prentice Hall. My collaborator once again showed himself a man of uncommon perseverance, enduring the usual array of "challenges from me. Peter, you are one of the good ones.

But the most special acknowledgement must go to Sharon, soon to be my wife. As with the first edition, her abilities as critic, as editor and as reader were unmatched. Without her, there would truly be no reader. there is no adequate way to thank you Sharon, other than to say I am blessed by our partnership. I love you! Thank you for being so good.

arp

Permission Acknowledgments and Sources

Chapter 1: Theories of American Government

1. *Democracy in America* by Alexis de Tocqueville, part II, ch. I and part I, ch. IV. Originally published in1835 (French) and 1840 (English). Translated and recised by Robert McTague. Copyright © 2000 by Robert McTague. Used by permission.
2. Copyright © 1993 from *Land of Idols* by Michael Parenti. Reprinted by permission of St. Martin's Press, Inc.
3. Reprinted with permission from *The American Prospect.* Number 46, September-October 1999.
4. Excerpts from *The Irony of Democracy: An Uncommon Introduction to American Politics,* Ninth Edition by Thomas R. Dye and Harmon Zeigler, copyright © 1993 by Harcourt Brace & Company, reprinted by permission of the publisher.
5. From *Who Governs?* Copyright © 1960 by Robert Dahl. Reprinted by permission of Yale University Press.
6. Reprinted by permission of Warner Books, Inc., New York, New York, U.S.A. From *Megatrends* by John Naisbitt. Copyright © 1982. All rights reserved.
7. *Pitfalls of Direct Democracy* by Daniel Smith. Copyright © 2000 by Daniel Smith. Used by permission.

Chapter 2: Political Culture and Ideology

8. Condensed and recised from *Second Treatise on Civil Government* by John Locke. Originally published 1690.
9. *The Mayflower Compact,* November 11, 1620.
10. From "American Political Thought and the American Revolution by Louis Hartz in the *American Political Science Review* (vol. XLVI, no. 2) 1952.
11. Delivered at Gettysburg, Pennsylvania, November 19, 1863.
12. From *The American Political System: A Radical Approach,* Fourth Edition by Edward S. Greenberg. Copyright © 1986 by Edward S. Greenberg. Reprinted by permission of Addison-Wesley Educational Publishers, Inc.
13. From "The Cultural War for the Soul of America" (speech) by Patrick J. Buchanan. Reprinted by permission of Patrick J. Buchanan.
14. *The Negotiable and Non-Negotiable in our Civic Conversation* by W. King Mott. Copyright © 2000 by W. King Mott. Used by permission.

Chapter 3: The Constitution and the Tradition of the Founders

15. From *A System of Politics* by James Harrington, edited by John Toland, London, 1700.
16. From *De L'Esprit des Lois* by Charles Louis de Secondat, baron de la Brede et de Montesquieu. Originally published in 1748. Translation and recision by Peter J. Woolley. Copyright © 1996 Peter J. Woolley.
17. *Federalist* No. 51 by James Madison appeared in the *New York Packet,* Friday, February 8, 1788.
18. From *An Economic Interpretation of the Constitution of the United States* by Charles Beard, MacMillan Co., 1913.
19. From "The Founding Fathers: A Reform Caucus in Action" by John P. Roche, *American Political Science Review,* Dec. 1961. Reprinted by permission of the *APSR.*
20. From "Democracy and *The Federalist*: a Reconsideration of the Framers' Intent" by Martin Diamond. *American Political Science Review,* vol. LIII, no. 1, 1959.
21. *Who Interprets? Judicial Review and "Departmentalism"* Copyright © 2000 by Bruce Peabody. Used by permission.
22. "Recast Judicial Supremacy" by Scott E. Gant. Copyright © 2000 Scott E. Gant. All Rights Reserved. An earlier and more expansive version of this article appeared as

"Judicial Supremacy and Nonjudicial Interpretation of the Constitution" in the *Hastings Constitutional Law Quarterly* (Winter 1997) (Copyright © 1997 Scott E. Gant. All Rights Reserved).

Chapter 4: The Tensions of Federalism

23. Speech to the Virginia Convention on June 4, 1788 by Patrick Henry as recorded by David Robertson.
24. From *Federalist* No. 39 by James Madison.
25. From *Democracy in America* by Alexis de Tocqueville. Originally published in 1835 (French) and 1840 (English).
26. From the *Congressional Record*: February 4, 1999, p. E141: [wais.access.gpo.gov] [DOCID:cr04fe99-22].
27. "Making the Grade: Federalism and National Education Reform" by John A. Donnangelo II. Copyright © 2000 by John A. Donnangelo II. Used by permission.

Chapter 5: Elections

28. From *Slate*. Posted Tuesday, Jan. 11, 2000, at 4:30 p.m. PT. Copyright © 2000 *Slate*. Distributed by The New York Times Special Features/Syndication Series.
29. Reprinted with the permission of Scribner, a Division of Simon & Schuster from *The Phantom Public* by Walter Lippman. Copyright 1925, renewed 1953 by Walter Lippmann.
30. From speech by the Honorable Spiro T. Agnew, Vice President of the United States, given at Midwest Republican Conference, Des Moines, Iowa, Nov. 13, 1969.
31. Reprinted with permission from *The American Prospect*. Number 21, Spring 1995.
32. From *The Culture of Fear* by Barry Glassner. Copyright © 1999 by Barry Glassner. Reprinted by permission of Basic Books, a member of Perseus Books, L.L.C.
33. Reprinted with permission from *The American Prospect*. Number 43, March-April 1999.

Chapter 6: Political Parties

34. From "The Crisis of Electoral Politics" as first published in the May 1997 issue of *The Atlantic Monthly*. Copyright © 1997 by Martin P. Wattenberg. Reprinted by permission of the author.
35. Reprinted with permission from *The American Prospect*. Number 39, July-August 1998.
36. From the "Farewell Address" by President George Washington originally published in *American Daily Advertiser*, (Sept. 19, 1796).
37. From *The Party's Just Begun: Shaping Political Parties for America's Future* by Larry J. Sabato. Copyright © 1988 by Larry J. Sabato. Reprinted by permission of Addison-Wesley Educational Publishers, Inc.
38. *Inevitable Losers: The Problem of Presidential Selection* by Albert R. Papa. Copyright © 1996 by Albert R. Papa.
39. From speech by the Honorable Adlai Stevenson, Governor of Illinois, given at the 1956 National Democratic Convention accepting the party's nomination for President of the United States.
40. Tucker Carlson in *The Weekly Standard,* November 8, 1999 /Volume 5, Number 8. Reprinted with permission of *The Weekly Standard*. Copyright © News America Incorporated.
41. From "The Southern Captivity of the GOP" as first published in the July 1997 issue of *The Atlantic Monthly*. Copyright © 1997 by Christopher Caldwell. Reprinted by permission of the author.
42. Reprinted by permission of *The New Republic*. Copyright © 1999 by The New Republic, Inc.

Chapter 7: Interest Groups

43. *Federalist* No. 10 by James Madison. From *The New York Packet.* Friday, November 23, 1787.
44. Scattered excerpts from *The Semisovereign People: A Realist's View of Democracy in America,* copyright © 1960 by E.E. Schattschneider and renewed 1988 by Frank W. Schattschneider, reprinted by permission of Holt, Rinehart and Winston.
45. From "The Public Philosophy: Interest Group Liberalism" by Theodore Lowi. Copyright © 1967 by the *American Political Science Review,* vol. 61(March, 1967): 5-24. Reprinted by permission.
46. Reprinted with permission from *The American Prospect,* Number 23, Fall 1995. Copyright © 1995 The American Prospect, P.O. Box 772, Boston MA 02102-0772. All rights reserved.
47. Reprinted with permission from *The American Prospect,* Number 30, January-February 1997. Copyright © 1997 The American Prospect, P.O. Box 772, Boston MA 02102-0772. All rights reserved.
48. *The Futile Quest for the Ideal Congressional Campaign Finance System* by Bruce A. Larson. Copyright © 2000 by Bruce A. Larson. Used by permission.

Chapter 8 Congress

49. From speech to his constituency by the Rt. Hon. Edmund Burke, M.P. given at Bristol, 1774.
50. Excerpt from chapter one from *Home Style: House Members in Their Districts* by Richard J. Fenno, Jr. Copyright © 1978 by Little, Brown and Company. Reprinted by permission of Addison-Wesley Educational Publishers, Inc.
51. From *Congress: The Electoral Connection* by David Mayhew, (Yale University Press). Coyright © 1974. All rights reserved. Reprinted by permission of Yale University Press.
52. From *Congress Against Itself.* Coyright © 1973 by Roger Davidson and Walter Oleszek. Reprinted by permission of the authors.
53. From *Congressional Government* by Woodrow Wilson. Originally published 1885.
54. Excerpted from "The Rise of the Public Speakership" by Douglas B. Harris from *Political Science Quarterly,* vol. 113, no. 2, dated 1998, pages 193 through 212. Reprinted with permission.
55. From "Newt's Legacy" in *The Weekly Standard* (September 13, 1999/Volume 4, Number 4). Copyright © 1999 by David Frum.

Chapter 9: The Presidency

56. From *Federalist* No. 70 by Alexander Hamilton.
57. From *Our Chief Magistrate and His Powers* by William Howard Taft, 1916.
58. "Rating the Presidents from Washington to Clinton" by Arthur M. Schlesinger, Jr. from *Political Science Quarterly,* vol. 112, no. 2, dated 1997, page 179 through 190. Reprinted with permission.
59. Reprinted with the permission of The Free Press, a division of Simon & Schuster from *Presidential Power and the Modern Presidency: The Politics of Leadership From Roosevelt to Reagan* by Richard E. Neustadt. Copyright © 1990 by Richard E. Neustadt.
60. From *The Presidential Character,* fourth ed., by James Barber. Copyright © 1992 by Prentice Hall, Inc.. Reprinted by permission of the author.
61. From Hearings before the House Committee on the Judiciary, 105th Congress, 2nd Session, 1998.
62. From Hearings before the House Committee on the Judiciary, 105th Congress, 2nd Session, 1998.

Chapter 10: The Bureaucracy

63. From speech by Herbert Hoover, given at New York, New York October 22, 1928.
64. From *The Jungle* by Upton Sinclair. Originally published 1905.
65. From "Bureaucracy and Constitutionalism: A Pluralist Case" by Norton E. Long in the *American Political Science Review* (Sept. 1952).
66. Excerpt from ch. 20 of *Bureaucracy and the American Regime: What Government Agencies Do & Why They Do It* by James Q. Wilson. Copyright © 1989 by Basic Books, Inc. Reprinted by permission of Basic Books, a division of HarperCollins Publishers, Inc.
67. *Privitization and Public Control: Why Make Public Management More Businesslike?* by Richard A. Loverd. Copyright © 2000 by Richard A. Loverd. Used by permission.

Chapter 11: The Judiciary

68. From *Federalist* No. 78 by Alexander Hamilton.
69. From "Brutus, No. 11," anonymous (Robert Yates or Thomas Treadwell), *New-York Journal and Weekly Register* (January 31, 1788).
70. From "The Origin and Scope of the American Doctrine of Constitutional Law" by James B. Thayer, *Harvard Law Review* (Oct. 25, 1893).
71. From "Judicial Self-Restraint" by John Roche, *American Political Science Review,* (Sept. 1955).
72. From *The Supreme Court: How it Was, How It Is* by William Rehnquist. Copyright © 1987 by William Rehnquist. Reprinted by permission of the author.
73. Speech by the Honorable William J. Brennan, October 1895, Washington, D.C.
74. From *The Confirmation Mess* by Stephen Carter. Copyright © 1994 by Stephen Carter. Reprinted by permission of Basic Books, a member of Perseus Books, L.L.C.
75. From "The Political Court" by Randall Kennedy. Reprinted with permission from *The American Prospect,* (Summer 1993). Copyright © New Prospect, Inc.

Chapter 12: Civil Rights and Liberties

76. Recised from *On Liberty* (London, 1859) by John Stuart Mill.
77. As proposed by Thomas Jefferson in 1779 and passed by the Virginia legislature in 1786.
78. Speech by Frederick Douglass at Rochester, July 5, 1852.
79. From Charles Fried, "Uneasy Preferences: Affirmative Action, in Retrospect," *The American Prospect* no. 46, September-October 1999. Copyright © 1999 by The American Prospect, Inc.
80. From "Abortion Politics: Writing for an Audience of One" by Susan Estrich and Kathleen Sullivan, *U. Pa. L. Rev.* 119 (1989). Copyright © 1989. All rights reserved. Reprinted by permission of the *University of Pennsylvania Law Review.*
81. *The Weekly Standard* Aug. 30/Sept. 6, 1999, Volume 4, Number 47.
82. Floor speech by Representative Clifford Stearns: *Congressional Record:* May 9, 2000 (House), pp. H2658-H2659.
83. *Privacy and Surveillance Technology: Do We Really Want the Police Seeing Through Our Clothing?* by Thomas C. Weisert. Copyright © 2000 by Thomas C. Weisert. Used by permission.

Chapter 13: Government and the Economy

84. From "Labor and Capital-Partners" by John D. Rockefeller, Jr., *Atlantic Monthly,* (January, 1916).
85. From speech to the Commonwealth Club of San Francisco by the Honorable Franklin D. Roosevelt, Governor of New York, given at San Francisco, September 23, 1931

86. Reprinted with the permission of Simon and Schuster from *Secrets of the Temple* by William Greider. Copyright © 1987 by William Greider.

87. Floor address by Representative Pete Sessions. From the *Congressional Record*: April 12, 2000, pp. H2128-H2147.

88. Speech by Secretary of Labor Robert B. Reich at the Center for National Policy, Washington, D.C., August 31, 1995.

89. *A Modest Suggestion for Modest Government* by Philip A. Mundo. Copyright © 2000 by Philip A. Mundo. Used by permission.

Chapter 14: International Relations

90. From the "Farewell Address" by President George Washington. Originally published in *American Daily Advertiser*, (Sept. 19, 1796).

91. Message of President James Monroe to Congress, 2 December 1823.

92. Woodrow Wilson, Message to Congress, 65 Congress, I Session, Senate Document No. 5.

93. Speech to the United States Senate. *Congressional Record*, 65 Congress, 1 Sess., pp. 223-236.

94. Inaugural Address of President John F. Kennedy, Friday, January 20, 1961.

95. Speech delivered in Chicago, February 8, 1968 as recorded in the *Chicago Sun-Times*, February 11, 1968.

96. Speech to the United States Senate, March 22, 1999. From the *Congressional Record*, pp. S3039-S3050.

97. Speech to the United States Senate, April 22, 1999. From the *Congressional Record*, pp. S4140-S4141.

American Politics

CHAPTER ONE

Competing Theories of American Government

OVERVIEW AND SUMMARY

Can there be a word with more positive connotations than *democracy*? Have you ever heard a speech or read an article in which the author argued against democracy? Consider all the things, foreign and domestic, that the American government and its people do and have done in democracy's name; from approving a local home-rule charter to intervening in the affairs of a foreign nation. Then consider if you have been asked (or have asked yourself) whether or not you live in a democratic nation and how you would go about proving it.

Serious writers who are looking at the same questions offer wildly divergent views about whether, to what extent, and how the American system is democratic. The belief that popular government is the means for the liberation of the human spirit, offering the promise that individuals can control their own destinies, holds a nearly universal appeal in the hearts of humankind. But whereas few dispute the desirability of democracy as an ideal, commentators invariably disagree over the standards by which democratic government should be measured.

Who really holds power in America? Can a representative form of government truly hold the powerful to account? Or must the citizenry directly affect policy outcomes for democracy to be effective? Is universal suffrage sufficient, or must the many actually vote and participate in other ways for democracy to flourish? How wide a choice must be offered by those who compete for power in a democratic polity? How wide a disparity of wealth and social standing among its citizens can a democracy accommodate? These are some of the questions that divide public officeholders, commentators, and political scientists, and these are the questions that you should ponder. Our answers to these questions become democratic standards—the signposts by which political reality is interpreted. Accordingly, this chapter offers the three traditional theories of American government as interpretations of that reality, and it ends with a discussion of direct democracy as a possible alternative.

What Is Theory?

At bottom, *a theory is a systematic and comprehensive representation of the reality it purports to describe.* Theories of government address the relationship between the ruling (those who decide who gets what) and the ruled (all of the rest of us) or, put another way, the relationship between elites and masses. Consequently, any theory must answer two essential questions—the *who question* and the *how question.* The first entails defining the elite: Who holds political power and in what manner is it exercised? The second refers to how (if at all) the elite are accountable to the larger mass public. The instruments of this accountability are often referred to as the democratic linkage. Theories may also be categorized as descriptive, describing what is, or normative, describing how things ought to be.

Of course, theorists differ greatly in answering both the *who* and *how* questions. Nevertheless, it is invariably true that anyone who thinks or writes about politics (even the common citizen who may intentionally keep such thoughts to a minimum), assumes answers to these two questions. Strictly speaking then, there are probably as many theories as there are political thinkers. Still, it is possible to capture the wide spectrum of theories of American government through the three presented here: the *civics book* model; the *elite* theory; and *pluralism.*

The Civics Book Model

The civics book model is one with which Americans are most familiar, reinforced as it has been through many years of civic education and vaguely approving messages from the popular media. Civics book "theology" holds that the framers of the Constitution formed a nearly perfect governmental system, one that both prevents the concentration of power through a variety of checking mechanisms and is adaptable to a system in which common citizens are able to affect governmental policy outputs. In this model the central questions of democracy are answered by assertion, and the theory is still best summarized by the work of **Alexis de Tocqueville**. The key points are as follows:

1. The true genius of the Constitution lies in its system of checks and balances. In setting "ambition against ambition," as James Madison put it, the founders dispersed power both within the federal government and between the federal and state governments. This is a structure in tune with "human nature" since it forces political elites into competition for their positions and for the vindication of their ideas—much as we compete in the classroom or the economic marketplace.
2. The institution of frequent, periodic, electoral competition is the instrument, nay, the guarantor, of public accountability. Although first extending only to elections for the House of Representatives (and that subject to state laws concerning the franchise), the inexorable logic of the constitutional system was an evolution to free elections at all levels of public office; for if it could be shown that elections ensured accountability at one level, then no objection could be raised to its extension. The genius of voting "by the clock" is that periodic elections removes from the hands of the elite the critical decision of *when* elections will be held.

3. This same logic extends to the expansion of the franchise, and the greater part of democratic history is the story of its extension. The struggles for women's suffrage and black voting rights are storied. Its heroes are majestic figures. And why not? The lesson of these struggles is that one need not be born into great wealth or prominence to participate meaningfully in a democratic system. We need not be consumed by politics nor be learned in its letters nor find solace in protest movements or group membership. Having been so hard won for so many, the right to vote is itself sufficient.

4. The tripartite virtues of divided power, limited government, and a universal franchise make possible the fourth virtue—*republican,* or representative, government. Representative democracy, while consigning citizens to an indirect role in policymaking, nevertheless offers the advantages of expert decision making without sacrificing accountability. It is in this spirit that Tocqueville can say that republican government offers citizens "no permanent obstacles from the exercise of perpetual influence on the daily conduct of affairs."

5. Augmenting this governmental system are the constitutional guarantees of free speech, press, religion, and dissent. These guarantee a meaningful civic dialogue without which popular decision making is not possible. Moreover, they provide protection from the arbitrary actions of governmental officials, as well as from short-lived and/or hot-tempered majorities.

6. Finally, the process of amending the Constitution, although difficult, is both ever present and critically important. Essentially, the Constitution's amendment process places the responsibility for the sustenance of the framework of government and these cherished liberties firmly in the hands of the public. And that is as it should be.

That the civics book model offers a governmental Shangri-La is not to suggest that its defenders turn a blind eye to democratic deficiencies. Indeed, popular criticism of the government is frequent and expected. The well-worn saying that "the price of freedom is eternal vigilance" shows the spirit of civics book democracy to be reformist. High school history curricula, although suggesting a record of progressive expansion of the franchise, do not fail to draw our attention to a time when the right to vote was denied to large numbers of our citizens for reasons that can be explained but not defended. Journalists are quick to point to governmental corruption, declining rates of voter turnout, an ineffectual party system, and entrenched "special interests" as causes for alarm. Nonetheless, these critiques suggest that democracy's deficiencies can be corrected within the system by finding the "right leaders," thus avoiding the need for structural reform.

Elite Theories of Government

Elite theory stands at quite the opposite theoretical pole from civics book theory, arguing that traditional American government is not and can never be democratic in fact. For elite theorists, there is no causal link between people and government and no significant competition among the elite.

When thinking about elite theory we must remember that we are actually talking about hundreds of distinct elite theories. These differences concern the *who* question, each theory offering different answers about the identity and size of the elite, their location in society, and the methods by which they control the mass public.

The divergences among elite theorists are noteworthy. Whereas some elite theorists concentrate on the machinations of elected officials, others deal almost entirely with nongovernmental actors (such as capitalists, corporate executives, or perhaps unnamed others who pull strings behind the scenes). Whereas some theorists focus on an elite that is conspiring to preserve its own power, others see elites as merely guardians of a sincerely held dominant ideology. Some elite theories present an interlocking network of elites, directing attention at those who divide their time among business, government, nonprofit institutions, and other facets of life. Others present different power centers for each sector. Some elite theories proffer a global elite; others confine their concerns to the United States. Some are economic theories, focusing on bankers or multinational corporations. Others are largely noneconomic, perhaps highlighting entrenched bureaucracies or a cultural elite. Any two elite theories may persuasively claim to identify those who pull the strings, yet, laid side by side, there may be no single person common to both lists. The reason we are able to consolidate this theoretical diversity under the single heading of elite theory becomes clear when we identify basic areas of agreement concerning the *how* question, the second critical democratic question.

Essentially, all elite theories have the following elements in common. First, they posit a two-class theory of society. No intermediate societal construct (such as a broad middle class) or linkage institution (such as elections or interest groups) can hide the basic fact that political society is divided into the ruling and the ruled. Second, the elite are bound together by a common educational and social background and, certainly, by a common mindset. These commonalities may have implications for the rest of us that are good or bad, but in no way can it be argued that the elite are representative of ordinary citizens. Third, whatever differences may exist among elites, they *do not compete* on fundamental policy matters. On these big issues—such matters as what type of economic system is best or what shall be the basic tenets of American foreign policy—there is no meaningful difference of opinion because the elites are dealing with questions fundamental to the preservation of the status quo. Finally, in viewing American politics, all elite theorists see a closed policymaking system. The masses may have the right to vote, but that right cannot be meaningful if those who run for office do not offer fundamental differences on important issues. For elite theorists, elections, like all linkage institutions, serve as sideshows. Even worse, elections may be inimical to democracy insofar as a sham process is elevated to the winning of a popular mandate. In sum, the elite theories differ on the method by which power is maintained but all agree that the masses are not meaningful participants.

We offer three selections as examples of the rich tradition of elite theories: **Michael Parenti**, who offers a Marxist theory of an economic elite; **Alan Wolfe**, commenting on **C. Wright Mills's** theory of a tripartite power elite; and **Robert Dye and R. Harmon Zeigler**, who describe a fluid elite, bound together to preserve dominant values. Dye and Zeigler's elite theory has the added interest of being both descriptive and normative.

One strength of the elite theory is its ability to direct our attention toward policies not debated and issues never considered. In so doing, elite theory exposes the narrow range of issues within which political discourse is often conducted in America and lays bare the assumptions of civics book democracy. For these reasons, students often find one elite theory or another an attractive alternative to the beliefs of their youth. Nonetheless, we ask you to hold elite theorists to the same stringent standard that they apply to the ruling class. Elite theorists often set up a series of straw men. For example, if the elite class emerges as the loser in some policy debate (and there are many such instances), elite theorists conclude that the elites did not see that policy debate as important enough to win. Likewise, if the public rejects some course of action that would have produced a fundamental change, their rejection becomes evidence that the elite has succeeded in manipulating mass opinion.

How, for instance, do the elite theorists explain the controversy surrounding the impeachment of President Clinton (1998–1999)? It is difficult to argue that the two sides of the impeachment question were not disputing a fundamental matter of governance. It is perhaps even more difficult to deny that a consistent and considered public opinion (holding that the President's behavior was squalid and disgraceful but did not constitute grounds for removal from office) was irrelevant to its outcome. The impeachment matter thus crystallizes a powerful critique of elite theorists. It is one thing to say that some hold more political power than others, but it is quite another thing to argue that the views of the powerful are invariably wrong or that vigorous debate occurs only on matters that are trivial.

The Pluralist Model

The last of our theories is pluralism. This model posits political life as a free market for the organization of influence. It begins with the assumption that individuals are interested in issues that directly affect their lifestyles, strongly held beliefs, or occupation. In a free society, all interests should be given their proverbial day in court. A funeral director, for example, may be uninterested and unknowledgable about policy issues *in general* but quite concerned about his or her own industry. Almost everyone believes that one's life's work is special, and all of us would want government to recognize this uniqueness insofar as its actions may confer a benefit or impose a burden on our own chosen profession or activity. Can an election possibly provide a means for this kind of communication? To be sure, the candidates' general position on taxation or regulation may cause a voter to be more favorably disposed to a particular candidate. But will this same businessperson believe that his or her interest is effectively represented as long as the right people are in office? In this sense, can there ever be a "funeral directors' candidate" for governor? As if by chemical reaction, the individual's response is to organize with other like-minded people to affect governmental actions concerning their interests. Once organized, the group then becomes a dynamic and continuing presence for representation of the particular concerns of that group. Thus, for pluralists, the *interest group* becomes the primary vehicle of linkage between the citizen and governmental policy.

Far from thinking that group advocacy is incompatible with democracy, most pluralists see group organization as the fullest expression of self-government in that it best provides the means for citizens' input. For a pluralist, the genius of the constitutional separation and division of powers is not only that it checks against the corruption of power but also that in so doing it gives the citizen many points at which to gain access to the political system. To begin, group pressures determine what issues will be on the agenda for debate, and even what issues will not be up for discussion. In addition, the group pressure system allows a very flexible means of pursuing issues on the agenda. For example, groups have many different means of influence: traditional lobbying, grassroots activity, litigation, and electoral influence. Groups can also press their issues in a myriad of different institutions: legislatures, bureaucracies, executive offices, and courts. Finally, groups can wield their influence at several different levels of society: national, state, and local, and in the public or private sector. The success of group organization naturally spawns further organization and counterpressures from those with differing points of view. In sum, the group process produces a competitive, open, and democratic method of policymaking.

The pluralist vision of democracy is well captured in the selection from **Robert Dahl**. Many power centers, representing concerns large and small, vie for the favor of hundreds of interested citizens. The group process is a regularized, peaceful, and open arena for the resolution of political conflict. It is a process in which people may bring a large number of resources to bear; those with little wealth may have the strengths of large numbers, a passionate following, or effective leadership. Resultant policy outcomes may not be perfect and often may seem sloppy; nevertheless, the process is one that guarantees a voice to all. And, to the pluralist mindset, this makes for the most democratic system possible.

Critics of pluralism are many and varied. However, two fundamental criticisms should be noted here. First, critics argue that pluralists exaggerate the degree to which individuals and interests will actually organize, and so they confuse the great increase in the number of groups with the fact that a relatively tiny percentage of Americans participate in these groups in any meaningful way. Moreover, political participation of any kind (particularly that denoted by active membership in interest groups) has always been associated with high socioeconomic status. Poor people, for instance, may number in the tens of millions but lack the political resources for effective representation and, additionally, have an agenda so diverse and far reaching that their wants are difficult to accommodate. A corporation that is seeking a specific tax break, on the other hand, is both better organized and is pursuing a benefit that is specific enough, as well as small enough, to be easily considered. In sum, these critics argue that pluralism is a system under which the haves will invariably have more.

The second fundamental criticism concerns government's inability to make basic choices in the face of numerous powerful groups. The unstated assumption of pluralism is that a substantive public interest cannot be defined for most issues, ergo the sum of all special interests is our best approximation therein. Since no one can precisely measure the effect on the ecosystem of clear-cutting timber in a certain forest, a pluralist might say that the best approach is to let the policy experts that are representing the affected groups fight it out in the policy arena. Rather than reaching a resolution of the question, policymakers often split the difference among the competing groups, leading to shifting, irrational decisions based more on which group can gain temporary political advantage than on the rightness of their positions. The upshot of this is a governmental system that simply doles out favors to all groups with a seat at the policy table. All decisions are up for grabs and all resolutions become temporary. The inevitable result is a government at cross purposes with itself. Many critics see pluralism as a fair approximation of reality but argue that this is not a democratic reality for the United States.

Direct Democracy

As frustration with the system becomes more pronounced, it is not surprising that more and more individuals have become interested in the possibility of alternatives. The U.S. Reform Party (founded in the wake of the 1992 presidential campaign of H. Ross Perot) is, ideologically speaking, a pastiche of disparate philosophical views. However, most of its followers do rally behind the banner of "opening up the system to allow citizens a direct voice in policy making."

Direct democracy is a system by which people directly approve or disapprove of specific policies rather than working through elected representatives. Twenty-three states offer an ever more free-flowing initiative and referenda process. Here, citizens vote directly on legislation that state and/or local representatives have been unable or unwilling to consider. Using referenda, voters have implemented and repealed gay rights initiatives, approved or turned down municipal stadiums, and rolled back auto insurance rates and local property taxes. Moreover, the prospect is that in the not too distant future citizens will have the ability to participate directly in policy decisions from the privacy of their own homes. In his 1992 and (to a lesser extent) 1996 campaigns, Perot touted the idea of an "electronic town hall." Others argue that the "information superhighway" may provide the means to both inform citizens and tabulate their votes.

In propounding their points, these "reformers" sometimes refer to our three theories of American government. They offer whatever reforms they propose as an antidote to the corruption of "entrenched elites" or "special interest groups"—in effect invoking both the various elite theories, as well as pluralism. In so doing, they pledge fealty to the founders of the Republic. But the framers of our government would turn over in their graves at the very idea of public initiative. As Tocqueville points out, the hallmark of popular government is democratic *accountability*, not policymaking by the masses.

The prospects for, as well as the desirability of, direct democracy form the basis of the current controversy in this chapter. The trend toward greater use of public initiative was both predicted and championed by **John Naisbitt**. While many cheer the prospect of direct public input, others are disquieted by these trends. As suggested by **Daniel Smith**, direct democracy raises troubling questions. These questions go not only to the capabilities of citizens as policymakers, but also the threat to the delicate balance struck by the framers of the Constituion, which made American democracy possible. In short, can true democracy be promoted by any proposed scheme of direct democracy?

1 | *Democracy in America*
Alexis de Tocqueville

This famous Frenchman came to American in 1831, as a relatively young man, to study the American penal system. Instead, he became fascinated by the entire political system. Tocqueville, whose aristocratic family suffered through the French revolution—a revolution that turned into a despotism—claimed that the "vices and weaknesses of democratic government were easy to see," but he nonetheless saw America as "eminently democratic." In his view the central features of American democracy were supported by the following observations: (1) The system is structurally democratic through representative organs; (2) accountability is ensured through the process of periodic elections; (3) self-government is achieved by a free people, with wide access to information, whose public opinion ultimately drives public policy.

In America, the people appoint those who make the laws and those who execute them; the people form the jury which punishes the violations of the law. The institutions are not only democratic in principle, but also in operation; thus, the people directly elect their representatives and usually select them every year, in order to keep them more completely in its dependence. Therefore, it is also the people who run things, and although the form of government is representative, it is obvious that the opinions, prejudices, interests, and even the passions of the people find no durable obstacles stopping them from participating in the daily direction of society.

In the United States, as in all countries where the people rule, the majority governs in the name of the people. This majority is mainly made up of peaceful citizens who, whether through taste or interest, honestly desire good for the country....

If there is one country in the world where a person can hope to appreciate the just value of the sovereignty of the people, study its application to society's affairs, and decide its advantages and dangers, America is most certainly that country.

I have previously said that from the outset the sovereignty of the people was the generating principle for most of England's American colonies.

However, it was as far from dominating the government of society then as it does these days.

Two obstacles, the one internal and the other one external, delayed its intrusive march.

It could not be conspicuously put in the laws, since the colonies were still forced to obey the home country; therefore, it had to remain concealed in the provincial assemblies and above all in the towns. From there it secretly spread.

American society then was not yet prepared to adopt it with all of its consequences. Education in New England and wealth south of the Hudson ... for a long time exerted a kind of aristocratic influence that tended to strengthen the exercise of social power in a few hands. It was still far from the practice that all public officials were elected and all citizens were voters. Everywhere voting rights were contained within certain limits, and subordinate to property qualification. That qualification was low in the North, but was more severe in the South.

Then the American Revolution broke out. The dogma of the sovereignty of the people came out of the town and seized the government; every class committed to its cause; they fought and won in its name; it became the supreme law.

A change nearly as rapidly was carried out within society. The inheritance law completed the breaking down of local influence.

Just as the effects of the laws and the Revolution were revealed to everyone, the victory of democracy had already been irrevocably proclaimed. By this event, power was in its hands. No longer was it even possible to fight against it. The upper classes submitted to an evil that was inevitable without fight or complaint. They arrived at the common fate of fallen powers: individual selfishness seized its members; as they could no longer tear power out of the people's hands, and as they did not sufficiently hate them to take pleasure in defying them, they only thought about winning their benevolence at any price. Therefore, the most democratic laws were passed by the same men whose interests were hurt the most. In this manner, the upper classes excited no popular passions against themselves; but they quickened the victory of the new order. Thus, this custom had the remarkable effect that the democratic surge was the most irresistible in those states where the aristocracy had the deepest roots.

Maryland, which had been founded by great lords, was the first to proclaim universal suffrage and introduced the most democratic forms within its entire government.

Once a people start to regulate the voting qualification, it is certain that sooner or later it will be completely eliminated. That concept is one of the most invariable rules governing society. As the limit on voting rights is reversed, the greater is the need to remove it even more; because after every new concession, the democratic forces are increased and its demands increase with its new power. The ambition of those who are left below the voting limit becomes inflamed in proportion to the large numbers above it. Finally, the ex-

ception becomes the rule; the concessions follow one another without break, and there is no stopping until universal suffrage has been reached.

Nowadays in the United States the sovereignty-of-the-people principle has been put into practice in every development that the imagination can conceive of. It has been cleared from every fiction in which elsewhere it has been connected to; it puts on every form successively that is necessary for each case. Sometimes the entire people make the laws, as in Athens; sometimes representatives, elected by universal suffrage, represent it and act for it under its almost immediate watch.

In some countries power is divided, being at the same time inside and outside of society. Nothing like that exists in the United States; there, society acts for and by itself. The only authority is society itself; it is extremely hard to find anyone who would dare to image or express the idea of seeking power somewhere else. The people contribute to the composition of the laws through their choice of legislators, and they participate in their application by the election of executive power agents; it could be said that they govern themselves, as the part left to the administration is so weak and limited, the popular origin of the administration is so vividly recalled, and the government is so obedient to its source of power. The people rule over the American political world like God rules over the universe. It is the cause and the end of all things; everything comes from it and is absorbed by it.

2 | *Class: America's Dirty Little Secret*
Michael Parenti

Marxism, once the most fashionable of elite theories, has declined to the point where you may be forgiven if you know little about it. Michael Parenti's career has spanned Marxism's various phases of respectability. In his most recent (1994) work, Parenti takes a fresh look at class theory, and shows himself the ever unrepentant social critic. For Parenti, American politics is explained by class structure, and that structure is built on the maldistribution of wealth.

There is a dirty little secret in America. It is not race or even sex; it is class. In this modern age, many formerly taboo subjects are now open to public purview. Be it abortion, child abuse, gay rights, wife battering, rape, sexual harassment, prurience in high places, or racial prejudice and hatred, such topics are now bandied about in the mass media—though rarely in a manner that do them justice. Not so with the subject of class. The expressions of *class* bigotry in our films and television, in our literature and textbooks, and in our institutions and daily lives remain largely unexamined, as do most of the important realities of class experience. If the subject of class is introduced, it is usually dismissed as an outworn "Marxist" notion having no relevance to modern America and increasingly less relevance everywhere else in the world.

THE FEW AND THE MANY

All of humanity may be divided into two groups, which I will call column A and column B. In column A are those who live principally off other people's labor ("principally" because they may themselves work and even draw a salary but this is not their paramount source of income). There are several hundred thousand adults in the United States who do not have to. They have what we call "private" or "independent" incomes; that is, they get enough money to live—usually quite well—from the money they possess.

The idea that wealth is constantly being transferred from the labor of many into the accounts of the few, from column B to column A, is widely at variance with the established notion in capitalist society that the relationship between rich and poor, owner and worker, is not exploitative but symbiotic and even providential. The question "Where would workers be without the company?" is more likely to be asked than "Where would the company be without the workers?" Worker and owner are supposedly engaged in mutually beneficial "teamwork." Such class collaboration is presumed beneficial to all. Conversely, class strife is seen as harmful to all.

The accepted wisdom is that, since the rich in this country are relatively few, their cumulative wealth is not very much. Supposedly the bulk of the nation's wealth is spread out among the middle class. But the statistics do not support that view. As of 1992, the rich in America had a net worth of $6.14 trillion. The richest one percent controlled more than 60 percent of the national wealth—and that includes only assets declared. In contrast, over 90 percent of American families have no net wealth. Wealth in the United States is highly concentrated. It is overwhelmingly under the control of organizations expressly designed to accumulate wealth: giant multinational corporations, banks, and other financial institutions.

The people in column A also have ... more financial resources with which to organize around their interests and a higher degree of unity and conscious awareness of what is at stake for them, being a class *for* itself rather than just a class *in* itself, as evidenced by the Trilateral Commission, the Bilderberg Conference, the Council on Foreign Relations, the Committee for Economic Development, the Business Roundtable, the Bohemian Grove, and other formally organized congregations of business and policy elites.

IDEOLOGISTS AGAINST CLASS CONSCIOUSNESS

While incarcerated in Mussolini's dungeons from 1928 to 1937, the great Italian communist Antonio Gramsci wrote about politics and culture in his prison notebooks. But he had to be careful to eliminate words or phrases like "Marx," "Marxist," "capitalism," or "class" for these might attract the attention of the fascist censor who would then stop him from doing any more writing. The fascists well understood their job was to suppress class consciousness wherever it might appear.

Today most of our intellectuals, journalists and social commentators avoid the use of the word "class" as carefully as did Gramsci. Unlike him, they are not in prison and there is no need for rulers to put them there. Throughout their schooling and professional training they are censored by superiors and more generally by the monopoly culture in which they live. Soon they learn to censor themselves. They still occasionally use "Marxism" and "Marxist" but it is usually in a dismissive, negative-labeling way. They don't need a fascist censor breathing down their necks because they have a mainstream one implanted in their heads. These internalized forms of suppression are far more effective than any state censor could hope to be. Gramsci knew he was being censored. Many of our intellectuals and pundits think they are as free as birds—and they are, as long as they fly in the right circles.

Class reality is obscured by a dominant ideology whose basic tenets might be listed as follows:

1. There are no real class divisions in this society. Save for some rich and poor, almost all of us are middle class.
2. The differences between rich and poor are a natural given, accumulated wealth being not a

cause of poverty. As the pie gets bigger, we all get more. It is not a zero sum situation.
3. If there are class divisions, they are not serious but secondary to the community of interests shared by us all. In modern-day America, class is greatly eclipsed by more salient factors like race, gender, region, nation, life-style, and culture.
4. Our social institutions and culture are autonomous entities in a pluralistic society, largely free of the influences of wealth and class power. To think otherwise is to entertain conspiracy theories.
5. Instead of class, it is individual human behavior that determines human performance and life chances. Therefore, existing social arrangements are not a matter of class power but a natural reflection of largely innate human proclivities.

THE MARXIST DEFINITION OF CLASS

To think critically about class power is a subversive but very democratic activity, a way of bringing the dirty little secret of class out into the open.

… Karl Marx's concept of class describes a relationship to the means of production, to the means of accumulating wealth and power and developing an entire social order known as capitalism (or feudalism or slavery). Hence, one cannot think of class as just existing unto itself, for any one class gets its definition from its relationship to another. There can be no slaveholders without slaves, no feudal lords without serfs, no capitalists without workers.…

… In the Marxist sense of class, the crucial axis of the relationship is not between the two classes as such, but the linkage to a third factor: the exploitative nature of the production process. Class gets its significance from its relationship to production and the process of surplus accumulation, that is, the process of producing and accumulating wealth from human labor.

Marxists have not invented this relationship out of their heads; they only recognize it and study its significance. For them, class is a relationship between those who own the means of production (the factories, refineries, agribusiness, investment houses, banks, law firms, shipping lines, airlines, hotels, hospitals, newspaper and magazine chains, television and radio stations, publishing houses, professional sports teams, department stores, shopping malls, supermarkets and so forth) and those who work for the owners. The relationship is an *exploitative* one, involving the constant transference of wealth from the worker who produces it to the owner who does not work. It explains how some people can get rich without working or with doing only a fraction of the work that enriches them....

Contrary to accepted notions, the working class is not withering away, certainly not as a social reality, not in numbers or potential strength. Part of the problem lies in what is meant by "working class." Those who apply the term only to the industrial proletariat are apt to see that class as being in relative, or even absolute, decline in the United States. But if we think of the working class as including service workers and most other employees who survive by selling their labor, then certainly there is a huge working class majority in the United States, one that is laboring harder to stay in the same place, underemployed, and downgraded in job levels, wages, and benefits.

PLURALISM AND THE MYTHS OF "DEMOCRATIC CAPITALISM"

Propagated by news pundits and academics, the myth of pluralism, or "democratic pluralism," tells us that power in U.S. society is widely distributed. All important interests have their say and get their way—at least some of the time. No social group or class consistently predominates. Policies are formulated by a multilateral interplay of interest groups. The government acts as a mediator of these conflicting demands, seeking to develop a workable consensus.

This image of a fluid pluralistic interplay begs the whole question of structured, insti-

tutionalized class power. While there certainly exists a wide diversity of interest groups, the resources of power actually are highly skewed in favor of those who represent wealthy interests and against those who represent impoverished or poorly organized ones. (S)eemingly, diverse institutions are linked to the same dominant class interests....

The capitalist system has its own myths as embodied in the free market ideology. There is the myth of individualism, which reduces human community to a conglomeration of atomized persons, each plotting his or her own gain, driven by a devotion to the cash nexus. Yet, the whole competition benefits everyone, thanks to the wonders of the free market as directed by Adam Smith's "invisible hand." Rather, everything *would* come out fine, conservatives argue, were it not for the intrusion of government regulations and social programs. For the conservative, public-interest programs represent the connivance of meddlesome bureaucrats rather than popular victories won after prolonged struggle. Corporate interests denounce government intrusion in the economy while themselves feeding gluttonously out of the public trough. At the same time, conservatives denounce government meddling in our lives, yet advocate the extension of state power in the control of personal morals and political dissent, and the suppression of national independence movements in the Third World.

CLASS INJURY: HATING THE POOR

... (W)ith class supremacy comes class bigotry. Poverty is seen not as only as the cause of vice but itself a vice. In societies that worship money and success, the losers become objects of scorn. Those who work hardest for the least are called lazy. Those who are forced to live in substandard housing are thought to be the authors of substandard lives. Those who do not finish high school or cannot afford to go to college are considered deficient or inept.

In sum, for centuries privileged persons have assumed that a lowly class position has been congruous with the limited needs and tastes of "lowly people," borne of their own personal deficiencies in character and ambition. Charity only undermines their self-reliance, and imposes a drain on society. Idleness is self-inflicted, for work is available for anyone who wants it. Poverty is a matter of volition. "They do not want to better themselves" is a commonly heard refrain to this day. The poor live poorly because that is their preference, and if not their preference, then certainly it is the result of their spendthrift ways, moral underdevelopment, indolence, unwillingness to pursue self-improvement, inability to defer gratification, weak or nonexistent family structures, and dislike for hard work and education. For the privileged classes the problem has not been the exploitation and mistreatment of the poor, but the difficulties caused by the poor's reactions to such mistreatment.

It is not only the affluent and their propagandists who ascribe to this class bigotry. The strength of the elite ideology lies in its dissemination among broader publics, made all the easier by the ideology's monopoly access to the mass media. Many persons of middle and lower-middle income status, struggling to maintain their standard of living, are among the most fervent haters of the poor, imagining themselves as the prime victims of lower-class criminal depravity and of the favoritism shown to the poor by "tax-spend do-gooders."

Some social scientists assert that the poor suffer from a "culture of poverty." By stressing "culture" ... the privileged apologists can ignore *economic* class realities, such as low wages, high unemployment, regressive taxes, rent-gouging landlords, overpriced goods, and substandard or nonexistent community services. To be sure, among the poor can be found many demoralized, disheartened people, who are seriously damaged by the conditions of their lives. But where does the "culture of poverty" come from? Do the poor create it, or are they created by it? Is it not caused by material deprivation and exploitation? Doesn't poverty have anything to do with the lack of money, or is it all a matter of attitude and personal habit? The "culture of poverty" does not float about in a social vacuum. How then is it linked to and affected by the lopsided distribution of economic resources and political power? "Culture of poverty" theorists do not answer these questions. In fact, they never ask them.

We hear that the poor must be made self-sufficient. But training programs designed to induce them to adopt a "work ethic" and develop employable skills are frequently misdirected because they assume the poor themselves are the problem, not the poverty and job market they face.

Workfare programs, like the pronouncements of conservative professors and economists, fail to address the social and material realities of single parents surviving on public assistance. Much "job training" is for jobs that do not exist. What is needed is massive investment in housing, education, day-care assistance, family health care, income support, public enterprises, and vigorous law enforcement and support systems to stop spouse abuse, child abuse, and drug infestation. The class bigotry and self-serving ideologies promoted by society's more affluent element do not themselves create inequitable economic conditions, but they do play a vital role in legitimating and disguising the class system. A new approach to the economically oppressed will come only after we develop a more realistic and critical understanding of the class society that produces them.

3 | *The Power Elite Now*
Alan Wolfe

The classic work on elite theory was developed by sociologist C. Wright Mills and positied a tripartite "power elite" of economic, military and political leaders. In this unique article, Boston University sociologist Alan Wolfe examines this power elite forty-three years later. Wolfe concludes that whereas the identity of the elites and the instrumentalities of their control may have changed, Mills's book retains its power both as an accurate representation of America in the 1950s and in its critique of the entire notion of pluralism.

C. Wright Mills's *The Power Elite* was published in 1956, a time, as Mills himself put it, when Americans were living through "a material boom, a nationalist celebration, a political vacuum." It is not hard to understand why Americans were as complacent as Mills charged.

Let's say you were a typical 35-year-old voter in 1956. When you were eight years old, the stock market crashed, and the resulting Great Depression began just as you started third or fourth grade. Hence your childhood was consumed with fighting off the poverty of the single greatest economic catastrophe in American history. When you were 20, the Japanese invaded Pearl Harbor, ensuring that your years as a young adult, especially if you were male, would be spent fighting on the ground in Europe or from island to island in Asia.

If you were lucky enough to survive that experience, you returned home at the ripe old age of 24, ready to resume some semblance of a normal life—only then to witness the Korean War, McCarthyism, and the beginning of the Cold War with the Soviet Union.

Into this milieu exploded *The Power Elite*. C. Wright Mills was one of the first intellectuals in America to write that the complacency of the Eisenhower years left much to be desired. His indictment was uncompromising.

On the one hand, he claimed, vast concentrations of power had coagulated in America, making a mockery of American democracy. On the other, he charged that his fellow intellectuals had sold out to the conservative mood in America, leaving their audience—the American people themselves—in a state of ignorance and apathy bearing shocking resemblance to the totalitarian regimes that America had defeated or was currently fighting.

One of the goals Mills set for himself in *The Power Elite* was to tell his readers again, assuming that they were roughly 35 years of age, how much the organization of power in America had changed during their lifetimes. In the 1920s, when this typical reader had been born, there existed what Mills called "local society," towns and small cities throughout America whose political and social life was dominated by resident businessmen. Small-town elites, usually Republican in their outlook, had a strong voice in Congress, for most of the congressmen who represented them were either members of the dominant families themselves or had close financial ties to them.

By the time Mills wrote his book, this world of local elites had become as obsolete as the Model T Ford. Power in America had become nationalized, Mills charged, and as a result had also become interconnected. *The Power Elite* called attention to three prongs of power in the United States. First, business had shifted its focus from corporations that were primarily regional in their workforces and customer bases to ones that sought products in national markets and developed national interests. What had once been a propertied class, tied to the ownership of real assets, had become a managerial class, rewarded for its ability to organize the vast scope of corporate enterprise into an engine for ever-expanding profits. No longer were the chief executive officers of these companies chosen because they were of the right social background. Connections still mattered, but so did bureaucratic skill. The men who possessed those skills were rewarded well for their efforts. Larded with expense accounts and paid handsomely, they could exercise national influence not only through their companies, but through the roles that they would be called upon to serve in "the national interest."

Similar changes had taken place in the military sector of American society. World War II, Mills argued, and the subsequent start of the Cold War, led to the establishment of "a permanent war economy" in the United States.... Given an unlimited checking account by politicians anxious to appear tough, buoyed by fantastic technological and scientific achievements, and sinking roots into America's educational institutions, the military, Mills believed, was becoming increasingly autonomous. Of all the prongs of the power elite, this "military ascendancy" possessed the most dangerous implications....

In addition to the military and corporate elites, Mills analyzed the role of what he called "the political directorate." Local elites had once been strongly represented in Congress, but Congress itself, Mills pointed out, had lost power to the executive branch. And within that branch, Mills could count roughly 50 people who, in his opinion, were "now in charge of the executive decisions made in the name of the United States of America." The very top positions—such as the secretaries of state or defense—were occupied by men with close ties to the leading national corporations in the United States. These people were not attracted to their positions for the money; often, they made less than they would have in the private sector. Rather they understood that running the Central Intelligence Agency or being Secretary of the Treasury gave one vast influence over the direction taken by the country. Firmly interlocked with the military and corporate sectors, the political leaders of the United States fashioned an agenda favorable to their class rather than one that might have been good for the nation as a whole.

Although written very much as a product of its time, *The Power Elite* has had remarkable staying power. The book has remained in print for 43 years in its original form, which means that the 35-year-old who read it when it first came out is now 78 years old. The names have changed since the book's appearance, younger readers will recognize hardly any of the corporate, military, and political leaders mentioned by Mills, but the underlying question of whether America is as democratic in practice as it is in theory continues to matter very much.

Changing Fortunes

The obvious question for any contemporary reader of *The Power Elite* is whether its conclusions apply to the United States today. Sorting out what is helpful in Mills's book from what has become obsolete seems a task worth undertaking.

Each year, *Fortune* publishes a list of the 500 leading American companies based on revenues. Roughly 30 of the 50 companies that dominated the economy when Mills wrote his book no longer do, including firms in once seemingly impregnable industries such as steel, rubber, and food. Putting it another way, the 1998 list contains the names of many corporations that would have been quite familiar to Mills: General Motors is ranked first, Ford second, and Exxon third. But the company immediately following these giants, "Wal-Mart Stores," did not even exist at the time Mills wrote; indeed, the idea that a chain of retail stores started by a folksy Arkansas merchant would someday outrank Mobil, General Electric, or Chrysler would have startled Mills. Furthermore, just as some industries have declined, whole new industries have appeared in America since 1956; IBM was fifty-ninth when Mills wrote, hardly the computer giant—sixth on the current Fortune 500 list—that it is now....

Despite these changes in the nature of corporate America, however, much of what Mills had to say about the corporate elite still applies. It is certainly still the case, for example, that those who run companies are very rich; the gap between what a CEO makes and what a worker makes is extraordinarily high. But there is one difference between the world described by Mills and the world of today that is so striking it cannot be passed over.

As odd as it may sound, Mills's understanding of capitalism was not radical enough. Heavily influenced by the sociology of its time, *The Power Elite* portrayed corporate executives as organization men who "must fit in with those already at the top." They had to be concerned with managing their impressions, as if the appearance of good results were more important than the actuality of them....

It may well have been true in the 1950s that corporate leaders were not especially inventive; but if so, that was because they faced relatively few challenges. If you were the head of General Motors in 1956, you knew that American automobile companies dominated your market; the last thing on your mind was the fact that someday cars called Toyotas or Hondas would be your biggest threat. You did not like the union which organized your workers, but if you were smart, you realized that an ever-growing economy would enable you to trade off high wages for your workers in return for labor market stability. Smaller companies that supplied you with parts were dependent on you for orders. Each year you wanted to outsell Ford and Chrysler, and yet you worked with them to create an elaborate set of signals so that they would not undercut your prices and you would not undercut theirs. Whatever your market share in 1956, in other words, you could be fairly sure that it would be the same in 1957. Why rock the boat? It made perfect sense for budding executives to do what Mills argued they did do: assume that the best way to get ahead was to get along and go along.

Very little of this picture remains accurate at the end of the twentieth century. Union membership as a percentage of the total workforce has declined dramatically, and while this means that companies can pay their workers less, it also means that they cannot expect to invest much in the training of their workers on the assumption that those workers will remain with the company for most of their lives. Foreign competition, once negligible, is now the rule of thumb for most American companies, leading many of them to move parts of their companies overseas and to create their own global marketing arrangements.... Often dominated by self-made men (another phenomenon about which Mills was doubtful), these firms are ruthlessly competitive, which upsets any possibility of forming gentlemen's agreements to control prices; indeed, among internet companies the idea is to provide the product with no price whatsoever, that is, "for free," in the hopes of winning future customer loyalty.

These radical changes in the competitive dynamics of American capitalism have important implications for any effort to characterize the power elite of today. C. Wright Mills was a translator and interpreter of the German sociologist Max Weber, and he borrowed from Weber the idea that a heavily bureaucratized society would also be a stable and conservative society. Only in a society which changes relatively little is it possible for an elite to have power in the first place, for if events change radically, then it tends to be the events controlling the people rather than the people controlling the events. There can be little doubt that those who hold the highest positions in America's corporate hierarchy remain, as they did in Mills's day, the most powerful Americans. But not even they can control rapid technological transformations, intense global competition, and ever-changing consumer tastes. American capitalism is simply too dynamic to be controlled for very long by anyone.

The Warlords

One of the crucial arguments Mills made in *The Power Elite* was that the emergence of the Cold War completely transformed the American public's historic opposition to a permanent military establishment in the United States. Indeed, he stressed that America's military elite was now linked to its economic and political elite. Personnel were constantly shifting back and forth from the corporate world to the military world. Big companies like General Motors had become dependent on military contracts. Scientific and technological innovations sponsored by the military helped fuel the growth of the economy. And while all these links between the economy and the military were being forged, the military had become an active political force. Members of Congress, once hostile to the military, now treated officers with great deference. And no president could hope to staff the Department of State, find intelligence officers, and appoint ambassadors without consulting with the military.

Mills believed that the emergence of the military as a key force in American life constituted a substantial attack on the isolationism which had once characterized public opinion. He argued that "the warlords, along with fellow travelers and spokesmen, are attempting to plant their metaphysics firmly among the population at large." Their goal was nothing less than a redefinition of "reality," one in which the American people would come to accept what Mills called "an emergency without a foreseeable end." "War or a high state of war preparedness is felt to be the normal and seemingly permanent condition of the United States," Mills wrote. In this state of constant war fever, America could no longer be considered a genuine democracy, for democracy thrives on dissent and disagreement, precisely what the military definition of reality forbids....

Much as Mills wrote, it remains true today that Congress is extremely friendly to the military, at least in part because the military has become so powerful in the districts of most congressmen. Military bases are an important source of jobs for many Americans, and government spending on the military is crucial to companies, such as Lockheed Martin and Boeing, which manufacture military equipment. American firms are the leaders in the world's global arms market, manufacturing and exporting weapons everywhere. Some weapons systems never seem to die, even if, as was the case with a "Star Wars" system de-

signed to destroy incoming missiles, there is no demonstrable military need for them.

Yet despite these similarities with the 1950s, both the world and the role that America plays in that world have changed. For one thing, the United States has been unable to muster its forces for any sustained use in any foreign conflict since Vietnam. Worried about the possibility of a public backlash against the loss of American lives, American presidents either refrain from pursuing military adventures abroad or confine them to rapid strikes, along the lines pursued by Presidents Bush and Clinton in Iraq. Since 1989, moreover, the collapse of communism in Russia and Eastern Europe has undermined the capacity of America's elites to mobilize support for military expenditures. China, which at the time Mills wrote was considered a serious threat, is now viewed by American businessmen as a source of great potential investment. Domestic political support for a large and permanent military establishment in the United States, in short, can no longer be taken for granted.

The immediate consequence of these changes in the world's balance of power has been a dramatic decrease in that proportion of the American economy devoted to defense.... By almost any account, Mills's prediction that both the economy and the political system of the United States would come to be ever more dominated by the military is not borne out by historical developments since his time.

And how could he have been right? Business firms, still the most powerful force in American life, are increasingly global in nature, more interested in protecting their profits wherever they are made than in the defense of the country in which perhaps only a minority of their employees live and work. Give most of the leaders of America's largest companies a choice between invading another country and investing in its industries and they will nearly always choose the latter over the former. Mills believed that in the 1950s, for the first time in American history, the military elite had formed a strong alliance with the economic elite. Now it would be more correct to say that America's economic elite finds more in common with economic elites in other countries than it does with the military elite of its own. *The Power Elite* failed to foresee a situation in which at least one of the key elements of the power elite would no longer identify its fate with the fate of the country which spawned it.

Mass Society and the Power Elite

Politicians and public officials who wield control over the executive and legislative branches of government constitute the third leg of the power elite. Mills believed that the politicians of his time were no longer required to serve a local apprenticeship before moving up the ladder to national politics. Because corporations and the military had become so interlocked with government, and because these were both national institutions, what might be called "the nationalization of politics" was bound to follow. The new breed of political figure likely to climb to the highest political positions in the land would be those who were cozy with generals and CEOs, not those who were on a first-name basis with real estate brokers and savings and loan officials.

For Mills, politics was primarily a facade. Historically speaking, American politics had been organized on the theory of balance: each branch of government would balance the other; competitive parties would ensure adequate representation; and interest groups like labor unions would serve as a counterweight to other interests like business. But the emergence of the power elite had transformed the theory of balance into a romantic, Jeffersonian myth. So antidemocratic had America become under the rule of the power elite, according to Mills, that most decisions were made behind the scenes. As a result, neither Congress nor the political parties had much substantive work to carry out. "In the absence of policy differences of consequence between the major parties," Mills wrote, "the professional party politician must invent themes about which to talk."

Mills was right to emphasize the irrelevance of eighteenth- and nineteenth-century images to the actualities of twentieth-century American political power. But he was not necessarily correct that politics would therefore become something of an empty theatrical show. Mills believed that in the absence of real substance, the parties would become more like each other. Yet today the ideological differences between Republicans and Democrats are severe.... Real substance may not be high on the American political agenda, but that does not mean that politics is unimportant. Through our political system, we make decisions about what kind of people we imagine ourselves to be, which is why it matters a great deal at the end of the twentieth century which political party is in power.

Contemporary commentators believe that Mills was an outstanding social critic but not necessarily a first-rate social scientist. Yet I believe that *The Power Elite* survives better as a work of social science than of social criticism....

...(N)ot much of the academic sociology of the 1950s has survived, while *The Power Elite*, in terms of longevity, is rivaled by very few books of its period. In his own way, Mills contributed much to the understanding of his era. Social scientists of the 1950s emphasized pluralism, a concept which Mills attacked in his criticisms of the theory of balance. The dominant idea of the day was that the concentration of power in America ought not be considered excessive because one group always balanced the power of others.

The biggest problem facing America was not concentrated power but what sociologists began to call "the end of ideology." America, they believed, had reached a point in which grand passions over ideas were exhausted. From now on, we would require technical expertise to solve our problems, not the musings of intellectuals.

Compared to such ideas, Mills's picture of American reality, for all its exaggerations, seems closer to the mark. If the test of science is to get reality right, the very passionate convictions of C. Wright Mills drove him to develop a better empirical grasp on American society than his more objective and clinical contemporaries. We can, therefore, read *The Power Elite* as a fairly good account of what was taking place in America at the time it was written.

As a social critic, however, Mills leaves something to be desired.... It is ... one thing to attack the power elite, yet another to extend his criticisms to other intellectuals—and even the public at large. When he does the latter, Mills runs the risk of becoming as antidemocratic as he believed America had become.... (T)he image he conveyed of what an American had become was thoroughly unattractive: "He loses his independence, and more importantly, he loses the desire to be independent; in fact, he does not have hold of the idea of being an independent individual with his own mind and his own worked-out way of life." Mills had become so persuaded of the power of the power elite that he seemed to have lost all hope that the American people could find themselves and put a stop to the abuses he detected.

One can only wonder, then, what Mills would have made of the failed attempt by Republican zealots to impeach and remove the President of the United States. At one level it makes one wish there really were a power elite, for surely such an elite would have prevented an extremist faction of an increasingly ideological political party from trying to overturn the results of two elections. And at another level, to the degree that America weathered this crisis, it did so precisely because the public did not act as if it were numbed by living in a mass society, for it refused to follow the lead of opinion makers, it made up its mind early and thoughtfully, and then it held tenaciously to its opinion until the end.

Whether or not America has a power elite at the top and a mass society at the bottom, however, it remains in desperate need of the blend of social science and social criticism which *The Power Elite* offered....

4 | *The Irony of Democracy*
Thomas R. Dye and L. Harmon Zeigler

Most elite theories present a system that, if not corrupt or exploitative, is surely contrary to the desires and sentiments of the majority. In this sense, most elite theorists describe a system they would not themselves choose. But in this excerpt from their popular textbook, Dye and Zeigler take a quite different tack. They argue that not only are elites better equipped to rule but also, considering the commitment of these elites to certain democratic principles—the rights of political dissenters, unpopular religious groups, criminal defendants, and the like—they are more likely to promote democratic values *than are the ill-informed, reactive, and frequently bigoted masses. In sum, America can be considered an elite system, and it is just as well that it is.*

Elites, not masses, govern America. In an industrial, scientific and nuclear age, life in a democracy, just as in a totalitarian society, is shaped by a handful of people. Despite differences in their approach to the study of power in America, political scientists and sociologists agree that "the key political, economic and social decisions are made by tiny minorities."

The central proposition of *elitism* (elite theory) is that all societies are divided into two classes: the few who govern and the many who are governed. Elites are not a product of capitalism or socialism or industrialization or technological development. All societies—socialist and capitalist, agricultural and industrial, traditional and advanced—are governed by elites. All societies require leaders, and leaders acquire a stake in preserving the organization and their position in it. This motive gives leaders a perspective different from that of the organization's members. An elite, then, is inevitable in any social organization. As the French political scientist Roberto Michels put it, "He who says organization, says oligarchy." The same is true for societies as a whole. According to political scientist Harold Lasswell, "The discovery that in all large scale societies the decisions at any given time are typically in the hands of a small number of people" confirms a basic fact: "Government is always government by the few, whether in the name of the few, the one, or the many."

Elitism also asserts that the few who govern are not typical of the masses who are governed. Elites control resources: power, wealth, education, prestige, status, skills of leadership, information, knowledge of political processes, ability to communicate, and organization. Elites in the United States are drawn disproportionately from wealthy, educated, prestigiously employed, socially prominent, white, Anglo-Saxon, and Protestant groups in society. They come from society's upper classes, those who own or control a disproportionate share of the societal institutions.

Elites share a general *consensus* about the fundamental norms of the social system. They agree on the basic rules of the game, as well as on the importance of preserving the social system. The stability of the system, and even its survival, depends upon this consensus. Elite consensus does not prevent elite members from disagreeing or competing with each other for preeminence. But competition takes place within a very narrow range of issues, and elites agree on more matters than they disagree on. Disagreement usually occurs over *means* rather than *ends*.... (Thus,) elitism implies that public policy does not reflect the demands of "the people" so much as it reflects the interests and values of the elites. Changes and innovations in public policy

come about when elites redefine their own values. However, the general conservatism of elites—that is, their interest in preserving the system—means that change in public policy will be incremental rather than revolutionary. Public policies are often modified but seldom replaced.

Finally, elitism assumes that the masses are largely passive, apathetic, and ill-informed. Mass sentiments are manipulated by elites more often than elite values are influenced by the sentiment of the masses. For the most part, communication between elites and masses flows downward. Masses seldom decide government policies through elections or through evaluation of political parties. For the most part, these "democratic" institutions—elections and parties—have only symbolic value: they help tie the masses into the political system by giving them a role to play on election day.

Elitism does not mean that those in power continually battle against the masses or that elites achieve their goals at the expense of the public interest. Elitism is not a conspiracy to oppress the masses. It does not imply that power is held by a single, impenetrable, monolithic body or that those in power always agree on public issues. It does not prevent power from shifting over time or prohibit the emergence of new elites. Elites may be more or less selfish and self-interested, or more or less enlightened and public-regarding. They may be more or less monolithic and cohesive, or more or less pluralistic and competitive.... Elitism does not deny the influence of the masses on elite behavior; it holds only that elites influence masses more than masses influence elites.

It is the irony of democracy that the survival of democratic values depends on enlightened elites. Despite a superficial commitment to the symbols of democracy, the American people have a surprisingly weak commitment to individual liberty, toleration of diversity, and freedom of expression when required to apply these principles to despised or obnoxious groups or individuals. In contrast, elites and the better-educated groups from which they are recruited are generally

more willing than the masses to apply democratic values to specific situation and to protect the freedoms of unpopular groups.

* * *

Clearly, the masses do not fully understand or
support the ideas and principles on which the
U.S. political system rests. We are left asking
why the system survives.

The distribution of antidemocratic attitudes among various social classes may provide part of an answer. Upper social classes
(from which members of elites are largely recruited) give greater, more consistent support
to democratic values than do lower social
classes.

The targets of intolerance change over
time, and attacks on freedom come from both
liberals and conservatives. Radical right
groups strive to control instruction and reading material in public schools by removing literature that they consider offensive. For
decades, such groups have sought to eliminate science books with an evolutionary bias,
sex education materials judged to be threatening to the institution of marriage, political
literature judged to be anti-American, and
economic material assessed as hostile to capitalism. Now, however, liberal groups are becoming equally vocal on behalf of censorship.
These groups seek to remove literature they
consider sexist and racist from schools and li-
braries, to ban pornography, and to reduce
the display of violence on television. Television networks and public schools both report
increased activity by liberal groups seeking to
impose their values.

In short, the targets of legitimate discrimination are changeable; they vary with the
times. In the 1950's when U.S. foreign policy
was vigorously anticommunist and the Cold
War was at its zenith, the masses' fear of communist activity led them to reject the legitimacy of communists speaking, writing, or
seeking public office. But by the 1960's many
people saw internal social protests as the
greatest threat. The percentage of people
who believed that members of the Communist party were harmful to the "American way
of life" decreased, while the percentage be-

lieving student demonstrators were harmful
increased. Later, increased fear of crime led
to growing mass willingness to curtail the
rights of accused criminals.

Public opinion is reactive: "Fear is transferred to new objects" as the political climate
and issues change. To discover the true nature of intolerance, one needs to know the
real targets of fear and hatred. One study allowed respondents to identify the group they
most strongly opposed and then asked them
whether a member of this group, whatever its
cause, should be allowed to seek political office, teach, make a speech, hold public rallies,
and the like. The conclusion was that "over
half of the respondents believe that their least
liked group should be outlawed, hardly consistent with the recent conclusion that the
mass public is increasingly tolerant."

Thus tolerance may not have declined but
simply found new targets. The public is more
tolerant of groups such as communists and
atheists that have faded from attention as
threats, but other targets have emerged to
take their place. This changeableness of mass
attitudes suggests that, given the right circumstances, effective counterelites could mobilize people against a particular scapegoat,
as has occurred in the past.

Ignorance and apathy also characterize
mass politics. Nearly half of eligible voters in
the United States stay away from the polls,
even in presidential elections. Voter turnout
is even lower in off-year congressional elections, when it falls to 35 percent of the voting-
age population. City and county elections,
when they are held separately from state or
national elections, usually produce turnouts
of 20 to 35 percent of eligible voters.

Political information is very scarce among
the masses. Ignorance extends not only to political issues but to the basic structures and
processes of government. Only about half the
public knows the elementary fact that each
state has two U.S. Senators; fewer still know
the terms of members of Congress or the
number of Supreme Court justices.

Ignorance breeds intolerance. Among the
masses, information about the various feared
and hated groups is not readily available. Not

having any clear appraisal of the probability that the feared and hated group will actually achieve its detested goals, the masses assume the worst. Among elites however, with greater information the true nature of the danger is more apparent, and fewer groups are feared. This point becomes important when we learn that when elites do feel threatened, they too become intolerant.

The irony of democracy is that democratic ideals survive because authoritarian masses are generally apathetic and inactive. Thus the lower classes' capacity for intolerance, authoritarianism, scapegoatism, racism, and violence seldom translates into organized, sustained political movements.

Moreover, the survival of democracy does not depend on mass support for democratic ideals. It is apparently not necessary that most people commit themselves to a democracy; all that is necessary is that they fail to commit themselves to an antidemocratic system. Though this fact suggests that American democracy is on shaky foundations, the masses' tendency to avoid political activity makes their antidemocratic attitudes less destructive. Those with the most dangerous attitudes are the least involved in politics.

5 | *Who Governs?*
Robert Dahl

It cannot often be said that an author has written the book on a subject. However, this 1961 study of New Haven city government is the seminal study of pluralism—the theory that the American system is made up of diverse institutions and organizations that compete for and share in the exercise of power. Robert Dahl's is a democratic pluralism in that he asserts that most can govern and many do, as long as they have the interest and wherewithal to participate. Criticized by many elite theorists for emphasizing the trivial and by some devotees of the civics book for being an elite theory, the continuing relevance of pluralism, democratic or not, is shown by the explosion of interest groups since Dahl's book was published.

In a political system where nearly every adult may vote but where knowledge, wealth, social positions, access to officials, and other resources are unequally distributed, who actually governs?

The question has been asked, I imagine, wherever popular government has developed and intelligent citizens have reached the stage of critical self-consciousness concerning their society. It must have been put many times in Athens even before it was posed by Plato and Aristotle.

Now it has always been held that if equality of power among citizens is possible at all—a point on which many political philosophers have had grave doubts—then surely consider-able equality of social conditions is a necessary prerequisite. But if, even in America, with its universal creed of democracy and equality, there are great inequalities in the conditions of different citizens, must there not also be great inequalities in the capacities of different citizens to influence the decisions of their various governments? And if, because they are unequal in other conditions, citizens of a democracy are unequal in power to control their government, then who in fact does govern? How does a "democratic" system work amid inequality of resources? These are the questions I want to explore by examining one urban American community, New Haven, Connecticut....

In the political system of the patrician oligarchy, political resources were marked by a cumulative inequality: when one individual was much better off than another in one resource, such as wealth, he was usually better off in almost every other resource— social standing, legitimacy, control over religious and educational institutions, knowledge, office. In the political system of today, inequalities in political resources remain, but they tend to be *noncumulative*. The political system of New Haven, then, is one of *dispersed inequalities....*

Within a century a political system dominated by one cohesive set of leaders had given way to a system dominated by many different sets of leaders, each having access to a different combination of political resources. It was, in short, a pluralist system. If the pluralist system was very far from being an oligarchy, it was also a long way from achieving the goal of political equality advocated by the philosophers of democracy and incorporated into the creed of democracy and equality practically every American professes to uphold.

One of the difficulties that confronts anyone who attempts to answer the question, "Who rules in a pluralist democracy?" is the ambiguous relationship of leaders to citizens.

Viewed from one position, leaders are enormously influential—so influential that if they are seen only in this perspective they might well be considered a kind of ruling elite. Viewed from another position, however, many influential leaders seem to be captive of their constituents. Like the blind men with the elephant, different analysts have meticulously examined different aspects of the body politic and arrived at radically different conclusions. To some, a pluralistic democracy is all head and no body; to others it is all body and no head.

Ambiguity in the relationship of leaders and constituents is generated by several closely connected obstacles both to observation and clear conceptualization. To begin with, the American creed of democracy and equality prescribes many forms and procedures from which the actual practices of leaders diverge. Consequently, to gain legitimacy for their actions leaders frequently surround their covert behavior with democratic rituals. These rituals not only serve to disguise reality and thus to complicate the task of observation and analysis, but—more important—in complex ways the very existence of democratic rituals, norms, and requirements of legitimacy based on a widely shared creed actually influences the behavior of both leaders and constituents even when democratic norms are violated. Thus the distinction between the rituals of power and the realities of power is frequently obscure.

Two additional factors help to account for this obscurity. First, among all the persons who influence a decision, some do so more directly than others in the sense that they are closer to the stage where concrete alternatives are initiated or vetoed in an explicit and immediate way. Indirect influence might be very great but comparatively difficult to observe and weigh. Yet to ignore indirect influence in analysis of the distribution of influence would be to exclude what might well prove to be a highly significant process of control in a pluralistic democracy.

Second, the relationship between leaders and citizens in a pluralistic democracy is frequently reciprocal: leaders influence the decisions of constituents, but the decisions of leaders are also determined in part by what they think are, will be, or have been the preferences of their constituents.

In New Haven, as in other political systems, a small stratum of individuals is much more highly involved in political thought, discussion, and action than the rest of the population. These citizens constitute the political stratum.

... (D)ifferences in the subcultures of the political and the apolitical strata are marked, particularly at the extremes. In the political stratum, politics is highly salient; among the apolitical strata, it is remote. In the political stratum, individuals tend to be calculating in their choice of strategies; members of the political stratum are, in a sense, relatively rational political beings. In the apolitical strata, people are notably less calculating; their political choices are more strongly influenced by inertia, habit, unexamined loyalties, personal attachments, emotions, transient impulses. In the political stratum, an individual's political beliefs tend to fall into patterns that have a relatively high degree of coherence and internal consistency; in the apolitical strata, political orientations are disorganized, disconnected, and unideological. In the political stratum, information about politics and the issues of the day is extensive; the apolitical strata are poorly informed. Individuals in the political stratum tend to participate rather actively in politics; in the apolitical strata citizens rarely go beyond voting and many do not even vote. Individuals in the political stratum exert a good deal of steady, direct, and active influence on government policy; in fact some individuals have a quite extraordinary amount of influence. Individuals in the apolitical strata, on the other hand, have much less direct or active influence on policies.

... The political strata of different communities and regions are linked in a national network of communications. Even in small towns, one or two members of the local political stratum are in touch with members of a state organization and certain members of the political stratum of a state or any large city maintain relations with members of organizations in other states and cities, or with national figures. Moreover, many channels of communication not designed specifically for political purposes—trade associations, professional associations, and labor organizations, for example—serve as part of the network of the political stratum.

In many pluralistic systems, however, the political stratum is far from being a closed or static group. In the United States the political stratum does not constitute a homogenous class with well-defined class interests. In New Haven, in fact, the political stratum is easily penetrable by anyone whose interests and concerns attract him to the distinctive political culture of the stratum. It is easily penetrated because (among other reasons) elections and competitive parties give politicians a powerful motive for expanding their coalitions and increasing their electoral followings.

Not only is the political stratum in New Haven not a closed group, but its "members" are far from united in their orientations and strategies. There are many lines of cleavage. The most apparent and probably the most durable are symbolized by affiliations with different political parties. Political parties are rival coalitions of leaders and subleaders drawn from the members of the political stratum. Leaders in a party coalition seek to win elections, capture the chief elective offices of government, and insure that government officials will legalize and enforce policies on which the coalition leaders can agree....

The goals and motives that animate leaders are evidently as varied as the dreams of men. They include greater wealth, economic security, power, social standing, fame, respect, affection, love, knowledge, curiosity, fun, the pleasure of exercising skill, delight in winning, esthetic satisfaction, morality, salvation, heroism, self-sacrifice, envy, jealousy, revenge, hate—whatever the whole wide range may be. Popular beliefs to the contrary, there is no convincing evidence at present that any single common denominator of motives can be singled out in leaders of associations ...

Ordinarily, the goals and strategies of leaders require services from other individuals.... To perform these services more or less regularly, reliably, and skillfully, auxiliaries or subleaders are needed....

Thus the survival of an association of leaders and subleaders depends on frequent transactions between the two groups in which the leaders pay off the subleaders in return for their services. To pay off the subleaders, leaders usually have to draw on resources available only outside the association.... Ordinarily ... the association must produce something that will appeal to outsiders, who then contribute resources that serve, directly or indirectly, to maintain the association. Probably the most important direct contribution of these outsiders—let us call them constituents is money; their most important indirect contribution is votes, which can be converted into office and thus into various other resources....

... (I)n each of a number of key sectors of public policy, a few persons have great *direct* influence on the choices that are made; most citizens by contrast would seem to have rather little direct influence. Yet it would be unwise to underestimate the extent to which voters may exert *indirect* influence on the decisions of leaders by means of elections.

In a political system where key offices are won by elections, where legality and constitutionality are highly valued in the political culture, and where nearly everyone in the political stratum publicly adheres to a doctrine of democracy, it is likely that the political culture, the prevailing attitudes of the political stratum, and the operation of the political system itself will be shaped by the role of elections. Leaders who in one context are enormously influential and even rather free from demands by their constituents may reveal themselves in another context to be involved in tireless efforts to adapt their policies to what they think their constituents want.

To be sure, in a pluralistic system with dispersed inequalities, the direct influence of leaders on policies extends well beyond the norms implied in the classical models of democracy developed by the political philosophers. But if the leaders lead, they are also led. Thus, the relations between leaders, subleaders, and constituents produce a stubborn and pervasive ambiguity that permeates the entire political system.

* * *

This system of dispersed inequalities is, I believe marked by the following six characteristics.

1. Many different kinds of resources for influencing officials are available to different citizens.
2. With few exceptions, these resources are unequally distributed.
3. Individuals best off in their access to one kind of resource are often badly off with respect to many other resources.
4. No one influence resource dominates all the others in all or even most key decisions.
5. With some exceptions, an influence resource is effective in some issue-areas or in some specific decisions but not in all.
6. Virtually no one, and certainly no group of more than a few individuals, is entirely lacking in some influence resource.

CURRENT CONTROVERSY

Is Direct Democracy a Better Way?

6 | From Representative Democracy to Participatory Democracy
John Naisbitt

The book Megatrends, *in one version or another, has long been a mainstay among best-selling books. Written by management consultant and social forecaster John Naisbitt, the book was a discussion of trends said to be "waves" of the next decade for American politics, business, and society. In this excerpt, Naisbitt turns his attention to democracy, with a discussion of trends toward greater direct citizen participation in policymaking through the state and local initiative process. The article's central point—that the communication revolution brings with it inexorable demands for direct democracy—may portend that teledemocracy and ever more direct forms of participatory government will be a megatrend of the next millennium.*

People whose lives are affected by a decision must be part of the process of arriving at that decision....

Politically, we are currently in the process of a massive shift from a representative to a participatory democracy. In a representative democracy, of course, we do not vote on issues directly; we elect someone to do the voting for us.

We created a representative system two hundred years ago when it was a practical way to organize a democracy. Direct citizen participation was simply not feasible, so we elected people to go off to the state capitals, represent us, vote, and then come back and tell us what happened. The representative who did a good job was reelected. The one who did not was turned out. For two hundred years, it worked quite well.

But along came the communication revolution, and with it an extremely well-educated electorate. Today, with instantaneously shared information, we know as much about what's going on as our representatives, and we know it just as quickly.

The fact is that we have outlived the historical usefulness of representative democracy and we all sense intuitively that it is obsolete. Furthermore, we have grown confident in our ability to make decisions about how institutions, including government and corporations, should operate.

We continue to elect representatives for two key reasons: (1) That is the way we've always done it, and, (2) it is politically expedient. We don't want to vote on *every* issue, only the ones that really make a difference in our lives.

Essentially, we are telling elected officials, "Okay, we've elected you to represent us, but if anything comes up that impacts our lives, you've got to check back with us."

The demise of representative democracy also signals the end of the traditional party system....

The political left and right are dead; all the action is being generated by a radical center.

The two-party system died because people gave up on it.

Writes (John) Herbers, "What has happened is that many people have given up trying to achieve goals through contests between Republicans and Democrats."

Politicians matter less and less. So there is a declining interest in national political elections. It is a natural consequence of the shift from a representative to a participatory democracy.

Political commentators and the media, of course, see this as anything but natural. We are constantly being upbraided for apathy and for taking democracy for granted. And by now we all even feel guilty about it.

We should not. Low voter turnout does not automatically signal trouble in democracy. It may mean that the people are more or less content whichever way an issue is settled, because it does not really impact on their lives.

Political analysts used to associate low turnout with apathy and ignorance. But as the electorate becomes better educated, more informed, and more assertive, that rationalization is becoming increasingly difficult to substantiate. Analysts are finally beginning to understand that voters are making a conscious decision *not* to participate.

Democratic Congressman George Danielson from California says (ironically, I hope): "We have leadership—there's just no followership."

Of course, that means there is no genuine leadership because *followers* create leaders.

What the people are saying is that they do not put much stock in either political office or the people filling it. By not voting they may be expressing the belief that politicians either cannot or will not do what the voters want done.

We have pulled the essence of political power out of the hands of our elected representatives and reinvested it into two main areas: (1) the direct ballot vote of initiatives and referenda and (2) grassroots political activity. In both cases citizens, not politicians, decide on a course of action and live with it.

Initiatives and referenda are the tools for the new democracy. These devices furnish direct access to political decision making, which is what informed, educated citizens want.

It is no wonder then that the popularity of initiatives exploded during the 1970's when we voted on 175 state-level initiatives, twice as many as in the 1960's. There were ten state initiatives in 1970 and forty in 1978. And there were hundreds of other local initiatives.

Yet there are signs the initiative trend is just beginning. The initiative is now legal in 23 states and in 100 cities, but pro-initiative groups are active in at least ten other states. The initiative process enjoys wide backing from virtually every political philosophy, from the Conservative party to Ralph Nader's Public Interest Research Group.

The difference between initiatives and referenda is that initiatives appear on the ballot through direct citizen action, while referenda are a means for citizens to approve of legislative action.

... (O)ne reason the referendum trend has taken hold recently is that people are demanding more accountability. The rise of the initiative, along with the referendum and the recall (which permits voters to recall an elected official and is legal in twelve states), represents an uncompromising demand on the part of voters for accountability from government. These new devices, the key instrumentalities in the new participatory democracy, enable the people to leapfrog traditional representative processes and mold the political system with their own hands.

Historically, the initiative has been used most frequently for political and governmental reform, according to political scientist Austin Ranney, the author of an American Enterprise Institute study on initiatives and referenda. State-passed initiatives were the driving force behind repealing the poll tax, woman suffrage, direct election of U.S. senators, and other important political changes.

But what is most interesting about the present initiative boom is the range of nontraditional issues that have popped up on initiative ballots—energy, the environment, health, values, foreign policy, and many more.

In 1978 California's Proposition 13, the tax-cut proposal by Howard Jarvis and Paul Gann, passed by a strong two-to-one margin and caught the country by storm. The proposal cut property taxes by 57 percent, to 1 percent of appraised value. For the state of California, its passage meant a $7 billion loss in property-tax revenue.

Even before the rest of the nation had a chance to see how California would cope with a multibillion dollar shortfall, the spirit of Proposition 13 inspired a flurry of tax-cutting all across the nation.

But only one year later, the tax revolution was already cooling. Two years later, newspaper accounts referred to the "tax revolt that never happened."

This all leads me to believe that Proposition 13 was greatly misunderstood. The tax revolt was not the important issue. Proposition 13 was really about the voter's discovery of the awesome power of the initiative.

I am not denying that Proposition 13 was a strong public demand for property-tax relief and accountability in government spending. It was all of that. But let us examine the process itself: The California legislature stalled for more than a year on a property-tax relief measure. In the meantime, tax-revolt groups had collected the 1.5 million signatures needed to bring their initiative to the voters. The legislature finally did pass a bill to reduce taxes somewhat, but by then the Jarvis proposal was already on the ballot. By that time, the voters had leapfrogged the state legislature and were so dazzled with the power of the initiative, few cared that the statehouse had finally delivered.

This discussion of initiatives has stressed the positive so far, the bottom-up victories won with initiatives. What has not been pointed out at all is that the initiative can create the monster as well as the genius.

Two negative considerations come to mind at once. First, all the standard dangers inherent in any electoral process—bribery, excessive campaign contributions, fraud—will emerge with greater use of initiatives. Second, and more threatening, the initiative can conceivably endanger the civil rights of minorities. In an initiative, there is the possibility that the majority will be voting on the rights of minorities.

There are some safeguards. Like any other legislation, successful initiatives are subject to judicial review; but if the rights of minorities are not already spelled out in national or state constitutions, those rights could be jeopardized.

It would be a travesty were the power of the initiative used to deny civil rights in a democracy. Yet, the initiative mechanism is far too valuable to abandon. In Washington, D.C., a city council proposal gets around the conflict by preventing voters from using any initiatives and referendum procedures to change human rights laws. It may become a model for other similar ordinances.

In other areas where the power of the initiative may be abused, traditional election reform is often the model for corrective practices.

For example, one of the original purposes of the initiative was to make it harder for well-monied groups to influence laws. Like the referendum, the initiative was supposed to discover the will of the people.

But as initiative use grew more frequent, it became apparent that money played a role in determining the outcome of initiative votes, just as it influenced other political contests. To the consternation of some, a 1978 Supreme Court ruling entitles corporations to spend as much money as they please to influence the outcome of initiatives.

But how to explain the 1976 Maine "bottle bill" or "Ban the can" initiative to require deposits on most beverage cans or bottles? Corporate opponents of the Maine bill outspent proponents thirty to one. But the bill passed by a three-to-one margin. In Massachusetts, labor and business interests opposed a similar bill and won—but by a meager half of 1 percent, although they spent $2 million on the campaign versus $10,000 on the other side.

I think the answer is this: When people really care about an issue, it doesn't matter how much is spent to influence their vote; they will go with their beliefs. When an issue is inconsequential to the voters, buying their vote is a snap.

Of course, advertisers, business interests, and politicians have worked together on numerous initiative campaigns, dipping into the whole bag of market research and advertising techniques. And business is winning many initiative votes. In Colorado, business interests campaigned against ballot initiatives on nuclear safety, throwaway beverage containers, establishment of a public advocate's office in the public utility commission, and other measures. They outspent proponents by huge amounts and they won.

Although I maintain that it occurred because people really didn't care that much, it is also clear that business's wins will provoke reexamination of initiative and referenda campaign practices and bring more cries for reform.

In the final analysis, initiatives, referenda, and recalls offer a tremendous safeguard in a democracy by enabling any aggrieved citizen or group to bypass the established representative system and submit a proposal to all citizens.

The high voter turnout (20 percent higher in states with initiatives than in states without them), which referenda and initiative produce, already justifies their existence. Yet there is another, stronger argument in favor of the participatory approach. Citizen initiatives frequently tackle the tough sensitive issues that legislators avoid to protect their popularity. Citizens do not. After all, the electorate need not concern itself with staying in office; it must only live with the results of its own decisions.

Participatory democracy, however, is not greeted enthusiastically in every quarter. Its detractors call it too radical and argue that representative democracy is safer because we ordinary people do not know enough to make decisions about complicated public policy issues. The voters will probably fall too easily for tricky, simplistic television advertising blitzes during the final week before an election, critics argue. If democracy has problems, we should improve representative democracy, they say, specifically, by electing better officials. But the visions of mob rule have remained simply visions. Most political scientists agree that referenda and initiatives have demonstrated, if anything, that voters are inherently conservative. The fear of radicalism is simply not justified.

The stand one takes on referenda and initiative depends on whether one is willing to trust the people. My Jeffersonian tendencies urge me to do that, provided civil and minority rights are safeguarded in the process.

---

7 | *Pitfalls of Direct Democracy*
Daniel A. Smith

This political scientist warns that all is neither new nor rosy when it comes to direct democracy. Ballot initiatives and referenda are more saturated with special-interest money than candidate races. It is even difficult in many cases to tell whose money is behind a given ballot question. Furthermore, there tends to be little public discussion of these referenda, and the ballot questions are often poorly worded, little publicized, and opposed in court afterward. Is direct democracy really purer and more democratic than representative democracy?

Direct democracy, a plebicitary process by which citizens make public policy on election day, grew out of the doctrines put forth by the Populist (People's) Party in the late 19th century. Two mechanisms—the initiative and the popular referendum—were highly prized by Progressive reformers in the early 1900s as instruments that could return government back to the people. Between 1898 and 1918, nearly two dozen states adopted either or both the popular referendum and the initiative. With the popular referendum, citizens are able to challenge laws passed by state legislatures by placing the measures to a popular vote; with the initiative, citizens and groups are able to propose laws and constitutional amendments that are then put up to a popular vote. In order to qualify initiatives or popular referendums for the ballot, citizens are required to collect a specified number of valid signatures for statutory measures or constitutional amendments, typically five to ten percent of the previous vote for a statewide office, such as Governor. While the popular referendum is rarely used in states today, the so-called "citizen" initiative has experienced a recent renaissance in the 24 states that permit the process.

Across the country, citizens in the two dozen states currently permitting the initiative are increasingly serving as election-day lawmakers. Ballot propositions have become an increasingly popular means of shifting decisions to voters that were once the exclusive province of legislatures. In recent years, citizens have voted on issues as varied as gambling, taxation and spending limits, education, welfare and environmental reforms, health, affirmative action, immigration, medical marijuana, term limits, abortion restrictions, gun control, growth controls, bans on mining, and bilingual education. The total number of statewide initiatives on the ballot has increased dramatically, with over 300 initiatives making it on the ballot in the 1990s. During the last decade of the 20th century, Californians cast their votes on more than 60 initiatives. In 1998 alone, voters in nearly 20 states considered 60 statewide initiatives. In the general election, citizens in Arizona cast their votes on 14 initiatives and referendums. Several other states—including Oregon, Florida, California, Colorado, and Nevada—had at least 10 statewide measures on their ballots.

Since its inception, the practice of direct democracy has garnered its share of defenders as well as critics. Progressive Era advocates of the procedural devices argued that referenda served as institutional checks on unresponsive state legislatures which were often under the thumb of corrosive special interests and party bosses. As political scientist Delos Wilcox wrote in 1912, the "pure" and unmediated procedures would incite "a great forward movement toward stability, justice, and public

spirit in American political institutions." Proponents argued that by serving as election-day legislators, "the people" could break the special interests' political stranglehold of state legislatures. Citing the clout of the California-based Southern Pacific Railroad and other corporate monopolies that often dominated state legislatures at the turn of the century, sympathetic observers contended that citizens could use the initiative and popular referendum to fight these vested interests.

Progressive Era critics of the process, who are frequently overlooked today, were not so sanguine about the process. Most scholarly observers of that epoch focused on the subject matters of measures on the ballot and tended not to detail how nascent initiative and referendum campaigns were actually conducted or the political and economic motivations of the financial supporters and opponents of the early measures. Yet special interests—namely railroads, utilities, mining operators, fishermen, school teachers, and even morticians—used the initiative and referendum during the alleged "Golden Age" of direct legislation. In many states, proponents and opponents during the formative years of direct democracy employed legal talent to draft petitions and paid solicitors to circulate petitions. In California, prior to the initiative process becoming centralized and industrialized, proponents and opponents spent over $1 million on seven measures on the 1922 ballot. In one ballot campaign alone—the Pacific Gas and Electric Company's effort to defeat the Water and Power Act—proponents and opponents spent over $660,000. In Colorado, proponents of initiatives were paying circulators upwards of 3 cents per name by 1926. While many ballot campaigns were indeed citizen-driven and "populist" during this early period, most were not as "amateur" and "grassroots" as the mythic narrative of direct democracy would suggest.

Today, direct democracy continues to flourish in most of the states that allow the procedural mechanism. It is clear that special interests have not relinquished their hold on state legislatures. Far from eliminating special interest money from the political process, special interests are increasingly utilizing the initiative to indirectly set the legislative agenda and pass legislation and even constitutional amendments. Indeed, ballot initiatives are no less susceptible to the influence of money than the representative system of government. This is not to say that money can outright "buy" ballot measure elections: average citizens still have some success using the initiative process to alter public policy in 24 states, and initiatives financed primarily by narrow economic interests have less than a 50% success rate. Nevertheless, wealthy, organized interests are able to assert their privileged position through the initiative process with relative ease, and certainly determine what measures qualify for the ballot.

It is likely that money will continue to dominate the initiative process in the future. Unlike candidate races in many of states, there are no restrictions on contributions or expenditures for ballot measure elections. This was not always the case. Prior to the 1970s, over half of the states that allowed direct democracy regulated the campaign finances of the groups that promoted and fought initiatives and referendums. Beginning with the Supreme Court's landmark 1976 decision, *Buckley v. Valeo,* and its subsequent 1978 ruling, *First National Bank of Boston v. Bellotti,* the Court has ruled out any form of campaign finance restrictions in ballot measure campaigns. In *Bellotti,* the Court struck down any campaign finance limits of ballot measure campaigns, ruling that there was no risk of *quid pro quo* corruption in issue campaigns. While several scholars since the *Bellotti* decision have shown that corporate spending does have a significant impact on ballot outcomes, the Court is unlikely to reverse its decision on First Amendment, specifically free speech, grounds.

While special interests have spent sizeable amounts of money on initiatives since the turn of the 20th century, the level of spending only increased after the Court's decisions. In 1998, issue committees across the country spent nearly $400 million promoting and opposing measures on the ballots in 44 states.

In comparison, the national Republican and Democratic parties raised *only* $193 million in "soft money" during the 1997–98 election cycle, and congressional committees raised another $92 million in "soft money" contributions. In California, spending on 1998 ballot measures broke several state campaign expenditure records. The $250 million spent on ballot measures broke the previous all-time state record of $141 million, set in 1996. Indian tribes spent over $63 million for their successful November 1998 ballot initiative, Proposition 5, which allowed the tribes to operate casinos on their reservations. Casino operators based in Nevada and organized labor opposed the measure, spending $25.4 million in their unsuccessful effort to defeat it. In addition, utility companies spent $38.1 million in their bid to defeat Proposition 9, a measure that would have deregulated the electric utility industry, and tobacco companies smoked $29.7 million (including more than $20 million from Phillip Morris) from their corporate coffers in their failed attempt to defeat Proposition 10, which raised taxes on cigarettes by 50 cents a pack to pay for early childhood education and health programs. In Florida, tax crusader David Biddulph, who drove around the state during his 1996 tax limitation campaign in a Winnebago plastered with tax cut slogans, claimed that his 1996 tax limitation initiative was "a healthy dose of democracy to put a check on runaway government." Although he asserted that the average contribution to his campaign was $18, Biddulph's Tax Cap Committee was principally bankrolled by Florida's powerful sugar industry; over a three year period, Biddulph raised more than $4.7 million dollars; $3.5 million of the total, roughly 75 percent, was contributed by sugar companies.

Smaller states too have witnessed a dramatic rise in spending on initiatives during the late 1980s and 1990s. In Colorado, for example, spending on ballot initiatives increased more than three-fold in the 1990s compared to the 1980s, rising to $29.8 million versus $9.2 million. Over $11 million was spent on eight ballot campaigns in 1998 in Colorado, nearly doubling the total spending on all statewide races, including the race for governor. In Montana in 1996, opponents of Initiative 122, a measure which would have required tougher water treatment standards in mine operations, spent nearly $9 per vote to defeat the measure. In Massachusetts, the backers of Question 2, the 1998 "clean money" and public financing measure, spent close to $1 million promoting their measure. In Washington, more than $5.6 million was spent in 1998 by the proponents and opponents of five ballot initiatives, and in Nebraska, AT&T spent $5.3 million in its successful campaign to defeat a single 1998 initiative that would have lowered long-distance access charges.

The direct impact of spending on ballot incomes is fairly clear. Without money, groups backing or opposing ballot measures are almost by definition excluded from the game. Furthermore, disproportionate spending by opponents of ballot measures is quite effective in defeating ballot measures, but not that helpful in getting measures passed. Since 1976, Colorado voters have passed one third of the 60 initiatives on the ballot. Of the seven initiatives where opponents outspent proponents by $500,000 or more, they defeated every single one. When opponents outspent proponents by $200,000 or more, they defeated 14 out of 17 initiatives. When opponents outspent proponents by *any amount,* they defeated 22 out of 28 initiatives—a 79 percent success rate. In 1994, backers of a measure that would have raised sale taxes on tobacco products raised $200,000 to promote their measure; opponents, specifically tobacco companies, spent $8 million to defeat the measure. Piling money on to pass initiatives, however, did not fair nearly as well. Proponents in Colorado who outspent opponents won only 14 out of 30 initiatives, a rate of 49 percent. Proponents who outspent opponents by $200,000 or more won only 4 out of 12 initiatives.

Besides the role of money in the initiative process, critics point to several other problems with direct democracy. Frequently, it is difficult to ascertain who is behind ballot measures. While voters certainly have the cognitive abilities to make rational decisions on ballot measures, it is not always easy for them to find out which vested interests are behind the measures. Cue taking, as a result, becomes a difficult task for voters. On most ballot questions, there is surprisingly little substantive debate that precedes an election. Initiative campaigns are often debated through the media, which tends to reduce complex debates over public policy to shallow, sound-bite posturing. There is no chance for iterative policymaking. Those measures that are successful on election day are often poorly worded and are difficult to implement and coordinate with other statutes or amendments. Subsequent litigation slows the implementation of public policies drives up the costs to the state that has to defend successful measures. It is even conceivable that the initiative process absolves legislatures from having to act. Rather than responding to the threat of ballot initiatives, state legislatures in initiative states can defer to "the people" to place a controversial issue to a popular vote. Finally, and most importantly, direct democracy procedurally foregoes the rights of the minority via the "winner-take-all" system of voting on ballot questions. As founder James Madison warned over 200 years ago, plebicitary decision-making can lead to majority tyranny by allowing the will of a majority (or minority) interest to run roughshod over the views of the community.

As journalist Peter Schrag warns, the initiative in California "has not just been integrated into the regular governmental-political system, but has begun to replace it." While this may not perfectly reflect the condition of other states with direct democracy, celebrants of the process see the process as springing from the only legitimate fountain of authority—the people. Nearly a century after it was first adopted, advocates of direct democracy still contend that it is a purer form of democracy than legislative governance, as voters are the ones directly deciding the fiscal authority of their state and local governments. But is direct democracy, and specifically the initiative, really a more democratic process than representative government? Many ballot initiatives are not emanating from "the people," but from the same special interests that critics of representative democracy so vociferously decry. Somehow, though, the American public has convinced itself that voting directly on ballot questions is more democratic than allowing its elected officials to make public policy. The cautionary words of political scientist E.E. Schattschneider ring truer today than ever: "The power of the people in a democracy depends on the importance of the decisions made by the electorate, not on the number of decisions they make."

CHAPTER TWO

Political Culture and Ideology

The Air We Breathe

OVERVIEW AND SUMMARIES

Embedded in every polity are beliefs, ideals, and just plain folk wisdom. These beliefs and ideals—when they are widely shared—subtly determine the boundaries of public debate: They shape peoples' views of public issues, they limit the acceptable solutions to public problems, and they guide people in their judgment of politicians and current events.

Many people may be unaware of the sources of these cultural beliefs, or are unable to defend them. They may not see what connection these beliefs have to the political behavior of themselves, their neighbors, or their representatives in Congress. Nonetheless, any serious political discussion or policy debate—whether about abortion, tax policy, or public education—is premised on some set of principles. These "givens" may include notions of equality, individual free choice, or the limits of governmental intervention in economic life. But whatever they may be, such ideas structure the policy debate, limiting or permitting a range of acceptable alternatives, and thus shape the outcome of any conflict. The principles of the American political culture exercise an enormous influence on the behavior of both government and individuals.

Ideology and Culture

Americans are said to be the philosophical stepchildren of **John Locke**, the seventeenth-century English philosopher who was so greatly admired by America's political founders. But like many children, we may not know our parents well at all. In fact, we may be unconscious of our intellectual heritage and the source of many of our ideals. The average person may never have heard of John Locke, though he or she would surely be familiar with many of Locke's ideas.

Locke's writings amount to an ideology that is widely embraced by Americans. But these same Americans may be unaware that other ideologies are available to which they can compare their own. They may simply refer to their own beliefs as "Americanism" or the "American way of life." In this way Locke's ideology, also known as *classical liberalism,* has clearly embedded itself in the American political culture.

So what is the difference between ideology and culture? *A political ideology is a systematic and internally consistent set of ideals that are meant to explain how governments should be run, by what standards government should be judged, and how people should behave.* Thus an ideology can be written down; its propositions can be examined; it can be taught in schools and publicly debated; and it can be embraced, criticized, or ignored. Locke's ideology was widely embraced by America's political philosophers, intellectuals, and practical politicians.

Political culture, not unlike ideology, *is a set of beliefs and understandings of the practical world.* But unlike ideology, the elements of a political culture are not necessarily consistent, are often unspoken, and are frequently unnoticed by a people who nevertheless universally adhere to its beliefs and perceptions. Whereas an ideology can be held at arm's length and examined, a culture envelops a people like the air they breathe and shapes the boundaries of their political existence although they are usually completely unaware of its effects.

Easily recognizable to Americans are the central tenets of classical liberalism, which are embedded in the American political culture: (1) *Individuals have natural rights,* which are inherent and precede the framing of any government; (2) *government is a social contract,* which is expressly or tacitly made by the people under that government; (3) the public good includes maximizing *the liberty of individuals*; (4) *property defines and protects individuals* and must therefore be protected by government; (5) no individual is inherently superior to any other, and therefore all people should have *equality under the law*; and (6) any individual should be free to conduct one's life as one sees fit so long as one does not encroach on the liberty of any other individual. You can see for yourself that these ideas are expressed in part or in full in two of the earliest and most of American documents: the Mayflower Compact and the Declaration of Independence (Appendix I).

The Mayflower Compact, written aboard the *Mayflower* in 1620 before its landing at Plymouth Rock, implies that government is necessary, the form of government is by mutual consent; laws apply equally to the members of the community; and there is a general good for which the government should act. The Declaration of Independence also reflects the values of individual liberty, equality under the law, the right to property, and government by collective consent. Indeed, the Declaration is primarily an enumeration of the many ways in which the British Crown had broken the contract between the government and the people.

A Mass of Contradictions

It was Alexis de Tocqueville, an aristocratic visitor to the United States, who pointed out in his now famous book, *Democracy in America,* how thoroughly the liberal ideology had infused the American political culture. Tocqueville was amazed that in America "all, from the beginning seemed destined to let freedom grow," and he expressed shock at this "vast multitude of people with roughly the same ideas about religion, history, science, political economy, legislation, and government." He admired how "a man who is not today one of the majority party may be so tomorrow" but claimed that in no other country is there "less independence of mind and true freedom of discussion than in America."

What explains Tocqueville's paradoxical observations? Perhaps it is that the United States never had any ideology to compete with classical liberalism. The ideology and the settlers arrived on America's shores at the same time. This belief system became as much a part of the North American landscape as wilderness, farms, and industry. Thus, the political scientist **Louis Hartz** concluded that the doctrine of classical "liberalism is a stranger in the land of its greatest realization and fulfillment."

Indeed, the use of the word *liberal* in present-day parlance has little or nothing to do with Locke's philosophy or with classical liberalism. In the spectrum of American public debate, we use the terms *liberal* and *conservative* to describe people who, almost without exception, would accept all the ideas of classical liberalism. In the classic sense of the word, all Americans are "liberal" and there has been no ideology that has seriously challenged Locke's ideas. America's so-called conservatives and liberals in fact all tend to appeal to the same Lockean values when they justify their policy positions. Public debate is usually concerned with the interpretation and application of those values or with competing values within the same ideology.

This does not mean that public debate is unimportant or frivolous, although some of it may be just that. It may be that since political debate is often not concerned with ideology but rather with a few difficult and sometimes complicated policy choices, voters prefer to focus on candidates' appearance, gaffes, sex life, and demeanor. But sometimes policy debates imply different views of the relative weight of one Lockean value to another. Tax policy, for example, implies a relative weighting of the sanctity of private property against the value of political equality. Debate over health-care reform may imply a relative weighting of personal liberty or the right to property against an inherent right to life. A debate over abortion pivots on a definition of individual rights that is different for each participant in the debate.

If public policy always implies a weighting of one Lockean value over another, then society sometimes leans in one direction or another, and as the weighting shifts the lines of public debate are slightly redrawn. For example, equality and the sanctity of private property were perhaps bound to come into conflict in a society that extolls the virtues of both and sometimes, if not often, suggests that equality means a fair chance of accumulating property—an equal right to be rich. But as long as private wealth is protected, clearly not everyone will be rich at any one moment, and some will exist in a state of privation. So, how much does private wealth make people unequal in the exercise of their public rights?

Does private wealth contribute to the public welfare by decentralizing influence, or does it hurt the public welfare by concentrating influence in the hands of a few? And what of the existence of a de facto class system? Do people have the opportunity to achieve class mobility? Or is the pursuit of happiness through the acquisition of money an illusory goal that merely preoccupies the masses without giving them any real power?

Many elite theorists stand ready to debunk the notion of a classless society in America. A professor and author of several texts on American government, **Edward S. Greenberg**, for one, has carried his class analysis to a radical conclusion, asserting that the ideology of classic liberalism is little more than propaganda, which reinforces an unequal distribution of property and power. Greenberg claims that we merely hold out the promise of individual liberty, and only a few really exercise it; we hold out the promise of equality under the law, even though some people have legal advantages; we protect property so that a few people can benefit greatly; and, in sum, we merely throw the crumbs of liberty and equality to the masses.

Divided We Stand?

Nearly all the classic commentators agree that Americans share roots in a common ideology, so why does it seem to contemporary pundits that we are so divided? In a speech delivered at the 1992 Republican National Convention, speechwriter-turned-columnist-turned-presidential candidate **Patrick Buchanan** stated flatly that American society was in the throes of a "cultural war," a fundamental disagreement over the most basic questions of morality. And even many who disagree with Buchanan's views have concluded that American political debate is in a crisis that can no longer be glossed over by an appeal to Lockean values. Issues of abortion or homosexuality, the public practice of religion, or even patriotism have become the battleground of these cultural warriors. On these issues there seems to be no room for compromise. The public debate is polarized. But why?

James Madison might claim that there is simply no end to disputes (see *Federalist* No. 10). **W. King Mott** reminds us also that Madison did not seek a perfect outcome in public debates. Rather, Madison and his Lockean colleagues wanted a system under which individual liberty might be maximized. Thus, Mott suggests that the cultural divide is as much a problem of *how* we argue as of *what* we argue.

For Mott, how we argue is not a question of mere style but a question of what we are willing to tolerate in other people's views and in other people's personal behavior. According to Mott, the warriors on all sides are too frequently tempted to call into question the legitimacy of the whole constitutional system when they don't get their way. The system, however, is one in which arguments are supposed to take place—whether or not we share the same philosophical stepparents—and one in which no debate is permanently resolved but can always be reopened.

8 | *Government as a Contract*
John Locke

The English philosopher John Locke is among the founders of the Age of Reason and perhaps merits the title of Philosopher of the American Revolution. His most famous work, Two Treatises of Government, *was published in 1690 and greatly admired by many of those who, almost a century later, wrote the Declaration of Independence and the Constitution. Locke argued that individuals possessed natural rights—including liberty, security of property, and equal treatment by the law—and formed governments to protect them.*

To understand political power aright, we must consider what estate all men are naturally in, and that is, a state of perfect freedom to order their actions, and dispose of their possessions and persons as they think fit without asking leave or depending upon the will of any other man. A state also of equality, wherein all the power is reciprocal, no one having more than another, there being nothing more evident than that creatures of the same species and rank, born to all the same advantages of nature, should also be equal one amongst another.

But though this be a state of liberty, yet it is not a state of license. The state of nature has a law which obliges everyone, and reason, which is that law, teaches all mankind that being all equal and independent, no one ought to harm another in his life, health, liberty, or possessions; for men being all the workmanship of one omnipotent and infinitely wise Maker; all the servants of one Master, sent into the world by His order and about His business; they are His property, whose workmanship they are made to last during His, not one another's pleasure. Every one as he is bound to preserve himself, so by like reason, ought as much as he can to preserve the rest of mankind, and not impair the life, the liberty, health, limb, or goods of another.

The liberty of man in society is to be under no other legislative power but that established by consent in the commonwealth. Freedom then is not: "A liberty for every one to do what he lists, to live as he pleases, and not to be tied by any laws"; but freedom of men under government is to have a standing rule to live by, common to every one of that society, and made by the legislative power erected in it. This freedom from absolute, arbitrary power is so necessary to a man's preservation that he cannot part with it but by what forfeits his preservation and life altogether.

God, who hath given the world to men in common, hath also given them reason to make use of it to the best advantage of life and convenience. Though the earth and all creatures be common to all men, yet every man has a "property" in his own "person." The "labor" of his body and the "work" of his hands are properly his. Whatsoever he removes out of the state that Nature hath left it in, he hath mixed his labor with it and thereby makes it his property. Though the water running in the fountain be everyone's, who can doubt that in the pitcher is his only who drew it out? Thus, this law of reason makes the deer that Indian's who hath killed it.

God, when He gave the world in common to all mankind, commanded man also to labor. God and his reason commanded him to subdue the earth—*i.e.*, improve it for the benefit of life and therein lay out something upon it that was his own, his labor. Thus labor, in the beginning, gave a right of property.

Though I have said "That all men by nature are equal," I cannot be supposed to understand all sorts of "equality." Age or virtue may give some men precedence. Excellency of merit may place others above the common level: the equality which all men are in being that equal right that every man hath to his natural freedom, without being subjected to the will or authority of any other man.

The law that was to govern Adam, was the same that was to govern all his posterity, the law of reason. For law, in its true notion, is not so much the limitation as the direction of a free and intelligent agent to his proper interest, and prescribes no farther than is for the general good of those under that law. Could they be happier without it, the law would of itself vanish. So that, however it may be mistaken, the end of law is not to abolish or restrain, but to preserve and enlarge freedom. For in all the states where there is no law there is no freedom. For liberty is to be free from restraint and violence from others. For who could be free, when every other man's humor might domineer over him?

The freedom of man is grounded on his having reason which is able to instruct him in that law he is to govern himself by. To turn him loose to an unrestrained liberty, before he has reason to guide him, is not allowing him the privilege of his nature to be free, but to thrust him out amongst brutes.

Men being by nature all free, equal, and independent, no one can be subjected to the political power of another with his own consent, which is done by agreeing with other men to join and unite into a community for their comfortable, safe, and peaceable living, one amongst another, in a secure enjoyment of their properties. When any number have so consented to make one community or government, they make one body politic, wherein the majority have a right to act and conclude the rest.

For when any number have, by the consent of every individual, made a community, they have thereby made that community one body, with a power to act as one body, which is only by the will of the majority. It is necessary the body should move whither the greater force carries it, which is the majority, or else it is impossible it should act or continue one body, one community. Thus every man, by consenting with others to make one body politic under one government, puts himself under an obligation to everyone of that society to submit to the determination of the majority,

else the original compact would signify nothing.

The objection, I find, against the beginning of polities in the way I have mentioned is this: "All men," they say, "are born under government, and therefore they cannot be at liberty to begin a new one." But it is plain governments themselves, understand it otherwise. There is a tacit consent. The difficulty is how far anyone shall be looked on to have consented and submitted to government, where he has made no expressions of it at all. And to this I say that every man that has any possession or enjoyment of any part of government doth hereby give his tacit consent and is obliged to obedience to the laws of that government during such enjoyment.

If man in the state of nature be so free, if he be absolute lord of his own person and possessions, equal to the greatest and subject to nobody, why will he part with his freedom?

To which it is obvious to answer, that though in the State of nature, the enjoyment of it is very uncertain and constantly exposed to the invasion of others. This makes him will to quit this condition which, however free, is full of fears and continual dangers; and he is willing to join in society with others for the mutual preservation of their lives, liberties, and estates. The great and chief end, therefore, of uniting into commonwealth is the preservation of property; in the state of Nature there are many things wanting.

Firstly, there wants an established, known law, by common consent to be the standard of right and wrong, and the common measure to decide all controversies between them.

Secondly, in the state of Nature there wants a known and indifferent judge. For men, being partial to themselves, passion and revenge is very apt to carry them too far, and with too much heat in their own cases, make them too remiss in other men's.

Thirdly, in the state of Nature there wants power to back and support the sentence when right, and to give it due execution. And so, whoever has the power of any commonwealth, is bound to govern by established standing laws, by upright judges, and to employ the force of the community only in the execution of such laws. And all this to be directed to no other end but the peace, safety, and public good of the people.

The great end of entering into society being the enjoyment of properties in peace and safety, the first and fundamental law of commonwealths is the establishing of the legislative power. The legislative is not only the supreme power of the commonwealth, but sacred and unalterable in the hands where the community has once placed it.

Though the legislative be the supreme power in every commonwealth; yet it is not absolutely arbitrary over the lives and fortunes of the people. The legislative power is limited to the public good of the society. It is a power that hath no other end but preservation, and therefore can never have a right to destroy, enslave, or designedly to impoverish the subjects.

Secondly, the legislative or supreme authority cannot rule by arbitrary decrees, but is bound to dispense justice and decide the rights of the subject by standing laws and known authorized judges.

Thirdly, the supreme power cannot take from any man any part of his property without his consent. For I have truly no property in that which another can by right take from me when he pleases against my consent. Hence it is a mistake to think that the supreme or legislative power can do what it will.

Fourthly, the legislative cannot transfer the power of making laws to any other hands, for it being but a delegated power from the people, they who have it cannot pass it over to others. The people alone can appoint the form of the commonwealth, which is by constituting the legislative, and appointing in whose hands that shall be.

To conclude. The power that every individual gave the society when he entered into it can never revert to the individuals again but will always remain in the community. But if they have set limits to the duration of their legislative and made this power temporary; or else, when, by the miscarriages of those in authority it is forfeited, it reverts to the society, and the people have a right to act as supreme, and continue the legislative in themselves or place it in a new form, or new hands, as they think good.

9 | *The Mayflower Compact*

The Mayflower *left England in September 1620 with about 100 passengers who intended to settle permanently in Virginia. Instead they landed in Massachusetts in November and would construct their private colony there. First, however, they made a governing accord. What may leap out in a first reading of this compact is that these were pious English people, loyal to the Crown. But inspect the agreement closely and find in some of its phrases the clear echoes of Lockean notions: Government is necessary, the form of government is by mutual consent, laws apply equally to the members of the community, and there is a general good for which the government should act.*

In the name of God, Amen. We, whose names are underwritten, the Loyal Subjects of our dread Sovereign Lord, King James, by the Grace of God, of England, France and Ireland, King, Defender of the Faith, &

Having undertaken for the Glory of God, and Advancement of the Christian Faith, and the Honour of our King and Country, a voyage to plant the first colony in the northern parts of Virginia; do by these presents, solemnly and mutually in the Presence of God and one of another, covenant and combine ourselves together into a civil Body Politick, for our better Ordering and Preservation, and Furtherance of the Ends aforesaid; And by Virtue hereof to enact, constitute, and frame, such just and equal Laws, Ordinances, Acts, Constitutions and Offices, from time to time, as shall be thought most meet and convenient for the General good of the Colony; unto which we promise all due submission and obedience.

In Witness whereof we have hereunto subscribed our names at Cape Cod the eleventh of November, in the Reign of our Sovereign Lord, King James of England, France and Ireland, the eighteenth, and of Scotland the fifty-fourth. Anno Domini, 1620.

10 | *Natural Liberalism*
Louis Hartz

Professor Hartz argued in several important articles and later in his book The Liberal Tradition in America *(1956) that American politics is impossible to understand without comparing it to that of the European nations whose politics the Americans rejected. According to Hartz, the keys to understanding the American government are as follows: (1) the founding Americans could embrace Locke's liberalism because of the unique circumstances of the time and place of settlement in North America, and (2) contemporary Americans embrace Locke's philosophy without knowing who Locke is.*

There are two sides to the Lockean argument: a defense of the state that is implicit, and a limitation of the state that is explicit.

The first is to be found in Locke's basic social norm, the concept of free individuals in a state of nature. This idea untangled men from the myriad associations of class, church, guild, and place, in terms of which feudal society defined their lives; and by doing so, it automatically gave to the state a much higher rank in relation to them than ever before. The state became the only association that might legitimately coerce them at all. That is why the liberals of France in the eighteenth century were able to substitute the concept of absolutism for Locke's conclusions of limited government and to believe that they were still his disciples in the deepest sense.

When Locke came to America, however, a change appeared. Because the basic feudal oppressions of Europe had not taken root, the fundamental social norm of Locke ceased in large part to look like a norm and began, of all things, to look like a sober description of fact. The effect was significant enough. When the Americans moved from that concept to the contractual idea of organizing the state, they were not conscious of having already done anything to fortify the state, but were conscious only that they were about to limit it. One side of Locke became virtually the whole of him.

It was a remarkable thing—this inversion of perspective that made the social norms of Europe the factual premises of America. History was on a lark, out to tease men, not by shattering their dreams, but by fulfilling them with a sort of satiric accuracy. In America one not only found a society sufficiently fluid to give a touch of meaning to the individualist norms of Locke, but one also found letter-perfect replicas of the very images he used.

There was a frontier that was a veritable state of nature. There were agreements, such as the Mayflower Compact, that were veritable social contracts. There were new communities springing up *in vacuis locis,* clear evidence that men were using their Lockean right of emigration, which Jefferson soberly appealed to as "universal" in his defense of colonial land claims in 1774. A purist could argue, of course, that even these phenomena were not enough to make a reality out of the presocial men that liberalism dreamt of in theory. But surely they came as close to doing so as anything history has ever seen. Locke and Rousseau themselves could not help lapsing into the empirical mood when they looked across the Atlantic. "Thus in the beginning," Locke wrote, "all the world was America...."

Here, then, is the master assumption of American political thought, the assumption from which all of the American attitudes discussed in this essay flow: the reality of atomistic social freedom. It is instinctive to the American mind, as in a sense the concept of the polis was instinctive to Platonic Athens or the concept of the church to the mind of the middle ages. Catastrophes have not been able to destroy it, proletariats have refused to give it up, and even our Progressive tradition, in its agonized clinging to a Jeffersonian world, has helped to keep it alive.

It might be appropriate to summarize with a single word, or even with a single sentence, the political outlook that this premise has produced. But where is the word and where is the sentence one might use? American political thought, as we have seen, is a veritable maze of polar contradictions, winding in and out of each other hopelessly: pragmatism and absolutism, historicism and rationalism, optimism and pessimism, materialism and idealism, individualism and conformism. But, after all, the human mind works by polar contradictions; and when we have evolved an interpretation of it which leads cleanly in a single direction, we may be sure that we have missed a lot. The task of the cultural analyst is not to discover simplicity, or even to discover unity, for simplicity and unity do not exist, but to drive a wedge of rationality through the pathetic indecisions of social thought. In the American case that wedge is not hard to find. It is not hidden in an obscure place. We find it in what the West as a whole has always recognized to be the distinctive element in American civilization: its social freedom, its social equality. And yet it is true, for all of our Jeffersonian nationalism, that the interpretation of American political thought has not been built around this idea. On the contrary, instead of interpreting the American revolution in terms of American freedom, we have interpreted it in terms of American oppression, and instead of studying the nineteenth century in terms of American equality, we have studied it in terms of a series of cosmic Beardian and Parringtonian struggles against class exploitation. We have missed what the rest of the world has seen and what we ourselves have seen whenever we have contrasted the New World with the Old.

The liberals of Europe in 1776 were obviously worshipping a very peculiar hero. If the average American had been suddenly thrust in their midst, he would have been embarrassed by the millennial enthusiasms that many of them had, would have found their talk of classes vastly overdone, and would have reacted to the Enlightenment synthesis of absolutism and liberty as if it were little short of dishonest doubletalk. Bred in a freer world, he had a different set of perspectives, was animated by a different set of passions, and looked forward to different goals.

But someone will ask, where did the liberal heritage of the Americans come from in the first place? Didn't they have to create it? And if they did, were they not at one time or another in much the same position as the Europeans?

These questions drive us back to the ultimate nature of the American experience, and, doing so, confront us with a queer twist in the problem of revolution. No one can deny that conscious purpose went into the making of the colonial world, and that the men of the seventeenth century who fled America from Europe were keenly aware of the oppressions of European life. But they were revolutionaries with a difference, and the fact of their fleeing is no minor fact: for it is one thing to stay at home and fight the "canon and feudal law," and it is another to leave it far behind. It is one thing to try to establish liberalism in the Old World, and it is another to establish it in the New. Revolution, to borrow the words of T. S. Eliot, means to murder and create, but the American experience has been projected strangely in the realm of creation alone. The destruction of forests and Indian tribes—heroic, bloody, legendary as it was—cannot be compared with the destruction of a social order to which one belongs oneself. The first experience is wholly external and, being external, can actually be completed; the second experience is an inner struggle as well as an outer struggle, like the slaying of a Freudian father, and goes on in a sense forever. Moreover, even the matter of creation is not in the American case a simple one. The New World, as Lord Baltimore's ill-fated experiment with feudalism in the seventeenth century illustrates, did not merely offer the Americans a virgin ground for the building of a liberal system; it conspired to help that system along. The abundance of land in America, as well as the need for a lure to settlers, entered so subtly into the shaping of America's liberal tradition, touched it so completely at every point, that Sumner was actually ready to say, "We have not made America, America has made us."

It is this business of destruction and creation which goes to the heart of the problem. For the point of departure of great revolutionary thought everywhere else in the world has been the effort to build a new society on the ruins of an old society, and this is an experience America has never had. Tocqueville saw the issue clearly.... "The great advantage of the American is that he has arrived at a state of democracy without having to endure a democratic revolution; *and that he is born free without having to become so.*

Born free without having to become so: this idea raises an obvious question. Can a people that is born free ever understand peoples elsewhere that have to become so? Can it ever lead them? Or to turn the issue around, can peoples struggling for a goal understand those who have inherited it.

11 | *The Gettysburg Address*
Abraham Lincoln

Given November 19, 1863, President Lincoln's speech was constructed as a classical funeral elegy but was much more powerful because of its brevity. To what date and event does Lincoln refer in the opening line? Indeed, Lincoln brought the Declaration of Independence into the popular conscience, and he shows that the Constitution does not stand alone as a contractual document but that Americans—Lockeans at the core—interpret the Constitution through the ideals of the Declaration.

Fourscore and seven years ago our fathers brought forth on this continent a new nation, conceived in liberty and dedicated to the proposition that all men are created equal. Now we are engaged in a great civil war, testing whether that nation or any nation so conceived and so dedicated can long endure. We are met on a great battlefield of that war. We have come to dedicate a portion of that field as a final resting-place for those who here gave their lives that that nation might live. It is altogether fitting and proper that we should do this. But in a larger sense, we cannot dedicate, we cannot consecrate, we cannot hallow this ground. The brave men, living and dead who struggled here have consecrated it far above our poor power to add or detract. The world will little note nor long remember what we say here, but it can never forget what they did here. It is for us the living rather to be dedicated here to the unfinished work which they who fought here have thus far so nobly advanced. It is rather for us to be here dedicated to the great task remaining before us— that from these honored dead we take increased devotion to that cause for which they gave the last full measure of devotion— that we here highly resolve that these dead shall not have died in vain, that this nation under God shall have a new birth of freedom, and that government of the people, by the people, for the people shall not perish from the earth.

12 | *Liberal Culture and Capitalist Society*
Edward S. Greenberg

Edward Greenberg argues in his textbooks that the dominant ideology of classic liberalism, which permeates American political behavior, is little more than cover for an elite political system based on the control of capital. Greenberg claims, in particular, that the Lockean emphasis on individualism and property gives people the illusion of control over their lives, whereas in fact control of the system is exercised by the corporate decisionmakers and government officials who act on behalf of corporate America.

One of the curious things about liberalism is the evolving divergence between its original theory and actual social reality. The contemporary United States hardly conforms to the Lockean world of small property holders, limited government, and open opportunity. On the contrary, it is a society of giant corporations, bureaucratized and centralized government, wage and salary earners, and limited social mobility. The correspondence between the dominant set of ideas and social reality seems increasingly tenuous.

The question then arises: if liberalism no longer helps citizens make sense of their world, why does it remain the repository for the dominant ideas in our political culture? While some would probably suggest *cultural lag* as an answer—that is, the long lead time required for ideas to change—I would suggest another: liberal ideas are consciously taught and reinforced, through the institutions of socialization, because liberal ideas support and sustain capitalism and those who control and most benefit from it.

In capitalist society, individualist values are dominant, not communal ones. Likewise, in contemporary socialist societies, individualistic values rank lower than collective ones. This fusion of culture and social structure is never left to chance. The dominant class or group in every society attempts to ensure that appropriate values, norms, and behaviors are taught to the population in general. In most societies, this is done through the main institutions of socialization—religion, education, and communications. The United States is no exception, for schools, churches, and the mass media continually bombard the American people with the tenets of liberal culture. Seen in this light, liberalism is neither "natural" nor "inevitable." It is carefully nurtured.

I would suggest that liberalism constitutes a major prop of the modern capitalist order. Liberalism helps to maintain the legitimacy of private business decision making. Contemporary capitalism is a system in which a handful of people occupying positions of industrial and financial power in the nation's corporations make decisions producing effects far beyond the walls of their particular enterprises. To the extent that liberalism encourages a respect for private property and a general hostility to government intervention in the affairs of private enterprise, it leaves the leaders of these dominant economic institutions free to act in their own interest.... The most important function that liberalism serves here is to establish an artificial separation between politics and economics, to buttress the claim that government has no business in economics (except when it can be of use to the corporation).

Capitalism cannot survive without selling an ever-expanding volume of goods and services. It must expand or wither: there are no alternatives. A steady-state, no growth capitalism is an entity that no one has yet seen and from which no credible theory has been advanced. No growth or diminishing rates of growth in the economy are always occasions for public expressions of worry by political leaders and government economists.

It is with respect to this recurrent problem of capitalist production that liberalism plays its supportive role. Liberalism, let us recall, emphasizes the values of individualism, competition, and striving toward success. At one time, these values helped a vigorous people tame a vast continent. In the modern era, however, in a world of giant bureaucratic organization, economic power concentrated in corporations, and the disappearance of cheap and plentiful land, liberal values can find few such outlets for their expression. The United States is no longer a place in which every person can aspire to be rich or to be president (if that were ever the case).

But one place remaining for Americans to express their individuality, their desire to better themselves and to prevail over their fellows, is in the realm of consumption. The individualistic energy of liberal society which once expressed itself in entrepreneurship is now redirected into the prodigious consumption of goods and services.

Liberalism undermines, in advance, collective definitions of problems and their collective solution by the American people. Although it may be reasonably argued that people are poor because they happen to have the wrong skill, or live in the wrong area, or to have been born the wrong sex or race, by and large people become unemployed because of the uncertainties of private investment and resultant fluctuations in the business cycle. Most economic problems that people suffer lie outside themselves. There is not much they personally can do about them. The most powerful function that liberalism performs for capitalism is to prevent people from realizing this. A people imbued with liberal values will not as a rule see their own situation as derived from the operations of the economy as a whole; rather, they will blame themselves. Such an outcome is useful for the overall system, since it shifts analysis of problems from criticism of dominant groups and institutions to criticism of self.

Given the pre-eminence of classical liberal ideas and values, moreover, it is inescapably the case that certain understandings of social justice and democracy have come to prevail in the United States. Given a society where values of individualism prevail over values of community, and where private interests take precedence over the public interest, moreover, it is hardly surprising that the direct, participatory form of democracy is not much in evidence. Such a culture strongly favors the indirect, representative form, where the ordinary citizen need not take undue time and attention from private pursuits in order to participate in the political process, as well as the pluralism form, where private interests are advanced in the formulation of public policy through the conflict, bargaining and agreement of interest groups.

Divided We Stand: How Deep Do Our Differences Run?

13 | *The Cultural War for the Soul of America*
Patrick J. Buchanan

A noted speech writer in the Nixon administration, a veteran commentator on national politics, a candidate for the Republican presidential nomination in 1992 and 1996, and the nominee of the Reform Party in 2000, Patrick Buchanan has long argued that there is a serious ideological rift in the United States. The central question around which the two sides gather in this culture war is "who are we and what do we believe?" This speech was offered by Buchanan in response to criticisms of him by Mario Cuomo, then the Democratic governor of New York.

As polarized as we have ever been, we Americans are locked in a cultural war for the soul of our country.

What is it all about? As columnist Sam Francis writes, it is about power; it is about who determines "the norms by which we live, and by which we define and govern ourselves." Who decides what is right and wrong, moral and immoral, beautiful and ugly, healthy and sick? Whose beliefs shall form the basis of law?

At Houston [site of the 1992 Republican Convention], William Rusher writes America heard "the first rumbles of a new storm ... fast approaching the American political arena, [a storm] that will quickly replace the old battles over the conduct of the cold war." Indeed, the storm has already hit the coast.

The Bosnia of the cultural war is abortion.

The Republican Party, in platform and ticket, is "pro-life." I.e. we hold abortion to be the unjust killing of a pre-born child. Bill Clinton's party rejoices in *Roe v. Wade.* To the one side, the 25 million abortions in 20 years are a testament to freedom and progress; to the other, they are the benchmark of a society literally hellbent on suicide. The conflicting positions can no more be reconciled than those of John Brown and John Calhoun.

Whose side is God on? In an angry letter to President Bush, the National Council of Churches wrote: "We need to be very clear that God belongs to no one side, for we believe all belong to God." Mr. Bush's effort to conscript Him, they wrote, is "blasphemous."

But was it blasphemous to enlist Him at Selma Bridge? Is the Creator truly neutral in the unequal struggle between his tiniest creatures and the abortionist with a knife and suction pump?

To those gathered at Madison Square Garden, a man's "sexual preference" and sexual conduct, so long as it is consensual, is irrelevant to moral character. To most of us in Houston, however, it is the codification of amorality to elevate gay liaisons to the same moral and legal plane as traditional marriage.

Americans are a tolerant people. But a majority believes that the sexual practices of gays, whether a result of nature or nurture, are both morally wrong and medically ruinous. Many consider this "reactionary" or "homophobic." But our beliefs are rooted in the Old and New Testament, in natural law and tradition, even in the writing of that paragon of the Enlightenment, Thomas Jefferson (who felt homosexuality should be punished as severely as rape).

Thirty years ago, both sides in today's cultural war shared the belief that homosexuals, be they 2 or 10 percent of the population, had the same constitutional rights as the rest of us, as well as a right to be let alone. We still do. Homosexuality was not an issue then. What makes it an issue now is the non-negotiable demand that this "lifestyle" be sanctioned by law, that gays be granted equal rights to marry, adopt and serve as troop leaders in the Boy Scouts.

Let me be blunt: We can't support this. To force it upon us is like forcing Christians to burn incense to the emperor.

But the cultural war is broader than two battlegrounds.

We see it in the altered calendar of holidays we are invited—nay, instructed—to celebrate. Washington's Birthday disappears into Presidents Day. States, like Arizona, that balk at declaring Martin Luther King's birthday a holiday face political censure and convention boycotts. Easter is displaced by Earth Day, Christmas becomes Winter break, Columbus day a day to reflect on the cultural imperialism and genocidal racism of the "dead white males" who raped this continent while exterminating its noblest inhabitants.

Secularism's Holy Days of Obligation were not demanded by us; they were imposed on us. And while Gov. Cuomo may plausibly plead ignorance of the culture war, the Hard Left has always understood its criticality.

Give me the child for six years, Lenin reportedly said, quoting the Jesuits, and he will be a Marxist forever. J. V. Stalin, who was partial to Chicago gangster films, thought that if only he had control of Hollywood, he could control the world.

Too many conservatives, writes art critic James Cooper, "never read Mao Tse Tung on waging cultural war against the West. [Mao's] essays were prescribed reading for the Herbert Marcuse-generation of the 1960's, who now run our cultural institutions.... Conservatives were oblivious to the fact that modern art—long ago separated from the idealism of Monet, Degas, Cezanne, and Rodin—had become the purveyor of a destructive, degenerate, ugly, pornographic, Marxist, anti-American ideology." While we were off aiding the Contras, a Fifth Column inside our own country was capturing the culture.

In wartime and postwar movies, the USA was a land worth fighting for, even dying for. But the distance from "The Sands of Iwo Jima" to "Born on the Fourth of July," from "The Song of Bernadette" to "The Last Temptation of Christ," which paints Jesus as a lustful, lying wimp, is more than four decades. Hollywood has crossed a cultural and religious divide—and left us on the other side.

In Eddie Murphy's new film, "Boomerang," every successful black has one obsession: having good sex, and lots of it. I left thinking this film could have been produced by the KKK, so thoroughly did it conform to old Klan propaganda about blacks being little more than sexual animals. From "The Cosby Show" to "Boomerang" is straight downhill; it is to travel from what is decent to what is decadent.

A sense of shame presupposes a set of standards. In the Old America, Ingrid Bergman, carrying the child of her lover, fled the country in scandal. Today, she would probably be asked to pose naked—and nine months' pregnant—on the cover of Vanity Fair.

Today, the standards are gone. Does it make a difference? Only if you believe books and plays and films and art make a difference in men's lives. Only if you believe ideas have consequences.

In *The End of Christendom*, the late Malcolm Muggeridge writes that Dostoyevsky, "in his astoundingly prophetic novel, *The Devils* ... makes his character Peter Vekovinsky ... say, 'A generation or two of debauchery followed by a little sweet bloodletting and the turmoil will begin.' So indeed it has."

Poets are the unacknowledged legislators of the world: wrote poet Shelley. Does it make a difference that school kids in LA, who never heard of Robert Frost, can recite the lyrics of Ice-T and 2 Live Crew? Ask the people of Koreatown.

Where did that LA mob come from?

It came out of the public schools from which the Bible and Ten Commandments were long ago expelled. It came out of drugstores where pornography is everywhere on the magazine rack. It came out of movie theaters and away from TV sets where sex and violence are romanticized. It came out of rock concerts where rap music extols raw lust and cop-killing. It came out of churches that long ago gave themselves up to social action, and it came out of families that never existed.

When the Rodney King verdict came down, and the rage boiled within, these young men had no answer within themselves to the question: Why not? Why not loot and burn? Why not settle accounts with the Koreans? Why not lynch somebody—and get even for Rodney King?

The secularists who have captured our culture have substituted a New Age Gospel, with its governing axioms: There are no absolute values in the universe; there are no fixed and objective standards of right and wrong. There is no God. It all begins here and ends here. Every man lives by his own moral code. Do your own thing. Well, the mob took them at their word, and it did its own thing.

"Of all the dispositions and habits which lead to prosperity," Washington said, "religion and morality are indispensable supports. In vain would that man seek the tribute of patriotism, who should labor to subvert these great pillars of human happiness."

Look at the works of "art" that ignited the controversy at the National Endowment. Almost all were desecrations of Christian images. Andreas Serrono submerged a crucifix in a vat of his own urine. Robert Mapplethorpe took a statue of the Virgin Mother of God and twisted it into a bloody tie rack.

Writing in an art catalog funded by NEA, an AIDS activist called Cardinal John O'Connor a "fat cannibal from that house of walking swastikas up on Fifth Avenue." That "house of walking swastikas" was St. Patrick's Cathedral, subsequently desecrated by militants who spat consecrated hosts on the floor at Sunday mass.

Yes, Mario, there is a connection.

The cultural war is already raging in our public schools. In history texts Benedict Arnold's treason at West Point has been dropped. So has the story of Nathan Hale, the boy-patriot who spied on the British and went to the gallows with the defiant cry, "I regret that I have but one life to give for my country." Elsewhere, they teach that our constitution was plagiarized from the Iroquois, that Western science was stolen from sub-Saharan Africa.

The name Custer has been stricken from the battlefield where his unit fell. Demands are heard throughout the South that replicas of the Battle Flag of the Confederacy be removed from state flags and public buildings. The old iron Confederate soldier who stood for decades in the town square must be removed; after all, he fought in an ignoble cause.

Slavery vs. freedom, that's what it was all about, they tell us. But go up to Gettysburg and park your car behind the union center. Look across that mile-long field and visualize 15,000 men and boys forming up at the tree line. See them walking across into the fire of cannon and gun, knowing they would never get back, never see home again. Nine of ten never even owned a slave. They were fighting for the things for which men have always fought: family, faith, friends, and country. For the ashes of their fathers and the temples of their Gods.

If a country forgets where it came from, how will its people know who they are? Will America one day become like that poor old man with Alzheimer's abandoned in the stadium, who did not know where he came from, or to what family he belonged? The battle over our schools is part of the war to separate parents from children, one generation from another, and all Americans from their heritage.

Our "common difficulties ... concern, thank God, only material things," FDR said at the nadir of the Depression. Our national quarrel goes much deeper. It is about "who we are" and "what we believe." Are we any longer "one nation under God," or has one-half already begun to secede from the other?

That, Mario, is what the cultural war is all about.

14 | The Negotiable and Non-negotiable in Our Civic Conversation

W. King Mott, Jr.

W. King Mott concludes that the "culture wars" of America stem from our confusion of privately held beliefs with the public will and the misguided identification of those beliefs with the public good. Mott believes that the culture warriors miss the founders' point: The public good consists of creating an order in which individuals have maximum liberty to practice their private beliefs, not impose them on others. And this can be achieved only through civic conversation, which requires tolerance, rather than political conversion, which requires imposition.

It is commonplace to come upon political conversations so polarized that it is impossible, in fact quite often unsafe, to engage in the discussion. The participants are not disposed towards negotiation. Ironically, inherent in the idea of conversation is the possibility for conversion. So, in this atmosphere of conversational hostility, are people who differ politically willing to change or consider their respective positions? If not, why might this be the case?

Let us acknowledge that there are single-issue political advocacy groups functioning in the American system. Often these groups promote one version of American culture—ultimately a singular notion of how the American person came to be. When different groups, motivated by unique definitions of culture, come forward to challenge one another, we have what has become known as our culture wars. In these wars Americans categorize themselves as true patriots, and the opposition as subversive malcontents. In a sense, those who position political conversation in this manner ask each of us to choose between believing in a defined culture or believing in ourselves.

This need not be the case and, in fact, it is peculiar to consider that all Americans fit into clearly defined groups. There is an alternative choice about American culture; one that recognizes that the distinction between our political choices and our private beliefs has become confused and that our Nation has never been monolithic. In conclusion, it seems that once this confusion is set right, we must return to conversation as opposed to confrontation.

Mark Gerzon in *A House Divided* presents a compelling start to this argument. Gerzon writes that "the struggle is no longer geographical, but ideological. The competition should not be between loyalty to the American nation versus loyalty to a particular state [group], but between fealty to our country and fighting for our personal beliefs." Previously personal loyalty could be attached to a region or local customs and quite often the enemy looked to be the monolithic national government. Now we have personalized the political; the contest has left the public forums where legal and institutional patterns establish methods of debate, compromise and resolution. It is now individual personal beliefs that must confront the *other*.

Consider how this idea works in our determinations of patriotism. An overwhelming number of Americans see themselves as very patriotic and, simultaneously, view most of their fellow citizens to be less than patriotic. This is possible because we all gauge loyalty independent of an objective benchmark—we each rely upon our personal beliefs to determine patriotism.

It is problematic to assume a singular perspective in defining culture or patriotism, not only now but also throughout our past. The notion of a singular American culture is a romantic one. Clearly we have experienced a dominant cultural impression, but individual impression is largely subjective. American history is full of different languages, religions and much conflict. Our past contains elements of both peaceful and warring dissent— beginning with the original settlers. The example set by Roger Williams leaving Massachusetts Bay for what would become Rhode Island in 1643 seems to have set in motion the American version of dispute resolution. Williams proved that one need only move away from the problem and found a new colony. This method worked until the frontier disappeared.

Somehow we must include prudential conversation in politics. Why is this so difficult? Partly because our *de facto* method of governing—pluralism—is almost exclusively subjective: as each interest group defines its own interest as the public interest. This subjectivity of politics adds to the confusion between public and private will. Special interest groups and contemporary political parties are inadequate purveyors of a collective intent. It is not unimportant to recognize that "industrial age pluralism" does satisfy the political demand of discerning "who gets what, when and how." The problem comes when those who lose in the allocation of resources believe that what is divided among us, however lawfully, is our very soul.

The prospect of losing what is most personal and precious calls the process that threatens this loss into question. William Greider, in *Who Will Tell the People*, writes that the "American democracy is in much deeper trouble than most people wish to acknowledge. Behind the reassuring façade, the regular election contests and so forth, the substantive meaning of self-government has been hollowed out."

Because our beliefs are made manifest in public conversation as special interest, we are personally vulnerable when the debate commences. This is where the trouble intensifies since pluralism is no longer strictly political, i.e., primarily concerned with the public interests. Compounding this confusion is the reality that many of us appear unaware of the commingling of public interest and private will. The result is a Democrat or Republican Party convention where delegates are promoting beliefs. These same delegates are confused and often violently offended when others outside their particular belief system do not understand. In fact, each opposing side will interpret the political outcome, the party platform as an example, as a personal violation and an attack upon the American body politic.

This sort of political drama is increasingly alienating and genuinely hurtful. How can a public airing of private beliefs be otherwise? The steps towards recovering a public conversation are difficult ones because they require each citizen to examine his or her private beliefs and to understand that others hold their beliefs as strongly. The conversation comes when this recognition begins to effect the sort of thing that is debated in our public forums. Legitimacy and efficacy come from a community, however diffuse, that shares a desire for the common or the public good.

In the end, a political conversation about the common good is one where the American prudential ethos dominates. The Founders were not impressed with the possibility of forming the ideal state. Perfection has always interfered with the practical. We are part of a working balance between order and liberty. It is no small thing to have a society where each can live private beliefs to the fullest within the context of a law that attends to the public good of all. Perhaps we are on our way to becoming better individuals when we keep our beliefs from public deliberation; and we are better citizens when we negotiate with what is negotiable.

CHAPTER THREE

The Constitution and Its Framers

OVERVIEW AND SUMMARIES

The Constitution of the United States is one of the world's most peculiar documents. It is peculiar for what it says and why it says it. It is peculiar because of its influence on constitutions elsewhere in the world. And it is peculiar most of all because it has continued to be the basic law of the land for over 200 years: As young as the United States is, it has the oldest, continuously functioning written constitution in the world.

But how did this document come to be written? What did the framers truly intend it to mean? Is it still a document worth the veneration it receives? These questions have no clear answers and continue to be debated with great fervor. The only fact we can count on is that there are widely differing interpretations both of what the Constitution should say and what it was intended to say.

The following readings are of three kinds. The first three authors in the chapter explicitly prescribe what kind of government is best. These include the English philosopher **James Harrington,** who lived and died in the seventeenth century but whose political ideas had great effect on the eighteenth century and beyond. Harrington is little remembered—the Constitution has come to be seen as a uniquely American document—but Harrington, like many of the framers, studied and wanted to correct the defects of political systems in Europe. In turn, Harrington's writings were closely studied by educated colonists, and he bequeathed any number of practical ideas to people he never met on a continent on which he never set foot.

The excerpt presented here is not from Harrington's most famous book, *The Commonwealth of Oceana* which is a bit too obtuse for our purposes. In that book, Harrington contrives a fictional country, compares it to real historical cases, and demonstrates how its government is superior. The book was popular in America a century later, but at the time it was published it was not as persuasive in England as its author had wished. Harrington spent the rest of his life trying to distill his arguments into shorter, more explicit, and more convincing explanations of the principles of good government. At the end of his life he went to prison at the order of a king who was definitely not an admirer of democratic principles. In the Tower of London, Harrington continued to write until he became insane and too ill. The excerpt here, from Harrington's *System of Politics*, was published after his death.

The French **Baron de Montesquieu** was born in 1689, twelve years after Harrington died. He, too, was interested in correcting the flaws of government and set about writing a comprehensive treatment of politics and government. Though he was greatly influenced by both John Locke and James Harrington, the Baron thought he could do better. Unlike Locke, Montesquieu set out to be specific about the mechanics of a good government, and unlike Harrington, Montesquieu did not construct a fictitious country. In fact, he thought he had already found a country that incorporated most, if not all, of the best principles of government—England (one wonders what Harrington would have said in reply). Nonetheless, the Americans contemplating independence from England thought the Baron had more than a few good arguments. Chief among these was the argument for the separation of government powers into three distinct departments or branches.

The third author is the American **James Madison,** who proved to be both a brilliant philosopher and an able practitioner. He is remembered most widely for being president during the War of 1812, but he is studied most vigorously for his ideas on the Constitution. He was perhaps a better philosopher and constitutional architect than president.

Madison's most famous arguments are contained in the *Federalist Papers*, a collection of eighty-five essays, of which Madison himself probably wrote twenty-six (Alexander Hamilton wrote fifty-one, John Jay wrote another five, and the authorship of three others is disputed). The *Federalist Papers* were originally published in New York newspapers and were meant primarily to persuade the voters of New York to pressure their state legislators to ratify the proposed Constitution. New York's legislature did ratify the Constitution, and the *Federalist Papers* lived on as the best explanation available of what was meant by the constitutional framers when they put that document together.

Note the similarity of Madison's arguments to both Harrington's and Montesquieu's. In *Federalist* No. 51, Madison takes up the theme of the separation of powers, echoing the great Montesquieu but with practical references to the mechanics of the newly proposed Constitution. In both *Federalist* Nos. 10 and 51, Madison parallels the philosophical assumptions of James Harrington: Where Harrington claims that the "lust for power is the greatest lust," Madison concludes in his more practical vein that "ambition must be made to counteract ambition" and that "if angels were to govern men, neither external nor internal controls on government would be necessary." Where Harrington asserts that the order of government must conform to "the necessities of human nature," Madison says that it is "a reflection on human nature that such devices should be necessary to control the abuses of government."

Madison's persuasiveness and influence have necessarily made him the focus of many critics in his century and the centuries following. These critics conclude that Madison is less democratic than his arguments would have the reader believe—or at least that the constitution is much less coherent in its philosophy than Madison claimed.

Chief among those critics of Madison were the antifederalists, a vaguely defined collection of people who argued against the ratification of the Constitution. For the most part, the antifederalists believed that the superimposition of a national government over the state governments would undermine and eventually suppress the vigorous and individualistic democracy that had developed in the towns, counties, and states. Some claimed that Madison's scheme was nothing more than the road back to aristocratic, European government. Some claimed that the proposed Constitution did not do as much as state governments to protect individual rights. Some merely claimed that a new order of things was unnecessary.

Although the antifederalists failed to stop the ratification of the Constitution, they did, at the very least, provide some alternative explanations of it to generations following. Those who would understand the "real meaning" of the framers and their famous document have found endlessly fascinating the opinions of all kinds of people and politicians at the debates at the Constitutional Convention and at the ratifying conventions in each state. This material has left plenty of room to argue over the original intentions of the framers and their real motives. Thus, we present three points of view from the twentieth century.

Among the most well known of the modern reinterpreters of the Constitution is **Charles Beard**. Indeed, rarely is the Constitution defended or attacked in any depth without some reference to him.

A professor of history at Columbia University, Beard published his *Economic Interpretation of the Constitution of the United States* in 1913. He took the view that the framers were an economic, as well as a political, elite who were protecting their own property interests by structuring the Constitution to stifle majority rule. Beard attempted to show that all the delegates to the Constitutional Convention had economic advantages, which were threatened by the lack of a centralized government and by too much democracy at the state level. Thus, Beard says, the delegates set out to construct a central government that would constrict democracy and protect private wealth.

For further evidence against the framers, Beard examines Madison's *Federalist Papers*. According to Beard, Madison was first and foremost concerned by the possibility that the majority might rule—and the many and the few were divided essentially by their ownership of property.

Beard's thesis, or one like it, might well have been inevitable, given the growing popularity of Marxist analysis at the turn of the twentieth century. (Beard wrote his analysis before the Bolshevik Revolution of 1917, which provoked a strong reaction to communism in the United States and elsewhere.) But Beard's argument continues to attract adherents to this day.

An equally engaging argument, partly in response to that of Charles Beard, is made by the political scientist **John Roche**. Professor Roche, like Beard, focuses on the framing elites, but Roche claims that these elites were democratic and that their decisions at the Constitutional Convention of 1787 were driven not by economic interests, or even abstract theories, but by the grueling business of getting a lot of people, including the public, to agree on something new and different.

Roche claims that what is most annoyingly overlooked by most commentators is that the framers were extremely practical, pragmatic, and savvy *politicians*; their main goal was to find some agreement that would ensure the unity of the many and rather diverse states.

Roche would prefer us to see the framers of the Constitution not as semidivine philosophers of democratic government and not as clever strategists of class warfare but as educated, experienced, democratic, and mortal politicians. These leaders, supported by various constituencies with various interests were bound together by only one thing: to improve or replace the Articles of Confederation (see Chapter Four). They agreed only that they should come to some agreement, and they differed on almost everything else. In this *pluralist* view (see Robert Dahl in Chapter One), Roche stops just short of describing the framers as competing elites, whose politics consisted most importantly of negotiation, compromise, bargaining, and accommodation. The Constitution, he concludes, "was a patchwork sewn together under the pressure of both time and events."

A more traditional defense of the Constitution is offered by another political scientist, **Martin Diamond**, who attempts to refute the idea that Madison and the other leaders were somehow less than democratic because they expressed so many reservations about the power of the majority. Indeed, when self-styled superdemocratic critics of the Constitution get down to the basics, it is this elite apprehension over majority rule that they cite as most damning evidence that the framers were less than democratic or were predemocratic or even antidemocratic.

Diamond asks a simple question: What if Madison is right? What if, in fact, "there are natural defects to a democracy"? If so, we must ask ourselves what those defects are and how they could be remedied. "The Madisonian solution involved a fundamental reliance on ceaseless striving after immediate interest," says Diamond. And we may well ask, like Diamond, do you have a better solution?

In fact, most people will say we can improve the Constitution—at least as it is currently interpreted. But how do we go about changing it? By some lights, the most sensible way to change the Constitution is to change the people who ultimately interpret the document: the justices of the Supreme Court. Thus, there is always substantial discussion about who is on the Court, who should be on the Court, and of course who the current president or next president may nominate for the Court. Others, some impatient with the glacial pace of change in the Constitution and some frustrated by rapid change, advocate new amendments to the Constitution. According to the advocates of various amendments, changing the actual language of the Constitution is far more effective a remedy than allowing liberal or conservative or elitist or populist judges to impose their own interpretations on the Constitution and from time to time to change them.

Bruce Peabody, professor of political science, presents a long-forgotten view of constitutional change. He argues that elective officeholders long ago gave up their obligation to participate in constitutional interpretation. It was common in the nineteenth century for presidents and legislators to justify their actions and to persuade the public by offering their own interpretations of the Constitution. But according to Peabody, in recent decades officeholders and the public have both submitted to "judicial supremacy": the idea that the Supreme Court is not only the ultimate arbiter of the Constitution but also the *only* arbiter. Peabody believes that our political discourse would be more edifying and the Constitution better served if only elected leaders would not shy from leadership in constitutional debates.

By contrast, **Scott E. Gant** concludes that the Supreme Court has not been the sole arbiter of the Constitution even during these recent decades of judicial supremacy. Instead, it is the *myth* of judicial supremacy that has been dominant, and the myth is useful to give the entire political system a measure of legitimacy. That is, whereas the myth is useful for the masses, Court watchers, if not all political activists, know well that the Court's decisions are shaped, at least indirectly, both by public opinion and by the other branches of government. Moreover, Gant claims, although the Court may make the final decision about interpretations of the Constitution, no decision is ever really final. Perhaps that is good news for those looking forward to constitutional changes.

15 | *System of Politics*
James Harrington

When the American Constitution was written, the work of the English philosopher James Harrington (1611–1677) was well known among the educated public, if not among the attentive public. In his most famous work, The Commonwealth of Oceana, *Harrington used a make-believe country to describe the perfectly balanced government. Many of his ideas were taken up by the Americans: a written Constitution, staggered membership in the Senate, and even freedom of religious practice. This excerpt comes from Harrington's* System of Politics *which he wrote in prison at the Tower of London, where he died. He had written in an earlier volume that "if this age fails me, the next will do me justice." He was quite right.*

1. That which gives the being, the action, and the denomination to a creature or thing is the form of that creature or thing.

2. There is in form something that is not elementary but divine.

3. The contemplation of form is astonishing to us and has a kind of trouble or impulse accompanying it that exalts our souls to God.

4. As the form of a person is the image of God, so the form of a government is the image of humankind.

5. A human is both a sensual and a philosophical creature.

6. Sensuality in humans is when they are led only as are the beasts, that is, by appetite.

7. Philosophy is the knowledge of divine and human things.

8. To preserve and defend oneself against violence is natural to a human as it is a sensual creature.

9. To have an impulse, or to be raised by the contemplation of natural things, to the adoration or worship of God is natural to a human as it is a philosophical creature.

10. Formation of government is the creation of a political creature after the image of a philosophical creature, or it is an infusion of the soul or faculties of a person into the body of a multitude of people.

11. The more the soul or faculties of a person (as they are infused into the body of a multitude of people) are refined or made incapable of passion, the more perfect is the form of government.

12. Not the refined spirit of a person, nor of some people, is a good form of government, but a good form of government is the refined spirit of a nation.

13. The spirit of a nation (whether refined or not) can never be wholly saint nor atheist: not saint because the far great part of the people is never able in matters of religion to be their own leaders, nor atheists because religion is every bit as indelible a character in man's nature as reason.

14. Language is not a more natural intercourse between the soul of one person and another than religion is between God and the soul of a person.

15. As not this language not that language, but some language, so not this religion not that religion, yet some religion is natural to every nation.

16. The soul of government as the true and perfect image of the human soul is every bit as necessarily religious as rational.

17. The body of a government as consisting of the sensual part of humans is every bit

as preservative and defensive of itself as sensual creatures are of themselves.

18. The body of a person, not actuated or led by the soul, is a dead thing out of pain and misery; but the body of a people, not actuated or led by the soul of government, is a living thing in pain and misery.

19. The body of a people, not led by the reason of the government, is not a people but a herd; not led by the religion of the government is at an inquiet and an uncomfortable loss; not disciplined by the conduct of the government is not an army for defense of itself but a rout; not directed by the laws of the government has not any rule of right; and without recourse to the justice or judicatories of the government has no remedy of wrongs.

20. In contemplation of, and in conformity to, the soul of humankind, as also for supply of human necessities which are not otherwise supplied or to be supplied by nature, the form of government consists necessarily of five parts: the civil, which is the reason of the people; the religious, which is the comfort of the people; the military, which is the captain of the people; the laws, which are the rights of the people; and the judicatories, which are the avengers of their wrongs.

21. The parts of form in government are as the offices in a house, and the orders of a form of government are as the orders of a house or family.

22. Good orders make evil people good and bad orders make good people evil.

23. Oligarchists (so that they may keep all others out of government) pretend to be saints, and pretend that others in whom lust reigns are not fit for government. But *libido dominandi*, the lust for power, is the greatest lust, which also reigns most in those that have least right to govern; for many a king and many a people have and had unquestionable right to govern, but an oligarchist never. Whence from their own argument, the lust for power reigning most in the oligarchists, it undeniably follows that oligarchists of all people are least fit for government.

24. As in houses not differing in the kinds of their offices, the orders of families differ much, so the difference of form in different governments consists not in the kinds or number of the parts, which in every one is alike, but in the different ways of ordering those parts. And as the different orders of a house arise for the most part from the quantity and quality of the estate by which it is defrayed or maintained, according as it is in one or more of the family as proprietors, so it is also in a government.

25. The orders of the form, which are the manners of the mind of the government, follow the temperament of the body or the distribution of the lands or territories and the interests thence arising.

26. The interest of arbitrary monarchy is the absoluteness of the monarch; the interest of regulated monarchy is the greatness of the nobility; the interest of democracy is the felicity of the people— for in democracy the government is for the use of the people, and in monarchy the people are for the use of the government, that is, of one lord or more.

27. The use of a horse without his nourishment or of the people without some regard to the necessities of human nature can be none at all; nor are those necessities of nature to be otherwise provided for than by those five parts of government already mentioned: the civil, the religious, the military, the laws, and the judicatories.

16 | *Laws Establishing Political Liberty in a Constitution*
Baron de Montesquieu

Born in 1689, a century before the beginning of the French Revolution, Montesquieu published The Spirit of the Laws *in 1748 and met with great success, not least of all among American intellectuals. The book was said to be the first systematic treatment of politics since Aristotle's, and it caused great controversy in Europe. Montesquieu was clearly influenced by both Locke and Harrington but was most noted for his novel exposition on the "separation of powers," claiming that power can be checked only by power and liberty can prevail only where no power is absolute. This theme was taken up by Madison in his* Federalist Papers.

What is liberty? It is true that in democracies the people may seem to do as they wish; but political liberty does not consist of doing whatever one pleases. In governments—that is to say in any society where there are laws—liberty consists of being allowed to do as one should want to do, and in not being forced to do things which one should not want to do.

It is necessary to keep in mind the difference between independence and liberty. Liberty is the right to do all that the laws permit; and if citizens could do that which is against the law, there would no longer be liberty, because everyone else would also have the same power.

Neither democratic nor aristocratic governments are free merely by their nature. Political liberty is to be found only in moderate governments, though it is not always found even in moderate governments. It is in fact found only where power is not abused. But it is an eternal truth that every person given power is likely to abuse it and will carry his authority as far as it will go. Who would have thought it! Even virtue itself has need of limits.

So to prevent the abuse of power, it is necessary, from the very nature of things, that power check power. A political constitution should be such that no one is forced to do things which the law does not require him to do, and one is not prevented from doing those things which the law permits.

To discover whether there is political liberty in a constitution does not require a great deal of work. There is in every state three sorts of power: the legislative power, the executive power which is concerned with the life of the nation among other nations, and the executive power which is concerned with civil rights.

With the first kind of power, the prince or magistrate makes either temporary or permanent laws and amends or removes laws already made. By the second power, the prince makes peace or war, sends and receives embassies, establishes security, and prevents invasions. By the third power, he punishes crimes, or judges disputes. (We shall call this third and last power, the judicial power and the other, or second, the executive power.)

The political liberty of any citizen is a tranquility of spirit which comes from the opinion that each person has safety. And in order to have this liberty, the government must be such that no citizen need fear the other citizens.

But when the same person, or the same institution, holds the legislative and the executive powers, there can be no liberty because one will necessarily fear that the king or the senate will make tyrannical laws and enforce the laws tyrannically.

Neither is there liberty when the power to adjudicate is not separated from the legislative or executive powers. If it is joined to the legislative functions, then power over life and liberty will be arbitrary because the judge is also the lawmaker. And if it is joined to the executive power, then the judge becomes an oppressor.

All is lost when the same person, or the same body of people, whether aristocratic or common folk, exercises all three powers: that is, to make the laws, to enforce these public resolutions, and to judge violations.

The Judiciary Power

The power to adjudicate ought not to be given to a standing senate, but should be exercised by persons drawn from among the people, in a manner prescribed by law, to form a tribunal which would last only as long as necessity requires. In this way, the power to judge, so terrible to mankind, not being attached to any particular class or profession, becomes invisible. One does not have the judges continually in view; and one can fear the office, but not the office holders.

But, even if tribunals ought not to be fixed and permanent, the judgments must be fixed so that they always conform precisely to the law. If judgments are merely the peculiar opinion of the judge, one would live in society without knowing exactly one's obligations.

Legislative Power

Since, in a free country, everyone who has a free soul should be governed by oneself, then it should be that the people have the power to make laws. But since this is impossible in large countries, and is very inconvenient even in small ones, it is necessary that the people accomplish through their representatives what they cannot accomplish themselves.

People know much better the needs of their own city than those of other cities; and are better judges of the abilities of their neighbors than of the rest of their compatriots. Therefore, the members of the legislature should not come from the population at-large but, rather, each region should select its own representative.

The great advantage of having representatives is that they are capable of discussing public affairs. The masses are not; and this is one of the great inconveniences of democracy.

There was a great vice in most of the ancient republics: this was that the people had the right to make referenda which required governmental action, something for which the masses are entirely unfit. They should not participate in government directly except to choose their representatives, something for which they are certainly fit. For, while few people are capable of determining exactly the abilities of a person, most are capable of knowing whether, in general, the person they choose is more enlightened than most others.

Neither should the legislators be given the power to enforce the law; for this they are not at all suited. But their task is better to make laws and to see that the laws are being properly administered; these things they can do very well and indeed they are in the best position to see to such things.

Now in every society there are some who are distinguished by their birth, their wealth, or their accomplishments, and if these are confused with the masses, if they had only the same voice as any other, the liberty of the masses would be like slavery to them, and they would have no interest in defending liberty because most popular legislation would be aimed against them. Their part in the legislative process should therefore reflect their position in society and this can only occur if they have an assembly which has the right to check the schemes of the people, just as the people have the right to check the schemes of the well-born.

Executive Power

The executive power ought to be left to a monarch because this part of government almost always has a need for momentary action, and is therefore better administered by one than by many; just as the law-making function is better performed by many than by one.

If there were no monarch and it happened that the executive function were performed by people selected by the legislature, then there would be an end to liberty because the two powers would be united, and the same people would be controlling both.

If the legislature went for some time without meeting, there would also be an end to liberty because one of two things would occur: either there would no longer be lawmaking and the state would fall into anarchy, or the lawmaking function would be assumed by the executive, who would then become absolute.

It is not necessary that the legislature be always assembled. That would be very inconvenient for the representatives but, moreover, they would interfere too much with the executive and the executive would spend most of his time merely defending his perogatives.

Once again, if the legislature were continually in session, it might eventually happen that they would be filling their own vacant seats and, in this case, once the legislature is corrupted, the evil is without remedy. When distinct legislatures succeed one another, the people, who have a poor opinion of one body of legislators, reasonably can harbor good hope for the next. But if it always happens to be the same group, then the people, seeing that it is corrupt, will no longer have hope in the laws, and they will become either enraged or despairing.

The legislative body should determine its own time of meeting; this is because an assembly should not have a will of its own except when it is already assembled; and if it is not unanimously assembled, it would be impossible to say which part is truly the legislature, the part that is meeting or the part absent. Likewise, if they have the right to prorogue themselves, it might happen that they would never adjourn; this would be extremely dangerous in case they decided to encroach on the executive's power. Moreover, some times are more appropriate than others for assembling the legislature and it should be the executive who regulates the time and duration of the legislative session according to circumstances.

Were the executive not able to resist the encroachments of the legislature, then the latter would become despotic because, it could give itself all the power it wanted, and it would extinguish the other powers.

Even if, in a free country, the legislative power must not encroach upon the executive power, the legislature must still have the ability to examine the manner in which laws are being enforced. But whatever might be the subject of this investigation, the legislature must not have the power to actually judge the executive and his conduct in office. His person should be sacred because it is necessary in a state that the legislature does not become tyrannical; and from the moment it can accuse and judge the executive, there will no longer be liberty. In this case, there would no longer be a monarchy but a republic that was not a free government.

Of course it can also happen that the citizen in public office violates the rights of the people and commits crimes which the judiciary either cannot or will not punish. But, in general, the legislative power should not try cases, much less this particular sort of case, where it represents the injured party, that is, the people. It can do no more than accuse. But what should become of the accusation? Before whom should it take such an accusation? Should it go before ordinary courts which are inferior to the legislative power and, moreover, are composed of ordinary people whose judgment would be swayed by an accuser so authoritative and powerful? No. In order to preserve the dignity of the people, and the safety of the accused, the popularly elected legislature should go before that part of the legislature which is composed of the nobility, people who have neither the same interests or passions as the people. This is an advantage this government has over most of the ancient republics where they had many abuses because the people were at the same time the accusers and the judge.

The executive power, as we have said, must take some part in legislation at least by being able to hinder the process; if not, the executive would soon be stripped of its perogatives. And if the legislature takes part in the administration, then the executive power would be just as lost.

If the executive were to take part in legislating by the ability to actually make statutes, then there would be an end to liberty. But since it is necessary that the executive take some part in legislating in order to defend its perogatives, this power should be the power to veto.

If the executive power can legislate the raising of public money other than by merely giving its consent, then liberty would also be at an end because the executive would be legislating on the most important matter of law.

Here is, then, the fundamental constitution of the government which we have been talking about. The legislature is composed of two parts, each one checking the other by the power of rejecting legislation, and the two legislatures kept in check by the executive which, in turn, is checked by the legislature.

Just as all things human come to an end, even the state of which we are speaking will one day lose its liberty and will perish. It will perish when the legislative power becomes more corrupt than the executive.

Harrington in his *Oceana* has also examined what kind of constitution provides the greatest degree of liberty. But one might say of him that not knowing liberty, he built a Chalcedon even though he had the shore of Byzantium before his eyes.

17 | *Obliging the Government to Control Itself (Federalist No. 51)*
James Madison

In this, one of the most famous of the Federalist Papers, *Madison explains both why government is necessary and how that government is to be prevented from becoming the preserve of an oligarchy, or a small number of people who would, as is the tendency of humankind, take and maintain power themselves. Remember, one of Madison's premises is that humans are flawed, and therefore government is necessary to control the people. Likewise, safeguards are needed to control people in government.*

To the People of the State of New York:

To what expedient, then, shall we finally resort, for maintaining in practice the necessary partition of power among the several departments, as laid down in the Constitution? The only answer that can be given is, that as all these exterior provisions are found to be inadequate, the defect must be supplied, by so contriving the interior structure of the government as that its several constituent parts may, by their mutual relations, be the means of keeping each other in their proper places. Without presuming to undertake a full development of this important idea, I will hazard a few general observations, which may perhaps place it in a clearer light, and enable us to form a more correct judgment of the principles and structure of the government planned by the convention.

In order to lay a due foundation for that separate and distinct exercise of the different powers of government, which to a certain extent is admitted on all hands to be essential to the preservation of liberty, it is evident that each department should have a will of its own; and consequently should be so constituted that the members of each should have as little agency as possible in the appointment of the members of the others. Were this principle rigorously adhered to, it would require that all the appointments for the supreme executive, legislative, and judiciary magistracies should be drawn from the same fountain of authority, the people, through channels having no communication whatever with one another. Perhaps such a plan of constructing the several departments would be less difficult in practice than it may in contemplation appear. Some difficulties, however, and some additional expense would attend the execution of it. Some deviations, therefore, from the principle must be admitted. In the constitution of the judiciary department in particular, it might be inexpedient to insist rigorously on the principle: first, because peculiar qualifications being essential in the members, the primary consideration ought to be to select that mode of choice which best secures these qualifications; secondly, because the permanent tenure by which the appointments are held in that department, must soon destroy all sense of dependence on the authority conferring them.

It is equally evident, that the members of each department should be as little dependent as possible on those of the others, for the emoluments annexed to their offices. Were the executive magistrate, or the judges, not independent of the legislature in this particular, their independence in every other would be merely nominal.

But the great security against a gradual concentration of the several powers in the same department, consists in giving to those who administer each department the necessary constitutional means and personal motives to resist encroachments of the others. The provision for defense must in this, as in all other cases, be made commensurate to the danger of attack. Ambition must be made to counteract ambition. The interest of the man must be connected with the constitutional rights of the place. It may be a reflection on human nature, that such devices should be necessary to control the abuses of government. But what is government itself, but the greatest of all reflections on human nature? If men were angels, no government would be necessary. If angels were to govern men, nei-

ther external nor internal controls on government would be necessary. In framing a government which is to be administered by men over men, the great difficulty lies in this: you must first enable the government to control the governed; and in the next place oblige it to control itself. A dependence on the people is, no doubt, the primary control on the government; but experience has taught mankind the necessity of auxiliary precautions.

This policy of supplying, by opposite and rival interests, the defect of better motives, might be traced through the whole system of human affairs, private as well as public. We see it particularly displayed in all the subordinate distributions of power, where the constant aim is to divide and arrange the several offices in such a manner as that each may be a check on the other that the private interest of every individual may be a sentinel over the public rights. These inventions of prudence cannot be less requisite in the distribution of the supreme powers of the State.

But it is not possible to give to each department an equal power of self-defense. In republican government, the legislative authority necessarily predominates. The remedy for this inconveniency is to divide the legislature into different branches; and to render them, by different modes of election and different principles of action, as little connected with each other as the nature of their common functions and their common dependence on the society will admit. It may even be necessary to guard against dangerous encroachments by still further precautions. As the weight of the legislative authority requires that it should be thus divided, the weakness of the executive may require, on the other hand, that it should be fortified. An absolute negative on the legislature appears, at first view, to be the natural defense with which the executive magistrate should be armed. But perhaps it would be neither altogether safe nor alone sufficient. On ordinary occasions it might not be exerted with the requisite firmness, and on extraordinary occasions it might be perfidiously abused. May not this defect of an absolute negative be supplied by some qualified connection between this weaker department and the weaker branch of the stronger department, by which the latter may be led to support the constitutional rights of the former, without being too much detached from the rights of its own department?

If the principles on which these observations are founded be just, as I persuade myself they are, and they be applied as a criterion to the several State constitutions, and to the federal Constitution it will be found that if the latter does not perfectly correspond with them, the former are infinitely less able to bear such a test.

There are, moreover, two considerations particularly applicable to the federal system of America, which place that system in a very interesting point of view.

First. In a single republic, all the power surrendered by the people is submitted to the administration of a single government; and the usurpations are guarded against by a division of the government into distinct and separate departments. In the compound republic of America, the power surrendered by the people is first divided between two distinct governments, and then the portion allotted to each subdivided among distinct and separate departments. Hence a double security arises to the rights of the people. The different governments will control each other, at the same time that each will be controlled by itself.

Second. It is of great importance in a republic not only to guard the society against the oppression of its rulers, but to guard one part of the society against the injustice of the other part. Different interests necessarily exist in different classes of citizens. If a majority be united by a common interest, the rights of the minority will be insecure. There are but two methods of providing against this evil: the one by creating a will in the community independent of the majority, that is, of the society itself; the other, by comprehending in the society so many separate descriptions of citizens as will render an unjust combination of a majority of the whole very improbable, if not impracticable. The first method prevails in all governments possessing an hereditary or self-

appointed authority. This, at best, is but a precarious security; because a power independent of the society may as well espouse the unjust views of the major, as the rightful interests of the minor party, and may possibly be turned against both parties. The second method will be exemplified in the federal republic of the United States. Whilst all authority in it will be derived from and dependent on the society, the society itself will be broken into so many parts, interests, and classes of citizens, that the rights of individuals, or of the minority, will be in little danger from interested combinations of the majority. In a free government the security for civil rights must be the same as that for religious rights. It consists in the one case in the multiplicity of interests, and in the other in the multiplicity of sects. The degree of security in both cases will depend on the number of interests and sects; and this may be presumed to depend on the extent of country and number of people comprehended under the same government. This view of the subject must particularly recommend a proper federal system to all the sincere and considerate friends of republican government, since it shows that in exact proportion as the territory of the Union may be formed into more circumscribed Confederacies, or States, oppressive combinations of a majority will be facilitated: the best security, under the republican forms, for the rights of every class of citizens, will be diminished: and consequently the stability and independence of some member of the government, the only other security, must be proportionately increased. Justice is the end of government. It is the end of civil society. It ever has been and ever will be pursued until it be obtained, or until liberty be lost in the pursuit. In a society under the forms of which the stronger faction can readily unite and oppress the weaker, anarchy may as truly be said to reign as in a state of nature, where the weaker individual is not secured against the violence of the stronger; and as, in the latter state, even the stronger individuals are prompted, by the uncertainty of their condition, to submit to a government which may protect the weak as well as themselves; so, in the former state, will the more powerful factions or parties be gradually induced, by a like motive, to wish for a government which will protect all parties, the weaker as well as the more powerful. It can be little doubted that if the State of Rhode Island was separated from the Confederacy and left to itself, the insecurity of rights under the popular form of government within such narrow limits would be displayed by such reiterated oppressions of factious majorities that some power altogether independent of the people would soon be called for by the voice of the very factions whose misrule had proved the necessity of it. In the extended republic of the United States, and among the great variety of interests, parties, and sects which it embraces, a coalition of a majority of the whole society could seldom take place on any other princi-

ples than those of justice and the general good; whilst there being thus less danger to a minor from the will of a major party, there must be less pretext, also, to provide for the security of the former, by introducing into the government a will not dependent on the latter, or, in other words, a will independent of the society itself. It is no less certain than it is important, notwithstanding the contrary opinions which have been entertained, that the larger the society, provided it lie within a practical sphere, the more duly capable it will be of self-government. And happily for the REPUBLICAN CAUSE, the practicable sphere may be carried to a very great extent, by a judicious modification and mixture of the FEDERAL PRINCIPLE.

PUBLIUS.

18 | An Economic Interpretation of the Constitution of the United States
Charles A. Beard

Charles Beard contends in his book, published in 1913, that the framers were preoccupied with "safeguards" against the worst tendencies of democracy only because the framers were actually antidemocratic. According to Beard, the Constitution was a device intended to protect their own economic advantages. The minority, which Madison and Hamilton wanted so dearly to protect, was an economic minority, with property interests. In this passage, Beard argues that the Federalist Papers *themselves demonstrate that the Constitutionalists were less concerned with constructing a democratic government than with protecting economic interests.*

It is difficult for the superficial student of the Constitution, who has read only the commentaries of the legists, to conceive of that instrument as an economic document. It places no property qualifications on voters or officers; it gives no outward recognition of any economic groups in society; it mentions no special privileges to be conferred upon any class. It betrays no feeling, such as vibrates through

the French constitution of 1791; its language is cold, formal, and severe.

The true inwardness of the Constitution is not revealed by an examination of its provisions as simple propositions of law; but by a long and careful study of the voluminous correspondence of the period, contemporary newspapers and pamphlets, the records of the debates in the Convention at Philadelphia and in the several state conventions, and particularly *The Federalist,* which was widely circulated during the struggle over ratification. The correspondence shows the exact character of the evils which the Constitution was intended to remedy; the records of the proceedings in the Philadelphia Convention reveal the successive steps in the building of the framework of the government under the pressure of economic interests; the pamphlets and newspapers disclose the ideas of the contestants over the ratification; and *The Federalist* presents the political science of the new system as conceived by three of the profoundest thinkers of the period, Hamilton, Madison, and Jay.

Doubtless, the most illuminating of these sources on the economic character of the Constitution are the records of the debates in the Convention, which have come down to us in fragmentary form; and a thorough treatment of material forces reflected in the several clauses of the instrument of government created by the grave assembly at Philadelphia would require a rewriting of the history of the proceedings in the light of the great interests represented there. But an entire volume would scarcely suffice to present the results of such a survey, and an undertaking of this character is accordingly impossible here.

The Federalist, on the other hand, presents in a relatively brief and systematic form an economic interpretation of the Constitution by the men best fitted, through an intimate knowledge of the ideals of the framers, to expound the political science of the new government. This wonderful piece of argumentation by Hamilton, Madison, and Jay is in fact the finest study in the economic interpretation of politics which exists in any language; and whoever would understand the Constitution as an economic document need hardly go beyond it. It is true that the tone of the writers is somewhat modified on account of the fact that they are appealing to the voters to ratify the Constitution, but at the same time they are, by the force of circumstances, compelled to convince large economic groups that safety and strength lie in the adoption of the new system.

Indeed, every fundamental appeal in it is to some material and substantial interest. Sometimes it is to the people at large in the name of protection against invading armies and European coalitions. Sometimes it is to the commercial classes whose business is represented as prostrate before the follies of the Confederation. Now it is to creditors seeking relief against paper money and the assaults of the agrarians in general; now it is to the holders of federal securities which are depreciating toward the vanishing point. But above all, it is to the owners of personality anxious to find a foil against the attacks of levelling democracy, that the authors of *The Federalist* address their most cogent arguments in favor of ratification. It is true there is much discussion of the details of the new framework of government, to which even some friends of reform took exceptions but Madison and Hamilton both knew that these were incidental matters when compared with the sound basis upon which the superstructure rested.

In reading the pages of this remarkable work as a study in political economy, it is important to bear in mind that the system, which the authors are describing, consisted of two fundamental parts—one positive, the other negative:

I. A government endowed with certain positive powers, but so constructed as to break the force of majority rule and prevent invasions of the property rights of minorities.
II. Restrictions on the state legislatures which had been so vigorous in their attacks on capital.

Under some circumstances, action is the immediate interest of the dominant party; and whenever it desires to make an economic gain through governmental functioning, it must have, of course, a system endowed with the requisite powers.

Examples of this are to be found in protective tariffs, in ship subsidies, in railway land grants, in river and harbor improvements, and so on through the catalogue of socalled "paternalistic" legislation. Of course it may be shown that the " general good " is the ostensible object of any particular act; but the general good is a passive force, and unless we know who are the several individuals that benefit in Its name, it has no meaning. When it is so analyzed, immediate and remote beneficiaries are discovered; and the former are usually found to have been the dynamic element in securing the legislation. Take for example, the economic interests of the advocates who appear in tariff hearings at Washington.

On the obverse side, dominant interests quite as often benefit from the prevention of governmental action as from positive assistance. They are able to take care of themselves if let alone within the circle of protection created by the law. Indeed, most owners of property have as much to fear from positive governmental action as from their inability to secure advantageous legislation. Particularly is this true where the field of private property is already extended to cover practically every form of tangible and intangible wealth. This was clearly set forth by Hamilton: "It may perhaps be said that the power of preventing bad laws includes that of preventing good ones.... But this objection will have little weight with those who can properly estimate the mischiefs of that inconstancy and mutability in the laws which form the greatest blemish in the character and genius of our governments. They will consider every institution calculated to restrain the excess of lawmaking, and to keep things in the same state in which they happen to be at any given period, as more likely to do good than harm.... The injury which may possibly be done by defeating a few good laws will be amply compensated by the advantage of preventing a number of bad ones."

19 | *The Founding Fathers: A Reform Caucus in Action*
John P. Roche

In his persuasive article from the American Political Science Review, *John Roche argues that most analysts of the Constitution attribute far too many motives to the framers and embue various clauses with far too much philosophical content. Roche argues that the framers' primary intention was to find agreement among themselves on how to construct a national government. One should see the finished document not as gilt with gold edges as some perverse conspiracy against the people but as the result of bargaining, negotiation, compromise, and accommodation among accomplished political figures, each of whom had his own ideas, interests, ambitions, constituencies, and pressures. In this excerpt, Roche offers two examples in support of his argument: the invention of the Electoral College and the regulation of slavery.*

There is a common rumor that the framers divided their time between philosophical discussions of government and reading the classics in political theory. Perhaps this is as good a time as any to note that their concerns were highly practical, that they spent little time canvassing abstractions. A number of them had some acquaintance with the history of political theory (probably gained from reading John Adams's monumental compilation *A Defense of the Constitutions of Government,* the first volume of which appeared in 1786), and it was a poor rhetorician indeed who could not cite Locke, Montesquieu, or Harrington *in support* of a desired goal. Yet up to this point in the deliberations, no one had expounded a defense of states' rights or the "separation of powers" on anything resembling a theoretical basis. It should be reiterated that the Madison model had no room either for the states or for the "separation of powers": effectively *all* governmental power was vested in the national legislature. The merits of Montesquieu did not turn up until *The Federalist,* and although a perverse argument could be made that Madison's ideal was truly in the tradition of John Locke's *Second Treatise of Government,* the Locke whom the American rebels treated as an honorary president was a pluralistic defender of vested rights, not of parliamentary supremacy.

It would be tedious to continue a blow-by-blow analysis of the work of the delegates; the critical fight was over representation of the states and once the Connecticut Compromise was adopted on July 17, the Convention was over the hump. Madison, James Wilson, and Gouverneur Morris of New York (who was there representing Pennsylvania!) fought the compromise all the way in a last-ditch effort to get a unitary state with parliamentary supremacy. But their allies deserted them and they demonstrated after their defeat the essential opportunist character of their objections—using "opportunist" here in a non-pejorative sense, to indicate a willingness to swallow their objections and get on with the business. Moreover, once the compromise had carried (by five states to four, with one state divided), its advocates threw themselves vigorously into the job of strengthening the general government's substantive powers—as might have been predicted, indeed, from Paterson's early statements. It nourishes an increased respect for Madison's devotion to the art of politics to realize that this dogged fighter could sit down six months later and prepare essays for *The Federalist* in contradiction to his basic convictions about the true course the Convention should have taken.

Two tricky issues will serve to illustrate the later process of accommodation. The first was the institutional position of the Execu-

tive. Madison argued for an executive chosen by the national legislature and on May 29 this had been adopted with a provision that after his seven-year term was concluded, the chief magistrate should not be eligible for re-election. In late July this was reopened and for a week the matter was argued from several different points of view. A good deal of desultory speech-making ensued, but the gist of the problem was the opposition from two sources to election by the legislature. One group felt that the states should have a hand in the process; another small but influential circle urged direct election by the people. There were a number of proposals: election by the people, election by state governors, by electors chosen by state legislatures, by the national legislature (James Wilson, perhaps ironically, proposed at one point that an Electoral College be chosen by lot from the national legislature!), and there was some resemblance to three-dimensional chess in the dispute because of the presence of two other variables, length of tenure and reeligibility. Finally, after opening, reopening, and re-reopening the debate, the thorny problem was consigned to a committee for absolution.

The Brearley Committee on Postponed Matters was a superb aggregation of talent and its compromise on the Executive was a masterpiece of political improvisation. (The Electoral College, its creation, however, had little in its favor as an *institution*—as the delegates well appreciated.) The point of departure for all discussion about the presidency in the Convention was that in immediate terms, the problem was nonexistent; in other words, everybody present knew that under any system devised, George Washington would be President. Thus they were dealing in the future tense and to a body of working politicians the merits of the Brearley proposal were obvious: everybody got a piece of cake. (Or to put it more academically, each viewpoint could leave the Convention and argue to its constituents that it had *really* won the day.) First, the state legislatures had the right to determine the mode of selection of the electors;

second, the small states received a bonus in the Electoral College in the form of a guaranteed minimum of three votes while the big states got acceptance of the principle of proportional power; third, if the state legislatures agreed (as six did in the first presidential election), the people could be involved directly in the choice of electors; and finally, if no candidate received a majority in the College, the right of decision passed to the national legislature with each state exercising equal strength. (In the Brearley recommendation, the election went to the Senate, but a motion from the floor substituted the House: this was accepted on the ground that the Senate already had enough authority over the executive in its treaty and appointment powers.)

This compromise was almost too good to be true, and the framers snapped it up with little debate or controversy. No one seemed to think well of the College as an *institution;* indeed, what evidence there is suggests that there was an assumption that once Washington had finished his tenure as President, the electors would cease to produce majorities and the Chief Executive would usually be chosen in the House. George Mason observed casually that the selection would be made in the House nineteen times in twenty and no one seriously disputed this point. The vital aspect of the Electoral College was that it got the Convention over the hurdle and protected everybody's interests. The future was left to cope with the problem of what to do with this Rube Goldberg mechanism.

In short, the framers did not in their wisdom endow the United States with a college of Cardinals— the Electoral College was neither an exercise in applied Platonism nor an experiment in indirect government based on elitist distrust of the masses. It was merely a jerry-rigged improvisation which has subsequently been endowed with a high theoretical content. When an elector from Oklahoma in 1960 refused to cast his vote for Nixon (naming Byrd and Goldwater instead) on the ground that the Founding Fathers intended him to exercise his great independent wisdom, he was indulging in historical fantasy. If

one were to indulge in counter-fantasy, he would be tempted to suggest that the Fathers would be startled to find the College still in operation—and perhaps even dismayed at their descendants' lack of judgment or inventiveness.

The second issue on which some substantial practical bargaining took place was slavery. The morality of slavery was, by design, not at issue; but in its other concrete aspects, slavery colored the arguments over taxation, commerce, and representation. The "Three-Fifths Compromise," that three-fifths of the slaves would be counted both for representation and for purposes of direct taxation (which was drawn from the past—it was a formula of Madison's utilized by Congress in 1783 to establish the basis of state contributions to the Confederation treasury) had allayed some Northern fears about Southern overrepresentation (no one then foresaw the trivial role that direct taxation would play in later federal financial policy), but doubts still remained. The Southerners, on the other hand, were afraid that Congressional control over commerce would lead to the exclusion of slaves or to their excessive taxation as imports. Moreover, the Southerners were disturbed over "navigation acts," i.e., tariffs, or special legislation providing, for example, that exports be carried only in American ships; as a section depending upon exports, they wanted protection from the potential voracity of their commercial brethren of the Eastern states. To achieve this end, Mason and others urged that the Constitution include a proviso that navigation and commercial laws should require a two-thirds vote in Congress.

These problems came to a head in late August and, as usual, were handed to a committee in the hope that, in Gouverneur Morris's words, "these things may form a bargain among the Northern and Southern States." The Committee reported its measures of reconciliation on August 25, and on August 29 the package was wrapped up and delivered. What occurred can best be described in George Mason's dour version (he anticipated

Calhoun in his conviction that permitting navigation acts to pass by majority vote would put the South in economic bondage to the North—it was mainly on this ground that he refused to sign the Constitution):

> The Constitution as agreed to till a fortnight before the Convention rose was such a one as he would have set his hand and heart to.... [Until that time] The 3 New England States were constantly with us in all questions ... so that it was these three States with the 5 Southern ones against Pennsylvania, Jersey and Delaware. With respect to the importation of slaves, [decision-making] was left to Congress. This disturbed the two Southern-most States who knew that Congress would immediately suppress the importation of slaves. Those two States therefore struck up a bargain with the three New England States. If they would join to admit slaves for some years, the two Southern-most States would join in changing the clause which required the 2/3 of the Legislature in any vote [on navigation acts]. It was done.

On the floor of the Convention there was a virtual love-feast on this happy occasion. Charles Pinckney of South Carolina attempted to overturn the committee's decision, when the compromise was reported to the Convention, by insisting that the South needed protection from the imperialism of the Northern states. But his Southern colleagues were not prepared to rock the boat and General C. C. Pinckney arose to spread oil on the suddenly ruffled waters; he admitted that:

> It was in the true interest of the S[outhern] States to have no regulation of commerce; but considering the loss brought on the commerce of the Eastern States by the Revolution, their liberal conduct towards the views of South Carolina [on the regulation of the slave trade] and the interests the weak Southern States had in being united with the strong Eastern states, he thought it proper that no fetters should be imposed on the power of making commercial regulations; *and that his constituents, though prejudiced against the Eastern States, would be rec-*

onciled to this liberality. He had himself prejudices against the Eastern States before he came here, but would acknowledge that he had found them as liberal and candid as any men whatever. (Emphasis added.)

Pierce Butler took the same tack, essentially arguing that he was not too happy about the possible consequences, but that a deal was a deal. Many Southern leaders were later—in the wake of the "Tariff of Abominations"—to rue this day of reconciliation; Calhoun's *Disquisition on Government* was little more than an extension of the argument in the Convention against permitting a Congressional majority to enact navigation acts.

Drawing on their vast collective political experience, utilizing every weapon in the politician's arsenal, looking constantly over their shoulders at their constituents, the delegates put together a Constitution. It was a makeshift affair; some sticky issues (for example, the qualification of voters) they ducked entirely; others they mastered with that ancient instrument of political sagacity, studied ambiguity (for example, citizenship); and some they just overlooked. In this last category, I suspect, fell the matter of the power of the federal courts to determine the constitutionality of acts of Congress. When the judicial article was formulated (Article III of the Constitution), deliberations were still in the stage where the legislature was endowed with broad power under the Randolph formulation, authority which by its own terms was scarcely amenable to judicial review. In essence, courts could hardly determine when "the separate States are incompetent or... the harmony of the United States may be interrupted"; the national legislature, as critics pointed out, was free to define its own jurisdiction. Later the definition of legislative authority was changed into the form we know, a series of stipulated powers, *but the delegates never seriously reexamined the jurisdiction of the Judiciary under this new limited formulation.* All arguments on the intention of the framers in this matter are thus deductive and *a posteriori,* though some obviously make more sense than others.

The framers were busy and distinguished men, anxious to get back to their families, their positions, and their constituents, not members of the French Academy devoting a lifetime to a dictionary. They were trying to do an important job, and do it in such a fashion that their handiwork would be acceptable to very diverse constituencies. No one was rhapsodic about the final document, but it was a beginning, a move in the right direction, and one they had reason to believe the people would endorse. In addition, since they had modified the impossible amendment provisions of the Articles (the requirement of unanimity which could always be frustrated by "Rogues Island") to one demanding approval by only three-quarters of the states, they seemed confident that gaps in the fabric which experience would reveal could be rewoven without undue difficulty....

The Constitution, then, was not an apotheosis of "constitutionalism," a triumph of architectonic genius; it was a patchwork sewn together under the pressure of both time and events by a group of extremely talented democratic politicians. They refused to attempt the establishment of a strong, centralized sovereignty on the principle of legislative supremacy for the excellent reason that the people would not accept it. They risked their political fortunes by opposing the established doctrines of state sovereignty because they were convinced that the existing system was leading to national impotence and probably foreign domination. For two years, they worked to get a convention established. For over three months, in what must have seemed to the faithful participants an endless process of give-and-take, they reasoned, cajoled, threatened, and bargained amongst themselves. The result was a Constitution which the people, in fact, by democratic processes, did accept, and a new and far better national government was established.

Beginning with the inspired propaganda of Hamilton, Madison, and Jay, the ideological build-up got under way. *The Federalist* had little impact on the ratification of the Constitution, except perhaps in New York, but this volume had enormous influence on the image of the Constitution in the minds of future generations, particularly on historians and political scientists who have an innate fondness for theoretical symmetry. Yet, while the shades of Locke and Montesquieu *may* have been hovering in the background, and the delegates *may* have been unconscious instruments of a transcendent *telos,* the careful observer of the day-to-day work of the Convention finds no overarching principles. The "separation of powers" to him seems to be a by-product of suspicion, and "federalism" he views as a *pis aller,* as the farthest point the delegates felt they could go in the destruction of state power without themselves inviting repudiation.

To conclude, the Constitution was neither a victory for abstract theory nor a great practical success. Well over half a million men had to die on the battlefields of the Civil War before certain constitutional principles could be defined, a baleful consideration which is somehow overlooked in our customary tributes to the farsighted genius of the framers and to the supposed American talent for "constitutionalism." The Constitution was, however, a vivid demonstration of effective democratic political action, and of the forging of a national elite which literally persuaded its countrymen to hoist themselves by their own boot straps. American pro-consuls would be wise not to translate the Constitution into Japanese, or Swahili, or treat it as a work of semi-Divine origin; but when students of comparative politics examine the process of nation-building in countries newly freed from colonial rule, they may find the American experience instructive as a classic example of the potentialities of a democratic elite.

20 | *A Reconsideration of the Framers' Intent*
Martin Diamond

A more traditional defense of the framers is offered by Martin Diamond, who asks, "What if Madison was right?" What if, because people are necessarily flawed, democracy must necessarily be flawed? In this case, the task of the Constitution's framers would have been exactly what Madison said it was: to mitigate the consequences of human nature by the provision of safeguards for democracy. In this case also, the Federalist Papers *can be taken at face value, and criticism should shift from "What were the framers really trying to do?" to "Are there any better solutions to these problems than those designed by the framers?"*

The Declaration [of Independence] has wrongly been converted into, as it were, a super-democratic document; has the Constitution wrongly been converted in the modern view into an insufficiently democratic document? The only basis for depreciating the democratic character of the Constitution lies in its framers' apprehensive diagnosis of the "diseases," "defects," or "evil propensities" of democracy, and in their remedies. But if what the Founders considered to be defects *are* genuine defects, and if the remedies, without violating the principles of popular government, *are* genuine remedies, then it would be unreasonable to call the Founders anti-or quasidemocrats. Rather, they would be the wise partisans of democracy; a man is not a better democrat but only a foolish democrat if he ignores real defects inherent in popular government. Then the question becomes: are there natural defects to democracy and, if there are, what are the best remedies?

In part, the Founding Fathers answered the question by employing a traditional mode or political analysis. They believed there were several basic possible regimes, each having several possible forms. Of these possible regimes they believed the best, or at least the best for America, to be popular government, but only if purged of its defects. At any rate, an unpurged popular government they believed to be indefensible. They believed there were several forms of popular government, crucial among these direct democracy and republican—or representative—government (the latter perhaps divisible into two distinct

forms, large and small republics). Their constitution and their defense of it constitute an argument for that form or popular government (large republic) in which the "evil propensities" would be weakest or most susceptible of remedy.

The whole of the thought of the Founding Fathers is intelligible and, especially, the evaluation of their claim to be wise partisans of popular government is possible, only if the words *"disease," "defect,"* and *"evil propensity"* are allowed their full force. Unlike modern "value-free" social scientists, the Founding Fathers believed that true knowledge of the good and bad in human conduct was possible, and that they themselves possessed sufficient knowledge to discern the really grave defects of popular government and their proper remedies. The modern relativistic or positivistic theories implicitly employed by most commentators on the Founding Fathers deny the possibility of such true knowledge and therefore deny that the Founding Fathers *could* have been actuated by knowledge of the good rather than by passion or interest (I deliberately employ the language of *Federalist* No. 10. Madison defined faction, in part, as a group "united and actuated by ... passion, or ... interest." That is, factions are groups *not*—as presumably the authors of *The Federalist* were—actuated by reason. How this modern view of the value problem supports the conception of the Constitution as less democratic than the Declaration is clear. The Founding Fathers did in fact seek to prejudice the outcome of democracy; they sought to alter, by certain restraints, the likelihood that the majority would decide certain political issues in bad ways. These restraints the Founders justified as mitigating the natural defects of democracy. But, say the moderns, there are no bad political decisions, wrong-in-themselves, from reaching which the majority ought to be restrained. Therefore, ultimately, nothing other than the specific interests of the Founders can explain their zeal in restraining democracy. And inasmuch as the restraints were typically placed on the many in the interest of the propertied, the departure of the Constitution is "anti-democratic" or "thermadorean." In short, according to this view, there cannot be what the Founders claimed to possess, "an *enlightened* view of the dangerous propensities against which [popular government] … ought to be guarded," the substantive goodness or badness of such propensities being a matter of opinion or taste on which reason can shed no light.

What are some of the arrangements which have been considered signs of "undemocratic" features of the Constitution? The process by which the Constitution may be amended is often cited in evidence. Everyone is familiar with the arithmetic which shows that a remarkably small minority could prevent passage of a Constitutional amendment supported by an overwhelming majority of the people. That is, bare majorities in the thirteen least populous states could prevent passage of an amendment desired by overwhelming majorities in the thirty-six most populous states. But let us, for a reason to be made clear in a moment, turn that arithmetic around. Bare majorities in the thirty-seven least populous states can pass amendments against the opposition of overwhelming majorities in the twelve most populous states. And this would mean in actual votes today (and would have meant for the thirteen original states) constitutional amendment by a minority against the opposition of a majority of citizens. My point is simply that, while the amending procedure does involve qualified majorities, the qualification is not of the kind that requires an especially large numerical majority for action.

I suggest that the real aim and practical effect of the complicated amending procedure was not at all to give power to minorities, but to ensure that passage of an amendment would require a *nationally* distributed majority, though one that legally could consist of a bare numerical majority. It was only adventitious that the procedure has the theoretical possibility of a minority blocking (or passing) an amendment. The aim of requiring nationally distributed majorities was, I think, to ensure that no amendment could be passed simply with the support of the few states or sections sufficiently numerous to provide a bare majority. No doubt it was also believed that it would be difficult for such a national majority to form or become effective save for the decent purposes that could command national agreement, and this difficulty was surely deemed a great virtue of the amending process. This is what I think *The Federalist* really means when it praises the amending process and says that "it guards equally against that extreme facility, which would render the Constitution too mutable; and that extreme difficulty, which might perpetuate its discovered faults." All I wish to emphasize here is that the actual method adopted, with respect to the numerical size of majorities, is meant to leave all legal power in the hands of ordinary majorities so long as they are national majorities. The departure from simple majoritarianism is, at least, not in an oligarchic or aristocratic direction. In this crucial respect, the amending procedure does conform strictly to the principles of republican (popular) government.

Consider next the suffrage question. It has long been assumed as proof of an anti-democratic element in the Constitution that the Founding Fathers depended for the working of their Constitution upon a substantially limited franchise. Just as the Constitution allegedly was ratified by a highly qualified electorate, so too, it is held, was the new government to be based upon a suffrage subject to substantial property qualifications. This view has only recently been seriously challenged, especially by Robert E. Brown, whose detailed researches convince him that the property qualifications in nearly all the original states were probably so small as to exclude never more than twenty-five per cent, and in most cases as little as only five to ten per cent, of the adult white male population. That is, the property qualifications were not designed to exclude the mass of the poor but only the small proportion which lacked a concrete—however small—stake in society, *i.e.*, primarily the transients or "idlers." The Constitution, of course, left the suffrage question to the decision of the individual states. What is the implication of that fact for deciding what sort of suffrage the Framers had in mind? The immediately popular branch of the national legislature was to be elected by voters who "shall have the qualifications requisite for electors of the most numerous branch of the State legislature." The mode of election to the electoral college for the Presidency and to the Senate is also left to "be prescribed in each State by the legislature thereof."

At a minimum, it may be stated that the Framers did not themselves attempt to reduce, or prevent the expansion of, the suffrage; that question was left wholly to the states—and these were, ironically, the very hotbeds of post-revolutionary democracy from the rule of which it is familiarly alleged that the Founders sought to escape.

In general, the conclusion seems inescapable that the states had a far broader suffrage than is ordinarily thought, and nothing in the actions of the Framers suggests any expectation or prospect of the reduction of the suffrage. Again, as in the question of the amending process, I suggest that the Constitution represented no departure whatsoever from the democratic standard of the Revolutionary period, or from any democratic standards then generally recognized.

What of the Senate? The organization of the Senate, its term of office and its staggered mode of replacement, its election by state legislatures rather than directly by the people, among other things, have been used to demonstrate the undemocratic character of the Senate as intended by the Framers. Was this not a device to represent property and not people, and was it not intended therefore

to be a non-popular element in the government? I suggest, on the contrary, that the really important thing is that the Framers thought they had found a way to protect property *without* representing it. That the Founders intended the Senate to be one of the crucial devices for remedying the defects of democracy is certainly true. But *The Federalist* argues that the Senate, as actually proposed in the Constitution, was calculated to be such a device as would operate only in a way that "will consist ... with the genuine principles of republican government." I believe that the claim is just.

Rather than viewing the Senate from the perspective of modern experience and opinions, consider how radically democratic the Senate appears when viewed from a premodern perspective. The model of a divided legislature that the Founders had most in mind was probably the English Parliament. There the House of Lords was thought to provide some of the beneficial checks upon the popular Commons which it was hoped the Senate would supply in the American Constitution. But the American Senate was to possess none of the qualities which permitted the House of Lords to fulfill its role; *i.e.*, its hereditary basis, or membership upon election by the Crown, or any of its other aristocratic characteristics. Yet the Founding Fathers knew that the advantages of having both a Senate and House could "be in proportion to the dissimilarity in the genius of the two bodies." What is remarkable is that, in seeking to secure this dissimilarity, they did not in any respect go beyond the limits permitted by the "genuine principles of republican government."

Not only is this dramatically demonstrated in comparison with the English House of Lords, but also in comparison with all earlier theory regarding the division of the legislative power. The aim of such a division in earlier thought is to secure a balance between the aristocratic and democratic elements of a polity. This is connected with the pre-modern preference for a *mixed* republic, which was rejected by the Founders in favor of a *democratic* republic. And the traditional way to secure this balance or mixture was to give one house or office to the suffrages of the few and one to the suffrages of the many. Nothing of the kind is involved in the American Senate. Indeed, on this issue, so often cited as evidence of the Founders' undemocratic predilections, the very opposite is the case. The Senate is a constitutional device which *par excellence* reveals the strategy of the Founders. They wanted something like the advantages earlier thinkers had seen in a mixed legislative power, but they thought this was possible (and perhaps preferable) without any introduction whatsoever of aristocratic power into their system. What pre-modern thought had seen in an aristocratic Senate—wisdom, nobility, manners, religion, etc.—the Founding Fathers converted into stability, enlightened self-interest, a "temperate and respectable body of citizens." The qualities of a Senate having thus been altered (involving perhaps comparable changes in the notion of the ends of government), it became possible to secure these advantages through a Senate based wholly upon popular principles. Or so I would characterize a Senate whose membership required no property qualification and which was appointed (or elected in the manner prescribed) by State legislatures which, in their own turn, were elected annually or biennially by a nearly universal manhood suffrage.

The great claim of *The Federalist* is that the Constitution represents the fulfillment of a truly novel experiment, of "a revolution" which has no parallel in the annals of society, and which is decisive for the happiness of "the whole human race." And the novelty, I argue, consisted in solving the problems of popular government by means which yet maintain the government "wholly popular." In defending that claim against the idea of the Constitution as a retreat from democracy I have dealt thus far only with the easier task: the demonstration that the constitutional devices and arrangements do not derogate from the legal power of majorities to rule. What remains is to examine the claim that the Constitution did in fact remedy the natural defects of democracy. Before any effort is made in this direction, it may be useful to summarize some of the implications and possible utility of the analysis thus far.

Above all, the merit of the suggestions I have made, if they are accurate in describing the intention and action of the Founders, is that it makes the Founders available to us for the study of modern problems. I have tried to restore to them their *bona fides* as partisans of democracy. This done, we may take seriously the question whether they were, as they claimed to be, wise partisans of democracy or popular government. If they were partisans of democracy and if the regime they created was decisively democratic, then they speak to us not merely about bygone problems, not from a viewpoint—in this regard—radically different from our own, but as men addressing themselves to problems identical in principle with our own. They are a source from within our own heritage which teaches us the way to put the question to democracy, a way which is rejected by certain prevailing modern ideas. But we cannot avail ourselves of their assistance if we consider American history to be a succession of democratizations which overcame the Founding Fathers' intentions. On that view it is easy to regard them as simply outmoded. If I am right regarding the extent of democracy in their thought and regime, then they are not outmoded by modern events "but rather are tested by them." American history, on this view, is not primarily the replacement of a predemocratic regime by a democratic regime, but is rather a continuing testimony to how the Founding Fathers' democratic regime has worked out in modern circumstances. The whole of our national experience thus becomes a way of judging the Founders' principles, of judging democracy itself, or of pondering the flaws of democracy and the means to its improvement....

21 | Who Interprets? Judicial Review and "Departmentalism"

Bruce Peabody

A professor of political science, Bruce Peabody asserts that the courts need not be the only arbiters of the Constitution. Congress, the president, and the public should participate in the debate over constitutional principles, rather than cede responsibility to an unelected body of judges.

Who, in the American political system, is empowered to interpret the Constitution? At one level, the question seems simplistic, perhaps even naive. Just as Congress passes laws and the President enforces them, surely it falls to the courts to interpret and apply our laws, including the fundamental law of the Constitution. As Chief Justice John Marshall famously argued in the Supreme Court case Marbury v. Madison, "it is emphatically the province and duty of the judicial department to say what the law is."

But naive questions, while sometimes just naive, frequently provide occasions to look at important issues anew, and such is the case with the question of who interprets the Constitution. While in numerous settings the courts, especially federal courts, take the lead in applying the Constitution's various clauses, in other important areas of American politics (such as during debates about pending legislation), primary responsibility for constitutional interpretation seems to fall to federal elected officials.

In addition to asking who actually does interpret the Constitution, we might also raise the question of who should determine the meaning of our preeminent political document. Even staunch defenders of the courts concede that judges make mistakes—the Supreme Court's support of slavery being an oft-cited example—and that there are areas of constitutional law beyond judicial expert-

ise. The seemingly straightforward issue of who can interpret the Constitution actually involves somewhat complex descriptive and normative questions.

One should note at the outset of this discussion a distinction between interpreting the Constitution directly and simply influencing this process. In a system of governance as open to external influences as ours, it would be surprising to find even the relatively insulated judiciary immune to political and popular pressures. Indeed, scholars have shown that public opinion, political control over the judicial appointment process, and various legislative mechanisms can shape judges' legal opinions and attenuate the force of unpopular decisions.

As important as these controls over the courts are, however, they do not serve as a substitute for independent non-judicial constitutional interpretation. Since the judiciary reviews only a finite number of cases and only ventures into certain areas of politics, indirect influence on the courts is inherently limited. In addition, notwithstanding the impact of political forces on judicial decision-making, there is not a complete correspondence between what even stable electoral majorities desire and the constitutional decisions of judges. Judges regularly exercise their counter-majoritarian power of judicial review to invalidate legislation and other political action that is perceived as unconstitutional. In

1997, for example, the Supreme Court struck down the Religious Freedom Restoration Act (RFRA), which provided heightened legal protection for religious groups, despite widespread support for the law from conservative as well as liberal interest groups and politicians. Elected officials and the public have, therefore, a strong interest in expressing their constitutional voices in settings and in language more closely under their control.

Constitutional Interpretation Outside of the Courts

Traditional accounts of constitutional law identify the judiciary as the supreme (and usually exclusive) expositor of the Constitution's meaning. In the course of deciding particular cases and controversies, judges analyze and construe the Constitution's individual provisions, overall structure, history, and underlying theory. The Supreme Court, in this view, sets out authoritative, general understandings of the constitutional text, which are then applied by lower courts and enforced by elected officials.

Over the past fifteen years or so, however, a group of scholars have argued that this understanding of constitutional interpretation is decidedly incomplete. Studies of what is sometimes called "departmentalism" or "coordinate construction" emphasize the role played by non-judicial actors, especially federal elected officials, in determining the Constitution's meaning and application to our political life. This revised account of constitutional interpretation assumes that each of the departments or branches of government have opportunities to form our understanding of the nation's highest law.

Where might we turn to find this non-judicial interpretation? To begin with, politicians and private citizens often articulate and attempt to advance their constitutional views in court. Members of Congress and the Solicitor General—the President's appointed representative before the Supreme Court—interpret the Constitution in presenting their arguments about why they should prevail in particular legal disputes. In addition, each

term hundreds of elected officials, interest groups, and private citizens present *amicus curiae* ("friend of the court") briefs as part of the judicial process, urging judges to adopt their respective constitutional positions.

Politicians also have opportunities to interpret the Constitution in settings far removed from courtrooms, and in ways unlikely to ever be reviewed by the judiciary. In these contexts, elected officials can develop their own conceptions of the Constitution's meaning, drawing from their distinctive experiences and perspectives. Consider, in this regard, a few of the ways in which U.S. Presidents can assert an independent understanding of the Constitution while performing various unique institutional duties. To begin with, a President might veto legislation on the grounds that it conflicts with the Constitution. In rejecting legislation rechartering the Bank of the United States, for example, President Andrew Jackson argued that a federal bank was beyond Congress's delegated constitutional powers. A President could also use his or her pardoning power to exonerate an individual convicted of a crime who did not, in the President's eyes, receive constitutional due process. Perhaps most dramatically, Presidents might direct the entire executive department to decline to enforce laws deemed unconstitutional; Thomas Jefferson ordered executive department attorneys not to prosecute individuals under the Sedition Act, on the grounds that the measure (which punished individuals for criticizing the federal government) violated the First Amendment's protection of free speech.

Congress can also evaluate constitutional questions in exercising its vital institutional powers and responsibilities. Members of Congress have engaged in constitutional analysis in examining proposed legislation, scrutinizing nominees to the federal courts, and in interbranch disputes about the operation of constitutional powers—such as congressional investigations or the power to go to war. Congress engages in constitutional interpretation when it determines the proper purposes and processes for presidential and judicial impeachments.

In short, there are numerous circumstances in which federal elected officials can engage in independent constitutional analysis, both inside and outside of the judicial process. But how much nonjudicial constitutional interpretation actually takes place? The modern acceptance of judicial supremacy, the doctrine that the courts have final authority over constitutional questions, has shifted attention away from federal officials as constitutional interpreters.

Today, politicians frequently avoid constitutional questions that come up in the course of policymaking, or—in the shadow of judicial supremacy—they engage these questions with an eye on the past and likely future decisions of the courts. Contemporary statutes that lawmakers believe raise significant constitutional questions (such as RFRA or the Line Item Veto Act of 1996) often contain "expedited review" provisions allowing these questions to be placed on a "fast track" for review by the federal courts, instead of legislators themselves.

Even in settings in which the courts possess limited influence or jurisdiction, independent non-judicial constitutional interpretation has receded. For example, throughout the nineteenth century, Presidents frequently cited constitutional concerns in vetoing bills, engaging in extensive and detailed constitutional analysis of their own making. In the twentieth century, however, Presidents were much more likely to raise policy and administrative concerns in vetoing legislation, and whatever constitutional arguments they surfaced were usually cursory and based on legal reasoning developed by judges.

Who Should Interpret?

Perhaps this state of affairs—in which the judiciary assumes near exclusive authority for examining constitutional issues—is precisely the way it should be. After all, elected officials are stretched thin as it is simply attending to their constituents and ordinary political duties, without assigning them the additional responsibility of regularly interpreting the Constitution. What, if anything, would be gained by fostering greater non-judicial constitutional interpretation?

To begin with, giving elected officials a greater role in our interpretive process would arguably better support the purposes of the American separation of powers system. Our Constitution allocates power somewhat inexactly between the three branches of government in order to promote the public interest in two distinct ways. First, it checks any one institution from assuming too much authority and becoming tyrannical. Secondly, it brings each department's distinctive perspectives, interests, and capacities to bear on the exercise of the powers and processes of government.

By giving the legislative and executive departments more of a hand in constructing the meaning of the Constitution, we would provide them with increased opportunities to check the judiciary. Instead of accepting a judge's decision as the "last word" on how to understand the Constitution, elected officials could challenge the interpretations of courts, or at least those rulings that threaten to encroach upon their autonomy or prerogatives (such as those involving the separation of powers or "political" institutions' internal procedures).

The alternative is to allow the Constitution's meaning to be largely restricted to the imagination and sentiments of the nine unelected members of the U.S. Supreme Court. As Abraham Lincoln cautioned in his First Inaugural Address, "the candid citizen must confess that if the policy of the government, upon vital questions, affecting the whole people, is to be irrevocably fixed by decisions of the Supreme Court . . . the people will have ceased to be their own rulers." Indeed, Lincoln acted upon this concern with judicial supremacy, forcefully arguing against the Court's decision, in *Dred Scott v. Sandford*, that slavery was constitutionally protected.

In addition to these observations, a shared, "departmentalist" view of constitutional interpretation would also encourage Members of Congress and Presidents to shape constitutional provisions according to their distinctive institutional expertise and views. This approach appears to be inherently desirable given that certain powers and processes fall under the particular purview of elected officials and are especially inappropriate for determination by the judiciary. Consider, in this regard, the case of presidential impeachments.

There are compelling reasons to believe that instead of looking to the judges for a model of what constitutes an impeachable offense, Congress must construct its own criteria. For example, in determining whether to impeach and convict a President, Congress might appropriately consider the potential for the President's ongoing effectiveness and overall capacity to fulfill his or her institutional and political duties—all factors that courts are most unsuited to evaluate.

By developing its own, independent sense of the impeachment power, Congress would also be able to exercise it with greater confidence, responsibility, and skill. Among the criticisms leveled against Congress during the impeachment trial of President Bill Clinton was that the legislature, engaged in a solemn constitutional duty, was uncertain how to proceed, and had great difficulty articulating a coherent account of the functions and limitations of the impeachment process. These difficulties might be at least mitigated if Congress more regularly took responsibility for its own constitutional interpretation.

In addition to helping elected officials more effectively exercise their institutional powers, non-judicial constitutional interpretation could also bolster the Constitution's legal authority. As James Thayer aptly reminds us, "much which is harmful and unconstitutional may take effect without any capacity in the courts to prevent it, since their whole power is [only] a judicial one." If we expect the law of the Constitution to be binding throughout our polity, and not just in the context of cases, political actors will need to have some hand in applying the constitutional text.

At the same time, however, non-judicial interpretation could help foster a collective sense that the Constitution is not simply a list of restrictive legal rules, but a blueprint for a just society and a reminder of the nation's highest political aspirations. By focusing exclusively on the legal analysis of the courts, we tend "to drive out questions of justice and right," filling our minds "with thoughts of mere legality of what the Constitution allows." By encouraging executive and legislative officials to interpret the Constitution, our constitutional principles would be given wider play by institutions with a more public and popular orientation, and in contexts (such as national policy debates) more likely to attract popular attention and discussion. In this way, constitutional interpretation might play an indispensable part of a general civic education about the polity's fundamental commitments, the basic values that infuse and bind our society together.

A Threat to Judicial Independence?

Despite the appeal of this vision of constitutional interpretation, perhaps it simply comes with too high a political price. Wouldn't expanding the role of non-judicial interpreters of the Constitution threaten our nation's carefully balanced allocation of powers? After all, doesn't the signature feature of the courts—protecting minority rights—depend upon their ability to interpret the Constitution without being encroached upon by political institutions? Moreover, recalling Hamilton's arguments in *Federalist* #78, don't we need an impartial, specially trained set of judges, protected from political influence, in order "to secure a steady, upright, and impartial administration of the laws"? Finally, wouldn't we compromise the special capacities judges bring to the interpretive process, and perhaps even threaten the rule of law, if Presidents, Members of Congress, and other political actors interpreted the Constitution?

Departmentalism need not, however, endanger the independence of American courts. Accepting that the judiciary contribute something distinctive and desirable to the development of our constitutional law does not lead to the conclusion that it should have exclusive authority over constitutional interpretation.

Even if we allow that judges can serve as a special bulwark in protecting rights, or provide an additional check on "political" actors, we do not have to concede the interpretive power to the courts alone.

There are at least two ways in which we could preserve the courts' special constitutional role while promoting non-judicial interpretation of the Constitution. First, we might simply call for a reinvigorated constitutional dialogue by political figures in those settings (such as legislative debates, or judicial confirmation battles) that do not regularly lead to controversies reviewable by judges. This approach would not challenge the ultimate authority of judges to interpret the Constitution, but would permit them to set their own limits.

Alternatively, we might encourage more robust and independent non-judicial constitutional interpretation by distinguishing different areas of interpretive competence for each department of government. Under this conception, each branch would have a specialized interpretive authority corresponding to its traditional constitutional prerogatives, responsibilities, and special capacities. Courts, for example, institutionally and historically disposed to identifying and protecting rights, would invoke the Constitution in pursuit of this end, while Members of Congress and Presidents would simultaneously apply their understanding of the constitutional text while attempting to fulfill their special functions and duties—such as passing and administering laws, and developing foreign policy.

Clearly, this second model of non-judicial interpretation would generate extensive interbranch conflict about the proper boundaries of constitutional powers and roles. But this conflict would itself be useful in raising diverse perspectives on the separation of powers and the different branches' claims to oversee various constitutional provisions. Moreover, conflict over these issues would be unlikely to persist indefinitely, given each department's incentives to work together to advance its institutional interests. As a federal appeals court once noted, "the resolution of conflict between the coordinate branches . . . [is] an opportunity for a constructive *modus vivendi*, which positively promotes the functioning of our system." Instead of reflexively turning to the courts for the resolution of their institutional differences, Members of Congress and Presidents would have to argue with each other about which department's constitutional understanding should prevail.

If each branch were required to articulate and defend both its constitutional views and the reasons why it was qualified to evaluate a particular constitutional question, we might even induce a greater sense of interbranch cooperation and respect, as each institution came to recognize the distinctive contributions and authority of its coordinate, rival departments.

Ironically, by making the power of constitutional interpretation a shared power, and not one exclusively utilized by courts, we might actually enhance judicial power by regularly and publicly legitimating, defending (and perhaps rethinking) the role of an unelected judiciary in a democratic system. As one scholar has explained, "the more the Court can be treated as a partner in the politics of American life and not as a superior external agent, the fewer will be our doubts about its contributions and the greater should be our willingness to see it exercise its functions without misgivings."

Constitutional Interpretation by States and Citizens?

In claiming that significant constitutional interpretation can and should take place outside of the courts, this argument has focused almost exclusively on the potential contributions of federal elected officials. While less prominent, private and state actors can and do engage in constitutional analysis both within and outside of the judicial process. In evaluating the performance of elected officials or the wisdom of popular initiatives, voters might consult the Constitution as a kind of political yardstick, and state politicians can and sometimes do invoke constitutional principles in a wide range of policy debates.

There are good reasons, however, to believe that state and popular constitutional interpretation should be carefully circumscribed. To begin with, the Constitution is primarily a charter of national political powers. As a result, it lodges a number of specific processes and responsibilities in the hands of federal officials. Thus, Presidents and Congresses need, at a minimum, some basic understanding of the institutional limits and prerogatives set out in the Constitution. Other political actors—with different responsibilities and capacities—ordinarily turn to different sources of power.

Moreover, in a political system in which federal law is supreme, it seems reasonable to assume that federal officials have a privileged oversight over that law. The Congress, the President, and the Supreme Court owe their existence to the U.S. Constitution, and in turn, they possess a distinctive responsibility to preserve that document through various methods, including constitutional interpretation. These issues were essentially settled as both a matter of politics and law by the Civil War and its aftermath.

Even if these arguments suggest that we need to limit constitutional interpretation by the states, surely the citizenry, as the source of the nation's political authority, should exercise a final, direct voice in constitutional interpretation? As Jefferson argued, there is "no safe depository of the ultimate powers of the society but the people themselves."

But ours is a constitutional democracy, not a direct democracy. Our government is founded on a cautious skepticism above human nature and popular rule, and is consequently committed to preserving certain political rights and restrictive procedures. While the people exercise ultimate political control over who serves in office, their governing power is indirect and tempered. If the Constitution's meaning could be regularly determined by the populace at large, we would compromise one of the primary purposes of American constitutionalism—protecting basic, enduring principles from the control of the shifting majorities and factions. We could imagine and even defend a "populist" approach to constitutional interpretation, but we could not readily square it with our existing constitutional structure or over 200 years of political practice.

The twin questions of who does and who should interpret the Constitution are often overlooked by even sophisticated observers of American politics. Given the symbolic power and supreme legal authority of our constitutional text, there are few political questions more deserving of our attention and study. While still widely accepted by politicians and the public, judicial supremacy is vulnerable to criticism from the civics book model of politics, elite theory, and pluralism. By ceding the responsibility to interpret the Constitution to the courts, and ultimately the Supreme Court, we turn over a central governing power to an unelected body of judges isolated from the interests of the electorate and the various political groups that comprise our heterogeneous society. Even when judicial opinions reflect a national consensus, they may be rejected or at least misunderstood by the people because of their often inscrutable legal language. And the formal, adversarial character of the judicial process tends to push aside the legitimization, compromise, and broad-based representation often associated with interest group politics. As a result of these factors, the courts' invocations of the Constitution may seem alien, imposed, or irrelevant, and may therefore be rejected by politicians and the citizenry alike.

In sum, we need to reevaluate the widely accepted doctrine of judicial supremacy and rethink how we structure the processes of constitutional interpretation. As citizens and as students of the American political order, we should be mindful of the words spoken by the Bishop of Bangor in 1717: "Whoever hath an absolute authority to interpret any written or spoken laws, it is he who is truly the lawgiver . . . and not the person who first spoke or wrote them."

22 | *Recast Judicial Supremacy*
Scott E. Gant

A scholar and practicing attorney, Scott Gant contends that, in fact, the Supreme Court is not and never has been the sole arbiter of the Constitution. Gant contends that the myth of judicial supremacy is just that, a myth. Congress, the president and the public have always helped shape constitutional interpretation. But, says Gant, we should preserve the myth....
Why?

This Article grapples with a fundamental question: Who other than the judiciary has responsibility for constitutional interpretation? This question has both a *descriptive* and a *normative* component; it asks who *does* interpret the Constitution, and who *should*. The answer to each part of the question is of great importance. Ascertaining who *does* interpret the Constitution is central to a full understanding of our political-legal culture. Developing an account of who *should* interpret the Constitution is essential to our vitality as a nation committed to constitutional governance.

Ultimately, I articulate and defend a revised model of judicial supremacy. It offers a way of thinking about judicial supremacy which accounts for the subtleties of the interpretive process and better explains who interprets the Constitution under our existing interpretive scheme.

The Judicial Roots of Judicial Supremacy

The Supreme Court's landmark decision in *Marbury v. Madison* is credited with providing the foundation for judicial review—the power of the Court to declare acts of Congress unconstitutional. At issue was whether Congress acted properly in conferring authority in the Court to issue original writs of mandamus in cases not "affecting Ambassadors, other public Ministers and Consuls [or] those in which a State [is] a party," the domains over which the Court had original jurisdiction under Article III. The Court held, in an opinion written by Chief Justice Marshall, that Congress

acted unconstitutionally in granting this power to the Court.

The argument that Marbury established judicial supremacy, quite apart from judicial review, was never more emphatically stated than by the Court itself in *Cooper v. Aaron*. In *Cooper* the court asserted: "Marbury . . . declared the basic principle that the federal judiciary is supreme in the exposition of the law of the Constitution, and [this] principle has ever been respected by this Court and the Country as a permanent and indispensable feature of our constitutional system."

On its face, this statement appears to be a ringing endorsement of judicial supremacy. One reading of Cooper is that the "Court's interpretation is itself the supreme law of the land." Many scholars identify Cooper as the moment when the Court truly declared itself the ultimate interpreter of the Constitution. Whether or not Cooper established judicial supremacy, the principle of judicial supremacy has been embraced by the Court several times since Cooper, and extended to cases involving Congress and the executive branch. As recently as 1992, the Court said that, in the minds of the people, it is "invested with the authority to decide . . . constitutional cases and speak before all others for [the people's] constitutional ideals."

Critics and Criticism of Judicial Supremacy

Notwithstanding the fact that the Supreme Court appears to have embraced judicial supremacy, the concept has its critics. If fact,

American history is replete with rejections of judicial supremacy by government actors outside the judiciary. For instance, many Presidents have challenged the rationale of judicial supremacy. Thomas Jefferson often criticized the notion that the judiciary is the ultimate arbiter of all constitutional questions. As President, Jefferson pardoned those prosecuted under the Sedition Act of 1798, which he viewed as unconstitutional, notwithstanding that it was upheld by the federal judiciary. Andrew Jackson was also a critic of judicial supremacy, as reflected in his challenge of the Court's judgment in *McCulloch v. Maryland* in his "Veto Message" of 1832.

A favorite President among critics of judicial supremacy is Abraham Lincoln. One of his stands against judicial supremacy was his contention that *Dred Scott v. Sandford* was an unconstitutional ruling which he was unwilling to allow to serve as a basis for nationalizing slavery. On another well-known occasion, Lincoln refused to obey the Court's order after it issued a writ of habeas corpus.

More recently, President Ronald Reagan's Attorney General, Edwin Meese, proclaimed in a speech: "[C]onstitutional interpretation is not the business of the Court only, but also properly the business of all branches of government." Other modern Presidents have bristled at aspects of judicial supremacy, and argued for their own authority to interpret the Constitution.

From a normative standpoint, there are several bases for criticizing judicial supremacy. Many interpreters look to the Framers' dispositions for guidance about how we ought to conduct our constitutional affairs today. Yet some claim that judicial supremacy is inconsistent with the Framers' intentions.

Other familiar complaints are that judicial supremacy effectively gives the judiciary the power to govern and that judicial supremacy conflates the Constitution and constitutional law. Critics further argue interpretation is too important to be left to a single branch. When interpretation is left to a single branch, there is a limited incentive for that branch to strive to persuade others of the appropriateness of its interpretations. Were other branches of the government vested with a substantial interpretive role, there would be an emphasis placed on "reason" in rendering interpretive judgments. The more it is necessary for one branch to convince other branches to accept its judgment, the more critical the quality of its analysis must be. Furthermore, the oft-made charge that judicial review is antidemocratic likewise can be made against judicial supremacy.

Standing in the shadow of these critiques of judicial supremacy, I concede that our current legal regime at times operates other than we would expect if judicial supremacy were an accurate descriptive account. What this suggests to me, however, is that it is our account of judicial supremacy, rather than the idea itself, which requires reconsideration. As for the normative critiques, judicial supremacy's shortcomings are not inherent ones. The perceived failings of judicial supremacy apply only to some visions of it. A modified model of judicial supremacy can avoid many of judicial supremacy's imagined defects while capturing the substantial virtues associated with it.

Judicial Supremacy Revisited

The particular model of revised judicial supremacy I propose is—for lack of a better term—recast judicial supremacy. At the core of recast judicial supremacy are three descriptive assertions. I will call these assertions recast judicial supremacy's "descriptive troika." They are: (1) the judiciary is the nonexclusive but "final" interpreter of what the Constitution means; (2) "final" does not mean insular; and (3) no interpretation is ever truly final.

This troika moves us closer to capturing how judicial supremacy really works, and in turn, how constitutional interpretation actually operates. This explanatory model of judicial supremacy also provides the basis for the normative program of recast judicial supremacy. The troika—these three features of our interpretive scheme—invite a diffusion of interpretive responsibility. They allow non-judicial actors to contribute their interpretive judgments while retaining the judiciary as the "final" arbiter of constitutional meaning. Such a diffusion of interpretive responsibility, operating with the advantages of judicial supremacy, would yield a distinct of advantages not available under an alternative model of interpretive authority.

Advantages of Judicial Supremacy

Judicial supremacy has numerous advantages. A familiar idea is that courts should deliver authoritative interpretations because they, unlike Congress or the executive, are apolitical, and because judges are granted life tenure. This argument has often been rephrased as one for a neutral umpire shielded from the passion of political life. A related view is that, as an institution, the judiciary is relatively resistant to majoritarian pressures. Any assignment of ultimate interpretive authority to the political branches is supposed to undermine the Constitution's own counter-majoritarian protections.

A second advantage of judicial supremacy concerns the principle of separation of powers. To the extent we remain committed to the principle, our tripartite system of government—featuring both overlapping functions and distinct powers—is served best by judicial supremacy. Without ultimate interpretive authority, the judiciary possesses no powers countervailing those of Congress or the President. Moreover, to allow branches of government to render authoritative judgments about interpretive issues affecting them is to engage in a kind of "double counting," by allowing them to wield interpretive powers as well as their already enumerated powers in pursuit of whatever interests they may have at a given time.

A third advantage begins as a conceptual point, but has far-reaching practical import. Under a scheme which denies a single branch the authority to vest the Constitution with meaning—like departmentalism—the Constitution "would not have an articulated meaning." At its core, the Constitution's meaning is social; it does not exist *a priori*. Without settled means for resolving interpretive conflicts, meaning becomes diffuse and arguments over meaning become unmanageable. The alternative is to settle conflicts through the rough-and-tumble of everyday politics. Yet not only does this stack the deck against judicial judgments, it encourages crises. Under such a scheme, political and constitutional strife would be too frequent. But this appears to be a dangerous method of dispute resolution. Constitutional discourse can, and ought to be, conducted according to more gentle and stability-engendering methods.

Judicial Supremacy: Myth, Legitimation and Social Solidarity

Some scholars have referred to the so-called "mystic function" of the Court, whereby its decisions upholding something as constitutional serve to legitimate the practice or action in question. But what of the Court's legitimacy—from what is it derived? I am unconvinced that legitimacy is necessarily self-actualizing.

Instead, affirmative steps must be taken to promote judicial legitimacy. Judicial supremacy, even in its current form, engenders broad popular support and promotes judicial legitimacy. Adherence to judicial supremacy as a foundational understanding of how our government works creates a "myth" of sorts—a cousin of the "mystic function." This myth is comprised of the unqualified idea that the courts authoritatively (although not exclusively) interpret the Constitution, and that the norms enunciated by courts as constitutional principles are to be given effect.

Why do we need such a myth? In America, constitutional law comprises a substantial part of our civic religion, and we have left it largely to the Supreme Court to fashion and concretize our image of the Constitution. A vision of political life without a clear sense of how to end conflicts about what the Constitution allows or proscribes would be unsettling to many citizens. The image of finality resting with the "dispassionate" judiciary, detached from the rough-and-tumble of daily politics, is easy to understand and embrace. The absence of at least short-term temporal finality, and of first-order conceptual finality, threatens to strip the Constitution of meaning. Therefore, it is imperative that judicial supremacy remain the popular account of our interpretive process.

The myth is useful despite that, in reality, judicial interpretation is neither insular nor truly final. We know that the myth is not "true," in the sense that it is not a sophisticated and comprehensive account which explains how dialogue and equilibrium unravel claims about interpretive finality. But it is "true" as a baseline political commitment, and it is capable of promoting support among the governed and of fostering social solidarity.

I imagine the myth operating something like the relationship between perceptions of the trial process and jury decision-making. We treasure our right to jury trials, and have "faith" in the "system." Yet we couple this with a set of rules designed to prevent knowledge of the way juries arrive at decisions. We know that juries operate in a manner far from our ideal, but we do not inquire further, for fear of undermining the legitimacy of the system. So too with constitutional interpretation. With less-than-rigorous probing we can know that the judiciary's "authoritative" interpretations are neither insular nor truly final; but there are virtues to be extracted from the image that courts have the final say. Therefore, we should preserve the myth, knowing full well what rests behind it. Abandoning judicial supremacy would jeopardize the vitality of the myth and invite more frequent crises—political and constitutional—in resolving interpretive disputes.

CHAPTER FOUR

The Tensions of Federalism

OVERVIEW AND SUMMARY

In 1781 the Continental Congress established the Articles of Confederation (see Appendix II), which were intended to maintain "a firm league of friendship" among the states. Under the articles, each state retained its sovereignty and independence; the national government exercised only the powers that the states were willing to give it. The central government could not levy taxes or regulate commerce among the states. Also, there was no national army—the central government was dependent on support from the state militias. Because of its weaknesses, the central government could not provide for national defense, it could not regularize commerce among the states, and it could not stop the states from pressing competing claims to land in the west. Subsequently, Pennsylvania and Virginia actually went to war near Pittsburgh over their land claims.

After a only few years of haphazard government under the articles, leaders such as George Washington and Alexander Hamilton concluded that a stronger central government was necessary. In 1785 a like-minded group met at Washington's Mt. Vernon home and called for a meeting to be held at Annapolis, Maryland, in September 1786 to discuss trade among the states. The meeting was not well attended; no one from New England participated. The group hoped for another meeting to be held the following spring. Then, in January 1787, Shays' Rebellion broke out.

Daniel Shays and other ex-Revolutionary War soldiers, suffering from debts and high taxes and worrying that they would lose their property, armed themselves and prevented local courts in western Massachusetts from meeting. The governor of Massachusetts asked the Continental Congress to send troops to suppress the insurrection, but every state except Virginia refused Congress's request for money. The governor then tried to raise a state militia, but his state treasury did not have sufficient funds to finance it. Finally, private funds were collected to hire a voluntary army, which quickly defeated the rebels.

Shays' Rebellion had a profound impact. The need for a stronger central government became clear. Consequently, a meeting in Philadelphia in May 1787 to consider revising the Articles of Confederation was well attended and included delegates from New England.

At this famous May meeting of the Constitutional Convention, some delegates quickly decided that revising the articles would not be sufficient: A new government was needed. They nonetheless feared a central government that was too strong and, what's more, knew that a strong central government would arouse insurmountable opposition from the very states that had empowered them as delegates to the convention. Hence, they compromised on a system they thought would ensure domestic tranquility; provide for the common defense; maintain substantial state power; and, most important, be embraced by the state legislatures. Indeed, the compromise was a new kind of government.

This was not a strongly centralized national government to which the regional governments were subordinate. Nor was it a typical federal form, or confederation, in which the central government was merely the servant of the existing state governments. This was a new kind of federal system, *one in which the subunits (i.e., the states) of a distinct national government had constitutional standing and retained some powers that could not be altered without their consent.* It was, in the words of **Alexis de Tocqueville**, an "incomplete national government" and a "great invention in modern political science." Ever since this inventive compromise, citizens, public officials, and theorists have argued over the appropriate relationship between the national and state governments.

Indeed, the wrangling over the meaning of the new federalism began immediately after the signing of the Constitution. **Patrick Henry**, a patriot of great renown, came out squarely against the plan. At the Virginia convention, called to decide whether Virginia would ratify the Constitution, the debate raged for weeks as each of Henry's arguments had to be addressed by supporters of the Constitution. Henry believed that the Articles of Confederation sufficiently protected the liberty of citizens because power was vested almost entirely in state governments and not in some lofty, remote, and unaccountable central government. Henry distrusted strong, centralized national power because he believed that such enormous power, vested in far-off elites, would sooner or later threaten individual liberty. He declared that if the Constitution were adopted "the republic may be lost forever."

For Henry, the states had to be the unrivaled elements of any national government: State government, the first and truest representative of the people, could never be replaced by a centralized, remote, and elite national government. Thus, he was very critical of the beginning phrase of the Constitution—"We the people...."—which claimed a direct relationship between the national government and the citizens. Henry asserted that the phrase should have been "We the states" to make clear that the national government was a union of states and that the state governments—the true representative organs of the people—held ultimate power.

Finally, Henry argued that the members of the Constitutional Convention were supposed to have assembled only to revise the Articles of Confederation, not to create a new government. The signers of the Constitution had gone well beyond their mandate. Henry saw no good reason for the drastic change of a new Constitution—there were disorders in other states, but in Virginia everything was tranquil and prosperous. In Henry's view, any danger to the existing state governments was minimal, and any change that introduced a strong central government was sure to threaten individual liberty.

James Madison answered Patrick Henry's arguments in the Virginia assembly and answered them again in *Federalist No. 39*. Madison asked two questions: (1) Was the proposed central government truly a *republican*, or representative, government, and (2) Was it a truly a *federal* system?

To answer the first question, Madison considered the distinctive characteristics of a republican, or popular, government. (Keep in mind that whereas the term *republic* is seldom used today, it connotes indirect or representative democracy.) He suggested that in a republic, the power of the government is derived from the people and exercised by representatives who are selected directly or indirectly by the people. These representatives serve for specific time periods and are held accountable by the people through regular elections. Madison then showed that the proposed Constitution met these criteria. Members of the House and Senate and the president would be elected for specific terms of office. Furthermore, members of the House would be elected directly by the people, whereas Senators, the President, and Supreme Court justices would be selected indirectly by the people.

Madison then considered the relation between the states and the national government. The terminology in his essay is confusing to the modern reader. We think of a confederacy as a form of government in which the central government has no power independent of that given to it by the member states. In a *confederacy*, for example such as that under the Articles of Confederation, the central government could not raise money by taxing citizens directly; it had to seek money from the states. But in *Federalist* No. 39, Madison used the terms *confederacy* and *federal government* interchangeably, and by either of those terms he meant a completely decentralized government. He contrasted the confederate, or federal, system with a *national* government, a completely centralized government. What he claimed the framers had produced was a combination of federal and national government; one in which both the states and the central government have independent sources of power. In American federalism, for example, both the states and the national government have the power to directly tax citizens. (If you are still confused, think of it this way: Madison was writing for people who understood only two possibilities, national government and state government. His Constitution was a blend of both, and there was no adequate word for it. It was both a national system and a system of state governments. Even his readers were confused.)

As Madison defended the proposed new government against the critics, he wanted to show that it was not strictly a national government and that it retained many important channels of influence by state governments. He carefully narrated the different "federal" (read: state) and "national" elements that had been mixed together to form a new kind of government altogether.

Madison explained that members of the House of Representatives would be elected directly by the people, and the number of representatives from each state would reflect the population of the state. This was a national element. However, senators would be selected by state governments and each state would have an equal number of senators. This federal element would give the state governments considerable power.

The election of the president, Madison explained, would be a complex process that combined federal elements with national ones. The president would be chosen by electors; the electors would come from the states, and they would be chosen by whatever method their state legislature chose. This was a federalized process, but each state would have a number of electors that reflected the state's relative population. This element reflected not equal states but equal citizenship, a national process. Then, if no candidate received an absolute majority of the electors' votes, the election would be decided by the House of Representatives (a national body) but each state's delegation of representatives would together cast just one vote.

In the ordinary operation of the new government, Madison explained that it would have the power to affect citizens directly by legislative, executive, and judicial decisions and, therefore, in this sense it would be a centralized and national government (see, for example, *McCulloch v. Maryland* in Appendix III). However, he insisted that these national powers would be limited and residual power given to citizens and states. He rightfully concluded that the Constitution was "in strictness neither a national nor a federal constitution; but a composition of both."

Alexis de Tocqueville, forever explaining things about the Americans, in 1835 showed how they successfully functioned within their still new and peculiar kind of federal state. He noted that any type of federal government must be a complicated system because it "brings two sovereignties face to face." He saw two problems in a federal system: (1) The member states and the central government are in constant conflict, and (2) The weakness of the central government often means that the country collapses in a crisis. Hence, a successful federal system would require not only good laws but also favorable circumstances—what we might call good luck.

Still, Tocqueville concluded that in the United States neither of these two problems of federalism had yet developed. First, Americans had not only the same interests but also the same kind of civilization. The Americans shared "a homogeneous civilization as well as common needs." It was almost always a comparatively easy matter for them to agree, and thus serious conflict between the states and national government had not yet developed. Second, war, which in history had always revealed the inherent weakness of federated governments, had not yet threatened the American federation. The Americans had the good luck to live on a vast continent insulated by oceans from the rest of the world.

Of course, the American Civil War showed Tocqueville to be right on several counts. Seventy-three years after the signing of the Constitution the state governments in the southern part of the United States decided that their quarrel with the central government and the other states in the federation was irreconcilable. They attempted to dissolve the union. What they did not count on was that the central government was willing and able to force the rebellious states back into the federation. In addition, the demands of the Civil War strengthened the national government's hand against the states. That central government was further tested and strengthened in the twentieth century in the course of two world wars and a severe economic depression. Nonetheless, the precise relation between the national government and the state governments continues to be debated.

Demonstrating that the tensions of federalism are still with us are any number of hotly debated national legislative initiatives at any given time. Here we have selected just one relatively noncontroversial topic—education—to show just how hard it can be to agree on the proper roles of the state and central governments.

Public education in the United States has long been under the direction of state and local governments. The regulation of public education is an issue that touches even the most apolitical people as school boards, parent associations, city councils and mayors, state legislatures, and governors wrestle over the costs and goals. But education is such a pervasive issue that the national government, too—both presidents and Congress—has frequently wanted to intervene and just as frequently has found the problems intractable and the politics complicated. Even a bill with widespread support, the Educate America Act, recently provoked deep suspicion and needed to be significantly modified before it could be passed. The bill essentially meant to force states and localities to raise their standards of education. But of course the devil was in the details, and there was plenty to complain about.

Bob Schaffer, representing a district in Colorado, sees in the Educate America Act the means by which Washington bureaucrats could, under the guise of enforcing standards, overthrow the wishes of parents and local boards. He finds the national government's attempt to intervene in local education to be antidemocratic in that national legislation removes the ability of the local boards to make decisions. Schaffer echoes the concerns of anti-federalists for 200 years: that the country is too diverse for Washington to make good decisions about local issues. Education is an issue as close to the everyday lives of people as an issue can get, and therefore decisions about education should be made as close to the source as possible. Power over education, as in many things, should reside primarily in the states because state governments are necessarily more responsive to citizens and more efficient than a remote, and often elitist, central government.

John Donnangelo argues to the contrary: First, education is not just a local issue but also a national one. The central government has an obligation to protect citizens from problems that are uncorrected by state and local governments. He asks, "[S]ince the states, in large part, are failing to provide adequate public education, what choice does the federal government have but to step in and help?" Second, he uses the Educate America Act to demonstrate that the federal system works just as Tocqueville said it would. It was not a national government that proposed and passed this education bill but was, as Tocqueville described, "an incomplete national government," whose members—elected in a variety of ways, coming from a diversity of circumstances, and advocating a variety of needs—hammered out a complicated, flexible bill that raised school standards, provided some extra money for education, and was sensitive to local concerns. Donnangelo concludes that the negotiations over the bill showed that the national government is not necessarily "the enemy of the state."

23 | *We the States:*
Against a Consolidated National Government
Patrick Henry

A fiery orator and passionate in favor of independence from Britain, Patrick Henry disapproved entirely of the constitutional movement that would have the states relinquish some, if not all, of their sovereignty to a consolidated national government. At the Virginia Convention in June 1788, called to ratify or reject the proposed Constitution, Henry stood repeatedly to air his criticism of the Constitution as contrary to both the interests of the states and the rights of the people. His speeches were followed by replies from Governor Edmund Randolph, George Mason, Edmund Pendleton, Richard Henry Lee, and of course James Madison.

MR. CHAIRMAN: The public mind, as well as my own is extremely uneasy at the proposed change of government. Give me leave to form one of the number of those who wish to be thoroughly acquainted with the reasons of this perilous and uneasy situation—and why we are brought hither to decide on this great national question. I consider myself as the servant of the people of this commonwealth, as a sentinel over their rights, liberty, and happiness. I represent their feelings when I say, that they are exceedingly uneasy, being brought from that state of full security, which they enjoyed, to the present delusive appearance of things.

A year ago the minds of our citizens were at perfect repose. Before the meeting of the late federal convention at Philadelphia, a general peace, and an universal tranquility prevailed in this country—but since that period they are exceedingly uneasy and disquieted. When I wished for an appointment to this convention, my mind was extremely agitated for the situation of public affairs. I conceive the republic to be in extreme danger.

If our situation be thus uneasy, whence has arisen this fearful jeopardy? It arises from this fatal system—it arises from a proposal to change our government—a proposal that goes to the utter annihilation of the most solemn engagements of the states, a proposal of establishing nine states into a confederacy, to the eventual exclusion of our states. It goes to the annihilation of those solemn treaties we have formed with foreign nations.

The present circumstances of France—the good offices rendered us by that kingdom, require our most faithful and most punctual adherence to our treaty with her. We are in alliance with the Spaniards, the Dutch, the Prussians: those treaties bound us as thirteen states, confederated together. Yet here is a proposal to sever that confederacy. Is it possible that we shall abandon all our treaties and national engagements? And for what?

I expected to have heard the reasons of an event so unexpected to my mind, and to many others. Was our civil polity, or public justice, endangered or sapped? Was the real existence of the country threatened—or was this preceded by a mournful progression of events?

This proposal of altering our federal government is of a most alarming nature: make the best of this new government—say it is composed by anything but inspiration—you ought to be extremely cautious, watchful, jealous of your liberty; for instead of securing your rights, you may lose them forever. If a wrong step be now made, the republic may be lost forever. If this new government will not come up to the expectation of the people, and they should be disappointed—their liberty will be lost, and tyranny must and will arise. I repeat it again, and I beg gentlemen to consider, that a wrong step made now will plunge us into misery, and our republic will be lost.

It will be necessary for this convention to have a faithful historical detail of the facts, that preceded the session of the federal convention, and the reasons that actuated its members in proposing an entire alteration of government—and to demonstrate the dangers that awaited us: if they were of such awful magnitude, as to warrant a proposal so extremely perilous as this, I must assert, that this convention has an absolute right to a thorough discovery of every circumstance relative to this great event. And here I would make this enquiry of those worthy characters who composed a part of the late federal convention. I am sure they were fully impressed with the necessity of forming a great consolidated government, instead of a confederation. That this is a consolidated government is demonstrably clear; and the danger of such a government is, to my mind, very striking.

I have the highest veneration for those gentlemen; but, sir, give me leave to demand, what right had they to say, *We, the People?* My political curiosity, exclusive of my anxious solicitude for the public welfare, leads me to ask, who authorized them to speak the language of, *We, the People,* instead of *We, the States?* States are the characteristics, and the soul of a confederation. If the states be not the agents of this compact, it must be one great consolidated national government of the people of all the states. I have the highest respect for those gentlemen who formed the convention, and were some of them not here, I would express some testimonial of esteem for them. America had on a former occasion put the utmost confidence in them; a confidence which was well placed: and I am sure, sir, I would give up anything to them; I would cheerfully confide in them as my representatives. But, sir, on this great occasion, I would demand the cause of their conduct. Even from that illustrious man, who saved us by his valor, I would have a reason for his conduct—that liberty which he has given us by his valor, tells me to ask this reason—and sure I am, were he here, he would give us that reason: but there are other gentlemen here, who can give us this information.

The people gave them no power to use their name. That they exceeded their power is perfectly clear. It is not mere curiosity that actuates me—I wish to hear the real actual existing danger, which should lead us to take those steps so dangerous in my conception. Disorders have arisen in other parts of America, but here, sir, no dangers, no insurrection nor tumult, has happened—everything has been calm and tranquil. But notwithstanding this, we are wandering on the great ocean of human affairs. I see no landmark to guide us. We are running we know not whither. Difference in opinion has gone to a degree of inflammatory resentment in different parts of the country—which has been occasioned by this perilous innovation.

The federal convention ought to have amended the old system—for this purpose they were solely delegated: the object of their mission extended to no other consideration. You must therefore forgive the solicitation of one unworthy member, to know what danger could have arisen under the present confederation, and what are the causes of this proposal to change our government.

24 | Federalist *No. 39*
James Madison

Attempting to answer criticisms that the proposed constitution was not sufficiently representative of the people and would usurp the rights of states, James Madison wrote this piece for the Independent Journal, *a New York newspaper. He first demonstrates that the Constitution strictly follows the prescription of representative democracy, or republicanism. He then shows that it would establish neither a national government to supersede state governments nor a confederacy of sovereign and independent states. Instead, the proposed Constitution would combine the two ideas to produce a new form of government altogether.*

To the People of the State of New York...

The first question that offers itself is whether the general form and aspect of the government be strictly republican. It is evident that no other form would be reconcilable with the genius of the people of America; with the fundamental principles of the Revolution; or with that honorable determination which animates every votary of freedom, to rest all our political experiments on the capacity of mankind for self-government. If the plan of the convention, therefore, be found to depart from the republican character, its advocates must abandon it as no longer defensible.

What, then, are the distinctive characters of the republican form?...

If we resort for a criterion to the different principles on which different forms of government are established, we may define a republic to be... a government which derives all its powers directly or indirectly from the great body of the people, and is administered by persons holding their offices during pleasure, for a limited period, or during good behavior. It is ESSENTIAL to such a government that it be derived from the great body of the society, not from an inconsiderable proportion, or a favored class of it; otherwise a handful of tyrannical nobles, exercising their oppressions by a delegation of their powers, might aspire to the rank of republicans, and claim for their government the honorable title of republic. It is SUFFICIENT for such a government that the persons administering it be appointed, either directly or indirectly, by the people; and that they hold their appointments by either of the tenures just specified; otherwise every government in the United States, as well as every other popular government that has been or can be well organized or well executed, would be degraded from the republican character. According to the constitution of every State in the Union, some or other of the officers of government are appointed indirectly only by the people. According to most of them, the chief magistrate himself is so appointed. And according to one, this mode of appointment is extended to one of the co-ordinate branches of the legislature. According to all the constitutions, also, the tenure of the highest offices is extended to a definite period, and in many instances, both within the legislative and executive departments, to a period of years. According to the provisions of most of the constitutions, again, as well as according to the most respectable and received opinions on the subject, the members of the judiciary department are to retain their offices by the firm tenure of good behavior.

On comparing the Constitution planned by the convention with the standard here fixed, we perceive at once that it is, in the most rigid sense, conformable to it. The House of Representatives, like that of one branch at least of all the State legislatures, is elected immediately by the great body of the people. The Senate, like the present Congress, and the Senate of Maryland, derives its appointment indirectly from the people. The President is indirectly derived from the choice of the people, according to the example in most of the States. Even the judges, with all other officers of the Union, will, as in the several States, be the choice, though a remote choice, of the people themselves, the duration of the appointments is equally conformable to the republican standard, and to the model of State constitutions. The House of Representatives is periodically elective, as in all the States; and for the period of two years, as in the State of South Carolina. The Senate is elective, for the period of six years; which is but one year more than the period of the Senate of Maryland, and but two more than that of the Senates of New York and Virginia. The President is to continue in office for the period of four years; as in New York and Delaware, the chief magistrate is elected for three years, and in South Carolina for two years. In the other States the election is annual. In several of the States, however, no constitutional provision is made for the impeachment of the chief magistrate. And in Delaware and Virginia he is not impeachable till out of office. The President of the United States is impeachable at any time during his continuance in office. The tenure by which the judges are to hold their places, is, as it unquestionably ought to be, that of good behavior. The tenure of the ministerial offices generally, will be a subject of legal regulation, conformably to the reason of the case and the example of the State constitutions.

Could any further proof be required of the republican complexion of this system, the most decisive one might be found in its absolute prohibition of titles of nobility, both under the federal and the State governments; and in its express guaranty of the republican form to each of the latter.

"But it was not sufficient," say the adversaries of the proposed Constitution, "for the convention to adhere to the republican form. They ought, with equal care, to have preserved the FEDERAL form, which regards the Union as a CONFEDERACY of sovereign states; instead of which, they have framed a NATIONAL government, which regards the Union as a CONSOLIDATION of the States." And it is asked by what authority this bold and radical innovation was undertaken? The handle which has been made of this objection requires that it should be examined with some precision.

Without inquiring into the accuracy of the distinction on which the objection is founded, it will be necessary to a just estimate of its force, first, to ascertain the real character of the government in question; secondly, to inquire how far the convention were authorized to propose such a government; and thirdly, how far the duty they owed to their country could supply any defect of regular authority.

First. In order to ascertain the real character of the government, it may be considered in relation to the foundation on which it is to be established; to the sources from which its ordinary powers are to be drawn; to the operation of those powers; to the extent of them; and to the authority by which future changes in the government are to be introduced.

On examining the first relation, it appears, on one hand, that the Constitution is to be founded on the assent and ratification of the people of America, given by deputies elected for the special purpose; but, on the other, that this assent and ratification is to be given by the people, not as individuals composing one entire nation, but as composing the distinct and independent States to which they respectively belong. It is to be the assent and ratification of the several States, derived from the supreme authority in each State,—the authority of the people themselves. The act, therefore, establishing the Constitution, will not be a NATIONAL, but a FEDERAL act.

That it will be a federal and not a national act, as these terms are understood by the objectors; the act of the people, as forming so many independent States, not as forming one aggregate nation, is obvious from this single consideration, that it is to result neither from the decision of a MAJORITY of the people of the Union, nor from that of a MAJORITY of the States. It must result from the UNANIMOUS assent of the several States that are parties to it, differing no otherwise from their ordinary assent than in its being expressed, not by the legislative authority, but by that of the people themselves. Were the people regarded in this transaction as forming one nation, the will of the majority of the whole people of the United States would bind the minority, in the same manner as the majority in each State must bind the minority; and the will of the majority must be determined either by a comparison of the individual votes, or by considering the will of the majority of the States as evidence of the will of a majority of the people of the United States. Neither of these rules have [sic] been adopted. Each State, in ratifying the Constitution, is considered as a sovereign body, independent of all others, and only to be bound by its own voluntary act. In this relation, then, the new Constitution will, if established, be a FEDERAL, and not a NATIONAL constitution.

The next relation is, to the sources from which the ordinary powers of government are to be derived. The House of Representatives will derive its powers from the people of America; and the people will be represented in the same proportion, and on the same principle, as they are in the legislature of a particular State. So far the government is NATIONAL, not FEDERAL. The Senate, on the other hand, will derive its powers from the States, as political and coequal societies; and these will be represented on the principle of equality in the Senate, as they now are in the existing Congress. So far the government is FEDERAL, not NATIONAL. The executive power will be derived from a very compound source. The immediate election of the President is to be made by the States in their political characters. The votes allotted to them are in a compound ratio, which considers them partly as distinct and coequal societies, partly as unequal members of the same society. The eventual election, again, is to be made by that branch of the legislature which consists of the national representatives; but in this particular act they are to be thrown into the form of individual delegations, from so many distinct and coequal bodies politic. From this aspect

of the government it appears to be of a mixed character, presenting at least as many FEDERAL as NATIONAL features.

The difference between a federal and national government, as it relates to the OPERATION OF THE GOVERNMENT, is supposed to consist in this, that in the former the powers operate on the political bodies composing the Confederacy, in their political capacities; in the latter, on the individual citizens composing the nation, in their individual capacities. On trying the Constitution by this criterion, it falls under the NATIONAL, not the FEDERAL character; though perhaps not so completely as has been understood. In several cases, and particularly in the trial of controversies to which States may be parties, they must be viewed and proceeded against in their collective and political capacities only. So far the national countenance of the government on this side seems to be disfigured by a few federal features. But this blemish is perhaps unavoidable in any plan; and the operation of the government on the people, in their individual capacities, in its ordinary and most essential proceedings, may, on the whole, designate it, in this relation, a NATIONAL government.

But if the government be national with regard to the OPERATION of its powers, it changes its aspect again when we contemplate it in relation to the EXTENT of its powers. The idea of a national government involves in it, not only an authority over the individual citizens, but an indefinite supremacy over all persons and things, so far as they are objects of lawful government. Among a people consolidated into one nation, this supremacy is completely vested in the national legislature. Among communities united for particular purposes, it is vested partly in the general and partly in the municipal legislatures. In the former case, all local authorities are subordinate to the supreme; and may be controlled, directed, or abolished by it at pleasure. In the latter, the local or municipal authorities form distinct and independent portions of the supremacy, no more subject, within their respective spheres, to the general authority, than the general authority is subject to them, within its own sphere. In this relation, then, the proposed government cannot be deemed a NATIONAL one; since its jurisdiction extends to certain enumerated objects only, and leaves to the several States a residuary and inviolable sovereignty over all other objects. It is true that in controversies relating to the boundary between the two jurisdictions, the tribunal which is ultimately to decide, is to be established under the general government. But this does not change the principle of the case. The decision is to be impartially made, according to the rules of the Constitution; and all the usual and most effectual precautions are taken to secure this impartiality. Some such tribunal is clearly essential to prevent an appeal to the sword and a dissolution of the compact; and that it ought to be established under the general rather than under the local governments, or, to speak more properly, that it could be safely established under the first alone, is a position not likely to be combated.

If we try the Constitution by its last relation to the authority by which amendments are to be made, we find it neither wholly NATIONAL nor wholly FEDERAL. Were it wholly national, the supreme and ultimate authority would reside in the MAJORITY of the people of the Union; and this authority would be competent at all times, like that of a majority of every national society, to alter or abolish its established government. Were it wholly federal, on the other hand, the concurrence of each State in the Union would be essential to every alteration that would be binding on all. The mode provided by the plan of the convention is not founded on either of these principles. In requiring more than a majority, and particularly in computing the proportion by STATES, not by CITIZENS, it departs from the NATIONAL and advances towards the FEDERAL character; in rendering the concurrence of less than the whole number of States sufficient, it loses again the FEDERAL and partakes of the NATIONAL character.

The proposed Constitution, therefore, is, in strictness, neither a national nor a federal Constitution, but a composition of both. In its foundation it is federal, not national; in the sources from which the ordinary powers of the government are drawn, it is partly federal and partly national; in the operation of these powers, it is national, not federal; in the extent of them, again, it is federal, not national; and, finally, in the authoritative mode of introducing amendments, it is neither wholly federal nor wholly national.

PUBLIUS.

25 | *An Incomplete National Government*
Alexis de Tocqueville

The aristocratic Frenchman who visited America in 1831 concluded that American federalism was unique not only because of its method of operation but also because it could not be easily imitated. According to Tocqueville, American federalism was complicated in theory, contained inherent tensions between the national and state governments and was imperfectly organized by definition. He suggested that the national government's weakness must either be corrected or lead to disastrous dissolution.

...This Constitution, which may at first sight be confounded with the federal constitutions which preceded it, rests upon a novel theory, which may be considered as a great invention in modern political science. In all the confederations which had been formed before the American Constitution of 1789 the allied States agreed to obey the laws of a Federal Government; but they reserved to themselves the right of enforcing the execution of the laws of the Union. The American States which combined in 1789 agreed that the Federal Government should not only dictate the laws, but that it should execute its own laws....

In all the confederations which had been formed before the American Union, the Federal Government demanded its supplies at the hands of the separate state Governments; and if the measure the central government prescribed was onerous to any one of those states, means were found to evade the central government's claims: if the State was powerful, it had recourse to arms; if it was weak, it connived... and resorted to inaction under the plea of inability. Under these circumstances one of two alternatives invariably occurred; either the most preponderant of the allied states assumed the privileges of the Federal authority and ruled all the States in its name, or the Federal Government was abandoned by its natural supporters, anarchy arose between the confederates, and the Union lost all powers of action....

In all former confederations the privileges of the Union furnished more elements of discord than of power, since they multiplied the claims of the nation without augmenting the means of enforcing them: and in accordance with this fact it may be remarked that the real weakness of federal governments has almost always been in the exact ratio of their nominal power. Such is not the case in the American Union, in which, as in ordinary governments, the Federal Government has the means of enforcing all it is empowered to demand.

...Here the term Federal Government is clearly no longer applicable to a state of things which must be styled an incomplete national Government: a form of government has been found out which is neither exactly national nor federal; but no further progress has been made, and the new word which will one day designate this novel invention does not yet exist....

Advantages of the Federal System: The law adapts itself to the exigencies of the population; population does not conform to the exigencies of the law

...The Federal system was created with the intention of combining the different advantages which result from the greater and the lesser extent of nations; and a single glance over the United States of America suffices to discover the advantages which they have derived from its adoption.

In great centralized nations the legislator is obliged to make uniform laws which do not always suit the diversity of customs and of localities; as he takes no cognizance of special cases, he can only proceed upon general principles; and the population is obliged to conform to the exigencies of the legislation, since the legislation cannot adapt itself to the exigencies and the customs of the population, which is the cause of endless trouble and misery. This disadvantage does not exist in confederations. The congress regulates the principal measures of the national Government, and all the details of the administration are reserved to the provincial legislatures. It is impossible to imagine how much this division of sovereignty contributes to the well-being of each of the States which compose the Union. In these small communities, which are never agitated by the desire of aggrandizement or the cares of self-defense, all public authority and private energy is employed in internal amelioration. The central government of each State, which is in immediate juxtaposition to the citizens, is daily apprised of the wants which arise in society; and new projects are proposed every year, which are discussed either at town meetings or by the legislature of the State, and which are transmitted by the press to stimulate the zeal and to excite the interest of the citizens. This spirit of amelioration is constantly alive in the American republics, without compromising their tranquillity; the ambition of power yields to the less refined and less dangerous love of comfort....

It is incontestably true that the love and the habits of republican government in the United States were engendered in the townships and in the provincial assemblies. In a small State, like that of Connecticut for instance, where cutting a canal or laying down a road is a momentous political question, where the State has no army to pay and no wars to carry on, and where much wealth and much honor cannot be bestowed upon the chief citizens, no form of government can be more natural or more appropriate than that of a republic. But it is this same republican spirit, it is these manners and customs of a free people, which are engendered and nurtured in the different States, to be afterwards applied to the country at large. The public spirit of the Union is, so to speak, nothing

more than an abstract of the patriotic zeal of the provinces. Every citizen of the United States transfuses his attachment to his little republic in the common store of American patriotism. In defending the Union he defends the increasing prosperity of his own district, the right of conducting its affairs, and the hope of causing measures of improvement to be adopted which may be favorable to his own interest; and these are motives which are wont to stir men more readily than the general interests of the country and the glory of the nation.

On the other hand, if the temper and the manners of the inhabitants especially fitted them to promote the welfare of a great republic, the Federal system smoothed the obstacles which they might have encountered. The confederation of all the American States presents none of the ordinary disadvantages resulting from great agglomerations of men.... As the sovereignty of the Union is limited and incomplete, its exercise is not incompatible with liberty; for it does not excite those insatiable desires of fame and power which have proved so fatal to great republics. As there is no common center to the country, vast capital cities, colossal wealth, abject poverty, and sudden revolutions are alike unknown; and political passion, instead of spreading over the land like a torrent of desolation, spends its strength against the interests and the individual passions of every State.

Nevertheless, all commodities and ideas circulate throughout the Union as freely as in a country inhabited by one people. Nothing checks the spirit of enterprise. Government avails itself of the assistance of all who have talents or knowledge to serve it. Within the frontiers of the Union the profoundest peace prevails, as within the heart of some great empire; abroad, it ranks with the most powerful nations of the earth; two thousand miles of coast are open to the commerce of the world; and as it possesses the keys of the globe, its flag is respected in the most remote seas. The Union is as happy and as free as a small people, and as glorious and as strong as a great nation.

Why the Federal System Is Not Adapted to All Peoples, and How the Anglo-Americans Were Enabled to Adopt It

...I have shown the advantages which the Americans derive from their federal system; it remains for me to point out the circumstances that enabled them to adopt it, as its benefits cannot be enjoyed by all nations. The incidental defects of the Federal system which originate in the laws may be corrected by the skill of the legislator, but there are further evils inherent in the system which cannot be corrected. The people must therefore find the strength necessary to support the natural imperfections of their Government.

The most prominent evil of all Federal systems is the very complex nature of the means they employ. Two sovereignties are necessarily in presence of each other. The legislator may simplify and equalize the action of these two sovereignties, by limiting each of them to a sphere of authority accurately defined; but he cannot combine them into one, or prevent them from coming into collision at certain points. The Federal system therefore rests upon a theory which is necessarily complicated, and which demands the daily exercise of a considerable share of discretion on the part of those it governs....

In examining the Constitution of the United States, which is the most perfect federal constitution that ever existed, one is startled, on the other hand, at the variety of information and the amount of discernment which it presupposes in the people whom it is meant to govern. The government of the Union depends entirely upon legal fictions; the Union is an ideal nation which only exists, so to speak, only in the mind, and whose limits and extent can only be discerned by the understanding.

Even when the general theory is comprehended, numberless difficulties remain to be solved in its application; for the sovereignty of the Union is so involved in that of the States that it is impossible to distinguish its boundaries at the first glance. The whole structure of the Government is artificial and conventional; and it would be ill adapted to a people which has not been long accustomed to conduct its own affairs, or to one in which the science of politics has not descended to the humblest classes of society. I have never been more struck by the good sense and the practical judgment of the Americans than in the ingenious devices by which they elude the numberless difficulties resulting from their Federal Constitution. I scarcely ever met with a plain American citizen who could not distinguish, with surprising facility, the obligations created by the laws of Congress from those created by the laws of his own State; and who, after having discriminated between the matters which come under the purview of the Union and those which the local legislature is competent to regulate, could not point out the exact limit of the several jurisdictions of the Federal courts and the tribunals of the State.

Yet, the Constitution of the United States is like those exquisite productions of human industry which ensure wealth and renown to their inventors, but which are profitless in any other hands. This truth is exemplified by the condition of Mexico at the present time. The Mexicans were desirous of establishing a federal system, and they took the Federal Constitution of their neighbors, the Anglo-Americans, as their model, and copied it with considerable accuracy. But although they had borrowed the letter of the law, they were unable to create or to introduce the spirit and the sense which give it life. They were involved in ceaseless embarrassments between the mechanism of their double government; the sovereignty of the States and that of the Union perpetually exceeded their respective privileges, and entered into collision; and to the present day Mexico is alternately the victim of anarchy and the slave of military despotism.

The second and the more fatal of the defects, and that which I believe to be inherent in the federal system, is the relative weakness of the government of the Union. The principle upon which all confederations rest is that of a divided sovereignty. The legislature may render this partition less perceptible, it may even conceal it for a time from the public eye, but it cannot prevent it from existing, and a divided sovereignty must always be less powerful than an entire one. The Constitution of the United States shows with what skill the Americans—while restraining the power of the Union—have nonetheless given their federal government the semblance, and to some extent the force, of a national government. By this means the constitution-makers diminished the natural danger of confederations but have not entirely obviated it....

Since legislators are unable to obviate such dangerous collisions as occur between the two sovereignties which coexist in the federal system, their first object must be, not only to dissuade the confederate States from warfare, but to encourage such institutions as may promote the maintenance of peace. Hence it results that the Federal compact cannot be lasting unless there exists in the communities which are leagued together a certain number of inducements to union which render their common dependence agreeable, and the task of the Government light, and that system cannot succeed without the presence of favorable circumstances added to the influence of good laws. All the peoples which have ever formed a confederation have been held together by a certain number of common interests, which served as the intellectual ties of association.

But the sentiments and the principles of people must be taken into consideration as well as their immediate interests. A certain uniformity of civilization is not less necessary to the durability of a confederation than a uniformity of interests in the states which compose it....

The circumstances which make it easy to maintain a Federal Government in America is that the states have not only similar interests, a common origin, and a common tongue, but that they have also arrived at the same stage of civilization; which almost always renders a union feasible. I do not know of any European nation, however small it may be, which does not present less uniformity in its

different provinces than the American people, which occupy a territory as extensive as one-half of Europe. The distance from the State of Maine to that of Georgia is reckoned at about one thousand miles; but the difference between the civilization of Maine and that of Georgia is slighter than the difference between the habits of Normandy and those of Brittany. Maine and Georgia, which are placed at the opposite extremities of a great empire, are consequently in the natural possession of more real inducements to form a confederation than Normandy and Brittany, which are only separated by a brook.

The geographical position of the country contributed to increase the facilities which the American legislators derived from the manners and customs of the inhabitants; and it is to this circumstance that the adoption and the maintenance of the Federal system are mainly attributable.

The most important occurrence which can mark the annals of a people is war. In war the people act as one against foreign nations in the defense of their very existence. The skill of a government, the good sense of the community, and the natural fondness which people have for their country, may suffice to maintain peace in the interior of a region, and to favor its internal prosperity; but a nation can only carry on a great war at the cost of more numerous and more painful sacrifices; and to suppose that a great number of people will of their own accord comply with these exigencies of the State is to betray an ignorance of mankind. All the peoples which have been obliged to sustain a long and serious warfare have consequently been led to augment the power of their government. Those who have not succeeded in this attempt have been subjugated. A long war almost always places nations in the wretched alternative of being abandoned to ruin by defeat or to despotism by success. War therefore renders the symptoms of the weakness of a government most palpable and most alarming; and I have shown that the inherent defeat of federal governments is that of being weak....

How does it happen then that the American Union, with all the relative perfection of its laws, is not dissolved by the occurrence of a great war? It is because it has no great wars to fear. Placed in the center of an immense continent, which offers a boundless field for human industry, the Union is almost as much insulated from the world as if its frontiers were girt by the ocean. Canada contains only a million of inhabitants, and its population is divided into two inimical nations. The rigor of the climate limits the extension of its territory, and shuts up its ports during the six months of winter. From Canada to the Gulf of Mexico a few savage tribes are to be met with, which retire, perishing in their retreat, before six thousand soldiers. To the South, the Union has a point of contact with the empire of Mexico; and it is thence that serious hostilities may one day be expected to arise. But for a long while to come the uncivilized state of the Mexican community, the depravity of its morals, and its extreme poverty, will prevent that country from ranking high amongst nations. As for the Powers of Europe, they are too distant to be formidable.

The great advantage of the United States does not, then, consist in a Federal Constitution which allows them to carry on great wars, but in a geographical position which renders such enterprises extremely improbable.

No one can be more inclined than I am myself to appreciate the advantages of the federal system, which I hold to be one of the combinations most favorable to the prosperity and freedom of man. I envy the lot of those nations which have been enabled to adopt it; but I cannot believe that any confederate peoples could maintain a long or an equal contest with a nation of similar strength in which the government should be centralized. A people which should divide its sovereignty into fractional powers, in the presence of the great military monarchies of Europe, would, in my opinion, by that very act, abdicate its power, and perhaps its existence and its name. But such is the admirable position of the New World that man has no other enemy than himself; and that, in order to be happy and to be free, he need only to determine that he will be so.

Should the National Government Enforce Education Standards for Local Communities?

26 | *Washington Bureaucrats versus Community and Parental Values*
| Bob Schaffer

Education has long been the exclusive purview of local authorities, and attempts to impose national goals or standards of any kind have long been viewed with deep skepticism, if not hostility. Representative Bob Schaffer of Colorado stood in the House to deliver this stinging reproach to the Department of Education and all the Washington bureaucrats who would attempt to shape school lessons for children across the country under the guise of setting standards. Schaffer questions who should determine the lessons of history, and the values children learn? Is it not safer to have local boards and parents determine what "standards" their children should live up to?

Mr. Speaker, ... Congress succeeded in blocking the president's efforts to consolidate national education standards and testing for local schools under the authority of the federal government.

Many parents and educators have been concerned about federalizing education measurements, content, and curriculum since the inception of Goals 2000 in 1994. While the need for standards and accountability is clear, concerns arise when one considers who will set the standards.

Under Goals 2000 legislation, unelected Washington bureaucrats set the standards. Although we hope the government will come up with reasonable and fair education benchmarks, in reality, there are big differences between what Washington experts prescribe and what parents want their kids to be taught.

This dilemma is no better illustrated than in the case of the National History Standards already developed under Goals 2000. Initial standards for American history did not mention some of the most prominent figures of

American history including Paul Revere, the Wright Brothers, or George Washington's presidency. They did, however, encourage the study of Mansa Musa, a West African king in the 14th Century.

Not surprisingly, the standards were unduly critical of capitalism and our European founders. Even members of the Clinton administration and the press found the standards objectionable. The standards have subsequently been revised.

Placing government in charge of standards is certain to include not only content requirements—the who, what, where, why, and how of history, science, math and so on—but also subjective standards such as "students must demonstrate high order thinking or appreciate diversity." Suppose students are held to a standard which defies lessons their parents have taught them? What if teachers are forced to teach what they know to be false or counterproductive? Will government curricula replace that which locally elected school boards have chosen?

If adopted, national education priorities will reflect not the community nor parental values, but those of Washington. Given the atmosphere of political and pervasive corruption in Washington, can we afford such influence in our classrooms?

Clearly, standards of behavior and content must be established and enforced at the state and local level by those who are directly elected and accountable to parents and the community. Federal cooption must give way to increased parental authority. Parents must insist lessons and reading materials state facts and relate values they know to be true. They should vote for school board members who hold their convictions and parents should attend board meetings to stay connected to the process.

The authority of parents to direct their children's education remains threatened however, at least until zeal for federalization is extinguished. The 105th Congress voted to keep education standards in hands of the parents and the community last year. Congress must continue to stand up for the freedom of local teachers to teach, and the liberty of our children to learn.

27 | *Making the Grade: Federalism and National Education Reform*
John A. Donnangelo II

How overbearing is the national (federal) government in regulating state and local governments? John Donnangelo argues that the national government can usefully intervene in local governments to help raise standards and services when local or state governments have been slow to reform or have failed altogether. He argues further that national intervention, as the case of the Educate America Act *shows, is sensitive and accommodating to the variety of local needs precisely because national legislation is made by a* federal *body. The two national legislatures, the House and Senate, are made up of elected officials from all over the country who represent competing interests and thus must carefully negotiate their differences to reach a broad consensus. Nonetheless, the author says, criticizing Washington bureaucrats makes for good press in local politics.*

"The powers not delegated to the United States by the Constitution, nor prohibited by it to the States, are reserved to the States respectively, or to the people." This Tenth Amendment to the *Constitution*, adopted in 1791, establishes a *federal* system in which the national government and individual states and localities share the powers of government. Thus, the framers of the *Constitution* accentuated an inherent tension and continual debate over who is best suited to decide various domestic issues, the national government, the states, or the people themselves. American political history is replete with conflicts over federalism. The Civil War, the establishment of the American Welfare State, and the Great Society are but a few significant examples. The continuing tension and debate over federalism is exemplified best by the debate over national education standards and federal programs, such as *Goals 2000*. However, ultimately, in education, as in many other policy areas, it is important to remember that questions of federalism are often disguised struggles of electoral politics.

THE CALL FOR NATIONAL STANDARDS

The current U.S. school age population of 53.2 million students is the largest it has ever been. Coupled with the nation's ever increasing economic need for highly trained workers in all economic sectors, the present size of the school age population makes the issue of quality education, and who can best provide it, extremely important to all. Washington's policy-makers generally view the issue of quality education as a national concern and the current problems related to providing a quality education—such as the serious shortage of qualified teachers—as requiring the overarching intervention and power of the national government.

In 1994, the Clinton administration's education crusade began with the passage of GOALS 2000, also known as the Educate America Act. The act is intended to provide federal support to states and localities for improving student performance by raising academic standards. It also intends to provide federal support to states and localities for enhancing teacher quality, expanding technology use in classrooms, and increasing parental involvement in the education of their children. Some of the key implementation measures in the Act are: (1) providing of federal incentive grants to states and schools to support effective approaches to improve students' academic performance; (2) providing of federal monies to be allotted to states and schools for better teacher training programs; and (3) allowing the Secretary of Education to waive particular federal regulations to assist states and schools in implementing various school improvements.

To many people, this type of federal intervention into the affairs of the various states is an effective primer and resource provider for badly needed education reforms. Others, however, such as Colorado Republican Congressman Bob Schaffer, argue that this kind of intervention by the national government erodes the states' individual sovereignty. These opponents point to GOALS 2000, and to national education reform in general, as infringements upon states' rights since the states must have their student performance enhancement programs, teacher education programs, and requests to dismiss particular federal regulations approved by the Department of Education in Washington. The opponents argue that this is tantamount to the federal government "dictating" to the states. Additionally, they ask "how can bureaucrats in Washington, D.C. know what initiatives, standards, or regulations will work best in Billings, Montana?"

On the other hand, since the states, in large part, are failing to provide adequate public education, what choice does the federal government have but to step in and help? While the current controversy over national education reform is fueled, in large part, by questions of federalism, it must not be forgotten that the current policy debates on education are also rooted in electoral politics. President Clinton came into office in 1993 behind a campaign message of "change." The "Republican Revolution" of 1994, which produced a Republican congressional majority for the first time in decades, also heralded "change." In an effort to maintain and, if possible, increase their respective political powers, President Clinton and congressional Republicans alike have each tried to show the voters that their "change" is superior and worthy of electoral support. The type of "change" that the Clinton administration tried to present is a federal government that can act effectively and responsibly without overstepping its bounds. On the other hand, the type of "change" that congressional Republicans after 1994 tried to present is rooted in the belief that states, localities, and individuals are better equipped than Washington politicians and bureaucrats to exercise political power and control.

In rebuttal to the states' rights argument, first, GOALS 2000 does NOT specify particular ("categorical") programs or standards that must be implemented with the use of federal funds, as was the case with federal grants made available to the states through the Great Society/War on Poverty programs of the mid and late 1960s. Quality education leading to the creation of a sizeable workforce able to compete in a fast paced, ever changing, technologically oriented global economy is a national goal too important to the nation as a whole for the federal government to simply say that education is a state issue and, therefore, individual states that are struggling to meet ever rising educational standards must go it alone. So, at least on the political surface, with GOALS 2000, the federal government is offering a partnership with the states, a partnership intended to meet essential national education goals without undue infringement upon the rights of the individual states.

Second, there is the misconception that GOALS 2000 is going to lead to a federal takeover of local education. On the contrary, Section 318 of GOALS 2000 clearly states: "Nothing in this Act shall be construed to authorize an officer or employee of the Federal Government to mandate, direct, or control a State, local educational agency, or school's curriculum, program of instruction, or allocation of State or local resources or mandate a State or any subdivision thereof to spend any funds or incur any costs not paid for under this Act."

Third, Section 319 states that Congress "reaffirms that the responsibility for control of education is reserved to the States and local school systems." And, most notably, state participation in GOALS 2000 is NOT federally mandated.

Fourth, another misconception is that our schools will henceforth be moved toward a philosophy known as Outcome-Based Education (OBE). The national government is certainly NOT out to have every school in the nation teach its students in exactly the same fashion and have every student know merely one set of standardized information to be measured by particular examinations. In fact, the 1996 Appropriations Act for GOALS 2000 mandates that the federal government cannot require states or localities to implement outcome-based education as a condition for receiving federal assistance under GOALS 2000.

Fifth, another misconception is the notion that GOALS 2000 is another burdensome federal program with a plethora of rules and regulations. As has already been mentioned, GOALS 2000 is not another Great Society/War on Poverty categorical grant in aid policy. It is a block grant program in keeping with the concept of New Federalism. The Department of Education emphasizes this point by describing the Act as a "responsible block grant" which sets broad educational objectives and goals, allowing states and localities to best determine how they can be reached in their particular schools. This seems to be clearly supported by Section 2 of the Educate America Act, which states the Act's purpose; the most important stated purpose of the act being "promoting coherent, nationwide, systemic education reform." How such a goal or purpose constitutes "federal overbearingness" is unclear to this author.

Further, among the major misconceptions about GOALS 2000 is the notion that it requires the use of national standards. This misconception exists despite the fact that the Department of Education clearly points out: "The use of national standards is voluntary. No funds are tied to the use of these standards, or of any subset of these standards. No law or regulation requires their use in any way."

Finally, among the major misconceptions about GOALS 2000 is the idea that the GOALS 2000 Act is a product of the liberal-education establishment's wish list, the product of powerful, liberal special interests in Washington getting their way and forcing their views upon every American. However, GOALS 2000 has received bipartisan gubernatorial political support across the country.

Ultimately, results are what count. Has GOALS 2000 produced educational improvement without undue federal infringements upon states' rights? The answer appears to be "Yes." By 1998, 47 states, plus Washington, D.C. and Puerto Rico, had developed comprehensive education reform plans. Additionally, 36 states put into place content standards, and 18 states, along with Puerto Rico, had defined performance standards. From 1994-1998, GOALS 2000 allocated in excess of $1.7 billion to various states, with 90% of each state's allotment being subgranted or given to local school districts to support local reforms, professional development, and preservice education (*without federal government mandates*).

State politicians and educators alike from across the country responded to GOALS 2000 with high praise. Governor Roemer of Colorado (D), for example, said that GOALS 2000 was a "flexible partnership" allowing states to "transform the federal grant into local action."

In Kentucky where the majority of GOALS 2000 awards went towards professional development and parental involvement, it was generally reported that "the districts receiving Goals 2000 funds performed at higher levels than districts that did not." Then there was Dr. Henry Marockie, the West Virginia Superintendent of Schools, who concluded that "the seemingly impossible dream of top down, bottom up reform [is] becoming a reality.... At last, the Feds finally got it right."

Finally, in New Jersey, as part of the NATIONAL impetus to improve education, Governor Whitman (R) announced budget plans in January of 2000 to upgrade the State's teacher mentoring program. Whitman's plan called for increasing new teacher mentoring by an experienced teacher from one year to two years while giving a pay increase and state funding for mentoring teachers. Subsequently, the New Jersey State Board of Education, upon the urging of Governor Whitman, voted to raise the college grade point average requirement for new teachers from 2.50 to 2.75.

President Clinton, with public opinion poll approval to continue federally supported education reform, was able to convince the Republican controlled Congress to further federal intervention in education through increased appropriations for education in the budget appropriations act for fiscal year 2000. At the Rose Garden bill signing ceremony, on November 29, 1999, the President summarized: "We value education and this budget truly puts education first, continuing our commitment to hire 100,000 highly-qualified teachers to lower class size in the early grades—which common sense and research both tells us leads to improved learning. The budget also helps to fulfill another promise made last winter to encourage more accountability for results in our nation's schools. Under this budget, for the first time, we will help states and school districts turn around or shut down their worst-performing schools—schools that year after year fail to give our most disadvantaged students the learning they need to escape poverty and reach their full potential. And the budget provides further help for students to reach higher standards by doubling funds for after-school and summer school programs...."

There is still an urgent need for education reform in the United States. However, the federal government has acted responsibly in priming states to take proper policy actions to enhance student performance, teacher competency, and parental involvement without "dictating" to the states what they should do, for doing so would violate the Tenth Amendment and the principles of federalism.

Whether or not the federal governments' actions to provide education reform through Goals 2000 has actually been the product of genuine concern for the principle of federalism with respect to this particular issue, or rather, simply has been the product of crafty electoral politics, is certainly a point for debate. However, some do still believe that the federal government has shown itself not to be the enemy of the state.

CHAPTER FIVE

Public Opinion and the Media
Prologue to a Democratic Farce?

OVERVIEW AND SUMMARY

"Thank God for public opinion!" This paean to vox populi (the voice of the people) was attributed to President Clinton after the Senate acquitted him in his 1999 impeachment trial. The president was expressing his view (as well as his gratitude) that the public made a considered judgment about his behavior during the Monica Lewinsky episode—that his President's actions, while hardly praiseworthy, did not rise to the level of an offense requiring his removal from office. But the voice of the people is a mercurial thing! It is unlikely that Clinton expressed similar approval in 1994 when his then largely lackluster public approval rating portended the Republican sweep of Congress. He may, at that time, even have attributed the 1994 debacle to a biased media serving as a handmaiden to a "disinformation campaign" by his political opponents.

This chapter is devoted to an examination of vox populi in a number of contexts. How can we measure public opinion? If we can accurately measure the public's policy preferences should we be bound by its dictates? In which contexts? Moreover, how is the public informed about policy choices? Is the media, as presently constituted, capable of providing the informational tools by which the mass public can exercise true democratic choice?

Measuring Public Opinion

George Gallup had a dream. As a young mathematician in the 1930s, Gallup turned his attention to the infant science of opinion measurement. He noticed that a host of people tried, unsuccessfully, to characterize and substantiate the popular will. For example, during the long congressional recesses of the prejet era, Congressman "Charlie" would aver that his constituents were saying thus and such about this or that policy issue. Editor Smith of the local newspaper in Charlie's district would weigh in on the same issue, perhaps disputing Charlie's characterization of local opinion. Both the congressman and the editor might be honest and earnest in their assessments. But in each case, their assessments were limited to the people they consulted—those who contacted the congressman's office or those who wrote letters to the editor of the newspaper.

Gallup was not necessarily an early supporter of direct democracy. Taking no express position on the normative question, he sought a method to accurately measure what the public actually thought. Could we determine the desires of people in cafés, barber shops, or rural American hamlets on the issues of the day? What did the common citizen think about the particulars of New Deal economic policy or the brewing war clouds in Europe?

In the 1930s, opinion science could best be described as going through the growing pains of a trial-and-error phase. "Opinion research" projects, some with surface professional credentials, came and went like nimbus clouds. Some projects operated under the assumption that the way to produce an accurate survey was to have the largest possible number of respondents. One such poll was undertaken by *Literary Digest* magazine to predict the results of the 1936 presidential election between President Franklin D. Roosevelt (then seeking a second term) and his Republican opponent, Governor Alfred M. Landon of Kansas. Questionnaires were sent en bloc to citizens whose names were culled from lists of subscribers, individuals who had home telephones, and from those who had purchased new automobiles in 1935-1936. More than 2 million Americans sent back responses. In tabulating the results, *Literary Digest* predicted that Landon would win a 55-45 percent victory over FDR the November election. In fact, President Roosevelt won by a margin of 61-37 percent, one of the largest landslides in American history.

The 1936 polling fiasco provided the spur for new research. The holy grail, as it were, of opinion measurement of this kind turned out to be random sampling. To simplify greatly, the principle of random sampling holds that a survey will be accurate to a high degree of confidence (within a small margin of error) *as long as everyone in a given population has an equal chance of being polled.* In other words, a poll of voters for the next American presidential election is accurate as long as (and assuming you are a voter) the person now reading this chapter is as likely to be surveyed as a person who is at this moment slopping hogs in Montana. As virtually every voter has access to a telephone, random phone surveys can capture an accurate picture of the American electorate with fewer than 1,000 respondents.

This is not to say that random digit-dialing eliminates all possible measurement problems, but the results of national opinion surveys from reputable polling organizations should be regarded as accurate. Nevertheless, a student cannot be blamed for being somewhat skeptical, given the rash of newspaper, radio, and television "talk back" polls that vie for our consideration today. These polls are accurate representations of nothing: They cannot even purport to give a true picture of the views held by readers of that particular newspaper or viewers of that particular program, much less stand as a reflection of vox populi. **Chris Suellentrop** puts a hot torch of skepticism to the recent trend of online polling. Such polls are often entertaining, but are, at most, a measurement of the idiosyncracies of visitors to particular web sites. We regard them as scientific at our peril.

Can the People Govern?

Assuming we can accurately gauge what the citizenry wants, are we best served by granting its wishes? This question, as discussed in Chapter One, does not necessarily imply a lack of faith in democracy. No writer during the founding of the American republic advocated government by public opinion. Even Tocqueville, who extolled the virtues of American democracy, would have looked askance at the notion. The sacred documents of the American *patriae* are, rather, paeans to republicanism. The civics book or republican model posits a view of the public good in which public opinion needs to be filtered by the representative process. Writing at the time when opinion research was in its infancy, **Walter Lippman** concluded that there were practical reasons for this filter. Indeed, Lippman suggested that the notion of government by public opinion would result either in tyranny or farce.

Lippman's argument is made from two perspectives. First, there is doubt whether the public—or even that segment of the public that could be said to be well informed—has sufficient knowledge from which to render a considered policy judgment. For instance, we now have a record of more than five decades of opinion research on the matter of health care in America. Throughout this period, the public has supported universal coverage, free prescription drug coverage, the right to choose one's own physician, and the necessity to maintain market incentives for breakthroughs in medical technology—with no apparent acknowledgement that these goals are in some sense contradictory. The public opposes "socialized medicine," yet, again in apparent contradiction, enthusiastically supports the federal Medicare program. No person can doubt the importance of health care in our constellation of national issues, but can public opinion, coherent enough to make public policy, be gleaned from the results of survey data? Would not national policy made on the basis of these surveys be the farce that Lippman suggests?

Then there is the matter of whether the public should, at all times, be given what it wants. If Congressman Charlie is convinced that President Clinton's behavior in the Lewinsky matter constituted an assault on the "rule of law" by the chief law enforcement officer of this nation, should Charlie feel bound by public opinion polls that suggest otherwise? Moreover, if impeachment seems to be a rather cut-and-dried matter in which vox populi should invariably prevail, can we say the same thing for the hundreds of policy areas that are too complex and/or esoteric for the average citizen to have a strong or considered opinion? If public opinion on health-care reform or national education standards or Social Security reform, measures nothing more than the not very well considered sum of public self-interest, would that not be the tyranny against which Lippman warns?

The Media and Public Information

James Madison wrote that "popular government without popular information is but a prologue to a farce." At the very least, it stands to reason that the formation of opinion is, in part, a function of the information the public receives. That public is bombarded by political messages from a variety of sources, each with a stake in its vote or expression of public support. But whether the message emanates from corporate public relations firms, a political candidate, or an interest group, many regard the messages as biased: We are all skeptical when someone is trying to sell us something. And as everyone seems to turn longingly to the Fourth Estate for "neutral" information, the media seem less and less able to deliver. Perhaps this is why many look first for an ideological basis to bias in the press.

Criticism of the media often consists of ruminations about "liberal" journalists. These critics cite as evidence such factors as the high percentage of media elites (editors and publishers of national, opinion-leading newspapers such as the *New York Times* and *Washington Post*, as well as editors and commentators on the major news networks) who tend to vote for the Democratic candidate in most presidential elections. Social issue conservatives cite the active influence of the "Hollywood elite" in support of liberal social causes—pro-choice on abortion or in favor of restrictions on handguns, for instance—and as the backbone of support for Clinton and Gore. Criticism of bias in the media goes back at least to the 1960's and famously found voice in a speech by Vice President **Spiro T. Agnew.**

Other commentators disagree, hastening to note that the media exist to serve the needs of corporate America. These critics argue that the media, almost by definition, guarantees the values of the status quo. **Jonathan Cohn** notes that national journalists, once comprised of up-through-the-ranks reporters with largely blue-collar roots, are today celebrities, earning high salaries and astronomical speaking fees. The result is an upper-class bias, which may evince itself in a liberal handling of cultural issues like abortion rights, gay rights, and gun control but is quite conservative on many other issues such as taxes, entitlements, and trade policy. In short, the press speaks for people much like themselves and their friends, and their reporting reflects the corresponding values of an elite class.

Without making light of these critiques, all of these quests to find a partisan or ideological bias in the media are ultimately fruitless. The word *media* is a plural noun, and multiple sources of information have always been available to citizens. The past two decades have seen a communications revolution, with several incarnations of distinctive new media—from local TV news (the minicam and "Live at Five" concepts) to nonstop cable news to national talk radio, desktop publishing, "infotainment" and the emergence of the news webpage entrepreneur. Thus, the new barons of the new media offer quite different political views and methods of reportage. And if the major newspapers and big three TV networks dominated the dissemination of information from the 1950s to the 1980s, so many new outlets of coverage have changed the arena entirely. Indeed, the next edition of this book may find CBS, NBC, and ABC largely out of the business of nightly news as we now know it.

The various media manipulation hypotheses also fail because they presuppose that people blindly follow the lead of biased commentators. Countless studies show that well-informed or even moderately informed citizens are not all that persuadable and that they are perfectly capable of ignoring, if not scorning, anything that Sam Donaldson or Rush Limbaugh might say. The less informed are often simply not interested in public affairs; most do not even vote. And those with some minimal level of interest are more likely to be persuaded by family, friends, and coworkers than by the media.

Journalistic Bias

The search for an ideological bias in the news media is perhaps most harmful because it may divert our attention from other, more substantial questions. That is, we perhaps need to turn our attention to the methods and processes of news gathering and processing. The media are first and foremost focused on entertainment, and their charge is to attract and hold audiences. Several journalistic biases—factors such as the propensity to personalize and to stress what is new, dramatic, or sensational—have had profound effects on the public dialogue.

Let us take a set of "news" stories that reached the highest level of saturation coverage in recent years—The OJ Simpson murder trial; the Oklahoma City bombing; the murder of Jon Benet Ramsey; the death of Princess Diana; the school shooting in Littleton, Colorado; and the events surrounding the plight of six-year-old Elian Gonzalez. Although the media sometimes attempted to graft issues of public policy onto these news stories, they were unquestionably sustained by the cult of celebrityhood, pop psychology, the tragic nature of the story, or its salacious or violent content. None of these stories broke new legal ground, and only the Colombine incident suggested consequences for public policy.

While the evidence is thin for the proposition that the media, in any systematic or successful way, tell us *how* to think, there is a broad scholarly consensus for the belief that they collectively influence what we think about. Journalistic bias thus becomes best understood when considered in the context of this agenda-setting role. The media can justify its focus on OJ or Elian Gonzalez by the degree of interest such stories generate. However, the press is much less persuasive when attempting to explain why precious time or space set aside for the discussion of public affairs is instead filled with psychological studies of Dylan Klebold, Timothy McVeigh, or Patsy Ramsey. The invariable effect is to crowd out substantial stories in favor of more immediate or more dramatic stories. No one can doubt that health care is more central to the lives of Americans than is history's verdict of OJ. But it is also true that health care may be seen as too complex, not personal or mediagenic enough, or simply too old a story to attract much of an audience. Fundamentally, these are the journalistic conventions that create a bias against the serious discussion of issues. Even when important public affairs are covered (such as election campaigns; see Chapter Six), the discussions must fit the strictures of those whose business is the news. And invariably, the public discourse is dumbed down by the media's need for conflict, drama personification, or strained topicality.

Our current controversy explores two facets of the journalistic bias. **Barry Glassner** sees the media as a handmaiden of a veritable "fear industry." News stories are selected for their potential to shock; exaggerated dangers, unfounded fears, and freakish occurrences are the rule. In a time of declining violence and falling crime rates, the news media still see the world as an ever more dangerous place.

The tabloidization of public affairs has even affected matters as serious as the impeachment of the president. **James Fallows** examines this media coverage of the Clinton-Lewinsky affair, depicting news media that eschewed all the potential constitutional issues presented by the case (e.g., what is an impeachable offense?) in pursuit of the next cigar, blue dress, or other salacious tidbit. Even serious news outlets lost all sense of proportion, crowding out scores of other concerns and compromising journalistic standards.

28 | *Why Online Polls Are Bunk*
Chris Suellentrop

A good way to acquaint oneself with opinion science is to present a negative example of an unscientific method of polling. Chris Suellentrop of "slate.com" offers a brief primer on the burgeoning "online poll." He argues that the online poll is, for all purposes of scientific accuracy, at best a grandchild of the newspaper, and talk radio/TV polls. What may be great entertainment does not even rise to the level of the infamous Literary Digest *poll in terms of predictive utility. Indeed, Suellentrop concludes that online polls are not polls at all.*

The weekly poll on the Web site of the Democratic National Committee asked visitors: "As the nation approaches a new millennium, what are the most important priorities facing our next president? Saving Social Security, strengthening Medicare and paying down the debt or implementing George W. Bush's $1.7 trillion risky tax scheme that overwhelmingly benefits the wealthy?"

Thanks to an organized Republican effort, more than two-thirds of the respondents favored Bush's tax cuts, prompting an embarrassed DNC to remove the poll from its site. News coverage of the incident explained that the poll was non-binding and non-scientific. But you could go further than that. Online polls aren't even polls.

A poll purports to tell you something about the population at large, or at least the population from which the sample was drawn (for example, likely Democratic voters in New Hampshire). Surprising though it may seem, the results of a scientific poll of a few hundred randomly sampled people can be extrapolated to the larger population (to a 95 percent degree of confidence and within a margin of error).... But the results of an online "poll" in which thousands or even millions of users participate cannot be extrapolated to anything, because those results tell you only about the opinions of those who participated. Online polls are actually elections, of a kind. And elections, while a fine way to pick a president, are a decidedly poor way to measure public sentiment.

Why aren't online polls an accurate measure of public opinion?

1. Respondents are not randomly selected. Online polls are a direct descendent of newspaper and magazine straw polls, which were popular in the 19th and early 20th centuries. The print-media straw polls (very different from today's political straw polls but equally inaccurate) featured clip-out coupons that readers sent in to cast ballots for their preferred candidate. Other organizers of straw polls mailed ballots to people on a list of names. The most infamous of these took place in 1936 when *Literary Digest* sent 10 million presidential ballots to people, based on telephone directories and automobile registration lists. More than 2 million of the ballots were returned, and based on the results, the magazine predicted Republican Alf Landon would carry 57 percent of the popular vote and defeat Franklin Delano Roosevelt in a landslide.

   Literary Digest was wrong, of course, and straw polls never recovered, at least as a predictive tool. Reader and viewer surveys continue to prosper, however, in magazine contests, on TV shows like CNN's TalkBack Live, and on Web sites.

2. Socioeconomic bias. Some of the common criticisms of online polling could be lobbed at the *Literary Digest* survey. In 1936, only a relatively small and wealthy portion of the electorate owned a telephone or an automobile. Likewise, many have criticized online polling because Internet users tend to be wealthier, more educated, and more male than the population at large. For this reason, many people assume Internet poll results to be biased in favor of the viewpoints of relatively wealthy, highly educated males.

But even saying that gives such polls too much credit. A scientific poll of the political opinions of Internet users would be subject to that socioeconomic bias (even random-digit telephone polls are only valid for the population of Americans owning telephones). An online poll—even one that eliminates the problem of multiple voting—doesn't tell you anything about Internet users as a whole, just about those users who participated in the poll.

3. Questions and answers are always given in the same order. Pollsters speak of both the "primacy effect" and the "recency effect," meaning that the first and last choices are more likely to be chosen, particularly when there is a long list of possible answers. In addition, the order in which questions are given can affect the respondents' answers. For example, a question about "the longest economic expansion in history" might affect respondents' answers to a subsequent question about the president's job approval. Scientific polls account for these effects by rotating the order of both the questions and the answers.

Of course, even scientific polls are subject to error, and not just to the standard "margin of error" that is due to assumed errors in sample selection. As in the DNC poll, questions can be biased. Errors can also be made by interviewers and by data processors. Despite these possibilities, scientific polling has a long, reliable history, whereas "straw polling" has a long history of total unreliability.

As long as they are meant as entertainment, and as long as users understand what their results communicate, there's no reason to lose much sleep over online polls. What is worrisome is the failure of pollsters themselves to learn from the history of their profession. Even if they bill themselves as "voting sites" rather than "polling sites," Web sites such as Dick Morris' Vote.com tacitly imply that the results of their online polls are reliable and valid. Otherwise, why would Morris bother to send Vote.com's results to members of Congress?

Another online pollster, Harris Interactive, is using its Harris Poll Online to learn about the public's views on the 2000 election. In order to overcome socioeconomic bias, Harris is using what is known as "quota sampling," which ensures that the poll's respondents are an accurate reflection of the population's demographics. Quota sampling assumes that the answers of a particular demographic group such as white, 18-to-25-year-old Internet users can be projected to describe the opinions of white 18-to-25-year-olds at large. This technique was in widespread use until 1948, when the major national polls based on this technique all predicted that Republican Thomas E. Dewey would defeat incumbent Democrat Harry S Truman.

29 | *The Disenchanted Man*
Walter Lippman

A real "publicist" is not an agent for a Hollywood star but someone who professionally comments on public affairs—such as Walter Lippman, who was a political scientist but also a prolific and accessible writer and an educator of both Washington insiders and the general public. In his enduring book on public opinion, Lippman paints a grim picture of the link between the people and their government, but note that he condemns neither the people nor the governors.

The private citizen today has come to feel rather like a deaf spectator in the back row, who ought to keep his mind on the mystery off there, but cannot quite manage to keep awake. He knows he is somehow affected by what is going on. Rules and regulations continually, taxes annually, and wars occasionally remind him that he is being swept along by great drifts of circumstance.

Yet these public affairs are in no convincing way his affairs. They are for the most part invisible. They are managed, if they are managed at all, at distant centers, from behind the scenes, by unnamed powers. As a private person he does not know for certain what is going on, or who is doing it, or where he is being carried. No newspaper reports his environment so that he can grasp it; no school has taught him how to imagine it; listening to speeches, uttering opinions and voting do not, he finds, enable him to govern it. He lives in a world which he cannot see, does not understand and is unable to direct.

In the cold light of experience he knows that his sovereignty is a fiction He reigns in theory, but in fact he does not govern. Contemplating himself and his actual accomplishments in public affairs, contrasting the influence he exerts with the influence he is supposed according to democratic theory to exert, he must say of his sovereignty what Bismarck said of Napoleon III: "At a distance it is something, but close to it is nothing at all." When, during an agitation of some sort, say a political campaign, he hears himself and some thirty million others described as the

source of all wisdom and power and righteousness, the prime mover and ultimate goal, the remnants of sanity in him protest....

It is well known that nothing like the whole people takes part in public affairs. Of the eligible voters in the United States less than half go to the polls even in a presidential year. During the campaign of 1924 a special effort was made to bring out more voters. They did not come out. The Constitution, the nation, the party system, the presidential succession, private property, all was supposed to be in danger. One party prophesied red ruin, another black corruption, a third tyranny and imperialism if the voters did not go to the polls in greater numbers. Half the citizenship was unmoved.

The students used to write books about voting. They are now beginning to write books about nonvoting. At the University of Chicago Professor Merriam and Mr. Gosnell have made an elaborate inquiry into the reason why, at the typical Chicago mayoral election of 1923, there were, out of 1,400,000 eligible electors, only 900,000 who registered, and out of those who registered there were only 723,000 who finally managed to vote. Thousands of persons were interviewed. About 30 per cent of the abstainers had, or at least claimed to have had, an insuperable difficulty about going to the polls. They were ill, they were absent from the city, they were women detained at home by a child or an invalid, they had had insufficient legal residence. The other 70 per cent, representing about half a million free and sovereign citizens of this

Republic, did not even pretend to have a reason for not voting, which, in effect, was not an admission that they did not care about voting. They were needed at their work, the polls were crowded, the polls were inconveniently located, they were afraid to tell their age… politics is rotten, elections are rotten, they were afraid to vote, they did not know there was an election. About a quarter of those who were interviewed had the honesty to say they were wholly uninterested.…

There is then nothing particularly new in the disenchantment which the private citizen expresses by not voting at all, by voting only for the head of the ticket, by staying away from the primaries, by not reading speeches and documents, by the whole list of sins of omission for which he is denounced. I shall not denounce him further. My sympathies are with him, for I believe he has been saddled with an impossible task and that he is asked to practice an unattainable ideal. I find it so myself for, although public business is my main interest and I give most of my time to watching it, I cannot find time to do what is expected of me in the theory of democracy; that is, to know what is going on and to have an opinion worth expressing on every question which confronts a self-governing community. And I have not happened to meet anybody, from a President of the United States to a professor of political science, who came anywhere near to embodying the accepted ideal of the sovereign and omnicompetent citizen.…

So I have been reading some of the new standard textbooks used to teach citizenship in schools and colleges. After reading one I do not see how any one can escape the conclusion that man must have the appetite of an encyclopaedist and infinite time ahead of him. To be sure he no longer is expected to remember the exact salary of the county clerk and the length of the coroner's term. In the new civics he studies the problems of government, and not the structural detail. He is told, in one textbook of five hundred pages, which I have been reading, about city problems, state problems, national problems, international problems, trust problems, labor prob-

lems, transportation problems, banking problems, rural problems, agricultural problems, and so on *ad infinitum*.…

But nowhere in this well-meant book is the sovereign citizen of the future given a hint as to how, while he is earning a living, rearing children and enjoying his life, he is to keep himself informed about the progress of this swarming confusion of problems.…

That is why the usual appeal to education as the remedy for the incompetence of democracy is so barren.… Democratic theorists in the nineteenth century had several… prescriptions which still influence the thinking of many hopeful persons.

One school based their reforms on the aphorism that the cure for the evils of democracy is more democracy. It was assumed that the popular will was wise and good if only you could get at it.… They begged the question, for it has never been proved that there exists the kind of public opinion which they presupposed.…

The individual man does not have opinions on all public affairs. He does not know how to direct public affairs. He does not know what is happening, why it is happening, what ought to happen. I cannot imagine how he could know, and there is not the least reason for thinking, as mystical democrats have thought, that the compounding of individual ignorances in masses of people can produce a continuous directing force in public affairs.

The actual governing is made up of a multitude of arrangements on specific questions by particular individuals. These rarely become visible to the private citizen. Government, in the long intervals between elections, is carried on by politicians, officeholders and influential men who make settlements with other politicians, officeholders and influential men. The mass of people see these settlements, judge them, and affect them only now and then. They are altogether too numerous, too complicated, too obscure in their effects to become the subject of any continuing exercise of public opinion.…

It may be objected at once that an election which turns one set of men out of office and installs another is an expression of public opinion which is neither secondary nor indirect. But what in fact is an election? We call it an expression of the popular will. But is it? We go into a polling booth and mark a cross on a piece of paper for one or two, or perhaps three or four names. Have we expressed our thought on the public policy of the United States? Presumably we have a number of thoughts on this and that with many buts and ifs and ors. Surely the cross on a piece of paper does not express them. It would take us hours to express our thoughts, and calling a vote the expression of our mind is an empty fiction....

I do not wish to labor the argument any further than may be necessary to establish the theory that what the public does is not to express its opinions but to align itself for or against a proposal....We must say that the popular will does not direct continuously but that it intervenes occasionally....

We must assume that the members of a public will not anticipate a problem much before its crisis has become obvious, not stay with the problem long after its crisis is past. They will not know the antecedent events, will not have seen the issue as it developed, will not have thought out or willed a program, and will not be able to predict the consequences of action on that program...

The public will arrive in the middle of the third act and will leave before the last curtain, having stayed just long enough perhaps to decide who is the hero and who the villain of the piece. Yet usually that judgment will necessarily be made apart from the intrinsic merits, on the basis of a sample of behavior, an aspect of a situation, by very rough external evidence.

30 | *The Nattering Nabobs of Negativism*
Spiro T. Agnew

If there is one thing that the public believes about the American media, it is the presence of systematic bias in the presentation of news and information about political affairs. Although both liberals and conservatives make their cases for bias, it is more often made by irate conservatives. It was never better stated than in Vice President Agnew's speech before the Midwest Republican Conference on November 13, 1969. Add a clause about Murphy Brown, and one can imagine Dan Quayle and many another politicians delivering the same speech today.

Tonight I want to discuss the importance of the television news medium to the American people. No nation depends more on the intelligent judgment of its citizens. No medium has a more profound influence over public opinion. Nowhere in our system are there fewer checks on vast power. So, nowhere should there be more conscientious responsibility exercised than by the news media. The question is, are we demanding enough of our television news presentations? And are the men of this medium demanding enough of themselves?

Monday night a week ago, President Nixon delivered the most important address of his Administration, one of the most important of our decade. His subject was Vietnam. His hope was to rally the American people to see the conflict through to a lasting and just peace in the Pacific. For 32 minutes, he reasoned with a nation that has suffered almost a third of a million casualties in the longest war in its history.

When the President completed his address—an address, incidentally, that he spent weeks in the preparation of—his words and policies were subjected to instant analysis and querulous criticism. The audience of 70 million Americans gathered to hear the President of the United States was inherited by a small band of network commentators and self-appointed analysts, the majority of whom expressed in one way or another their hostility to what he had to say.

It was obvious that their minds were made up in advance. Those who recall the fumbling and groping that followed President Johnson's dramatic disclosure of his intention not to seek another term have seen these men in a genuine state of nonpreparedness. This was not it.

One commentator twice contradicted the President's statement about the exchange of correspondence with Ho Chi Minh. Another challenged the President's abilities as a politician. A third asserted that the President was following a Pentagon line. Others, by the expression on their faces, the tone of their questions and the sarcasm of their responses, made clear their sharp disapproval....

Now every American has a right to disagree with the President of the United States and to express publicly that disagreement. But the President of the United States has a right to communicate directly with the people who elected him, and the people of this country have the right to make up their own minds and form their own opinions about a Presidential address without having a President's words and thoughts characterized through the prejudices of hostile critics before they can even be digested....

The purpose of my remarks tonight is to focus your attention on this little group of men who not only enjoy a right of instant rebuttal to every Presidential address, but, more importantly, wield a free hand in selecting, presenting and interpreting the great issues in our nation.

First, let's define that power. At least 40 million Americans every night, it's estimated, watch the network news. Seven million of them view ABC, the remainder being divided between NBC and CBS.

According to Harris polls and other studies, for millions of Americans the networks are the sole source of national and world news. In Will Roger's observation, what you knew was what you read in the newspaper. Today for growing millions of Americans, it's what they see and hear on their television sets.

Now how is this network news determined? A small group of men, numbering perhaps no more than a dozen anchormen, commentators, and executive producers, settle upon the 20 minutes or so of film and commentary that's to reach the public. This selection is made from the 90 to 180 minutes that may be available. Their powers of choice are broad.

They decide what 40 to 50 million Americans will learn of the day's events in the nation and in the world.

We cannot measure this power and influence by the traditional democratic standards, for these men can create national issues overnight.

They can make or break by their coverage and commentary a moratorium on the war.

They can elevate men from obscurity to national prominence within a week. They can reward some politicians with national exposure and ignore others....

Nor is their power confined to the substantive. A raised eyebrow, an inflection of the voice, a caustic remark dropped in the middle of a broadcast can raise doubts in a million minds about the veracity of a public official or the wisdom of a Government policy.

One Federal Communications Commissioner considers the powers of the networks equal to that of local, state, and Federal Governments all combined. Certainly it represents a concentration of power over American public opinion unknown in history.

Now what do Americans know of the men who wield this power? Of the men who produce and direct the network news, the nation knows practically nothing. Of the commentators, most Americans know little other than that they reflect an urbane and assured presence seemingly well-informed on every important matter.

We do know that to a man these commentators and producers live and work in the geographical and intellectual confines of Washington, D.C., or New York City, the latter of which James Reston terms the most unrepresentative community in the entire United States.

Both communities bask in their own provincialism, their own parochialism.

We can deduce that these men read the same newspapers. They draw their political and social views from the same sources. Worse, they talk constantly to one another, thereby providing artificial reinforcement to their shared viewpoints....

The American people would rightly not tolerate this concentration of power in Government.

Is it not fair and relevant to question its concentration in the hands of a tiny enclosed fraternity of privileged men elected by no one and enjoying a monopoly sanctioned and licensed by Government?

The views of the majority of this fraternity do not—and I repeat, not—represent the views of America.

That is why such a great gulf existed between how the nation received the President's address and how the networks reviewed it....

As with other American institutions, perhaps it is time that the networks were made more responsive to the views of the nation and more responsible to the people they serve.

Now I want to make myself perfectly clear. I'm not asking for Government censorship or any other kind of censorship. I'm asking whether a form of censorship already exists when the news that 40 million Americans receive each night is determined by a handful of men responsible only to their corporate employers and is filtered through a handful of commentators who admit to their own set of biases.

The questions I'm raising here tonight should have been raised by others long ago. They should have been raised by those Americans who have traditionally considered the preservation of freedom of speech and freedom of the press their special provinces of responsibility....

Normality has become the nemesis of the network news. Now the upshot of all this controversy is that a narrow and distorted picture of America often emerges from the televised news....

Perhaps the place to start looking for a credibility gap is not in the offices of the Government in Washington but in the studios of the networks in New York....

By way of conclusion, let me say that every elected leader in the United States depends on these men of the media. Whether what I've said to you tonight will be heard and seen at all by the nation is not my decision, it's not your decision, it's their decision.

In tomorrow's edition of *The Des Moines Register*, you'll be able to read a news story detailing what I've said tonight. Editorial comment will be reserved for the editorial page, where it belongs.

Should not the same wall of separation exist between news and comment on the nation's networks?

Now, my friends, we'd never trust such power, as I've described, over public opinion in the hands of an elected Government. It's time we questioned it in the hands of a small and unelected elite.

The great networks have dominated America's airwaves for decades. The people are entitled to a full accounting of their stewardship.

31 | *Perrier in the Newsroom*
Jonathan Cohn

Jonathan Cohn offers us this insight on the partisan bias of the media: "If Washington's elite tend to champion most liberal cultural causes, their financial self-interest often translates into a conspicuous sympathy for conservative doctrines on economics and government activism."

There was a day not far distant, you know, just before World War II, when nearly all of us news people, although perhaps white collar by profession, earned blue-collar salaries. We were part of the "common people." We suffered the same budgetary restraints, the same bureaucratic indignities, waited in the same lines, suffered the same bad service. We could identify with the average man because we were him.

For at least a generation conservative politicians have accused the Washington press corps of being part of the liberal elite. The accusation is half right. Better educated and better paid than at any time in history, reporters and editors at America's major news institutions are members of the privileged class. Gone are the familiar blue-collar trappings of newspapering, and with them have frayed the bonds between reporters and working-class readers. Once the common man's watchdog over the establishment, the national media has become part of it.

But while Newt Gingrich has been the one registering this complaint lately, liberals have more reason to worry. If Washington's elite tend to champion most liberal cultural causes, their financial self-interest often translates into a conspicuous sympathy for conservative doctrines on economics and government activism. As long as this sensibility defines the boundaries of political debate in the media, liberals will struggle in their attempt to promote an agenda of expanding economic opportunity for the working class....

As recently as 25 years ago, journalism was still a predominantly blue-collar occupation, at least in spirit. Although college graduates were in the business as early as the turn of the century, not until the 1970s did they account for the majority. Even among those who had college degrees in generations past, there was still a high proportion of social misfits and underachievers: kids who were smart and made it to college, but couldn't quite cut it in a "real" profession like law or medicine. Describing his colleagues at the *Nashville Tennessean* in the 1950s, former *New York Times*man David Halberstam wrote in a recent issue of the *Columbia Journalism Review:*

> There was nothing about us, in our past performances, in our personal style, in our dress code and our personal grooming that would lead anyone to think we were candidates to be Most Likely to Succeed.... The normally ambitious young men of our time (there were no women in those days) wanted to make as much money as possible with as large a company as possible. We, by contrast, were doing something that not only paid very little in the present, but promised to pay not very much more in the future.

At many small to mid-size newspapers, one still finds traces of grimier days: Cub reporters still struggle to make $20,000 a year, and they still prefer Bud to Perrier. Even at some of the larger papers, staff rarely make more than $50,000, more than the national average, yes, but middle class by any definition.

The same can't be said of senior staff at the largest dailies, the newsweeklies, and the networks, where salaries can climb past $100,000 and clever journalists parlay their visibility into lucrative speaking and television engagements. As Ken Auletta recently wrote in the *New Yorker*, celebrity journalists can double or even triple their base salaries solely through paid appearances: *ABC News*'s Cokie Roberts, for example, made more than $300,000 in outside income last year, or nearly ten times what the average American took home, according to Auletta.

A number of Washington media critics, chief among them the *Washington Post*'s Howard Kurtz and the *Chicago Tribune*'s Jim Warren, have hammered away at the honoraria issue for some time, with particular attention to how corporate speaking engagements can create conflicts of interest. Yet while the conflict-of-interest question has sparked some soul-searching within the media community, surprisingly few journalists seem conscious of the more subtle ways that celebrity status and salary inflation have tainted their worldview. Though these folks still consider themselves part of the "working press," they have no more to do with the working man than do the officials they cover. They inevitably live in such places as the Upper West Side or Bethesda, and send their kids to Groton Academy or maybe Sidwell Friends. Legend has it reporters at the *Boston Globe* cheered when the stock market crashed in 1929; when it crashed in 1987, the story goes, they called their stockbrokers.

Many of today's high-profile reporters also came to Washington via a different route. A generation ago, even the most ambitious and well-educated young scribes cut their teeth on city beats at daily newspapers, an experience that could be as much an exercise in class awareness as an apprenticeship in writing. "It didn't matter who you were or what graduate degrees you were loaded with," recalls Pulitzer-winner J. Anthony Lukas of his stint covering cops for the *Baltimore Sun*. "That's where you started."

To make matters worse, the new fast track screens out aspiring scribes who lack independent financial means. The breeding grounds for many Washington reporters, such as the *New Republic* or the *Washington Monthly*, now pay their entry-level writers anywhere from $10,000 to $13,000 a year; the same goes for internships at think tanks and other stepping-stone organizations. Though this bout with near-poverty can help breed working-class sympathy, it also has the perverse effect of attracting to the field primarily those people who don't owe college loans but still went to college and those who can get by with occasional cash stipends from Mom or Dad....

[T]he cumulative effect of these trends has been the creation of an elite class of reporters with a conspicuously upper-middle-class sympathy. Sometimes this instinct manifests itself as a sympathy for liberal causes such as abortion rights, gay rights, and the like. But the same bias also expresses itself as an uncritical faith in conservative doctrines about inflation, trade, taxes, and government spending, and it is these attitudes that most directly shaped the coverage of politics during... the Clinton administration.

One vivid illustration was the coverage of the North American Free Trade Agreement (NAFTA). Whether or not the treaty was in the nation's best interests, it threatened the short-term employment prospects of thousands of American workers. Yet, as Howard Kurtz has argued in the *Post,* the vast majority of stories on the issue treated projections of job losses as just more abstract studies to be cited as context and then dispelled by experts. When NAFTA was in trouble on Capitol Hill, most political reporters played it as just another case of parochial legislators, beholden to labor unions, looking to cripple a visionary initiative. "Most journalists simply don't know personally anybody whose job might have been threatened by NAFTA," says Kurtz, who has been a lone but persistent critic of elite journalism for years. "Journalists get real upset when a handful of jobs are lost at a newspaper, but when it's factory workers in the Midwest, it's easy to treat it as just another statistic."

The coverage of NAFTA, with its heavy reliance on economists as experts, was indicative of another problem. Elite journalists who are more comfortable in the lecture hall than the precinct house often rely on professorial talking heads. By magnificent coincidence, these authorities often validate the writers' own analytical theories and make it unnecessary for them to bother with the traditional, on-the-ground reporting that might encourage a working-class perspective. News is treated in the abstract; reporters inquire what it means for the system, not for the people.

A more blatant pattern of class bias, one that more clearly worked to the Clinton administration's disadvantage, emerged in the debates over the 1993 budget. Recall that while the president proposed to raise some $305 billion in taxes, nearly all of it was to come from the very wealthy. For 15 million working Americans he offered a tax break (in the form of an expanded earned income tax credit); the middle class would pay an energy tax costing the average family only $200 a year. The gas tax was eventually reduced to a pittance, yet polls show[ed] as many as 70 percent of Americans (thought) Clinton raised taxes on the middle class.

The *New Republic*'s Michael Kinsley, among others, has suggested that the nation's intellectual and media elite may have been the source of this misconception; after all, many of them were among the 1.2 percent of Americans hit by the income tax hike....

The same can be said for the press's obsession with entitlements and the deficit, which helped stymie the administration's early attempts to increase public investment.... [T]he press ... measured every Clinton initiative by its likely impact on the deficit.... "You have a lot of reporters talking about getting entitlements under control," says one correspondent. "You don't hear them talking about getting rid of the home mortgage deduction."

Health care coverage, too, fell prey to this mentality. "I defy you to ask any reporter to name five people he knows who don't have health insurance or even some who might lose it," steams political svengali James

Carville. Indeed, it often seemed that the press establishment's primary concern was whether the blue-chip coverage of most reporters might suffer under reform....

But for a majority of Americans, the Clinton plan would have expanded options. Employers are now shifting their workers into health maintenance organizations and preferred provider plans that limit their choice of doctor, and about half of employees who receive health benefits have no choice of plan. The Clinton proposal, in contrast, would have guaranteed Americans access to a broad slate of plans in their communities, including fee-for-service options that many are now losing entirely....

Now and again prominent journalists still manage to crash through class barriers.... But promoting such coverage is difficult because other trends in the media business reinforce the gentrification of news. As newspapers use zoned editions to cultivate affluent suburban readers, the pressure to cater to that audience grows stronger. Omnipresent, too, are the fiscally conservative sentiments of corporate advertisers and media chain moguls. Yet it is not the publishers but the editors and writers who make most of the daily calls on content and the framing of coverage; the power to right the pro-establishment tilt remains theirs. Most journalists, of course, don't like to think of themselves as anybody's advocate. But that's most likely because advocacy of elite interests comes so easily that it scarcely seems like bias at all. Media executives constantly wonder why so many poor or working-class Americans would rather watch the distortions of trash television than pick up a newspaper. Perhaps it's because many of these people no longer see the front page as true to their experience.

A CURRENT CONTROVERSY

The Media: Friend, Foe, or Fake?

32 | *Culture of Fear*
Barry Glassner

What is the real bias of the media? Barry Glassner reminds us not to believe everything we hear, as the media, especially television, cultivate fear in order to cultivate consumer interest. Moreover, interest groups and other political actors are often willing to use this media bias to their own advantage. The problem? The public is informed, and the political agenda made, through this culture of fear.

Why are so many fears in the air and so many of them unfounded? Why, as crime rates plunged throughout the 1990s did two-thirds of Americans believe they were soaring? How did it come about that by mid-decade 62 percent of us described ourselves as "truly desperate" about crime—almost twice as many as in the late 1980s when crime rates were higher?...

In the late 1990s the number of drug users had decreased by half compared to a decade earlier; almost two-thirds of high school seniors had never used any illegal drugs, even marijuana. So why did a majority of adults rank drug abuse as the greatest danger to America's youth?...

Give us a happy ending and we write a new disaster story. In the late 1990s the unemployment rate was below 5 percent for the first time in a quarter century. People who had been pounding the pavement for years could finally get work. Yet pundits warned of imminent economic disaster. They predicted inflation would take off, just as they had a few years earlier—also erroneously—when the unemployment rate dipped below 6 percent....

[A] popular explanation blames the news media. We have so many fears, many of them off-base, the argument goes, because the media bombard us with sensationalistic stories designed to increase ratings. This explanation, sometimes called the media-effects theory, is less simplistic than the millennium hypothesis and contains sizable kernels of truth. When researchers from Emory University computed the levels of coverage of various health dangers in popular magazines and newspapers they discovered an inverse relationship: much less space was devoted to several of the major causes of death than to some uncommon causes. The leading cause of death, heart disease, received approximately the same amount of coverage as the eleventh-ranked cause of death, homicide. They found a similar inverse relationship in coverage of risk factors associated with serious illness and death. The lowest-ranking factor, drug use, received nearly as much attention as the second-ranked factor, diet and exercise.

Disproportionate coverage in the news media plainly had effect on readers and viewers. When Esther Madriz, a professor at Hunter College, interviewed women in New York City about their fears of crime they frequently responded with the phrase "I saw it in the news." The interviewees identified the news media as both the source of their fears and the reason they believed those fears were valid. Asked in a national poll why they believe the country has a serious crime problem, 76 percent of people cited stories they had seen in the media. Only 22 percent cited personal experience.

When professors Robert Blendon and John Young of Harvard analyzed forty-seven surveys about drug abuse conducted between 1978 and 1997, they too discovered that the news media, rather than personal experience, provide Americans with their predominant fears. Eight out of ten adults say that drug abuse has never caused problems in their family, and the vast majority report relatively little direct experience with problems related to drug abuse. Widespread concern about drug problems emanates, Blendon and Young determined, from scares in the news media, television in particular.

Television news programs survive on scares. On local newscasts, where producers live by the dictum "if it bleeds, it leads," drug, crime, and disaster stories make up most of the news portion of the broadcasts. Evening newscasts on the major networks are somewhat less bloody, but between 1990 and 1998, when the nation's murder rate declined by 20 percent, the number of murder stories on network newscasts increased 600 percent (not counting stories about O.J. Simpson).

After dinnertime newscasts the networks broadcast news-magazines, whose guiding principle seems to be that no danger is too small to magnify into a national nightmare. Some of the risks reported by such programs would be merely laughable were they not hyped with so much fanfare: "Don't miss *Dateline* tonight or YOU could be the next victim!" Competing for ratings with drama programs and movies during prime-time evening hours, news-magazines feature story lines that would make a writer for "Homicide" or "ER" wince.

"It can happen in a flash. Fire breaks out on the operating table. The patient is surrounded by flames," Barbara Walters exclaimed on ABC's "20/20" in 1998. The problem—oxygen from a face mask ignited by a surgical instrument—occurs "more often than you might think," she cautioned in her introduction, even though reporter Arnold Diaz would note later, during the actual report, that out of 27 million surgeries each year the situation arises only about a hundred times. No matter, Diaz effectively nullified the

reassuring numbers as soon as they left his mouth. To those who "may say it's too small a risk to worry about" he presented distraught victims: a woman with permanent scars on her face and a man whose son had died.

The gambit is common. Producers of TV news-magazines routinely let emotional accounts trump objective information. In 1994 medical authorities attempted to cut short the brouhaha over flesh-eating bacteria by publicizing the fact that an American is fifty-five times more likely to be struck by lightening than die of the suddenly celebrated microbe. Yet TV journalists brushed this fact aside with remarks like, "whatever the statistics, it's devastating to the victims" (Catherine Crier on "20/20"), accompanied by stomach-turning videos of disfigured patients.

… To blame the media is to oversimplify the complex role that journalists play as both proponents and doubters of popular fears. It is also to beg… the key issue… why particular anxieties take hold when they do. Why do news organizations and their audiences find themselves drawn to one hazard rather than another?

May Douglas, the eminent anthropologist who devoted much of her career to studying how people interpret risk, pointed out that every society has an almost infinite quantity of potential dangers from which to choose. Societies differ both in the types of dangers they select and the number. Dangers get selected for special emphasis, Douglas showed, either because they offend the basic moral principles of the society or because they enable criticism of disliked groups and institutions. In *Risk and Culture*, a book she wrote with Aaron Wildavsky, the authors give an example from fourteenth century Europe. Impure water had been a health danger long before that time, but only after it became convenient to accuse Jews of poisoning the wells did people become preoccupied with it.

Or take a more recent institutional example. In the first half of the 1990s U.S. cities spent at least $10 billion to purge asbestos from public schools, even though removing asbestos from buildings posed a greater health hazard than leaving it in place. At a time when about one-third of the nation's schools were in need of extensive repairs the money might have been spent to renovate dilapidated buildings. But hazards posed by seeping asbestos are morally repugnant. A product that was supposed to protect children from fires might be giving them cancer. By directing our worries and dollars at asbestos we express outrage at technology and industry run afoul.

From a psychological point of view extreme fear and outrage are often projections. Consider, for example, the panic over violence against children. By failing to provide adequate education, nutrition, housing, parenting, medical services, and child care over the past couple of decades we have done the nation's children immense harm. Yet we project our guilt onto a cavalcade of bogeypeople—pedophile preschool teachers, preteen mass murderers, and homicidal au pairs, to name only a few....

Diverse groups used the ritual-abuse scares to diverse ends. Well-known feminists such as Gloria Steinem and Catharine MacKinnon took up the cause, depicting ritually abused children as living proof of the ravages of patriarchy and the need for fundamental social reform.

This was far from the only time feminist spokeswomen have mongered fears about sinister breeds of men who exist in nowhere near the high numbers they allege. Another example occurred a few years ago when teen pregnancy was much in the news. Feminists helped popularize the frightful but erroneous statistic that two out of three teen mothers had been seduced and abandoned by adult men. The true figure is more like one in ten, but some feminists continued to cultivate the

scare well after the bogus stat had been definitively debunked.

Within public discourse fears proliferate through a process of exchange. It is from crosscurrents of scares and counterscares that the culture of fear swells ever larger. Even as feminists disparage large classes of men, they themselves are a staple of fear mongering by conservatives. To hear conservatives tell it, feminists are not only "anti-child and anti-family" (Arianna Huffington) but through women's studies programs on college campuses they have fomented an "anti-science and anti-reason movement" (Christina Hoff-Sommers).

Conservatives also like to spread fears about liberals, who respond in kind. Among other pet scares, they accuse liberals of creating "children without consciences" by keeping prayer out of schools—to which liberals rejoin with warnings that right-wing extremists intend to turn youngsters into Christian soldiers.

Samuel Taylor Coleridge was right when he claimed, "In politics, what begins in fear usually ends up in folly." Political activists are more inclined, though, to heed an observation from Richard Nixon: "People react to fear, not love. They don't teach that in Sunday school, but it's true." That principle, which guided the late president's political strategy throughout his career, is the sine qua non of contemporary political campaigning. Marketers of products and services ranging from car alarms to TV news programs have taken it to heart as well.

The short answer to why Americans harbor so many misbegotten fears is that immense power and money await those who tap into our moral insecurities and supply us with symbolic substitutes....

33 | *Rush from Judgment:*
How the Media Lost Their Bearings

James Fallows

Long-time reporter and commentator James Fallows offers his analysis of the media coverage of the Lewinsky-Impeachment story of 1998–1999. What was striking to Fallows was the degree of predictability about the coverage. This article allows us to apply what we know about the journalistic biases of the media to see the cause of this predictability.

The main question left from the Monica era is: Was it inevitable? Not the trysts themselves—whether they were psychologically inevitable, apart from being insane, can now be left to various Clintons in their future books. Nor is it really worth pondering at the moment whether Kenneth Starr's fixation on the case, or the Republican Congress's exploitation of it in the drive to impeachment, was inevitable. Their responses were logical extensions of the scorched-earth party politics of the last 15 years. We could say that Starr, Newt Gingrich, Tom DeLay, and the others resembled Bill Clinton (and Bob Livingston) in not being able to restrain their least attractive but apparently strongest drives.

The interesting question concerns the press.... [F]rom the weekend of January 19, 1998, when the three network news anchors began scrambling back from Havana, leaving Fidel Castro and the pope to meet in relative privacy, until the revving up of the impeachment hearings just after the congressional elections—Monica dominated coverage more completely than Watergate did until its final months, and more than the Vietnam War did through most of the 1960s. It was like nothing since . . . well, since the Diana story of the preceding fall, and the O. J. story before that. And while Monica resembled Diana and O. J. in the degree of media saturation, it differed in that the press could claim to have "won" the Monica fight. Reporters (especially *Newsweek's* Michael Isikoff) did win in a technical sense—rumors that sounded far-fetched at the beginning of the year were part of the stipulated body of fact by the end.... And the

segments of the press that pushed the story hardest won in a larger sense: there is no denying that the episode has now taken on historic gravity, forever bracketing Clinton at least with Andrew Johnson and conceivably with Richard Nixon. But neither the Clintonian self-indulgence that started the story nor the Republican determination that may end it mean we can just forget about everything that happened in between. Through much of the year, polls indicated that people thought Clinton had behaved like an idiot—but that didn't keep them from also being skeptical of Starr. The press should be capable of at least as complex a view. A volley of our shots finally hit a target, but it is still worth asking how many were fired, what they were aimed at, and who else got killed.

If Clinton's excesses were depressing for their familiarity, exactly the same is true of the press's. The most surprising aspect of the Monica excesses was how unsurprising—how perfectly predictable—they were... as the months went on, it was as if every media hand-wringing session held in the aftermath of the Rodney King coverage, every bit of press introspection after the era of O. J., every purported lesson of the Diana orgy, had never occurred—notwithstanding that, again, the press "won" in the sense that Clinton ended up getting impeached. The fundamental and predictable problem was a return of an "all or nothing" mentality, in which the running spectacle-story of the moment squeezes everything else out of the news.... Even if we stipulate that every accusation against Clinton was true, even if we assume (as I do not) that he should have been impeached, it's still hard to contend that the story should have forced out so many other subjects for such a long time.

So, was this all inevitable—the press's recapitulation of its past excesses? The answer is surprisingly significant, no matter what you think the correct answer is. If reporters, editors, and broadcasters really had no choice in the matter and were forced to overplay Monica for commercial reasons—or because of the rise of the Internet, or whatever—then journalism is in a worse predicament than even Newt Gingrich might think. But if, on the other hand, reporters and editors had more room to maneuver than most now claim, and were able to shape the coverage by their own choice, then it's worth wondering how they might make different choices the next time.

What Went Wrong

For the record, what exactly was embarrassing about the press's performance in this case? For half a dozen years critics inside and outside the press have worked up a standard list of complaints about Media Gone Wrong. Nearly everything that was generally thought to be a problem proved to be a problem when exposed to Monica.

No sense of proportion. This was the big one. It is reassuring to go back to an old newspaper or newsmagazine and see that events considered important in retrospect got attention at the time. ("Hitler Invades Poland.") It is intriguing but less heartening to go back and see saturation coverage for trends or events that seem like sideshows once they are done. (Banner headlines about the departure of Bert Lance from the Carter administration, for one example; or the mere existence of the Menendez brothers, for another.)...

Journalists aren't supposed to be historians, but if we have any claim to expertise over the typical guy in a bar, it should lie in our ability to say: This event is more significant than that one, and I'm going to explain why. That ability is what the famed "nose for news" is all about. The Monica frenzy will, I suspect, be seen in the long run as a Bert Lance/Menendez brothers moment rather than a Watergate moment in press coverage—or more precisely, as an Andrew Johnson rather than a Richard Nixon event. That is, as an episode whose heavy media coverage illustrates the mood of its times rather than reflecting the magnitude of the story itself. The problem with all-out saturation coverage, whether about Diana or Monica, is what gets left out— all the things that aren't written about, published, or placed into public awareness because of the obsession of the moment. It may seem that in the age of cable TV, talk radio, and the Internet there is a limitless amount of space for news. But two journalistic vehicles remain incredibly short on space—network TV broadcasts, and weekly newsmagazines—and only so many stories can fit on a newspaper's front page. Anyone who's worked in a big news organization knows that when a Monica– or O. J.–style frenzy begins, other news simply gives way. The foreign correspondents take long(er) lunches, the people writing about science or the economy leave work early, the "news hole" for non-scandal news disappears. You can see the effect on shows designed to add perspective—*Nightline*, even *Crossfire* or *Larry King Live*. When there's no O. J.–style story, their producers have to think up new topics. During a frenzy they stop trying, and thereby magnify rather than offset the impression that only one thing matters in the world.

Prediction rather than explanation. It is now clear that, apart from lucky-number psychics, political pundits have the worst track record of any group that presumes to tell the future.... Two days before the 1998 election, every pundit who went on record on the talk shows and opinion sections foresaw that the Republicans would gain seats in both the Senate and the House. The complaint is not that their guesses were wrong.... It is instead that the journalistic culture now places so much emphasis on something it can't do—guessing—rather than on the interpretation and explanation it could presumably do better if it tried.

This habit was on full display during the Monica era, starting with the immediate "This presidency is over!" pronunciamentos on the Sunday shows. Through the next ten months, as if by reflex, pundits and "normal" reporters alike turned each day's events into an opportunity for speculation about what they thought would happen a day, a week, a year from now. With their emphasis on why Politician X might adopt Strategy Y, talk shows began to resemble the Chris Farley/George Wendt "Da Bears" skits on *Saturday Night Live*, in which beery sports fans compare predictions of who would win if Godzilla and Mike Ditka had a fight. The one exercise in prediction that proved to be useful—Slate's "Clintometer," assessing the day-by-day probability of Clinton leaving office—was the exception proving the rule, since in the guise of a forecast it was actually an analysis, explaining the impact of recent events....

Why spend so much time prognosticating, when the current evidence—Clinton still in office, no Republican gains at the polls—suggests we might as well have been gassing about Da Bears? There is a possible high-road answer: since Washington politics involves constant reassessment of who is stronger than whom, there's a point in discussing who might win the next election or the next test of strength. There is a low-road answer too: this kind of speculation is unbelievably easy, because it requires no extensive reporting or research. And there is a real answer, which is that the barroom forecasting has become so prominent precisely because no one in the media takes it seriously. If they did take it seriously, then like racing touts or investment strategists who made chronically bad calls, they'd risk being out of business. Instead, it's a pro wrestling exercise, a lark....

Internally driven stories. Institutions fall apart when they start doing what's convenient for internal reasons, rather than addressing the outside world—the customer who has to be wooed, the enemy who needs to be fought, the mystery that has to be solved.

Monica was an "internal" story from the start. It was interesting to people in Washington because it was about people in Washington. The sense of zip in the whole city picked up—as you drove through town, you saw crowds of cameramen outside the grand jury site; pundits, lawyers, and politicians scooted from studio to studio to give their latest views. Meanwhile, in sharp contrast to the O. J. and Diana stories, Monica was not doing much for newsstand sales or viewership. When the Starr Report was finally released, cigar and all, it sold strongly; and niche cable outlets could attract larger-than-normal audiences by concentrating on Monica news. But most weeks the story did not do well for newsmagazines or network news—and yet the media kept dishing it out.

Journalists are not, of course, just shopkeepers meeting market demand. The highest achievement of the trade is to make people care about and understand events or subjects they had not previously been interested in. This requires journalists to be internally guided to a large degree—but not just by parochial, insider obsessions....

Use by leakers. Leaks are inevitable, and so is relying on them in reporting. But since leakers always have a motive, journalists serve their readers by suggesting the context in which leaked information should be seen. Failure to do so was rampant during the first six months of the Monica saga. Many of the incredible-seeming, leaked claims of the first few weeks turned out to be true.... A few did not.... What seems clear about nearly all the claims is that they came from sources with an ax to grind against the White House—Lucianne Goldberg, the Paula Jones defense team, and (circumstantial evidence strongly suggests) the independent counsel's staff.

Merger of entertainment and news. For a decade or more the news business has been trapped in a vicious cycle. Nervousness about falling market share leads to more tabloid-style gore-and-celebrities emphasis in the news. This higher tabloid quotient puts normal news more in head-to-head competition with real tabloids (*Hard Copy*) or real entertainment coverage (*People, Entertainment Week-*

ly), and its market share shrinks further still. If this is the news, even the natural audience for the news thinks: Who needs it? Within a week or two, the tabloid-entertainment component of the Monica story overtook its other meanings, and the cycle continued...

The Press Is Nuts

But wait! Maybe we are being too negative. Maybe in remaining true to past traits the press did the job it was meant to do. That is one of several ways to view the Monica record. Let's consider four hypotheses, each with different implications for what is inevitable in the future of journalism.

The press went nuts, but that's how the press is, so calm down. This might be called the Lewis Lapham hypothesis. In the last few years Lapham, the editor of *Harper's*, has written wry essays saying that we are but a band of jesters, and that it's pompous to expect anything more than tabloid-mindedness from the press.

For the real tabloids, this is a completely convincing defense. I love reading *Weekly World News* and the *National Enquirer*, because they are true to their mission. But that mission hardly fits the pretensions of the punditariat that kept the Monica story alive.

The press went nuts, and that's the price of liberty. We can call this the Maureen Dowd hypothesis, after the *New York Times* columnist who wrote countless screeds against Clinton before turning against Starr late in the year. When the election was over—but the impeachment vote had not yet re-legitimized the emphasis on Monica—she conceded that she was tired of the Monica story, and that the press had run amok in various ways. But: despite public hostility, reporters had just been doing their essential job. "The impure history of modern America—Vietnam, Watergate, Iran-contra—proves that reporters have a duty to dig for the truth, whatever the public thinks."...

OK: When it is about life and death, reporters should dig like crazy—as a few did during Watergate, more during Vietnam, not enough during Iran-Contra (nor during the financial life and death savings and loan scandal). The whole idea behind "news judgment" is that reporters and editors can draw such distinctions: certain misdeeds are truly ominous, others are merely disgusting. If anything, the press's power to draw attention to genuine life and death problems is diminished if it treats every passing scandal as a "cry wolf" cataclysm....

The press went nuts, and things will only get worse. Here we return to inevitability, and what might be called the Marvin Kalb hypothesis. Just before last fall's election, Kalb, a longtime TV newsman and more recently the director of the Joan Shorenstein Center at Harvard, published an essay on the rise of the "New News." Monica coverage was indeed rushed, sloppy, and disproportionate, Kalb said. And in these failings it reflected deeper structural changes in the press, especially these two developments:

- runaway technology, ranging from internet "publishers" like Matt Drudge, to portable news-cams that allow live coverage of countless local disasters, to the proliferation of cable channels that keep the news cycle running 24 hours a day. The cumulative effect of these changes, Kalb says, has been to make it harder for journalists to exercise judgment even if they wanted to....

- a shift in the underlying business model, away from the complicated mixture of goals a generation ago and toward a simple emphasis on profitability and ratings. When TV and newspapers were covering the Watergate story, many significant outlets were not even expected to turn a profit (the network news divisions were run as loss leaders), and the main newspapers were family-dominated businesses with an expressed mission beyond quarterly profit. By the time of the Monica story, the only main not-for-profit outlets were NPR and PBS, while the corporate quarterly profit model was in place at the broadcast networks and most newspapers....

As the quarterly profit model spreads, there are familiar ripple effects: fewer foreign bureaus, less investment in reporting, more tabloid stories, and news as pure product rather than as a business with a major impact on public life.

These trends are real. But emphasizing them has a peculiar consequence: in the short term, it excuses journalists their excesses in the Monica (or Diana, or O. J.) case. But in the long term it should make reasonable people wonder: Why stay in this business at all? If the worst parts of the New News really do represent the inevitable future, then perhaps sane reporters should drop the First Amendment folderol, stop pretending that their role is to help us understand what's going on in the world, and start describing themselves as "content providers," and nothing more. Some content providers will provide sophisticated news to an upscale readership, via the *Financial Times* and online services. Others will provide mass fare, as network programmers or entertainment-magazine editors do. But the idea that this "content" is at all special—that it deserves its unique protection from government control—is a stretch....

The Geriatric Punditariat. This being America, there is a fourth, happier alternative. Despite the business and technological pressures, despite the nuttiness of the year just past, there are two good reasons to think, or hope, that the press can do a better job next time.

One is that some of the press did a better job this time. After the frenzied first month, some editors began reasserting their responsibility—just because a rumor was "out there," via Matt Drudge, they didn't have to carry it themselves until they'd satisfied their own standards of proof. By midsummer, there were fewer stories based on purely anonymous sources (perhaps because there were fewer juicy nuggets left to report). Some news organizations kept the story in perspective— "perspective" meaning the recognition that other things were going on in the world....

The other source of hope is less high-minded and perhaps therefore more reliable. The media culture that produced these effects may be described in various ways—experienced, isolated, sophisticated, cynical, articulate, pompous, the list goes on. But for our purposes its most salient trait is that it is old....

... [T]here is such a thing as an old, complacent establishment. And today's press hierarchy looks very much like it. Unlike Tom Wolfe, it is not constantly searching for new worlds or experiences. Unlike itself a generation ago, it seems less fascinated by testing, improving, and expanding the possibilities of its craft than in (often harrumphingly) exercising the power it enjoys.

Discouraging? Yes, but only in the short run. The thing about old orders is that, inevitably, they pass.

CHAPTER SIX

Parties and Elections
The Crisis of Electoral Politics

OVERVIEW AND SUMMARY

In the civics book model of democracy, elections assume the importance of a talisman: They are the mechanism that drives government. For pluralists, elections exist for the purpose of selecting political leaders, a minimal means of participation. Elite theorists hold the ballot box in still less regard, as elections serve no higher purpose than to provide a psychic balm or democratic facade for the mass public. But for those who still hold the republican model dear, elections are the essence of effective popular government. For the republicans, having eschewed models of direct democracy as being more democratic in form than in substance, effective representative government becomes paramount. From this premise it follows that republican government can be no more democratic than the election process allows it to be.

The mere existence of elections does not necessarily realize the republican goals of the civics book model or answer the barbs of its critics. Traditionally, political scientists evaluate the democratic sufficiency of elections by three broad sets of questions:

1. *Voter turnout*: Is the level of voter participation sufficiently broad to satisfy minimal requirements of a democratic republic? Is the pool of voters broadly representative of all the diverse elements of society?

2. *Party system:* Are political parties sufficiently strong and well organized to present clear alternatives on important matters of public policy to the citizenry?

3. *Voting behavior:* Do voters react to the policy alternatives the parties have offered and make their selections on the basis of issues rather than personality? Does the electoral victory thus convey a mandate to govern on the basis of these critical issues?

This chapter begins with a foundational article by **Martin Wattenberg**, examining these three questions. Wattenberg (as well as some of the other authors in this chapter) believes that there is cause to severely question whether the election system, as presently constituted, satisfies the minimal strictures of republican government. Hence he concludes that there is a crisis in electoral politics.

The Crisis of Declining Voter Turnout

What is the level of participation in U.S. elections? Are those who turn out to vote representative of the larger population? The answers to these questions do not appear to auger well for the health of American democracy. To begin, U.S. voter turnout lags behind that of almost all other nations in the democratic world. In the 1990s, voter turnout in the United States was not much more than 40 percent of the eligible electorate for the midterm congressional elections and a little more than one-half for presidential elections. Furthermore, turnout is usually much lower for local and municipal elections. Not only does U.S. voter turnout lag behind our democratic brethren, but also the rate has declined nearly 25 percent from its twentieth-century high, attained in 1960. These facts almost stand alone as an indictment of U.S. elections.

Moveover, turnout is a class-based activity. Participation has historically been, and continues to be, skewed toward better educated, upper-middle-class, and high-income citizens. Unemployed persons, members of minority groups, and young voters are among those groups consistently underrepresented at the voting booth. As **David Callahan** suggests, this problem of the chronic nonvoter has proven intractable, resisting even well-intentioned registration "reforms" at the state level, as well as the national Motor Voter Law, and has only intensified in the past four decades. Callahan argues that this crisis needs to be addressed lest a de facto disenfranchisement of the poor be further perpetuated.

Few commentators would suggest that low voter turnout is a good thing. But many would not agree that by itself it warrants the conclusions suggested by Callahan. There is little evidence that turnout is related to alienation or that an increase in turnout would have affected the outcome of any recent national election. It could also be argued that our "tapestry of turnout" is beneficial to democracy in America and that voting is a "high skill," which requires from the voter an investment in time, reflection, and research. Would democracy be improved by adding a pool of largely uninterested citizens to the lines at the voting booths?

The Crisis of Party Decline

It is said that we live in an antiparty age. Although this is true, we should also note that, metaphorically speaking, the parties have never been regarded as political bathing beauties.

There are at least three reasons for the historical unpopularity of parties. The first is the age-old fear of *faction* in republican governments, a fear given voice by

President **George Washington** in his Farewell Address. The second reason is the traditional American fear of "bigness." Whether we are discussing multinational business conglomerates, elephantine labor organizations, large government bureaucracies, or the electronic network of Christian churches, Americans believe that "big is bad." Third, parties strike us as vague labels. Although supposedly standing for certain enduring principles, *parties in fact exist primarily to win political office.* Hence, to many citizens, there is a certain hat-in-hand quality in the way parties present themselves to the voters.

Nevertheless, most scholars believe that parties virtually invented "government by the people" as it has come to be known. The beginnings of party government came from Washington's own cabinet in the dispute between Alexander Hamilton and Thomas Jefferson over the proper size and scope of the federal government. From these natural beginnings, parties have served three broad democratic functions: (1) *organizers of elections*: registering voters, getting out the vote, and overseeing the machinery of elections; (2) *cue givers*: identifying where office seekers stand on basic issues; (3) *coordinators of government*: ensuring that the winners have the opportunity to bring their policies to fruition. As noted political scientist Maurice Duverger first demonstrated, the structure of the American election system (using *single-member districts*) both presupposes and promotes a two-party system.

Nonetheless, in a system of fragmented powers, American parties have never been as strong as the party organizations in European parliamentary systems. To make matters worse for American parties, the progressive reform movement of the early twentieth century emasculated what strength the party system ever had by successfully pushing a number of "good government" reforms through national and state legislatures. These reforms—including such things as nonpartisan local elections, the "long ballot" (which increased the number of local elected offices), and the initiative and referendum process—had the intended effect of weakening party organizations. While these reforms helped to destroy state and urban party machines, they left nothing systematic in their place to mobilize voters.

The most important and long-lasting progressive reform was the institution of the direct party primary. This reform offered voters the opportunity to select party nominees directly, thus eliminating the power of the machine bosses to handpick candidates. This may be a democratic reform, but it has had several harmful effects. For instance, by allowing any person who merely proclaimed himself to be a Republican, say, to run for, and even win, the party's nomination, the primary also allows the platform and principles of the party to be defined piecemeal by candidates rather than by party regulars who might present a coherent ideological viewpoint. Past party discipline is now replaced by entrepreneurial candidacies, wherein each office seeker becomes a sort of ad hoc, one-time only "political machine." Once elected, the winning entrepreneur becomes a free agent in office, under no obligation to work with fellow partisans.

At the same time, voter turnout in primary elections is far lower than in general elections and even more heavily skewed toward the better educated, higher income policy activists among us. **Albert R. Papa** points out that in presidential elections, party reforms have created a crazy-quilt system of nomination. In this new system of direct primaries, factors such as which candidate is most viable or which candidate best reflects a party's abiding philosophy are less important than momentum, front-runner status, and the ability to gratify the concerns of small numbers of issue activists.

Party woes are made even worse by modernity. In an era of instant electronic communication, the door-to-door mobilization that was the stock and trade of parties has gone the way of the horse and buggy. Parties are low-tech institutions in a high-tech age. We now expect candidates to come into our living rooms as individuals—through television or computer screens. Meanwhile, the political party has become antiquated, representing little more than a label and a vague set of images. Party organizations cannot compete with the "up-close and personal" style of modern day campaigning.

However, this new form of entrepreneurial campaigning suggests to many that strong parties are needed now more than ever. **Larry Sabato** argues that the parties' loss has come at the gain of interest groups, celebrity candidates, and well-financed campaigns. Lacking adequate information, voters require some intermediary to structure democratic choice. Parties can stress a candidate's ideology and policy positions much better than the celebrity campaigns, electronic media, or interest groups. Our antiparty neurosis may come at the expense of effective democratic representation.

Although it can be difficult to separate cause from effect in this area, the conclusion of party decline is unmistakable. Lacking organizational strength, parties are less able to fulfill their mobilization role, hence adulterating their cue-giving function and, ultimately, retarding their ability to coordinate government. Whatever the causal chain, the result is a level of party identification less than half of that of two generations ago—a trend that shows no signs of abating. In the last three presidential elections, the combined minor party vote exceeded 10 percent. This had occurred in only four elections between 1864 and 1988. Finally, the decline of parties has been implicated in the decline of voter turnout as well. Parties, as Wattenberg suggests, exist to make elections user-friendly. In this, the parties have notably failed.

The Crisis of Elections Without Mandates

What kind of information do the voters bring with them to the voting booth? Do they understand the important issues that candidates for public office present, or are they vulnerable to emotional appeals, character assaults, and media packaging? Does the electorate cast their ballots on important issue choices so that the mandate theory is vindicated?

Surely, the influence of the mass media has created a very different election process in recent years. The journalistic biases of the media (see Chapter Five) have had their impact in structuring electoral choice. In its quest for drama, contention, and making the news personal, the news business extols conflict over sober discussion. The need to present pictorial images does not often dovetail with the needs of the perceptibly verbal enterprise of electing candidates to office. In their mania to present their readers and viewers with "objective" information, the media offer a plethora of polls (many of which are developed and financed by news organizations). Many believe that polling is a prime example of "make news," which devalues the public dialogue of the election process in favor of covering the "horse race."

Into this information breach have stepped the candidates themselves. The successful office seeker often seems to be the one who has best mastered the communicative arts, has hired the best political consultants, and who has been best able to fill the campaign coffers. **Adlai E. Stevenson,** a twice-failed candidate for president, saw these problems brewing as early as the 1950s, as his 1956 speech will tell. Since then, the trend has only intensified, and many see the present-day elections as little more than battles between the candidates' public relations and money machines. As **Tucker Carlson** points out, money cannot always buy electoral success, but the perception that it can and the occasional showings that it does have damaged very concept of democratic elections (see Chapter Seven).

Many also decry the increasingly negative tone of election campaigns. Even more remarkable is the triviality of electronic campaigns, whereby personal scandal and character concerns are offered as substitutes for dialogue. As disconcerting as such developments are, some analysts do not believe they represent a cause for serious concern. They say that the voters have done a good job of sifting through the rubble of negativity and triviality, as well as money and media, to make rational choices.

Which view is correct? Few political subjects are as mysterious as what drives the voting decision. We can nonetheless offer a number of suggestions. Judging from presidential election returns, about three-fourths of the vote is safe for one or the other major party. This so-called safe, or normal, vote promotes stability in our electoral system. Also, party voters tend to be the best informed, casting their ballots largely on the basis of broad issue differences between candidates and parties. However, this normal vote tends to split evenly between Democrats and Republicans, leaving the outcome of the election to the remaining one-fourth of the voting pool. These swing voters cast votes according to performance in office or candidates' character (and/or other candidate preference factors) in far greater measure than the consideration of issues. When an incumbent is on the ballot, the performance factor comes to the fore, as in the 1992 defeat of President Bush or the reelection of President Clinton in 1996. In the past four decades, only two presidential elections (1988 and 2000) were run without an incumbent on the ballot. Not surprisingly, these character elections were notable for larger measures of negative attack and personal invective than the norm. Consequently, they are often considered the most baneful campaigns of recent history.

In the face of multioffice ballots, weak party cues, vacuous news coverage, a campaign finance system run amok, attack ads and "blow-dried" candidates, it is no surprise that a majority of voters cast split decisions on election day. Even the normal presidential voter routinely selects an opposition party candidate or several at the congressional, state, or local level. The split-ticket voters may see their voting behavior as a show of independence of thought; and they may be right. However, the result of such independence means that in twenty-six of the preceeding thirty-two years a president faced at least one house of Congress that was dominated by the other political party. Wattenberg notes the consequences of rampant ticket splitting on policymaking—the declining ability of the president to exert legislative leadership, governmental gridlock and ultimately elections without mandates. And how can it be otherwise? It would be as if a corporation allowed obstreperous minority stockholders to elect the company's CEO.

We close this chapter with a discussion of the recent trends in and the future direction of party politics in America. The 1990s saw some profound changes, as Bill Clinton's "new Democrat" philosophy moderated the historic economic approach of the party, combined with a basically liberal thrust on social and cultural issues. Clinton won two electoral college landslide victories by positioning himself as a centrist, falling ideologically between his own party and the Republican opposition. (This was Clinton's famous "triangulation" strategy.) But his approach was neither widely imitated by down-ballot Democrats nor famously successful. In fact, Clinton's moderation was seen as watering down what many Democratic voters saw as the party's historic commitment to the less fortunate in society. Thus, discouraged, traditional Democratic voters stayed away from the polls in millions; and the success of Clinton's message in 1992 presaged the failure of congressional Democrats thereafter, as well as the Republican ascendency in 1994.

Christopher Caldwell notes the effect of Clinton's career on the Republican Party. The election results of the 1990s defined Republicans (the GOP) as the party of the South and Mountain West; in effect, the GOP coalition mirrors that of the Democrats of a century ago. This southern, conservative "captivity" became problematic after the 1994 GOP victory. The need to forge governing majorities, combined with the need to reach out to more diverse national constituencies, has resulted in George W. Bush's "compassionate conservatism." Conservative Republicans decry this as the "Clintonization of the Republican Party," perhaps as squishy and unprincipled as Clinton's adoption of the "New Democrat" cloak.

Sean Willentz discusses the travails and bleak future of the Reform Party at the turn of the century. He argues that the 19 percent garnered by Ross Perot in 1992 (the second-highest showing for a third party in this century) came largely from the failure of the two major parties to address the issue of balancing the budget. The 1996 election saw both President Clinton and the new Republican majority committed to debt reduction and the elimination of annual deficits. Perot's vote was cut by more than half—which is unsurprising given that historically third-party challenges have withered away when their big issue is coopted by one or both of the major parties. With Perot's departure, the Reform Party's existence is sustained by campaign laws that guarantee funding to any party whose vote in the previous election exceeded 5 percent. The Reform Party's haphazard organizational structure in the summer of 2000 was captured by former Republican candidate Patrick J. Buchanan, who pulled the party in a direction at odds with its founding principles.

Perhaps each of the major parties' movement to centrist politics is both salutary and in keeping with the desires of the voters. Maybe the ultimate decline of the Reform party is a sign of the nascent strength of the two majors. Perhaps there is still some kick remaining in the donkey and roar in the elephant. Perhaps—but also perhaps not. As of this writing, America is at peace and is enjoying prosperous times. Even antigovernment sentiment is at a low. Two-party hegemony is part of the basic structure of our elections, and the challengers to this hegemony seem both fractious and eccentric. With all this apparent good news, voter turnout and party identification continue to decline, governmental gridlock continues to reign, and more and more citizens view the parties with indifference. One can only speculate about what the future for the parties will be when the environment is not quite so favorable.

34 | *The Crisis of Electoral Politics*
Martin P. Wattenberg

In his review of the classic political science study The American Voter *and its recent counterpart,* The New American Voter, *Martin Wattenberg examines the three critical components of democratic elections: voter turnout, party identification, and voting behavior. His findings may be disquieting: Are you satisfied "with elections in which the majority of the population stays home and those who go to the polls rarely confer power on either party"?*

The publication of the classic work *The American Voter*, in 1960, led many to question whether Americans were living up to democratic theory's expectations of a well-informed and active electorate. The critical findings of this first in-depth examination of national survey data were startling, especially in light of indicators that contentment with politics was widespread at the time. Back then three quarters of the public trusted the government to do what was right all or most of the time, people were generally satisfied with the party system, and the national turnout rate was at its highest since 1908.

If the message of *The American Voter* was that not all was well with American democracy, *The New American Voter* bears the opposite message. Warren E. Miller (one of the authors of the original work) and J. Merrill Shanks have produced a three-part book that provides an analysis of declining turnout rates, an examination of changing patterns of party identification, and a comprehensive model of voting behavior, which they apply to the 1992 election. After 500 pages of analysis of survey data the authors complacently conclude that "nothing we have learned suggests that the basic institutions in our system of choosing a president are in need of repair, other than that which can be provided by wise and effective leaders." Many observers of the 1996 presidential campaign might wonder whether they were looking at the same country as Miller and Shanks.

Once again in 1996 the turnout rate of Americans was nothing for our leaders to brag about at G7 meetings. As Miller and Shanks rightly point out, the first decision cit-izens must make on Election Day is whether or not to go to the polls.... Over the past several decades no other G7 country has ever had a turnout in an election for its lower legislative house as low as our 49 percent turnout in 1996, let alone the abysmal 39 percent in 1994. And if this weren't embarrassing enough, newly emerging democracies have surpassed our turnout rates. Recent presidential elections in Taiwan, Russia, and Poland produced turnouts of 76, 69, and 67 percent respectively. Millions of South Africans stood in line for hours to vote in their country's first election open to all races, in which 87 percent of the eligible electorate took part. Of course, after the initial enthusiasm for democracy wears off, turnout should fall somewhat in these new democracies. Such a pattern has occurred in the former Soviet satellites, but their turnout rates have remained high in comparison to ours.

Americans once had a reasonable excuse for relatively low turnout rates: the aftermath of the Civil War. For more than a century the states of the old Confederacy were a major drag on the nation's turnout rate, owing to racial discrimination, the poll tax, and lack of party competition. In the contest between John F. Kennedy and Richard Nixon only 40 percent of adults in those southern states voted, whereas the turnout in the rest of the nation was a respectable 70 percent. By 1996 turnout had risen in the states of the former Confederacy to 46 percent, but had fallen in the rest of the country to 50 percent.

Some analysts have interpreted this precipitous drop outside the South as reflecting growing alienation, and thus widespread disengagement, from government. Miller and Shanks take issue with this view. Focusing on generational patterns in turnout from 1960 to 1988, they find that whereas those who were of voting age by 1964 maintained consistently high levels of turnout, Baby Boomers and post–Boomers have voted at lower rates. Inquiring minds will naturally want to know what has kept the post–Second World War generations from going to the polls. Miller and Shanks fail to find any answers to this key question in the survey data. They simply surmise that the turmoil of the 1960s and afterward must have discouraged many of these citizens from getting into the voting habit.

Though the authors stress the importance of common generational experiences, they neglect the one factor that most altered socialization for these younger generations: the introduction of television. A regular scholarly finding is that people acquire less information about politics from television than from newspapers and talking to others. TV's fast-paced and superficial view of the political world has led to a generation of voters who are underinformed about politics. For example, a Gallup poll in June of last year found that 75 percent of people born after the Second World War could identify the host of *The Tonight Show*, but only 50 percent could name the current speaker of the House—the most visible in recent memory.

Miller and Shanks write that asking why the politically uninterested don't vote is like asking "why those who have never heard an opera don't sing operatic arias." But comparisons of survey data from around the world show that Americans actually report relatively high levels of interest in politics. So why do people in other countries vote more often? Walter Dean Burnham, a noted elections analyst, has long argued that socialist parties elsewhere mobilize the working classes in a manner unknown in the American environment of competition between two middle-class parties. There is clearly some truth to this—but even as leftist parties like the British Labour and the German SPD have moved away from class-based appeals, turnout has remained relatively high. Other fundamental differences between politics in the United States and in the other G7 countries must be at the root of the American phenomenon of low turnout. One such factor is the overwhelming range of offices and referenda about which Americans must make decisions. In the most recent election, for example, I was asked to make thirty-six marks on my California ballot. Other countries may have many parties to choose from, but their citizens have to make only one or two choices on Election Day. Surely it is not coincidental that the only established democracy with turnout rates as low as ours—Switzerland—has also inundated its citizens with voting opportunities. Build a user-friendly electoral system and voters will come; build a complex system and they'll stay away. The recent "Motor Voter" Act and other reforms may have made it easier to register, but voter turnout remains low because America's political system is non-user-friendly.

Ever since the publication of *The American Voter* scholars have looked to party identification as the major means for making the voting process user-friendly. As Miller and Shanks observe, one role of party affiliation is to provide a framework for understanding the political world. Therefore many observers have bemoaned the recent decline of party identification, fearing that voters are being set adrift in a sea of political volatility. Miller and Shanks believe that such fears are overblown. Again, the crux of their critique is a generational analysis. They find that people born before the Second World War have not rejected partisan labels at all. But new voters are more likely than voters of previous generations to call themselves Independents.

However, just because older voters have retained their partisan labels doesn't necessarily mean that such labels continue to be important. Miller and Shanks draw an analogy between party identification and religion: both often have origins in the family and are learned early in life. But just as people who stop attending religious services usually still call themselves members of a particular faith, many Democrats and Republicans have kept these labels long after their meaning has withered. My favorite piece of evidence concerning the current lack of relevance of political parties comes from a set of open-ended questions about them, which are regularly asked in the National Election Study conducted biennially at the University of Michigan. In both 1992 and 1994, three out of ten people responded as follows:

Q. Is there anything in particular that you like about the Democratic Party?
A. No.

Q. Is there anything in particular that you dislike about the Democratic Party?
A. No.

Q. Is there anything in particular that you like about the Republican Party?
A. No.

Q. Is there anything in particular that you dislike about the Republican Party?
A. No.

When these questions were first asked, in the 1952 election study, only one out of ten people interviewed responded in this fashion. Back then people who felt this way about the parties had little to say about the candidates either, and few of them voted. Today people who have tuned out the parties are frequently well versed in the candidates and the issues. Many observers consider these people to be the most important group in American electoral politics—the floating voters.

Miller and Shanks try to lay to rest any concern that the pool of floating voters is increasing. Their best evidence is that party identification was more strongly related to the presidential vote in the 1980s than in previous decades. However, they ignore powerful counterevidence by ending this part of their analysis with 1988 and focusing solely on the votes for one office.

In the hundred years from 1864 to 1964 there were only three elections in which the presidential candidate of a minor party received more than five percent of the vote. Since then this threshold has been exceeded by George Wallace, John Anderson, and Ross Perot. Recently, for the first time ever, a third-party candidate—Perot—garnered more than five percent in two consecutive elections: 19 percent in 1992 and eight percent in 1996.

Another historically unprecedented facet of recent American elections is the split decisions they have regularly yielded. Historians typically identify political eras according to the dominant party of the times. The Republican Party of Abraham Lincoln was the dominant party in national elections over the three decades after the Civil War. Then William McKinley's brand of pro-business Republicanism was ascendant for nearly forty years. A Democratic era followed in which New Deal policies were in favor. But since the election of 1968 neither party has really been in control, because Presidents have typically been faced with opposition majorities in Congress. Computing presidential batting averages based on success in achieving partisan majorities in the House and the Senate yields the following numbers for each historical period:

	House	*Senate*
The Era of Divided Government 1969–present	.200	.400
The New Deal & the Great Society 1933–1968	.778	.778
McKinley Republicanism 1897–1932	.778	.944
Lincoln Republicanism 1861–1896	.667	.722

If batting averages had fallen so dramatically in baseball, there would be an uproar demanding something to restore the historical balance between hitters and pitchers. In American politics something does need to be done to restore the electoral link between the President and Congress. The situation that Bill Clinton face(d) in his second term, with the opposition party controlling the House and Senate, is now the norm rather than the exception. In 1996 many voters again split their tickets. For example, in Maine, Clinton garnered 21 percent more of the vote than Bob Dole, while Susan Collins—who disavowed Dole's tax-cut plan—won a Senate seat for the Republicans. At the opposite end of Interstate 95 Clinton won Florida but the Republicans won fifteen of the state's twenty-three seats in the House. Such results have become increasingly common in an electorate in which 71 percent of voters say they usually split their tickets and 92 percent say they vote for the person, not the party. If you wonder why American government often seems paralyzed, one major reason is that ticket-splitting often gives us a President without much clout in Congress.

Perhaps the best way to evaluate this book, which was published on the eve of the 1996 presidential election, is to see how well it helps us to understand recent voting behavior. Miller and Shanks say in their conclusion that "it seems reasonable to expect voting turnout to continue to rise." Instead the decline in turnout from 1992 to 1996 was the largest since the Second World War. Rather than taking the authors' advice not to worry about turnout rates, political observers will probably be devoting much discussion over the next four years to why the majority of Americans are not voting.

The one aspect of the party system that Miller and Shanks single out for future investigation also seems off target in light of recent results. They make much of the fact that through the 1980s Democrats had lower loyalty rates at the polls than Republicans—especially in the South. "The explanation for Democratic variation and Republican constancy should rank high on electoral researchers' agenda for future research," they write. However, in both 1992 and 1996 Democratic identifiers were more loyal to their presidential nominee than Republicans were. Also contrary to Miller and Shanks's earlier findings, 1996 exit polls revealed no significant difference in defection rates between

northern and southern Democrats. Rather, a regional split can now be found in the Republican Party. Southern Republicans were seven percent more likely to vote for Dole than Republicans outside the South. The tough task facing the Republican Party is how to get supporters of Christine Todd Whitman, Pete Wilson, George Pataki, and the like to unite behind a presidential nominee about whom supporters of Jesse Helms and Phil Gramm will be enthusiastic as well. Given the predominance of southern conservatives in the Republican congressional leadership, and the great influence of the new Christian right in Republican primaries, this is likely to be a substantial obstacle to the party's hopes of regaining the White House.

In contrast, Republican congressional prospects look better than they have in at least forty years. The party is almost certain to gain House seats in 1998, given the historical pattern in which the President's party has lost seats in every off-year election since 1934. And it is hard to see how the Democratic senators who were elected in 1992 can do as well in the unfavorable midterm environment they are likely to face in 1998. The prospects are therefore good that the Republican Party will enter the election of 2000 with a substantially stronger hold on Congress than it enjoyed in 1996—one that even a Democratic presidential landslide might not be able to overcome. In sum, the era of divided government is likely to be with us for some time.

If one is satisfied with elections in which the majority of the population stays home and those who go to the polls rarely confer power on either party, then the conclusion of *The New American Voter* will ring true. For many others, though, this book will serve as a reminder that scholarly consensus has yet to be reached about the gravity of America's problems of declining turnout, a weakening party system, and the absence of mandates in elections.

35 | Ballot Blocks: What Gets the Poor to the Polls?

David Callahan

Why don't people vote—or why don't SOME people vote? At root, the enduring problem of U.S. voter turnout remains one of getting the urban poor to the polls. The many dimensions of, and possible solutions to, this seemingly intractable problem are little studied, and various efforts to increase turn-out have little success. Why?

Election day in New York City.... A cold wind whips through the streets of East Harlem, but sun peeks through billowy clouds and rain is nowhere in sight. A chipper young campaign worker stands on the corner of 125th Street handing out flyers for a city council candidate. She's hopeful about turnout. "I think people are going to vote because the weather is nice," she predicts. A few blocks away, on 120th Street, dutiful citizens—most of them older—trickle into a dilapidated elementary school that serves as a polling place.

This year, as in years past, those voting will be a minority in Harlem. As the Democratic candidate for mayor, Ruth Messinger, is defeated by Rudolph Giuliani, the vast majority of adults in Harlem—natural supporters of the reliably liberal Messinger—are staying away from the polls. "I don't like Giuliani, but I'm not excited about anyone else," says a young woman who is registered but not voting. Many others aren't even registered. "I ain't never got the paper," says William, a young man with an intelligent manner and thick glasses who is hanging out with a friend at the corner of Lexington and 123rd Street. "I just never voted." William wonders why these questions are being asked. Because it's election day, his friend explains.

One week after the election, a desultory meeting is underway at the New York League of Women Voters. The night's topic is "Making Democracy Work." Twelve members of the league have shown up, out of a citywide membership of 1,000. The principal item on the table is raising turnout, and everyone is bemoaning the figures from the election.

Returns indicate that only 38 percent of registered voters went to the polls—about 1.5 million New Yorkers in a city where nearly four million people are eligible to vote. From past experience, members of the league know that when final data come in they will show turnout in poor neighborhoods like Harlem lagging far behind that of the rest of the city. In a modest response, the league is developing a plan to increase voting in one impoverished city council district in Brooklyn where turnout in recent elections has been particularly dismal. Members discuss civic education in the neighborhood, trying to reach young people in the high schools, going door to door to raise voter awareness. Nobody is very hopeful about success: the task of raising turnout in even a single poor neighborhood seems Herculean....

New York City is unique in its vast numbers of nonvoters; there are more nonvoters in New York than the entire population of Chicago. But in terms of turnout by percentage of registered voters, New York is actually doing better than many other cities. In Boston's most recent mayoral race, a paltry 28 percent of registered voters bothered to cast ballots. In Atlanta, last November's mayoral contest attracted 29 percent of voters, despite nearly $5 million in campaign spending. In Los Angeles, turnout in last April's mayoral contest was only half as great as turnouts recorded in the 1969 and 1973 mayoral contests. In all cities throughout the United States, those who participate the least are poor people.

The political disengagement of many urban Americans matters at several levels. In

142

terms of social and economic policy, the implications are bitterly ironic. Few groups have more at stake in public policy than the urban poor. Low-income city dwellers are more likely to rely on public assistance, live in subsidized housing, send their children to public school, and rely on public hospitals than others in the United States. When the urban poor don't vote, they worsen their precarious situation by giving politicians little reason to care about them. This pattern is repeated nationwide: in a country where tens of millions of low-income people don't vote, politicians face few penalties when they cut poverty programs and redistribute income upward.

Nonvoting in cities also has major ramifications for the larger prospects of urban America. In the 1992 presidential election, suburban voters outnumbered urban voters for the first time. This shift capped long-apparent trends in which cities have lost clout in national and state politics. In New York State, for example, New York City's percentage of the total state vote has fallen by more than 15 percent since 1952. This declining influence has meant less aid for cities even as urban woes have mounted in many places. Funding has fallen for such purposes as infrastructure, the arts, and public parks. While higher voter turnout in cities would not reverse the suburbanization of American life, it might at least help urban areas secure a larger share of state and national budgetary pies.

A vicious circle is at work here: urban poor people are disengaged from a politics in which nobody seems to speak for them. Political leaders, in turn, see no incentive to represent the views of dropouts and instead tailor their appeals to suit more affluent (and centrist) voters. Ending this pattern will not be easy, but the payoff could be significant, especially for the liberal wing of the Democratic Party. Mobilized in large numbers, poor urban voters could decisively aid progressive candidates in citywide races, have a major impact on senatorial and gubernatorial contests in many states, and also influence presidential elections.

Given all that is at stake, one would think that urban nonvoting would be a heavily studied topic. Strangely, it is not, and investigation into this matter meets with obstacles at every turn. The vast scholarly literature on voting has little to say about the urban poor, and data that break down participation by income are notoriously hard to come by. Most city election agencies cannot even say for certain what percentage of a city's eligible adult population is registered to vote, much less specify the unregistered by class or race. Analysis of possible remedies is fragmentary, and little research exists about what works best to get poor city people to the polls. Voting is just one way for the urban poor to influence the public institutions that so strongly affect their lives. Still, while voting rates are an imperfect measure of overall political empowerment, no other indicator tells a more vivid story about the shortcomings of democracy in America's cities.

Why the Urban Poor Don't Vote

The nonvoting of the urban poor takes place in a broader context: all Americans are voting less than they used to, and all poor people—wherever they live—vote at lower rates than wealthier Americans. Between 1960 and 1988, according to National Election Study data, turnout among eligible voters making less than $7,500 fell from 65.4 percent to 45.2 percent. Meanwhile, turnout among Americans making more than $50,000 only fell from 94.3 percent to 86.5 percent....

One particularly depressing chapter in the story of nonvoting among low-income Americans was written in 1994. Perhaps no other election in the past 60 years has carried greater significance for poor people. Yet even as Republicans announced an attack on entitlement programs in the Contract with America, low-income people stayed away from the polls in huge numbers. A census report issued in June 1995 showed that turnout among eligible citizens earning less than $5,000 a year had fallen to 20 percent in 1994 from 32 percent in 1990. For those with incomes between $5,000 and $10,000, voter turnout dropped to 23 percent from 31 percent. In contrast, voter turnout among those earning at least $50,000 climbed to 60 percent from 59 percent. Overall, those in the higher income brackets made up 23 percent of the voting population in 1994, up from 18 percent in 1990. In 1996, after the intentions of the Republican Congress had been amply demonstrated and with a presidential race at stake, poor voters again turned out at much lower levels than wealthier voters. In the 20 poorest congressional districts an average of only 42 percent of voters turned out compared to 57 percent of voters in the 20 richest districts.

Poor Americans vote less than wealthier Americans for various reasons, most of which are unsurprising. First, political scientists agree that the poor vote less because they have fewer resources to spare. All forms of civic participation, even the simple act of voting, exact a cost whether measured in time, energy, or money. Those with more income are better positioned to pay this cost. Second, the poor are less educated, and education levels correlate closely with voting. Educated citizens have more skills with which to participate, in terms of obtaining information about the mechanics of voting and becoming familiar with public policy issues. According to a 1993 study by Steven J. Rosenstone and John Mark Hansen, college graduates are 16.6 percent more likely to vote in presidential elections than those who have no more than an eighth-grade education. The poor are also more likely to be young and unmarried, other factors that correlate with low turnout.

Moving beyond socioeconomic influences, the picture gets more complicated. Political alienation, changing campaign tactics, and the decline of parties each play a role in falling participation among low-income Americans. Measuring these factors with any precision is difficult. Alienation is clearly the most important of the three; the literature on voting stresses that feelings of "political efficacy" are centrally related to participation. People are more likely to vote if they think that people like them can influence what the government does. Numerous studies confirm that the poor and less educated believe in their own political efficacy less than wealthier Americans do. This is hardly surprising.

Yet being poor and living in an inner city doesn't guarantee low electoral participation. Historically, different minority groups have viewed the franchise in different ways, with blacks most likely to invest voting with symbolic importance and see it as a path to improved circumstances. In Los Angeles and New York, poverty rates for both blacks and Hispanics are extremely high, yet blacks are registered and vote at higher rates than other poor minorities. Poor Asians have even lower registration rates than Hispanics. Variation also exists between different cities and different neighborhoods within the same cities. In a 1997 study of voting in New York City, political scientist David Olson documents wide variation in turnout among poor people. Olson suggests that "neighborhood stability" is critically important in predicting turnout. Homeowners and long-term residents, says Olson, are more likely to vote than people who are equally poor but who rent and have a less permanent connection to their neighborhood. Similarly, Jeffrey Berry, Kent Portnoy, and Ken Thomson argue in a 1991 essay that feelings of efficacy among the urban poor are closely related to the sense of community in the neighborhoods in which they live. A 1993 study by the same scholars showed that government efforts to involve city residents in the political process by creating strong "participation structures" also affect feelings of efficacy among the poor. Likewise, churches and political machines can cultivate a sense of political empowerment. Some inner-city black churches have made politics a central focus of their activities, and the leader who plays both political and religious roles is a familiar sight in inner cities. Contemporary urban political machines are often based in social-services empires and are well poised to mobilize poor supporters.

Besides the influence of such institutional arrangements, interest in politics varies widely from election to election, with certain candidates and elections triggering far higher levels of participation by the urban poor than others. All potential voters, regardless of income, are more likely to go to the polls if they strongly prefer a given candidate or view the election as important. Likewise, all voters are more likely to vote if they are directly contacted by a political party or candidate. Finally, electoral participation is affected by the ease with which poor urban voters can get registered and the information that is provided to them about voting—although how much these factors matter is a source of some controversy, since voting has declined over recent decades even as administrative obstacles to participation have dwindled....

New York, Miami, San Francisco

New York, Miami, and San Francisco could hardly be more different from one another. Yet in all three cities one finds wide variations in the voting behavior of poor people—from election to election and from neighborhood to neighborhood—and clear indications as to why these variations exist. For the most part, voting rates and income correlate with near mathematical certainty in all three cities. [In matching] up census tract data from 1990 and turnout reports at the precinct or assembly district level, a clear pattern is evident that parallels national trends: the poorest registered city dwellers vote by 15 to 25 percentage points less than the wealthiest....

The Miami neighborhoods of Liberty City and Overtown share many characteristics. Both are predominantly black and extremely poor. The unemployment rate in each is far above the citywide average, while rates of high school graduation are far below average. According to the 1990 census, Liberty City and Overtown are home to the two poorest population tracts in all of Dade County.... But here the similarities end. Once the center of black Miami, Overtown was effectively destroyed as a neighborhood when urban renewal projects crisscrossed it with highways and overpasses. Several thousand families still live in Over-

town, but most other poor blacks migrated to Liberty City long ago.

The contrast in electoral participation between Liberty City and Overtown is striking. In the 1996 election, the two poorest precincts in Liberty City had a turnout rate of 54 percent of registered voters—13 points below the average turnout in Dade County, but 6 points higher than the national average. The picture was very different in Overtown. In Overtown's poorest precinct, only 15 percent of registered voters showed up at the polls, the lowest rate anywhere in Dade County. In Overtown's next poorest precinct, turnout was higher but still only 32 percent. And this gap was not a one-time fluke: during the 1994 election, turnout in Overtown's poorest precinct also lagged nearly 35 points behind turnout in Liberty City's poorest precinct.

San Francisco also shows major discrepancies among poor neighborhoods. Visitacion Valley, a ghetto located far from downtown, is the poorest black neighborhood in San Francisco. Across the city, near the bustle of the financial district, is Chinatown, a neighborhood with equally intense poverty. In the 1996 election, turnout in Visitacion Valley as a whole was 41 percent, and this neighborhood contained the precinct with the lowest turnout rate in all of San Francisco, with only 28 percent of voters going to the polls. In Chinatown, however, registered voters participated at rates above the national average, with 54 percent going to the polls....

Clearly in this city, as in Miami, a neighborhood's impact on participation can be more powerful than that of socioeconomic status. For all their differences, San Francisco's Chinatown and Miami's Liberty City are both more cohesive and viable neighborhoods than the marginal areas of Overtown and Visitacion Valley. David Olson's study of voting in New York reaches a similar conclusion. "A low turnout rate is often a sign of an unstable neighborhood," he observes. Olson's work is of particular value because it controls for ethnicity and looks at several different elections....

... [S]ome electoral contests mobilize poorer urban voters at higher rates than better-off voters. In New York City, Jesse Jackson's candidacy during the 1988 Democratic presidential primary particularly raised turnout among poor black voters. A few months later, however, during the lackluster general election that pitted Dukakis against Bush, whites voted at much higher rates than blacks did. The 1989 mayoral candidacy of David Dinkins also had a mobilizing effect among black New York voters....

In Search of Remedies

There is good news and bad news in the large variations in the voting behavior of the urban poor. The good news is that these voters are not uniformly indifferent: they can be aroused to participate at levels comparable to other voters. The bad news is that no simple remedy can raise voting rates.

As a matter of either activism or policy-making, it is no easy feat to create cohesive neighborhoods and strong "participation structures" or to otherwise increase feelings of political efficacy among the urban poor. As a matter of partisan political strategy, there are costs that come with appealing to the urban poor by running candidates that excite them, tailoring policy platforms to their interests, or expending campaign resources to contact them. In contemplating the prospects for reclaiming America's abandoned urban voters, the pitfalls and promises of both policy proposals and political approaches must be clearly understood.... Increasing the political efficacy felt by the poor is difficult but not impossible.... The basic approach of community organizing groups is to empower poor people by helping them to achieve victories that directly affect their neighborhoods and thus to see that political involvement is not pointless....

Community organizing efforts to increase electoral participation often do work, but they have limited potential to raise turnout dramatically among the urban poor.... In recent years, Jesse Jackson's 1984 and 1988 pres-

idential campaigns have demonstrated a more successful model for mass mobilization. These efforts gave poor citizens the sense of participating in an historic moment. New voters registered and voted in huge numbers. Jackson was particularly successful in energizing inner-city churches to play a role in registering people and getting them to vote on election day. Unfortunately, the Jackson campaign's gains proved difficult to sustain. In New York, Jackson's 1988 campaign helped to lay the groundwork for David Dinkins's mayoral victory in 1989. But four years later, Dinkins lost to Giuliani by a mere 57,000 votes as large numbers of Jackson voters stayed away from the polls....

... [T]he most important recent development in the area of voter registration has been the 1994 National Voter Registration Act, popularly called "Motor Voter," which enables people to register during the course of routine government transactions such as applying for public assistance or a driver's license. At this point, the jury is still out on how Motor Voter will affect participation by the poor. Recent studies suggest that many of the citizens registered through Motor Voter have not voted. Overall, the fall in voter turnout in the 1996 election suggests that political motivation is more important than simple registration. At the same time, a true test of Motor Voter's impact will not be seen until there is a competitive and exciting election. In addition, there is no question that by enlarging the base of registered voters among the urban poor, Motor Voter provides a boon to both long-term community organizing efforts and ad hoc mobilization campaigns. If fewer resources need to be spent registering people, more can be used to get them to the polls.

Beyond Motor Voter, it is possible to imagine other measures to increase the turnout rate among the urban poor. Foremost among these are electoral reform initiatives such as public financing of campaigns, which would make it easier for leaders from poor city neighborhoods to run for office. Other often discussed steps for increasing turnout in the United States overall include mandatory voting laws of the kind that exist in Australia; allowing people to vote by phone or computer; holding elections on weekends; and making election day a national holiday...

Efforts to register, empower, and mobilize poor urban voters can all yield results. Yet to be truly transformative, these approaches must be linked to a political strategy by the Democrats to consistently reach out to the urban poor. (Republicans have shown little interest in these voters.) Such a strategy carries major risks, but it also is crucial for stemming mounting erosion of the Democratic Party's electoral base....

These conditions have produced a standard game plan for Democratic politicians at all levels in recent years: do the absolute minimum to shore up support of base Democratic constituencies in the cities, while targeting appeals at those voters who might defect to the Republicans. The result is the vicious circle mentioned at the outset of this article: the Democrats neglect poor urban residents be-

cause they don't vote in great enough numbers to wield electoral clout, and the risk of courting them seems to outweigh the gain. Feeling neglected, these citizens see little reason to participate in a system that does not address their concerns. Centrist Democrats may be able to live with this state of affairs, but the party's liberal wing has historically relied upon urban voters for much of its support. As this base shrinks in relation to the rest of the electorate, strategies to awaken dormant urban voters will become more important to liberal Democrats....

There are no silver bullets that can slay electoral estrangement in the inner cities. But this estrangement need not remain an immutable feature of American politics. If political leaders pay attention to neglected urban voters, chances are greater that these voters will pay attention to them. Above all, we need public ideas and candidates who inspire poor people to believe that politics can make a difference in their lives.

36 | *The Scourge of Parties*
George Washington

This excerpt from the Farewell Address is the best example of the traditional antiparty argument. As George Washington faced a burgeoning party system, springing from different camps in his own cabinet, he resorted to the "danger of faction" argument.

I have already intimated to you the danger of parties in the state, with particular reference to the founding of them on geographical discriminations. Let me now take a more comprehensive view and warn you in the most solemn manner against the baneful effects of the spirit of party generally.

The spirit, unfortunately, is inseparable from our nature, having its root in the strongest passions of the human mind. It exists under different shapes in all govern-

ments, more or less stifled, controlled, or repressed; but, in those of the popular form, it is seen in its greatest rankness and is truly their worst enemy.

The alternate domination of one faction over another, sharpened by the spirit of revenge natural to party dissension, which in different ages and countries has perpetrated the most horrid enormities, is itself a frightful despotism. But this leads at length to a more formal and permanent despotism. The disorders and miseries which result gradually incline the minds of men to seek security and repose in the absolute power of an individual; and sooner or later the chief of some prevailing faction, more able or more fortunate than his competitors, turns this disposition to the purposes of his own elevation on the ruins of public liberty.

Without looking forward to an extremity of this kind (which nevertheless ought not to be entirely out of sight), the common and continual mischiefs of the spirit of party are sufficient to make it the interest and duty of a wise people to discourage and restrain it

It serves always to distract the public councils and enfeeble the public administration. It agitates the community with ill-founded jealousies and false alarms, kindles the animosity of one part against another, foments occasionally riot and insurrection. It opens the door to foreign influence and corruption, which find a facilitated access to the government itself through the channels of party passions. Thus the policy and the will of one country are subjected to the policy and will of another.

There is an opinion that parties in free countries are useful checks upon the administration of the government and serve to keep alive the spirit of liberty. This within certain limits is probably true, and, in governments of a monarchical cast, patriotism may look with indulgence, if not with favor, upon the spirit of party. But in those of the popular character, in governments purely elective, it is a spirit not to be encouraged. From their natural tendency, it is certain there will always be enough of that spirit for every salutary purpose. And there being constant danger of excess, the effort ought to be, by force of public opinion, to mitigate and assuage it. A fire not to be quenched, it demands a uniform vigilance to prevent its bursting into a flame, lest instead of warming it should consume.

37 | *When Parties Lose, Who Wins?*
Larry J. Sabato

Despite the traditional American suspicion of bigness, something is necessary to structure the choices of voters. Larry Sabato points out which institutions and entities will provide structure in the absence of a strong party system. His answer may recommend the rebirth of the two parties.

There are no more unappreciated institutions in America than the two major political parties. Often maligned by citizens and politicians alike as the repositories of corrupt bosses and smoke-filled rooms, the parties nonetheless perform essential electoral functions for our society. Not only do they operate (in part) the machinery for nomination to most public offices, but the two parties serve as vital, umbrella-like, consensus-forming institutions that help counteract the powerful centrifugal forces in a country teeming with hundreds of racial, economic, social, religious, and political groups. The parties are often accused of dividing us; on the contrary, they assist in uniting us as few other institutions do. Just as important, they permit leaders to be successful by marshalling citizens and legislators around a common standard that elected executives can use to create and implement a public agenda.

The grand partnership of the Democratic and Republican parties has endured for thirty-two presidential elections, much longer than almost all the regimes around the world that existed when the association began. Yet the parties command precious little respect in some quarters. Many members of the press, especially those in television, frequently deride the parties and characterize them as archaic, undemocratic institutions. The judiciary has sometimes treated them as political outcasts and legal stepchildren. Presidents have frequently ignored them, choosing to run their election campaigns wholly apart from the party organization. Many congressional and gubernatorial contenders have run *against* the party, presenting themselves as worthy of public office precisely because they lacked party endorsement or experience. But the greatest scorn for parties—and the residual source of all the other indignities borne by the parties— has been expressed by the American electorate. Politics in general is held in low regard by the voters, and party politics lower still....

... [W]hat would ... life be like without a strong two-party system? Surely, even the parties' severest critics would agree that our politics will be the poorer for any further weakening of the party system. We have only to look at who and what gains as parties decline.

Special Interest Groups and PACs Gain.
Their money, labels, and organizational power can serve as a substitute for the parties' own. Yet instead of fealty to the national interest or a broad coalitional party platform, the candidates' loyalties would be pledged to narrow, special interest agendas instead. "Pressure groups may destroy party government but they cannot create a substitute for it," observed E. E. Schattschneider.

Wealthy and Celebrity Candidates Gain.
Their financial resources or fame can provide name identification to replace party affiliation as a voting cue. Already at least a third of the United States Senate seats are filled by millionaires, and the number of inexperienced but successful candidates drawn from the entertainment and sports worlds seems to grow each year.

Incumbents Gain.
The value of incumbency increases where party labels are absent or less important, since the free exposure incumbents receive raises their name identification level. There would also be extra value for candidates endorsed by incumbents or those who run on slates with incumbents.

The News Media, Particularly Television News, Gains.
Party affiliation is one of the most powerful checks on the news media, not only because the voting cue of the party level is in itself a countervailing force but also because the "perceptual screen" erected by party identification filters media commentary. (People tend to hear, see, and remember the news items that reinforce their party attitudes and biases.)

Political Consultants Gain.
The independent entrepreneurs of new campaign technologies (such as polling, television advertising, and direct mail) secure more influence in any system of party decline. Already they have become (along with some large PACs) the main institutional rivals of the parties, luring candidates away from their party moorings and using the campaign technologies to supplant parties as the intermediary between candidates and the voters.

Many thoughtful citizens are deeply troubled by these prospects. Most Americans are concerned about the growth in single-issue politics and special interest financing of political campaigns, and most want public office available to able citizens of modest means and those who are respected for knowledge more than fame. Few average voters, or anyone else, favor empowering the news media still further, and with good reason. The news industry's influence is already overweening and government conducted through the media inherently dangerous without the unifying and stabilizing influence of party identification. Moreover, is there anyone in or around politics who would not cringe at the assertion made by prominent Democratic political consultant Robert Squier, "The television set has become the political party of the future"? The personality-cult politics encouraged by television is abhorrent; it is unaccountable, aloof from average voters, and prone to stylistic gimmickry. This disturbing development has been lovingly patterned by the very consultants who hail the medium of television and advance their interests at the parties' expense. The consultants' main alliance, of course, is with incumbent officeholders whose power they help preserve and who also electorally benefit in some ways from party woes. With 80 to 90 percent of incumbent officeholders at all levels regularly reelected, the last trend we ought to encourage is any weakening of party. Vigorous parties help to produce competition which, to judge from the ridiculously high incumbent reelection rates, our politics desperately needs.

There are many other unfortunate and debilitating side effects to party decline. Without the linkage provided by political parties, the Federalist division and the separation of powers in the American system leads to gridlock among the competing branches and layers of government. As Clifton McCleskey writes: "Dividing political power to prevent its abuse is the heart of constitutionalism, but it is as well an invitation to immobilism, endangering the capacity of government to act at all unless some bridging mechanism(s) can be found." Only the political parties, says McCleskey, are "capable of generating political power from the people and transmitting it to public officials, so as to overcome the fragmentation within the government." The disturbingly frequent inability of our government to deal with seemingly in-

tractable problems from massive budget deficits to the balance of trade may be due to a mismanaged presidency or an irresponsible Congress—but the ultimate cause can be found in what McCleskey believes is the inability of weakened political parties "to generate sufficient political power to turn the constitutional mill."

With atrophied parties, public officials have more difficulty developing popular support for their programs, and they have to expend more energy to do it. The most vital connection they have to voters and to other officeholders is devalued. Compromise becomes more elusive, both in government and among political groups in elections. Consensus is forged less easily, and effective action to combat whatever problems are plaguing society cannot be taken, serious inadequacies persist for too long, dissatisfaction and instability would inevitably grow, perhaps producing the volatility and divisive fragmentation of a multiparty system that features transient, emotional issues and colorful personalities but little hope of competent, successful government.

Citizens lose mightily under such conditions, and in fact suffer whenever parties are incapacitated to any great degree, since they cannot use the parties as a tool to influence officeholders. Accountability without parties is impossible in a system as multifaceted as America's. After all, under the separation of powers arrangement, no one—not even the president—can individually be held responsible for fixing a major problem because no one alone has the power to do so. Collective responsibility by means of a common party label is the only way for voters to ensure that officials are held accountable for the performance of the government.

Any diminution of party strength is also likely to lead to a further decline in voter turnout, something the United States can hardly afford since it already has one of the lowest voter participation rates in the democratic world. The parties currently provide the organizational stimulus for the volunteer involvement of millions. Additionally, their get-out-the-vote efforts on election day increase turnout by at least several percent in most cases, amounting to several million extra voters in national contests. Without the parties' work, many fewer citizens would cast a ballot and take an interest in politics. Those who did would be more easily swept up by the political tides of the moment, and a necessary element of stability would be removed from the electoral system.

Already, as party ties weaken, increasing volatility can be observed in the electorate.... It can be dangerous when important elections hinge on one or two developments in a campaign's waning hours; the vote should be based on a broad evaluation of individual and national interest, coupled with retrospective judgment of a party's performance in office and speculation on the promise of party candidates. Strong party identification once prevented this pronounced volatility by anchoring a voter during late-developing political storms.

If these are the increasingly visible results of party decline, what forces arrayed against the parties have produced the deterioration? Perhaps the problem stems from the individualism that is so much a part of the American character. This "don't fence me in" attitude held by most voters is supplemented by a natural suspicion of aggregated power in big organizations. In one of our polls, we asked respondents how they viewed the "many large institutions such as government, labor unions, corporations, and utilities in America today." Only 24 percent agreed with the statement "Being big is *good* because it allows these institutions to work better and get more done," while 58 percent chose the alternate position, "Big is *bad* because these institutions are wasteful and have too much power."

Historically, the government's assumption of important functions previously performed by the parties, such as printing ballots, conducting elections, and providing social welfare services, had a major impact. In the large cities, particularly, party organizations once were a central element of life for millions, sponsoring community events and entertainment, helping new immigrants to settle in, giving food and temporary housing to those in immediate need—all in exchange for votes, of course. But as these social services began to be seen as a right of citizenship rather than a privilege extended in exchange for a person's support of a party, and as the flow of immigrants slowed dramatically in the 1920s, party organizations gradually withered in most places.

Simultaneously, the Progressive-inspired direct primary usurped the power of nomination from party leaders and workers, giving it instead to a much broader and more independent electorate and thus loosening the tie between the party nominee and the party organization. Progressive civil service laws also removed much of the patronage used by the parties to reward their loyal followers....

Fortunately for those who see the compelling need for stronger parties, there are also winds at the parties' backs today, forces that are helping to reverse decades of decline. None may be more important than the growing realization of the worth of political parties by many journalists and officeholders, as well as the continued advocacy of party-building reforms by many academics and political practitioners.... Additionally, the application of new campaign technologies to help *parties* (not just individual candidates) raise money, advertise, and contact supporters has been a healthful if insufficient tonic, with potential for even greater good.

38 | *Inevitable Losers:*
The Problem of Presidential Selection

Albert R. Papa

If you believe something is wrong with presidential elections, perhaps you should reexamine the way presidential candidates are nominated. Albert Papa argues that the parties nominate "losers" because the nomination process is beset by four problems: the frontrunner problem, the calendar problem, the activist problem, and the dreaded "X" factor.

The results were predicted many months before the 1992 vote. The election of William Jefferson Clinton as the 43rd President of the United States surprised no one. But surely we have lost the capacity to be astounded if we take as commonplace a fifty point fall in the approval rating of the sitting president whom Clinton defeated. More important, we need to ask why the Democrats would nominate Bill Clinton in 1992; for on its face, Clinton's nomination was even more mystifying than his eventual victory over President Bush. Consider that dozens of Democrats had wider name recognition and greater fund raising capabilities than Clinton, a then little-known governor of a small southern state. Consider also that many other Democrats could claim greater expertise in foreign, domestic, and administrative affairs than could the Governor of Arkansas.

Similarly, Bob Dole may have been the perfect Republican standard bearer—in 1988! An experienced leader and policy craftsman, Dole seemed a perfect stand-in for a third Reagan term, offering the kind of policy continuity that voters sought in that election year. But George Bush was first in line, and Dole had to wait eight more years, until 1996, for his turn. Of all of the explanations of Dole's defeat in the general election of 1996, one stands out: Dole, for all his positive attributes, was unable to present himself as an agent of change, the strategy of choice for anyone who would unseat an incumbent—particularly one with the potential vulnerabilities of President Clinton. Just as we ask how could the Democrats nominate Clinton in 1992, we ask how could the Republicans have nominated Bob Dole in 1996?

This article shows some of the ways in which the parties have lost control of the process of nominating presidential candidates. The reforms which followed the 1968 conventions took the power of nomination out of the hands of the convention system (which had served the nation since 1832), and entrusted it, instead, to voters in a series of sequential primaries and caucuses compressed into a period of a few weeks in late winter and early spring. Since that time, the "out party" has been forced into a quadrennial farce, pandering to a relative handful of voters, and emerging with a safe, yet (notwithstanding the fact that some of these candidates will invariably win) inevitable loser as party nominee. This "loser syndrome" is explained by four problems of the nominating process: the frontrunner problem, the calendar problem, the activist problem, and the X Factor (multi-candidate) problem.

The Frontrunner Problem: The contours of each presidential primary are structured around the question, "who is the front running candidate?" This front running candidate is determined, often by media pundits, on the basis of (1) name recognition; (2) fund-raising advantages; and/or, (3) access to top tier party political consultants. Even when there is no obvious front runner, a front runner is always found—even if by default. Michael Dukakis in 1988 as well as Bill Clinton in 1992 attained their front running status merely by being the "best" of a very weak lot.

The problem here is that certain types of challengers have little ability to break through the pack to defeat the said front runner. A particular kind of challenger, who I will refer to as a "traditional contender," is particularly disadvantaged. A contender will often be a well-known or well-regarded candidate who is yet not a front runner—Senator John Glenn in 1984, Senator Bob Dole in 1988, Senator Bob Kerrey in 1992, Senator Phil Gramm and Governor Lamar Alexander in 1996, or Senator Bill Bradley in 2000. Such candidates, due to their invariably ideological similarity to the front runner, have never gained the party's nomination; even though, in many of the above examples, the contender would have made a stronger nominee than the winning frontrunner.

In fact, the contender rarely gets beyond the early primaries. The more enduring challenges to the front runner come from the ranks of "renegade" candidates—Gary Hart in 1984, Jesse Jackson in 1988, Gerry Brown in 1992, Pat Buchanan in 1992 and 1996, and John McCain in 2000. This is because these insurgents draw sharp ideological distinctions between themselves and the ineluctable mainstream front runner. Successful "renegades" exhort their party to "change," thus inheriting the "antiestablishment" vote within the party and casting the race in terms of themselves versus the staid politics of the past represented by the frontrunner. At some point early in the primary season, the traditional contenders fall away, creating a two person race.

The Calendar Problem: Think of the primary season as a football schedule with the first two games being at Iowa and New Hampshire. These early tests (an open caucus, and then the first direct primary) have been designated as "test markets" for the candidates. However, candidates who do not do well in those two tests, or those who do not perform "better than expected," do not win the nomination. Given a poor perfomance in either of these states, candidates are expected to drop out of the race even if they have viable prospects in other, larger states. By this logic,

the 1994 Super Bowl Champion Dallas Cowboys should have had the rest of their schedule cancelled because they lost their first two games.

As test markets, Iowa and New Hampshire are among the two least representative states. Both are small. Neither have diversity in employment or in their population. Iowa, dominated by agricultural and rural issues and containing not a single military installation or contractor, would rarely be selected by any business enterprise to test market anything. For its part, New Hampshire is the only state in the union with neither a state income tax nor a state sales tax. The pressure, particularly on Republican candidates, to take the infamous "pledge" not to raise taxes is responsible for many a political *faux pas*, such as George Bush's 1988 "read my lips" pledge. Notwithstanding, the media judges the results of these two early contests as significant. Winners get to trudge along, while those who do not do well go home.

In fact, the Iowa and New Hampshire tests are not even indicative of how Iowa and New Hampshire will vote in the general presidential election. Michael Dukakis ran third in the 1988 Iowa Caucus, yet won a whopping victory in the Hawkeye State in November. Bill Clinton, bedeviled by the Gennifer Flowers scandal ran an unimpressive second to an unimpressive Paul Tsongas in the 1992 New Hampshire primary, yet in the general election Clinton became the first Democrat to win the Granite State since 1964.

The Activist Problem: The activist problem is a consequence of abysmally low turnout in presidential primaries. Excepting New Hampshire, voter turnout even in critical primaries and caucuses rarely exceeds fifteen to twenty percent. Turnout is not only low, but it almost always reflects the exclusive participation of activist, "cause" people and is not a representative sample of the party at large. For the Democrats, these primary activists tend to be far more liberal than the average Democratic voter; for the Republicans, more conservative. These self-appointed keepers of the parties' ideological flame have the tendency to demand candidate fealty to sometimes esoteric or far out positions. In Iowa for instance, candidates are expected to support ethanol subsidies (the corn into oil alchemy condemned as a classic "boondoggle" by most independent analysts). Elderly activists are particularly prized. Democratic electorates tend to be dominated by labor union activists, pro-choice supporters, and others dovish on foreign policy issues. Social conservatives on issues such as abortion, school prayer, and gun control tend to hold sway against Republican candidates. Inside both parties, candidates are forced to placate these groups because turnouts are so low that the activists will dominate the early primary states. Thus, in order to win these early primaries, the would-be winner is forced to take positions that will brand that candidate an inevitable loser in the fall.

The Problem of Multiple Candidacies (a.k.a. the X factor): When an electorate is divided among a number of contenders, there is no way of knowing whether the plurality winner could have defeated any of the other candidates had they been in a one-on-one contest. For instance, Jimmy Carter finished first in the 1976 New Hampshire primary with 29% of the vote. That result could have been interpreted as: "Lone moderate, in a field of unknown liberals, performs less well than he should have." But, according to most media reports, Carter "won" New Hampshire. With this publicity, the momentum from the 29% victory propelled Carter to the Democratic nomination for President. In sum, multi-candidacies throw open the possibility for weak candidates to capture the party nomination. Jimmy Carter was certainly a weak nominee. In 1976, a year when the Democrats almost could not lose, Carter nearly lost.

In a more recent example of the effect of multiple candidacies, Pat Buchanan's 26% "victory" in New Hampshire in 1996 had the effect of cinching the nomination for Bob Dole. Buchanan received approximately the same base vote in every primary state, but

could only "win" primaries when the electorate was divided among candidates Dole, Alexander, Forbes, and sundry others. In this case, Republican "regulars" coalesced around Senator Dole in lieu of possibly having to nominate the unacceptable Buchanan. Dole, for his part, said that he would have dropped out of the race had he finished third to Buchanan and Alexander in New Hampshire. He came only a few thousand votes from so doing.

Like a game of musical chairs, multiple candidacies mean that primary results hinge on who is there (and not there) when the music stops. The effect of Jesse Jackson on Democratic nominations presents a good example. If electability is a valued standard, then, like Buchanan, Jackson has no business running for President. But while unable to capture the nomination for himself, Jackson's presence and nonpresence has been the critical factor in defining the contours of the Democratic race. Gary Hart provided a strong challenge to Walter Mondale in 1984 because, in large measure, Jackson took away a bloc of votes that almost certainly would have gone to Mondale had Jackson not run. In 1988, Jackson split the Southern vote with Al Gore in the Southern "Super Tuesday" primaries, thus denying Gore a sweeping victory on that day. Jackson's performance had the effect of swinging the nomination to Michael Dukakis, who on Super Tuesday won two critical 35% "victories" in Texas and Florida, states that were hopeless for him in November. Like Al Gore before him, Bill Clinton could well have been denied the momentum of a Southern sweep if Jesse Jackson had decided to be a three-time siphon. But Jackson did not run in 1992; and that fact, as much as any other, may explain Clinton's victory.

The parties are not guilty of *nominating* these candidates—they are guilty of *losing control of the nominating process.* The Democrats did not nominate their string of inevitable losers in the '70's and '80's unless one defines the Democratic Party as the handful of activists who participated in early primaries and caucuses. While primary voters are greater in number than the party bosses of the old convention system, they are far less reflective of the desires of the great mass of general election voters than were the convention delegates in days of yore. The party bosses at least cared about winning. Now, we have nominations turning on a few thousand votes in small, unrepresentative states.

Frontrunners generally prevail, but they are nevertheless damaged by the vagaries of the process. The nomination is decided by the minor candidates who are, or who are not, in the field, rather than on the merits of the eventual winner. Bob Dole's year was 1988, but it was not his turn. In 1996, it was his turn, but not his year. President Clinton, too, was nominated with only guarded optimism in 1992; but he and his party were the beneficiaries of the implicit rule that dictates when an election is called, someone has to win.

2000 and the Inevitable Loser Syndrome

An interesting development in the year 2000 was the extent to which the Republican Party used the frontrunner status of George W. Bush as an attempt to revive a bastardized form of the old "smoke-filled room" method of nominating presidential candidates. In the pre-primary period, Bush built upon his name to establish not only an impressive money raising apparatus, but to win endorsements of virtually every Republican pol in the nation. So impressive was the Bush machine, that the traditional contenders for the Republican nod—Dan Quayle, Elizabeth Dole, and Lamar Alexander–dropped out months before any primary contests were held. This was all heady stuff for George W., a five year governor of a "weak Governor" state, and utterly devoid of national policy experience.

Entering the 2000 contests, John McCain appeared to be a more obscure version of John Glenn, circa 1984—a traditional partisan best known for the heroics of his pre-political career. But when Quayle, Dole, and

Alexander withdrew, McCain saw an opening. He repackaged himself as a renegade, trumpeting a reformist agenda (especially with regard to campaign finance) and offering a somewhat more moderate version of Republican economic orthodoxy. He did not contest Iowa, instead training all of his resources on New Hampshire. McCain mounted a bus (dubbed the "Straight Talk Express") and held more than 140 town meetings in the Granite State. His engaging personal style and witty candor made McCain a favorite of the media as well. In any event, the Arizona Senator rode the bus to a 49%–30% victory over Bush in New Hampshire. This erstwhile John Glenn had become more comparable to Glenn's 1984 rival, Gary Hart; a "centrist renegade" who rose to be the only alternative to the frontrunner.

As impressive as McCain's New Hampshire gambit proved to be, it did nothing to enhance his overall prospects for the GOP nomination. Given Bush's frontrunner advantages, McCain needed nothing less than an unbroken string of primary victories. Unfortunately for the Senator, he was next forced to compete in the GOP-only South Carolina primary—a primary first conceived in 1988 to serve as a "firewall" to protect "establishment" candidates from the quirky vagaries of New Hampshire. George W. ran a counterattack in South Carolina. With the help of top-advisor Ralph Reed (a former head of the Christian Coalition), conservative Christians eschewed their early flirtations with Steve Forbes and others. Bush became the beneficiary of a substantial independent expenditure campaign of anti-McCain negative ads put out by Christian groups fearful of the Senator's reform agenda and worried about losing their role of predominance in the GOP. Bush even made a controversial appearance at Bob Jones University in Greenville to rally the social issue conservatives. Bush's resultant eight point plurality in South Carolina proved to be the Waterloo of the McCain campaign. He managed to upset Bush in Michigan three days later, but the rash of closed and dual party primaries in the coming weeks proved to be too high a hurdle. McCain's popularity proved to be among Independent and crossover Democratic voters. Bush's domination of regular Republican voters led Bush to a sweep of these states, outside of New England.

For the Democrats, 2000 started out with promise for former New Jersey Senator Bill Bradley. He amassed a considerable campaign war chest and faced a primary calendar that enhanced his competitive prospects. However, Bradley's campaign never found its sea legs. Notwithstanding his promised panoply of "big ideas," he never effectively distinguished himself from Al Gore in terms of policy or ideology. With this failure, he reverted to the tired (and unsuccessful) bromides of the traditional contender—attempting to separate himself from the Vice President in terms of leadership, character, and other personal qualities. Bradley spent heavily in Iowa despite the fact that union and other Democratic activists gave strong support to Gore; thus, his two-to-one defeat there embarassed him. Competing with the VP for Democratic regulars and John McCain for Independents, Bradley lost 52%-47% in "must-win" New Hampshire. This loss effectively ended Bradley's run for the White House.

What does 2000 tell us about the state of our selection process? Despite the hopes of the GOP establishment, the frontrunner problem is where it has been—the frontrunner wins nomination, but does so at some considerable price to his reputation, his prospects for November, and for his future presidency should he win election. As for the calendar problem, the GOP continues to seek ways to devalue the importance of the New Hampshire primary in future election years. However, their "firewall solution" is problematic in that South Carolina is, if anything, *less* representative of the national electorate than New Hampshire. The South Carolina experience also shows that the activist problem remains extant. The press vaunted the "record turnout" of the 2000 primary season. But

while turnout doubled in some state primaries, it reached only 20% of the voting age population in South Carolina, and did marginally better in only a few other states outside of New Hampshire. In any case, the mutual embrace of George W. Bush and the Christian conservatives continued to plague the Bush campaign throughout the year.

In the post-1968 presidential nomination system, 2000 marks the first year that each of the two major parties nominated the "establishment favorite." Of course, one of the two candidates had to win in November. But did either party nominate their "best" candidate? A good case could be made that, given his strong showing among Independent and crossover Democrats in the primaries, John McCain was, at least electorally, the better GOP standard bearer. If this is true, we should ponder the consequences of the fact that Senator McCain could not possibly have won nomination under the present system. As for the Vice President, the relative ease in which Bill Bradley was dispatched belied underlying problems with the Gore candidacy. Many of the delegates who gathered in Los Angeles in August, 2000 evinced a sense of foreboding for the Fall. Perhaps many of these skeptics would have looked wistfully upon the opportunity to have a measure of deliberation brought to their proceedings.

Political parties serve democracy insofar as they contest elections, appealing to a broad electorate on relevant, far-reaching concerns. But our nomination system has bequeathed us a process where this "sense of the whole" cannot be grasped; where instead the narrow concerns of a candidacy, an interest, a constituency, or an event hold primacy. We may not be able to return to the days when presidential nominations were the preserve of party professionals. But we might find ways to increase the influence of those whose concerns are about the future direction of the party rather than those whose interests are narrow or parochial. Until then, the inevitable loser is the American voter.

39 | *Selling Politicians Like Breakfast Cereal*
Adlai E. Stevenson

The 1952 presidential campaign was the first to use television extensively. Dwight D. Eisenhower, procuring the services of advertising maven Rosser Reeves, won a smashing victory built on simple imagery, slogans such as "I Like Ike," and state-of-the-art animation, all backed with the heaviest campaign spending to that time. The loser of the 1952 campaign, outspent at every turn, nonetheless accepted the 1956 Democratic nomination and then, in this speech, warned his partisans and countrymen that more of the same lay ahead. Calling the "merchandising" of candidates for high office the "ultimate indignity to the democratic process," Governor Stevenson was answered by the landslide reelection of President Eisenhower. It is, however, doubtful that even Stevenson could predict the "indignities" that lay ahead.

I come here on a solemn mission. I accept your nomination and your program....

I don't propose the coming campaign to make political capital out of the President's illness.... As we all do, I wish deeply for the President's health and well-being. But if the condition of President Eisenhower is not an issue, as far as I am concerned the condition of the conduct of the President's office and of the administration he heads is very much an issue. The men who run the Eisenhower Administration evidently believe that the minds of Americans can be manipulated by shows and slogans and the arts of advertising; and that conviction, I dare say will be backed up by the greatest torrent of money ever poured out to influence an American election. Poured out by men who fear nothing so much as change and who want everything to stay the way it is, only more so. Now this idea that you can merchandise candidates for high office like breakfast cereal, that you can gather votes like box tops is, I think, the ultimate indignity to the democratic process.

But we Democrats must also face the fact that no President and no administration has ever before enjoyed such an uncritical and enthusiastic support from so much of the press and the organs of comment as this one. Let us, however, ask the people of our country what great purpose for the republic has the President's popularity and this unrivaled opportunity for leadership gotten us? Has the Eisenhower Administration used this opportunity to elevate us? To enlighten us? To inspire us? Did it, in a time of headlong, worldwide revolutionary change, prepare us for stern decisions and for great risks? Did it, in short, give men and women a glimpse of the nobility and vision without which people and nations perish? Or did it, on the other hand, just assure us that all is well, that everything is all right, that everyone is prosperous and safe, that no great decisions are challenging us, that even the presidency of the United States has somehow become an easy job....

I say they have smothered us in smiles and complacency while our social and our economic advancement has ground to a halt, and while our leadership and security in the world have been imperiled.... I say, my friends, that what this country needs is not propaganda and a personality cult. What this country needs is leadership and truth and that is what we mean to give it...

40 | Money Can't Buy You Love
Tucker Carlson

If money, as California Democrat Jess Unruh once said, is the "mother's milk" of American politics, magazine publisher Steve Forbes should have been one big bambino. Instead, his well-funded campaign for president in 2000 crashed and burned in particularly inept fashion. Is the Forbes campaign a refutation of the usual money and politics theory? Tucker Carlson offers a humorous inside look at the early days of this doomed effort—a campaign in which everyone, except the jovial candidate and his stoic staff well knew the outcome.

... Forbes has been running for president more or less continuously since the fall of 1995. Since then he has spent—depending on how you count it—anywhere from $60 to $75 million. The vast majority has been his own money—money that Forbes, rich as he is, didn't have sitting in his checking account. An investigation by the *New York Times* found that Forbes has relatively few liquid assets, and that in order to finance his career in politics he has had to sell off part of his stake in his family-owned company. After four years of campaigning, Steve Forbes is no longer the majority shareholder of Forbes Inc....

For Forbes, politics has been an expensive hobby. Except, as has become abundantly clear, Forbes doesn't consider it a hobby. In contrast to Hatch and Keyes, Forbes isn't running on a lark or as a form of protest. He's not attempting to prove a point, or make a statement, or drive up his speaking fees after the election. Steve Forbes is running for president so he can become president. That's the only reason. And perhaps the strangest reason.

You get the sense that Forbes isn't kidding the moment you walk into his campaign headquarters in Northern Virginia. The first thing you notice about the place is how different it is from Forbes's former, real-life office in New York. The *Forbes* magazine building in Manhattan, where Forbes spent his professional life until the last election, is grand but surprisingly homey. Though the company maintains a large display of rare documents and Fabergé eggs on the first floor, there are no obvious security cameras or armed guards. The bath-

rooms off the lobby are wood-paneled, unlocked and open to the public. When he ran the magazine, Forbes routinely walked down to the reception desk himself to escort visitors back to his office. In person, he was charming in a self-deprecating way. He laughed and grinned and giggled a lot, often at himself. He talked enthusiastically about baseball. He returned his own phone calls without the usual "please-hold-for-Mr.-Forbes" power displays. He had a funny haircut. He did not, in short, seem like the kind of guy who would blow his family fortune ego-tripping through a midlife crisis.

His campaign headquarters, on the other hand, looks like something designed by Ross Perot. A humorless uniformed guard with a buzz cut sits at a table outside the door taking names and handing out electronic passes, which visitors are instructed to wear around their necks. "Sign your name," demands the guard, thrusting forward a log book; ("do not initial"). Inside, the campaign office—which takes up an entire floor of a sizable building...—seems more like a large corporation than the headquarters of a third-tier candidate. There are divisions upon divisions, with weirdly bureaucratic labels: "Office of Coalitions," "Political Ops.," "Polling Division," "Budgeting," "Ballot Operations," "Legal Office," "Finance," "Candidate Operations," (It's difficult to imagine that the Keyes campaign has a similar organizational chart.) On the walls are dozens, maybe hundreds, of pictures of Steve Forbes.

Then there is the staff. Forbes 2000 may be doomed, but no one seems to have told the people who work there. Forbes spokesmen churn out an amazing amount of propaganda, much of it about as subtle as a head injury. The campaign is famous for badgering television news producers (I get to work and I've already got three messages from them on my machine, sighs one) as well as for the relentlessly pedantic, overbearing spin. The morning after Forbes gave a notably mediocre performance in a New Hampshire forum with other second-string GOP candidates, campaign flack Keith Appell sent an e-mail to reporters clumsily declaring victory. "The inaugural debate of campaign 2000 showed why Steve Forbes is going to win," Appell wrote in a message dripping with the campaign's signature irony-free fervor. "The big loser: George Bush."

Laughably ineffective as this is, there is nothing cut-rate or unprofessional about most of Forbes's staff. In 1995, Forbes hired campaign manager Bill DalCol, who has subsequently brought on a number of well-regarded Republican campaign operatives, many with experience in previous presidential races.... As of last week, Forbes 2000 had 12 campaign offices around the country, staffed by 113 full-time employees, not including consultants and paid advisers.

All of them seem to be working hard, though none harder than the candidate himself. In contrast to Ross Perot, who spent wildly but rarely left his compound in Dallas, Forbes has hit the campaign trail like a man half his age and five tax brackets poorer. He happily accepts any and all offers to talk to reporters. (For this story, Forbes called me back, personally, four times.) His staff estimates he has done 3,500 interviews since the latest campaign began. He tapes a daily radio commentary, gives speeches constantly, spends virtually his entire life on buses and commercial airplanes (he no longer has his own). Since early spring he has traveled to more than 40 states. In the first three weeks of October alone, Forbes made campaign appearances in Wyoming, New Jersey, Missouri, Louisiana, Washington, South Carolina, Seattle, Atlanta, Delaware, California, Alabama, and London. He made three separate trips to

Iowa and two to New Hampshire. At one point he flew from England to an event in California in the space of a single day.

Forbes admits that he hasn't taken a day off since sometime in August (he can't seem to remember exactly when) and doesn't plan to again until Thanksgiving, but claims he isn't exhausted or even particularly tired. Bill DalCol, who oversees his schedule, doesn't seem to care if he is. "He understands the mission at hand," DalCol says with no hint of a smile. "He only has to keep it up through April or May."

The question is, Why would he want to? Despite his best efforts, his campaign seems to be going nowhere at great expense. Why not hang it up now and with dignity, take early retirement to a private island and spend the next 30 years sipping fruity cocktails and making targeted campaign donations? Or, better yet, why not use what has become a formidable campaign organization to run for and win the open Senate seat in New Jersey? Forbes won't even dignify the question with an answer. "The Bush people have been fanning that for weeks," he says. "My feeling is that if Hillary can run in New York, I'd be very supportive if Governor Bush was to run in New Jersey." Forbes has delivered the line countless times, but he still snorts with what sounds like genuine laughter as he says it.

His staff, however, doesn't see the humor. Ask why Forbes is still in the race and you'll get blank stares followed by a patient lecture explaining that everything is going precisely according to plan, down to the 4 percent *USA Today* poll. "We're right where we need to be," says DalCol. "I don't know that we'd want to be in any stronger position right now."...

How can smart people say things like this? For starters, the Forbes people dismiss national polls as meaningless in a Republican primary.... Rather, they claim (with some justification) that the only people who matter in a primary are the Republican faithful, the fabled Base, who for the most part are conservatives. And conservatives prefer Forbes who, since the implosion of the Quayle, Buchanan, and Bob Smith campaigns, is the only true conservative left in the race.

That's the idea. Never mind that it ignores the existence of Gary Bauer, another true conservative whose presence poses a real threat to Forbes's performance in the Iowa caucus. (In public, Forbes staffers pretend to be not quite sure who Bauer is. John McCain, meanwhile, is written off as moderate and therefore irrelevant to the strategy.) The real problem with the Forbes scenario is that it ends there. Forbes strategists can go on for hours about the weaknesses of the Bush campaign "too liberal, wildly bloated, insufferably arrogant," etc., etc., but ask them how, exactly, their candidate is going to win the nomination and they become notably inarticulate.

They are particularly vague when it comes to individual primaries. All point out that in past elections underdogs have frequently done better than expected, while a long list of front-runners have crashed and burned. Pollster John McLaughlin likes to remind reporters that in the fall of 1979, Sen. Ted Kennedy was far and away the favorite in the 1980 election, beating Ronald Reagan in surveys by two to one. Others resurrect the memory of Pat Buchanan, who months before the 1996 New Hampshire primary was trailing Bob Dole by 40 points. Buchanan, of course, wound up winning.

You might assume that the moral of the story is that Steve Forbes has a real chance to take New Hampshire. But no. Forbes staffers don't seem to expect a victory there. Or, for that matter, in Iowa, the state where Forbes has spent the most time and money. In fact, it's not clear what state the Forbes campaign expects to win. At first, Bill DalCol seems to suggest a Bush rout will come early. "We've got to take Bush out within the first eight," he says. Asked how and where this will take place, DalCol hedges. "It would be helpful if we won one," he explains. Forbes himself indicates that losing the first eight primaries would not necessarily be enough to force him from the race. "It depends on the circumstances at the time," he says.

After a while it becomes clear that Forbes plans to stay in the race for a long, long time, regardless of how he fares in the early primaries. And, in fact, staying in for a long time is at the heart of what passes for his strategy. Even if Forbes were to lose eight primaries in a row, even if John McCain were to win New Hampshire, thereby becoming the undisputed alternative to Bush, the Forbes people argue that their candidate would still be the only credible challenger, simply because he has the most money. And once everyone but Bush drops out for lack of cash, Forbes will still have the reserves to hammer the front-runner with negative ads... and ultimately topple him.

Just about every political professional outside the Forbes campaign regards this scenario as borderline crackpot. In fact, early victories are crucial. In 1996, Forbes's surprisingly poor showing in Iowa (he was expected to place second; he came in fourth) cost him 10 points in New Hampshire overnight. He never recovered. Forbes strategists don't seem to understand that if McCain (or, for that matter, Bauer) actually won an upset victory in an early primary state, his fund-raising would jump accordingly. More important even, an upset winner gets so much free media attention, it can catapult him ahead in other states. Winning primaries, in other words, is the only way to win primaries. Which one do the Forbes people think he can win? If they have one in mind, it's a closely held secret.

Instead of victories, they would rather talk about money, a subject on which Forbes and his staff appear to have bought their own spin. "He's Lamar with money," says Steve Schmidt, who, as the former communications director of Alexander 2000, ought to know. "Steve Forbes is not going to be president of the United States," declares James Carville, a connoisseur... of strategy and technical skill in politics. "I think you or I would have a better chance of winning. I know of no other political person—Republican or Democrat—who doesn't agree with me."

The Forbes campaign, of course, doesn't agree. Bill DalCol dismisses doubts about Forbes as a symptom of insular, inside-the-Beltway thinking. Or of something more sinister. The national media, DalCol says, are members of the same "club"—a club from which Steve Forbes, as an outsider, is excluded. "A lot of these [reporters] socialize with the establishment players," DalCol explains. "The establishment players are all with Bush." Moreover, he says, Forbes is a magazine publisher. If you're a journalist, who is the enemy? The publisher, the company. He happens to come out of the publishing industry. That's something we have to overcome."

It's easy to mock conspiracy theories like this. But they have been of great use to the Forbes campaign. For one thing, they allow Forbes's staff to ignore the biting coverage their boss often receives. And they allow Forbes himself to continue his bid for the presidency unhampered by doubts that perhaps the critics are right. All of which may explain why Forbes, at 4 percent in national polls, sometimes behaves like the front-runner.

For instance, when he issues slightly pompous statements on matters of concern to the International Community.... Or when he faxes out press releases about subjects so trivial that it's hard to believe a human being actually sat down and typed them out ("FBI Veteran Named Forbes Security Director"). Or when, as he does every day, he acts as if at some point soon he will be president of the United States.

CURRENT CONTROVERSY

Wither the Parties?

41 | *The Southern Captivity of the GOP*
Christopher Caldwell

A senior editor for the Weekly Standard *tells the story of how the Republicans became captives of their own constituent groups in a way reminiscent of the Democrats in the 1970s and 1980s. This captivity has had ramifications for the electoral map of American politics as the two parties have swapped their regional bases of fifty years ago. The GOP has become the party of the South and the Mountain West, but it is no longer competitive in the states on both coasts that once formed its base. At the same time, Caldwell argues, the party has turned its back on its goal of small government in its quest to service its constituency and hold on to its slender majorities.*

... Since the 1960s Republican gains at the national level have been built on two trends. One is regional—the capture of more and more southern seats. The other is sociological—the tendency of suburbanites to vote Republican. The party's 1994 [Congressional] majority came thanks to a gain of nineteen seats in the South. In 1996 Republicans picked up another six seats in the Old Confederacy. But that only makes their repudiation in the rest of the country the more dramatic. The party has been all but obliterated in its historical bastion of New England, where it now holds just four of twenty-three congressional seats. The Democrats, in fact, dominate virtually the entire Northeast. The

Republicans lost seats in 1996 all over the upper Midwest—Michigan, Wisconsin (two seats), Iowa, and Ohio (two seats). Fatally, they lost seats in all the states on the West Coast. Their justifiable optimism about the South aside, in 1996 it became clear that the Democratic Party was acquiring regional strongholds of equal or greater strength.

As Walter Dean Burnham, a political scientist at the University of Texas, has noted, the 1996 elections almost diametrically oppose those of 1896. Anyone who is today middle-aged or older was born in a country with a solidly Democratic South and a predominantly Republican Midwest and Northeast, and probably will die in a country in which the Republicans hold the Old Confederacy and the Democrats dominate from the Great Lakes to the Atlantic. In effect, the two parties have spent the twentieth century swapping regional power bases....

The Republican Party is increasingly a party of the South and the mountains. The southernness of its congressional leaders... only heightens the identification. There is a big problem with having a southern, as opposed to a midwestern or a California, base. Southern interests diverge from those of the rest of the country, and the southern presence in the Republican Party has passed a "tipping point," at which it began to alienate voters from other regions.

As southern control over the Republican agenda grows, the party alienates even conservative voters in other regions. The prevalence of right-to-work laws in southern states may be depriving Republicans of the socially conservative midwestern trade unionists whom they managed to split in the Reagan years, and sending Reagan Democrats back to their ancestral party in the process. Anti-government sentiment makes little sense in New England, where government, as even those who hate it will concede, is neither remote nor unresponsive.

The most profound clash between the South and everyone else, of course, is a cultural one. It arises from the southern tradition of putting values—particularly Christian

values—at the center of politics. This is not the same as saying that the Republican Party is "too far right"; Americans consistently tell pollsters that they are conservative on values issues. It is, rather, that the Republicans have narrowly defined "values" as the folkways of one regional subculture, and have urged their imposition on the rest of the country. Again, the nonsoutherners who object to this style of politics may be just as conservative as those who practice it. But they are put off to see that "traditional" values are now defined by the majority party as the values of the U-Haul-renting denizens of two-year-old churches and three-year-old shopping malls.

Southerners now wag the Republican dog. How did the party let that happen?

The Party George McGovern Built

Throughout the 1980s the Reagan coalition—economic and social libertarians on the one hand, and largely Christian "social issues" voters on the other—were in rough balance. If anything, southern Christians were the low men on the Reaganite totem pole, coddled far less than tax activists in the prosperous coastal cities. That Reagan paid only lip service to pro-life activists during their annual Washington marches still rankles the party's southern wing. Although he several times sent a message by phone hookup, he never once greeted them on the Mall....

There has always been tension between the Republicans' constituent wings. What long masked it was the Cold War. The Reaganite party was never a two-part but always a three-part coalition, of social conservatives, economic conservatives, and foreign-policy hawks. The hawks' group was minuscule, but it happened that their passion (anti-communism) was shared by Christians and capitalists alike. This was a passion that Democrats... were renouncing by the mid-1970s. Foreign-policy hawkishness became a permanent electoral advantage for the Republicans, but just as important, it became the party's internal glue. When the Cold War ended, the coalition lost its last point of common ground. As one Republican consultant says, "In 1992 we go to Houston, and Jack Kemp and Pat Buchanan look up at one another and say, 'What the hell are you doing in *my* party?'"

The Republicans have been, in a word, "McGovernized." We think of McGovernization as a Democratic problem, largely because George McGovern was a South Dakota Democrat when he led a commission that reformed party structures three decades ago, increasing the importance of state primaries and thus shifting power away from compromise-oriented national conventions. Not incidentally, McGovern went on to suffer electoral humiliation in the first presidential election conducted under the reforms. The Republicans, too, soon adopted boss-proof electoral rules. These reforms were implemented just when money and television were driving politics away from "local" issues (that is, bread-and-butter ones) and toward "national" issues (that is, ideological ones). One party was bound to win and one to lose. In retrospect—and it was only the aftermath of Richard Nixon's disgrace that blinded people to it at the time—the ideological configuration of the country in the 1970s gave the Republican right a monumental advantage over the Democratic left. What was the 1976 Reagan movement if not a McGovernized groundswell?

Now the shoe is on the other foot. Overideologization is beginning to work against the Republicans. At the 1996 convention Christian conservatives moved to make their intraparty advantage permanent and institutional, much as racial and social liberals had done before the 1972 Democratic convention. Control over appointments to the Resolutions Committee was wrested from the national chairman and given to the (largely hard-line) delegates. Organized interest groups of the values right thus grew strong enough to bend the party to their own interests, at the expense of the party's. An unstoppable McGovernesque radicalization was under way....

In this sense, conservative Christians are to the Republican Party what blacks were to the Democrats in the 1970s: its most loyal troops, the source of its most talented activists, its moral core. For that reason they are also the main source of radicalization and overreach. The activists who in the 1970s married the Democratic Party to a caricature of black interests burdened the party with busing, affirmative action, leniency on crime—all unpopular issues. As voters began to drift away, Democrats resorted to ever-more-preposterous accusations of Republican "racism." From there it was easy for the Republicans to taunt the Democrats into pursuing policies that taxed the patience even of moderate voters. Attacks on the Democrats for coddling "welfare queens" worked politically less because of their substance than because they goaded the Democrats into defending the worst kind of welfare abuse.

But there is an easily overlooked difference between southern Christian Republicans and black Democrats—or any Democratic group, for that matter. The great Democratic electoral liability has always been that the party is a congeries of constituencies—blacks, the welfare-dependent, Jews, union members, feminists, teachers—the loss of any one of which can cost an election. None of the individual Democratic constituencies can produce a commanding majority on its own, but for that reason none is particularly frightening, either. Southern-style Christians are a powerful bloc in a way that none of the Democratic blocs is....

... [I]f Christians are the blacks of the Republican coalition, then the NRA is its ACLU... Rabidly pro-gun rhetoric has succeeded in putting the Democrats on the side of the cops and crime control, Republicans on the side of criminals and crime. Suddenly, in the wake of Oklahoma City, Americans noticed that it was conservatives, not liberals, who assailed the FBI and railed against putting 100,000 cops on the streets. It was the NRA, not the ACLU, that was raising money by attacking the Bureau of Alcohol, Tobacco and Firearms as "jackbooted thugs." Today it is the right, not the left, on which suspicion falls first whenever a bomb goes off....

The Forbes Postcard

It is taxes and spending, the Republicans' bread and butter, that best show how superannuated the party's agenda is. Just as the Democratic Party fell apart in the seventies and eighties when it could add no more to its proudest achievement, the social safety net, the Republicans are finding that their tax revolution is complete and they have no more reforms to offer the public that are sensible even on their own terms.

However much the Democrats may have derided Reaganomics, and however haphazardly it may have been implemented, its central insight—that beyond a certain level taxes retard investment, hinder economic growth, and lead to declining tax revenues—was merely common sense. At the beginning of the Reagan Administration taxes were indeed at such a level—70 percent for top earners. Today, with top marginal rates in the 30s, they're not. In a climate like this not only do tax cuts always produce less revenue, but modest tax hikes, such as the ones in Clinton's 1993 budget, produce more. Particularly now that U.S. interest rates are highly competitive in a rapidly globalizing capital market, tax cuts can no longer be justified on supply-side grounds. With the budget back in balance (owing partly to Clinton's rate hikes for top earners), and with voters leery of going back into the red, tax cuts are hard to defend on political grounds, too.

There is, however, a way that Republicans can keep promising to cut taxes. The old-fashioned way: by cutting spending. This should play to a Republican strength, because cutting spending means shrinking government, which has always been the noblest and most stirring part of the Republican philosophy, because it means giving people more freedom—and, arguably, not just economic freedom. In 1994 the Republicans promised exactly that with the Contract with America....

It was the small-government part of the contract that Gingrich publicized and pursued most forcefully. In a series of maneuvers that owed much to his dismal tactical judgment, the new Republican majority frightened voters with what appeared to be a recklessly anti-government agenda. Most famous were the two government shutdowns in the winter of 1995-1996, but there were smaller confrontations as well: over school lunches, whose federal subsidies the Republicans wanted to eliminate; over disaster relief to the flooded Midwest, which Republicans held up to win budget concessions; over tax cuts that almost exactly matched Medicare cuts.... These minor incidents mobilized much of the American public on behalf of a cause it didn't know it espoused: keeping government roughly the same size....

The Republicans have been on the defensive ever since. If they would abandon in a matter of months what they had proclaimed to be the heart and soul of their mission, then either they had been disgraceful panderers all along or they were just as reckless as their opponents had said. They suddenly had the worst of both worlds. They were indeed too far to the right for much of the country on social issues. But they were too far to the left for the base that had sacrificed so much to bring them to this point.

To be fair, even if the Republicans were serious about shrinking government (and they're not), there are good structural reasons that people would begin to desert the party despite accepting its small-government message. There must be a reason that countries all over the world have demanded reforms in their welfare states—and entrusted the *more statist* parties, which created the rickety structures in the first place, to enact those reforms. The reason may be this: A welfare state that funds itself on a pay-as-you-go basis, as all welfare states do, creates a "vesting problem." Voters, even voters who think of the Great Society as a con game and a wretched investment, are on the hook for somewhere between a quarter and half of the money they've earned in their lives. The costs are already sunk. The benefits, however, are in most cases delayed until retirement. Voters will thus be inclined to look kindly on the party that promises to defend the benefits they've already paid for, and to look askance at the party that says, "Just trust me."...

The Republicans' loss on the Contract with America set up a chain reaction of political catastrophe. When they gave up small government, they gave up any credible tax plan as well. Too bad: tax cuts were the part of Republicanism that *everyone* loved, provided the deficit was kept in check. When the Republicans can no longer promise tax cuts, they're left with only the most abrasive aspects of the Reagan message, kept under wraps throughout the 1980s: the southern morals business. If the Republicans didn't believe in shrinking government, they didn't believe in the freedom that it was supposed to promote—which made it much harder to argue that their moral agenda was being advanced in the name of live and let live. And what did they have besides the moral agenda?...

So the Republicans, unable to promise tax cuts credibly, have decided to promise them *in*credibly. What's new is the language: regressivizing taxes is now couched in terms of abolishing the IRS and instituting a flat tax that you can file by filling out a postcard. Of course, since investment income is exempt from taxes under most flat-tax plans, the program is destined to be popular only until some Democratic strategist writes an ad showing that Steve Forbes would pay zero taxes on his enormous stock portfolio. The old Republican program to abolish estate taxes is advanced as the abolition of the "death tax." Even on entitlement reform, Gingrich's talk of "privatizing" Social Security has now yielded to rhetoric about giving taxpayers "personal accounts."

This is little more than a marriage of Reaganite issues... to Clintonite sweet talk. The Republicans would like to think that Americans are the dupes of a lecherous Arkansas sleazeball, just as the Democrats in the 1980s saw voters as gulled by a senile B-movie warmonger. But Clinton's success, like Reagan's, has to do with American beliefs and the extent to which he embodies them and his opponents do not.

The Hillary Cluster

There is an ideological component to Clinton's success and the Republicans' failure. The end of the Cold War, the increasing significance of information technology, and the growth of identity politics have caused a social revolution since the badly misunderstood 1980s. It's difficult to tell exactly what is going on, but in today's politics such subjects for discussion as Communist imperialism and welfare queens have been replaced by gay rights, women in the workplace, environmentalism, and smoking. On those issues the country has moved leftward. In 1984 the Republicans held a convention that was at times cheerily antihomosexual, and triumphed at the polls. In 1992 the party was punished for a Houston convention at which Pat Buchanan made his ostensibly less controversial remarks about culture war....

This is in part a story of how successful parties create their own monsters. Just as Roosevelt's and Truman's labor legislation helped Irish and Polish and Italian members of the working class move to the suburbs (where they became Republicans), Reaganomics helped to create a mass upper-middle class, a national culture of childless yuppies who want gay rights, bike trails, and smoke-free restaurants. One top Republican consultant estimates that 35 to 40 percent of the electorate now votes on a cluster of issues created by "New Class" professionals—abortion rights, women's rights, the environment, health care, and education. He calls it the "Hillary cluster." The political theorist Jean Bethke Elshtain calls it, more revealingly, "real politics."

And with this new landscape of issues Republicans aren't even on the map. Because of the Reagan victory, the Democrats went through the period of globalization and the end of communism amid self-doubt and soul-searching. The experience left them a supple party that quickly became familiar with the Hillary cluster. Bill Clinton's ideology here is necessarily an inchoate one, and in his heart of hearts he may be to the left of where the country is. But he is the first President to understand that the Hillary cluster is not on one side or the other of a partisan fault line (and that is his greatest contribution to American politics). The American people are not "for" or "against" gay rights. They overwhelmingly say they favor equal rights for gays—but then draw the line at gays in the military. They're for AIDS-research funding—but think gays are pushing their agenda too fast. Americans aren't "for" or "against" environmentalism. They believe that global warming is going on—but waffle on whether major steps should be taken to block it. They have shown a tolerance for paying more taxes to protect the environment, but few list it as their No.1 concern when asked by pollsters.

Such jagged political fault lines make Americans' ideology look ambiguous by old definitions. In fact, the Boston University sociologist Alan Wolfe doubts whether the old polarity of "conservatives" and "liberals" is any longer meaningful, at least on the increasingly important cultural issues. The big question is whether this blending of conservatives and liberals is happening at the party level—whether President Clinton has effected a wholesale change in his party....

To the Republicans, it doesn't much matter. They've missed all of this, and continue to campaign against the Democrats they wish they were contesting: against Jimmy Carter and his economy, against George McGovern and his foreign policy, against Jesse Jackson and his urban policy. They treat the ('92 and '96) presidential elections... as aberrations, much as certain Democrats throughout the eighties insisted that the only "typical" elections since Truman were in 1960 and 1976. According to Jim Chapin, for decades a New York Democratic activist... "Republicans remind me of us in the late seventies and early eighties. They say, 'If you lay our policies out without telling people whose policies they are, they approve of them.' So what! Voters are merely making judgments based on the credibility of the party as an institution. And they're right. In 1980 I knew if people understood what many liberal Democrats *really* wanted, our vote would go down."

People are finding out that the Republicans don't want anything at all, other than to re-elect enough of their members to keep enjoying the fruits of a congressional majority. Lacking a voice on the new 1990s issues, the Republicans are retreating to the issues on which they used to have a voice. In this they resemble those "boomerang kids" who after their first career reversal return home in their late twenties to live with their parents. Republicans are going home to Ronald Reagan but are finding that theirs is no longer the only house on the block promoting the most popular part of his agenda—free-market economics. They're finding that there's nothing to do around the house except dress up their old ideas in the clothes of Clintonite insincerity. Where is the broad argument of a "natural majority" here?

There is none. The Republicans are too conservative: their deference to their southern base is persuading much of the country that their vision is a sour and crabbed one. But they're too liberal, too, as their all-out retreat from shrinking the government indicates. At the same time, the Republicans have passed none of the reforms that ingratiated the party with the "radical middle." The Republicans' biggest problem is not their ideology but their lack of one. Stigmatized as rightists, behaving like leftists, and ultimately standing for nothing, they're in the worst of all possible worlds....

... [R]epublicans, like the Democrats of the 1970s, ... are now the party with a stake in institutional disruption and bad news. And their resemblance to the corrupt dynasty they overthrew does not stop there. Their party is now directionless, with only two skills to recommend it: first, identifying and prosecuting the excesses of its opponents; second, rigging the campaign-finance system to protect its incumbency long after it has ceased having any ideas that would justify incumbency. The Republican Party is an obsolescent one. It may continue to rule, disguised as a majority by electoral legerdemain. But it will be a long time before the party is again able to rule from a place in Americans' hearts.

42 | Third Out: Why the Reform Party's Best Days Are Behind It

Sean Wilentz

The difficulties of the Reform Party at the beginning of a new century seem insurmountable. Sean Wilentz hightlights these obstacles as well as the barriers facing all third parties in American history. Voters who are seeking a "third way" may be disappointed. But are the two major parties invincible?

American politics isn't physics, but it has rules nonetheless. And one of the clearest has to do with third parties. Since the nation's founding, no third party has knocked off one of the reigning two, and none has taken power. (The Republican Party of the 1850s, sometimes cited as an exception, actually emerged as a major party after the Whig Party expired.) That's not to say third parties always fail; they just succeed in a different way. When third parties succeed, it's because they change the terms of debate. They take a cry from the margins of American life—an issue, or an interest, or a prejudice—and force it onto the agenda of the political elite. When the cry is powerful enough—for instance, Prohibition in the 1910s—the two parties adapt, and the political landscape alters. But then the messenger is no longer needed. And so ideological success presages political failure. As the great historian Richard Hofstadter put it in *The Age of Reform*, "Third parties are like bees: once they have stung, they die."

Has anyone mentioned this to America's pundits? To hear the chattering on the nation's cable stations, you'd think the Reform Party is taking off. Sure, everyone makes fun of Pat Buchanan and Donald Trump and Jesse Ventura, but they're getting almost as much press as George W. Bush, Al Gore, and Bill Bradley. And, behind the mockery, the underlying theme is clear: in 1992, Ross Perot's presidential candidacy was just one man's ego writ large; in 1996, it was just one man's ego writ smaller; but, in the 2000 election, America has a real third party. It has enticed a serious Republican presidential contender and elected a governor. It has wads of cash at its disposal. It has activists and counteractivists and flacks. Most important, it's becoming the repository of deep, hitherto unexpressed yearnings from the heartland. Never mind that these yearnings are contradictory; they're authentic and fresh—the stuff of which paradigm shifts are made.

It's an intriguing idea in what looks to be an otherwise boring campaign season. And it's nonsense. In fact, the Reform Party is proof positive of Hofstadter's theorem. Perot in 1992 was the movement's zenith. Coming out of nowhere and running a makeshift, largely self-financed presidential campaign, Perot won 19 percent of the popular vote—the largest total for any American third-party candidate since Theodore Roosevelt's Progressive Party campaign in 1912. And it wasn't because of his personality. Perot had a cause—deficit reduction—that perfectly symbolized what many recession-weary Americans felt: that government was irresponsible, arrogant, and beyond their control. Before Perot, the conventional wisdom held that deficit reduction was a dry-as-dust issue, capable of mobilizing only the nerdiest of wonks and goo-goos. After Perot's 19 percent, both major parties made deficit reduction their own. The Clinton administration famously chose Rubinomics over Reichonomics in 1993, and the Republicans in 1994 tried to do the administration one better. Upon winning Congress, they pledged that by a date certain they would not merely cut the deficit but end it. When Perot first proposed that idea, it seemed like political and fiscal lunacy. In two years it was on the mainstream policy agenda. In six years it was reality. That is how successful third parties work.

Today, by contrast, the Reform Party is all buzz and no sting. It survives because of a quirk in the campaign laws: the $12.6 million in federal matching funds waiting for its presidential nominee next year. It survives because the expansion—and dumbing down—of the broadcast media has blurred distinctions between the political mainstream and the political margin, turning the latter into a plausible simulacrum of the former. (Imagine what might have happened in 1912 if the schismatic Theodore Roosevelt or, for that matter, the socialist Eugene V. Debs could have schmoozed on camera with Larry King.) And it survives because it has become a Rorschach test. There are discontents in America, and discontented Americans of all stripes like to think of themselves as reformers. But this does not add up to a political future. The Reform Party of 1999, unlike the Perot movement of 1992, does not have a compelling issue all its own. Its closest thing to an issue, campaign finance reform, has already been picked up by mainstream presidential contenders, in the time-honored American manner. In fact, none of its leaders has anywhere near as much credibility on the issue as does Republican John McCain.

What the Reform Party has is aging crusaders, each in desperate search of some political fountain of youth. The crusaders, notably the supporters of Minnesota Governor Jesse Ventura, may be young compared to the electorate as a whole, but their ideas are old and spent. They have a history in American politics—a history of coming to nothing. The Reform Party is fast evolving into a museum of quixotic causes tricked out in the latest telegenic gear.... It will not elect anyone president, and, more important, it will not change the way American government addresses the major issues of the day.

... [T]here are really three Reform Parties, led, respectively (from right to left), by Buchanan, Ventura, and the (comparatively) obscure New York-based radical Lenora Fulani.

Buchanan has the backing of Perot's crony (and 1996 vice presidential running mate) Pat Choate; Buchanan has apparently also struck an alliance with Fulani. Ventura hopes to keep the party from falling to the extremists; along those lines, he's helping promote Trump's candidacy while leaving open the possibility that he might enter the ring himself, so to speak. Perot, down in Dallas, is said to be leaning toward Buchanan, but the Texan has been known to change his mind, and it's by no means clear that Perot still controls the contraption he built. Anything could happen. And, no matter what happens, the Reform candidate will represent an earlier, failed political sensibility.

Buchanan would represent the biggest regression, at least in terms of chronology. Some of his dark apprehensions about the future are rooted in the deep, pre-American classical past. (The title, if not the content, of his new book, *A Republic, Not an Empire*, conveys much the same message as Thucydides's *History of the Peloponnesian War:* that a government overextended by military adventures will collapse of its own weight.) Moving closer to the present, Buchanan lays claim to the highly diverse legacies of Henry Clay (as a high-tariff protectionist), John C. Calhoun (as a prudent, not imperial, expansionist), and Andrew Jackson (ditto). But, more than anything, Buchanan harkens back to the 1930s—and to a brand of nationalist pseudo-populism that, then as now, had a curious appeal at either end of the political spectrum.

At heart, Buchanan is a man of the old Catholic right—echoing the anti-New Deal catechism popularized by the "radio priest," Father Charles Coughlin, and the muscular, pietistic, corporatist anti-communism that found a hero in Generalissimo Francisco Franco during the Spanish Civil War. (To call Buchanan a Hitlerite, as some of his opponents have, is unfair; Francoist comes closer to the mark.) He detests the welfare state, which he sees as an intrusive secularist force. He regards the world beyond our shores as a tempest of savage tribalism, and he would like, on that account, both to halt immigration and to pull the United States out of the United Nations. He has a penchant for conspiratorial thinking, illustrated by his remarks about the devilish "foreign policy elites" and the pro-Israel "amen corner" that supposedly control our policies abroad and corrupt our politics at home.

The pundits who believe that Buchanan represents a genuinely new synthesis often say that his politics confound customary right-left distinctions. They point to his success among blue-collar Democrats and his ties to Teamster head James Hoffa Jr. But, if Buchanan's politics transcend right-left divisions, they transcend them in awfully familiar ways. The nostalgic view of America as a once-noble republic corrupted by special interests, the instinctive distrust of foreign involvements (and of foreigners), the economic nationalism that would enshrine nineteenth-century protectionism for all time—this has a long pedigree among supposed liberals and radicals as well as among conservatives and reactionaries. Sixty years ago, such ideas propelled the rise of the isolationist group America First, which Buchanan defends in his new book as a sort of forerunner of his own political insurgency. Although dominated, as Buchanan writes, by "small-government Republicans," America Firstism won over any number of leftist intellectuals... No one should be surprised, then, that Buchanan has gained a respectful hearing in some pro-labor and erstwhile "anti-imperialist" circles, where his opposition to free trade and his polemics against the traitorous rich and the new world order outweigh his right-wing moralism.

Nor should anyone be surprised when Buchananism amounts to little or nothing. Isolationism, as commentators love to say, has a deep history in this country. But it is a history of failure. Isolationism has been a powerful force in twentieth-century America only once—after World War I, when phobias about entangling alliances defeated Woodrow Wilson's plans for American entrance into the League of Nations. America First dissolved for good on December 8, 1941, as soon as war be-

came unavoidable. Some of its spirit lived on after 1945 in the Robert Taft conservative wing of the Republican Party, but it was quickly overwhelmed by the imperatives of the cold war.

The cold war, of course, is now over, which makes Buchananism possible. But 1999 is not 1919. World War II and the struggle with the Soviet Union have invested American internationalism with a moral dimension that it did not have in the aftermath of World War I. The cost-benefit argument for isolationism may retain wide appeal, but, early in [the twentieth century], its defenders could claim that isolationism was also moral. In an America whose citizens remember Hitler, Stalin, and Milosevic, Buchanan has lost that argument before his campaign even starts.

Buchanan's crossover appeal may explain his weird alliance with the pro-Fulani Reformers. Or it may be a marriage of convenience. But, either way, the alliance brings into play yet another familiar fringe—what might be called the psycho-left. Fulani first attracted public notice in the early '80s as a perennial candidate of the New Alliance Party, based in New York.... [L]ate in 1994, after years of getting nowhere with the electorate, Fulani and her supporters shut down the NAP—only to moderate their rhetoric and refocus their abundant energies and tactical know-how on capturing various pro-Perot grassroots organizations....

Tactically, Fulani's insurgency also represents the old, parasitic Marxist tradition of "boring from within"—camouflaging its actual political agenda behind anodyne talk of ending racism and democratizing the political system. Back in the '80s, for example, NAP partisans tried to confuse voters and potential donors by calling themselves members of the "Rainbow Alliance" and the "Rainbow Lobby," as if they were nothing more than Jesse Jacksonians. In their latest, even more moderate incarnation, the Fulanites have suppressed their socialism and posed as hardnosed welfare reformers to fit in with the more conservative Perotistas. Yet none of these efforts shows any greater likelihood of success than the Communists' infiltration tactics of the 1920s or their mendacious, pro-New Deal posturing in the mid-'30s. Even in the Reform Party itself, which is considerably more tolerant of marginal agendas than is the electorate as a whole, the Fulanites are being exposed. At a recent party convention in Dearborn, Michigan, Perotistas dismissed them as Reds.

The sight of Fulani joining forces with Buchanan is almost enough to make one sympathize with Ventura. The Minnesota governor does not truck in protectionist dogma, anti-immigration demagoguery, or left-wing psychobabble. More than that, he strikes many observers as a refreshing force in our national life—an anti-political politician, a down-to-earth man unafraid to call 'em the way he sees 'em. Yet Venturaism only seems new. It, too, has a history, and, like that of its Reform Party rivals, its history is not marked by success.

Nearly forgotten amid the hoopla over Ventura's rise to power is one of the chief reasons he won his election: the implementation of Election Day voter registration in Minnesota. To encourage the masses of stay-at-homes to exercise their civic duty, in 1973 Minnesotans enacted a law that permitted unregistered residents to sign up just before they cast their ballots. The reform, like the federal "motor voter" law linking driver's license registration with voting registration, was meant to amplify the voice of poorer and younger voters. And so it did—as swarms of Minnesotans (many young wrestling fans among them) showed up to vote for "the Body" instead of his staid, mainstream opponents. Ventura's improbable victory, in short, was an unintended consequence of his home state's high-minded progressive impulses.

Those impulses have a venerable history, especially across the nation's northern tier. Since the end of the last century, from the upper Midwest to the Pacific Northwest, all sorts of structural political reforms—including the ballot initiative, the recall, and the referendum—have flourished. If the technical aspects of the political system could be perfected, the reformers presumed, then the voice of the people would prevail, and good policy would reign. Ventura apparently agrees: His most audacious political effort since coming to office has been to try to abolish Minnesota's bicameral legislature and replace it with a single house.

Compared to the Buchanan-Fulani combine's machinations, Ventura's neo-Progressivism is encouraging. But it's hardly the vehicle for an independent political insurgency. Structural reforms may well benefit the political system, making it more efficient and responsible, as the turn-of-the-century Progressives hoped they would. But they can carry a political movement only so far. Eventually, the politics of clashing interests kick in, and the question of who gets what from whom overwhelms procedure. In other words, it's not enough to have beliefs about means. Eventually you must have beliefs about ends, as well.

Progressivism had mass appeal as a third party in 1912, when it combined good-government reforms with Theodore Roosevelt's "new nationalist" conception of a regulatory state that stood up to big business. Twelve years later, the Progressive Party revived under Wisconsin Senator Robert La Follette because of its strong labor support, winning 17 percent of the popular vote against Calvin Coolidge. Ventura, by contrast, lacks the compelling economic ideology that powered his Progressive predecessors. Insofar as he gets beyond structural reform, he seems to favor fiscal responsibility and social laissez-faire. Ten years ago that would have made him an unusual figure in American politics; today, however, he fits fairly easily into the New Democrat camp of Bill Clinton and Al Gore. So Ventura's Reform Party is caught. If it focuses only on process, it will be a distinctive force, but one without a compelling message. If it combines process reformism with social liberalism and pro-business moderation, it will be redundant.

The Reform Party will produce a lot of sound and fury over the coming twelve months. It will keep talk-show hosts in business, and it will cause the major parties headaches. A Buchanan candidacy, in particular, could sap the Republican nominee of support, which might prove decisive in a close race. Furthermore, the two-party system is not invincible. There has been a steady decline in partisan loyalty over the past three decades. According to one recent poll, two-thirds of the electorate now favors the existence of a third party, more than double the figure of 30 years ago. Somewhere down the line, a new movement will almost certainly do again what Perot did early this decade: knock our political system for a loop.

But the Reform Party will not. The two major parties have absorbed its best issues. What remains is a strange reunion of lost causes, causes that historically have caught fire only in circumstances that neither America nor the Reform Party can replicate. After their auspicious debut in 1992, the Perotistas had reasons to feel heady; and there is still some lingering headiness surrounding the Reform Party. But that bee has stung. The buzz you hear is its death rattle.

CHAPTER SEVEN

Interest Groups
Democratic Duty or the Devil's Work?

OVERVIEW AND SUMMARY

Of all things that can be said about interest groups, the simplest and starkest is that they have proliferated. Fostered by the growing complexities of societal problems, the concentration of power in Washington, and the weakening of the party system, the growth in the sheer number of groups appears to be inevitable. As the complexity of political problems increases, so does the need for information. And like attorneys arguing a case for their clients, group advocates (for tobacco growers, cable TV companies, or high school teachers) provide both information and representation on behalf of their members. The growth of federal power makes the nation's capital the locus of influence for the fate of each one of us. So too, it has naturally become the headquarters for influencing the influential. Finally, in a decentralized system with multiple sources of power and no strong party system, organization becomes necessary for the survival of group interests. An interest without an organized group is an interest unrepresented.

As noted in Chapter One, it is pluralist theory that champions the organized group as a democratic necessity. Whereas for many of us the proliferation of groups is as welcome as a swarm of locusts, the pluralists' philosophy is "let a million flowers bloom." The pluralists believe that group leadership provides what was the missing link of public access to the councils of government.

A pluralist might explain the linkage in this way. Citizens have many points of view, which they might hold with varying degrees of intensity. It is natural that they will wish to focus their energies on those causes in which they are most interested, such as those issues related to their livelihood or the feelings they hold dear. It is also likely that they will join with others who hold similar priorities and positions. Their group will attempt to influence policymakers to see things in the same way, perhaps through such direct lobbying techniques as providing information for and building personal relationships with legislators. Their group may also engage in community outreach and education activities to promote the group's ends to a public audience. This is grassroots lobbying. And, quite naturally, the group will support the electoral aims (through campaign contributions) of those officials who have promoted the group's ends. These three major group activities are ordinary and natural.

Through this peaceful, regularized, and legally monitored process of group influence, each citizen has a direct voice in policymaking, particularly for those issues with which they have the most concern. For any opinion a person might hold, there is likely to be a group to advocate that view. If there is not such a group, one can be formed; hence the notion of *potential groups*: Organization begets organization, and the competition generated by the push and pull of interest groups provides the best store of information by which policymakers can rationally choose between alternatives.

The civics book view of American government has always regarded interest groups with some suspicion. On the one hand, the First Amendment's "right of the people to petition the government for redress of grievances" is hallowed. On the other hand, group influence is seen as something of a virus in the American body politic. Indeed, interest groups are the best contemporary cognate to **James Madison's** notion of *faction*, explicated in the famous *Federalist* No. 10 and treated by Madison very much as a virus.

Madison's key point is to distinguish between the interest of any part of society—whether a numerical minority or majority—and the "aggregate and permanent interest" of the whole society. Madison assumes, as any person of the Enlightenment Age would, that there is a public interest that is apart and above what anyone in the society might actually discern or want. The trick, then, according to Madison, is to construct a political system that at least gives well-meaning representatives the opportunity to decide matters in the whole society's interest.

Pluralists say that the usual criticism of interest groups is simplistic, if not altogether wrongheaded; that interest group leaders hold the whole political system hostage to special interests, that interest group money skews the political process; and that lobbyists engage in strong-arm tactics. Such criticisms, pluralists say, miss the mark in several ways.

Outside of issues such as public safety, a healthy economy, and the like, there are few interests on which any sizable majority of the public can be said to agree. Who, a pluralist might ask, should be empowered to resolve competing claims of companies that advocate economic development, on the one hand, and those that seek to protect the environment or endangered species, on the other hand? The president, whose mandate had nothing to do with endangered species? A council of policy experts? Who would appoint such experts? From where would they come? To whom would they be accountable?

Since most interests are in some fundamental sense decidedly "special," pluralists find the perjorative notion of "special interests" quite difficult to understand. Pluralists likewise view the "public interest" as essentially undefinable. Such an overarching interest can only be "discovered" after a process that allows all the disparate voices and interests to be heard.

As for group tactics, the truism "work with your friends; don't stir up your enemies" is an accurate description of how the overwhelming majority of lobbyists do business. It is quite clear that elected officials eschew any overwrought, threatening, or ham-fisted tactics from those who try to influence them. Most groups represent mainstream interests and can find ready adherents in congressional offices. So, too, the financial and other support that interest groups lend to the political system can be said to enhance the election process in an American society that clearly does not want public support for its campaigns. Talk of twisting arms and buying votes with $500 contributions simply misses the mark, particularly as it obscures the real problems groups may pose for democratic society.

Nevertheless, all is not well in a pluralist world. The critique of **E. E. Schattschneider** may be the most devastating. The bias of the pressure system, according to Schattschneider, is that "in the pluralist heaven ... the heavenly chorus sings with a strong upper-class accent." That is, group joiners and activists tend to be self-recruited from the ranks of the best educated and wealthiest members of society. Indeed, the difference between those who participate in interest group activity and those who stand at the sidelines is much greater than that between voters and nonvoters. The policy desires of business groups and other upper-middle-class concerns will invariably be heard in the political system. But as Senator Bob Dole once noted, there is no interest group for food stamp recipients. Advocacy for the interests of the homeless are, in most cities, confined to rather forlorn figures, staging "hunger strikes." Consequently, the interest group system, far from leveling the playing field for the less well off, is a forum for those who already have a lot to get more.

Another deficiency of the group theory is to be found in the problem of the "free rider." That is, when political conflict involves public goods, organizing an interest group becomes very difficult. The shared interests of taxpayers, consumers, poor people, and the like become problematic as no one in the group will personally benefit to such a degree as to make participation in the group essential. For example, a Cleveland pharmacist can pony up some cash for his local pharmacy PAC (political action committee), knowing that his contribution will benefit himself and other druggists. But why should that same pharmacist join a (hypothetical) group named Clevelanders for Clean Air, when he knows that the air over his pharmacy will be no cleaner for his contribution? So, in many cases such groups never form. The problem of free riders means that in some cases the interests of the largest number of people often go unorganized, or underorganized, and quite probably unvindicated.

A third problem with interest groups entails their effect on the political system as a whole. **Theodore Lowi** argues that government officials (wrongly) treat groups according to the political power that they wield. Any group, representing anything at all, is dealt with and judged according to the political resources it brings to the table and not for the moral or rationalist strength of its interest. This creates what Lowi refers to as "interest group liberalism," wherein government benefits are ladled out to all those who have a plate at the policy table. This explains the rationality of a political system at cross purposes with itself, such as a federal government that both creates programs aimed at getting people not to smoke, and at the same time subsidizes those who raise tobacco. Moreover, Lowi says, interest group liberalism harms the political system by depriving officials of the ability to make choices based on the validity of claims rather than on who is present to make these claims.

These critiques strike at the heart of pluralist assumptions. There is, critics of the group theory contend, a notion of the common good that is sufficient to show that all interests are not special. There is, further, a difference in the effectiveness of participation and in the resources that various groups bring to the table. Thus, critics insist, group activity is no antidote to the problem of representing the common good and may in reality be inimical to a properly functioning democratic system

Complicating the critique of pluralism is the fact that it can be difficult to distinguish among its critics. Some resent the pluralist system; many others resent specific interest groups. After all, what is a "special" interest? Pluralists might respond that a special interest is one you happen to disagree with.

We present one critic of one powerful interest group who is clearly not sympathetic to it or its goals. **Robert Dreyfuss** skewers the National Rifle Association (NRA) for exercising undue influence on politicians, elections, and policy. His intent is to show that the NRA not only mishapes public policy but also misrepresents its own members. But he also suggests that the NRA will eventually, by its own success, engender opposition and its own defeat. His conclusion, then, is a pluralist's one—that the system of group politics is self-correcting and will, in the end, balance all the interests of society. In the meantime, the reader can decide whether the NRA's organization is exerting unfair influence or whether the group is simply better than most at exercising its First Amendment rights.

On the one hand, groups do allow interested citizens to have direct access to the policy process in a way that is not found in any other system in the world. On the other hand, the bias in the type of participants, the fact that some interests are difficult to mobilize, and the weak link between group demands and public desires raise the question of whether the proliferation of interest groups has done anything to promote a more democratic society. This paradox also raises the question of whether group influence should be controlled and, if so, how it might best be done.

When it comes to curbing the power of interest groups, perhaps no issue is as controversial as that of campaign finance reform. **Ellen Miller**, among others, has had enough of elections awash in interest-group money. Miller, asserting that the American public has had enough as well, provides a forthright plan to curb interest-group money and thus interest-group pressure on candidates and national policy—public financing of elections.

Bruce Larson concludes that most reform plans simply create new and different problems for democracy. He doubts whether limiting the flow of interest group contributions (assuming it can be done in a manner consistent with the Constitution) would really limit the influence of interest groups on elections. His own suggestion for reform runs counter to most reform plans insofar as they attempt to limit campaign contributions or expenditures. Larson suggests that it might be a more honest approach to raise the limits for contributions and give the public a more accurate accounting of who is paying for whom.

Whatever the solution, the problem of campaign finance reflects the problem of interest groups, as it raises all the perennial democratic questions. Should group influence be limited in a democratic society? Can it be? Will the cure be worse than the disease?

43 | Federalist *No. 10*
James Madison

In his classic statement on the danger of factions, James Madison makes a distinction that few interest group leaders accept: that there is, above and beyond any combination of personal and group interests, a national interest, a common good. For Madison, "the permanent and aggregate interest of the community" is necessarily different from the pluralists' idea that the public good is the sum of all interests in a community.

To the People of the State of New York:

Among the numerous advantages promised by a well constructed Union, none deserves to be more accurately developed than its tendency to break and control the violence of faction. The friend of popular governments never finds himself so much alarmed for their character and fate, as when he contemplates their propensity to this dangerous vice. He will not fail, therefore, to set a due value on any plan which, without violating the principles to which he is attached, provides a proper cure for it. The instability, injustice, and confusion introduced into the public councils, have, in truth, been the mortal diseases under which popular governments have everywhere perished; as they continue to be the favorite and fruitful topics from which the adversaries to liberty derive their most specious declamations. The valuable improvements made by the American constitutions on the popular models, both ancient and modern, cannot certainly be too much admired; but it would be an unwarrantable partiality, to contend that they have as effectually obviated the danger on this side, as was wished and expected. Complaints are everywhere heard from our most considerate and virtuous citizens, equally the friends of public and private faith, and of public and personal liberty, that our governments are too unstable, that the public good is disregarded in the conflicts of rival parties, and that measures are too often decided, not according to the rules of justice and the rights of the minor party, but by the superior force of an interested and overbearing majority. However anxiously we may wish that these complaints had no foundation, the evidence, of known facts will not permit us to deny that they are in some degree true. It will be found, indeed, on a candid review of our situation, that some of the distresses under which we labor have been erroneously charged on the operation of our governments; but it will be found, at the same time, that other causes will not alone account for many of our heaviest misfortunes; and, particularly, for that prevailing and increasing distrust of public engagements, and alarm for private rights, which are echoed from one end of the continent to the other. These must be chiefly, if not wholly, effects of the unsteadiness and injustice with which a factious spirit has tainted our public administrations.

By a faction, I understand a number of citizens, whether amounting to a majority or a minority of the whole, who are united and actuated by some common impulse of passion, or of interest, adverse to the rights of other citizens, or to the permanent and aggregate interests of the community.

There are two methods of curing the mischiefs of faction: the one, by removing its causes; the other, by controlling its effects.

There are again two methods of removing the causes of faction: the one, by destroying the liberty which is essential to its existence; the other, by giving to every citizen the same opinions, the same passions, and the same interests.

It could never be more truly said than of the first remedy, that it was worse than the disease. Liberty is to faction what air is to fire, an aliment without which it instantly expires. But it could not be less folly to abolish liberty, which is essential to political life, because it nourishes faction, than it would be to wish the annihilation of air, which is essential to animal life, because it imparts to fire its destructive agency.

The second expedient is as impracticable as the first would be unwise. As long as the reason of man continues fallible, and he is at liberty to exercise it, different opinions will be formed. As long as the connection subsists between his reason and his self-love, his opinions and his passions will have a reciprocal influence on each other; and the former will be objects to which the latter will attach themselves. The diversity in the faculties of men, from which the rights of property originate, is not less an insuperable obstacle to a uniformity of interests. The protection of these faculties is the first object of government. From the protection of different and unequal faculties of acquiring property, the possession of different degrees and kinds of property immediately results; and from the influence of these on the sentiments and views of the respective proprietors, ensues a division of the society into different interests and parties.

The latent causes of faction are thus sown in the nature of man; and we see them everywhere brought into different degrees of activity, according to the different circumstances of civil society. A zeal for different opinions concerning religion, concerning government, and many other points, as well of speculation as of practice; an attachment to different leaders ambitiously contending for pre-eminence and power; or to persons of other descriptions whose fortunes have been interesting to the human passions, have, in turn, divided mankind into parties, inflamed them with mutual animosity, and rendered them much more disposed to vex and oppress each other than to co-operate for their common good. So strong is this propensity of mankind to fall into mutual animosities, that where no substantial occasion presents itself, the most frivolous and fanciful distinctions have been sufficient to kindle their unfriendly passions and excite their most violent conflicts. But the most common and durable source of factions has been the various and unequal distribution of property. Those who hold and those who are without property have ever formed distinct interests in society. Those who are creditors, and those who are debtors, fall under a like discrimination. A landed interest, a manufacturing interest, a mercantile interest, a moneyed interest, with many lesser interests, grow up of necessity in civilized nations, and divide them into different classes, actuated by different sentiments and views. The regulation of these various and interfering interests forms the principal task of modern legislation, and involves the spirit of party and faction in the necessary and ordinary operations of the government.

No man is allowed to be a judge in his own cause, because his interest would certainly bias his judgment, and, not improbably, corrupt his integrity. With equal, nay with greater reason, a body of men are unfit to be both judges and parties at the same time; yet what are many of the most important acts of legislation, but so many judicial determinations, not indeed concerning the rights of single persons, but concerning the rights of large bodies of citizens? And what are the different classes of legislators but advocates and parties to the causes which they determine? Is a law proposed concerning private debts? It is a question to which the creditors are parties on one side and the debtors on the other. Justice ought to hold the balance between them. Yet the parties are, and must be, themselves the judges; and the most numerous party, or, in other words, the most powerful faction must be expected to prevail. Shall domestic manufactures be encouraged, and in what degree, by restrictions on foreign manufactures? Are questions which would be differently decided by the landed and the manufacturing classes, and probably by neither with a sole regard to justice and the public good. The apportionment of taxes on the various descriptions of property is an act which seems to require the most exact impartiality; yet there is, perhaps, no legislative act in which greater opportunity and temptation are given to a predominant party to trample on the rules of justice. Every shilling with which they overburden the inferior number, is a shilling saved to their own pockets.

It is in vain to say that enlightened statesmen will be able to adjust these clashing interests, and render them all subservient to the public good. Enlightened statesmen will not always be at the helm. Nor, in many cases, can such an adjustment be made at all without taking into view indirect and remote considerations, which will rarely prevail over the immediate interest which one party may find in disregarding the rights of another or the good of the whole.

The inference to which we are brought is, that the CAUSES of faction cannot be removed, and that relief is only to be sought in the means of controlling its EFFECTS.

If a faction consists of less than a majority, relief is supplied by the republican principle, which enables the majority to defeat its sinister views by regular vote. It may clog the administration, it may convulse the society; but it will be unable to execute and mask its violence under the forms of the Constitution. When a majority is included in a faction, the form of popular government, on the other hand, enables it to sacrifice to its ruling passion or interest both the public good and the rights of other citizens. To secure the public good and private rights against the danger of such a faction, and at the same time to preserve the spirit and the form of popular government, is then the great object to which our inquiries are directed. Let me add that it is the great desideratum by which this form of government can be rescued from the opprobrium under which it has so long labored, and be recommended to the esteem and adoption of mankind.

By what means is this object attainable? Evidently by one of two only. Either the existence of the same passion or interest in a majority at the same time must be prevented, or the majority, having such coexistent passion or interest, must be rendered, by their number and local situation, unable to concert and carry into effect schemes of oppression. If the impulse and the opportunity be suffered to coincide, we well know that neither moral nor religious motives can be relied on as an adequate control. They are not found to be such on the injustice and violence of individuals, and lose their efficacy in proportion to the number combined together, that is, in proportion as their efficacy becomes needful.

From this view of the subject it may be concluded that a pure democracy, by which I mean a society consisting of a small number of citizens, who assemble and administer the government in person, can admit of no cure for the mischiefs of faction. A common passion or interest will, in almost every case, be felt by a majority of the whole; a communication and concert result from the form of government itself; and there is nothing to check the inducements to sacrifice the weaker party or an obnoxious individual. Hence it is that such democracies have ever been spectacles of turbulence and contention; have ever been found incompatible with personal security or the rights of property; and have in general been as short in their lives as they have been violent in their deaths. Theoretic politicians, who have patronized this species of government, have erroneously supposed that by reducing mankind to a perfect equality in their political rights, they would, at the same time, be perfectly equalized and assimilated in their possessions, their opinions, and their passions.

A republic, by which I mean a government in which the scheme of representation takes place, opens a different prospect, and promises the cure for which we are seeking. Let us examine the points in which it varies from pure democracy, and we shall comprehend both the nature of the cure and the efficacy which it must derive from the Union.

The two great points of difference between a democracy and a republic are: first, the delegation of the government, in the latter, to a small number of citizens elected by the rest; secondly, the greater number of citizens, and greater sphere of country, over which the latter may be extended.

The effect of the first difference is, on the one hand, to refine and enlarge the public views, by passing them through the medium of a chosen body of citizens, whose wisdom may best discern the true interest of their country, and whose patriotism and love of justice will be least likely to sacrifice it to temporary or partial considerations. Under such a regulation, it may well happen that the public voice, pronounced by the representatives of the people, will be more consonant to the public good than if pronounced by the people themselves, convened for the purpose. On the other hand, the effect may be inverted. Men of factious tempers, of local prejudices, or of sinister designs, may, by intrigue, by corruption, or by other means, first obtain the suffrages, and then betray the interest, of the people. The question resulting is, whether small or extensive republics are more favorable to the election of proper guardians of the public weal; and it is clearly decided in favor of the latter by two obvious considerations:

In the first place, it is to be remarked that, however small the republic may be, the representatives must be raised to a certain number, in order to guard against the cabals of a few; and that, however large it may be, they must be limited to a certain number, in order to guard against the confusion of a multitude. Hence, the number of representatives in the two cases not being in proportion to that of the two constituents, and being proportionally greater in the small republic, it follows that, if the proportion of fit characters be not less in the large than in the small republic, the former will present a greater option, and consequently a greater probability of a fit choice.

In the next place, as each representative will be chosen by a greater number of citizens in the large than in the small republic, it will be more difficult for unworthy candidates to practice with success the vicious arts by which elections are too often carried; and the suffrages of the people being more free, will be more likely to centre in men who possess the most attractive merit and the most diffusive and established characters.

It must be confessed that in this, as in most other cases, there is a mean, on both sides of which inconveniences will be found to lie. By enlarging too much the number of electors, you render the representatives too little acquainted with all their local circumstances and lesser interests; as by reducing it too much, you render him unduly attached to these, and too little fit to comprehend and pursue great and national objects. The federal Constitution forms a happy combination in this respect; the great and aggregate interests being referred to the national, the local and particular to the State legislatures.

The other point of difference is, the greater number of citizens and extent of territory which may be brought within the compass of republican than of democratic government; and it is this circumstance principally which renders factious combinations less to be dreaded in the former than in the latter. The smaller the society, the fewer probably will be the distinct parties and interests composing it; the fewer the distinct parties and interests, the more frequently will a majority be found of the same party; and the smaller the number of individuals composing a majority, and the smaller the compass within which they are placed, the more easily will they concert and execute their plans of oppression. Extend the sphere, and you take in a greater variety of parties and interests; you make it less probable that a majority of the whole will have a common motive to invade the rights of other citizens; or if such a common motive exists, it will be more difficult for all who feel it to discover their own strength, and to act in unison with each other. Besides other impediments, it may be remarked that, where there is a consciousness of unjust or dishonorable purposes, communication is always checked by distrust in proportion to the number whose concurrence is necessary.

Hence, it clearly appears, that the same advantage which a republic has over a democracy, in controlling the effects of faction, is enjoyed by a large over a small republic,—is enjoyed by the Union over the States composing it. Does the advantage consist in the substitution of representatives whose enlightened views and virtuous sentiments render them superior to local prejudices and schemes of injustice? It will not be denied that the representation of the Union will be most likely to possess these requisite endowments. Does it consist in the greater security afforded by a greater variety of parties, against the event of any one party being able to outnumber and oppress the rest? In an equal degree does the increased variety of parties comprised within the Union, increase this security. Does it, in fine, consist in the greater obstacles opposed to the concert and accomplishment of the secret wishes of an unjust and interested majority? Here, again, the extent of the Union gives it the most palpable advantage.

The influence of factious leaders may kindle a flame within their particular States, but will be unable to spread a general conflagration through the other States. A religious sect may degenerate into a political faction in a part of the Confederacy; but the variety of sects dispersed over the entire face of it must secure the national councils against any danger from that source. A rage for paper money, for an abolition of debts, for an equal division of property, or for any other improper or wicked project, will be less apt to pervade the whole body of the Union than a particular member of it; in the same proportion as such a malady is more likely to taint a particular county or district, than an entire State.

In the extent and proper structure of the Union, therefore, we behold a republican remedy for the diseases most incident to republican government. And according to the degree of pleasure and pride we feel in being republicans, ought to be our zeal in cherishing the spirit and supporting the character of Federalists.

PUBLIUS.

44 | *The Scope and Bias of the Pressure System*
E. E. Schattschneider

The classic critique of pluralist theory came from the late E.E. Schattschneider. In his book The Semi Sovereign People, *he distinguishes between public interests and special interests, and thus between party politics and pressure politics. In addition, he identifies the upper-class bias in interest group participants and in the types of issues they advocate.*

The scope of conflict is an aspect of the scale of political organization and the extent of political competition. The size of the constituencies being mobilized, the inclusiveness or exclusiveness of the conflicts people expect to develop have a bearing on all theories about how politics is or should be organized. In other words, nearly all theories about politics have something to do with the question of who can get into the fight and who is to be excluded.

Every regime is a testing ground for theories of this sort. More than any other system American politics provides the raw materials for testing the organizational assumptions of two contrasting kinds of politics, *pressure politics* and *party politics*. The concepts that underlie these forms of politics constitute the raw stuff of a general theory of political action. The basic issue between the two patterns of organization is one of size and scope of conflict; pressure groups are small-scale organizations while political parties are very large-scale organizations. One need not be surprised, therefore, that the partisans of large-scale and small-scale organizations differ passionately, because the outcome of the political game depends on the scale on which it is played.

To understand the controversy about the scale of political organization it is necessary first to take a look at some theories about interest-group politics. Pressure groups have played a remarkable role in American politics, but they have played an even more remarkable role in American political theory. Considering the political condition of the country in the first third of the twentieth century, it was probably inevitable that the discussion of special interest pressure groups should lead to development of "group" theories of politics in which an attempt is made to explain everything in terms of group activity, i.e., an attempt to formulate a universal group theory. Since one of the best ways to test an idea is to ride it into the ground, political theory has unquestionably been improved by the heroic attempt to create a political universe revolving about the group. Now that we have a number of drastic statements of the group theory of politics pushed to a great extreme, we ought to be able to see what the limitations of the idea are....

Nevertheless, in spite of the excellent and provocative scholarly work done by Beard, Latham, Truman, Leiserson, Dahl, Lindbloom, Laski and others, the group theory of politics is beset with difficulties that are theoretical, growing in part out of sheer over-statements of the idea and in part out of some confusion about the nature of modern government.

One difficulty running through the literature of the subject results from the attempt to explain *everything* in terms of the group theory. On general grounds it would be remarkable indeed if a single hypothesis explained everything about so complex a subject as American politics....

As a matter of fact, the distinction between *public* and *private* interests is a thoroughly re-spectable one; it is one of the oldest known to political theory. In the literature of the subject the public interest refers to general or common interests shared by all or by substantially all members of the community. Presumably no community exists unless there is some kind of community of interests, just as there is no nation without some notion of national interests. If it is really impossible to distinguish between private and public interests the group theorists have produced a revolution in political thought so great that it is impossible to foresee its consequences. For this reason the distinction ought to be explored with great care....

The reality of the common interest is suggested by demonstrated capacity of the community to survive. There must be something that holds people together.

In contrast with the common interests are the special interests. The implication of this term is that these are interests shared by only a few people or a fraction of the community; they *exclude* others and may be *adverse* to them. A special interest is exclusive in about the same way as private property is exclusive. In a complex society it is not surprising that there are some interests that are shared by all or substantially all members of the community and some interests that are not shared so widely. The distinction is useful precisely because conflicting claims are made by people about the nature of their interests in controversial matters....

Since one function of theory is to explain reality, it is reasonable to add that it is a good deal easier to explain what is going on in politics by making a distinction between public and private interests than it is to attempt to explain *everything* in terms of special interests. The attempts to prove that all interests are special forces us into circumlocutions such as those involved in the argument that people have special interests in the common good. The argument can be made, but it seems a long way around to avoid a useful distinction....

All public discussion is addressed to the general community. To describe the conflict of special-interest groups as a form of politics means that the conflict has become generalized, has become a matter involving the broader public. In the nature of things a *political conflict among special interests is never restricted to the groups most immediately interested.* Indeed, it is an appeal (initiated by relatively small numbers of people) for the support of vast numbers of people who are sufficiently remote to have a somewhat different perspective on the controversy....

We can now examine the second distinction, the distinction between organized and unorganized groups. The question here is not whether the distinction can be made but whether or not it is worth making. Organization has been described as "merely a stage or degree of interaction" in the development of a group.

The proposition is a good one, but what conclusions do we draw from it? We do not dispose of the matter by calling the distinction between organized and unorganized groups a "mere" difference of degree because some of the greatest differences in the world are differences of degree.... At this point we have a distinction that makes a difference. The distinction between organized and unorganized groups is worth making because it ought to alert us against an analysis which begins as a general group theory of politics but ends with a defense of pressure politics as inherent, universal, permanent and inevitable. This kind of confusion comes from the loosening of categories involved in the universalization of group concepts....

If we are able, therefore, to distinguish between public and private interests and between organized and unorganized groups we have marked out the major boundaries of the subject; *we have given the subject shape and scope.* We are now in a position to attempt to define the area we want to explore. Having cut the pie into four pieces, we can now appropriate the piece we want and leave the rest to someone else. For a multitude of reasons *the most likely field of study is that of the organized, special-interest groups.* The advantage of concentrating on organized groups is that they are

known, identifiable and recognizable. The advantage of concentrating on special-interest groups is that they have one important characteristic in common: they are all exclusive. This piece of the pie (the organized special-interest groups) we shall call the *pressure system.* The pressure system has boundaries we can define; we can fix its scope and make an attempt to estimate its bias....

By the time a group has developed the kind of interest that leads it to organize it may be assumed that it has also developed some kind of political bias because *organization is itself a mobilization of bias in preparation for action.* Since these groups can be identified and since they have memberships (i.e., they include and exclude people), it is possible to think of the *scope* of the system.

When lists of these organizations are examined, the fact that strikes the student most forcibly is that *the system is very small.* The range of organized, identifiable, known groups is amazingly narrow; there is nothing remotely universal about it....

The business or upper-class bias of the pressure system shows up everywhere. Businessmen are four or five times as likely to write to their congressmen as manual laborers are. College graduates are far more apt to write to their congressmen than people in the lowest educational category are....

The bias of the system is shown by the fact *that even nonbusiness organizations reflect an upper-class tendency....*

The class bias of associational activity gives meaning to the limited scope of the pressure system, because *scope and bias are aspects of the same tendency.* The data raise a serious question about the validity of the proposition that special-interest groups are a universal form of political organization reflecting *all* interests. As a matter of fact, to suppose that everyone participates in pressure-group activity and that all interests get themselves organized in the pressure system is to destroy the meaning of this form of politics. The pressure system makes sense only as the political instrument of a segment of the community. It gets results by being selective and biased; *if everybody got into the act the unique advantages of this form of organization would be destroyed, for it is possible that if all interests could be mobilized the result would be a stalemate.*

Special-interest organizations are most easily formed when they deal with small numbers of individuals who are acutely aware of their exclusive interests. To describe the conditions of pressure-group organization in this way is, however, to say that it is primarily a business phenomenon. Aside from a few very large organizations (the churches, organized labor, farm organizations, and veterans' organizations) the residue is a small segment of the population. *Pressure politics is essentially the politics of small groups.*

The vice of the groupist theory is that it conceals the most significant aspects of the system. The flaw in the pluralist heaven is that the heavenly chorus sings with a strong upper-class accent. Probably about 90 percent of the people cannot get into the pressure system.

The notion that the pressure system is automatically representative of the whole community is a myth fostered by the universalizing tendency of modern group theories. *Pressure politics is a selective process ill designed to serve diffuse interests. The system is skewed, loaded and unbalanced in favor of a fraction of a minority.*

45 | *Interest Group Liberalism*
Theodore Lowi

In this classic 1967 work, Theodore Lowi finds in the interest group explosion the emergence of a new and dangerous public philosophy. Interest group liberalism is the belief that people who organize into pressure groups should receive public benefits by the mere dint of their presence, not withstanding the interests they represent. The result is a political system unable to make either choices or rational policy.

In the constitutional epoch immediately preceding our own, ending in 1937, the perennial issue underlying all debate on public policy—and therefore the key to public philosophy in that period—was the question of the nature of government itself and whether expansion or contraction best produced public good. Liberal and conservative regimes derived their principles and rationalizations of governing and policy formulation from their positions on the question. Expansion of government was demanded by liberals as the only means of combating the injustices of a brutal

physical and social world that would not change as long as it was taken as natural. Favoring government expansion became the mark of the contemporary liberal. His underlying assumption was that the instruments of government provided the means for conscious induction of social change; without capacity for such change no experimentation with any new institutional norms or means of expanding rights would be possible. Opposition to such means, but not necessarily those forms or those rights, became the mark of the contemporary conservative....

The old dialogue has passed into the grave-yard of consensus. Yet it persists. Since it has no real, operable meaning any more, it is almost purely ritualistic. However, its persistence has had its real effects. The persistence of this state of affairs so far beyond its own day, has been responsible for two pathological conditions in the 1960s. The first is that the empty rhetoric has produced a crisis of public authority. Without a basis for meaningful adversary proceedings, there has been little, if any, conflict among political actors at the level where each is forced regularly into formlulating general rules, applicable to individual acts of state and at one and the same time ethically plausible to the individual citizen. The tendency of individuals to accept governmental decisions because they are good has probably at no time in this century been less intense and less widely distributed in the United States. This is producing many problems of political cynicism and irresponsibility in everyday political processes; and these problems, in turn, have tended toward the second pathological condition, the emergence of an ersatz public philosophy that seeks to justify power and to end the crisis of public authority by parceling out public authority to private parties. That is, the emerging public philosophy seeks to solve the problem of public authority by defining it away. A most maladaptive "political formula," it will inevitably exacerbate rather than end the crisis, even though its short-run effect is one of consensus and stabilization.

Out of the developing crisis in public authority has developed an ersatz political formula that does, for all its problems, offer the public man some guidance and some justification in his efforts to shape, form and provide for the administration of positive laws in the positive state. There are several possible names for this contemporary replacement of liberalism-conservatism. A strong possibility would be *corporatism,* but its history as a concept gives it several unwanted connotations, such as conservative Catholicism or Italian fascism, that keep it from being quite suitable. Another is *syndicalism,* but among many ob-jections is the connotation of anarchy too far removed from American experience or intentions. However, the new American public philosophy is a variant of those two alien philosophies.

The most clinically accurate term to describe the American variant is *interest-group liberalism.* It may be called liberalism because it expects to use government in a positive and expansive role, it is motivated by the highest sentiments, and it possesses strong faith that what is good for government is good for the society. It is "interest-group liberalism" because it sees as both necessary and good that the policy agenda and the public interest be defined in terms of the organized interests in society. In a brief sketch, the working model of the interest-group liberal is a vulgarized version of the pluralist model of modern political science. It assumes: (1) Organized interests are homogeneous and easy to define, sometimes monolithic. Any "duly elected" spokesman for any interest is taken as speaking in close approximation for each and every member. (2) Organized interests pretty much fill up and adequately represent most of the sectors of our lives, so that one organized group can be found effectively answering and checking some other organized group as it seeks to prosecute its claims against society. And (3) the role of government is one of ensuring access particularly to the most effectively organized, and of ratifying the agreements and adjustments worked out among the competing leaders and their claims. This last assumption is supposed to be a statement of how our democracy works and how it ought to work. Taken together, these assumptions constitute the Adam Smith "hidden hand" model applied to groups. Ironically, it is embraced most strongly by the very people most likely to reject the Smith model applied in its original form to firms in the market.

These assumptions are the basis of the new public philosophy. The policy behaviors of old-school liberals and conservatives, of Republicans and Democrats, so inconsistent with liberalism-conservatism criteria, are fully consistent with the criteria drawn from interest-group liberalism: *The most important difference between liberals and conservatives, Republicans and Democrats—however they define themselves—is to be found in the interest groups they identify with. Congressmen are guided in their votes, Presidents in their programs, and administrators in this discretion, by whatever organized interests they have taken by themselves as the most legitimate; and that is the measure of the legitimacy of demands....*

The fact that a doctrine has some support in the realities of power certainly helps to explain its appeal as a doctrine. But there were also several strongly positive reasons for the emergence of this particular doctrine. The first, and once perhaps the only, is that it has helped flank the constitutional problems of federalism. Manifestations of the corporate state were once limited primarily to the Extension Service of the Department of Agriculture, with self-administration by the land grant colleges and the local farmers and commerce associations. Self-administration by organized groups was an attractive technique precisely because it could be justified as so decentralized and permissive as to be hardly federal at all. Here began the ethical and conceptual mingling of the notion of organized private groups with the notions of "local government" and "self-government." Ultimately direct interest group participation in government became synonymous with self-government, first for reasons of strategy, then by belief that the two were indeed synonymous. As a propaganda strategy it eased acceptance in the courts, then among the locals who still believed the farmer was and should be independent. Success as strategy increased usage; usage helped elevate strategy to doctrine. The users began to believe in their own symbols.

A second positive appeal of interest-group liberalism is strongly related to the first. Interest-group liberalism helps solve a problem for the democratic politician in the modern state where the stakes are so high. This is the problem of enhanced conflict and how to avoid it. The politician's contribution to society is his skill in resolving conflict. However, direct confrontations are sought only by the zealous ideologues and "outsiders." The typical American politician displaces and defers and delegates conflict where possible; he squarely faces conflict only when he must. Interest-group liberalism offers a justification for keeping major combatants apart. It provides a theoretical basis for giving to each according to his claim, the price for which is a reduction of concern for what others are claiming. In other words, it transforms logrolling from necessary evil to great good. This is the basis for the "consensus" so often claimed these days. It is also the basis for President Kennedy's faith that in our day ideology has given over to administration....

The third positive appeal of interest-group liberalism is that it is a direct, even if pathological, response to the crisis of public authority. The practice of dealing only with organized claims in formulating policy, and of dealing exclusively through organized claims in implementing programs, helps create the sense that power need not be power at all, nor control. If sovereignty is parceled out among the groups, then who's out anything? ... *If* the groups to be controlled control the controls, *then* "to administer does not always mean to rule." The inequality of power, ultimately the involvement of coercion in government decisions, is always a gnawing problem in a democratic culture. Rousseau's General Will stopped at the boundary of a Swiss canton. The myth of the group and the group will is becoming the answer to Rousseau in the big democracy....

For all the political advantages interest-group liberals have in their ideology, there are high *costs* involved. Unfortunately, these costs are not strongly apparent at the time of the creation of a group-based program. As Wallace Sayre once observed, the gains of a change tend to be immediate, the *costs* tend to be cumulative. However, it takes no long-run patience or the spinning of fine webs to capture and assess the consequences of group-based policy solutions. Three major consequences are suggested and assessed here: (I) the atrophy of institutions of popular control; (2) the maintenance of old and creation of new structures of privilege; and (3) conservatism, in several senses of the word.

... In his *The Public Philosophy*, Lippmann was rightfully concerned over the "derangement of power" whereby modern democracies tend first toward unchecked elective leadership and then toward drainage of public authority from elective leaders down into their constituencies. However, Lippmann erred if he thought of constituencies only as voting constituencies. Drainage has tended toward "support group constituencies," and with special consequence. Parceling out policy-making power to the most interested parties destroys political responsibility. A program split off with a special imperium to govern itself is not merely an administrative unit. It is a structure of power with impressive capacities to resist central political control.

Besides making conflict-of-interest a principle of government rather than a criminal act, participatory programs shut out the public. To be more precise, programs of this sort tend to cut out all that part of the mass that is not specifically organized around values strongly salient to the goals of the program. They shut out the public, first, at the most creative phase of policy making—the phase where the problem is first defined. Once problems are defined, alliances form accordingly and the outcome is both a policy and a reflection of superior power. If the definition is laid out by groups along lines of established group organization, there is always great difficulty for an amorphous public to be organized in any other terms. The public is shut out, secondly, at the phase of accountability. In programs in which group self-administration is legitimate, the administrators are accountable primarily to the groups, only secondarily to President or Congress as institutions. In brief, to the extent that organized interests legitimately control a program there is functional rather than substantive accountability. This means questions of equity, balance and equilibrium to the exclusion of questions of overall social policy

and questions of whether or not the program should be maintained or discontinued. It also means accountability to experts first and amateurs last; and an expert is a man trained and skilled in the mysterious and technologies of the program....

Finally, the public is shut out by tendencies toward conspiracy to shut the public out. One of the assumptions underlying direct group representation is that on the boards and in the staff and among the recognized outside consultants there will be regular countervailing and checks and balances. In Schattschneider's terms, this would be expected to expand the "scope of conflict." But there is nothing inevitable about that, and the safer assumption might well be the converse....

... Government by and through interest groups is in impact conservative in almost every sense of that term. Part of its conservatism can be seen in another look at the two foregoing objections: Weakening of popular government and support of privilege are, in other words, two aspects of conservatism. It is beside the point to argue that these consequences are not intended. A third dimension of conservatism, stressed here separately, is the simple conservatism of resistance to change. David Truman, who has not been a strong critic of self-government by interest groups, has, all the same, identified a general tendency of established agency-group relationships to be "highly resistant to disturbance." ... If there is already a tendency in a pluralistic system, then agency-group relationships must be all the more inflexible to the extent that the relationship is official and legitimate....

No individual interest group can be expected to take fullest account of the consequences of its own claims. This is what Presidents and Congresses are for, and this is what will continue to be delegated away as long as the ideology of interest-group liberalism allows. In effect this means that restoring pluralism as an effective principle of democratic politics requires destroying it as a principle of government. If this is to be accomplished, reform must begin with the replacement of interest-group liberalism with some contemporary version of the rule of law. The program of reform must include at least: debate that centers upon the actual consequences of public policies and of their forms of implementation; a legislative process that regularly treats enabling legislation rather

than revision; political brokers that have to deal in substantive as well as functional issues; and adaptation of public controls to local needs through choice of appropriate level of government rather than through delegation of the choice to the most interested parties.

46 | *Political Snipers*
Robert Dreyfuss

Here is one close look at just one interest group. In his case study, Robert Dreyfuss intends to show how one group can exercise an outsized influence on the political system. Still, the question remains, is the group merely doing its rightful best to defend its common interest under the First Amendment? Or, is the entire point of organization to exploit the democratic system even at the cost of Madison's "aggregate and permanent interest of the community."

…This is the story of how the NRA [National Rifle Association] managed to accumulate so much influence over the democratic process. It is an unnerving ride through the loopholes in federal election law, which allow a powerful special interest to bring almost overwhelming force to bear in a single congressional district. It is the story of how the firearms lobby bludgeoned its opponents with slashing, near-anonymous attack commercials and buried them with bulk mailings on hot-button themes unrelated to guns. It is the story of how conservative financiers and the Republican Party used the NRA to do some of their dirty work, and the price the NRA is now extracting for those services.

This story leads to the question of how the NRA gets its money in the first place, and here, too, there is more than first meets the eye. Despite its image as a membership organization subsisting entirely on $35 membership dues, the NRA actually collects much of its money in large donations from upper-

middle-class and even wealthy supporters. Big contributors, bequests, fundraising dinners, and backing from the gun industry have combined to provide the NRA with a substantial block of funds. The NRA uses that money for direct-mail solicitations, in effect converting large contributions into many smaller ones, which it then channels into political campaigns.…

Lawyers, Guns, and Money

What made the NRA such a useful tool to conservatives, of course, was its ability to raise and spend vast amounts of money. In 1994 the NRA was the nation's single biggest spender on elections. But how did it raise all the cash? Although the NRA's closemouthed tradition makes answering that question somewhat difficult, interviews with many current and former NRA officials, along with experts on the pro-gun movement, provide a fairly detailed picture—a picture that looks somewhat different from the grass roots, middle-American image NRA officials have nurtured for years.

It is true that like most direct-mail operations, the bulk of the NRA's daily operating revenue comes from small contributions, averaging about $18 per donor, and from annual dues of $35. Not surprisingly, most of this money comes from the ranks of American gun owners, who at last count were some 70 million strong. But that is not the entire story. Like the Republican and Democratic parties, which tout the fact that their average giver sends them between $10 and $25, the small average can obscure the presence of large backers. The NRA maintains an additional base of big contributors, who are clearly a few income levels above the typical working-class NRA member. This list includes the nation's 20,000 gun dealers and manufacturers and a small group of wealthy conservative financiers....

The NRA conducts a broad fundraising campaign for several of its organizations, from the NRA itself to the ILA, the NRA Foundation, and the Political Victory Fund PAC. In a column in the *American Rifleman,* the NRA's monthly, NRA President Thomas L. Washington cited a single dinner held in Corpus Christi, Texas, where 907 people donated more than $175,000 to the NRA. And the NRA recently published a list of 214 "Friends of the NRA" fundraising events scheduled between April and October 1995.

The *American Rifleman* routinely lists the names of groups and individuals around the country who give the NRA at least $1,000 at a time; until earlier this year, the magazine listed those who donated special, onetime gifts of $250 or more but dropped that practice because of space limitations. And some NRA members have left the NRA bequests in the hundreds of thousands of dollars—their parting shot, so to speak.

Finally, there is the gun industry... the NRA in 1993 earned $8.6 million from advertising income, largely through ads from the gun industry in NRA magazines. And the NRA has arranged with gun dealers around the country to help the NRA solicit contributions from gun buyers. According to Tom Washington's "The President's Column" in the *American Rifleman,* just one dealer—Midway Arms of Columbia, Missouri—raised more than $678,000 for the NRA in four years. "It isn't just individual volunteers who benefit our Association," wrote Washington. "Many businesses donate their time and efforts as well."

Thanks to the Federal Election Commission [FEC}, those millions raised by the NRA cannot be spent on federal campaigns. The FEC carefully regulates how a PAC, in this case the Political Victory Fund (PVF) of the NRA, raises or spends its cash.

Or does it?

The answer is: It does, but not very well. There are so many loopholes in the FEC rules that an organization like the NRA can do just about anything it wants to do for political objectives. Here's how.

A glance at the NRA's PAC records on file at the FEC, provided by the Center for Responsive Politics, shows that the overwhelming bulk of the NRA's PAC money comes into the PVF in donations of less than $200. Anything more than $200 must be reported to the FEC on an itemized basis. Yet over the six-year period ending December 31, 1994, the PVF reported itemized donations of only $278,631. During the same period, the PVF raised a total of $16,499,000.

One might conclude that large donors stay away from the PVF. But the FEC is not required to verify the accuracy of the NRA's filing. The forms that the NRA fills out simply list the itemized gifts as a line item, then present a lump-sum total for the bulk of the PVF income under the nonitemized heading. Even if the FEC suspects that there is something fishy about the lopsided nature of the PVF's income, it cannot investigate on its own without evidence of wrongdoing. The FEC takes the NRA's report on faith, just as it does with every other PAC.

More important, though, the FEC does not regulate the so-called "administrative and fundraising" costs associated with a PAC. That means that the NRA can spend unlimited sums, millions of dollars, to raise PAC funds, paying for repeated mailings to the NRA's 3.4 million members—and it does not have to report a single cent of those fundraising costs to the FEC. (That is also true for all other PACs, but it is particularly important for a large organization that can harvest small contributions, as opposed to, say, a trade association with a few dozen members whose executives kick in big bucks.)

And that is exactly what the NRA does. Using its corporate treasury, which is "soft money," that is, not regulated by the FEC, the NRA in 1994 spent at least $2 million—and probably much more—asking NRA members to contribute to the PVF. That, in turn, is what raised the PVF's $6.83 million during 1993–94. Through the science of direct mail, the NRA can estimate how much each dollar spent on soliciting donations to the PVF will bring in. So, while the FEC rules prevent a wealthy donor from giving more than $1,000 to a PAC, nothing prevents that donor from giving the NRA $5,000 in soft money, which the NRA then plows into PVF fundraising. A direct donation of $5,000 in soft money suddenly becomes $5,000, $10,000, or more in "hard money"—in other words, legally usable, reportable PAC cash....

Not-So-Independent Expenditures

Those who have found themselves in the NRA's sights, however, are generally more familiar with the organization's use of another legal loophole that allows the NRA to support candidates well beyond the limits on direct donations to campaigns.

Because the FEC cannot regulate free speech (thank goodness), the NRA—like any individual, corporation, or group—can spend unlimited amounts of money to promote its cause, even during an election, as long as the NRA does not engage in what is called "express advocacy." Express advocacy means that the NRA must cross a fuzzy line by explicit,

campaign-style promotion of a particular candidate. If a promotion crosses that line, the thinking goes, the money spent on it ought to count as a direct political contribution, thus subject to the limits set by the FEC.

But the line is so fuzzy that the NRA can run television commercials criticizing a candidate and supporting the NRA's laissez-faire attitude toward semiautomatic weapons without falling under FEC regulations at all. In the 1992 Synar race, the NRA liberally took advantage of this loophole, running one attack advertisement with "hard" PVF money blasting Synar and then, sandwiched around another commercial, following up with a second spot that used the same spokesman, Charlton Heston, yet did not mention Synar by name. That second commercial was paid for by the NRA's corporate account, not by its PAC—thus giving the NRA a double bang for its buck.

All of these loopholes, including the biggest one of all, the use of independent expenditures, were used expertly by the NRA in 1994. To put the NRA's use of independent expenditures in perspective, consider this: In 1993-94, the NRA accounted for fully one-third of all independent expenditures by all groups during the election....

Self-Inflicted Wounds

Stricter campaign finance law or tougher FEC regulation of the NRA seems an unlikely possibility as long as Republicans control Congress. But the NRA's coziness with the Republican Party may yet cost the organization some loyalty among its many lower and middle-class members, many of whom find the Republican stances on economics less appealing than the party's opposition to gun control.

In the past the NRA has been able to whipsaw organized labor, many of whose members oppose gun control. But the trade union rank-and-file is only beginning to appreciate that the NRA is an ally of bitterly anti-union legislators. Already, the AFL-CIO is launching a labor counteroffensive against the NRA. That movement is starting in the West, where key AFL-CIO state presidents and affiliates are studying the NRA's role in the 1994 elections. Don Judge, president of the Montana AFL-CIO, in a state where the NRA and the militia movement are powerful side-by-side forces, says that his organization is trying to educate union members that the candidates supported by the NRA are precisely the ones who, once in office, vote against labor on every issue from the minimum wage to right-to-work to safety and health provisions. "Many of us have decided, what have we got to lose in confronting this?" asks Judge. "The kind of people being promoted by the NRA, with rare exceptions, typically do not support the kinds of things that are important to working people, beyond the issue of gun ownership."

In Pennsylvania, the AFL-CIO was rocked by the Democrats' rout in 1994, and Rick Bloomingdale, president of the AFL-CIO there, is ready to confront the NRA. Bloomingdale points out that the NRA backed the victorious Republican Representative Tom Ridge in Pennsylvania's governor's race last year, even though Ridge had voted for the assault weapon ban in Congress in 1994. Says Bloomingdale, "We finally know what the NRA-PAC stands for: the National Republican Association." When the Pennsylvania AFL-CIO began running ads last year featuring a union member and the slogan, "I'm the NRA and I'm supporting Harris Wofford," the NRA's lawyers hit them with a cease and desist order because "I'm the NRA" is copyrighted by the organization. Adds Bloomingdale, "The same people who support the NRA are the people trying to bust unions."

A study by Professor Paul Clark of Pennsylvania State University shows that the NRA consistently backs candidates whose positions on economic issues are far to the right. "While [the NRA] claims not to take positions on overtly economic issues, the candidates they support clearly do," he says. "Significant-

ly, they have had some success at convincing union members to support their organizations and their candidates."

Warren Cassidy, a former NRA executive vice president... worries openly that the NRA's lurch to the right may involve a quid pro quo to support the Republicans on issues that have nothing to do with guns. "When does that quid pro quo begin to hurt your organization?" he asks. "With all the connections to a strong conservative movement, NRA got caught up in that tide and they might not be able to extricate themselves." He warns: "It isn't necessarily true that all those chits should fall to one party, the Republican Party ... because we have always had a strong, strong blue-collar element, both rural and urban, in the NRA. And many, many, many of these people are union members."...

In the meantime, NRA officials have more immediate concerns. In its single-minded fervor to defeat even the most hesitant supporters of gun control, the NRA may have recklessly stretched its spending to the breaking point. The direct-mail scheme upon which the NRA has built its empire has been costly, and the organization recently traded a sizeable chunk of its inheritance for a posh new headquarters building. All of this has led many former NRA officials to say that the organization will crash in the near future. Reports of financial difficulties have attracted the scrutiny of the Internal Revenue Service.

Still, on Capitol Hill a healthy symbiosis between the Republicans and the NRA continues to thrive. While a good number of mainstream Republicans see the NRA as a loose cannon and an organization of zealots flirting with the far right, these Republicans still want the NRA's money and grassroots army at election time, and they still worry that any misstep—even in the course of the routine give-and-take that occurs in a legislative session—could bring the NRA down on their heads....

CURRENT CONTROVERSY

What Should Be Done about Campaign Finance?

47 | *Clean Elections: How To*
Ellen Miller

Most citizens agree that the current system of financing our campaigns is so costly and so dependent on special interest money that it represents a perversion of democracy. Ellen Miller, a member of the advocacy group Public Campaign, offers a solution to these woes. She argues that the problem with past reforms (and most of the popular current plans) is their piecemeal approach. Hence, she points to the need to rally public support behind a comprehensive solution: the "Clean Money Option." Would it work?

...We now have a rare political opportunity as Congress reconvenes to revisit proposals and strategies for campaign finance reform.

- But beware "bipartisan" reforms. Both parties have colluded in a system that has generated record sums of special-interest money. A better concept is nonpartisan reform. And we know that for truly far-reaching and clean-sweeping reform to be enacted, the public must be fully mobilized to support it.
- The record of failed reform attempts in Congress over the last 20 years offers a clear lesson: Packages of piecemeal reforms do not generate the requisite public enthusiasm. The first task is to frame the outcome we seek, to define where reform ultimately has to take us, and to find a solution that directly confronts the real problems. And the real problems are too much money; too much time spent raising money; the money's influence over lawmakers by the special interests who contribute it; and the reality that good people don't have a fair chance of winning without the money....

The "Clean Money Option"

The Working Group on Electoral Democracy, an informal association of longtime public policy activists from various parts of the country, developed the Clean Money model reform for congressional elections several years ago. It has been adapted by state-based campaign finance reform activists and was the basis of a proposal for state elections that was enacted by Maine voters, by a margin of 56 to 44. Under this system, once candidates pass a carefully determined qualification threshold, they receive a fixed amount of public money for their campaigns. (For example, candidates for the U.S. House of Representatives would receive $150,000 for the primary and $200,000 for the general election, with additional money available to protect against excessive private spending.) This would eliminate the need to raise private money, and thus eliminate the inherent conflicts of interest that arise when the campaigns of public servants are privately financed.

Public financing is made available for a candidate's entire campaign, beginning with the primary and running through the general election and any runoff. To be eligible for this "Clean Money," congressional candidates would be required to raise a relatively large number of five-dollar "qualifying contributions" from within his or her election district. Eligibility would also be conditioned on candidates' agreement not to raise or spend any private money whatsoever during the primary and general election periods, and thus to limit their spending to the fixed amount of public funding they receive.

Prior to the beginning of the primary, however, prospective congressional candidates would be allowed to raise a limited amount of private, "seed" money, with a $100 per donor limitation on contributions. This money could only be spent on the start-up costs of qualifying for public financing, and couldn't be spent during the primary or general election periods. All the candidates running for the same office who met the qualifying test would receive equal amounts of public financing.

This system would be strictly voluntary, to conform to the Supreme Court's 1976 *Buckley v. Valeo* decision, which allows candidates to spend unlimited amounts of their own money. Candidates would be free to reject the Clean Money Option and raise private money, or to use their own money to finance their campaigns. However, judging from the participation rate in the system of partial public financing for presidential elections, the great majority of congressional candidates capable of financing their own campaigns are very likely to choose public financing instead, once such an option is in place....

As part of a Clean Money Option, soft money of the kind that now undermines the integrity of the presidential system (because it is used not for generic "party-building" purposes as officially intended, but to support particular federal candidates) would be banned. In addition, with a Clean Money Option, publicly financed candidates who are outspent by privately financed opponents receive additional, "equalizing" funds. In the version just approved by Maine voters, the additional funding is capped at 100 percent of the original amount received, but a higher cap could be set for federal elections. This cap protects the Clean Money Fund from being depleted by "the sky's the limit" private spending.

The problem of independent expenditures is addressed in a similar way. Candidates

targeted by such expenditures, as determined by the Federal Election Commission, would receive the same kind of equalizing funds. This, of course, does not mean the disappearance of independent expenditures, including those the political parties are now making on behalf of their own candidates thanks to a new loophole recently opened up by the Supreme Court in Colorado *Republican Campaign Committee v. Federal Election Commission.* (In this controversial June 1996 decision, the Court declared that political parties should have the same right to make independent expenditures that individuals and other political committees enjoy, so long as there is no coordination or communication between the parties and their candidates.) However, there is a high likelihood that the equalizing provision will reduce these expenditures because opponents will be able to match them with public money. Also, in a Clean Money Option environment in which all candidates have the opportunity to "just say no" to special-interest money and receive full and equal amounts of public financing, there is likely to be strong voter disapproval of independent spenders who try to circumvent the new system and also disapproval of the candidates they are trying to help.

Failure of Other Approaches

Several alternative approaches have lately been proposed, ranging from a constitutional amendment overturning *Buckley v. Valeo* to a variety of piecemeal strategies. But there is no viable alternative that would bring down the cost of campaigns, free candidates and elected officials from the incessant "money chase," and, most importantly, end their dependency on special-interest contributors.

Establishing low limits on individual contributions has popular appeal and has been approved by voters for state elections in several states. This approach commendably pushes wealthy donors away from candidates, but it forces candidates to spend even more time raising money. In the two locales where it has actually been tried, Washington, D.C., and Oregon, it appears to have led to an explosion of independent expenditures and other methods of end-running the system. Federal courts have subsequently declared unconstitutional both the Washington, D.C., law and a similar measure that was passed by ballot initiative, but never put into effect, in Missouri.

Attempts to provide only partial public financing have not been very successful either. Twenty-three states have some form of partial public financing on their books, but in practice only nine states are able to provide even limited funds to statewide candidates, and only three states provide partial public financing to legislative candidates. The partial public financing system for presidential races that provides matching public financing in the primary and purportedly full public financing for the general election is equally ineffective. Of the approximate $800 million spent on this year's presidential contest, more than $225 million came from "soft" (unregulated) contributions by large private donors, including some possibly illegal sources.

Unfortunately, the McCain-Feingold bill, which went down to resounding bipartisan defeat earlier this year and which its co-sponsors stand ready to reintroduce in January, is another such package. Its complex combination of limits and incentives—seen by many inside the Beltway as the most possible winnable reform—does not represent a compelling, or even comprehensible, solution. No one thinks that the McCain-Feingold bill goes far enough—not even its sponsors. The bill is incomplete because the most pernicious influence of money—the checks handed over by special interests to candidates—isn't dealt with comprehensively.

Although McCain-Feingold provides discounted television advertising and mail rates to candidates who agree to various voluntary limits, it offers no public financing and thus perpetuates a system in which candidates will spend lots of time raising money from the same private interests as before. In addition, the voluntary limits on overall campaign spending and the percentage of money candidates can receive from PACs and out-of-state contributors are set at above the average amounts currently being spent or raised.

The McCain-Feingold provisions for limiting soft money and tightening the definition of "independent expenditures" are important and worthy. But by focusing primarily on restricting PAC and out-of-state contributions, the bill ignores a basic reality—namely, that in a society in which wealth is so unevenly distributed, any campaign finance system that requires candidates to raise large sums of private money is bound to be rife with conflicts of interest and unfair to people without access to wealth.

Buckley v. Valeo makes reform difficult, by forbidding mandatory limits on overall campaign spending and by granting constitutional "free speech" protections to contributions by wealthy candidates to their own campaigns, as well as independent expenditures. It is for this reason that former Senator Bill Bradley and many others see the need for a constitutional amendment to overturn Buckley. But the road to achieving a constitutional amendment is long and arduous, and for most who have tried to go down it—including, in recent times, advocates of term limits, equal rights for women and men, and a ban on flag burning—the result has been failure. Moreover, an amendment that truly limited all independent expenditures could well threaten legitimate First Amendment rights, such as the right of a newspaper to endorse or oppose a candidate or the rights of citizen groups to run paid advertisements on public issues.

The Clean Money Option provides the best solution to the core problem of money in politics—the influence of private money given directly to candidates for public office. Not only is it constitutional (because it is voluntary), but it is also both comprehensive and comprehensible, enjoying a combination of sweeping effect and simplicity of design that is rare in public policy debates. Limiting campaign spending, reducing government favors to special interests, and leveling the playing field to give good candidates a fair chance of being elected are the goals that drive public support for this proposal....

No solution closes all channels of monied influence, but the Clean Money Option blocks the most destructive path, that of large sums of money changing hands directly between special interests and candidates. Piecemeal steps leave this channel open, ultimately reducing reform to little more than minor legislative obstacles for special interests to avoid.

48 | *The Futile Quest for the Ideal Congressional Campaign Finance System*
Bruce Larson

Beware any campaign finance reform that seems to good too be true—it just might be. This survey shows that most schemes dam up the rushing waters of political money in one place, only to divert it elsewhere. Whereas the ideal system may not be attainable by sweeping reform, political scientist Bruce Larson concludes that the system can certainly be improved—perhaps by raising contribution limits rather than trying to stifle them.

In reforming congressional campaign finance, the temptation is to reach for ideals. Reform advocates—such as Ellen Miller— want a congressional campaign finance system that minimizes the influence of special interest money, keeps campaign spending at sensible levels, fosters healthy electoral competition, encourages a more grass-roots system of campaign finance, doesn't advantage wealthy candidates, and doesn't require candidates to spend all of their waking hours raising money. Although Miller's reform plan brings the quest for an ideal campaign finance system to new heights, she is by no means alone in believing that we can fashion a campaign finance system that achieves all of these desirable goals.

Indeed, the much-maligned congressional campaign finance system we now have is itself a product of well-intended reform efforts passed by Congress in the early 1970s. More recently, as weaknesses in the present laws have become evident, reform advocates and reform-minded members of Congress, armed with a multitude of reform plans, remain convinced that a perfect congressional campaign finance system is within reach. Yet no reform scheme, however well intended, is likely to produce an ideal congressional campaign finance system because no plan is likely to surmount the considerable obstacles in the way of doing so—namely, the constraints of the First Amendment, the impracticality of public financing for congressional elections, and the propensities of those with a stake in election outcomes to find innovative ways around even the tightest of regulations.

The present congressional campaign finance laws provide an exemplary case study of how even the most well-meaning reforms can fall victim to such obstacles. In the early 1970s, in response to the Watergate Scandal and increasing campaign spending, Congress passed a series of campaign finance regulations designed to replace the various (and largely unenforced) laws enacted earlier in the century. The most comprehensive of the new laws, which continue to govern federal campaign finance practices today, were passed as a series of amendments in 1974 and 1976 to the Federal Election Campaign Act (FECA).

Contribution and expenditure limits were the primary components of the FECA amendments regulating congressional campaign finance. Contribution limits restricted individuals to giving $1,000 per candidate per election, whereas multicandidate committees (what we now know as political action committees, or PACs) were limited to contributions of $5,000 per candidate per election. Since candidates run in primary and general elections, both of these limits were effectively doubled. The 1974 FECA also limited to $5,000 per candidate per election the sum that political parties could contribute to candidates and to $10,000 per election cycle the amount that parties could spend on behalf of their candidates. (Party expenditure limits, but not contribution limits, were indexed to inflation). Finally, the new law limited to $25,000 per calendar year the total sum of money that individuals could contribute to federal candidates, PACs, and national party committees combined. The FECA's contribution limits were intended to reduce the influence of wealthy individuals and organized interests in the political system.

Congress also included a menu of spending limits in the FECA Amendments that were intended to limit the overall sums of money spent in federal elections and reduce the electoral advantage enjoyed by wealthy candidates. These restrictions limited House candidates (and their families) to spending $25,000 per year of their own money in their campaigns; the limit for Senate candidates was $35,000. Both limits were indexed for inflation. The FECA also limited House candidates' campaigns to $70,000 in total spending, whereas total spending by Senate campaigns was limited to $100,000 or 8 cents times the voting-age population of a state,

whichever was greater. As with restrictions on the use of candidates' own money, spending limits for both House and Senate campaigns were indexed for inflation. Finally, independent spending by groups and individuals to support or oppose federal candidates was limited to $1,000 per candidate per election. Limits on independent spending were intended to reduce the ability of organized interests and wealthy individuals to exert an undue influence on the electoral process.

Although the amendments were scheduled to take effect in 1976, the regulations were never fully implemented. Instead, challenged in the federal courts by an unlikely alliance of politicians across the ideological spectrum, the new law collided with what would become one of the foremost obstacles to campaign finance reform: the First Amendment. In a landmark ruling that would indelibly shape the future course of federal campaign finance law, the Supreme Court in *Buckley v. Valeo* struck down all of the FECA's *expenditure* limits (except those that applied to political parties) while leaving intact the law's *contribution* limits.

The difference in the Court's treatment of contribution and expenditure limits ultimately rested on a subtle distinction that the Court drew between these two types of political activity. In the Court's view, limits on campaign *expenditures* violated a candidate's First Amendment protections because such limits "reduce the quantity of expression by restricting the number of issues discussed, the depth of their exploration, and the size of the audience reached." By contrast, the Court stated that *contribution* limits "entail only a marginal restriction upon the contributor's ability to engage in free communication." Contributing to a candidate or a group is a symbolic expression of support, the Court reasoned, and contribution limits do not infringe upon the ability of a person to express support, nor do contribution limits infringe upon the contributor's freedom to discuss political issues. Thus, before Congress's 1974 reform could be implemented, the Court, armed with the First Amendment, placed beyond reach various ingredients of an ideal congressional campaign finance system. What ultimately became law, then, was a regulatory structure in which campaign contributions *to* candidates would be strictly limited but campaign spending *by* candidates would be permitted to grow without limits. The results were not especially conducive to the requirements of an ideal campaign finance system.

Without legal limits on campaign expenditures, the level of spending in congressional campaigns continued to increase sharply. The rise in campaign spending reflected the growing professionalization of congressional campaigns (which are now typically media-driven affairs directed by high-priced political consultants), the heightened volatility of the electorate (caused by a weakening of partisan attachments among voters), and the perception of electoral uncertainty that this volatility created for incumbents (reinforced by increasingly large swings in incumbents' vote margins from election to election). Indeed, even *after* adjusting for inflation, total campaign spending in House contests more than doubled between 1972 and 1998, and total spending in Senate campaigns nearly tripled. To make matters worse, congressional candidates were forced to raise these ever-increasing sums of money under the FECA's restrictive contribution limits, which were set in 1974 and never indexed for inflation. (By 1996, a $1,000 contribution had a real value of only $362 in 1976 dollars.) One congressional candidate observed that fundraising in the post-*Buckley* era had become like attempting to fill a large swimming pool using a tablespoon.

The fate of the FECA reforms provides vivid illustration that many of the requirements of an ideal congressional campaign finance system may be out of reach. With candidates forced to raise more and more campaign money under static contribution limits, they have been pressured either to increase the number of donors giving to their campaigns or to cajole their regular supporters into giving larger amounts. Both strategies have required candidates to spend *more* time

fundraising. Pressure to raise increasing sums of campaign money under restrictive limits has also given increasing political influence to new players—those who can effectively organize and mobilize large numbers of contributors. Chief among these players are the "bundlers"—the lobbyists and political entrepreneurs who gather checks written by others, present them in a "bundle" to a candidate, and earn political credit from the candidate for the entire package. As political scientist Frank J. Sorauf observes in his book *Inside Campaign Finance,* these bundlers are in many ways nothing more than a new breed of political "fat cat" that the reforms sought to eliminate in the first place. Finally, with large sums of money so difficult to raise under the FECA's restrictive contribution limits, the post-*Buckley* congressional campaign finance system has benefited wealthy candidates who don't need to solicit donations in order to wage a competitive campaign.

Quite clearly, then, the reforms passed by Congress have failed to achieve their objectives. They have neither curbed the influence of organized money, lessened the electoral advantage of wealthy candidates, nor reduced the amount of time candidates need to spend fundraising.

As if these problems weren't bad enough, the shrinking margin of partisan control in the House during the 1990s motivated the national parties (especially the congressional campaign committees) to find new ways of funneling resources into campaigns likely to be won or lost at the margins. By far the most important development along these lines was the growing use of unregulated "soft money" by the parties on "issue-advocacy" advertisements—a development which some political observers argue represents the final and complete meltdown of the post-*Buckley* campaign finance system.

In the late 1970s, a series of Federal Election Commission advisory opinions allowed party committees to raise money in unlimited sums from individuals, corporations, unions, and other interest groups—to pay for the non-federal portion of their campaign activities. As a result of these opinions and a complicated 1979 amendment to the FECA, the parties began using these unregulated funds—coined "soft" money by journalist Elizabeth Drew—to help finance generic party advertisements (such as "Vote Republican, for a change"), state and local party building activities (such as get-out-the-vote drives), and national party administrative and overhead expenses (such as rent, personnel, salaries).

More recently, however, the parties have begun pushing the boundaries of permissible soft money expenditures by using these funds to help finance "issue-advocacy" advertisements. Issue-advocacy ads resemble traditional "election-advocacy" advertisements in almost every way; they typically show images of the candidate being supported or opposed and make reference to his or her legislative record. What sets issue-advocacy advertisements apart from election-advocacy advertisements is that issue-advocacy ads never technically advocate the election or defeat of a specific candidate by using words such as "vote for," "vote against," "support," or "oppose." Although the difference may seem trivial, it has major consequences for the way issue-advocacy advertisements are financed. Because issue-advocacy ads do not technically advocate the election or defeat of a federal candidate, they may be partially financed with money raised outside the federal restrictions (i.e., soft money). The national parties typically transfer the funds to state party committees that then make the media buys in accordance with the national party's wishes.

The result of these developments is that unions, corporations, and wealthy individuals now regularly contribute six-figure sums to the soft money accounts of the national party committees, which turn around and spend unlimited sums on thinly disguised campaign ads designed unmistakably to help or hurt specific candidates. Following the lead of the parties, interest groups—and more recently several congressional party leaders—have also begun raising and spending large sums of unregulated soft money. Like no other develop-

ment, the advent of soft money illustrates that we have come full circle—that despite the best efforts of reformers during the 1970s to eliminate big money from the political system, big money has found its way back in. Indeed, the metaphor that political money is like rushing water—dam it up in one place and it will come out somewhere else—has never seemed so apt.

Although there is no shortage of reform plans that attempt to remedy the problems with the present congressional campaign finance system, there is also nothing to indicate that any of these plans can produce a better campaign finance system than the one we currently have. The problem is that most of the campaign reform schemes presently being touted by reform advocates are either blatantly unconstitutional, politically infeasible, practically unworkable, substantively misguided, or all of the above.

Consider first the reform plan advocated by Ellen Miller and her reform advocacy group Public Campaign. Miller proposes a system in which congressional candidates who meet certain qualification thresholds would receive full public funding in exchange for voluntarily complying with spending limits. Under these arrangements, House candidates would receive $150,000 in public funds for primary elections and $200,000 for general elections. Presumably, Senate candidates would receive larger subsidies. In both House and Senate races, candidates would voluntarily agree to spend no more than the amount of the public subsidy. Moreover, additional "equalizing" funding would be available to candidates outspent by opponents who opt out of the public funding program and to candidates negatively targeted by independent expenditure campaigns. Miller's plan would also ban the national parties from raising soft money, which would prevent special interests from contributing six-figure sums to the national parties and limit the parties' ability to run expensive issue-advocacy advertisements. Finally, Miller notes that her plan is fully constitutional because candidates would be free to reject the public funding/spending limits option and raise private funds for their campaigns instead.

At first glance, Miller's scheme seems like a good idea, and her plan has the virtue of having been passed in several states, mostly via state ballot initiative. But as a means of financing congressional campaigns, Miller's plan is politically unrealistic, financially and administratively impractical, and unlikely to achieve the goals to which it aspires.

First, from a political perspective, any congressional campaign finance plan that includes a provision for public funding would be dead-on-arrival in Congress. Simply put, a majority of representatives and senators—and probably a majority of American voters as well—object philosophically to the idea of using taxpayer money to fund congressional campaigns. As political scientist Frank J. Sorauf has noted in his book *Inside Campaign Finance*, the public may want the *results* of public funding (that is, getting interested money out of the political system), but it has shown no inclination to pay for such programs. Indeed, the United States already has public funding for presidential elections, and the lack of public support for the program is illustrated by the declining percentage of people who use the check-off box on their tax returns to contribute to the presidential election fund.

In addition to being politically unrealistic, the Miller plan is also highly impractical. Although it may be financially possible to provide public funding for a handful of presidential candidates every four years (and even this has been a challenge), it is another matter entirely to provide public funding for the multitude of candidates who compete in 435 House contests and 33 or 34 Senate contests every two years. (In 1998, a total of 2,100 candidates competed in House and Senate primary and general elections!) Moreover, even if the public was willing to foot the bill for such an expense, the chronically underfunded and understaffed Federal Election Commission would be thoroughly unequipped to administer the program unless it was radically overhauled and enlarged.

Political and practical concerns aside, it is also doubtful that Ellen Miller's plan would achieve two of her most important stated goals: eliminating private money from the political system and limiting overall campaign spending in congressional elections. Consider first the goal of eliminating private money from the political system.

Although Miller's plan includes a ban on soft money contributions to the national parties, no law could constitutionally prohibit political parties or interest groups from running costly independent expenditure campaigns on behalf of their favored candidates. Indeed, the Supreme Court has jealously guarded the rights of interest groups, and more recently political parties, to spend unlimited sums of money on behalf of candidates, so long as the money being spent is raised in accordance with federal laws and the spending is done independently of candidates. Moreover, while the Supreme Court may uphold a ban on soft money contributions to the national parties, it would almost certainly view unfavorably laws banning interest groups and state parties from raising soft money. As such, interest groups and state parties would be free to continue running issue-advocacy advertisements, financed with unregulated soft money and designed to benefit or harm specific federal candidates.

Clearly, then, the First Amendment makes it virtually certain that private interests would continue to play an important financial role in any system of publicly funded congressional campaigns. Indeed, as evidence of this, one need look no further than the presidential campaign finance system, where, despite public funding and voluntary spending limits, private money has once again become increasingly important.

In theory, Miller's plan *could* help to reduce overall candidate spending in congressional elections, though even here the outcome is far from guaranteed. For the Miller plan to succeed in limiting overall candidate spending in congressional elections, a significant portion of congressional candidates would need to accept the public funding/voluntary spending limits option. Miller is confident that there would be widespread participation among congressional candidates. After all, she reasons, almost all presidential candidates have accepted the public funding/spending limits option since it became available in 1976. But such reasoning is suspect.

Congressional campaigns are entirely different affairs than presidential campaigns, and a congressional candidate's decision to accept public funding will be based not on what presidential candidates do but rather on the candidate's strategic calculation as to whether accepting such a package will help her win the election. Put in these terms, it is possible to imagine scenarios in which candidates opt out of the public funding/spending limit package, even if doing so results in an increased flow of public "equalizing" money for their opponents. For example, a House Republican candidate with a highly conservative support base might opt out of the public funding program because his core supporters object philosophically to publicly funded campaigns. In fact, at the state level, such a scenario appears to be more than purely hypothetical. In their work *The Day After Reform*, political scientists Michael J. Malbin and Thomas Gais have shown that Republicans have participated at much lower rates than Democrats in public funding programs for state legislative elections. The point here is that Miller's plan will not *necessarily* reduce overall candidate spending in congressional elections. Rather, such an outcome depends on high levels of participation among those competing in congressional elections, and such participation is far from guaranteed.

While the ambitiousness of Ellen Miller's plan renders it particularly vulnerable to criticism, most of the more mainstream campaign finance fixes presently being touted withstand scrutiny no better. Consider, for example, the Shays-Meehan Bipartisan Campaign Finance Reform Act. As passed by the House in September 1999 (but not the Senate) the Shays-Meehan bill attempts primarily to provide two major repairs to the present congressional campaign finance system.

First, as with the Miller plan discussed above, the Shays-Meehan bill provides for a ban on the raising of soft money by the national party committees. Second, the bill broadens the definition of election advocacy to include any advertisements that feature the name or image of a specific candidate. This definition of election advocacy contrasts with the present, more narrow definition articulated by the federal courts, which have defined election advocacy as any advertisement that uses explicit and unequivocal *words*—such as "vote for," "vote against," "support," or "oppose"—to urge viewers to elect or defeat a clearly identified federal candidate. The goal of the issue-advocacy reform is to force groups running advertisements that are clearly designed to help or hurt a specific candidate to pay for these advertisements with hard (regulated) money rather than with soft (unregulated) money.

As attractive as these fixes sound, there are still problems. First, there is no reason to think that the federal courts, which have consistently adhered (on First Amendment grounds) to a narrow definition of election advocacy, will uphold the broadening of that definition in the Shays-Meehan bill. Second, while the ban on soft money contributions would stop the national parties from raising soft money, the ban aims at the symptoms of a problem while doing nothing to remedy the problem's causes: overly restrictive limits on *hard* money contributions in a system without spending limits. Without an increase in hard money contribution limits to reduce the gap between candidates' fundraising needs and their fundraising abilities—and with partisan competition for control of Congress likely to remain intense— the national parties will undoubtedly develop other innovative ways to spend resources on behalf of their candidates.

Even the most innovative campaign finance reform plans have their flaws. Without doubt, the most interesting and tantalizing reform idea to emerge in recent years is the "blind" trust model devised by law professors Ian Ayres of Yale and Jeremy Bulow of Stanford. In their model, any individual or group could contribute any sum of money to any candidate. Importantly, however, candidates wouldn't know the identities of their contributors. Instead, all campaign contributions to candidates would flow through blind trusts designated for them, from which candidates could draw money to spend on their elections. (To be sure, a contributor could secretly notify a candidate of his financial support, but so could a non-contributor.) At first glance, this is a truly appealing idea. Unlike other reform plans, the effectiveness of the blind trust idea does not depend on halting the flow of big money—a seemingly impossible task, if our experience with such a quest is any meter. Moreover, the plan seems on its face to be fully constitutional, since contributors could continue to contribute and candidates could continue to spend as much as they can raise. (As *New York Times* journalist Jack Hitt put it, any court that struck down the law would be forced to explain why the secret ballot isn't also unconstitutional, since the secret ballot, in concealing a candidate's political supporters from her, does essentially the same thing as the contribution trust fund.) Finally, the plan doesn't rely on the administratively impractical and the politically unrealistic idea of public funding.

Tantalizing as it sounds, even the trust fund model has the potential for some unhappy consequences. First, the plan might well result in a collapse of fundraising. After all, individuals who contribute to members would be reluctant to contribute if a member couldn't find out about their support. Such a result may sound appealing to people intent on ridding the political system of interested money. Yet absent public funding or spending limits, a campaign finance system that makes it difficult for candidates to raise campaign money is a system that inevitably benefits wealthy candidates—who don't need to raise funds from others to foot the bill for their campaigns. The trust fund model also re-introduces the obstacles to campaign finance reform presented by the First Amendment. That is, no constitutionally valid law could stop an interest group from waging a

very public campaign on behalf of a candidate—a campaign replete with expensive television advertisements and all the other accoutrements of modern electoral politics. Such a campaign, run completely independently of the benefited candidate, would nevertheless garner for the interest group significant thanks from the candidate. And the trust fund model, it seems logical to think, might well amplify the importance of such campaigns in American politics. Thus, even the trust fund model, ideal as it first appears conceptually, would likely run into some major difficulties in practice.

Underlying much of this essay is the argument that an ideal campaign finance system will never be attainable. Such an argument does not imply, however, that the present congressional campaign finance system cannot be *improved*. It can be. The problem is that in their quest for unattainable ideals, reform advocates have overlooked more modest—but more workable—reforms that would improve the system.

With ideals beyond reach, the best course of action would be to make a few remedial modifications to the present system. Most importantly, Congress should provide for across-the-board *increases* in hard money contribution limits—that is, increases in the sums that individuals may contribute to PACs, parties, and candidates, and increases in the sums that PACs and parties may contribute to candidates. While reform advocates would likely fret about this recommendation, increasing hard money contribution limits would create a better fit between candidates' fundraising needs and their fundraising abilities, perhaps reducing the incentives for candidates and donors to find innovative ways of sidestepping the laws. At the very least, increasing hard money contributions would have the benefit of keeping campaign finance transactions in full public view, since, unlike bundling activity and most soft money transactions, hard money contributions must be fully disclosed in a timely manner to the FEC.

Any congressional campaign finance reform bill should also take extra care not to weaken the national parties' ability to help candidates. Although most reform advocates complain relentlessly about the campaign activities of the newly revitalized national parties, strong parties may be the best means we have of ensuring a healthy degree of competition in congressional elections. This seems especially true when we consider how political parties offset the incumbent-based contribution strategies of most PACs. A major barrier to competitive congressional elections is that PACs, which provide a significant bulk of candidates' campaign receipts, contribute mostly to congressional incumbents. This contribution strategy reflects PAC goals. Most PACs make campaign contributions to gain access to officeholders. From the perspective of a PAC director, therefore, a campaign contribution to a losing candidate is a wasted contribution. Yet in any congressional race featuring an incumbent and a challenger, the incumbent is, all other things being equal, always more likely to win. (Incumbents have an array of official resources at their disposal to benefit their reelection bids, and they typically have much greater name recognition than do challengers.) Hence, the safest way for PACs to maintain their access is by contributing to incumbents—which they do with remarkable regularity. The result is that challengers attempting to unseat incumbents are typically starved for resources, while incumbents, already more likely to win than challengers, usually have more resources than they can possibly use. This scenario greatly reduces the level of competition in congressional elections.

Political parties, however, tend to offset the incumbent-based strategies of PACs. Parties make financial contributions to candidates not to maintain access with officeholders but rather to maximize the number of seats the party holds in Congress. Their ultimate goal is to capture and maintain majorities. Thus, rather than contribute overwhelmingly to incumbents, as PACs do, the national parties direct the bulk of their resources to incumbent *and* non-incumbent candidates in close races, where their re-

sources are most likely to affect the electoral outcomes and on which majority party control hinges. Importantly, then, by getting campaign money to competitive candidates who need it—especially non-incumbents— parties help to offset the incumbent-based strategies of most PACs and, in doing so, serve to make congressional elections more competitive. Reformers seeking to make congressional races more competitive, therefore, should consider raising the limits on what parties may contribute to candidates even beyond the limits that govern individual and PAC contributions to candidates. At the very least, the desirability of healthy national parties suggests that any ban on soft money contributions to the parties should be accompanied by significant increases in the amount of hard money that the parties may solicit from individuals and interest groups. Alternatively, the special role played by political parties in democracies justifies providing the national party committees with public subsidies as several states presently do.

The FEC should also be made a much more effective watchdog agency. In its current make-up, the agency consists of six commissioners, three Democrats and three Republicans, and it can take no enforcement action (even on minor matters) without the consent of four commissioners. This leads to considerable deadlocks, especially on controversial cases. One helpful reform, therefore, would be to reduce the commission to five members: two Democrats, two Republicans, and one independent. Yet perhaps most importantly, the FEC should be given a substantially larger budget. Unfortunately, the FEC is a public agency without much of a constituency, and it is the only public agency whose funding is allocated directly by those it regulates. As we would expect given these arrangements, the FEC is chronically underfunded and micro-managed by Congress. Despite the ever-increasing workload of the FEC, the agency's budget (in inflation-adjusted dollars) has increased only minimally since it was created. Moreover, when Congress has appropriated additional funds for the agency, the money has typically been earmarked for specific uses (greater enforcement rarely being one of them). As an indicator of how serious the agency's money woes have become, the FEC dumped 41 percent of the cases on its docket in 1997 because it did not have sufficient resources to handle them. Indeed, the public should be highly suspect of any campaign finance reform plan that does nothing to remedy the FEC's chronic shortage of resources.

These admittedly modest recommendations may be understandably difficult for most Americans to accept. As a people, we have always reached for ideals, and we have always had great faith in the ability of legal reforms (such as campaign finance reform and term limits) to solve what we perceive as problems of corruption in government and politics. Still, legal solutions to the campaign finance thicket have not inspired confidence. Moreover, as with many problems in republican governments, the best antidote is greater political attentiveness on the part of the public. In this sense, the most effective way to ensure that our representatives act the way we want them to act is not by passing yet another series of reforms but rather by letting our representatives know that we are paying attention to their actions.

CHAPTER EIGHT

Congress

A Question of Representation

OVERVIEW AND SUMMARY

Congress is often referred to as the "broken branch" of government. Its popularity and public approval almost always lag far behind that of both the president and the courts. Such a popularity lag has existed for most of the time in which public opinion has been measured. It seems that the public has long believed that Congress fails to be truly representative.

The reflexive anti-Congress sentiment may be the primary reason that the Republican majority (who stoked the coals of anti-Congress sentiment when the party was in the minority) withered a bit in subsequent election years. Indeed, the Republican takeover of Congress in 1994 may have been the main cause of the resuscitation of the Clinton presidency and of the president's reelection in 1996.

Much of the public sees Congress as self-interested, out of touch with the concerns of the average citizen, and far too dependent on the money and support of "special" interests. And because both Congress and special interests have been so persistently unpopular, calls for campaign finance reform have become more persistent. Some of the articles in this section suggest that this case against Congress is exaggerated, if not wholly distorted. Nevertheless, the question of who and what Congress represents continues to be at the core of the movement for campaign finance reform.

The core readings in this chapter focus on the evolution of the concept of representation and on how that concept has affected the legislative product of the U.S. Congress. Traditionally, representational theory has focused on how closely a member reflects the opinion of his or her district and, more generally, on how accurately the body of representatives reflects public opinion as a whole. *Delegate* behavior denotes a member who is voting in accordance with the specific wishes of his or her constituency. This recalls the question raised in Chapter Five: Can the people govern? Although some may assume that the delegate role is expected by the civics book theory, a troubling question remains in that the voice of the people may be nonexistent, uninformed, or simply wrongheaded. In this case, how should a member cast his or her vote?

Edmund Burke, the great eighteenth-century British Parliamentarian, argued that a member of the legislature should not be merely a delegate but rather a *trustee*. According to Burke, legislators have a duty to exercise their best judgment in pursuit of the interests of the whole society, not just the interests of the narrow constituency that elected them. The blending of the two roles, delegate and trustee, is known as the *politico* role. Least popular among the public, the politico nonetheless describes many legislators who exercise some independent judgment while "horse-trading" in order to satisfy the parochial interests of their constituency.

Scholarship in the 1970s broadened our understanding of the role of representatives by synthesizing their behavior in their district with their behavior in Washington, D.C. For example, **Richard Fenno** explains that a member of Congress seeks reelection as the prerequisite for the attainment of influence in Washington and for the making of good public policy. Members cannot attain these goals if they regard the district that elected them as no more than an amorphous blob of citizenry to be shown fealty, to be educated, or to be handed goodies. According to Fenno, the astute member discerns different constituencies among the people in the district and distinguishes among core interests (the geographic constituency), active participants (the primary constituency), and the marginally attentive voting citizenry (the reelection constituency). These three (of Fenno's "four constituencies") roughly translate into the politico, delegate, and trustee roles, respectively.

Fenno's insight that the member of Congress sees multiple, distinct constituencies has ramifications for both the representational role and the behavior of the representative as legislator. The needs of the geographic constituency (meaning "vital services" if you live in that district, and "pork" if you do not) are crucial to the member's career and the easiest to gratify. Primary constituents, on the other hand, will not be so easily assuaged. They are politically sophisticated and demand access to their members of Congress. They are the Rotarians, the letter writers, and the participants in group activity. They can be either a base of support and a work force for Congressman "Charlie" or they can be bane of his existence.

David Mayhew highlights the several ways in which members deal with the reelection constituency. He identifies three "tools" of the incumbent representative: advertising (the building of a member's "brand name" within the constituency), credit claiming (for providing casework and particular benefits for the district), and position taking (the making of pleasing judgmental statements with little policy content, such as railing against drugs or crime). Fenno and Mayhew would agree that representatives' interaction with the marginally attentive constituents is directed at building trust rather than communicating agreement on policy issues.

Mayhew's "tools" explain the incumbency advantage better than the oft-cited advantages of money, staff allowances, and other financial benefits. Essentially, members are reelected because they are members and have access to the forum of Congress and to the advantages the institution offers to enrich a member's district. Voters, for their part, seem quite content with their representatives as long as they see them as "one of us," delivering specific benefits to the district. This has led to the aphorism that voters love their individual member of Congress, although they hate the institution.

Roger Davidson and **Walter Oleszek** expand this concept, discussing ways in which the needs of the successful representative come into conflict with the legislature as an institution. Citizens appreciate a member's attentiveness but often do not understand that it comes at the price of policy coherence. Insofar as every member of the legislature is focused on his or her district, the legislature as a whole must have difficulty in agreeing on a common purpose. Congress thus gets bad press as parochial pothole patchers whereas other institutions of government receive credit for policy accomplishments—even when they have to piggyback on Congressional spadework to do so. Meanwhile, crosscurrents in the caucuses of both political parties make coalition building and legislative agenda setting difficult, if not impossible. In sum, whereas Congress has the best democratic credentials to lead the governing process, the institutionalized demands placed on representatives all but prevent Congress from performing its critical function. Many people say that Congress cannot govern, but few look at the citizenry itself for why this may be so.

Still, if you find yourself unconvinced by these explanations and defenses of Congressional behavior, you find yourself in a great company of Congress-bashers, including President **Woodrow Wilson**. Wilson is notable for criticizing Congress when he was eminent professor of political science, long before he became president. He was sympathetic to the citizen who thinks, having watched Congress operate, that government is a "haphazard affair." Much like the critical public of today, Wilson decried an institution in which the ridicule and discrediting of fellow members is rampant and whose members grandstand, meddle, and generally seek to avoid responsibility for their actions.

Congressional Leadership and its Discontents

As one might imagine, the task of providing leadership to this collective of often unruly free agents can be daunting. Two developments in the 1970s increased the capabilities of the speaker of the house in his role of party leader. First, the desire of members to strip autocratic committee chairs of absolute power over their fiefdoms led to some increase in the formal powers of the speaker. Second, speakers began to take public relations seriously.

Presidents since Franklin D. Roosevelt had taken advantage of their media opportunities (initially on radio, later on television). Congressional leaders, however, were more used to exercising a backroom style of leadership, and their sole concern was within their institution. Even a strong speaker such as Samuel Rayburn refused to appear on "Meet the Press," explaining only that if he accepted one invitation he could not refuse others. This changed in the 1970s with the speakerships of Tip O'Neill (1977-1987), Jim Wright (1987-1989), and Tom Foley (1989-1995). Each of these Democratic speakers served mainly under Republican presidents. Although none of these men was naturally mediagenic, each was able to become a major spokesman for the congressional opposition through a frequent use of television.

However, the quantum leap in the emergence of the public speakership came with Newt Gingrich (1995-1998), who rose to prominence through his role in exposing the scandal that toppled Speaker Wright. Assuming the GOP leadership, he was the architect of the stunning victory that in 1994 put the Republicans in the majority for the first time since the 1950s and installed him as speaker. He had nationalized the 1994 elections through the "Contract with America," an agenda for congressional reform and conservative governance. However, almost at once, he ran into trouble. Gingrich spoke of himself as a "prime minister" and took great store in confronting (and often scorning) President Clinton. He first lost a series of legislative battles with the White House, notably with the "government shutdown" of 1995. These defeats occurred in no small part because of the public image of a pompous and pedantic speaker. Making matters worse, he then became mired in his own ethical scandals. Thus chastened, Gingrich had to retreat inside his institution for support but found his plans for congressional government had crashed on the rocks of the often parochial demands of his party's fractious caucus. Some members urged the speaker to compromise and soften the rough edges of his rhetoric for the sake of preserving the GOP majority. Other, younger Republicans decried Gingrich's "sellout" of their conservative revolution. When, on Election Day in 1998, the Democrats gained five House seats (marking the first time that the president's party had gained House seats in an off-year election since 1934) the logic of the Gingrich era became irrelevant. He resigned three days after the election and was replaced by a less public and far less controversial Speaker.

The Gingrich experience suggests a question that will inform our current controversy for this chapter: Can effective national leadership be exercised from the podium of the parochial institution of the House? **Douglas Harris** chronicles the rise of the public speakership, from the days when the House leader was expected to be the "man of the House" to the Gingrich "prime ministership." Harris sees the public speakership as an evolutionary step and bound to endure. Conservative commenator **David Frum** examines the Gingrich speakership in particular. Whereas Frum believes that most of Gingrich's wounds were self-inflicted, he also suggests that national leadership by legislative leaders is not possible, and not even desirable.

49 | *The Trusteeship Theory of Representation*

Edmund Burke

The noted British parliamentarian and conservative hero made the following remarks to his Bristol constituents in 1774. Burke's speech is the classic statement that the common good is best attained through a deliberative process of reason and judgment.

… Certainly, gentlemen it ought to be the happiness and the glory of a representative to live in the strictest union, the closest correspondence, and the most unreserved communication with his constituents. Their wishes ought to have great weight with him; their opinions high respect, their business unremitted attention…. But his unbiased opinion, his mature judgment, his enlightened conscience, he ought not to sacrifice to you, to any man, or to any set of men living…. Your representative owes you, not his industry only, but his judgment; and he betrays you instead of serving you, if he sacrifices it to your opinion….

If government were a matter of will upon any side, yours, without question, ought to be superior. But government and legislation are matters of reason and judgment, and not of inclination; and what sort of reason is that in which the determination precedes the discussion, in which one set of men deliberate and another decide, and where those who form the conclusion are perhaps three hundred miles distant from those who hear the arguments?…

Parliament is not a congress of ambassadors from different and hostile interests, which interests each must maintain, as an agent and advocate, but Parliament is a deliberative assembly of one nation, with one interest, that of the whole—where not local purposes, not local prejudices, ought to guide, but the general good, resulting from the general reason of the whole. You choose a member, indeed; but when you have chosen him, he is not a member of Bristol, but he is a member of Parliament.

50 | Perceptions of Constituency
Richard J. Fenno, Jr.

The 1978 book Home Style: House Members and Their Districts *is a ground-breaking study of Congress. To write it, Richard Fenno traveled with sixteen members of the House of Representatives through their districts over a period of three years, attempting to see the world of representation through their eyes. This method of investigation produced several critical insights into how members of Congress see their districts as made up of several constituencies.*

What does a House member see when looking at his or her constituency? Kaleidoscopic variety, no doubt. That is why there can be no one "correct" way of slicing up and classifying member perceptions—only "helpful" ways. Most helpful to me has been the member's view of a constituency as a nest of concentric circles. In one form or another, in one expression or another, in one degree or another, this bullseye perception is shared by all House members. It is helpful to us for the same reason it is common to them. It is a perception constructed out of the necessities of political life.

THE GEOGRAPHICAL CONSTITUENCY: THE DISTRICT

The largest of the concentric circles represents the House member's most encompassing view of his or her constituency. It is "the district," the entity to which, from which, and within which the member travels. It is the entity whose boundaries have been fixed by state legislative enactment or by court decision. It includes the entire population within those boundaries. Because it is a legal entity, we could refer to it as the legal constituency. We capture more of what the member has in mind when conjuring up "my district," however, if we think of it as the *geographical constituency*. We then retain the idea that the district is a legally bounded space, and emphasize that it is located in a particular place....

If one essential aspect of "the geographical constituency" is seen as its location and boundaries, another is its internal makeup. And House members describe their districts' internal makeup using political science's most familiar demographic and political variables: socioeconomic structure, ideology, ethnicity, residential patterns, religion, partisanship, stability, diversity, etc. Every congressman, in his mind's eye, sees his geographical constituency in terms of some special configuration of such variables.... Some internal configurations are more complex than others. But no congressman sees, within his district's boundaries, an undifferentiated glob. And the rest of us should not talk about his relations with his "constituency" as if he did....

Of all the internal characteristics of the district, the one that best illuminates subsequent member perceptions and behavior is district homogeneity or heterogeneity. As the following answers to the question "What kind of district do you have?" suggest, representatives do think in terms of the relative homogeneity or heterogeneity of their districts....

... All we can say, for sure, is that the less conflict a congressman perceives among district interests, the more likely he is to see his district as homogeneous, and the more conflict he perceives among district interests, the more likely he is to see his district as heterogeneous.

Whether by design or by accident, the most homogeneous districts are likely to have boundaries which incorporate pre-existing communities of interest. Among the most heterogeneous districts, on the other hand, are those with boundaries determined by partisan interests or mathematical design....

Still another kind of heterogeneous district contains groups that, while potentially in conflict, have little actual interest in or contact with one another's problems. Were they not so insulated, these elements would very likely be at odds with one another. Most such districts cover a good deal of territory, and distance acts as a barrier to contact and to interest. We have called them *segmented* districts. It is characteristic of homogeneous districts that new controversies are highly contagious. Soon after they break out, these controversies affect and engage almost everyone in the district. It is characteristic of segmented districts, however, that new controversy remains localized.

THE REELECTION CONSTITUENCY: THE SUPPORTERS

Each congressman does perceive an explicitly political constituency nested within his geographical constituency. It is composed of those people in the district who he thinks vote for him. We shall call it his *reelection constituency*. The idea is the same as John Kingdon's "supporting coalition." But, because all members do not perceive their support in coalitional terms and because all members do see support in reelection terms, we shall use the more universal language. As they move about "the district," House members continually draw the distinction between those people who vote for them and those who do not: "I do well here"; "I run poorly here"; "This group supports me"; "This group does not." By distinguishing supporters from nonsupporters, they articulate their fundamental political perception.

House members use two reference points—one cross-sectional, the other longitudinal—in shaping this perception. First, by a process of inclusion and exclusion, they come to a rough approximation of the upper and lower ranges of the reelection constituency. That is to say, there are some votes a member believes he nearly always gets. There are other votes he believes he almost never gets. Among those he thinks he usually gets, the perceived partisan component of the electorate is always a basic element. Every member begins with a perception of his partisan support—estimated by registration figures or poll data, and by political demography....

In thinking about his reelection constituency, he is helped by a second, more time-related perception, of who voted for him "last time" and of how well he did overall "last time." Starting with that calculation, he adds or subtracts incrementally on the basis of changes that will have taken place, or could be made to take place, between "last time" and "this time" or "next time." The results of previous elections give every member a baseline against which to estimate future results. "Last time we lost the northern area by 5000 votes. This time we should at least break even." "I'll be a much stronger candidate than I was last time. 1970 was an exceptionally good year for Democrats in the Midwest. And incumbency counts for something." Earlier elections are particularly useful in giving members a basis for estimating the achievable size of their reelection constituencies....

Thinking about "last time's" electoral margin, if it was an apparently safe one, should assuage a good deal of a representative's uncertainty about his reelection constituency. And it does. But it does not produce certainty. Far from it. Most House members will have experienced, at some point in their careers, "the fight of my life"—a testing election they felt especially hard pressed to win. When members recall their testing elections they dwell on the immense organizational and personal efforts required to win. Frequently, the severest test is the first....

Representatives worry about vote drop-offs much smaller than 20 points. They believe that there is always a good bit of latent opposition in the district that will surface if it appears they are losing their electoral grip.

People can be mad at you, but if they don't see a chance of beating you, they will keep it inside.

If I looked vulnerable, the right-to-life people would be on me like a hen on a junie bug. And the gun control people, too.

Similarly, there are potential opponents out there waiting for signs of slippage.

It's important for me to show strength to keep the young state representatives and city councilmen away. If they have the feeling that I'm invincible, they won't try. That reputation is very intangible. [But] your vote margin is part of it.

"Last time's" election margin, therefore, must be maintained—however lopsided or statistically "safe" it may be—to discourage potential adversaries. Big reelection constituencies may be far more worrisome to a member than an outsider, ignorant of political dynamics, would have imagined....

Members of Congress do have an idea of who votes for them and who does not. And their perceptions are probably more accurate more often than are the perceptions of anyone else in their districts, though we have no way of checking. Our assumption is that because their jobs depend on it, the members will work harder than others to achieve a reasonable level of perceptual accuracy....They worry a lot. They exhibit great caution in making perceptual judgments. Their favorite electoral exercise is "worst case analysis." They rarely allow themselves the luxury of feeling "safe" electorally. They do not take their reelection constituency for granted. Political scientists cannot know these things by reading election statistics. When we generalize about their electoral situations, we must supplement our statistical perspective with a perceptual one.

THE PRIMARY CONSTITUENCY: THE STRONGEST SUPPORTERS

In thinking about their political condition, House members make distinctions *within* their reelection constituency, thus giving us a third, still smaller perceptual circle. Having distinguished between their nonsupporters and their supporters, they further distinguish between their weak supporters and their strong supporters. Weak supporters come in both the routine and the temporary varieties. Routine supporters do no more than vote for the member, often simply following party identification. Temporary supporters back the member as the best available alternative "this time," as "the lesser of two evils." Strong supporters display an intensity capable of producing additional political activity, and they tender their support "through thick and thin," regardless of who the challenger may be. Within each reelection constituency, then, nests a smaller constituency perceived as "my strongest supporters," "my loyalists," "my true believers," "my political base," "my hard core," "my nucleus," "my tough nut," "my bread basket." We shall think of these people as the ones each congressman believes would provide his last line of electoral defense in a primary contest, and label them the *primary constituency.* We do not mean this label to include all the people who vote for him in a primary, only those from whom he expects a special solidity of support in a primary election....

THE PERSONAL CONSTITUENCY: THE INTIMATES

Within the primary constituency, House members perceive still a fourth, and final, concentric circle. These are the few individuals whose relationship with the member is so personal and so intimate that their relevance cannot be captured by any description of "very strongest supporters." Some of them are his closest political advisers and confidants. Others are people from whom he draws emotional sustenance for his political work. They are all people with whom the congressman has shared some crucial experience—usually early in his career, and often the "testing election." Times of relaxation are thick with reminiscence. Fellow feeling is heavily "we few, we happy few, we band of brothers." Sometimes a staff assistant is among these intimates;

sometimes not. Sometimes the member's spouse is involved, but not always. These are the people, if any, to whom he has entrusted his political career. He can meet with all of them in one place, face to face, as he cannot with any of his other constituencies. He knows them by name, as individuals. He thinks of them as friends....

CONCLUSION

Each member of Congress perceives four concentric constituencies: geographic, reelection, primary, and personal. This is not the only way a member sees his or her "constituency"; but it is one way. It is a set of perceptions that emphasizes the context in which, and the strategies by which, the House member seeks electoral support. It is a complicated context, one featuring varying scopes of support and varying intensities of support. The strategies developed for getting and keeping electoral support involve the manipulation of these scopes and intensities....

A perceptual analysis of congressional constituencies both complicates and clarifies efforts of political science to understand the relationship between congressman and constituency. It complicates matters both conceptually and statistically. For example, political scientists have a heavy investment in role conceptions that distinguish between the "trustee" who follows his independent judgment and the "delegate" who follows the wishes of his constituency. But we now must ask, which constituency? And we cannot be content with a conceptual scheme that provides only two answers to this question: "the district" and "the nation." More frequent, we think, than this kind of choice is one in which the congressman must choose among constituencies *within* the district. Also, when studies of party voting conclude that a member of Congress can vote independently because he or she "knows the constituency isn't looking," we need to ask again, which constituency?

One of the several constituencies may very well be looking.

Similarly, the variables we have used as surrogates for "the constituency" in our statistical analyses (for instance, in relating roll calls to constituency characteristics) have described only the geographical constituency—typically derived from census data. Rarely have we used variables capable of differentiating the other three constituencies, individually or collectively. A perceptual analysis warns us of the hazards of these oversimplified conceptualizations and representations of "the constituency." The most useful "first difference" to incorporate into our studies is that between the geographical constituency and the other three *supportive constituencies.* That is a distinction and a terminology we shall try to retain throughout, making added refinements where possible.

A perceptual analysis clarifies most by including the tremendous amount of uncertainty surrounding the House member's view of his or her electoral situation. Political scientists using the idea of electoral marginality to explain behavior, for example, will underestimate the effect of this uncertainty so long as they rely wholly on numerical indicators of electoral safety. Similarly, although political scientists may ask, in the manner of a regression analysis, which campaign activity contributed how much to the election results, a view from over the member's shoulder may reveal that he or she does not think in terms of the weights of variables. We might help ourselves by seeing the electoral situation the way the members see it, to ask ourselves the questions they ask: How much did I win by? Who supported me? Who worked especially hard for me? What net effect did the changes from last time have on the outcome this time? If members of Congress are more uncertain than we think they are and if they calculate more configuratively than we think they do, we might find these altered perspectives worth assimilating into our knowledge.

51 | Congress: The Electoral Connection
David Mayhew

David Mayhew identifies reelection as the preeminent motivation of members of Congress. He explains three activities—advertising, credit claiming, and position taking—that all members employ in pursuit of reelection. His insights are more prescient today than when his book was published in 1974. Today, for instance, members have several additional ways of position taking, including the use of the parties' "TV galleries" and of C-SPAN. Mayhew's three reelection activities tend to explain better than any other factors the nearly automatic victories of incumbents over the last several decades.

Whether they are safe or marginal, cautious or audacious, congressmen must constantly engage in activities related to reelection. There will be differences in emphasis, but all members share the root need to do things—indeed, to do things day in and day out during their terms. The next step here is to present a typology, a short list of the *kinds* of activities congressmen find it electorally useful to engage in. The case will be that there are three basic kinds of activities....

One activity is *advertising,* defined here as any effort to disseminate one's name among constituents in such a fashion as to create a favorable image but in messages having little or no issue content. A successful congressman builds what amounts to a brand name, which may have a generalized electoral value for other politicians in the same family. The personal qualities to emphasize are experience, knowledge, responsiveness, concern, sincerity, independence, and the like. Just getting one's name across is difficult enough; only about half the electorate, if asked, can supply their House members' names. It helps a congressman to be known. "In the main, recognition carries a positive valence; to be perceived at all is to be perceived favorably." A vital advantage enjoyed by House incumbents is that they are much better known among voters than their November challengers. They are better known because they spend a great deal of time, energy, and money trying to make themselves better known. There are standard routines—frequent visits

to the constituency, nonpolitical speeches to home audiences, the sending out of infant care booklets and letters of condolence and congratulation....

... There are some differences between House and Senate members in the ways they go about getting their names across. House members are free to blanket their constituencies with mailings for all boxholders; senators are not. But senators find it easier to appear on national television—for example, in short reaction statements on the nightly news shows. Advertising is a staple congressional activity, and there is no end to it. For each member there are always new voters to be apprised of his worthiness and old voters to be reminded of it.

A second activity may be called *credit claiming,* defined here as acting so as to generate a belief in a relevant political actor (or actors) that one is personally responsible for causing the government, or some unit thereof, to do something that the actor (or actors) considers desirable. The political logic of this, from the congressman's point of view, is that an actor who believes that a member can make pleasing things happen will no doubt wish to keep him in office so that he can make pleasing things happen in the future. The emphasis here is on individual accomplishment (rather than, say, party or governmental accomplishment) and on the congressman as doer (rather than as, say, expounder of constituency views). Credit claiming is highly important to congressmen, with the consequence that much of congressional life is a relentless search for opportunities to engage in it.

Where can credit be found? If there were only one congressman rather than 535, the answer would in principle be simple enough. Credit (or blame) would attach in Downsian fashion to the doings of the government as a whole. But there are 535. Hence it becomes necessary for each congressman to try to peel off pieces of governmental accomplishment for which he can believably generate a sense of responsibility. For the average congressman the staple way of doing this is to traffic in what may be called "particularized benefits." Particularized governmental benefits, as the term will be used here, have two properties: (1) Each benefit is given out to a specific individual, group, or geographical constituency, the recipient unit being of a scale that allows a single congressman to be recognized (by relevant political actors and other congressmen) as the claimant for the benefit (other congressmen being perceived as indifferent or hostile). (2) Each benefit is given out in apparently ad hoc fashion (unlike, say, social security checks) with a congressman apparently having a hand in the allocation. A particularized benefit can normally be regarded as a member of a class. That is, a benefit given out to an individual, group, or constituency can normally be looked upon by congressmen as one of a class of similar benefits given out to sizable numbers of individuals, groups, or constituencies. Hence the impression can arise that a congressman is getting "his share" of whatever it is the government is offering....

In sheer volume the bulk of particularized benefits come under the heading of "casework"—the thousands of favors congressional offices perform for supplicants in ways that normally do not require legislative action. High school students ask for essay materials, soldiers for emergency leaves, pensioners for location of missing checks, local governments for grant information, and on and on. Each office has skilled professionals who can play the bureaucracy like an organ—pushing the right pedals to produce the desired effects.

But many benefits require new legislation, or at least they require important allocative decisions on matters covered by existent legislation. Here the congressman fills the traditional role of supplier of goods to the home district. It is a believable role; when a member claims credit for a benefit on the order of a dam, he may well receive it. Shiny construction projects seem especially useful....

How much particularized benefits count for at the polls is extraordinarily difficult to say. But it would be hard to find a congressman who thinks he can afford to wait around until precise information is available. The lore is that they count—furthermore, given home expectations, that they must be supplied in regular quantities for a member to stay electorally even with the board. Awareness of favors may spread beyond their recipients, building for a member a general reputation as a good provider....

The third activity congressmen engage in may be called *position taking*, defined here as the public enunciation of a judgmental statement on anything likely to be of interest to political actors. The statement may take the form of a roll call vote. The most important classes of judgmental statements are those prescribing American governmental ends (a vote cast against the war; a statement that "the war should be ended immediately") or governmental means (a statement that "the way to end the war is to take it to the United Nations"). The judgments may be implicit rather than explicit, as in: "I will support the president on this matter." ... The congressman as position taker is a speaker rather than a doer. The electoral requirement is not that he make pleasing things happen but that he make pleasing judgmental statements. The position itself is the political commodity. Especially on matters where governmental responsibility is widely diffused it is not surprising that political actors should fall back on positions as tests of incumbent virtue. For voters ignorant of congressional processes the recourse is an easy one....

The ways in which positions can be registered are numerous and often imaginative.

There are floor addresses ranging from weighty orations to mass-produced "nationality day statements." There are speeches before home groups, television appearances, letters, newsletters, press releases, ghostwritten books, *Playboy* articles, even interviews with political scientists. On occasion congressmen generate what amount to petitions; whether or not to sign the 1956 Southern Manifesto defying school desegregation rulings was an important decision for southern members. Outside the roll call process the congressman is usually able to tailor his positions to suit his audiences....

... On a controversial issue a Capitol Hill office normally prepares two form letters to send out to constituent letter writers—one for the pros and one (not directly contradictory) for the antis. Handling discrete audiences in person requires simple agility....

> "You may find this difficult to understand," said Democrat Edward R. Roybal, the Mexican-American representative from California's thirtieth district, "but sometimes I wind up making a patriotic speech one afternoon and later on that same day an anti-war speech. In the patriotic speech I speak of past wars but I also speak of the need to prevent more wars. My positions are not inconsistent; I just approach different people differently."

Roybal went on to depict the diversity of crowds he speaks to: one afternoon he is surrounded by balding men wearing Veterans' caps and holding American flags; a few hours later he speaks to a crowd of Chicano youths, angry over American involvement in Vietnam. Such a diverse constituency, Roybal believes, calls for different methods of expressing one's convictions.

Indeed it does. Versatility of this sort is occasionally possible in roll call voting. For example a congressman may vote one way on recommittal and the other on final passage, leaving it unclear just how he stands on a bill. Members who cast identical votes on a measure may give different reasons for having done so. Yet it is on roll calls that the crunch comes; there is no way for a member to avoid making a record on hundreds of issues, some of which are controversial in the home constituencies. Of course, most roll call positions considered in isolation are not likely to cause much of a ripple at home. But broad voting patterns can and do; member "ratings" calculated by the Americans for Democratic Action, Americans for Constitutional Action, and other outfits are used as guidelines in the deploying of electoral resources. And particular issues often have their alert publics....

Probably the best position-taking strategy for most congressmen at most times is to be conservative—to cling to their own positions of the past where possible and to reach for new ones with great caution where necessary....

There can be no doubt that congressmen believe that positions make a difference. An important consequence of this belief is their custom of watching each other's elections to try to figure out what positions are salable. Nothing is more important in Capitol Hill politics than the shared conviction that election returns have proven a point. Thus the 1950 returns were read not only as a rejection of health insurance but as a ratification of McCarthyism. When two North Carolina nonsigners of the 1956 Southern Manifesto immediately lost their primaries, the message was clear to southern members that there could be no straying from a hard line on the school desegregation issue....

These, then, are the three kinds of electorally oriented activities congressmen engage in—advertising, credit claiming, and position taking.... No deterministic statements can be made; within limits each member has freedom to build his own electoral coalition and hence freedom to choose the means of doing it. Yet there are broad patterns. For one thing senators, with their access to the media, seem to put more emphasis on position taking than House members; probably House members rely more heavily on particularized benefits. But there are important differences among House members. Congressmen from the traditional parts of old machine cities rarely advertise and seldom take positions on anything (except on roll calls), but devote a great deal of time and energy to the distribution of benefits. In fact they use their office resources to plug themselves into their local party organizations....

Another kind of difference appears if the initial assumption of a reelection quest is relaxed to take into account the "progressive" ambitions of some members—the aspirations of some to move up to higher electoral offices rather than keep the ones they have. There are two important subsets of climbers in the Congress—House members who would like to be senators (over the years about a quarter of the senators have come up directly from the House), and senators who would like to be presidents or vice presidents (in the Ninety-third Congress about a quarter of the senators had at one time or another run for these

offices or been seriously "mentioned" for them). In both cases higher aspirations seem to produce the same distinctive mix of activities. For one thing credit claiming is all but useless. It does little good to talk about the bacon you have brought back to a district you are trying to abandon. And, as Lyndon Johnson found in 1960, claiming credit on legislative maneuvers is no way to reach a new mass audience; it baffles rather than persuades. Office advancement seems to require a judicious mixture of advertising and position taking. Thus a House member aiming for the Senate heralds his quest with press releases; there must be a new "image," sometimes an ideological overhaul to make ready for the new constituency. Senators aiming for the White House do more or less the same thing.

52 | *Congress Against Itself*
Roger Davidson and Walter Oleszek

Roger Davidson and Walter Oleszek seek to explain why Congress has such a bad problem with its public image. In fact, the members' success as representatives explains their bad press as lawmakers. Many members run for Congress by running against the institution itself.

Historically, Congress has been a traditional whipping boy of the press and the public. Several considerations help to explain the poor public image of Congress. First, Congress' decision-making process is more open to public view than that of the executive branch or judiciary. Accordingly, if a representative or senator sounds ill-informed or advances an outrageous proposal during committee or floor debate, then representatives of the media are likely to stress that newsworthy event rather than the substance of the overall debate. While inanities also exist in the other branches of government ... re-

porters usually lack access to the early stages of executive or judicial planning.

A second consideration is the bad press received by Congress. No doubt part of this is Congress' fault. The President has learned to utilize the media to get his message across to the American people while Congress generally has not. Equally important, many important legislative events are simply ignored by broadcasters and reporters. Obviously covering the White House is both easier and more glamorous, but significant legislative events that go unreported have serious consequences, not the least of which is public ignorance about the roles and responsibilities of Congress....

Third, there appears to be general public misunderstanding about the role of Congress. Public approbation is often high when Congress appears to agree with a popular President. During the first session of the 89th Congress, for example, 71 percent of the American people approved of Congress' performance. That can be partially explained by Congress' approval of many of President Johnson's "Great Society" programs. In our achievement-oriented society, the legislative record looked good to the public. But if Congress approves too many of the President's proposals, it is not long before detractors call it a rubber stamp. On the other hand, if Congress works its will in a deliberative fashion, and amends or proposes alternatives to presidential suggestions, then Congress may be labeled the obstructionist body.

Many citizens fail to appreciate that Congress is a co-equal branch of government with authority both to formulate public policies of its own and to ensure that the laws that it enacts are properly administered. Congress is not paid for piecework. Its productivity cannot be measured in terms of the number of public laws it enacts. By design and structure, Congress is a slow institution in comparison with the presidency and, perhaps, the judiciary. (On occasion, of course, it may act too quickly.) Congress is a consensus-building institution, which helps ensure that critical public policies will be accepted by the people. Hence, it may be unrealistic to criticize Congress for functioning as it was intended.

Fourth, Congress has often been criticized by its own members. This, too, helps to create a poor public image of the legislative branch. Legislators who attack the institution, but are unwilling to reform it, ought to be held accountable by the citizenry. In that regard, constituents might ask what their representatives are doing to improve the performance of the legislative branch, and then hold them accountable for the failures of Congress. Consequently, the performance of Congress as a whole might be strengthened.

Fifth, Congress is also criticized because it lacks sufficient modern technology to assist it in making informed policy judgments. Compared to the executive branch, Congress seems far behind....

Sixth, the various legislative party structures have failed to procure enough staff and other assistance to critique executive branch proposals, or to develop an independent party program. Numerous scholars have argued that disciplined political parties should formulate public policies, which could then be implemented through centralized congressional party structures. The goal of party government, so they hold, would facilitate national actions to meet national needs. However, party structures in Congress have traditionally been weak, although this may be changing in view of the revitalized party caucuses in both chambers. The dilemma, however, is how to reconcile the presumed need for party discipline with a legislator's obligation to his constituents and his conscience.

Seventh, numerous jurisdictional overlaps among standing committees inhibit the formulation of coherent and coordinated national policies.... While efforts have been made, through party task forces and ad hoc arrangements, to resolve some jurisdictional duplications in the committee system, much more could still be done to facilitate the development of comprehensive policies by standing committees.

Eighth, with its multiplicity of voices, Congress has no single spokesman to articulate the congressional viewpoint. What, indeed, is the congressional viewpoint, and who defines it? The Speaker, the majority or minority leaders, the party caucuses, the committee chairmen, or others? As a result, a serious communications imbalance has developed between the branches. While the President can communicate quickly to the American people concerning his goals and programs, Congress lacks such capabilities. A legitimate question is, "Who speaks for Congress?" Hence, the legislative viewpoint on public problems receives scant attention by the American people. To remedy this serious problem, Congress has been exploring various methods to improve its ability to communicate with the public.

Ninth, Congress is often criticized because it lacks the ability to initiate policies. As the textbooks have so often stated, "The President initiates and Congress responds." However, where does the President often get many of his "innovations" before he initiates them? Often creative ideas are born and kept alive through the years and even decades within Congress by such devices as hearings and floor debate. The President, too, often tailors his proposals to meet anticipated congressional responses to them. Hence, Congress often sets the framework within which the President functions. Moreover, in numerous policy areas Congress has either taken the lead or reformulated and revised presidential proposals to make them its own.

Finally, some legislative procedures limit Congress' consideration of legislation in committee and on the floor. Some observers claim that such devices, practices, or entities as the filibuster, the House Rules Committee, or inadequate scheduling of committee and floor sessions all act to limit individual legislators' and the legislative branch's obligation to develop or enact legislation. However, numerous recent procedural changes (allowing the Speaker to nominate members to the Rules Committee, reducing the number of senators required to invoke cloture, and others) have underscored the legislative branch's willingness to reform its organization and procedures to meet new circumstances.

53 | *Congressional Government*
Woodrow Wilson

Most presidents learn to become Congress-bashers as soon as their legislative program falters. But Woodrow Wilson, as a professor of political science, attacked Congress long before he became president. Do his criticisms resonate with you today?

Congress always makes what haste it can to legislate. It is the prime object of its rules to expedite law-making. Its customs are fruits of its characteristic diligence in enactment. Be the matters small or great, frivolous or grave, which busy it, its aim is to have laws always a-making. Its temper is strenuously legislative....

Legislation unquestionably generates legislation. Every statute may be said to have a long lineage of statutes behind it; and whether that lineage be honorable or of ill repute is as much a question as to each individual statute as it can be with regard to the ancestry of each individual legislator. Every statute in its turn has a numerous progeny, and only time and opportunity can decide whether its offspring will bring it honor or shame. Once begin the dance of legislation, and you must struggle through its mazes as best you can to its breathless end,—if any end there be.

It is not surprising, therefore, that the enacting, revising, tinkering, repealing of laws should engross the attention and engage the entire energy of such a body as Congress. It is, however, easy to see how it might be better employed; or, at least, how it might add others to this overshadowing function, to the infinite advantage of the government. Quite as important as legislation is vigilant oversight of administration; and even more important than legislation is the instruction and guidance in political affairs which the people might receive from a body which kept all national concerns suffused in a broad daylight of discussion. There is no similar legislature in existence which is so shut up to the one business of law-making as is our Congress. As I have said, it in a way superintends administration by the exercise of semi-judicial powers of investigation, whose limitations and insufficiency are manifest....

An effective representative body, gifted with the power to rule, ought, it would seem, not only to speak the will of the nation, which Congress does, but also to lead it to its conclusions, to utter the voice of its opinions, and to serve as its eyes in superintending all matters of government,—which Congress does not do. The discussions which take place in Congress are aimed at random. They now and again strike rather sharply the tender spots in this, that, or the other measure; but, as I have said, no two measures consciously join in purpose or agree in character, and so debate must wander as widely as the subjects of debate. Since there is little coherency about the legislation agreed upon, there can be little coherency about the debates. There is not one policy to be attacked or defended, but only a score or two of separate bills. To attend to such discussions is uninteresting; to be instructed by them is impossible....

Congress could not be too diligent about such talking; whereas it may easily be too diligent in legislation. It often overdoes that business. It already sends to its committees bills too many by the thousand to be given even a hasty thought; but its immense committee facilities and the absence of all other duties but that of legislation make it omnivorous in its appetite for new subjects of consideration. It is greedy to have a taste of every possible dish that may be put upon its table, as an "extra" to the constitutional bill of fare....

As at present constituted, the federal government lacks strength because its powers are divided, lacks promptness because its authorities are multiplied, lacks wieldiness because its processes are roundabout, lacks efficiency because its responsibility is indistinct and its action without competent direction. It is a government in which every officer may talk about every other officer's duty without having to render strict account for not doing his own, and in which the masters are held in check and offered contradiction by the servants.... Talk is not sobered by any necessity imposed upon those who utter it to suit their actions to their words. There is no day of reckoning for words spoken. The speakers of congressional majority may, without risk of incurring ridicule or discredit, condemn what their own Committees are doing; and the spokesmen of a minority may urge what contrary courses they please with a well-grounded assurance that what they say will be forgotten before they can be called upon to put it into practice. Nobody stands sponsor for the policy of the government. A dozen men originate it; a dozen compromises twist and alter it; a dozen offices whose names are scarcely known outside of Washington put it into execution....

... The average citizen may be excused for esteeming government at best but a haphazard affair, upon which his vote and all of his influence can have but little effect. How is his choice of a representative in Congress to affect the policy of the country as regards the questions in which he is most interested, if the man for whom he votes has no chance of getting on the Standing Committee which has virtual charge of those questions? How is it to make any difference who is chosen President? Has the President any very great authority in matters of vital policy? It seems almost a thing of despair to get any assurance that any vote he may cast will even in an infinitesimal degree affect the essential courses of administration. There are so many cooks mixing their ingredients in the national broth that it seems hopeless, this thing of changing one cook at a time.

The Dilemma of Congressional Leadership

54 | *The Rise of the Public Speakership*
Douglas B. Harris

Historically, the speaker of the House has been alternately a dictator, a backroom facilitator, or even a servant. Douglas Harris chronicles the recent evolution of the speaker as a public symbol, a person with a public, as well as an institutional, role. With both the rise and the fall of Speaker Newt Gingrich (1995-1998) and his replacement by the taciturn Dennis Hastert, will the speakership again be so public?

In the 1994 elections, the Republican party won a majority in the House of Representatives, the first time since a Republican House majority was swept into office with the election of Dwight Eisenhower in 1952. Attention to this historic change centered on the Speaker of the House. Newt Gingrich (R-GA) was the most "public" speaker in memory. The House Republican agenda in the 104th Congress was based on the well publicized "Contract with America." On 7 April 1995, Speaker Gingrich delivered a nationally televised address to the American people, and on 11 June 1995, Gingrich shared a stage in New Hampshire with President Bill Clinton to debate various national issues. NBC congressional correspondent Lisa Myers said, "Newt is the star. Newt's setting the agenda." In each of these events, Speaker Gingrich was defying the traditional understanding of what a congressional party leader does. Scholars have long argued that congressional party leadership is primarily internal. But to accept that Gingrich's speakership was more public and external than the speakerships of Joe Martin (R-MA), Sam Rayburn (D-TX), John McCormack (D-MA), and Carl Albert (D-OK)- the four Speakers from 1940 until 1976- -is not to say that Gingrich is unique in his public role. In fact, there has

been a growth in the public nature of the speakership over the last two decades with Tip O'Neill (D-MA), Jim Wright (D-TX), Tom Foley (D-WA), as well as Gingrich. Just as presidents had perceived and exploited an opportunity to use mass media to build coalitions in Congress, congressional party leaders, most notably Speakers of the House, were "going public" too.

HISTORICAL PERSPECTIVE

As both a partisan office and a constitutionally dictated institutional position, the speakership conjoins the power of the House majority party and the institutional resources of the House itself. At times, the speakership has been a very potent office. Speakers Henry Clay, Thomas Brackett Reed, and Joseph Cannon each enjoyed considerable power primarily because of the unity of the congressional parties they led. But as the strength of political parties declined, so too did the strength of the speakership. Comparing Speaker Rayburn to Reed and Cannon, one finds that "Rayburn was not and could not be as powerful a speaker as Cannon or Reed. His sources of leverage in the formal and party systems were simply not comparable."

This public, media-oriented congressional leadership would have been foreign to Rayburn in whose House there was a distinction between showhorses and workhorses. He would say, "Damn the fellow who's always seeking publicity." Rayburn saw media as counterproductive and even a direct challenge to his party leadership efforts... Rayburn's effectiveness rested on his personal relationships with key House members (most notably committee chairs) and his ability to keep muted the ideological divisions that challenged the unity of southern and northern Democrats. Media had the potential to undermine the feudal power of committee chairs while simultaneously highlighting those policy issues that would divide the fragile House majority....

A MORE PUBLIC SPEAKERSHIP

Speakers on the Nightly News—One measure of the extent to which the speakership has become a more public office is the amount of coverage speakers of the House receive on the three networks' nightly news programs as well as the amount of coverage they get relative to other House members... In 1969, Speaker John McCormack was mentioned on the three networks' nightly news programs only seventeen times. In fact, five other House members—minority leader Gerald Ford (R-MI) and four of McCormack's fellow Democrats—were mentioned more often than the speaker. In 1972, Speaker Albert was mentioned only twelve times, and ten House members received more television attention than he.

By 1977, the first year of the O'Neill speakership, the Speaker would receive more television coverage than both his predecessors and any other House member that year. O'Neill was mentioned in ninety-eight television stories in 1977 and as many as 184 in 1981. In 1984, O'Neill was mentioned 168 times—exceeding the combined number of mentions for the nine House members who immediately followed O'Neill on the most televised list. Although Speakers Wright and

Foley were less visible than O'Neill, they were still more visible than the Speakers who preceded O'Neill. And mentions of speaker Gingrich surpassed the number of mentions of even Speaker O'Neill; in the first three months of the 104th Congress alone, the three networks broadcast 114 stories in which Gingrich was mentioned.

Besides appearing on the nightly news, speakers and other party leaders have turned to Sunday morning talk shows to help disseminate their messages. When Sam Rayburn was asked to appear on Sunday morning television, he rarely complied. When asked to appear on *Meet the Press* in 1957, Rayburn replied: "I do appreciate your wanting me to be on Meet the Press, but I never go on programs such as yours.... The trouble about my going on one program is then I would have no excuse to say to others that I could not go on their program...."

This practice seems to hold true for the speakerships of McCormack and Albert as well as for the more open, public speakership of Tip O'Neill.... Speakers Wright and Foley, however, made frequent use of the Sunday morning format.... Speaker Foley seemed to prefer the Sunday talk format to other media outlets....

Foley's ... routine policy of accepting invitations to appear on Sunday morning talk shows suggests more evidence that the media role of party leaders has become institutionalized and routine. Contemporary speakers are more likely to appear on Sunday talk shows than were earlier speakers, and this activity fits a broader pattern of increased media presence throughout the congressional party leadership.

Speakers' Responses to Presidential Addresses—Since the early 1970s, during periods of divided government, Democratic congressional leaders have sought network access to reply to the president's State of the Union address as well as other major speeches. Particularly during the O'Neill and Wright speakerships, the Democratic congressional leadership evinced an increasing sophistication in securing congressional response time and performing once that time had been secured. Speakers Wright and Foley continued to secure response time to the State of the Union address while becoming more sophisticated in the technical aspects of their responses by preparing speeches extensively and hiring technical consultants. Moreover, speakers in this era often give the opposition's response to the president's weekly radio address. These activities by House Democratic leaders pale in comparison to those of Speaker Gingrich in the104th Congress. His opening day speech to the House, his April address to the nation, and his New Hampshire debate with Clinton were covered widely by broadcast as well as print reporters.

Whether one views the punctuated change in nightly news appearances or the secular growth of appearances on *Meet the Press,* one thing is clear: the contemporary speakership (as well as the congressional party leadership) is a more public, media-oriented office than in the Rayburn era.

ORGANIZATIONAL SUPPORT

As speakers became more public figures, the office of Speaker changed to accommodate that more public role. Moreover, the multiple institutions that comprise the House majority party leadership apparatus began to change as well as to provide support for the public speakership and congressional leadership. The most notable organizational changes are in the speaker's daily press conference, media relations staff allocations in the speakership and the broader party leadership, and the role and function of House party organizations.

The Speaker's Daily Press Conference—
All speakers since Rayburn have had daily meetings with the press, but the tone and purpose of these meetings has changed considerably with the rise of the public speakership. In Rayburn's press briefings, the topic was always the upcoming schedule, and discussion centered on arcane legislative procedure. One observer noted: "Speaker Rayburn per-

ceived relationships with reporters as an advantage internally within the House rather than a conduit to a national constituency. He was far more concerned with what his colleagues read than with what the general public read."...

O'Neill's press conferences, however, represented a marked contrast to those of his predecessors. One reporter described the "vaudevillian overtones" of an O'Neill press conference: "O'Neill responds to questions with a mixture of routine business, political analysis, humor, partisan sniping and social commentary."... Besides the stylistic changes, reporters detected a marked contrast to previous speakers in the value and purpose of O'Neill's press conferences. One wrote...that "for the first time. . . a speaker's press conference has become a place where reporters can really find out what House Democrats are up to."...

Speaker Wright's daily press conferences were even more sophisticated than O'Neill's. Prior to each press conference, Wright would meet with other top Democratic leaders to coordinate the message for the day. Upon completion of the press conference, the other party leaders would remain to talk to reporters in an effort to reinforce Wright's points. Wright also extended contacts to broadcast reporters immediately following the daily print meeting. In the beginning of the 104th Congress, Gingrich opened up the traditionally pen-and-pad press session to the broadcast media, thus formalizing and extending the attention to broadcast journalists that Wright and Foley had pioneered on an informal basis.

Congressional Party Press Secretaries—
In the postreform House of Representatives, public speakers and other congressional party leaders have increasingly recognized the need for media expertise in the form of press secretaries, assistants, and communications directors. Neither Rayburn nor McCormack had a press secretary. In fact, the speakership did not include such a position until 1972, when Carl Albert hired J. Roddy Keiser as press secretary. Speaker press secretaries have

increased in number, prestige, and experience since Albert's speakership. O'Neill made press secretary Christopher Matthews co-administrative assistant (the highest position within a congressional office) in the Speaker's office. And speakers since O'Neill have allocated multiple staff positions to media relations. Both Wright and Foley had as many as three press assistants in their leadership offices, and by 1996, Gingrich had four media staff positions, the titles of which were "Press Secretary," "Deputy Press Secretary," "Press Assistant," and "Communications Coordinator."

Role and Function of House Party Organizations—Evidence of the press/communications efforts of the House parties goes beyond staff allocations. First of all, there has been an increased integration of press/communications activities as communications staff from the speaker's office, the majority leader's office, the whip operation, and the caucus or conference have regularized meetings with one another. Furthermore, the stated mission of the various party organizations has changed. During the 104th and 105th Congresses, the House Republican Conference's mission statement listed four chief goals, the last of which stated that the conference "Organizes and implements an internal and external communication plan."...

Similarly, the House Democratic minority leadership put an emphasis on communications strategy in the new Republican Congresses. Representative David Bonior (D-MI) described his role as minority whip: "My new role will not only be counting the votes by which we are going to lose. My role will be to emphasize the message which we are trying to convey to the American people." To accomplish this goal, House Democrats established a communications team to "run the Democrat floor show for one-minutes, morning business, and special orders, trying to coordinate Members' speeches to hit on themes that the party wants to emphasize." Moreover, House Democrats and Republicans created Message Groups, Message Boards, Theme Teams, and Communications Strategy teams

(dubbed CommStrat by House Republicans) to coordinate and disseminate messages to the media. And like the offices of the top party leaders, the Democratic Caucus, the Republican Conference, and both parties' whip offices have hired increasingly large communications staffs.

CAUSES AND CONSEQUENCES OF THE PUBLIC SPEAKERSHIP

In terms of both their visibility and the institutional support they have erected to support this new leadership style, speakers and their party leadership colleagues have been forging new strategies of leadership strategically avoided by Rayburn, McCormack, and Albert. What might explain this change in House leadership from a strictly inside game to a more public, media-oriented congressional leadership? And, what are the possible consequences of this public role for the speakership? ...

Causes—Possible explanations of this more public speakership range from changes in the political system, such as changes in the nature of mass media and the prevalence of divided party control of the national government, to changes in Congress itself. Certainly the nature of mass media has changed since the time of Rayburn. Television news expanded from fifteen minutes to half an hour to twenty-four hours a day; cable television has provided for both an expansion of congressional coverage through C-SPAN and C-SPAN II and news coverage more generally; and the growth of alternative media such as talk radio and the Internet has provided more media outlets for politicians. Like changes in media, the prevalence of divided government is supportive of the rise of the public speakership as well. Indeed, in almost two-thirds of the period from 1960 to 1996 there was divided party control of the Congress and the presidency. Coupled with the use of media by presidents, this intuitively seems to explain the rise of the speaker's position as public spokesperson....

The prevalence of divided government and the fact that presidents were increasingly using media are important factors in the rise of the public speakership. Indeed, those changes that led presidents to believe that going public would help them build legislative coalitions likely affected congressional leaders as well.... Members' independence of political parties relative to earlier eras and their increasing sense of exposure to the public (and the consequent sense of vulnerability) made their support of legislative proposals increasingly contingent on public perceptions and sentiment. The importance of media politics to building legislative coalitions was likely impressed upon O'Neill and other House party leaders by President Reagan's successful use of media to build support for his legislative program in 1981. In many ways, divided government increased the incentives for both congressional party leaders to go public and for reporters to focus on them.

A more complete explanation of the rise of the public speakership requires attention not only to the changing environmental factors of increasing media outlets and divided government but also attention to changes within the House. Joseph Cooper and David Brady demonstrate that changes in congressional leadership strength, activity, and style are most likely due to changes in the institutional context of the House. This contextualist theory suggests that the impetus for a new leadership style for speakers is most likely found in a new type of House member. There is considerable evidence that members' individual and collective styles and expectations were significantly different in the Rayburn era from the era of the public speakership. Individually, members in the postreform, post-Watergate Congress had more power within the House due to reforms which distributed power, were more comfortable with media politics, and felt increasingly vulnerable electorally and sought cover from their leaders. Collectively, recent House majorities have been more ideologically homogeneous. Taken together, these changes increased the benefits of leaders' use of media while reducing the perceived costs of such public leadership.... Moreover, both the obstacles of feudalist committee chairs threatened by media politics and ideological divisions within the majority party were lessened as committee reforms broke up the feudal system and the ideological divisions between northern and southern Democrats waned.

Leadership style changed because members' expectations of leaders changed. In both the leaders they select and the expectations that shape current leaders' activities, members have increasingly not only allowed, but expected a more public congressional party leadership... Not only did the challenges to media politics of the Rayburn era wane, but members now demanded media leadership from their party leaders.

Consequences—As the rise of media leadership represents a fundamental change within the House of Representatives, it has had an impact on many elements of American politics. First of all, by equipping the House majority to compete in media politics, this change could have an effect on the relative balance of power between the Congress and the presidency.... Just as the use of media gave rise to the strong presidency in the twentieth century, its use by congressional leaders has empowered Congress as well. Certainly, Congress does not enjoy the extensive coverage the president receives, but it increasingly has opportunities to counter messages emanating from the White House. And at times, Congress and not the president has dominated the policy agenda. By coupling their internal and external roles, Speakers Wright and Gingrich came to dominate not only the House agenda but, in many ways, the nation's agenda as well during the 100th and 104th Congresses respectively. At a 1995 conference on congressional leadership, Gingrich outlined his view of a prime ministerial speakership. In short, Congress is no longer a defenseless victim of media politics.

Where this public role has made Speakers more potent leaders, it has also made them more powerful symbols for the opposition. In different ways, Wright, Foley, and Gingrich were made symbols of their parties' programs and faced challenges to their position as a result. For Wright and Gingrich, ethics charges were brought in part because of the political advantage seen by the minority party. For Foley, his public leadership on key issues of congressional term limits and gun control made him more vulnerable in his district.

Besides changing the power of the Speaker and the Congress, this change represents a profound change in the nature of the speakership and congressional party leadership.... For public Speakers, leadership is often based on mediated rather than face-to-face communication with followers....

In the more open House since the O'Neill speakership, party leaders must deal with a vastly larger number of members with powers of consequence. These members are largely independent of party leaders for reelection. To complicate matters further, party leaders have fewer opportunities to meet with members face to face because there are so many important members; and members visit the floor less frequently, because they are now able to monitor floor activities on C-SPAN in their offices. As a result, mediated congressional leadership is more ideological and less pragmatic. Indeed, public Speakers are neither the boss of their House colleagues as Cannon was nor are they chief bargainers as Rayburn was. The types of arguments most persuasive to members are less likely to be promises of favor-trading or cash as in Rayburn's day, but rather those arguments likely to persuade interest-group supporters and constituents are most persuasive to members.

For these reasons, public Speakers increasingly use media in conjunction with the mobilization of groups and the shaping of public opinion to build legislative coalitions from outside Congress.... Including organized interest group leaders in strategy is important to leaders who will call upon these groups to help them persuade members. To similar effect, since the 1980s, congressional leaders have increasingly employed polling to shape media messages and monitor the success of their media efforts.... [I]n the 104th Congress, polls were important to the marketing strategy of the "Contract with America." Moreover, poll results can be used by leaders to persuade members. For example, while he was House majority whip, Representative Tony Coelho (D-CA) convinced other House leaders to conduct regular polls. But "Coelho suggested keeping the polling operation secret; that way they could make results public when they showed good news, and could avoid releasing them when they carried bad news."

In the new style of legislative leadership—including the use of media strategies, group coalitions, and polling—leaders do not simply bargain within the confines of the Capitol and within the constraints of the legislative environment, but rather they seek to shape the environment in which they and other legislators must act. As majority whip and future Speaker, Tom Foley said in 1986: "Sometimes to pass a bill you have to change the attitude of the country." Where public Speakers probably balance the old style with the new, there are signs that the new style is increasingly supplanting the old. In 1996, Gingrich handed over the daily operations of the House to Majority Leader Dick Armey, "free[ing] Gingrich to travel around the country to promote the Republican congressional message."

This new style of leadership does raise questions about the quality of Congress's contribution to policy making in American politics. Students of media politics often question the ability of the media to facilitate sound deliberation on public policy matters, and those institutions within Congress that help foster sound, responsible deliberation (that is, committees and bargaining) are undermined by attempts to publicize legislative proposals and market congressional parties.... Increasingly, it seems, party leaders are packaging legislative proposals for media and public consumption. Leaders use polling and media to change the ways they talk about proposals in addition to changing the legislation. In reshaping Clinton health care proposals in 1994, congressional leaders had as their chief objective to convince the public that their proposal was not "the Clinton bill," despite the remarkable similarities that remained. When engaging in the Medicare debate in

1995, House Republican leaders would cry foul when reporters and Democrats would use the seemingly innocuous words "cut" and "change" to describe Republican proposals. Pollsters had told Republicans that those words hurt their popularity....

In all, Congress is more important to the constitutional system than previously, but its contribution is potentially less deliberative. Thus, this change in congressional party leadership has not only changed the balance of power between the Congress and the president, but it also has the potential of lowering the quality of Congress's contribution to policy making....

55 | *Newt's Legacy*
David Frum

The smashing Republican congressional victory in 1994 brought Newt Gingrich (R-GA) to the speakership flush with the goals of a new movement and armed with an agenda for a conservative governance. Four years later, bedeviled by scandal and caricatured as a heartless pedant, he was deposed by his own slender, factious GOP coalition. In this critique of the Gingrich years, conservative commentator David Frum perhaps puts his finger not only on Gingrich's greatest failure but also on the dilemma of congressional leadership: "A leader who seeks to attain national power by building a congressional majority is naturally going to be inclined to shun the grand themes... and instead try to identify issues that could move particular and local blocs of voters."

It can seem so terribly unfair. Newt Gingrich led the Republicans to their first majority in the House of Representatives since 1955, and then to two successive majorities for the first time since the 1920s. He forced welfare reform and a balanced budget onto President Clinton. His reward for this record of accomplishment? Spurious ethics charges, anonymous quotes in the *Washington Post* from Republican congressmen about how much better things have worked since he quit the speakership, and a Republican front-runner for the presidential nomination that Gingrich coveted whose rhetoric is very largely intended to separate himself as widely as possible from the once all-conquering Newt. On the other hand, it all seemed rather less terribly unfair last week, when C-SPAN broadcast its three-segment interview with Gingrich.

By unfortunate coincidence, C-SPAN broadcast the third and final segment only four hours after it carried a major policy address by George W. Bush, a speech on education to the Latino Business Expo in Los Angeles. Bush called for enlarging the federal Department of Education, imposing stricter federal supervision on state and local school systems, and limiting the role of vouchers to an emergency treatment for the worst-functioning districts. Four years ago, and certainly eight, a Republican candidate who took such a New Democrat approach to schooling would have provoked a mutiny on the right, but Bush has already pocketed the conservative vote.

The abject disarray of the once-formidable conservative wing of the party is not entirely Gingrich's fault. But it is very largely his fault, and his interview nicely reminded viewers of how he led conservatives to their present unhappy pass.

Through most of the 1980s, Gingrich had been just one of dozens of clever young congressmen who identified themselves with the excitement of the Reagan revolution. In those long-ago days, a Vin Weber or Jim Courter would have seemed as good a bet to recapture the speakership for the GOP—actually a better bet than Newt, since Gingrich was then widely seen as a flighty and undisciplined free-lancer. But time and chance worked in his favor. Congressmen from swing states, like Courter's New Jersey, lost their seats. Congressmen from solid Republican states, like Mississippi's Trent Lott, ascended to the Senate. Others despaired of perpetual minority status and quit politics altogether. By 1990, Gingrich had become the unquestioned leader of the conservatives in the House. The Bush budget deal promoted him to conservative national leadership. Jack Kemp's decision to seek a cabinet seat in the Bush administration—rather than challenge Mario Cuomo for the governorship of New York in 1990—and Kemp's unwillingness to resign that seat silenced the supply-sider when the senior Bush broke his no-new-taxes pledge. Gingrich denounced Bush, and with that act positioned himself to lead the opposition to Bill Clinton after 1992.

Every leader remakes his movement in his own image, and between 1990 and 1998, Gingrich reshaped Republican conservatism. Unlike his deal-making elders in the House leadership, Gingrich was a fighter, and he imbued conservatism with his own fierce combativeness. Gingrich's concept of fighting was the scoring of parliamentary victories to expose the high-handedness and corruption of the Democratic majority. In the C-SPAN interviews, Gingrich discusses at some length how he used television (C-SPAN, actually) as a weapon against Tip O'Neill. Gingrich, Bob Walker, and other allies would use the quiet hours of special orders to give one-minute speeches in the well of the House denouncing the Democratic leadership....

Gingrich's greatest parliamentary victory, of course, was his more or less single-handed bringing down of Democratic Speaker Jim Wright on corruption charges. Gingrich dutifully acknowledges that it was the errors of the Clinton administration—the health care plan, the tax increases, and gays in the military—that toppled the Democratic Congress in 1994, but he does not really believe it. After the perfunctory acknowledgment, he devotes most of his airtime to talking about what he imagines really did the trick: the discrediting of the Democratic leadership through scandals like Wright's.

There may be some truth to this, although one wonders whether ethics charges could really produce the 10 million vote shift of 1994. Believing in the truth of it had, however, immense consequences for the Gingrich-led conservative movement. In trying to upend the congressional Democrats through procedural victories in Congress, Gingrich directed the reforming zeal of conservatives toward the procedures of Congress. Instead of tax cuts, the building of a post-Communist world order, equal justice under law regardless of race, the cultural and linguistic unity of the United States, or any of the dozen other powerful potential issues available to them in the mid-1990s, conservatives found themselves talking about term limits, a balanced budget amendment, House members' bank, the line-item veto, and a series of other issues equally remote from Americans' everyday concerns. The logical culmination of this way of thinking was the Contract With America, which spent the energies of the biggest Republican congressional swing since 1894 on six months of votes on the internal governance of the House of Representatives.

Throughout his C-SPAN interview, Gingrich referred to his passion for "ideas." But in the procedural politics that Gingrich sold to conservatives, ideas had only a weak independent existence. (Even now, Gingrich's idea of an idea is, as he repeatedly stressed, delivering better health care at a lower cost. Until one has some notion of how the job can be done, that is an aspiration, not an idea.) Gingrich's indifference to the grand themes of a Ronald Reagan followed naturally from his approach to politics. Grand themes appeal to national electorates. Congressmen, obviously, don't have national electorates. Their electorates are particular and local. A leader who seeks to attain national power by building a congressional majority is naturally going to be inclined to shun the grand themes of a presidential candidate and instead try to identify issues that could move particular and local blocs of voters out of his opponent's coalition and into his own. That's how proposals like the repeal of the so-called marriage penalty (the higher tax rates faced by married couples with two incomes as compared to two equivalent single filers) and treating western water-use rights as private property protected by the Fifth Amendment came to move ahead of Reagan-style grand initiatives on the Republican agenda.

This made considerable tactical sense, but it left Republicans speechless and defenseless in their 1995-1996 battles with Bill Clinton. As the president framed his defense of Medicare in the broad language of ideals, Republicans were left sputtering that their so-called "cuts" amounted to barely a couple of dollars a month. Clinton had a big idea about Medicare; Gingrich never did. It was the Reagan-Carter fight in reverse—principle vs. technicalities. To this day, conservatives have not recovered from Gingrich's downgrading of thematics. In 1999, for the first time since the 1940s, there is no generally accepted conservative agenda. Conservatives have dozens, even hundreds, of projects and concepts. But the clarity and power that comes from saying first we'll do this, then we'll do that, when this and that speak to the values and interests of tens of millions of people—that has been lost.

Because Gingrich lacked a unifying political vision of his own, he was susceptible to the sort of populism that postulates some hypothetical "will of the people" that politicians must detect and serve. This susceptibility explains why Gingrich got so caught up in fads and trends: He felt that if he squinted hard enough at them, he could detect the people's wishes. In his 1984 book *Window of Opportunity*, he interpreted the success of the Star Wars movies as proof that Americans yearned for a renaissance of the space program. In his 1992 speech to the Republican convention, he interpreted rising quality standards in the private sector as proof that the public had wearied of the bureaucratic welfare state. Gingrich taught a generation of conservative intellectuals to sleuth out the potential political implications of the success of particular movies, songs, and television shows. It was an amusing parlor game, but it dangerously disparaged the importance of political leadership. In truth, nothing in politics happens spontaneously—which is why it proved such a catastrophe when Gingrich made the fateful decision in early 1998 to let the electorate lead Congress on the Lewinsky scandal, postponing action on Clinton's perjury for the eight fateful months until Ken Starr delivered his report.

As Clinton again and again bested Gingrich, conservatives lost faith in the political appeal of their message. As Gingrich's parliamentary tactics proved useless against the agenda-setting power of the president, conservatives came to doubt not merely their tactics, but their doctrines. And once Clinton escaped punishment for his crimes, conservatives' uncontainable rage convinced them that his successor must be defeated, even at the price of nominating a Republican presidential candidate who owed conservatives little and liked them even less. Much fun has been made of Gingrich's self-comparison to Henry Clay. But what was dismaying about Gingrich's interview was not the reappearance of his familiar fondness for grandiose historical self-comparisons, but the reminder of how much he once promised conservatives—and how low they have since fallen.

CHAPTER NINE

The Presidency
A Question of Leadership

OVERVIEW AND SUMMARY

Richard Nixon was innovative and secretive. His out-of-the-limelight approach was responsible for diplomatic openings to the Soviet Union and China, as well as the events that brought an end to American involvement in Vietnam. However, this same style led him to paranoid activities such as illegally gathering political intelligence during the Watergate affair. He was forced to resign.

Jimmy Carter was folksy, self-reflective, and attentive to detail. His style spurred a new openness in government. He made extensive plans to reform health care and energy policy. But in times of crisis—such as the Arab oil embargo and the Iranian hostage crisis—that same folksy, hands-on style mired him in details and rendered him unable to make hard decisions. He was defeated for reelection.

Ronald Reagan was the "Great Communicator," amiable and single-minded. His "Reagan Revolution" instituted sweeping changes in tax and budgetary policy in his first months in office. Yet his inattentiveness led to policy drift and nearly total lack of domestic accomplishment during his last years in office. The administration became mired in scandal. Although he retired with a high approval rating, he is rarely regarded, even among supporters, as a great president.

George Bush was self-effacing and directed. These traits served him well during the Persian Gulf war. Yet in his foreign policy accomplishments lay the seeds of his demise. His casual approach to the economy made him appear out of touch and even uncaring. His was a one-term presidency.

Bill Clinton was engaging and engaged, flexible, hard-working, and adept in matters of domestic policy. He presided over an unprecedented economic expansion and left office with a high job approval rating. Yet he failed to enact the fundamentals of his reform proposals, and his direct accomplishments appear to be at the margins of policy. Moreover, Americans appeared to reject his agenda in 1994. His 1996 reelection and 1999 victory in the trial of impeachment seemed to be the result of the public's revulsion toward his adversaries. His legacy may well be that he marred the presidency.

In 1996, historian **Arthur Schlesinger** reported on a poll (first commissioned by his father in 1948) of fellow historians in rating the presidents. The recent presidents noted above did not fare well. The Watergate scandal and other events that caused his resignation led the historians to rate President Nixon a "failure." Ronald Reagan's sometimes sharp ideological tones led scholars to rate his presidency at both extremes and resulted in an "average" evaluation. The four other recent presidents also earned only average ratings. None of the recent presidents even finished in the top half of the forty-one men who have held the nation's highest office. Considering that the poll was taken before the impeachment crisis, President Clinton seems unlikely to rise to the pantheon of greats.

With the possible exception of President Reagan, the public's judgment mirrors that of the historians. What is noteworthy is that these were presidents who were similar only in their differences. That is, these were men who were very different as leaders—in personality and temperament, in judgment and policy, in energy and activity, and in the political circumstances they faced. In short, these were five different men with five distinct presidencies, none notable for its success. This leads to a number of questions that informs our consideration of the office. How can the office at once seem so unfettered and so limited? How can it be the scene of such amazing triumph and such abject failure? Is the problem of leadership inherent to the modern presidency, or have we simply had the bad fortune of selecting mediocre people to the world's most important office?

One thing for certain is that the framers of the Constitution did not have the contemporary presidency in mind when they established the office. The standard view that the president proposes and the Congress disposes is quite opposite the original intention. In fact, during the drafting of the Constitution, the notion of an independent executive—that is, a president selected separately from Congress—was hotly debated. An independent executive brought to mind absolute monarchy. Hence, the founders took great pains to see that the office was limited. Their fear was of a factional power in Congress, and the office of president was meant to be a check against the legislature rather than the other way around.

Article II of the Constitution provides very few specifically enumerated presidential powers. Aside from the role of commander-in-chief, most of the enumerated powers are either ministerial ("he shall take care that the laws be faithfully executed") or negative (the veto power).

That the office was meant primarily as a check is made clear by the institution of the Electoral College. Not anticipating the emergence of a two-party system, the founders expected the Congress to select the president from among a few candidates proposed by the states through the Electoral College.

According to **Alexander Hamilton**, the chief executive was to provide the necessary energy and coordination when extraordinary times required a single, vigorous policy. In ordinary times, the presidency would more closely resemble a clerkship than any kind of monarchy. As a prognostication of the immediate future, Hamiliton's conception of the presidency was not far off the mark. In the nineteenth century, presidents routinely did the family grocery shopping. With few exceptions, such as the Civil War, the president's stock-in-trade was doling out patronage to his supporters. (That particular responsibility got the best of President James Garfield, who was assassinated by a crazed office seeker in 1881.) From the 1840s on, presidents were beholden for their nominations to potentates of local parties, and presidential candidates were selected largely for the regional advantages they offered. As late as 1916, President **William Howard Taft** argued that any notion of an activist presidency was a usurpation of constitutional design, the founders having believed that presidents should exercise only specifically enumerated powers.

Crises, economic and foreign, led to enormous change in the presidential office in the twentieth century. Franklin D. Roosevelt accelerated the trend toward an activist presidency, a trend begun early in the century by Theodore Roosevelt and Woodrow Wilson. Economic depression and world war were the extraodinary events during which F.D.R. centralized presidential power, thus creating an informal presidential role as crisis manager. He was the first president to exploit the potential of mass media by using radio to broadcast his "fireside chats." It was during his administration that Washington, D.C. truly became the locus of national affairs, just as the White House became the focal point of national policy.

As the century progressed, the public came to expect that the president could and should respond to nearly every crisis, as well as to almost any situation. In the 1950s, with the advent of the Cold War and the nuclear age, the president's primary role in foreign affairs led to further centralization of authority in the White House. In the 1960s and 1970s, supposed abuses of power during the Johnson and Nixon administrations caused some to wonder whether circumstance and ambition had not created an "imperial" presidency—an executive power totally at odds with the intentions of the founders and one that threatened the very foundation of democracy.

In the 1990s, few continued to look at the presidency in such majestic terms. As the powers of the presidency grew, so did the expectations of and demands on the executive office. As **Richard Neustadt** points out, those other Washingtonians (Congress, the president's partisans, public opinion, bureaucrats, and foreign leaders) have retained their independent bases of power and their ability to say no to the president. Lacking the power to command, the president can rely only on his persuasive abilities for success. Neustadt's claim is supported by several recent presidents, who were bedeviled by falling or uneven public approval ratings, policy gridlock, and public expectations that could not possibly be fulfilled.

It seems, then, that today's presidency combines the expectations of a leader with the power of a clerk. With the end of the Cold War, the primacy of the commander-in-chief and chief diplomat roles have been diminished. And with this decline, some argue that the stature of the presidency itself has been diminished accordingly. On the other hand, presidential success seems to rise and fall with the health of the American economy. Those who think the presidency has become easier without the imminent specter of nuclear war can consider that the expectation and evaluation of the president are now premised on the dicey proposition that the economy can be managed from the White House.

Many other presidential "raters" turn to the evaluation of the personal presidency. In the media age, communication skills hold the chief executive in good stead. At least, good communications cures a multitude of sins. This emphasis on the personal suggests that perhaps the presidency is what the president makes it. Hence, there is the recurring claim that character is the best measure and predictor of both presidential power and performance.

One famous approach to assessing presidential character is presented by **James David Barber**, who offers a four-part typology of presidential character-in-office. He suggests that if we can understand the backgrounds of presidential candidates, ways and means of predicting presidential performance can also be found. Many students may want to quarrel with Barber's emphasis on energy and enthusiasm as indicators of great leadership, or even of presidential character. For example, President Clinton would surely fall under Barber's ideal type ("active-positive"), but the rating will be bereft of the measurement of specific accomplishments, moral leadership, or the articulation of a vision for the nation's future. Barber's analysis is useful in that it channels our thoughts toward a systematic evaluation of the personal presidency.

The public seemed to take the impeachment of William Jefferson Clinton rather in stride. Large portions of both the House impeachment hearings and floor proceedings and the subsequent Senate trial were not even covered by the three major networks. The portions covered tended to be the titillating elements of the saga—such as President Clinton's affair with a young White House intern.

Nearly lost in the discussion was a consideration of the political and constitutional issues at stake. The Constitution denotes two specific impeachable offenses (treason and bribery) but adds the phrase "or other high Crimes and Misdemeanors." As there is little consensus on what this phrase means, there is also little guidance on how to apply it to a situation such as the one that faced President Clinton. Are all criminal acts impeachable? Are some noncriminal acts impeachable? If we say that President Clinton's acts were impeachable, do we need to specify which ones and how? And how do we present boundaries for the "charges" to provide guidance for future presidential acts? In this century, presidents have had extended periods of incapacity (and subsequently lied about the fact or its severity). Are these acts impeachable? Some have slept through long portions of the day. Some have refused to put very much time into their duties. Some have engaged in clear violations of law in pursuit of policy goals. Are these impeachable? If Congress knew of these past acts and refused to impeach (or even investigate the matter in terms of impeachment), is that relevant to the Clinton case? Is Congress required to follow public opinion on the matter? If the House cannot form a bipartisan consensus for impeachment (thus making a two-thirds vote for conviction in the Senate impossible), what end is promoted by proceding? The case raised these and many more questions, which need to be examined in the luxuries of time and perspective.

The current controversy in this chapter attempts to sort out these and other dilemmas surrounding the nature of impeachable offenses by offering an example of the scholarly testimony delivered before Congress. **Gary McDowell** argues that the "rule of law" sets the parameters for impeachable offenses. Clear and convincing evidence of perjury or criminal obstruction of justice provides the House with an affirmative obligation to impeach and turn the matter over to the Senate for trial. **Cass R. Sunstein** and **Lawrence H. Tribe** assert that, historically and logically, the basis of the impeachment clause are acts and offenses against the American state or system of government. They conclude that Clinton's behavior didn't even approach this standard. But perhaps it is future generations who will return the verdict.

56 | Energy in the Executive (Federalist No. 70)

Alexander Hamilton

Alexander Hamilton, patriot and statesman, discusses the advantages of a strong, independent executive and addresses fears of a too-powerful presidency.

To the People of the State of New York:

There is an idea, which is not without its advocates, that a vigorous Executive is inconsistent with the genius of republican government. The enlightened well-wishers to this species of government must at least hope that the supposition is destitute of foundation; since they can never admit its truth, without at the same time admitting the condemnation of their own principles. Energy in the Executive is a leading character in the definition of good government. It is essential to the protection of the community against foreign attacks; it is not less essential to the steady administration of the laws; to the protection of property against those irregular and high-handed combinations which sometimes interrupt the ordinary course of justice; to the security of liberty against the enterprises and assaults of ambition, of faction, and of anarchy. Every man the least conversant in Roman story, knows how often that republic was obliged to take refuge in the absolute power of a single man, under the formidable title of Dictator, as well against the intrigues of ambitious individuals who aspired to the tyranny, and the seditions of whole classes of the community whose conduct threatened the existence of all government, as against the invasions of external enemies who menaced the conquest and destruction of Rome.

There can be no need, however, to multiply arguments or examples on this head. A feeble Executive implies a feeble execution of the government. A feeble execution is but another phrase for a bad execution; and a government ill executed, whatever it may be in theory, must be, in practice, a bad government.

Taking it for granted, therefore, that all men of sense will agree in the necessity of an energetic Executive, it will only remain to inquire, what are the ingredients which constitute this energy? How far can they be combined with those other ingredients which constitute safety in the republican sense? And how far does this combination characterize the plan which has been reported by the convention?

The ingredients which constitute energy in the Executive are, first, unity; secondly, duration; thirdly, an adequate provision for its support; fourthly, competent powers.

The ingredients which constitute safety in the republican sense are, first, a due dependence on the people; secondly, a due responsibility.

Those politicians and statesmen who have been the most celebrated for the soundness of their principles and for the justice of their views, have declared in favor of a single Executive and a numerous legislature. They have with great propriety, considered energy as the most necessary qualification of the former, and have regarded this as most applicable to power in a single hand, while they have, with equal propriety, considered the latter as best adapted to deliberation and wisdom, and best calculated to conciliate the confidence of the people and to secure their privileges and interests.

That unity is conducive to energy will not be disputed. Decision, activity, secrecy, and despatch will generally characterize the pro-

ceedings of one man in a much more eminent degree than the proceedings of any
greater number; and in proportion as the
number is increased, these qualities will be diminished....

Men often oppose a thing, merely because
they have had no agency in planning it, or because it may have been planned by those
whom they dislike. But if they have been consulted, and have happened to disapprove, opposition then becomes, in their estimation,
an indispensable duty of self-love. They seem
to think themselves bound in honor, and by
all the motives of personal infallibility, to defeat the success of what has been resolved
upon contrary to their sentiments. Men of
upright, benevolent tempers have too many
opportunities of remarking, with horror, to
what desperate lengths this disposition is
sometimes carried, and how often the great
interests of society are sacrificed to the vanity,
to the conceit, and to the obstinacy of individuals, who have credit enough to make
their passions and their caprices interesting
to mankind. Perhaps the question now before
the public may, in its consequences, afford
melancholy proofs of the effects of this despi-
cable frailty, or rather detestable vice, in the
human character.

Upon the principles of a free government,
inconveniences from the source just mentioned must necessarily be submitted to in the
formation of the legislature; but it is unnecessary, and therefore unwise, to introduce
them into the constitution of the Executive.
It is here too that they may be most pernicious. In the legislature, promptitude of decision is oftener an evil than a benefit. The
differences of opinion, and the jarrings of
parties in that department of the government, though they may sometimes obstruct
salutary plans, yet often promote deliberation
and circumspection, and serve to check excesses in the majority. When a resolution too
is once taken, the opposition must be at an
end. That resolution is a law, and resistance
to it punishable. But no favorable circumstances palliate or atone for the disadvantages
of dissension in the executive department.
Here, they are pure and unmixed. There is

no point at which they cease to operate. They
serve to embarrass and weaken the execution
of the plan or measure to which they relate,
from the first step to the final conclusion of
it. They constantly counteract those qualities
in the Executive which are the most necessary
ingredients in its composition, vigor and ex-
pedition, and this without any counterbalanc-
ing good. In the conduct of war, in which the
energy of the Executive is the bulwark of the
national security, every thing would be to be
apprehended from its plurality....

But one of the weightiest objections to a
plurality in the Executive, and which lies as
much against the last as the first plan, is, that
it tends to conceal faults and destroy responsibility. Responsibility is of two kinds to censure and to punishment. The first is the more
important of the two, especially in an elective
office. Man, in public trust, will much oftener act in such a manner as to render him unworthy of being any longer trusted, than in
such a manner as to make him obnoxious to
legal punishment. But the multiplication of
the Executive adds to the difficulty of detection in either case. It often becomes impossible, amidst mutual accusations, to determine
on whom the blame or the punishment of a
pernicious measure, or series of pernicious
measures, ought really to fall. It is shifted
from one to another with so much dexterity,
and under such plausible appearances, that
the public opinion is left in suspense about
the real author. The circumstances which may
have led to any national miscarriage or misfortune are sometimes so complicated that,
where there are a number of actors who may
have had different degrees and kinds of
agency, though we may clearly see upon the
whole that there has been mismanagement,
yet it may be impracticable to pronounce to
whose account the evil which may have been
incurred is truly chargeable....

It is evident from these considerations, that
the plurality of the Executive tends to deprive
the people of the two greatest securities they
can have for the faithful exercise of any delegated power, first, the restraints of public
opinion, which lose their efficacy, as well on
account of the division of the censure atten-

dant on bad measures among a number, as on account of the uncertainty on whom it ought to fall; and, secondly, the opportunity of discovering with facility and clearness the misconduct of the persons they trust, in order either to their removal from office or to their actual punishment in cases which admit of it....

... I will only add that, prior to the appearance of the Constitution, I rarely met with an intelligent man from any of the States, who did not admit, as the result of experience, that the UNITY of the executive of this State was one of the best of the distinguishing features of our constitution.

57 | Buchanan Presidents, Lincoln Presidents, and Taft Presidents
William Howard Taft

The character and personality of a president is clearly related to the success of his presidency. But to what extent? In his autobiography, Theodore Roosevelt attacked President Taft, his successor in the White House, as passive and disengaged: a Buchanan president rather than a Lincoln president. Responding to Roosevelt in a series of lectures at Columbia University in 1915 and 1916, Taft argued for a conservative presidency. He claimed that the office was intended to be one of limited powers and not a vehicle for the president's personality.

The true view of the executive functions is, as I conceive it, that the President can exercise no power which cannot be fairly and reasonably traced to some specific grant of power or justly implied and included within such express grant as proper and necessary to its exercise. Such specific grant must be either in the federal Constitution or in an act of Congress passed in pursuance thereof. There is no undefined residuum of power which he can exercise because it seems to him to be in the public interest.... The grants of executive power are necessarily in general terms in order not to embarrass the executive within the field of action plainly marked for him, but his jurisdiction must be justified and vindicated by affirmative constitutional or statutory provision, or it does not exist.

There have not been wanting, however, eminent men in high public office holding a different view and who have insisted upon the necessity for an undefined residuum of executive power in the public interest....

... Mr. Roosevelt in his *Notes for a Possible Autobiography* on the subject of Executive Powers ... says:

The most important factor in getting the right spirit in my administration, next to insistence upon courage, honesty, and a genuine democracy of desire to serve the plain people, was my insistence upon the theory that the executive power was limited only by specific restrictions and prohibitions appearing in the Constitution or imposed by Congress under its constitutional powers. My view was that every executive officer and, above all, every executive officer in high position was a steward of the people, bound actively and affirmatively to do all he could for the people and not to content himself with the negative merit of keeping his talents undamaged in a napkin. I declined to adopt this view that what was imperatively necessary for the nation could not be done by the president unless he could find some specific authorization to do it.

My belief was that it was not only his right but his duty to do anything that the needs of the nation demanded unless such action was forbidden by the Constitution or by the laws. Under this interpretation of executive power I did and caused to be done many things not previously done by the President and the heads of the departments. I did not usurp power but I did greatly broaden the use of executive power. In other words, I acted for the common well-being of all our people whenever and in whatever measure was necessary, unless prevented by direct constitutional or legislative prohibition.

I may add that Mr. Roosevelt, by way of illustrating his meaning as to the differing usefulness of Presidents, divides the presidents into two classes and designates them as "Lincoln Presidents" and "Buchanan Presidents." In order more fully to illustrate his division of Presidents on their merits, he places himself in the Lincoln class of Presidents and me in the Buchanan class. The identification of Mr. Roosevelt with Mr. Lincoln might otherwise have escaped notice, because there are many differences between the two, presumably superficial, which would give the impartial student of history a different impression.

It suggests a story which a friend of mine told of his little daughter Mary. As he came walking home after a business day, she ran out from the house to greet him, all aglow with the importance of what she wished to tell him. She said, "Papa, I am the best scholar in the 10 class. " The father's heart throbbed with pleasure as he inquired, "Why, Mary, you surprise me. When did the teacher tell you? This afternoon?" "Oh, no," Mary's reply was, "the teacher didn't tell me—I just noticed it myself."

My judgment is that the view of Mr. Garfield and Mr. Roosevelt, ascribing an un-

defined residuum of power to the President, is an unsafe doctrine and that it might lead under emergencies to results of an arbitrary character, doing irremediable injustice to private right. The mainspring of such a view is that the executive is charged with responsibility for the welfare of all the people in a general way, that he is to play the part of a universal Providence and set all things right, and that anything that in his judgment will help the people he ought to do, unless he is expressly forbidden not to do it. The wide field of action that this would give to the executive, one can hardly limit....

There is little danger to the public weal from the tyranny or reckless character of a president who is not sustained by the people. The absence of popular support will certainly in the course of two years withdraw from him the sympathetic action of at least one House of Congress, and by the control that House has over appropriations, the executive arm can be paralyzed, unless he resorts to a coup d'etat, which means impeachment, conviction, and deposition. The only danger in the action of the executive under the present limitations and lack of limitation of his powers is when his popularity is such that he can be sure of the support of the electorate and therefore of Congress, and when the majority in the legislative halls respond with alacrity and sycophancy to his will. This condition cannot probably be long continued. We have had Presidents who felt the public pulse with accuracy, who played their parts upon the political stage with histrionic genius and commanded the people almost as if they were an army and the President their commander in chief. Yet, in all these cases, the good sense of the people has ultimately prevailed and no danger has been done to our political structure and the reign of law has continued. In such times when the executive power seems to be all prevailing, there have always been men in this free and intelligent people of ours who, apparently courting political humiliation and disaster, have registered protest against this undue executive domination and this use of the executive power and popular support to perpetuate itself.

The cry of executive domination is often entirely unjustified, as when the President's commanding influence only grows out of a proper cohesion of a party and its recognition of the necessity for political leadership; but the fact that executive domination is regarded as a useful ground for attack upon a successful administration, even when there is no ground for it, is itself proof of the dependence we may properly place upon the sanity and clear perceptions of the people in avoiding its baneful effects when there is real danger. Even if a vicious precedent is set by the Executive and injustice done, it does not have the same bad effect that an improper precedent of a court may have; for one President does not consider himself bound by the policies or constitutional views of his predecessors.

58 | *Rating the Presidents*
Arthur M. Schlesinger, Jr.

What makes a president great, almost great, or just plain horrid? Historian Arthur Schlesinger discusses a recent poll of scholars, rating U.S. presidents, following the model of polls taken by his father in 1948 and 1962. Schlesinger's respondents considered intelligence, maturity, the existence of war and/or internal crisis during a president's term, and many more variables. Although many factors had some degree of predictive power, the factors that stood out were that the "Great" or "Near Great" Presidents were bold, visionary, and eschewed middle-of-the-road solutions to problems. These factors did not augur well for President Clinton's rating even before the impeachment crisis.

My father, the historian Arthur M. Schlesinger, started it all nearly half a century ago. In 1948 he asked fifty-five leading historians how they rated the American presidents. The results, published in *Life* magazine just before Harry Truman confounded the prophets and won reelection, excited much interest and also much controversy. In 1962 the *New York Times Magazine* prevailed upon my father to repeat the poll. Again much interest and much controversy. In 1996 the *New York Times Magazine* asked a less eminent historian, Arthur M. Schlesinger, Jr., to replicate his father's poll.…

The Schlesinger polls asked historians to place each president (omitting William Henry Harrison and James A. Garfield because they died so soon after taking office) in one of five categories: Great, Near Great, Average, Below Average, and Failure. The standard was not lifetime achievement but performance in the White House. As to how presidential performance was to be judged, the scholars were left to decide for themselves. It was assumed that historians would recognize greatness—or failure—when they saw it, as Justice Potter Stewart once proposed to recognize pornography.

Presidents might well have wondered (and some did): who are historians to arrogate to themselves the judging of presidential performance? Dwight D. Eisenhower, who did badly in the Schlesinger 1962 poll, accused the scholars of equating "an individual's strength of dedication with oratorical bombast; determination, with public repetition of a catchy phrase; achievement, with the exaggerated use of the vertical pronoun." "History will treat me fairly," said Richard M. Nixon, drawing an odd distinction. "Historians probably won't. They are mostly on the left."…

John F. Kennedy too came to doubt whether the quality of the presidential experience could be understood by those who had not shared it. My father sent his 1962 questionnaire to the historian who had written *Profiles in Courage* and *A Nation of Immigrants*. Kennedy started to fill it out; then changed his mind. "A year ago," he wrote my father, "I would have responded with confidence . . . but now I am not so sure. After being in the office for a year, I feel that a good deal more study is required to make my judgment sufficiently informed. There is a tendency to mark the obvious names. I would like to subject those not so well known to a long scrutiny after I have left this office."

He said to me later, "How the hell can you tell? Only the president himself can know what his real pressures and real alternatives are. If you don't know that, how can you judge performance?" Some of his greatest predecessors, he went on, were given credit for doing things when they could have done nothing else; only detailed inquiry could disclose what difference a president made by his individual contribution. War, he observed, made it easier for a president to achieve greatness. But would Abraham Lincoln have been judged so great a president if he had had to face the almost insoluble problem of Reconstruction?

For all his skepticism, Kennedy read the results of my father's 1962 poll with fascination. He was greatly pleased that Truman was voted a Near Great, nor was he displeased that Eisenhower came in twenty-second, near the bottom of the Averages. Later, jokingly or half-jokingly, he blamed Eisenhower's vigorous entry into the 1962 congressional elections on the historians. "It's all your father's poll," he said. "Eisenhower has been going

along for years, basking in the glow of applause he has always had. Then he saw that poll and realized how he stood before the cold eye of history—way below Truman; even below Hoover. Now he's mad to save his reputation."…

Kennedy was surprised that the historians voted Woodrow Wilson a Great, placing him number four after Abraham Lincoln, George Washington, and Franklin D. Roosevelt, while ranking Andrew Jackson only number six and a Near Great. Though a fine speaker and writer, Wilson, in Kennedy's view, had failed in a number of cherished objectives. Why did professors admire him so much? (I suggested that he was, after all, the only professor to make the White House.)

Kennedy was surprised too by Theodore Roosevelt's ranking—number seven and a Near Great; TR had really got very little significant legislation through Congress. Why should Wilson and TR rate ahead of achievers like James K. Polk (number eight) or Truman (number nine)? For Kennedy, the measure of presidential success was evidently concrete accomplishment. Presidents who raised the consciousness of the nation without achieving their specific objectives ought, he seemed to think, to rate below those, like Polk and Truman, who achieved their objectives even if they did little to inspire or illuminate the nation. Ironically, historians feel that Kennedy himself comes off better when measured by the TR-Wilson rather than by the Polk-Truman standard.…

Meanwhile, scholars continued to play the rating game. Some felt that ratings on the Schlesinger basis were unduly impressionistic and subjective. Quantitative history was coming into vogue. Also political scientists, with their faith in typologies and models, were joining the fun. Would not the results be more "scientific" if presidents were given numerical scores against stated criteria? Then feed the figures into the computer.…

But the yardsticks were mostly too general to warrant mathematical precision or to escape subjective judgment. Their proliferation only produced lengthy and intimidating questionnaires. And, to judge by the results, the refinement of standards made little difference. However simple or complex the method, the final ratings turned out to be much the same....

There have been nine Greats and Near Greats in nearly all the scholarly reckonings. Lincoln, Washington and F. D. Roosevelt are always at the top, followed always, though in varying order, by Jefferson, Jackson, Polk, Theodore Roosevelt, Wilson, and Truman. Occasionally John Adams, Cleveland, and Eisenhower join the top nine. The Failures have always been Grant and Harding, with Buchanan, Pierce, Fillmore, Taylor, and Coolidge always near the bottom.

The scholars' lists not seldom provoke popular as well as presidential indignation. For a long time FDR's top standing enraged many who had opposed his New Deal. "To rank him with Lincoln and Washington," the Detroit editor Malcolm Bingay wrote in 1948 about the first Schlesinger poll, "hits me as historical sacrilege." As late as 1982, Robert K. Murray of Penn State, a leading scholar of presidential ratings, polled 846 historians. When they placed Franklin Roosevelt slightly ahead of George Washington (though still behind Lincoln), Murray was deluged with angry letters, "many being from the fanatic right," he wrote me, "whose fulminations know no bounds." People today forget that Roosevelt was the most hated as well as the best loved president of the twentieth century. But now that even Newt Gingrich pronounces FDR the greatest president of the century, conservatives accept FDR at the top with stoic calm.

The choice of best and worst presidents has remained relatively stable through the years. There is much more fluctuation in between. Some presidents—particularly J. Q. Adams, Buchanan, Andrew Johnson, and Cleveland—have declined in the later polls, but the most striking change has been the steady rise of Eisenhower from twenty-second place in the Schlesinger 1962 poll to twelfth in David Porter's 1981 poll, to eleventh in the poll taken by Robert Murray and Tim Blessing in 1982, to ninth in Steve Neal's *Chicago Tribune* poll the same year and ninth again in

Neal's *Chicago Sun-Times* poll in 1996. Had he lived long enough, Eisenhower might have raged less over the verdicts of scholars.

Several factors account for Eisenhower's ascent. The opening of his papers showed that the mask of genial affability Ike wore in the White House concealed an astute, crafty, confident, and purposeful leader. As Nixon typically put it, Eisenhower was "a far more complex and devious man than most people realized, and in the best sense of those words." Moreover, the FDR model and the yardsticks in earlier polls contained a bias in favor of an activist presidency. After Vietnam and Watergate showed that presidential activism could go too far, Eisenhower appeared in a better light. The peace and harmony sentimentally recollected from Ozzie-and-Harriet days shone well against the turbulence of the 1960s and 1970s. The more his successors got into trouble, the better Eisenhower looked. Presidents sometimes do more for the reputations of their predecessors than they do for their own.

Over the years it has been periodically suggested that I replicate my father's polls. But the difficulty of making overall judgments about some of the presidents since Eisenhower stumped me -in the cases of Kennedy and Gerald Ford, because of the brevity of their time in office; in the cases of Lyndon Johnson, Nixon, and George Bush, because their foreign and domestic records are so discordant. Scholars, for example, might be inclined to rate Johnson higher in domestic than in foreign affairs and do the reverse for Nixon and Bush. And the most recent presidents always seem more controversial and harder to classify. Still the passage of time permits appraisals to crystallize. So in 1996 the *New York Times Magazine* took a new poll.

The question of disjunction still nags. "I find three cases," Walter Dean Burnham said, "which one could describe as having dichotomous or schizoid profiles. On some very important dimensions, both Wilson and L. B. Johnson were outright failures in my view; while on others they rank very high indeed. Similarly with Nixon." Alan Brinkley said: "There are presidents who could be considered both failures and great or near great (for example, Wilson, Johnson, Nixon)." James MacGregor Burns observed of Nixon, "How can one evaluate such an idiosyncratic president, so brilliant and so morally lacking? . . . so I guess to average out he would be average."...

Yet the 1996 poll still shows a high degree of continuing scholarly consensus.

In nearly all the polls since 1948, the same nine men top the list. Lincoln, with a unanimous Great vote, comes in first in 1996. Washington and FDR, as usual, are next; each had one Near Great vote. The big three are followed, as usual, by the Near Greats—Jefferson, Jackson, Theodore Roosevelt, Wilson, Truman, and Polk. Steve Neal's 1996 poll, with five yardsticks (political leadership, foreign policy, domestic policy, character, impact on history) and fifty-eight respondents, came up with the same nine men, plus Eisenhower and Ronald Reagan, who edged out Polk.

Polk's high ranking is always a puzzle for laymen. "Of all our array of presidents," James Thurber once imprudently wrote, "there was none less memorable than James K. Polk." But Polk at 49 was the youngest man up to that time, and the only Speaker of the House of Representatives ever, to make the White House. He specified his objectives early on—to reduce the tariff, establish the independent treasury system, settle the Oregon boundary question, and acquire California—and worked efficiently and relentlessly to achieve them. His objectives have been criticized but not his ability. Besides, he kept the most complete of presidential diaries, which endears him to scholars.

The next batch, the High Averages, are led in the 1996 Schlesinger poll by Eisenhower, whose one Great vote and ten Near Greats are outweighed by a host of Averages. The same fate befalls John Adams with ten Near Greats and Kennedy with nine. Lyndon Johnson receives fifteen Near Greats from scholars who seem to have forgotten about Vietnam, but low ratings and two Failures awarded by those who remember Vietnam bring his score down below Kennedy's. Monroe and McKinley complete the High Averages.

Most presidents fall into the Average class. Recent presidents, too close for historical perspective, are likely to rise or fall in polls to come. Carter has one Near Great and two Failures, with the rest of his votes in between. Some admire his accomplishment in putting human rights on the world's agenda; others deplore his political ineptitude and the absence of any clear direction in his handling of domestic affairs.

Reagan, on the other hand, has seven Near Great votes, including some from liberal scholars impressed by his success in restoring the prestige of the presidency, in negotiating the last phases of the cold war, and in imposing his priorities on the country. But he also receives nine Below Averages and four Failures from those who consider his priorities—his attack on government as the root of all evil and his tax reductions that increased disparities between rich and poor while tripling the national debt—a disaster for the republic.

His score averages out a shade below that of George Bush, who receives no Near Greats but more Averages than Reagan and only one Failure. Bush's skill in putting together the coalition that won the Gulf War outweighs for many his seeming lack of purpose in domestic policy. Some respondents thought it premature to judge Clinton, but two vote him Near Great and two more a Failure, and he ends up Average....

Some exception has been taken to Reagan's rating as number twenty-five, placing him between Bush and Arthur and below Clinton. According to the March-April 1997 *Policy Review*, this "low assessment" was "the most astonishing part of Schlesinger's poll."... [T]hey then picked its own panel...—a group that invites the same suspicion roused in Policy Review by my panel— and they joined seven of my respondents in putting Reagan in the Near Great category....

The list of Failures shows a slight shift from past polls. Harding and Grant are, as usual, favorite Failures. Do they really deserve it? They are marked down because of the scandal and corruption that disgraced their administrations. But they were careless and negligent rather than villainous. Their sin was excessive loyalty to crooked friends. "Harding was not a bad man," as Theodore Roosevelt's daughter, Alice Roosevelt Longworth, put it. "He was just a slob."... Scandal and corruption are indefensible, but they may injure the general welfare less than misconceived policies.

In the new poll the ineffectual Franklin Pierce and the rigidly dogmatic Herbert Hoover tie with Grant as the best among the Failures. Next down the list comes Nixon. Most respondents, while recognizing Nixon's intelligence and drive, resolve the "schizoid profile" by concluding that his impressive ability is negated by his rather more impressive offenses against the Constitution.

It is perhaps hard to demonstrate that the only president forced to resign from the office was not a Failure....

The nation's belated awakening to racial injustice explains why two presidents receive more Failure votes this time than in earlier polls: James Buchanan, whose irresolution encouraged the secession of the Confederate states; and Andrew Johnson, who, while a Unionist, was a stout believer in white supremacy. It seems reasonable to suggest that Buchanan, Andrew Johnson, Hoover, and Nixon damaged the republic a good deal more than did the hapless Grant and the feckless Harding.

Nine men, we have seen, have led the list from the first Schlesinger poll of historians nearly half a century ago. What do Washington, Jefferson, Jackson, Polk, Lincoln, Theodore Roosevelt, Wilson, Franklin Roosevelt, and Truman have in common? What do they, and Eisenhower too, who arrived too late for the 1948 poll, tell us about the qualities necessary for success in the White House?

Well, half were over six feet tall. The exceptions were Polk (5'8"), Theodore Roosevelt (5'10"), Wilson (5'11"), Truman (5'9") and Eisenhower (5'10-½"). On the other hand, James Monroe, John Tyler, Buchanan, Chester A. Arthur, Taft, Harding, Kennedy, Lyndon Johnson, Gerald Ford, Reagan, Bush, and Clinton were also six feet or more; so height by itself is no guarantee of greatness in the White House. Nor is education. Nearly

half the prize group—Washington, Jackson, Lincoln, and Truman—never attended college. As for age, the average age of the nine at inauguration or succession was 54 years; so youth is a comparative advantage.

Height and age are minor considerations. Intelligence helps, though Reagan with his seven Near Greats shows that an influential president need not have much. Maturity? The British ambassador called Theodore Roosevelt an arrested 11-year-old. Unflinching honesty? Deviousness is a presidential characteristic not confined to Eisenhower. Loyalty? This can be a presidential defect: remember Grant and Harding. Private virtues do not guarantee public effectiveness.

More to the point is the test proposed 125 years ago by our most brilliant historian, Henry Adams. The American president, he wrote, "resembles the commander of a ship at sea. He must have a helm to grasp, a course to steer, a port to seek." The Constitution offers every president a helm, but the course and the port constitute the first requirement for presidential greatness. Great presidents possess, or are possessed by, a vision of an ideal America. Their passion is to make sure the ship of state sails on the right course....

To succeed, presidents must have a port to seek and must convince Congress and the electorate of the rightness of their course. Politics in a democracy is ultimately an educational process, an adventure in persuasion and consent. Every president stands in Theodore Roosevelt's bully pulpit. National crisis widens his range of options but does not automatically make a man great. The crisis of rebellion did not spur Buchanan to leadership, nor did the crisis of depression turn Hoover into a bold and imaginative president. Their inadequacies in the face of crisis allowed Lincoln and the second Roosevelt to show the difference that individuals can make to history.

Of national crises, war is the most fateful, and all the top ten save Jefferson were involved in war either before or during their presidencies. As Robert Higgs has noted, five (Polk, Lincoln, Wilson, Franklin Roosevelt, and Truman) were commanders-in-chief when the republic was at war, and four more (Washington, Jackson, Theodore Roosevelt, and Eisenhower) made pre-presidential reputations on the battlefield....

Crisis helps those who can rise to it, and the association of war with presidential greatness has its ominous aspect. Still, two of the immortals, it should be noted, made their mark without benefit of first-order crisis. Jackson and Theodore Roosevelt forced the nation through sheer power of personality to recognize incipient problems- Jackson in vindicating the national authority against the state of South Carolina and against the Second Bank of the United States; the first Roosevelt in vindicating the national authority against the great corporations and against raids on the people's natural resources. As the historian Elting Morison admirably described this quality of noncrisis leadership: "Theodore Roosevelt could get the attention of his fellow citizens and make them think. He knew how to put the hard questions a little before they became obvious to others; how to make the search for sensible answers exciting; how to startle the country into informing debate; and how to move people into their thinking beyond short-run self-interest toward some longer view of the general welfare."

We hear much these days about the virtues of the middle of the road. But not one of the top nine can be described as a middle-roader. Middle-roading may be fine for campaigning, but it is a sure road to mediocrity in governing.

The succession of middle-roaders after the Civil War inspired James Bryce to write the notorious chapter in *The American Commonwealth* entitled "Why Great Men Are Not Chosen President." "The middle of the road is not the vital center: it is the dead center."

The Greats and Near Greats all recognized, in the aphorism of Pierre Mendes-France, that "to govern is to choose." They all took risks in pursuit of their ideals. They all provoked intense controversy. They all, except Washington, divided the nation before reuniting it on a new level of national understanding.

Presidents who seek to change the nation's direction know that they are bound to alienate those who profit from the status quo. Great presidents go ahead anyway. "Judge me," FDR said, "by the enemies I have made." Truman's approval rating at the end of his presidency was down to 31 percent. Look where he ranks now....

Clinton brings to the bar of history a rare combination of talents and infirmities. He is a man of penetrating intelligence. He has impressive technical mastery of complicated issues. He has genuine intellectual curiosity and listens as well as talks. He is a skilled and resilient politician. When the spirit moves him, he is capable of real eloquence, and the spirit moves him most of all when he confronts the supreme American problem—race. Racial justice appears to be his most authentic concern.

On the other hand, he lacks self-discipline. His judgment of people is erratic. His political resilience strikes many as flagrant opportunism. His reactions are instinctively placatory, perhaps from growing up in a household where the wrong words might provoke an alcoholic stepfather to violence. He rushes to propitiate the audience before him, often at his own long-term expense. His scandals and cover-ups are ripe for exploitation by a vindictive opposition. Who can tell how this combination of talents and infirmities will play out?...

59 | *Leader or Clerk?*
Richard Neustadt

Richard Neustadt's Presidential Power *is sometimes said to be the most important book on the presidency. First published in 1960 and updated frequently, the thesis is that constituency pressures on and high expectations of the president make effective presidential leadership problematic. The presidential power is not to command but to persuade.*

In the United States we like to "rate" a president. We measure him as "weak " or "strong" and call what we are measuring his "leadership." We do not wait until a man is dead; we rate him from the moment he takes office. We are quite right to do so. His office has become the focal point of politics and policy in our political system. Our commentators and our politicians make a specialty of taking the man's measurements. The rest of us join in when we feel "government" impinging on our private lives....

We deal here with the President himself and with his influence on governmental action. In institutional terms the Presidency now includes two thousand men and women. The President is only one of them. But his performance scarcely can be measured without focusing on him. In terms of party, or of country, or the West, so-called, his leadership involves far more than governmental action. But the sharpening of spirit and of values and of purposes is not done in a vacuum. Although governmental action may not be the whole of leadership, all else is nurtured by it and gains meaning from it....

In form all Presidents are leaders nowadays. In fact this guarantees no more than that they will be clerks. Everybody now expects the man inside the White House to do something about everything. Laws and customs now reflect acceptance of him as the great initiator, an acceptance quite as widespread at the Capitol as at his end of Pennsylvania Avenue. But such acceptance does not signify that all the rest of government is at his feet. It merely signifies that other men have found it practically impossible to do their jobs without assurance of initiatives from him. Service for themselves, not power for the President, has brought them to accept his leadership in form. They find his actions useful in their business. The transformation of his routine obligations testifies to their dependence on an active White House. A President, these days, is an invaluable clerk. His services are in demand all over Washington. His influence, however, is a very different matter. Laws and customs tell us little about leadership in fact.

Why have our Presidents been honored with this clerkship? The answer is that no one else's services suffice. Our Constitution, our traditions, and our politics provide no better source for the initiatives a President can take. Executive officials need decisions, and political protection, and a referee for fights. Where are these to come from but the White House? Congressmen need an agenda from outside, something with high status to respond to or react against. What provides it better than the program of the President? Party politicians need a record to defend in the next national campaign. How can it be made except by "their" administration? Private persons with a public ax to grind may need a helping hand or they may need a grinding stone. In either case, who gives more satisfaction than a President? And outside the United States, in every country where our policies and postures influence home politics, there will be people needing just the "right" thing said and done or just the "wrong" thing stopped in Washington. What symbolizes Washington more nearly than the White House?

A modern President is bound to face demands for aid and service from five more or less distinguishable sources: from executive officialdom, from Congress, from his partisans, from citizens at large, and from abroad. The Presidency's clerkship is expressive of these pressures. In effect they are constituency pressures, and each President has five sets of constituents. The five are not distinguished by their membership; membership is obviously an overlapping matter. And taken one by one they do not match the man's electorate; one of them, indeed, is outside his electorate. They are distinguished, rather, by their different claims upon him. Initiatives are what they want, for five distinctive reasons. Since government and politics have offered no alternative, our laws and customs turn those wants into his obligations.

Why, then, is the President not guaranteed an influence commensurate with services performed? Constituent relations are relations of dependence. Everyone with any share in governing this country will belong to one (or two, or three) of his constituencies. Since everyone depends on him, why is he not assured of everyone's support? The answer is that no one else sits where he sits or sees quite as he sees; no one else feels the full weight of his obligations. Those obligations are a tribute to his unique place in our political system. But just because it is unique they fall on him alone. *The same conditions that promote his leadership in form preclude a guarantee of leadership in fact.* No man or group at either end of Pennsylvania Avenue shares his peculiar status in our government and politics. That is why his services are in demand. By the same token, though, the obligations of all other men are different from his own. His cabinet officers have departmental duties and constituents. His legislative leaders head Congressional parties, one in either house. His national party organization stands apart from his official family. His political allies in the states need not face Washington or one another. The private groups that seek him out are not compelled to govern. And friends abroad are not compelled to run in our elections. Lacking his position and prerogatives,

these men cannot regard his obligations as their own. They have their jobs to do; none is the same as his. As they perceive their duty they may find it right to follow him, in fact, or they may not. Whether they will feel obliged on their responsibility to do what he wants done remains an open question....

In the early summer of 1952, before the heat of the campaign, President Truman used to contemplate the problems of the general-become-President should Eisenhower win the forthcoming election. "He'll sit here," Truman would remark (tapping his desk for emphasis), "and he'll say, 'Do this! Do that!' *And nothing will happen.* Poor Ike—it won't be a bit like the Army. He'll find it very frustrating."

Eisenhower evidently found it so. "In the face of the continuing dissidence and disunity, the President sometimes simply exploded with exasperation," wrote Robert Donovan in comment on the early months of Eisenhower's first term. "What was the use, he demanded to know, of his trying to lead the Republican Party...." And this reaction was not limited to early months alone, or to his party only. "The President still feels," an Eisenhower aide remarked to me in 1958, "that when he's decided something, that *ought* to be the end of it... and when it bounces back undone or done wrong, he tends to react with shocked surprise. "

Truman knew whereof he spoke. With "resignation" in the place of "shocked surprise," the aide's description would have fitted Truman. The former senator may have been less shocked than the former general, but he was no less subjected to that painful and repetitive experience: "Do this, do that, and nothing will happen." Long before he came to talk of Eisenhower he had put his own experience in other words: "I sit here all day trying to persuade people to do the things they ought to have sense enough to do without my persuading them....That's all the powers of the President amount to."

In these words of a President, spoken on the job, one finds the essence of the problem now before us: "powers" are no guarantee of power; clerkship is no guarantee of leadership. The President of the United States has an extraordinary range of formal powers, of authority in statute law and in the Constitution. Here is testimony that despite his "powers" he does not obtain results by giving orders—or not, at any rate, merely by giving orders. He also has extraordinary status, ex officio, according to the customs of our government and politics. Here is testimony that despite his status he does not get action without argument. Presidential power is the power to persuade....

The limits on command suggest the structure of our government. The Constitutional Convention of 1787 is supposed to have created a government of "separated powers." It did nothing of the sort. Rather, it created a government of separated institutions *sharing* powers. "1 am part of the legislative process," Eisenhower often said in 1959 as a reminder of his veto. Congress, the dispenser of authority and funds, is no less part of the administrative process. Federalism adds another set of separated institutions. The Bill of Rights adds others. Many public purposes can only be achieved by voluntary acts of private institutions; the press, for one, in Douglass Cater's phrase, is a "fourth branch of government." And with the coming of alliances abroad, the separate institutions of a London, or a Bonn, share in the making of American public policy.

What the Constitution separates our political parties do not combine. The parties are themselves composed of separated organizations sharing public authority. The authority consists of nominating powers. Our national parties are confederations of state and local party institutions, with a headquarters that represents the White House, more or less, if the party has a President in office. These confederacies manage presidential nominations. All other public offices depend upon electorates confined within the states. All other nominations are controlled within the states. The President and congressmen who bear one party's label are divided by dependence upon different sets of voters. The differences are sharpest at the stage of nomination. The

White House has too small a share in nominating congressmen, and Congress has too little weight in nominating presidents for parties to erase their constitutional separation. Party links are stronger than is frequently supposed, but nominating processes assure the separation.

The separateness of institutions and the sharing of authority prescribe the terms on which a President persuades. When one man shares authority with another, but does not gain or lose his job upon the other's whim, his willingness to act upon the urging of the other turns on whether he conceives the action right for him. The essence of a President's persuasive task is to convince such men that what the White House wants of them is what they ought to do for their sake and on their authority. (Sex matters not at all; for *man* read *woman*.)

Persuasive power, thus defined, amounts to more than charm or reasoned argument. These have their uses for a President, but these are not the whole of his resources. For the individuals he would induce to do what he wants done on their own responsibility will need or fear some acts by him on his responsibility. If they share his authority, he has some share in theirs. Presidential "powers" may be inconclusive when a President commands, but always remain relevant as he persuades. The status and authority inherent in his office reinforce his logic and his charm....

The power to persuade is the power to bargain. Status and authority yield bargaining advantages. But in a government of "separated institutions sharing powers," they yield them to all sides. With the array of vantage points at his disposal, a President may be far more persuasive than his logic or his charm could make him. But outcomes are not guaranteed by his advantages. There remain the counter pressures those whom he would influence can bring to bear on him from vantage points at their disposal. Command has limited utility; persuasion becomes give-and-take. It is well that the White House holds the vantage points it does. In such a business any President may need them all—and more.

60 | *The Presidential Character*
James David Barber

James David Barber's four presidential character types is one way to consider the makeup of a successful president. If nothing else, putting recent presidents on the couch may be thought provoking, as well as fun. But can we cast presidents as types? What types are desirable? Under what circumstances? Can presidential performance be accurately predicted?

When we citizens vote for a Presidential candidate, we make, in effect, a prediction. We choose from among the contenders the one we think (or feel or guess) would be the best President. We operate in a situation of immense uncertainty. If we have already been voting for years, we can recall time and time again when we guessed wrong. We listen to the commentators, the politicians, and our friends, then add it all up in some rough way to produce our prediction and our vote. Earlier in the game, our anticipations have been taken into account, either directly in the polls and primaries or indirectly in the minds of politicians who want to nominate someone we will like. But we must choose in the midst of a cloud of confusion, a rain of phony advertising, a storm of sermons, a hail of complex issues, a fog of charisma and boredom, and a thunder of accusation and defense. In the face of this chaos, a great many citizens fall back on the past, vote their old allegiances, and let it go at that. Nevertheless, the citizens' vote says that on balance we expect Candidate X would outshine Candidate Y in the presidency.

... To understand what actual Presidents do and what potential Presidents might do, the first need is to know the whole person— not as some abstract embodiment of civic virtue, some scorecard of issue stands, or some reflection of a faction, but as a human being like the rest of us, a person trying to cope with a difficult environment. To that task, the candidate brings an individual character, worldview, and political style. None of that is new at campaign time. If we can see the pattern set already for the candidate's political life, we can, I contend, estimate better

the pattern this person brings forth to the stresses and chances of the Presidency.

The Presidency is a peculiar office. The Founding Fathers left it extraordinarily loose in definition, partly because they trusted George Washington to invent a tradition as he went along. It is an institution made a piece at a time by successive men (so far) in the White House. Jefferson reached out to Congress to put together the beginnings of political parties; Jackson's dramatic force extended electoral partisanship to its mass base; Lincoln vastly expanded the administrative reach of the office; Wilson and the Roosevelts showed its rhetorical possibilities—in fact every President's mind and demeanor has left its mark on a heritage still in lively development.

But the Presidency is much more than an institution. It is a focus of feelings. In general, popular feelings about politics are low-key, shallow, casual. For example, the vast majority of Americans knows virtually nothing of what Congress is doing and cares less. The Presidency is different. The Presidency is the focus for the most intense and persistent emotions in the American polity. The President is a symbolic leader, the one figure who draws together the people's hopes and fears for the political future. On top of all his routine duties. he has to carry that off—or fail.

Our emotional attachment to Presidents shows up when one dies in office. People were not just disappointed or worried when President Kennedy was killed; people wept at the loss of a man most had never even met. Kennedy was young and charismatic—but history shows that whenever a President dies in office, heroic Lincoln or debased Harding, McKinley or Garfield, the same wave of deep emotion sweeps across the country. On the other hand, the death of an ex-President brings forth no such intense emotional reaction….

The President helps people make sense of politics. Congress is a tangle of committees, the bureaucracy is a maze of agencies. The President is one man trying to do a job—a picture much more understandable to the mass of people who find themselves in the same boat. Furthermore, he is the top man. He ought to know what is going on and set it right. So when the economy goes sour, or war drags on, or domestic violence erupts, the President is available to take the blame. Then when things go right, it seems the President must have had a hand in it. Indeed, the flow of political life is marked off by Presidents: the "Eisenhower Era," the "Kennedy Years."

What all this means is that the President's *main* responsibilities reach far beyond administering the Executive Branch or commanding the armed forces. The White House is first and foremost a place of public leadership. That inevitably brings to bear on the President intense moral, sentimental, and quasi-religious pressures which can, if he lets them, distort his own thinking and feeling. If there is such a thing as extraordinary sanity, it is needed nowhere so much as in the White House.

Who the President is at a given time can make a profound difference in the whole thrust and direction of national politics. Since we have only one President at a time, we can never prove this by comparison, but even the most superficial speculation confirms the commonsense view that the man himself weighs heavily among other historical factors. A Wilson re-elected in 1920, a Hoover in 1932, a John F. Kennedy in 1964 would, it seems very likely, have guided the body politic along rather different paths from those their actual successors chose. Or try to imagine a Theodore Roosevelt ensconced behind today's "bully pulpit" of a Presidency, or Lyndon Johnson as President in the age of McKinley. Only someone mesmerized by the lures of historical inevitability can suppose that it would have made little or no difference to government policy had Alf Landon replaced FDR in 1936, had Dewey beaten Truman in 1948, or Adlai Stevenson reigned through the 1950s. Not only would these alternative Presidents have advocated different policies—they would have approached the office from very different psychological angles. It stretches credibility to think that Eugene McCarthy would have run the institution the way Lyndon Johnson did….

My argument comes in layers.

First, a President's personality is an important shaper of his Presidential behavior on nontrivial matters.

Second, Presidential personality is patterned. His character, world view, and style fit together in a dynamic package understandable in psychological terms . Third, a President's personality interacts with the power situation he faces and the national "climate of expectations" dominant at the time he serves. The tuning, the resonance—or lack of it—between these external factors and his personality sets in motion the dynamic of his Presidency.

Fourth, the best way to predict a president's character, world view, and style is to see how they were put together in the first place. That happened in his early life, culminating in his first independent political success.

But the core of the argument…is that Presidential character—the basic stance a man takes toward his Presidential experience—comes in four varieties. The most important thing to know about a President or candidate is where he fits among these types, defined according to (a) how active he is and (b) whether or not he gives the impression he enjoys his political life….

PERSONALITY SHAPES PERFORMANCE

I am not about to argue that once you know a President's personality you know everything. But… the degree and quality of a President's emotional involvement in an issue are powerful influences on how he defines the issue itself, how much attention he pays to it, which facts and persons he sees as relevant to its resolution, and, finally, what principles and purposes he associates with the issue. Every story of Presidential decision-making is really two stories: an outer one in which a rational man calculates and an inner one in which an emotional man feels. The two are forever connected. Any real President is one whole man and his deeds reflect his wholeness.

As for personality, it is a matter of tendencies. It is not that one President "has" some basic characteristics that another President does not "have." That old way of treating a trait as a possession, like a rock in a basket, ignores the universality of aggressiveness, compliancy, detachment, and other human drives. We all have all of them, but in different amounts and in different combinations.

THE PATTERN OF CHARACTER, WORLD VIEW, AND STYLE

The most visible part of the pattern is style. *Style is the President's habitual way of performing his three political roles: rhetoric, personal relations, and homework.* Not to be confused with "stylishness," charisma, or appearance, style is how the President goes about doing what the office requires him to do—to speak, directly or through media, to large audiences; to deal face to face with other politicians, individually and in small, relatively private groups; and to read, write, and calculate by himself in order to manage the endless flow of details that stream onto his desk. No President can escape doing at least some of each. But there are marked differences in stylistic emphasis from President to President. The *balance* among the three style elements varies; one President may put most of himself into rhetoric, another may stress close, informal dealing, while still another may devote his energies mainly to study and cogitation. Beyond the balance, we want to see each President's peculiar habits of style, his mode of coping with and adapting to these Presidential demands....

A President's *world view consists of his primary, politically relevant beliefs, particularly his conceptions of social causality, human nature, and the central moral conflicts of the time.* This is how he sees the world, and what his lasting opinions are about what he sees. Style is his way of acting; world view is his way of seeing. Like the rest of us, a President develops over a lifetime certain conceptions of reality—how things work in politics, what people are like, what the main purposes are. These assumptions or conceptions help him make sense of his world, give some semblance of order to the chaos of existence. Perhaps most important, a man's world view affects what he pays attention to, and a great deal of politics is about paying attention. The name of the game for many politicians is not so much "Do this, do that" as it is "Look here!"

"Character" comes from the Greek word for engraving; in one sense it is what life has marked into a man's being. As used here, *character is the way the President orients himself toward life*—not for the moment, but enduringly. Character is the person's stance as he confronts experience. And at the core of character, a man confronts himself. The President's fundamental self-esteem is his prime personal resource; to defend and advance that, he will sacrifice much else he values. Down there in the privacy of his heart, does he find himself superb, or ordinary, or debased, or in some intermediate range? No President has been utterly paralyzed by self-doubt and none has been utterly free of midnight self-mockery. In between, the real Presidents move out on life from positions of relative strength or weakness. Equally important are the criteria by which they judge themselves. A President who rates himself by the standard of achievement, for instance, may be little affected by losses of affection.

Character, world view, and style are abstractions from the reality of the whole individual. In every case they form an integrated pattern: the man develops a combination which makes psychological sense for him, a dynamic arrangement of motives, beliefs, and habits in the services of his need for self-esteem.

THE POWER SITUATION AND "CLIMATE OF EXPECTATIONS"

Presidential character resonates with the political situation the President faces. It adapts him as he tries to adapt it. The support he has from the public and interest groups, the party balance in Congress, the thrust of Supreme Court opinion, together set the basic power situation he must deal with. An activist President may run smack into a brick wall of resistance, then pull back and wait for a better moment. On the other hand, a President who sees himself as a quiet caretaker may not try to exploit even the most favorable power situation. So it is the relations between President and the political configuration that make the system tick.

Even before public opinion polls, the President's real or supposed popularity is a large factor in his performance. Besides the power mix in Washington, the President has to deal with a national climate of expectations, the predominant needs thrust up to him by the people. There are at least three recurrent themes around which these needs are focused.

People look to the President for *reassurance*, a feeling that things will be all right, that the President will take care of his people. The psychological request is for a surcease of anxiety. Obviously, modern life in America involves considerable doses of fear, tensions, anxiety, worry; from time to time, the public mood calls for a rest, a time of peace, a breathing space, a "return to normalcy."

Another theme is the demand for a *sense of progress and action*. The President ought to do something to direct the nation's course or at least be in there pitching for the people. The President is looked to as a take-charge man, a doer, a turner of the wheels, a producer of progress—even if that means some sacrifice of serenity.

A third type of climate of expectations is the public need for a sense of *legitimacy* from, and in, the Presidency. The President should be a master politician who is above politics. He should have a right to his place and a rightful way of acting in it. The respectability—even religiosity—of the office has to be protected by a man who presents himself as defender of the faith. There is more to this than dignity, more than propriety. The President is expected to personify our betterness in an inspiring way, to express in what he does and is (not just in what he says) a moral idealism which, in much of the public mind, is the very opposite of "politics."

Over time, the climate of expectations shifts and changes. Wars, depressions, and other national events contribute to that change, but there also is a rough cycle, from an emphasis on action (which begins to look too "political") to an emphasis on legitimacy (the moral uplift of which creates its own strains) to an emphasis on reassurance and rest (which comes to seem like drift) and back to action again. One need not be astrological about it. The point is that the climate of expectations at any given time is the political air the President has to breathe. Relating to this climate is a large part of his task.

PREDICTING PRESIDENTS

The best way to predict a President's character, world view, and style is to see how he constructed them in the first place. Especially in the early stages life is experimental; consciously or not, a person tries out various ways of defining and maintaining and raising self-esteem. He looks to his environment for clues as to who he is and how well he is doing. These lessons of life slowly sink in: certain self-images and evaluations, certain ways of looking at the world, certain styles of action get confirmed by his experience and he gradually adopts them as his own. If we can see that process of development, we can understand the product. The features to note are those bearing on Presidential performance.

Experimental development continues all the way to death; we will not blind ourselves to midlife changes, particularly in the full-scale prediction cases. But it is often much easier to see the basic patterns in early life histories. Later on a whole host of distractions—especially the image-making all politicians learn to practice—clouds the picture.

In general, character has its *main* development in childhood, world view in adolescence, style in early adulthood. The stance toward life I call character grows out of the child's experiments in relating to parents, brothers and sisters, and peers at play and in school, as well as to his own body and the objects around it. Slowly the child defines an orientation toward experience; once established, that tends to last despite much subsequent contradiction. By adolescence, the child has been hearing and seeing how people make their worlds meaningful, and now he is moved to relate himself—his own meanings—to those around him. His focus of attention shifts toward the future; he senses that decisions about his fate are coming and he looks into the premises for those decisions. Thoughts about the way the world works and how one might work in it, about what people are like and how one might be like them or not, and about the values people share and how one might share in them too—these are typical concerns for the post-child, pre-adult mind of the adolescent.

These themes come together strongly in early adulthood, when the person moves from contemplation to responsible action and adopts a style. In most biographical accounts, this period stands out in stark clarity—the time of emergence, the time the young man found himself. I call it his first independent political success. It was then he moved beyond the detailed guidance of his family; then his self-esteem was dramatically boosted; then he came forth as a person to be reckoned with by other people. The *way* he did that is profoundly important to him. Typically he grasps that style and hangs onto it. Much later, coming into the Presidency, something in him remembers this earlier victory and re-emphasizes the style that made it happen....

FOUR TYPES OF PRESIDENTIAL CHARACTER

The five concepts—character, world view, style, power situation, and climate of expectations—run through the accounts of Presidents in the chapters to follow, which cluster the Presidents since Theodore Roosevelt into four types. This is the fundamental scheme of the study. It offers a way to move past the complexities to the main contrasts and comparisons.

The first baseline in defining Presidential types is *activity-passivity*. How much energy does the man invest in his Presidency? Lyndon Johnson went at his day like a human cyclone, coming to rest long after the sun went down. Calvin Coolidge often slept eleven hours a night and still needed a nap in the middle of the day. In between, the Presidents array themselves on the high or low side of the activity line.

The second baseline is *positive-negative* affect toward one's activity—that is, how he feels about what he does. Relatively speaking, does he seem to experience his political life as happy or sad, enjoyable or discouraging, positive or negative in its main effect? The feeling I am after here is not grim satisfaction in a job well done, not some philosophical conclusion. The idea is this: is he someone who, on the surfaces we can see, gives forth the feeling that he has fun in political life? Franklin Roosevelt's Secretary of War, Henry L. Stimson, wrote that the Roosevelts "not only understood the *use* of power, they knew the *enjoyment* of power too.... Whether a man is burdened by power or enjoys power; whether he is trapped by responsibility or made free by it; whether he is moved by other people and outer forces or moves them—that is the essence of leadership."

The positive-negative baseline, then, is a general symptom of the fit between the man and his experience, a kind of register of *felt* satisfaction.

Why might we expect these two simple dimensions to outline the main character types? Because they stand for two central features of anyone's orientation toward life. In nearly every study of personality, some form of the active-passive contrast is critical; the general tendency to act or be acted upon is evident in such concepts as dominance-submission, extraversion-introversion, aggression-timidity, attack-defense, fight-flight, engagement-withdrawal, approach-avoidance. In everyday life we sense quickly the general energy output of the people we deal with. Similarly, we catch on fairly quickly to the affect dimension—whether the person seems to be optimistic or pessimistic, hopeful or skeptical, happy or sad. The two baselines are clear and they are also independent of one another: all of us know people who are very active but seem discouraged, others who are quite passive but seem happy, and so forth. The activity baseline refers to what one does, the affect baseline to how one feels about what he does.

Both are crude clues to character. They are leads into four basic character patterns long familiar in psychological research. In summary form, these are the main configurations:

Active-Positive

There is a congruence, a consistency, between being very active and the enjoyment of it, indicating relatively high self-esteem and relative success in relating to the environment. The man shows an orientation toward productiveness as a value, and an ability to use his styles flexibly, adaptively, suiting the dance to the music. He sees himself as developing over time toward relatively well-defined personal goals—growing toward his image of himself as he might yet be. There is an emphasis on rational mastery, and on using the brain to move the feet. This may get him into trouble; he may fail to take account of the irrational in politics. Not everyone he deals with sees things his way and he may find it hard to understand why.

Active-Negative

The contradiction here is between relatively intense effort and relatively low emotional reward for that effort. The activity has a compulsive quality, as if the man were trying to make up for something or to escape from anxiety into hard work. He seems ambitious, striving upward and seeking power. His stance toward the environment is aggressive and he has a persistent problem in managing his aggressive feelings. His self-image is vague and discontinuous. Life is a hard struggle to achieve and hold power, hampered by the condemnations of a perfectionistic conscience. Active-negative types pour energy into the political system, but it is an energy distorted from within.

Passive-Positive

This is the receptive, compliant, other-directed character whose life is a search for attention as a reward for being agreeable and cooperative rather than personally assertive. The contradiction is between low self-esteem (on grounds of being unlovable, unattractive) and a superficial optimism. A hopeful attitude helps dispel doubt and elicits encouragement from others. Passive-positive types help soften the harsh edges of politics. But their dependence and the fragility of their hopes and enjoyments make disappointment in politics likely.

Passive-Negative

The factors are consistent—but how are we to account for the man's *political* role-taking? Why is someone who does little in politics and enjoys it less there at all? The answer lies in the passive-negative's character-rooted orientation toward doing dutiful service; this compensates for low self-esteem based on a sense of uselessness. Passive-negative types are in politics because they think they ought to be. They may be well adapted to certain non-political roles, but they lack the experience and flexibility to perform effectively as political leaders. Their tendency is to withdraw, to escape from the conflict and uncertainty of politics by emphasizing vague principles (especially prohibitions) and procedural arrangements. They become guardians of the right and proper way, above the sordid politicking of lesser men.

Active-positive Presidents want to achieve results. Active-negatives aim to get and keep power. Passive-positives are after love. Passive-negatives emphasize their civic virtue. The relation of activity to enjoyment in a President thus tends to outline a cluster of characteristics, to set apart the well adapted from the compulsive, compliant, and withdrawn types.

The first four Presidents of the United States, conveniently, ran through this gamut of character types. (Remember, we are talking about tendencies and broad directions; no individual man exactly fits a category.) George Washington—clearly the most important President in the pantheon—established the fundamental legitimacy of an American government at a time when this was a matter in considerable question. Washington's dignity, judiciousness, his aloof air of reserve and dedication to duty, fit the passive-negative or withdrawing type best. Washington did not seek innovation, he sought stability. He longed to retire to Mount Vernon, but fortunately was persuaded to stay on through a second term, in which, by rising above the political conflict between Hamilton and Jefferson and inspiring confidence in his own integrity, he gave the nation time to develop the organized means for peaceful change.

John Adams followed, a dour New England Puritan, much given to work and worry, an impatient and irascible man—an active-negative President, a compulsive type. Adams was far more partisan than Washington; the survival of the system through his Presidency demonstrated that the nation could tolerate, for a time, domination by one of its nascent political parties. As President, an angry Adams brought the United States to the brink of war with France, and presided over the new nation's first experiment in political repression: the Alien and Sedition Acts, forbidding, among other things, unlawful combinations "with intent to oppose any measure or measures of the government of the United States," or "any false, scandalous, and malicious writing or writings against the United States, or the President of the United States, with intent to defame...or to bring them or either of them, into contempt or disrepute."

Then came Jefferson. He too, had his troubles and failures—in the design of national defense, for example. As for his presidential character (only one element in success or failure), Jefferson was clearly active-positive. A child of the Enlightenment, he applied his reason to organizing connections with Congress aimed at strengthening the more popular forces. A man of catholic interests and delightful humor, Jefferson combined a clear and open vision of what the country could be with a profound political sense, expressed in his famous phrase, "Every difference of opinion is not a difference of principle."

The fourth President was James Madison, "little Jemmy," the constitutional philosopher thrown into the White House at a time of great international turmoil. Madison comes closest to the passive-positive, or compliant, type; he suffered from irresolution, tried to compromise his way out, and gave in too readily to the "war-hawks" urging combat with Britain. The nation drifted into war, and Madison wound up ineptly commanding his collection of amateur generals in the streets of Washington. General Jackson's victory at New Orleans saved the Madison administration's historical reputation, but he left the Presidency with the United States close to bankruptcy and secession.

These four Presidents—like all Presidents—were persons trying to cope with the roles they had won by using the equipment they had built over a lifetime. The President is not some shapeless organism in a flood of novelties, but a man with a memory in a system with a history. Like all of us, he draws on his past to shape his future. The pathetic hope that the White House will turn a Caligula into a Marcus Aurelius is as naive as the fear that ultimate power inevitably corrupts. The problem is to understand—and to state understandably—what in the personal past foreshadows the Presidential future.

CURRENT CONTROVERSY

High Crimes and Misdemeanors?

61 | *For Impeachment*
Gary L. Mc Dowell

Gary McDowell argues that "willful and corrupt perjury" as a direct contravention of the rule of law fits comfortably under the framers' notion of "high crimes and misdemeanors." It is the gravity of perjury itself, not the question of whether the perjury refers to "official" or "private" acts, that should control the decision of the House to impeach.

I begin by stating the obvious: Under the logic of our written Constitution of enumerated and limited powers, it is inconceivable that the sole power of impeachment is given to the House of Representatives without restraint. As a result, the most important question to this committee is the meaning of "high Crimes and Misdemeanors." Those words were not mindlessly crafted or chosen because they could be endlessly manipulated. Rather, they constituted one of "those expressions that were most easy to be understood and least equivocal in their meaning."... Their constant use in numerous impeachments stretches back to 1386.

Thus, there is an obligation to determine exactly what "high Crimes and Misdemeanors" meant to those who framed and ratified our Constitution because the ascertainable content of that phrase, as Raoul Berger has pointed out, furnishes the boundaries of power. What was clear to the Founders has become less so to the current generation.

This confusion was best expressed by Gerald Ford's insistence that "an impeachable offense is whatever a majority of the House of Representatives considers it to be at a given moment to history." This is simply not true. To adopt such an understanding, as Joseph Story said, would be to grant Congress an arbitrary discretion incompatible with the genius of our institutions. It would create an absolute despotism of opinion and practice which might make that a crime at one time or in one person which would be deemed innocent at another time.

Impeachment is not to be initiated simply for any reason that might occur to this distinguished House, but only for "Treason, Bribery or other high Crimes and Misdemeanors." It is important to remember that the word "high" in "high Crimes and Misdemeanors" was used to emphasize that it was a crime or misdemeanor against the commonwealth. The objects of impeachment, Alexander Hamilton explained, "are those offenses which proceed from the misconduct of public men, or in other words from the abuse or violation of some public trust. They are of a nature which may with peculiar propriety be denominated POLITICAL, as they relate chiefly to the injuries done immediately to society itself."...

A survey of the common law authorities to whom the Founders looked for guidance, such as Sir William Blackstone, indicates that such crimes against public justice as "obstructing the execution of lawful process" and "willful and corrupt perjury" would have been understood by the Founders as constituting "high Crimes and Misdemeanors" as that phrase was used in the Constitution. Of all of the major common law writers, they saw perjury as one of the most serious offenses against the commonwealth....

Because a witness swears that he will "speak the truth, the whole truth and nothing but the truth," a person under oath cannot cleverly lie and not commit perjury. If the witness conceals any truth, Paley writes, that relates to the matter in adjudication, that "is as much a violation of the oath, as to testify a positive falsehood." It is no excuse for the witness to say he was not forthcoming "because it was never asked of me." An oath obliges to tell all one knows, whether asked or not.

Nor ... can ... [s]hame or embarrassment.. .."justify his concealment of truth, unless it could be shown, that the law which imposes the oath, intended to allow this indulgence to such motives."

The moral and legal inheritance of the founding generation saw the violation of an oath, in Algernon Sidney's words, "as nothing less than treachery." Based on a review of the historical record, the expressed intent of the framers, the voting of the Constitution, the writings of the principal legal authorities known to the framers, and the common law, the conclusion is inescapable that perjury and subornation of perjury must certainly be included as "high Crimes and Misdemeanors" and thus impeachable offenses under the United States Constitution.

Further, the record fails to support the claim that impeachable offenses are limited to only those abuses that occur in the official exercise of executive power. As seen in the authorities, impeachable offenses, in both English and American history, have been understood to extend to, and I quote, "personal misconduct, violations of trust, and im-

morality and imbecility," among other charges of a more private nature. Thus, perjury to conceal private misconduct is still perjury.

The Founders' success in creating the impeachment power to be both politically effective and safe to republican government is reflected in the few instances of its use. Lord Bryce described the power of impeachment over a century ago as "the heaviest piece of artillery in the congressional arsenal," and thus "unfit for ordinary use." The constitutional provisions for impeachment were designed to prevent the President from being driven from office for mere partisan reasons. To get rid of a president, or to try to, Congress has to have good cause. As Bryce said, one does not use impeachment for light and transient reasons, "as one does not use steam hammers to crack nuts."...

You gather here to consider whether to exercise what Hamilton called the "awful discretion" of the impeachment process. In the end, the determination of whether presidential misconduct rises to the level of "high Crimes and Misdemeanors" is left to the discretion and deliberation of this distinguished House.

No small part of that deliberation, guided as it must be by the history and meaning of "high Crimes and Misdemeanors," must weigh what effect the exercise of this extraordinary constitutional sanction would have on the health of the Republic, as against the necessity of making clear that in America no one, not even a popular President, is above the law. In the end, that is what matters most, and that is what must bear most heavily on the Members of this House as you consider what you must do in the weeks ahead. What you decide here, one way or the other, will echo through our history.

62 | *Against Impeachment*
Carl R. Sunstein and Lawrence H. Tribe

Unlike Mc Dowell, Carl Sunstein and Lawrence Tribe believe that context is all important. Their separate testimonies argue that, to be impeachable, a presidential act must be one directed against the American system of government and must ordinarily be an act committed in the official capacity of the president. In short, lies about sex may be prosecutable but cannot and must not be impeachable.

CARL R. SUNSTEIN

My basic submission is that the great function of the Impeachment Clause of the Constitution, not just in the 20th century, not just in the 19th, but in the 18th too, is to allow the country to remove from office those Presidents who have abused public office by using their distinctly presidential powers in a manner that involves egregious or large-scale abuse. This is a suggestion that the President, in order to be impeachable, must as a general rule have misused powers that exist by virtue of the fact that he is the President of the United States.

Under that test, the actions alleged by Judge Starr and others involving President Clinton do not make out an impeachable offense under the Constitution, and an impeachment by the House of Representatives would violate the Constitution of the United States on the allegations as they currently exist....

The text of the Constitution is often ambiguous. With respect to the Due Process Clause and Equal Protection Clause, we may not know a lot, what it means, if we just read it. The text of the Impeachment Clause has a lot more weight and texture in it than these other clauses. It refers to Treason, Bribery or other high Crimes and Misdemeanors....

The word "other" suggests we need acts of the same magnitude and the same nature as treason and bribery. Treason and bribery are terms that go to misuse of distinctly public office, and the word "other" is a clear signal that that is what the framers had in mind.

The word "misdemeanor" is not a reference to small crimes as opposed to felonies. It is a reference to bad conduct of the same kind that would justify removal of a high officer because that is bad conduct of the officer exercised as an officer. The debates on the Constitution are very clear on this. This was not something that just passed by the framers....

Contrary to the draft of the House majority report which is now circulating and has it exactly— bad words—the word "maladministration" was suggested and eliminated, in favor of high Crimes and Misdemeanors, not to expand the power to impeach, as the draft suggests, but just the opposite, to specify and decrease the power. That is what the framers wanted to do with the words "high Crimes and Misdemeanors."...

In the Nation's entire history, only one President has been impeached and only one other President has been subject to serious impeachment inquiry. What is important to underline about this is the dogs that haven't barked in the night. That is, the numerous cases in which Presidents of the United States, sad to say, were engaged in unlawful activity or lying or even criminal activity, and Congress did not choose to impeach. That is even more indicative of a tradition of restraint and forbearance than the two little number cases that we have actually had.

President Nixon was alleged to have been engaged in unlawful tax evasion. The Democrats decided by a healthy majority not to call that an impeachable offense. President Johnson, Presidents Reagan and Bush, even

President Lincoln, who suspended the writ of habeas corpus; President Roosevelt, who lied to the country and violated the law with respect to the Lend-Lease Program for a period of 2 months, none of these, thank goodness, were subject to serious impeachment inquiries as they would have been under the standard suggested today....

I suggest that this case is not close to the line that would be raised by a case involving misuse of distinctly presidential power or imaginable horrendous cases, such as those involving murder or rape and the like.

It is not the case that the Take-Care Clause, the oath of office or the commission of a crime could plausibly justify removal of the President from office. President Truman violated the Take-Care Clause. A majority of the Supreme Court said so in the steel seizure case. President Truman ought not to have been impeachable.

The oath of office has been violated by many Presidents, not by criminal conduct necessarily, but by conduct in violation of civil statutes. That is true with respect to President Roosevelt and President Lincoln, two of our greatest Presidents. They ought not to have been subject to impeachment hearings because they behaved inconsistently with their oath of office....

My concern about using perjury and obstruction of justice as a basis for impeachment here is that surely whether perjury and obstruction of justice are a legitimate basis for impeachment depends on what the perjury and obstruction of justice are about. If the President of the United States perjured himself in defending a friend in connection with a negligence action in an automobile tort suit, there would be no legitimate basis for impeachment.

The ominous fact is that the invocation of impeachment for this kind of perjury makes it very hard to distinguish conceptually numerous cases in which the Congress of the United States has behaved with forbearance and restraint involving Presidents Reagan and Bush and Johnson and Nixon and Lincoln and Roosevelt. The question is whether this can meaningfully be distinguished from

some of those, even if it can conceptually, and people of good faith think it can, conceptually; in practice we are unleashing a terrible caged lion....

Laurence H. Tribe

Nearly everyone who has studied the impeachment clause and its history... has concluded that criminal acts are neither necessary nor sufficient for impeachment, whose central purpose is not to punish, but to protect the functioning of our constitutional system from injury at the hands of Federal officials who turn against the Nation or who corrupt its processes. I think that much is clear from the constitutional text itself, "treason, bribery, or other high Crimes and Misdemeanors."

The decision to exemplify impeachable acts with two of the offenses most threatening to our system of government, treason and bribery, identifies the three great accuracies of impeachable conduct. The high level to which it must rise, and either the end, grave damage to the Nation, or the means, serious corruption of office and abuse of power, that it must entail....

... (B)ribery always, by definition, involves the corrupt use of official government powers, the powers of whoever is getting bribed. The fact that the officer being impeached acted privately as the briber, and not publicly as the bribee, is irrelevant, because the person who bribes is a full partner in a grave corruption and abuse of government power.

I don't think that can be said of perjury, however serious. And I certainly think it is a serious offense, because if perjury succeeds, an indictable wrong has occurred, but it has occurred by concealing the truth from another government body and not by co-opting that body in a scheme to abuse power....

I don't think we can ignore what Professor Sunstein called "all the dogs that didn't bark," the things the House didn't impeach Presidents like Lincoln, Roosevelt, Truman, Johnson, Reagan and Bush for doing.

I also don't think we can ignore the pattern of impeachments voted by the House of

Representatives from 1797 to the present. It is not hard to summarize them. There were only 15. One of a President, one of a Senator, one of a Secretary of War, 12 judges. Fourteen of those 15 cases involved either the gravest abuses of official power, like taking a bribe to use that power for personal benefit, or the most obscene attacks on our Nation and its system of government, like armed rebellion against the United States or military assault upon our allies. There were two cases of the 14 that involved perjury, but they actually dealt with perjury to cover up taking a bribe in a judge's official capacity....

Now, I take very seriously the President's oath to take care that the laws be faithfully executed. But that does not involve the hands-on presiding at trials where telling the truth under oath is the whole point. We have to remember that the President is unlike a judge who serves for life, but wields an authority that evaporates once his veracity can no longer be accepted. The President derives his legitimacy and his capacity to govern 4 years at a time from the electorate, and yes, some people did predict some months ago that a President could no longer lead the Nation or even govern if he had been caught lying under oath. Who would believe him? Knowing that he might, when he leaves office, be subject to prosecution for perjury, how could we govern?

The prediction seems to have been wrong, and I think that the American people, sophisticated or not, do compartmentalize lies about sex affairs and do not equate them with lies about affairs of state. The whole argument about the presidential oath and the Take-Care Clause of the rule of law which Chairman Hyde spoke about so eloquently a while ago, ultimately comes down to the proposition that if we let the Nation's chief law enforcer get away with breaking the law, we will be unable to justify enforcing that law against anyone, and our whole legal system will break down. I call that, with all respect, the "chicken little" argument, "the sky is falling." I don't think any of us really believes it....

(I)f you buy that line of argument, let me underscore this. It would follow, since the theory would be that any law violation by a sitting President is a violation of his oath and of the take-care clause, it would follow that you can impeach the President of the United States more easily than any other civil officer of the government. And making the President uniquely vulnerable to removal, especially on a fuzzy standard like virtue, seems to me to be profoundly unwise. We have only one President at a time; we have 1,200 or 1,300 judges.

Removing a President, even just impeaching him, paralyzes the country. Removing him decapitates a coordinate branch. And remember that the President's limited term provides a kind of check, and if the check fails, he can be prosecuted when he leaves.

To impeach on the novel basis suggested here when we have impeached only one President in our history, and we have lived to see that action universally condemned; and when we have the wisdom not to impeach Presidents Reagan or Bush over Iran-Contra; and when we have come close to impeaching only one other President for the most wide-ranging abuse of presidential power subversive of the Constitution would lower the bar dramatically, would trivialize a vital check. It may be a caged lion, but it will lose its fangs if we use it too promiscuously and would permanently weaken the President and the Nation, leaving a legacy all of us in time would come to regret deeply....

CHAPTER TEN

Bureaucracy
Responding to Whom?

OVERVIEW AND SUMMARY

You are not the only one who thinks that bureaucracy is the problem. Most people find bureaucracy to be a convenient target. There is no shortage of amusing stories that seem to demonstrate that bureaucrats are incompetent. However, more serious political questions underlie criticisms of the bureaucratic branch. The issue is not the mere inconvenience of dealing with a surly clerk at the local bureau of motor vehicles.

How much power do administrators have? Do they do what they want regardless of how they are instructed to behave by the legislature or the elected executive? Do they naturally abuse their power in an attempt to gain more power? In whose interest do they work? These questions are as old as bureaucracy itself.

Indeed, **Herbert Hoover**, on the eve of his election to the presidency, made the case against a growing government and stifling bureaucracy. The increasing regulation of private economic and social behavior, he argued, leads inevitably to less and less freedom of political action. Since liberalism is about the freedoms of speech, press, and assembly, as well as equality of opportunity, liberalism's goal cannot be to introduce more government regulation and bureaucracy; to the contrary, its goal must be to set limits of government power.

What Hoover and other critics of government bureaucracy might sometimes overlook is that, to be fair, government sometimes has to intervene in private behavior. Thus, the American novelist **Upton Sinclair** tried to show that government intervention was often needed to modify the ill effects of private behavior. In Sinclair's novel about immigrants to the United States, his characters attempt to pursue the American dream in the bustling industrial town of Chicago. In *The Jungle* (1905), everything goes wrong for everyone despite hard work and honesty. Everything goes wrong because private individuals and businesses lie, cheat, and steal at every opportunity.

Sinclair, a socialist and a political activist who nearly became governor of California in 1934, was trying to make the point that government was sorely needed to provide a fair structure of equality and opportunity for individuals. Much to Sinclair's chagrin, the nation took a different view than his novel. The main characters in *The Jungle* happened to work for the nasty and greedy capitalists in a meat-packing plant. Sinclair's entirely realistic description of what went on in the meat-packing industry disgusted his readers and prompted an outcry for government intervention only in that specific industry. (The meat packers contemplated their prospects of successfully suing Sinclair for libel but never acted.) And thus was a new bureaucracy born, which became the Federal Food and Drug Administration (FDA). Even if the FDA is sometimes criticized for being too slow and too exacting in its standards, there are few people who would care to return to the days of unregulated and unsupervised food production. Like many other agencies and departments, the FDA bureaucracy lives on because it performs a function that much of the public thinks is beneficial.

If there is support for the *functions* of bureaucracy, perhaps the problem is not the functions themselves but the people who actually perform them, that is, the *bureaucrats*. Perhaps it is the bureaucrats themselves who are incompetent or lazy or merely self-serving seekers of higher salaries, larger offices, and more functions to perform. Perhaps too much power has been delegated to them. In fact, one of the enduring criticisms of bureaucracy by both citizens and elected officials is that the bureaucrats seem to have a mind and an agenda of their own, that they exercise too much influence over the way in which the details of the political process work out.

It is true that bureaucrats, especially high-level administrators and their politically chosen bosses, do have a substantial influence on any legislation that affects their bureau. Many agencies also have a great deal of discretion and influence because they are allowed, by authority of Congress, to make public regulations (as well as to enforce them). For example, the Internal Revenue Service (IRS) makes rulings on the tax code; the Occupational Safety and Hazard Administration (OSHA) makes rules about safety in the workplace; the Environmental Protection Agency (EPA) regulates the disposal of toxic wastes, air emissions, and discharges into waterways. In this way, such bureaus are actually going beyond the laws made by Congress; and thus they are strongly suspected of being malicious rivals of the elective organs of democracy and of substituting their own will for that of the people. However, **Norton E. Long**, a pluralist theorist, argues to the contrary.

Long claims that the bureaucracy, rather than being an upstart "fourth branch of government," is actually a crucial part of the intricate democratic and constitutional organism. According to Long, the massive bureaucracy softens the hard edges of electoral competition. Long points out, for example, that bureaucrats as a group are more representative of the American people than are members of Congress when one compares their demographic characteristics. This is especially true when one compares the income and assets of members of Congress to the income of bureaucrats. Moreover, says Long, these bureaucrats are more likely to take a broad and far-reaching view of issues than are elected representatives, who answer to narrow constituencies in their peculiar geographical districts.

In short, elected officials are forced by elections to take the short and narrow view of things based on the loud demands of a small number of politically active people; bureaucrats have the expertise and the careerist's commitment to take the long and broad view of the same issues. For Long, bureaucracy is an important contributor to that dynamic equilibrium of truly representative democracy in which public policy approximates all the interests of society.

Like Long, **James Q. Wilson** defends the American bureaucracy as a democratic affair. Wilson does not, however, resort to pluralist theory to make his defense. He points out that most Americans think of the bureaucracy problem in *a*political terms: one of improper management or administrative inefficiency. They also think that the solution involves getting the right people to run the bureaucracy or redesigning administrative channels of authority or finding the right technical solution to social problems.

Wilson says, however, that to the extent there is a bureaucracy problem it is a consequence of the American Constitution, which at its conception made no provision for how things were to be administrated. The framers were concerned not with making the administration of government "efficient and powerful" but with making it "tolerable and malleable." To deal with the bureaucracy problem, then, would require a radical alteration of the Constitution—an unacceptable sacrifice that would result in a more efficient administration but also in bigger and less accessible government. Thus Wilson concludes that however frustrating the bureaucracy problem seems, the system is in fact open to the redress of grievances and does essentially work.

Richard A. Loverd, a professor of public administration, offers a balanced answer to the popular question, why can't government be more like business? Having private companies perform tasks once done by public bureaucracies has met with at least some modicum of success in many places and sectors. A little success, naturally, has led both policymakers and the public to wonder how far the experiment can go.

Whereas Loverd acknowledges that some discreet tasks, such as sanitation or mass transit, can be contracted to private companies, he concludes that asking government managers to act like private managers is not possible. Public managers of public trusts are naturally different from their counterparts in the private world precisely because government is not a business. Government departments are, by design, diffuse, political, bureaucratic, and very public. Thus, whereas government, too, aims to get things done, and whereas efficiency in government is desirable, government is not centralized, it has no profit motive, and its organs and agencies exist to promote equality of opportunity and to protect people. In sum, the privitization of government functions has natural limits as long as citizens in a democracy demand some measure of equality, access to government decisions, and accountability.

63 | *The Liberal Principles of Decentralized Self-Government*

Herbert Hoover

On the campaign trail a month before he would be elected the thirty-first president of the United States, Herbert Hoover spoke against excessive government regulation and control of business. Bureaucratic control, he argued, necessarily limits individual freedom. This self-made millionaire who grew up on a farm noted that big business, too, can transgress and that some government regulation is necessary. However, a truly liberal system should not expand government bureaucracy but set limits to it.

... Bureaucracy is ever desirous of spreading its influence and its power. You cannot extend the mastery of the government over the daily working life of a people without at the same time making it the master of the people's souls and thoughts. Every expansion of government in business means that government in order to protect itself from the political consequences of its errors and wrongs is driven irresistibly without peace to greater and greater control of the nation's press and platform. Free speech does not live many hours after free industry and free commerce die.

It is a false liberalism that interprets itself into the government operation of commercial business. Every step of bureaucratizing of the business of our country poisons the very roots of liberalism—that is, political equality, free speech, free assembly, free press, and equality of opportunity. It is the road not to more liberty, but to less liberty. Liberalism should be found not striving to spread bureaucracy but striving to set bounds to it. True liberalism seeks all legitimate freedom first in the confident belief that without such freedom the pursuit of all other blessings and benefits is vain. That belief is the foundation of all American progress, political as well as economic.

Liberalism is a force truly of the spirit, a force proceeding from the deep realization that economic freedom cannot be sacrificed if political freedom is to be preserved. Even if governmental conduct of business could give us more efficiency instead of less efficiency, the fundamental objection to it would remain unaltered and unabated. It would destroy political equality. It would increase rather than decrease abuse and corruption. It would stifle initiative and invention. It would undermine the development of leadership. It would cramp and cripple the mental and spiritual energies of our people. It would extinguish equality and opportunity. It would dry up the spirit of liberty and progress. For these reasons primarily it must be resisted. For 150 years liberalism has found its true spirit in the American system, not in the European systems.

I do not wish to be misunderstood in this statement. I am defining a general policy. It does not mean that our government is to part with one iota of its national resources without complete protection to the public interest. I have already stated that where the government is engaged in public works for purposes of flood control, of navigation, of irrigation, of scientific research or national defense, or in pioneering a new art, it will at times necessarily produce power or commodities as a by-product. But they must be a by-product of the major purpose, not the major purpose itself.

Nor do I wish to be misinterpreted as believing that the United States is a free-for-all and devil-take-the-hindmost. The very essence of equality of opportunity and of American individualism is that there shall be no domination by any group or combination in this republic, whether it be business or political. On the contrary, it demands economic justice as well as political and social justice. It is no system of laissez faire.

I feel deeply on this subject because during the war I had some practical experience with governmental operation and control. I have witnessed not only at home but abroad the many failures of government in business. I have seen its tyrannies, its injustices, its destructions of self-government, its undermining of the very instincts which carry our people forward to progress. I have witnessed the lack of advance, the lowered standards of living, the depressed spirits of people working under such a system. My objection is based not upon theory or upon a failure to recognize wrong or abuse, but I know the adoption of such methods would strike at the very roots of American life and would destroy the very basis of American progress.

Our people have the right to know whether we can continue to solve our great problems without abandonment of our American system. I know we can. We have demonstrated that our system is responsive enough to meet any new and intricate development in our economic and business life. We have demonstrated that we can meet any economic problem and still maintain our democracy as master in its own house, and that we can at the same time preserve equality of opportunity and individual freedom.

In the last fifty years we have discovered that mass production will produce articles for us at half the cost they required previously. We have seen the resultant growth of large units of production and distribution. This is big business. Many businesses must be bigger, for our tools are bigger, our country is bigger. We now build a single dynamo of 100,000 horsepower. Even fifteen years ago that would have been a big business all by itself. Yet today advance in production requires that we set ten of these units together in a row.

The American people from bitter experience have a rightful fear that great business units might be used to dominate our industrial life and by illegal and unethical practices destroy equality of opportunity. Years ago the Republican administration established the principle that such evils could be corrected by regulation. It developed methods by which abuses could be prevented while the full value of industrial progress could be retained for the public. It insisted upon the principle that when great public utilities were clothed with the security of partial monopoly, whether it be railways, power plants, telephones, or what not, then there must be the fullest and most complete control of rates, services, and finances by government or local agencies. It declared that these businesses must be conducted with glass pockets.

As to our great manufacturing and distributing industries, the Republican Party insisted upon the enactment of laws that not only would maintain competition but would destroy conspiracies to destroy the smaller units or dominate and limit the equality of opportunity among our people.

One of the great problems of government is to determine to what extent the government shall regulate and control commerce and industry and how much it shall leave it alone. No system is perfect. We have had many abuses in the private conduct of business. That every good citizen resents. It is just as important that business keep out of government as that government keep out of business.

Nor am I setting up the contention that our institutions are perfect. No human ideal is ever perfectly attained, since humanity itself is not perfect.

The wisdom of our forefathers in their conception that progress can only be attained as the sum of the accomplishment of free individuals has been reinforced by all of the great leaders of the country since that day. Jackson, Lincoln, Cleveland, McKinley, Roosevelt, Wilson, and Coolidge have stood unalterably for these principles.

And what have been the results of our American system? Our country has become the land of opportunity to those born without inheritance, not merely because of the wealth of its resources and industry but because of this freedom of initiative and enterprise. Russia has natural resources equal to ours. Her people are equally industrious, but she has not had the blessing of 150 years of our form of government and of our social system.

By adherence to the principles of decentralized self-government, ordered liberty, equal opportunity, and freedom to the individual, our American experiment in human welfare has yielded a degree of well-being unparalleled in all the world. It has come nearer to the abolition of poverty, to the abolition of fear of want than humanity has ever reached before. Progress of the past seven years has been the proof of it. This alone furnishes the answer to our opponents, who ask us to introduce destructive elements into the system by which this has been accomplished.

64 | *The Jungle*
Upton Sinclair

Upton Sinclair was a prolific writer and one of a few well-known American socialists. He nearly won the governorship of California in 1934 but is best remembered for The Jungle, *a novel he intended as an indictment of the predatory nature of capitalism. Instead, he seemed only to indict the meat-packing industry. The Food and Drug Administration was formed by a government whose people were sick to their stomach after reading Sinclair's book.*

Little Kotrina was like most children of the poor, prematurely old; she had to take care of her little brother, who was a cripple, and also of the baby; she had to cook the meals and wash the dishes and clean house, and have supper ready when the workers came home in the evening. She was only thirteen, and small for her age, but she did all this without a murmur; and her mother went out, and after trudging a couple days about the yards, settled down as a servant of a "sausage machine."

Elzbieta was used to working, but she found this change a hard one, for the reason that she had to stand motionless upon her feet from seven o'clock in the morning till half-past twelve, and again from one till half-past five. For the first few days it seemed to her that she could not stand it, and would come out at sundown with her head fairly reeling. Besides this, she was working in one of the dark holes, by electric light, and the dampness, too, was deadly—there were always puddles of water on the floor, and a sickening odor of moist flesh in the room. The people who worked here followed the ancient custom of nature, whereby the ptarmigan is the color of dead leaves in the fall and of snow in the winter, and the chameleon, who is black when he lies upon a stump and turns green when he moves to a leaf. The men and women who worked in this department were precisely the color of the "fresh country sausage" they made.

The sausage room was an interesting place to visit, for two or three minutes, and provided that you did not look at the people; the machines were perhaps the most wonderful things in the entire plant. Presumably sausages were once chopped and stuffed by hand, and if so it would be interesting to know how many workers had been displaced by these inventions. On one side of the room were the hoppers, into which men shovelled loads of meat and wheelbarrows full of spices; in these great bowls were whirling knives that made two thousand revolutions a minute, and when the meat was ground fine and adulterated with potato flour, and well mixed with water, it was forced to the stuffing machines on the other side of the room. The latter were tended by women; there was a sort of spout, like the nozzle of a hose, and one of the women would take a long string of "casing" and put the end over the nozzle and then work the whole thing on, as one works on the finger of a tight glove. This string would be twenty or thirty feet long, but the woman would have it all on in a jiffy; and when she had several on, she would press a lever, and a stream of sausage meat would be shot out, taking the casing with it as it came. Thus one might stand and see appear, miraculously born from the machine, a wriggling snake of sausage of incredible length. In front was a big pan which caught these creatures, and two more women who seized them as fast as they appeared and twisted them into links. This was for the uninitiated the most perplexing work of all, for all that the woman had to give was a single turn of the wrist; and in some way she contrived to give it so that instead of an endless chain of sausages, one after another, there grew under her hands a bunch of strings, all dangling from a single center. It was quite like the feat of a prestidigitator—for the woman worked so fast that the eye could literally not follow her, and there was only a mist of motion, and tangle after tangle of sausages appearing. In the midst of the mist, however, the visitor would suddenly notice the tense set face, with the two wrinkles graven in the forehead, and the ghastly pallor of the cheeks; and then he would suddenly recollect that it was time he was going on. The woman did not go on: she stayed right there—hour after hour, day after day, year after year, twisting sausage links and racing with death. It was piece work, and she was apt to have a family to keep alive; and stern and ruthless economic laws had arranged it that she could only do this by working just as she did, with all her soul upon her work, and with never an instant for a glance at the well-dressed ladies and gentlemen who came to stare at her, as at some wild beast in a menagerie.

With one member trimming beef in a cannery, and another working in a sausage factory, the family had a first-hand knowledge of the great majority of Packingtown swindles. For it was the custom, as they found, whenever meat was so spoiled that it could not be used for anything else, either to can it or else to chop it up into sausage. With what had been told them by Jonas, who had worked in the pickle rooms, they could now study the whole of the spoiled-meat industry on the inside, and read a new and grim meaning into that old Packingtown jest—that they use everything of the pig except the squeal.

Jonas had told them how the meat that was taken out of pickle would often be found sour, and how they would rub it up with soda to take away the smell, and sell it to be eaten on free-lunch counters; also of all the miracles of chemistry which they performed, giving to any sort of meat, fresh or salted, whole or chopped, any color and any flavor and any odor they chose. In the pickling of hams they had an ingenious apparatus, by which they saved time and increased the capacity of the plant—a machine consisting of a hollow needle attached to a pump; by plunging this needle into the meat and working with his foot a man could fill a ham with pickle in a few seconds. And yet, in spite of this, there would be hams found spoiled, some of them with an odor so bad that a man could hardly bear to be in the room with them. To pump into these the packers had a second and much stronger pickle which destroyed the odor—a process known to the workers as "giving them thirty per cent." Also, after the hams had been smoked, there would be found some that had gone to the bad. Formerly these had been sold as "Number Three Grade," but later on some ingenious person had hit upon a new device, and now they would extract the bone, about which the bad part generally lay, and insert in the hole a white-hot iron. After this invention there was no longer Number One, Two, and Three Grade—there was only Number One Grade. The packers were always originating such schemes—they had what they called "boneless hams," which were all the odds and ends of pork stuffed into casings; and "California hams," which were the shoulders, with big knuckle joints, and nearly all the meat cut out; and fancy "skinned hams" which were made of the oldest hogs, whose skins were so heavy and coarse that no one would buy them—that is, until they had been cooked and chopped fine and labelled "head cheese."

It was only when the whole ham was spoiled that it came into the department of Elzbieta. Cut up by the two-thousand-revolution-a-minute-flyers, and mixed with half a ton of other meat, no odor that ever was in a ham could make any difference. There was never the least attention paid to what was cut up for sausage; there would come all the way back from Europe old sausage that had been rejected, and that was mouldy and white—it would be dosed with borax and glycerine, and dumped into the hoppers, and made over again for home consumption. There would be meat that had tumbled out on the floor, in the dirt and sawdust where the workers had tramped and spit uncounted billions of tubercular germs. There would be meat stored in great piles in rooms; and the water from leaky roofs would drip over it, and thousands of rats would race about on it. It was too dark in these storage places to see well, but a man could run his hand over these piles of meat and sweep off handfuls of the dried dung of rats. These rats were nuisances, and the packers would put poisoned bread out for them, they would die, and then rats, bread, and meat would go into the hoppers together. This is no fairy story and no joke; the meat would be shovelled into carts, and the man who did the shoveling would not trouble to lift out a rat even when he saw one—there were things that went into the sausage in comparison with which a poisoned rat was a tidbit. There was no place for the men to wash their hands before they ate their dinner, and so they made a practice of washing them in the water that was to be ladled into the sausage. There were the butt-ends of smoked meat, and the scraps of corned beef, and all the odds and ends of the waste of the plants, that would be dumped into old barrels in the cellar and left there. Under the system of rigid economy which the packers enforced, there were some jobs that it only paid to do once in a long time, and among these was the cleaning out of the waste barrels. Every spring they did it; and in the barrels would be dirt and rust and old nails and stale water—and cart load after cart load of it would be taken up and dumped into the hoppers with fresh meat, and sent out to the public's breakfast. Some of it they would make into "smoked sausage"—but as the smoking took time, and was therefore expensive, they would call upon their chemistry department, and preserve it with borax and color it with gelatine to make it brown. All of their sausage came out of the same bowl, but when they came to wrap it they would stamp some of it "special" and for this they would charge two cents more a pound.

Such were the new surroundings in which Elzbieta was placed, and such was the work she was compelled to do. It was stupefying, brutalizing work; it left her no time to think, no strength, for anything. She was part of the machine she tended, and every faculty that was not needed for the machine was doomed to be crushed out of existence. There was only one mercy about the cruel grind—that it gave her the gift of insensibility. Little by little she sank into a torpor—she fell silent. She would meet Jurgis, and Ona in the evening, and the three of them would walk home together, often without saying a word. Ona, too, was falling into a habit of silence—Ona, who had once gone about singing like a bird. She was sick and miserable, and often she would barely have strength enough to drag herself home. And there they would eat what they had to eat, and afterwards, because there was only their misery to talk of, they would crawl into bed and fall into a stupor and never stir until it was time to get up again, and dress by candlelight, and go back to the machines. They were so numbed that they did not even suffer much from hunger, now; only the children continued to fret when the food ran short.

65 | *Bureaucracy and Constitutionalism: A Pluralist Case*
Norton E. Long

Some have suggested that the bureaucracy has become the fourth branch of government, and Norton E. Long argues that it should be the fourth branch. The bureaucracy, he claims, is far more representative than Congress. Bureaucracy represents and advocates positions that would otherwise be lost among the electioneering influences that drive the members of congressional committees. Long's bureaucracy fosters a pluralist, and therefore more democratic, government.

The role of the legislature and of the political executive may come to consist largely of encouraging, discouraging and passing on policy which wells up from the agencies of administration. All of this is because the bureaucracy is not just an instrument to carry out a will formed by the elected Congress and President. It is itself a medium for registering the diverse wills that make up the people's will and for transmuting them into responsible proposals for public policy.

Growth in the power of the bureaucracy is looked upon as a menace to Constitutionalism. By some it is seen as a dangerous enhancement of the power of the President, by others as an alarming accretion of power to a non-elective part of the government. The logic of *either-or* sees a cumulative process in which the supremacy of the elected legislative is replaced by the supremacy of an appointed bureaucracy. Given the alternative, the choice of the supremacy of an elected legislature would be clear, but that choice is an unreal bogy. To meet our needs, we have worked out a complex system in which the bureaucracy and legislature perform complementary and interlocking functions. Both are necessary, and the supremacy of either would be a constitutional misfortune.

Others have argued that the essence of Constitutionalism is the division of power in such a way as to provide a system of effective regularized restraints upon governmental action. The purpose of this division of power is not to create some mechanical equipoise among the organs of government but so to represent the diversity of the community that its own pluralism is reflected in a pluralism within the government. Now it is extremely clear that our Congress fails to do this and that the bureaucracy in considerable measure compensates for its deficiency. Important and vital interests in the United States are unrepresented, underrepresented, or malrepresented in Congress. These interests receive more effective and more responsible representation through administrative channels than through the legislature.

To the modern student of government, Aristotle's characterization of an election as an oligarchical device always comes somewhat as a shock. Nonetheless, its implications for representative democracy are significant. If one were to set forth in law the facts of life of the American Congress, it would appear that, to be eligible, overwhelmingly a candidate had first to be in the upper, upper-income bracket or second, either personally or through his associates, to be able to command substantial sums of money.

While the Jacksonian conception of the civil service as a domain for the common man was not expressly designed as a balance to the inevitably oligarchical aspects of an elected legislature, it has been influential in that direction. Accustomed as we are to the identification of election with both representation and democracy, it seems strange at first to consider that the non-elected civil service may be both more representative of the country and more democratic in its composition than the Congress.

As it operates in the civil service, the recruitment process brings into federal employment and positions of national power, persons whose previous affiliations, training, and background cause them to conceive of themselves as representing constituencies that are relatively uninfluential in Congress. These constituencies, like that of the presidency, are in the aggregate numerically very large; and in speaking for them as self-appointed, or frequently actually appointed, representatives, the bureaucrats fill in the deficiencies of the process of representation in the legislature. The importance of this representation lies not only in offsetting such defects as rural overrepresentation, the self-contained district, and other vagaries of our system that leave many without a voice, but in the qualitative representation of science, the professions, the institutions of learning, and the conscience of society as it is expressed in churches, civil liberties groups, and a host of others.

The democratic character of the civil service stems from its origin, income level, and associations. The process of selection of the civil service, its contacts, milieu, and income level after induction make the civil service as a body a better sample of the mass of the people than Congress. Lacking a caste system to wall them off from their fellows, the members of this sample are likely to be more responsive to the desires and needs of the broad public than a highly selected slice whose responsiveness is enforced by a mechanism of elections that frequently places more power in the hands of campaign-backers than voters. Furthermore, it is unlikely that any overhauling of our system of representation in Congress will remove the need for supplementary representation through the bureaucracy. The working interaction of President, Congress, courts, and the administrative branch makes the constitutional system a going concern—not the legal supremacy of anyone of them.

It is not by any means sure that the people think that what they want is the same as what Congress wants. In fact there is considerable evidence that the ordinary person views Congress members, if not Congress as an institution, with considerable skepticism. The retort that the people elected the Congress falls somewhat wide of the mark. Given the system of parties and primaries, rural overrepresentation, seniority rule, interest-dominated committees, and all the devices that give potent minorities a disproportionate say, it should occasion no surprise if Congress' claim exclusively to voice what the people want be taken with reservations.

If one rejects the view that election is the *sine qua non* of representation, the bureaucracy now has a very real claim to be considered much more representative of the American people in its composition than the Congress. This is not merely the case with respect to the class structure of the country but, equally significantly, with respect to the learned groups, skills, economic interests, races, nationalities, and religions. The rich diversity that makes up the United States is better represented in its civil service than anywhere else.

Responsibility is a product of responsible institutions; and with all their deficiencies—which are many indeed—the departments of administration come closer than any other organs of government to achieving responsible behavior by virtue of the breadth and depth of their consideration of the relevant facts and because of the representative character of their personnel. As continuing organizations, they can learn from their mistakes. They can even make their mistakes meaningful. That is, they can make explicit to themselves the hypotheses on which they act and so make failure itself a source of knowledge. In however limited a form, these agencies are organized to make self-corrective behavior possible.

The difficulties of arriving at self-corrective behavior in the disorganized and heatedly partisan atmosphere of Congress are all too apparent. In the absence of a disciplined party system with reasonable continuity of leadership, conditions are too anarchical in our Congress to permit that body to try to organize its experience for the production of knowledge. The conditions of political success do not encourage the cooperative corporate endeavor that characterizes our successful disciplines dedicated to the discovery of fact and the testing of hypothesis.

Through the breadth of the interests represented in its composition, the bureaucracy provides a significant constitutionalizing element of pluralism in our government. Through its structure, permanence, and processes, it provides a medium in which the conditions requisite for the national interpretation of experience can develop. Thus it has a substantial part to play in the working constitution as representative organ and as a source of rationality.

Given the views and composition of Congress, it is a fortunate fact of our working constitution that it is complemented by a bureaucracy indoctrinated with the fundamental ideals of Constitutionalism. This varied group, rooted in the diversity of the country, can be counted on to provide important representation for its pluralism. In a real and important sense, it provides a constitutional check on both legislature and executive.

It is high time that the administrative branch is recognized as an actual and potentially great addition to the forces of Constitutionalism. The advice of the devotees of Locke would make it a neutral instrument, a gun for hire by any party. Fortunately, such advice cannot be taken. Far better would be to recognize that, by appropriate recruitment, structure, and processes, the bureaucracy can be made a vital part of a functioning constitutional democracy, filling out the deficiencies of the Congress and the political executive. The theory of our constitution needs to recognize and understand the working and the potential of our great fourth branch of government, taking a rightful place beside President, Congress, and Courts.

66 | *Bureaucracy and the American Regime*
James Q. Wilson

A political scientist and professor of management at UCLA, James Q. Wilson argues that insofar as there is a bureaucracy problem, it is not a management problem but a political consequence of our Constitution's separation of powers. Our political system was not designed to be efficient "but to be tolerable and malleable." The bureaucracy may be more unwieldly or more costly or less efficient than we would like it to be, says Wilson, but it is open to citizen participation, critisism, investigation, and change—and as such, is a very democratic affair.

In short, you can have less bureaucracy only if you have less government. Many, if not most, of the difficulties we experience in dealing with government agencies arise from the agencies being part of a fragmented and open political system. If an agency is to have a sense of mission, if constraints are to be minimized, if authority is to be decentralized, if officials are to be judged on the basis of the outputs they produce rather than the inputs they consume, then legislators, judges, and lobbyists will have to act against their own interests. They will have to say "no" to influential constituents, forgo the opportunity to expand their own influence, and take seriously the task of judging the organizational feasibility as well as the political popularity of a proposed new program. It is hard to imagine this happening, partly because politicians and judges have no incentive to make it happen and partly because there are certain tasks a democratic government must undertake even if they cannot be performed efficiently. The greatest mistake citizens can make when they complain of "the bureaucracy" is to suppose that their frustrations arise simply out of management problems; they do not—they arise out of governance problems.

The central feature of the American constitutional system—the separation of powers—exacerbates many of these problems. The governments of the United States were not designed to be efficient or powerful, but to be tolerable and malleable. Those who devised these arrangements always assumed that the federal government would exercise few and limited powers. As long as that assumption was correct (which it was for a century and a half) the quality of public administration was not a serious problem except in the minds of those reformers (Woodrow Wilson was probably the first) who desired to rationalize government in order to rationalize society. The founders knew that the separation of powers would make it so difficult to start a new program or to create a new agency that it was hardly necessary to think about how those agencies would be administered. As a result, the Constitution is virtually silent on what kind of administration we should have. At least until the Civil War thrust the problem on us, scarcely anyone in the country would have known what you were talking about if you spoke of the "problem of administration."

Matters were very different in much of Europe. Kings and princes long had ruled; when their authority was captured by parliaments, the tradition of ruling was already well established. From the first the ministers of the parliamentary regimes thought about the problems of administration because in those countries there was something to administer. The centralization of executive authority in the hands of a prime minister and the exclusion (by and large) of parliament from much say in executive affairs facilitated the process of controlling the administrative agencies and bending them to some central will. The constitutions of many European states easily could have been written by a school of management.

Today, the United States at every level has big and active governments. Some people worry that a constitutional system well-designed to preserve liberty when governments were small is poorly designed to implement policy now that governments are large. The contrast between how the United States and the nations of Western Europe manage environmental and industrial regulation is illuminating: Here the separation of powers insures, if not causes, clumsy and adversarial regulation; there the unification of powers permits, if not causes, smooth and consensual regulation.

I am not convinced that the choice is that simple, however. It would take another book to judge the advantages and disadvantages of the separation of powers. The balance sheet on both sides of the ledger would contain many more entries than those that derive from a discussion of public administration. But even confining our attention to administration, there is more to be said for the American system than many of its critics admit.

America has a paradoxical bureaucracy unlike that found in almost any other advanced nation. The paradox is the existence in one set of institutions of two qualities ordinarily quite separate: the multiplication of rules and the opportunity for access. We have a system laden with rules; elsewhere that is a sure sign that the bureaucracy is aloof from the people, distant from their concerns, and preoccupied with the power and privileges of the bureaucrats—an elaborate, grinding machine that can crush the spirit of any who dare oppose it. We also have a system suffused with participation: advisory boards, citizen groups, neighborhood councils, congressional investigators, crusading journalists, and lawyers serving writs; elsewhere this popular involvement would be taken as evidence that the administrative system is no system at all, but a bungling, jerry-built contraption wallowing in inefficiency and shot through with corruption and favoritism.

That these two traits, rules and openness, could coexist would have astonished Max Weber and continues to astonish (or elude)

many contemporary students of the subject. Public bureaucracy in this country is neither as rational and predictable as Weber hoped nor as crushing and mechanistic as he feared. It is rule-bound without being overpowering, participatory without being corrupt. This paradox exists partly because of the character of mores of the American people: They are too informal, spontaneous, and other-directed to be either neutral arbiters or passionless Gradgrinds. And partly it exists because of the nature of the regime: Our constitutional system, and above all the exceptional power enjoyed by the legislative branch, makes it impossible for us to have anything like a government by appointed experts but easy for individual citizens to obtain redress from the abuses of power. Anyone who wishes it otherwise would have to produce a wholly different regime, and curing the mischiefs of bureaucracy seems an inadequate reason for doing that. Parliamentary regimes that supply more consistent direction to their bureaucracies also supply more bureaucracy to their citizens. The fragmented American regime may produce chaotic government, but the coherent European regimes produce bigger governments.

In the meantime we live in a country that despite its baffling array of rules and regulations and the insatiable desire of some people to use government to rationalize society still makes it possible to get drinkable water instantly, put through a telephone call in seconds, deliver a letter in a day, and obtain a passport in a week. Our Social Security checks arrive on time. Some state prisons, and most of the federal ones, are reasonably decent and humane institutions. The great majority of Americans, cursing all the while, pay their taxes. One can stand on the deck of an aircraft carrier during night flight operations and watch two thousand nineteen-year-old boys faultlessly operate one of the most complex organizational systems ever created. There are not many places where all this happens. It is astonishing it can be made to happen at all.

Can We Run Government Like a Business?

67 | *Privitization and Public Control: Why Make Public Management More Businesslike?*

Richard A. Loverd

A professor of public administration, Richard A. Loverd questions how much public management can emulate private, corporate management. Government bureaucracy is different from private business because by its design and nature it is (1) diffuse, (2) political, (3) bureaucratic, and (4) very public. And although private contractors can provide some public services, one must be aware that a private contractor has less, not more, public accountability.

About a century ago, in a less known passage from his classic essay, "The Study of Administration," Woodrow Wilson noted that in public bureaucracies the same administrative means can be used for any number of fair or foul purposes. As an example, the future president pointed out that "If I see a murderous fellow sharpening a knife cleverly, I can borrow his way of sharpening the knife without borrowing his probable intention to commit murder with it."

In much the same way, private sector approaches in public management can be viewed from a variety of perspectives. For some observers, they are considered as something akin to a murderous weapon destructive of public practice. Others view them as a blunt instrument with largely irrelevant effects. And still others judge them as above reproach, since business techniques are thought to be so far superior to those of government. In this article, we first consider why it is so difficult for the government to be more "businesslike" in its management, and then examine whether business should instead take on the government's work through what has come to known as "privatization."

Why Can't the Government Be More Businesslike?

Public sector management is far from easy. It requires a good deal of competence, courage, tact and tenacity for those who try it. There are few easy victories.

In no small part this lack of ease in management is due to the constraints which surround public officials and provide them with an environment which is *diffuse, political, bureaucratic, very public* and therefore more challenging than the private sector.

(1) It's Diffuse. At base, our system of government was designed to be anything but manageable; it is purposefully, indeed constitutionally, difficult and diffuse. Such ideas are echoed in the words of political scientist Graham Allison: "In business, the functions of the general management are centralized in a single individual: the Chief Executive Officer.... In contrast, in the U.S. government, the functions of general management are constitutionally spread among competing institutions: the executive, two houses of Congress, and the courts." Thus, as Justice

Brandeis observed, the constitutional goal was "not to promote efficiency but to preclude the exercise of arbitrary power." And, again, as *The Federalist Papers* make clear, the aim of the founders was very different from that of setting up a business. It was "to prevent concentration of the several powers in the same branch" by "giving those who administer each branch the constitutional means and personal motives to resist encroachment of the others."

Furthermore, the view is expanded beyond constitutional boundaries by political scientist Jonathan Brock who notes that "in public employment, the separation of personnel authority does not stop with the constitutional separation of powers.... Typically a [public sector] manager shares authority and influence with personnel officers, classifiers, job analysts, budget officers, civil service boards and commissions, selection panels, and a host of others who have technical or other roles to play in personnel selection, compensation and other matters." Indeed, with power divided and ambition pitted against ambition, it is sometimes a wonder that such managers respond as well as they do!

(2) It's Political. Of course, the very diffusion of power, pitting ambition against ambition, encourages political activity as managers try to marshal forces which will help them accomplish tasks, protect prerogatives and, where possible, expand their power bases. In so doing, in addition to the power vested in their formal positions, they might use rules, funds, jobs, expertise, tradition, charisma, information, timing, group pressure and any number of other power sources to influence those within and around their immediate work settings.

As an especially instructive example, jobs have served as a source of power, particularly political party power, throughout the history of American public management. During the 1800's, from around the time of Presidents Jackson to Garfield, government jobs were viewed as "spoils" or prizes to be given to those who worked for the party and helped victorious candidates win public office. Con-

sequently, partisan service, rather than individual competence, was used as the basis for awarding public jobs; and the jobs themselves were deemed of little importance except as they contributed to party power.

Unfortunately, the spoils system soon became a two-edged sword, sharper on one side than the other. Although it proved helpful to the party leadership, it became quite harmful to the country. Because their jobs tended to last only as long as their party candidates were in office, appointees were tempted to follow the advice as expressed by New York City Tammany Ward boss George Washington Plunkett and "see their opportunities and take 'em," plundering their public trusts for personal gain.

Thus, the use of jobs as a political means for enhancing party power came to be associated with a lack of competence and an excess of corruption in the government. And when a disappointed office seeker named Charles Guiteau assassinated President James Garfield in 1881, that use was associated with murder as well. Obviously, something had to be done.

(3) It's Bureaucratic. To curb the excesses of party interests and restore some measure of responsibility and competence to public servants, bureaucratic reforms were initiated through legislation, first at the federal level, with the passage of the Civil Service Act of 1883, and soon after by states and localities.

These reforms, by being bureaucratic, stressed the use of a rational-legal rather than a partisan political approach to public management. In so doing, to use Max Weber's terms, impersonal "calculable rules," rather than personal partisan preferences, were used to provide the basis for uniform, evenhanded judgments about public employees; and, with no pejorative overtones intended, public managers were to "go by the book" and see that others did the same within their specified spheres of authority, responsibility and competence. Indeed, competence itself would be judged on the basis of technical proficiency rather than political affiliation or social status; and as much as possible, employees would be kept away from the corrupting, debilitating influences of partisan politics.

The bulk of these bureaucratic ideas are included in what has come to be known as the "merit system concept" of civil service reform, a concept which provides the cornerstone for civil service policies and processes. At base, as Virginia McMurty notes, this concept includes three fundamental tenets set forth for civil servants (i.e. public bureaucrats): competitive examinations, the absence of arbitrary removals, and political neutrality. Thus, competent people are selected through open, competitive examinations instead of partisan politics, and subsequently protected from politically motivated removal by job tenure. And in exchange for that tenure, they are expected to remain politically neutral by making their competence available to the political party leaders of the day.

While the notions of competence and tenure seem straightforward enough, political neutrality has caused problems from the start. Might not merit employees be tempted to resist the wishes of the political party machinery, prove unresponsive and attend to their own bureaucratic machinery instead?

Indeed, according to a report by the Committee for Economic Development just such bureaucratic merit system problems have come to pass, including 1) bureaucratic delays which prevent the prompt filling of job vacancies, many times leading to the loss of top applicants to other job opportunities; 2) recruitment by personnel offices which is often slow, unimaginative and unaggressive; 3) rigid classification systems which impede the efficient assignment of work; 4) excessive reliance on written examinations, seniority and other criteria that have little or no relation to job performance; and 5) a lack of authority available to managers to reward superior performers and discipline or fire non-performers.

Of course, not all bureaucratic difficulties can be attributed to problems with merit system techniques. The very culture of bureaucracy can nurture behavior which can get in the way of constructive public sector management. As Anthony Downs observes in his famous book, *Inside Bureaucracy*, bureaucratic culture produces five distinct types of behavior—climbers, conservers, zealots, advocates and statesmen—and one is far more in evidence than the others.

In describing these different types, Downs notes that the *climbers* are individuals who are interested in acquiring power, income and prestige as the motivating forces in their value systems. In a very real sense, the stereotypical example of today's young, upwardly mobile professionals, dubbed "Yuppies," comes to mind. The *conservers*, on the other hand, are more committed to convenience and security. Unlike the climbers, they would like to hold on to power, income and prestige they already have, instead of seeking to maximize them further. Consequently, these sorts of people are inclined to manifest a form of "35-10-2 syndrome" thinking (which reflects those who are at least 35 years old with 10 years on the job and 2 children) and "turf protecting" (which only seeks to keep ground gained) pursuing gradual, conservative, "don't rock the boat" behavior.

The next three bureaucratic types have progressively less self-interested and more magnanimous views. The *zealots* are obsessed with narrow policies or concepts, which they treat as "sacred" and pursue with a vengeance which attacks the status quo and can "antagonize their superiors to a surprising degree." Examples include Admiral Hyman Rickover and his pursuit of a nuclear submarine fleet after World War II, and General William "Billy" Mitchell and desire for a strong air force after World War I. Rickover's obsession proved successful, while Mitchell's ended in demotion and court martial. Although these types of individuals are obviously not the best liked people in public service, their willingness to support any organizational changes, however radical, that advance their sacred policies is, according to Downs, critically important because they help to overcome bureaucratic inertia and foster long run reform.

In contrast, the *advocates* are loyal to a broader set of functions or to a broader organization than zealots. Unlike zealots, they are less inclined to be loners or gadflies and more likely to try to marshal the support of their colleagues in their efforts. In so doing, they are more prone to be influenced by their superiors, peers and subordinates as they pursue their attempts to gain more control over the policies and actions that interest them.

The fifth and final bureaucratic type, the *statesmen*, are the most magnanimous of all. "Big picture types," their loyalties are to society as a whole and to the general welfare as they see it. But do their views carry much weight? Unfortunately, in most cases, the specialized nature of the bureaucratic workplace forces them to become something else, usually advocates. For if they remain broad-based statesmen, they are likely to be viewed as grandiose misfits in their own offices, misfits who may antagonize others and win few resources with their Olympian views.

Having reviewed this cast of characters, which of the five bureaucratic types is the most prevalent in public organizations? According to Downs, the *conserver* stands out, and hangs on, above the rest, a phenomenon which he stresses through his "Law of Increasing Conservatism." In that law, he states that "In every bureau, there is an inherent pressure upon the vast majority of officials to become conservers in the long run." Therefore, particularly among merit civil servants whose fates are protected from one change in partisan administration to the next and whose tenure extends toward the long term, we would expect to (and do) see a preponderance on conservative behavior, behavior which can get in the way of positive public management.

(4) It's Very Public. James Forrestal, the nation's first Secretary of Defense after World War II, once stressed that "the difficulty of government work is that it not only has to be well done, but the public has to be convinced that it is being well done. In other words, there is a necessity both for competence and exposition, and I hold it is extremely difficult to combine the two in the same person."

This need for exposition, to have the public's business openly conducted and judged for all to see, can prove quite challenging to managers in government, particularly those used to the privacy of the business world. In the private sector, far more of its managerial activities are, by definition, private: more internal, less visible and less subject to public and media scrutiny. By contrast, in the public sector, with instant global communications and an intrusive press, managers can expect to be placed in a goldfish bowl, scrutinized about anything and everything that can or may come their way.

Having Business Do the Government's Work

Given the constraints on government being more businesslike, why not have business do the government's work? In a word, why not "privatize?"

Such a transfer of functions from the public to the private spheres can be seen in an increasing number of areas, from the provision of school lunches and garbage collection to waste water treatment and mass transit. So too are fire protection, custodial work, vehicle towing, park maintenance and numerous other public services being shifted to the private realm. Indeed, some state and local governments have even privatized parts of their justice systems through such means as private security forces, private adjudication and mediation services, and private institutionalization of public offenders. And last, but far from least, even such high tech tasks as the building of nuclear reactors and the manufacture of military weapons are being done by private companies.

In choosing privatization, efficiency is the main attraction. But is efficiency always improved through privatization and, for that matter, should efficiency be the only value used in measuring public service success? Critics and analysts have their doubts.

First of all, recent studies suggest that not all areas of public activity are equally amenable to improved efficiency. For example, in instances where a good or service, such as trash collection or bus transit, is relatively straightforward, simple to measure and technological, more efficient performance is likely to be achieved. But when an activity, such as education or human services, is complex, long-term and sociological in nature, more caution is needed because the efficiencies are less clear to measure and more difficult to achieve (i.e. what is a quality education, or how do we determine social well-being?).

Furthermore, beyond efficiency, other values need to be considered. In particular, the notion of public accountability is paramount. As Ronald Moe stresses, "while a government agency is directly accountable to elected officials, a private entity under contract has only an indirect and tenuous relationship to elected officials." By having what amounts to a form of "third-party government" through privatization, the government strains its line of authority and can lose much of its public control of activities to the private sector.

Along with strained lines of authority, notions of citizen access, social equity and corruption need to be considered when addressing the concern of public accountability. With privatization, citizen access is diminished as decisions once made in public through open discussion fall into the private realm of private companies. And in that less visible, private realm, their choices may not always be right. For example, benefits to the poorest and neediest clients in society may be curtailed by business in the name of efficiency even though this may be unfair as a matter of social equity. Moreover, under the cloak of privacy with less public control and more discretion, opportunities abound for corruption.

In sum, public management is indeed a challenge, one involving a government workplace with a great many constraints and a business realm with perhaps too few. Given the constraints in the government workplace, the business realm looks very tempting. After all, if we wish to have public management more businesslike, why not go to business itself? Why not privatize? Unfortunately, that too is not without drawbacks. For while it may prove more efficient in some instances, it can also prove less accountable to the public, with strained lines of authority, less citizen access, questionable equity and substantial instances of corruption. These factors should give public managers pause before embracing privatization too freely.

At the start of our republic, James Madison observed that "In framing a government which is to be administered by men over men, the great difficulty lies in this: you must first enable the government to control the governed; and in the next place oblige it to control itself." Therefore, while governmental constraints on our public managers are substantial, perhaps too much public control may be given away if we turn to privatization.

CHAPTER ELEVEN

The Judiciary

A Question of Legitimacy

OVERVIEW AND SUMMARY

The democratic question in this chapter concerns the nature of judicial power generally and of judicial review in particular. Judicial review is the power of courts to declare acts of Congress, of the president and other executive officers, of bureaucratic agencies, of state and local officials, and of lesser courts violative of the Constitution and, as such, null and void. The democratic question is put squarely before us when we consider the countermajoritarian nature of the Supreme Court and the federal judiciary. Nowhere else in the world is this power more extensive.

The first thing to know about judicial review is that it is nowhere made explicit in the Constitution. At best, the power is implied by the supremacy clause and through the argument in *Federalist Paper* No. 78 by **Alexander Hamilton**. Hamilton's argument is that, bereft of "purse or sword," the court might qualify as primary arbiter of the Constitution by virtue of the fact that it is "the least dangerous branch" of government.

The power of judicial review was later claimed by the Court itself in an opinion by Chief Justice John Marshall in *Marbury v. Madison* in 1803. Marshall was able to establish the power of judicial review at the same time as he avoided issuing a judicial order that almost certainly would have been defied by President Thomas Jefferson, damaging the prestige of the Court. At the time Marshall wrote his opinion, judicial review—now the fundamental power of the court—was generally not recognized. Indeed, the antifederalists (see the article by **Brutus**) and other critics took exception to the whole of **Alexander Hamilton**'s analysis, as well as Marshall's opinion. The Court was not again to declare an act of Congress unconstitutional until 1857, in the *Dred Scott* decision.

Judicial review slowly gained acceptance through the years as an adjunct to democratic government. Judicial review is necessary, in the words of **James Thayer**, to fix the "outside border" of reasonable legislative action. The idea was that the judicial department could check the worse excesses of majoritarian government.

The difficult part was to reconcile judicial review with government by majority rule and to define the nature and limits of judicial power. In essence, courts needed somehow to be restrained in their exercise of constitutional interpretation.

Thayer says that the doctrine of judicial self-restraint comes as one of the few antidotes to the counter-majoritarian nature of the federal judiciary. That is, justices must restrain themselves. After all, they are appointed for "life under good behaviour" and they are removable only by the unwieldy tool of impeachment. The danger is therefore apparent. What is to stop an unrestrained court from usurping the powers of the popularly elected branches?

Critics of the Supreme Court have noted many examples of what can be considered judicial legislation. For instance, in *Roe v. Wade* (1973) the Court employed the unenumerated "right to privacy" to pronounce a fundamental right to abortion, notwithstanding state laws to the contrary. And in *Miranda v. Arizona* (1968), the Court required police departments to read a list of rights to all criminal suspects.

The wisdom of these actions can be debated in policy terms. It is one thing for an elected representative to stand in the well of Congress and wax philosophical on the right to choose abortion or on protecting citizens from abusive police tactics. It is quite another thing for far-reaching policies to be proclaimed by "nine old men" (now seven old men and two old women) in the marble temple on Constitution Avenue. Each time the Court has made such a proclamation, some loudly protest that the Court has overreached its bounds. (In the 1962 case of *Engel v. Vitale*, the Court unleashed a never-ending debate when it overturned the widespread practice of reading prayers in public schools.) With each controversial decision, some call for limiting the powers of the Court, through extraordinary means if necessary.

In a majoritarian system, by what right does the Court exercise such authority? Do judges have special expertise in medical and moral issues or on the intricacies of police procedures? They may have the power to make these things stick, but do they really have the democratic credentials to legislate on them?

In most respects, however, the courts are inherently restrained. Institutionally, they are vulnerable to the powers of the other branches. It is Congress and not the courts that determines the pay scale for judges, the number of lower federal courts, and even the number of justices on the Supreme Court. And Congress can by simple legislation limit the jurisdiction of the Supreme Court by the terms of Article III of the Constitution. These congressional powers provide a powerful incentive for restraint, and not surprisingly the doctrine of self-restraint is judicially imposed. As **John Roche** explains, there are a number of tools the Court has historically employed as a means of institutional self-preservation. The Court's control of its docket, its rules of standing, its adherence to precedent, its political question doctrine, and its rule of parsimony are among the ways in which it avoids no-win entreaties into political thickets. Restraint, then, provides the critical core by which the Court preserves its prestige, its independence, and its standing as a co-equal branch of government.

Although few would accept the notion of a runaway judiciary, some suggest that courts should take a more active role in constitutional adjudication. The argument for judicial activism proceeds from the nature of the rights that courts exist to protect. Fundamental rights such as freedom of speech and equal protection of the laws are thought to be inviolable, and the courts are uniquely situated to protect them. For instance, the First Amendment is not needed to protect popular speech. Indeed, the Bill of Rights exists to protect the damned, the despised, the malcontented, and the unconventional. It is not intended by the Constitution that these liberties be subject to popular referenda. And it is the nature of the court system—the fact that it is unelected and not accountable to a sometimes shortsighted electorate—that makes it best able to vindicate individual rights. The argument for a more active judiciary thus turns the restraint argument on its head. Following this activist logic, Justice **William J. Brennan** (1956-1989) argues for what might be called a "living Constitution." "The genius of the Constitution," says Brennan, "rests not in any static meaning it might have had in a world that is dead and gone, but in the adaptability of its great principles to cope with current problems and current needs."

The processes of the Supreme Court can seem almost Byzantine to the casual viewer. In the majesty of its proceedings and the secretive nature of its deliberations, the judiciary is a far cry from the often excessively open processes of Congress or of a presidency under the seemingly constant scrutiny of the press. Nevertheless, the nuts and bolts of the judiciary—how a case is heard; oral argument; conference of the justices; and majority, concurring, and dissenting opinions—proceed under rules that are quite regular if not exactly static. As a young law clerk in 1952, **William Rehnquist** was witness to these procedures in the politically supercharged "steel seizure case." The reflections of the Chief Justice will help us understand these ways of the Supreme Court.

In any case, the final arbiter, the Supreme Court, has come to be focused on the most contentious areas of social policy in America—abortion, affirmative action, free speech and press, and the like. Supreme Court appointments represent a large part of the "legacy" of every president. Voters show little interest in considering judicial appointments in casting their presidential vote, but given the nature of the issues the Court handles, it is small wonder that presidential appointments and the Senate confirmation process has grown to be a very public process. Add the likelihood of a split control of the White House and Congress, and all the elements of a political donnybrook are present

In the recent past, white-hot confirmation battles accompanied the appointments of Robert Bork (1987) and Clarence Thomas (1991). These confirmations resembled election campaigns insofar as interest groups produced simplistic TV commercials and generated a torrent of mail to senators in hopes of influencing their votes. In the case of Justice Thomas, the proceedings degenerated into a media circus, involving charges of sexual harassment. For both cases, it can be argued that the institution of the judiciary and the doctrine of judicial independence lose when a seat on the Supreme Court is treated as a local sheriff's race.

Stephen Carter suggests that the atmosphere of recent confirmation battles places the legitimacy of the Court at stake. If, as Carter argues, courts exist in part to protect the rights of numerical minorities, how can a confirmation process that resembles an election campaign produce justices who will vindicate minority rights? If reforms are not instituted, the day will soon come when we might as well elect these judges. In contrast, **Randall Kennedy** argues that the process of confirmation has always been and must always be political. Nothing can stop the president from leaving his mark on the Court, as he believes his election demands, nor will the the Senate give up its own prerogatives. That nomination hearings have recently resembled a public argument about the meaning of constitutional rights is both inevitable and, given the importance of this argument, not to be undervalued.

68 | The Least Dangerous Branch (Federalist No. 78)

Alexander Hamilton

Patriot, statesman, and agitator for national government, Alexander Hamilton argues for the necessity of an independent judiciary and makes the case that there is no realistic possibility of a tyrannical court system.

To the People of the State of New York:

WE PROCEED now to an examination of the judiciary department of the proposed government.

… As to the tenure by which the judges are to hold their places; this chiefly concerns their duration in office; the provisions for their support; the precautions for their responsibility.

According to the plan of the convention, all judges who may be appointed by the United States are to hold their offices DURING GOOD BEHAVIOR; which is conformable to the most approved of the State constitutions and among the rest, to that of this State. Its propriety having been drawn into question by the adversaries of that plan, is no light symptom of the rage for objection, which disorders their imaginations and judgments. The standard of good behavior for the continuance in office of the judicial magistracy, is certainly one of the most valuable of the modern improvements in the practice of government. In monarchy it is an excellent barrier to the despotism of the prince; in a republic it is a no less excellent barrier to the encroachments and oppressions of the representative body. And it is the best expedient which can be devised in any government, to secure a steady, upright, and impartial administration of the laws.

Whoever attentively considers the different departments of power must perceive, that, in a government in which they are separated from each other, the judiciary, from the nature of its functions, will always be the least dangerous to the political rights of the Constitution; because it will be least in a capacity to annoy or injure them. The Executive not only dispenses the honors, but holds the sword of the community. The legislature not only commands the purse, but prescribes the rules by which the duties and rights of every citizen are to be regulated. The judiciary, on the contrary, has no influence over either the sword or the purse; no direction either of the strength or of the wealth of the society; and can take no active resolution whatever. It may truly be said to have neither FORCE nor WILL, but merely judgment; and must ultimately depend upon the aid of the executive arm even for the efficacy of its judgments.

This simple view of the matter suggests several important consequences. It proves incontestably, that the judiciary is beyond comparison the weakest of the three departments of power; that it can never attack with success either of the other two; and that all possible care is requisite to enable it to defend itself against their attacks. It equally proves, that though individual oppression may now and then proceed from the courts of justice, the general liberty of the people can never be endangered from that quarter; I mean so long as the judiciary remains truly distinct from both the legislature and the Executive. For I agree, that "there is no liberty, if the power of judging be not separated from the legislative and executive powers." And it proves, in the last place, that as liberty can have nothing to fear from the judiciary alone, but would have every thing to fear from its union with either of the other departments; that as all the effects of such a union must ensue from a dependence of the former on the latter, notwithstanding a nominal and apparent separation; that as, from the natural feebleness of the judiciary, it is in continual jeopardy of being overpowered, awed, or influenced by its co-ordinate branches; and that as nothing can contribute so much to its firmness and independence as permanency in office, this quality may therefore be justly regarded as an indispensable ingredient in its constitution, and, in a great measure, as the citadel of the public justice and the public security.

The complete independence of the courts of justice is peculiarly essential in a limited Constitution. By a limited Constitution, I understand one which contains certain specified exceptions to the legislative authority; such, for instance, as that it shall pass no bills of attainder, no *ex-post-facto* laws, and the like. Limitations of this kind can be preserved in practice no other way than through the medium of courts of justice, whose duty it must be to declare all acts contrary to the manifest tenor of the Constitution void. Without this, all the reservations of particular rights or privileges would amount to nothing.

Some perplexity respecting the rights of the courts to pronounce legislative acts void, because contrary to the Constitution, has arisen from an imagination that the doctrine would imply a superiority of the judiciary to the legislative power. It is urged that the authority which can declare the acts of another void, must necessarily be superior to the one whose acts may be declared void. As this doctrine is of great importance in all the American constitutions, a brief discussion of the ground on which it rests cannot be unacceptable.

There is no position which depends on clearer principles, than that every act of a delegated authority, contrary to the tenor of the commission under which it is exercised, is void. No legislative act, therefore, contrary to the Constitution, can be valid. To deny this, would be to affirm, that the deputy is greater than his principal; that the servant is above his master; that the representatives of the people are superior to the people themselves; that men acting by virtue of powers, may do not only what their powers do not authorize, but what they forbid.

If it be said that the legislative body are themselves the constitutional judges of their own powers, and that the construction they put upon them is conclusive upon the other departments, it may be answered, that this cannot be the natural presumption, where it is not to be collected from any particular provisions in the Constitution. It is not otherwise to be supposed, that the Constitution could intend to enable the representatives of the people to substitute their WILL to that of their constituents. It is far more rational to suppose, that the courts were designed to be an intermediate body between the people and the legislature, in order, among other things, to keep the latter within the limits assigned to their authority. The interpretation of the laws is the proper and peculiar province of the courts. A constitution is, in fact, and must be regarded by the judges, as a fundamental law. It therefore belongs to them to ascertain its meaning, as well as the meaning of any particular act proceeding from the legislative body. If there should happen to be an irreconcilable variance between the two, that which has the superior obligation and validity ought, of course, to be preferred; or, in other words, the Constitution ought to be preferred to the statute, the intention of the people to the intention of their agents.

Nor does this conclusion by any means suppose a superiority of the judicial to the legislative power. It only supposes that the power of the people is superior to both; and that where the will of the legislature, declared in its statutes, stands in opposition to that of the people, declared in the Constitution, the judges ought to be governed by the latter rather than the former. They ought to regulate their decisions by the fundamental laws, rather than by those which are not fundamental....

It can be of no weight to say that the courts, on the pretense of a repugnancy, may substitute their own pleasure to the constitutional intentions of the legislature. This might as well happen in the case of two contradictory statutes; or it might as well happen in every adjudication upon any single statute. The courts must declare the sense of the law; and if they should be disposed to exercise WILL instead of JUDGMENT, the consequence would equally be the substitution of their pleasure to that of the legislative body. The observation, if it prove any thing, would prove that there ought to be no judges distinct from that body.

If, then, the courts of justice are to be considered as the bulwarks of a limited Constitution against legislative encroachments, this consideration will afford a strong argument for the permanent tenure of judicial offices, since nothing will contribute so much as this to that independent spirit in the judges which must be essential to the faithful performance of so arduous a duty....

This independence of the judges is equally requisite to guard the Constitution and the rights of individuals from the effects of those ill humors, which the arts of designing men, or the influence of particular conjunctures, sometimes disseminate among the people themselves, and which, though they speedily give place to better information, and more deliberate reflection, have a tendency, in the meantime, to occasion dangerous innovations in the government, and serious oppressions of the minor party in the community. Though I trust the friends of the proposed Constitution will never concur with its enemies in questioning that fundamental principle of republican government, which admits the right of the people to alter or abolish the established Constitution, whenever they find it inconsistent with their happiness, yet it is not to be inferred from this principle, that the representatives of the people, whenever a momentary inclination happens to lay hold of a majority of their constituents, incompatible with the provisions in the existing Constitution, would, on that account, be justifiable in a violation of those provisions; or that the courts would be under a greater obligation to connive at infractions in this shape, than when they had proceeded wholly from the cabals of the representative body. Until the people have, by some solemn and authoritative act, annulled or changed the es-

tablished form, it is binding upon themselves collectively, as well as individually; and no presumption, or even knowledge, of their sentiments, can warrant their representatives in a departure from it, prior to such an act. But it is easy to see, that it would require an uncommon portion of fortitude in the judges to do their duty as faithful guardians of the Constitution, where legislative invasions of it had been instigated by the major voice of the community....

That inflexible and uniform adherence to the rights of the Constitution, and of individuals, which we perceive to be indispensable in the courts of justice, can certainly not be expected from judges who hold their offices by a temporary commission. Periodical appointments, however regulated, or by whomsoever made, would, in some way or other, be fatal to their necessary independence. If the power of making them was committed either to the Executive or legislature, there would be danger of an improper complaisance to the branch which possessed it; if to both, there would be an unwillingness to hazard the displeasure of either; if to the people, or to persons chosen by them for the special purpose, there would be too great a disposition to consult popularity, to justify a reliance that nothing would be consulted but the Constitution and the laws.

There is yet a further and a weightier reason for the permanency of the judicial offices, which is deducible from the nature of the qualifications they require. It has been frequently remarked, with great propriety, that a voluminous code of laws is one of the inconveniences necessarily connected with the advantages of a free government. To avoid an arbitrary discretion in the courts, it is indispensable that they should be bound down by strict rules and precedents, which serve to define and point out their duty in every particular case that comes before them; and it will readily be conceived from the variety of controversies which grow out of the folly and wickedness of mankind, that the records of those precedents must unavoidably swell to a very considerable bulk, and must demand long and laborious study to acquire a competent knowledge of them. Hence it is, that there can be but few men in the society who will have sufficient skill in the laws to qualify them for the stations of judges. And making the proper deductions for the ordinary depravity of human nature, the number must be still smaller of those who unite the requisite integrity with the requisite knowledge. These considerations apprise us, that the government can have no great option between fit character; and that a temporary duration in office, which would naturally discourage such characters from quitting a lucrative line of practice to accept a seat on the bench, would have a tendency to throw the administration of justice into hands less able, and less well qualified, to conduct it with utility and dignity....

PUBLIUS.

69 | The Judiciary's Power to Mold the Government
Brutus

From among the less well-known antifederalists, this anonymous author takes direct exception to Alexander Hamilton's contention that the judiciary cannot pose a threat to democratic government. The argument mirrors that of Charles Evans Hughes a century and a half later, who said that "we are under a Constitution, but the Constitution is what the judges say it is."

Much has been said and written upon the subject of this new system, on both sides, but I have not met with any writer who has discussed the judicial powers with any degree of accuracy. And yet it is obvious that we can form but very imperfect ideas of the manner in which this government will work or the effect it will have in changing the internal police and mode of distributing justice at present subsisting in the respective states without a thorough investigation of the powers of the judiciary and of the manner in which they will operate. This government is a complete system, not only for making but for executing laws. And the courts of law which will be constituted by it are not only to decide upon the Constitution and the laws made in pursuance of it but by officers subordinate to them to execute all their decisions. The real effect of this system of government will therefore be brought home to the feelings of the people through the medium of the judicial power. It is, moreover, of great importance to examine with care the nature and extent of the judicial power, because those who are to be vested with it are to be placed in a situation altogether unprecedented in a free country. They are to be rendered totally independent, both of the people and the legislature, both with respect to their offices and salaries. No errors they may commit can be corrected by any power above them, if any such power there be, nor can they be removed from office for making ever so many erroneous adjudications.

The only causes for which they can be displaced [are] conviction of treason, bribery, and high crimes and misdemeanors.

This part of the plan is so modeled as to authorize the courts not only to carry into execution the powers expressly given but, where these are wanting or ambiguously expressed, to supply what is wanting by their own decisions.

That we may be enabled to form a just opinion on this subject, I shall, in considering it, (I) examine the nature and extent of the judicial powers; and (2) inquire whether the courts who are to exercise them are so constituted as to afford reasonable ground of confidence that they will exercise them for the general good....

... This article, therefore, vests the judicial with a power to resolve all questions that may arise on any case on the construction of the Constitution, either in law or in equity.

First, they are authorized to determine all questions that may arise upon the meaning of the Constitution either in law or in equity. This article vests the courts with authority to give the Constitution a legal construction, or to explain it according to the rules laid down for construing a law. These rules give a certain degree of latitude of explanation....

Second, the judicial are not only to decide questions arising upon the meaning of the Constitution in law but also in equity. By this they are empowered to explain the Constitution according to the reasoning spirit of it, without being confined to the words or letter....

They will give the sense of every article of the Constitution that may from time to time come before them. And in their decisions they will not confine themselves to any fixed or established rules but will determine, according to what appears to them, the reason and spirit of the Constitution. The opinions of the Supreme Court, whatever they may be, will have the force of law because there is no power provided in the Constitution that can correct their errors or control their adjudications. From this court there is no appeal. And I conceive the legislature themselves cannot set aside a judgment of this court because they are authorized by the Constitution to decide in the last resort. The legislature must be

controlled by the Constitution, and not the Constitution by them. They have therefore no more right to set aside any judgment pronounced upon the construction of the constitution than they have to take from the President the chief command of the Army and Navy and commit it to some other person. The reason is plain—the judicial and executive derive their authority from the same source that the legislature do theirs; and, therefore in all cases where the Constitution does not make the one responsible to or controllable by the other, they are altogether independent of each other.

The judicial power will operate to effect, in the most certain but yet silent and imperceptible manner, what is evidently the tendency of the Constitution: I mean, an entire subversion of the legislative, executive, and judicial powers of the individual states. Every adjudication of the Supreme Court on any question that may arise upon the nature and extent of the general government will affect the limits of the state jurisdiction. In proportion as the former enlarge the exercise of their powers will that of the latter be restricted.

That the judicial power of the United States will lean strongly in favor of the general government, and will give such an explanation to the Constitution as will favor an extension of its jurisdiction....

... [T] he Constitution itself strongly countenances such a mode of construction. Most of the articles in this system which convey powers of any considerable importance are conceived in general and indefinite terms, which are either equivocal, ambiguous, or which require long definitions to unfold the extent of their meaning....

... [N]ot only will the Constitution justify the courts in inclining to this mode of explaining it but they will be interested in using this latitude of interpretation. Every body of men invested with office are tenacious of power; they feel interested, and hence it has become a kind of maxim to hand down their offices, with all its rights and privileges unimpaired, to their successors. The same principle will influence them to extend their power and increase their rights; this of itself will operate strongly upon the courts to give such a meaning to the Constitution, in all cases where it can possibly be done, as will enlarge the sphere of their own authority. Every extension of the power of the general legislature, as well as of the judicial powers, will increase the powers of the courts; and the dignity and importance of the judges will be in proportion to the extent and magnitude of the powers they exercise.... From these considerations the judges will be interested to extend the powers of the courts, and to construe the constitution as much as possible in such a way as to favor it; and that they will do it appears probable....

When the courts will have a precedent before them of a court which extended its jurisdiction in opposition to an act of the legislature, is it not to be expected that they will extend theirs, especially when there is nothing in the Constitution expressly against it? And they are authorized to construe its meaning, and are not under any control?

This power in the judicial will enable them to mold the government into almost any shape they please.

70 | *The Doctrine of Judicial Review*
James Thayer

One of the leading judicial scholars of the nineteenth century, James Thayer expounds the American doctrine of judicial review in a manner that remains fresh to this day. Called by Justice Felix Frankfurter the single most important essay in constitutional law, Thayer's work argues that courts are uniquely qualified to fill in the gaps of the legislative process and that the inherent limits in the doctrine of judicial review obviate any fears of judicial tyranny.

How did our American doctrine, which allows to the judiciary the power to declare legislative acts unconstitutional and to treat them as null, come about, and what is the true scope of it?

It is plain that where a power so momentous as this primary authority to interpret is given, the actual determinations of the body to whom it is entrusted are entitled to a corresponding respect; and this is not on mere grounds of courtesy or conventional respect but on very solid and significant grounds of policy and law. The judiciary may well reflect that if they had been regarded by the people as the chief protection against legislative violation of the Constitution, they would not have been allowed merely this incidental and postponed control. They would have been let in, and it was sometimes endeavoured in the conventions to let them in, to a revision of the laws before they began to operate. As the opportunity of the judges to check and correct unconstitutional acts is so limited, it may help us to understand why the extent of their control, when they do have the opportunity, should also be narrow.

It was, then, all along true, and it was foreseen, that much which is harmful and unconstitutional may take effect without any capacity in the courts to prevent it, since their whole power is a judicial one. Their interference was but one of many safeguards, and its scope was narrow....

Let us observe the course which the courts, in point of fact, have taken in administering this interesting jurisdiction.

They began by resting it upon the very simple ground that the legislature had only a delegated and limited authority under the constitutions; that these restraints, in order to be operative, must be regarded as so much law; and, as being law, that they must be interpreted and applied by the court. This was put as a mere matter of course. The reasoning was simple and narrow....

The people, as it was said, have established written limitations upon the legislature; these control all repugnant legislative acts; such acts are not law; this theory is essentially attached to a written constitution; it is for the judiciary to say what the law is, and if two rules conflict, to say which governs; the judiciary are to declare a legislative act void which conflicts with the constitution or else that instrument is reduced to nothing. And then, it was added, in the federal instrument, this power is expressly given....

Having ascertained all this, yet there remains a question—the really momentous question—whether, after all, the court can disregard the act. It cannot do this as a mere matter of course, merely because it is concluded that upon a just and true construction the law is unconstitutional. That is precisely the significance of the rule of administration that the courts lay down. It can only disregard the act when those who have the right to make laws have not merely made a mistake but have made a very clear one—so clear that it is not open to rational question. That is the standard of duty to which the courts bring legislative acts; that is the test which they apply, not merely their own judgment as to constitutionality but their conclusion as to

what judgment is permissible to another department which the Constitution has charged with the duty of making it....

What really took place in adopting our theory of constitutional law was this: We introduced for the first time into the conduct of government through its great departments a judicial sanction, as among these departments—not full and complete, but partial. The judges were allowed, indirectly and in a degree, the power to revise the action of other departments and to pronounce it null. In simple truth, while this is a mere judicial function, it involves, owing to the subject matter with which it deals, taking a part, a secondary part, in the political conduct of government. If that be so, then the judges must apply methods and principles that befit their task....

The view which has thus been presented seems to me highly important. I am not stating a new doctrine, but attempting to restate more exactly and truly an admitted one. If what I have said be sound, it is greatly to be desired that it should be more emphasized by our courts, in its full significance. It has been often remarked that private rights are more respected by the legislatures of some countries which have no written constitution than by ours. No doubt our doctrine of constitutional law has had a tendency to drive out questions of justice and right and to fill the mind of legislators with thoughts of mere legality of what the Constitution allows. And moreover, even in the matter of legality, they have felt little responsibility; if we are wrong, they say, the courts will correct it. If what I have been saying is true, the safe and permanent road toward reform is that of impressing upon our people a far stronger sense than they have of the great range of possible harm and evil that our system leaves open, and must leave open, to the legislatures and of the clear limits of judicial power; so that responsibility may be brought sharply home where it belongs.

71 | *Judicial Self-Restraint*
John Roche

Courts are political institutions. However, those who fear a runaway judiciary must come to terms with the institutional vulnerability of the Supreme Court. Dependent on Congress for everything from creature comforts to jurisdiction and necessarily beholden to the executive branch that appoints its members, the Court must zealously protect its independence. John Roche discusses the tools of self-restraint, showing how the Court acts to protect itself and flourish in a sometimes hostile political environment. Issues may change, but the institutional needs of the Court remain the same.

... The fact is that the United States Supreme Court, and the inferior federal courts under the oversight of the high Court, have enormous policy-making functions. Unlike their British and French counterparts, federal judges are not merely technicians who live in the shadow of a supreme legislature, but are fully equipped to intervene in the process of political decision-making. In theory, they are limited by the Constitution and the jurisdiction it confers, but, in practice, it would be a clumsy judge indeed who could not, by a little skillful exegesis, adapt the Constitution to a necessary end. This statement is in no sense intended as a condemnation; on the contrary, it has been this perpetual reinvigoration by reinterpretation, in which the legislature and the executive as well as the courts play a part, that has given the Constitution its survival power. Applying a Constitution which contains at key points inspired ambiguity, the courts have been able to pour the new wine in the old bottle....

Thus it is naive to assert that the Supreme Court is limited by the Constitution, and we must turn elsewhere for the sources of judicial restraint. The great power exercised by the Court has carried with it great risks, so it is not surprising that American political history has been sprinkled with demands that the judiciary be emasculated. The really startling thing is that, with the notable exception of the McCardle incident in 1869, the Supreme Court has emerged intact from each of these encounters. Despite the plenary power that Congress, under Article III of the Constitution, can exercise over the appellate jurisdiction of the high Court, the national legislature has never taken sustained and effective action against its House of Lords. It is beyond the purview of this analysis to examine the reasons for congressional inaction; suffice it here to say that the most significant form of judicial limitation has remained self-limitation....

TECHNIQUES OF JUDICIAL SELF-RESTRAINT

The major techniques of judicial self-restraint appear to fall under the two familiar rubrics: procedural and substantive. Under the former fall the various techniques by which the Court can avoid coming to grips with substantive issues, while under the latter would fall those methods by which the Court, in a substantive holding, finds that the matter at issue in the litigation is not properly one for judicial settlement. Let us examine these two categories in some detail.

Procedural Self-Restraint. Since the passage of the Judiciary Act of 1925, the Supreme Court has had almost complete control over its business. United States Supreme Court *Rule* 38, which governs the certiorari policy, states that discretionary review will be granted only "where there are special and important reasons therefor." Professor Fowler

Harper has suggested in a series of detailed and persuasive articles on the application of this discretion that the Court has used it in such a fashion as to duck certain significant but controversial problems. While one must be extremely careful about generalizing in this area, since the reasons for denying certiorari are many and complex, Harper's evidence does suggest that the Court in the period since 1949 has refused to review cases involving important civil liberties problems which on their merits appeared to warrant adjudication....

Furthermore, the Supreme Court can issue certiorari on its own terms. Thus in *Dennis v. United States,* appealing the Smith Act convictions of the American Communist leadership, the Court accepted the evidential findings of the Second Circuit as final and limited its review to two narrow constitutional issues. This, in effect, burked the basic problem: whether the evidence was sufficient to demonstrate that the Communist party, U.S.A., was *in fact* a clear and present danger to the security of the nation, or whether the Communists were merely shouting "Fire!" in an empty theater.

Other related procedural techniques are applicable in some situations. Simple delay can be employed, perhaps in the spirit of the Croatian proverb that "delay is the handmaiden of justice." ...The Japanese-Americans, attempting to get a judicial ruling on the validity of their detainment in relocation centers, met with the same Kafka-esque treatment. However, the technique of procedural self-restraint is founded on the essentially simple gadget of refusing jurisdiction, or of procrastinating the acceptance of jurisdiction, and need not concern us further here.

Substantive Self-Restraint. Once a case has come before the Court on its merits, the justices are forced to give some explanation for whatever action they may take. Here self-restraint can take many forms, notably, the doctrine of political questions, the operation of judicial parsimony, and—particularly with respect to the actions of administrative officers or agencies—the theory of judicial inexpertise.

The doctrine of political questions is too familiar to require much elaboration here. Suffice it to say that if the Court feels that a question before it, *e.g.,* the legitimacy of a state government, the validity of a legislative apportionment, or the correctness of executive action in the field of foreign relations, is one that is not properly amenable to judicial settlement, it will refer the plaintiff to the "political" organs of government for any possible relief. The extent to which this doctrine is applied seems to be a direct coefficient of judicial egotism, for the definition of a political question can be expanded or contracted in accordion-like fashion to meet the exigencies of the times. A juridical definition of the term is impossible, for at root the logic that supports it is circular: political questions are matters not soluble by the judicial process; matters not soluble by the judicial process are political questions. As an early dictionary explained, violins are small cellos, and cellos are large violins.

Nor do examples help much in definition. While it is certainly true that the Court cannot mandamus a legislature to apportion a state in equitable fashion, it seems equally true that the Court is without the authority to force state legislators to implement unsegregated public education. Yet in the former instance the Court genuflected to the "political" organs and took no action, while in the latter it struck down segregation as violative of the Constitution.

Judicial parsimony is another major technique of substantive self-restraint. In what is essentially a legal application of Occam's razor, the Court has held that it will not apply any more principles to the settlement of a case than are absolutely necessary, *e.g.,* it will not discuss the constitutionality of a law if it can settle the instant case by statutory construction. Furthermore, if an action is found to rest on erroneous statutory construction, the review terminates at that point: the Court will not go on to discuss whether the statute, properly construed, would be constitutional. A variant form of this doctrine, and a most important one, employs the "case or controversy" approach, to wit, the Court, admitting the importance of the issue, inquires as to whether the litigant actually has standing to bring the matter up....

A third method of utilizing substantive self-restraint is particularly useful in connection with the activities of executive departments or regulatory agencies, both state and federal. I have entitled it the doctrine of judicial *inexpertise,* for it is founded on the unwillingness of the Court to revise the findings of experts. The earmarks of this form of restraint are great deference to the holdings of the expert agency usually coupled with such a statement as "It is not for the federal courts to supplant the Commission's judgment even in the face of convincing proof that a different result would have been better." In this tradition, the Court has refused to question *some* exercises of discretion by the National Labor Relations Board, the Federal Trade Commission, and other federal and state agencies. But the emphasis on *some* gives the point away: in other cases, apparently on all fours with those in which it pleads its technical *inexpertise,* the Court feels free to assess evidence *de novo* and reach independent judgment on the technical issues involved....In short, with respect to expert agencies, the Court is equipped with both offensive and defensive gambits. If it chooses to intervene, one set of precedents is brought out, while if it decides to hold back, another set of equal validity is invoked....

This does not pretend to be an exhaustive analysis of the techniques of judicial self-restraint; on the contrary, others will probably find many which are not given adequate discussion here. The remainder of this paper, however, is devoted to the second area of concern: the conditions under which the Court refrains from acting.

THE CONDITIONS OF JUDICIAL SELF-RESTRAINT

The conditions which lead the Supreme Court to exercise auto-limitation are many and varied. In the great bulk of cases, this restraint is an outgrowth of sound and quasi-automatic legal maxims which defy teleological interpretation. It would take a master of the conspiracy theory of history to assign meaning, for example, to the great majority of certiorari denials; the simple fact is that these cases do not merit review. However, in a small proportion of cases, purpose does appear to enter the picture, sometimes with a vengeance. It is perhaps unjust to the Court to center our attention on this small proportion, but it should be said in extenuation that these cases often involve extremely significant political and social issues. In the broad picture, the refusal to grant certiorari in 1943 to the Minneaeolis Trotskyites convicted under the Smith Act is far more meaningful than the similar refusal to grant five hundred petitions to prison "lawyers" who have suddenly discovered the writ of habeas corpus....

What we must therefore seek are the conditions under which the Court holds back *in this designated category of cases.* Furthermore, it is important to realize that there are positive consequences of negative action: as Charles Warren has implied, the post-Civil War Court's emphasis on self-restraint was a judicial concomitant of the resurgence of states' rights. Thus self-restraint may, as in wartime, be an outgrowth of judicial caution, or it may be part of a purposeful pattern of abdicating national power to the states.

Ever since the first political scientist discovered Mr. Dooley, the changes have been rung on the aphorism that the Supreme Court "follows the election returns," and I see no particular point in ringing my variation on this theme through again. Therefore, referring those who would like a more detailed explanation to earlier analyses, the discussion here will be confined to the bare bones of my hypothesis.

The power of the Supreme Court to invade the decision-making arena, I submit, is a consequence of that fragmentation of political power which is normal in the United States. No cohesive majority, such as normally exists in Britain, would permit a politically irresponsible judiciary to usurp decision-making functions, but, for complex social and institutional reasons, there are few issues in the

United States on which cohesive majorities exist. The guerrilla warfare which usually rages between Congress and the President, as well as the internal civil wars which are endemic in both the legislature and the administration, give the judiciary considerable room for maneuver. If, for example, the Court strikes down a controversial decision of the Federal Power Commission, it will be supported by a substantial bloc of congressmen; if it supports the FPC's decision, it will also receive considerable congressional support. But the important point is that *either* way it decides the case, there is no possibility that Congress will exact any vengeance on the Court for its action. A disciplined majority would be necessary to clip the judicial wings, and such a majority does not exist on this issue.

On the other hand, when monolithic majorities do exist on issues, the Court is likely to resort to judicial self-restraint. A good case here is the current tidal wave of anti-communist legislation and administrative action, the latter particularly with regard to aliens, which the Court has treated most gingerly. About the only issues on which there can be found cohesive majorities are those relating to national defense, and the Court has… traditionally avoided problems arising in this area irrespective of their constitutional merits.

Like the slave who accompanied a Roman consul on his triumph whispering "You too are mortal," the shade of Thad Stevens haunts the Supreme Court chamber to remind the justices what an angry Congress can do.

To state the proposition in this brief compass is to oversimplify it considerably. I have, for instance, ignored the crucial question of how the Court knows when a majority *does* exist, and I recognize that certain aspects of judicial behavior cannot be jammed into my hypothesis without creating essentially spurious epicycles. However, I am not trying to establish a monistic theory of judicial action; group action, like that of individuals, is motivated by many factors, some often contradictory, and my objective is to elucidate what seems to be one tradition of judicial motivation. In short, judicial self-restraint and judicial power seem to be opposite sides of the same coin; it has been by judicious application of the former that the latter has been maintained. A tradition beginning with Marshall's *coup* in *Marbury v. Madison* and running through *Mississippi v. Johnson* and *Ex Parte Vallandigham* to *Dennis v. United States* suggests that the Court's power has been maintained by a wise refusal to employ it in unequal combat.

72 | *The Vision of Our Time*
William J. Brennan

Long-time justice of the Supreme Court and long considered the Court's most liberal member, William Brennan makes the case for judicial activism. It is not possible to know the framers' intent, he argues, nor is it possible, or even desirable, for the Constitution to be static.

… The text I have chosen for exploration is the amended Constitution of the United States, which, of course, entrenches the Bill of Rights and the Civil War amendments, and draws sustenance from the bedrock principles of another great text, the Magna Carta. So fashioned, the Constitution embodies the aspiration to social justice, brotherhood, and human dignity that brought this nation into being. The Declaration of Independence, the Constitution and the Bill of Rights solemnly committed the United States to be a country where the dignity and rights of all persons were equal before all authority. In all candor we must concede that part of this egalitarianism in America has been more pretension than realized fact. But we are an aspiring people, a people with faith in progress. Our amended Constitution is the lodestar for our aspirations. Like every text worth reading, it is not crystalline. The phrasing is broad and the limitations of its provisions are not clearly marked. Its majestic generalities and ennobling pronouncements are both luminous and obscure. This ambiguity of course calls forth interpretation, the interaction of reader and text….

There are those who find legitimacy in fidelity to what they call "the intentions of the Framers." In its most doctrinaire incarnation, this view demands that Justices discern exactly what the Framers thought about the question under consideration and simply follow that intention in resolving the case before them. It is a view that feigns self-effacing deference to the specific judgments of those who forged our original social compact. But in truth it is little more than arrogance cloaked as humility. It is arrogant to pretend that from our vantage we can gauge accurately the intent of the Framers on application of principle to specific, contemporary questions. All too often, sources of potential enlightenment such as records of the ratification debates provide sparse or ambiguous evidence of the original intention. Typically, all that can be gleaned is that the Framers themselves did not agree about the application or meaning of particular constitutional provisions, and hid their differences in cloaks of generality. Indeed, it is far from clear whose intention is relevant—that of the drafters, the congressional disputants, or the ratifiers in the states?—or even whether the idea of an original intention is a coherent way of thinking about a jointly drafted document drawing its authority from a general assent of the states. And apart from the problematic nature of the sources, our distance of two centuries cannot but work as a prism refracting all we perceive. One cannot help but speculate that the chorus of lamentations calling for interpretation faithful to "original intention"—and proposing nullification of interpretations that fail this quick litmus test—must inevitably come from persons who have no familiarity with the historical record.

Perhaps most importantly, while proponents of this facile historicism justify it as a depoliticization of the judiciary, the political underpinnings of such a choice should not escape notice. A position that upholds constitutional claims only if they were within the specific contemplation of the Framers in effect establishes a presumption of resolving textual ambiguities against the claim of constitutional right. It is far from clear what justifies such a presumption against claims of right. Nothing intrinsic in the nature of interpretation—if there is such a thing as the "nature" of interpretation—commands such a passive approach to ambiguity. This is a choice no less political than any other; it expresses antipathy to claims of the minority to rights against the majority. Those who would restrict claims of right to the values of 1789 specifically articulated in the Constitution turn a blind eye to social progress and eschew adaptation of overarching principles to changes of social circumstance.

Another, perhaps more sophisticated, response to the potential power of judicial interpretation stresses democratic theory: because ours is a government of the people's elected representatives, substantive value choices should by and large be left to them. This view emphasizes not the transcendent historical authority of the Framers but the predominant contemporary authority of the elected branches of government. Yet it has similar consequences for the nature of proper judicial interpretation. Faith in the majoritarian process counsels restraint. Even under more expansive formulations of this approach, judicial review is appropriate only to the extent of ensuring that our democratic process functions smoothly. Thus, for example, we would protect freedom of speech merely to ensure that the people are heard by their representatives, rather than as a separate, substantive value. When, by contrast, society tosses up to the Supreme Court a dispute that would require invalidation of a legislature's substantive policy choice, the Court generally would stay its hand because the Constitution was meant as a plan of government and not as an embodiment of fundamental substantive values.

The view that all matters of substantive policy should be resolved through the majoritarian process has appeal under some circumstances, but I think it ultimately will not do. Unabashed enshrinement of majority will would permit the imposition of a social caste system or wholesale confiscation of property so long as a majority of the authorized legislative body, fairly elected, approved. Our Constitution could not abide such a situation. It is the very purpose of a Constitution—and particularly of the Bill of Rights—to declare certain values transcendent, beyond the reach of temporary political majorities: The majoritarian process cannot be expected to rectify claims of minority right that arise as a response to the outcomes of that very majoritarian process. As James Madison put it:

> The prescriptions in favor of liberty ought to be levelled against that quarter where the greatest danger lies, namely, that which possesses the highest prerogative of power. But this is not found in either the Executive or Legislative departments of Government, but in the body of the people, operating by the majority against the minority.

Faith in democracy is one thing, blind faith quite another. Those who drafted our constitution understood the difference. One cannot read the text without admitting that it embodies substantive value choices; it places certain values beyond the power of any legislature. Obvious are the separation of powers; the privilege of the Writ of Habeas Corpus; prohibition of Bills of Attainder and ex post facto laws; prohibition of cruel and unusual punishments; the requirement of just compensation for official taking of property; the prohibition of laws tending to establish religion or enjoining the free exercise of religion; and since the Civil War, the banishment of slavery and official race discrimination. With respect to at least such principles, we simply have not constituted ourselves as strict utilitarians. While the Constitution may be amended, such amendments require an immense effort by the People as a whole....

We current Justices read the Constitution in the only way that we can: as Twentieth Century Americans. We look to the history of the time of framing and to the intervening history of interpretation. But the ultimate question must be, What do the words of the text mean in our time? For the genius of the Constitution rests not in any static meaning it might have had in a world that is dead and gone, but in the adaptability of its great principles to cope with current problems and current needs: What the constitutional fundamentals meant to the wisdom of other times cannot be their measure to the vision of our time. Similarly, what those fundamentals mean for us, our descendants will learn, cannot be the measure to the vision of their time. This realization is not, I assure you, a novel one of my own creation. Permit me to quote from one of the opinions of our Court, *Weems v. United States,* written nearly a century ago:

Time works changes, brings into existence new conditions and purposes. Therefore, a principle to be vital must be capable of wider application than the mischief which gave it birth. This is peculiarly true of constitutions. They are not ephemeral enactments, designed to meet passing occasions. They are, to use the words of Chief Justice John Marshall, "designed to approach immortality as nearly as human institutions can approach it." The future is their care and provision for events of good and bad tendencies of which no prophesy can be made. In the application of a constitution, therefore, our contemplation cannot be only of what has been, but of what may be....

73 | *The Steel Seizure Case*
William Rehnquist

How political are the judges of the Supreme Court? Do they bow to public opinion? Chief Justice William Rehnquist was once a clerk for the Court. He witnessed and retold his observations of court politics during the landmark case Youngstown Sheet and Tube Co. et. al. v. Sawyer. *The case came to the Court after President Truman ordered a government takeover of steel mills during the Korean War as mill workers were about to strike.*

My instincts favored the position of the steel companies, though I can't give any very cogent explanation of why. I think that during my years as a graduate student... I had gotten the impression that the balance of power within the federal establishment had shifted markedly away from Congress and toward the president during the preceding fifteen years, and that this trend was not a healthy one. But when I asked myself how I felt the Court would decide the case, rather than how I wished it would be decided, I thought the odds were rather heavily in favor of the government....

When I contemplated the nine individuals who would make this decision, the thought uppermost in my mind was that all nine of them has been appointed by two Democratic presidents, Roosevelt and Truman. Eight of them had been at one time or another active in Democratic politics. I was sufficiently new as a law clerk that I had not had a chance to form an opinion as to whether these sorts of considerations entered into a decision, but I had the suspicion that at the very least a tie would count for the runner—the runner in this case being President Truman....

The Chief Justice's extensive experience in government—first fourteen years in Congress, and then three years of high-level executive branch service during a critical time in the nation's history—undoubtedly gave him a feel for the way government works that some of his colleagues did not possess....

It seemed to me as I pondered how the justices might vote in the Steel Seizure Case that this very sort of experience was bound to incline the Chief Justice toward the government's position. He had served three demanding years trying to manage difficult situations on behalf of the government, an experience that is bound to incline one toward a practical rather than a theoretical approach. President Truman would not have seized the steel mills unless he had thought it absolutely necessary to maintain the production of these mills in the national interest, and that the courts therefore should bend over backward to uphold his "best effort" in the difficult situation.

To law clerks who didn't work for him, I think the Chief Justice appeared distant and old; a good deal older, for example, than did Frankfurter, who was in fact eight years his senior. Law clerks who did work for him spoke of his ready wit and fund of stories based on nearly thirty years' life in Washington. He, Tom Clark, and Sherman Minton managed to get out to a few of the Washington Senators baseball games in the spring of the years and rumor had it that Vinson remained an intimate "crony" of the President and participated in regular poker games at the White House.

Hugo Lafayette Black was the senior associate justice on the Court. He had one of the most mellifluous voices and delightful accents that I, a northerner, had ever heard. Not for nothing had he been a renowned stump speaker in his two victorious campaigns to be elected United States Senator from Alabama. I can still remember him beginning his announcement of a dissenting opinion in a rather technical and uninteresting case involving administrative law by saying that the case involved a fight between "large corporate truckers" and "little independent truckers"; the correct result, in Justice Black's eyes, seemed foreordained by that description of the parties....

On the Court, Black, as expected, became a champion of "judicial restraint" when deal-

ing with social and economic legislation of the kind he had actively fought for in the Senate—laws, for example, regulating the minimum wages and maximum hours of workers in interstate commerce, and laws regulating the relationship between management and labor. This came as a surprise to no one. But after he had been on the Court for a few years, he began to differentiate sharply between this kind of law on the one hand, and on the other hand, laws that tended to infringe rights he thought to be guaranteed in specific language by the Bill of Rights. He became a strong upholder of the constitutional rights of criminal defendants and political dissidents; as to them he was not an apostle of judicial restraint. He had dissented in both of the two recent cases written by Vinson upholding governmental authority to prosecute Communists and to require non-Communist affidavits....

One year after President Roosevelt appointed Black to the Court, Justice George Sutherland announced his retirement and to replace him the President chose Stanley Forman Reed of Kentucky. By the time I saw him when I was a law clerk, Justice Reed was in his late sixties and bald as an egg. To me he looked more like a doctor than a lawyer, although I cannot say why. His visage in the formal picture of the Court taken about that time makes him look quite avuncular, with broad shoulders and large ears.

He was thought of as the quintessential moderate. In the late 1940s, when there had been four liberals on the Court, he often provided them with a fifth vote to vindicate their views of constitutional law. But in recent years he had sided with Chief Justice Vinson in rejecting civil-liberties claims....

One year after Franklin Roosevelt appointed Stanley Reed to the Court, he filled the vacancy resulting from the death of Justice Cardozo by appointing his long-time adviser and confidant, Professor Felix Frankfurter of the Harvard Law School....

Frankfurter was probably the preeminent academic student of the Supreme Court for much of the time he taught at Harvard Law School; he contributed major volumes analyzing its work, and significant articles dealing with various aspects of that work. He had been an adviser to Franklin Roosevelt when the latter was governor of New York from 1929 to 1933, and retained that role in a totally unofficial capacity when Roosevelt became President....

Frankfurter had been a forceful and vigorous critic of the "Old Court" and its propensity to declare unconstitutional state and federal legislation designed to improve the lot of working people by regulating business in one way or another. In this respect he was a disciple of Justice Brandeis, who retired from the Supreme Court after serving twenty-three years a month after Frankfurter's appointment. Frankfurter continued, after his appointment, to adhere to his broad view of governmental power to regulate economic and social matters.

But during the 1940s, the cutting edge of the debate over constitutional law shifted from the constitutional validity of economic and social regulation such as the Fair Labor Standards Act and the National Labor Relations Act to claims of civil liberties violations on behalf of various kinds of dissidents. Several of the Roosevelt appointees to the Court, led by Justices Black and William O. Douglas, drew a distinction between the constitutional limitation on the government's authority to regulate economic and social affairs, and its authority to regulate freedom of speech and of the press. They likewise were very receptive to claims by criminal defendants that the government had impinged on some constitutional right in the course of prosecuting them for the commission of a crime. But Frankfurter adhered to the belief that judicial restraint was required in one area as much as another, and therefore, as the 1940s drew to a close, he found himself allied with the conservative wing of the Court against its liberal wing....

The fourth Roosevelt appointment to the Supreme Court had come only a month after Frankfurter's upon the retirement of Justice Brandeis. For this vacancy President Roosevelt selected William O. Douglas, who had grown up in the state of Washington. Douglas

was only forty when he was appointed to the Court in April 1939, the youngest man to be appointed since Joseph Story had been chosen by President James Madison in 1811. When I first saw him in the spring of 1952, he was in his early fifties, spare and rangy, with sandy hair and a craggy face....

On the Court, Douglas had joined with the other Roosevelt appointees to solidly establish the validity of both state and federal regulation of business. But when in the 1940s the split among the Roosevelt appointees occurred on civil-rights issues, Douglas along with Black championed the claims of civil-rights litigants who sought to impose constitutional limits upon governmental power in that area....

He had been considered for the vice-presidential nomination of the Democratic party in both 1944 and 1948, and some thought that he might be available for the ticket in the November election of 1952. Due to a strange set of circumstances he had barely missed succeeding Franklin Roosevelt when the latter died in office in 1945. During Roosevelt's third term Henry A. Wallace was the Vice-President, but while the Democratic National Convention meeting in Chicago was willing to nominate Roosevelt for a fourth term as President, it was unwilling to nominate Wallace for a second term as Vice-President. Roosevelt sent word to the convention that he would prefer to see Wallace renominated as Vice-President, but that if it was not to be Wallace, he would be happy to run on a ticket with either Bill Douglas or Harry Truman. Douglas recounts that this message was relayed through D.N.C. Chairman Robert Hannegan. When the message came from Roosevelt it placed Douglas's name before Truman's, but by the time it was read to the convention Truman's name was in first position. Truman, of course, was nominated to run with Roosevelt. Were it not for this quirk of fate, perhaps it might have been President William O. Douglas, and not President Harry S Truman, who seized the steel mills.

The most junior of the five Roosevelt appointees to the Court at this time was my boss, Robert H. Jackson.... In 1938 he was promoted to the office of solicitor general and proved such an able advocate for the government that Justice Brandeis commented, "Jackson should be solicitor general for life." In 1940 he was named attorney general, and was at one time thought to be Franklin Roosevelt's choice to succeed him as President. In the event, however, it proved that Roosevelt did not want any candidate groomed to succeed him; he ran for a third term in 1940 and was elected by a large majority, and the following year he named Jackson to the Supreme Court. Jackson was viewed as an ardent New Dealer at the time of his nomination, but his votes proved to be a good deal less predictable than those of Justices Black and Douglas....

Truman had been in office only a few months when the retirement of Justice Roberts gave him a vacancy to fill on the Supreme Court.

Considerable public sentiment was expressed that the new justice ought to be a Republican; Roberts was a Republican who had been appointed by Herbert Hoover, and the remaining eight justices had all been placed in their present position by Franklin Roosevelt. Truman, moved by this sentiment, nominated Harold H. Burton, Republican senator from Ohio, and he was of course promptly confirmed by the Senate....

Burton tended to side with the conservative wing of the Court in cases involving governmental power.... He was not thought to be either a brilliant lawyer or an interesting writer but he was greatly respected for the total detachment with which he approached the cases he was obliged to decide.

For four years after Burton's appointment, the Court functioned without any change of personnel. Then, quite suddenly, Justice Frank Murphy died in July 1949, and Justice Wiley Rutledge in September 1949. Appointed by Roosevelt, both had been staunch allies of Justices Black and Douglas in the liberal bloc on the Court, and their sudden departure had a marked effect on the Court's alignment. This was because President Truman, now in his second term, chose Tom C. Clark

of Texas and Sherman Minton of Indiana to replace them....

Harry Truman [had] appointed Clark his attorney general. Clark was active in promoting the government's "loyalty program" during the beginning of the cold-war period, and was the first compiler of the then famous "Attorney General's list" of subversive organizations. He argued several cases before the Supreme Court during his tenure as attorney general, and his nomination by Truman to the vacancy in 1949 came as no surprise. Clark's nomination was opposed in the Senate by liberals who disliked his support of the government's loyalty program, but he was confirmed with little difficulty....

To fill the second of the two vacancies occurring in the fall of 1949, Truman named Sherman Minton, then a judge of the Court of Appeals for the Seventh Circuit in Chicago, and before that United States senator from Indiana....

Minton's enry into the Senate in 1934 coincided with that of the freshman senator from Missouri, the newly elected Harry S Truman. Minton had been considered for the vacancy to which Roosevelt ultimately appointed Hugo Black, and with Truman's penchant for appointing friends to high office it was quite natural for him to name Minton to the High Court.

These, then, were the nine justices who were going to decide whether or not President Truman had acted lawfully when he seized the steel mills. The time they had allowed the parties and themselves to prepare for oral argument was remarkably short; on Saturday, May 3, the Court had entered its order granting certiorari, and only nine days later the case was set for oral argument....

Shortly before 12:30 p.m., John W. Davis, who was to argue for the steel companies, rose to the make what was his one-hundred and twenty-eighth argument before the Supreme Court. Now nearing eighty, he had been successively a congressman from West Virginia, solicitor general in the administration of President Woodrow Wilson, founding partner of the firm of Davis, Polk, Sunderland, Ward and Kiendl, Democratic candidate for president in 1924, and a Supreme Court advocate whose reputation was matched only by Charles Evans Hughes before he became Chief Justice in 1930.

Davis's argument was a polished performance, which I thought was masterful. Naturally the law clerks debated the merits of the various lawyers arguing the case, and some of them thought that he appeared over the hill. I did not. He sat down after about an hour and a half, and the solicitor general, Philip B. Perlman, addressed the Court on behalf of the government. There was little dispute among the law clerks that Perlman was not a particularly effective advocate. Justice Jackson complained after the argument that he treated the Court like a jury, and it seemed to me that there was much merit in this complaint. While the Court had appeared to be almost in awe of Davis, and asked him only one question during his ninety minutes of argument, Perlman was virtually peppered with questions from the justices.

The solicitor general relied heavily in his brief and also in his oral argument on the opinion that Justice Jackson had written when he was attorney general, affirming President Roosevelt's authority to seize the North American Aviation Plant shortly before Pearl Harbor. Jackson commented from the bench that he was afraid that a lot of the basis for the government's seizure was being laid at his doorstep, and Perlman agreed. Jackson then responded, "I claimed everything, of course, like every other Attorney General does. It was a custom that didn't leave the Department of Justice when I did."

Every law clerk likes to see his own boss look "sharp" on the bench, as if the justice's performance somehow reflected credit upon the law clerk. I virtually glowed with satisfaction at Justice Jackson's comment, not only because I thought it was both relevant and witty, but because it seemed to me to suggest that he did not agree with the government's position.

The Court rose at 4:30 on Monday, and at noon on Tuesday resumed with the solicitor

general's argument. In closing, Perlman became somewhat hortatory, and insisted to the Court, "This is wartime." Both Jackson and Frankfurter questioned him sharply on this point, pointing out that Congress had indicated rather strongly that it did not regard the present situation in Korea as war. John W. Davis closed with a predictably rhetorical, but nonetheless effective, peroration, and the Court left the bench. The conference on the case was scheduled for noon on Friday, and speculation was intense on the part of the press, the legal community, and needless to say, the law clerks, as to what the result would be....

As I look back now, I wonder if a case cannot be made for some sort of "geographic determinism" so far as the votes of the dissenters are concerned. Fred Vinson, Stanley Reed, and Sherman Minton had all grown up in towns along the Ohio River not more than two hundred miles apart. Vinson and Reed were from Kentucky, Minton from Indiana. I don't know what this proves but it nonetheless seems to me an interesting fact.

Justice Jackson told us that Justice Black, who was the senior justice, would assign the opinion to himself, but that probably several opinions would be written. I don't know whether the justices had set themselves any sort of tentative deadline for circulating opinions in the case, but in a space of less than three weeks seven separate opinions had been written. Justice Black wrote an opinion for the Court, which was joined by Justices Frankfurter, Douglas, Jackson, and Burton; Justice Clark wrote separately, because although he agreed that the President had acted unconstitutionally, he did not agree with the analysis in Justice Black's opinion. When one reads the separate opinions written by Justices Jackson, Frankfurter, Douglas, and Burton, it is apparent that they, too, did not fully subscribe to the view set forth in Justice Black's opinion. But they nonetheless joined it. There simply does not seem to have been enough time for the negotiation that often goes on in order to enable those who disagree with minor parts of a proposed Court opinion, but not with the result, to effect some sort of compromise that will enable them to join the principal opinion.

Justice Black's opinion dealt rather shortly—one is tempted to say almost summarily—with the equitable arguments upon which the government had relied in urging the Court not to reach the constitutional question of the President's power to seize the mills. Black's opinion said that because the damages the mills might suffer if the seizure was invalid would be very difficult to calculate, they were entitled to an injunction against the seizure. At the time this seemed to me a fine example of cutting through a lot of red tape to get to the real issue in the case, but reflection in later years had made me think that there was a lot more to the government's arguments on these issues than the Court gave credit for. On the merits, Justice Black's opinion was quite logical, but also quite abstract. He reasoned that the Constitution has given the lawmaking power to Congress, and has given to the executive certain other powers, which do not include the lawmaking power. Since the seizure of the steel mills was an exercise of what Black described as the lawmaking power, it was beyond the president's authority unless Congress had authorized it.

This very neat analysis obviously bothered most of the justices who joined Black's opinion, and it certainly bothered Justice Jackson. He prepared an opinion that was really more like an essay than a standard judicial opinion, but it is an opinion that proved valuable to subsequent courts and lawyers in discussing the relationship between the president and the Congress. Jackson took the position, not surprisingly, that the president's powers are at their zenith when exercised to execute a law that Congress had enacted; here the legislative and executive powers are combined, and they are potent indeed. The president occupies a middle ground when he seeks to use the executive power to accomplish a goal in an area where Congress has not legislated, and therefore where Congress cannot be said to have either approved or disapproved of the use of presidential power for the purpose for which it is used. The president's authority is

at its nadir when the president acts to accomplish a goal in an area where Congress had already legislated, and when the president's authority is exercised in such a manner as to be inconsistent with the legislation of Congress.

The shortness of time would have precluded much participation by the law clerks in the drafting of Justice Jackson's opinion in any event, but I am sure that this was the sort of opinion in which he felt no need for the help of law clerks. We were shown the opinion in draft form, and as I recall, asked to find citations for some of the propositions it contained, but that was about the extent of our participation....

I had been quite surprised when Justice Jackson told us, "Boys, the President got licked." I thought about the outcome of the Steel Seizure Case some at the time, and I have thought about it a good deal more while writing this book. The law on the equitable issues was clearly in favor of the government, and while the law on the constitutional question was more or less up for grabs, the whole trend of the Court's decisions in the preceding fifteen years leaned toward the government. Why, then, did six members of the Court vote against the government in this case? I think that this is one of those celebrated constitutional cases where what might be called the tide of public opinion suddenly began to run against government, for a number of reasons, and that this tide of public opinion had a considerable influence on the Court.

This was a case that unfurled in the newspapers before the very eyes of the justices long before any papers were filed in the Supreme Court. The members of the Court began learning about it in the morning after President Truman's announcement of his seizure of the steel mills, when the press reported that the steel companies' attorneys had gone to Judge Bastian's home late in the evening to attempt to secure a temporary restraining order against the government. From beginning to end, the facts of the case and its progress through the court were very much of a local event in Washington, heavily covered by the Washington newspapers....

But I also think another, more deeply seated factor played a part in the rides of public opinion that were running at this time. There was a profound ambivalence on the part of much of the public about the Korean War, which was the principal basis upon which President Truman justified his seizure of the steel mills. When North Korea invaded South Korea, President Truman and his top advisers deliberately refrained from asking Congress for a declaration of war, and the United States continued to refer to the Korean conflict as a "police action" under the aegis of the United Nations rather than as a war. But in fact it seemed indistinguishable to most people from a war, in which the fortunes of the United States contrasted rather sharply with the success of that country and its Allies in the Second World War....

The Korean conflict was quite different The initial momentum of the North Koreans carried them far into South Korean territory, but then General MacArthur's landing at Inchon had regained the initiative for the allies and they victoriously crossed back over the thirty-eight parallel boundary. But then the Chinese entered the war, and the allies were forced back from their earlier gains at great cost in men and material. In the spring of 1952, the Korean conflict appeared to be pretty much of a stalemate; the result was an erosion of public willingness to sacrifice. We had a draft, we had price controls, we had rent controls, we had production controls, but these measures during the Second World War, were borne less resolutely and with considerably more grumbling during the Korean conflict. After President Truman forbade

General MacArthur to authorize air strikes beyond the Yalu River, which separated North Korea from China, it seemed very difficult to figure out how the United States could "win" in Korea, and sacrifices that will be cheerfully borne when related to a clearly defined objective will not be so cheerfully borne when the objective seems confused and uncertain. I think that if the steel seizure had take place during the Second World War, the government probably would have won the case under the constitutional grant to the president of the war power, but I also have the distinct feeling that if the American objectives and strategy in Korea had been less uncertain, the government probably would have fared better in the Supreme Court even without being able to resort to the president's war power....

... I was recently asked at a meeting with some people in Washington, who were spending a year studying various aspects of the government, whether the justices were able to isolate themselves from the tides of public opinion. My answer was that we are not able to do so, and it would probably be unwise to try. We read newspapers and magazines, we watch news on television, we talk to our friends about current events. No judge worthy of his salt would ever cast his vote in a particular case simply because he thought the majority of the public wanted him to vote that way, but that is quite a different thing from saying that no judge is ever influenced by the great tides of public opinion that tun in a country such as ours. Judges are influenced by them, and I think that such influence played an appreciable part in causing the Steel Seizure Case to be decided the way it was.

How Political Must Judicial Appointments Be?

74 | *The Confirmation Mess*
Stephen Carter

*How can we prevent the process of confirming judges from hinging on trivial issues and de-
generating into a media circus, as did the confirmations of Robert Bork and Clarence
Thomas? Stephen Carter argues that this problem strikes at the heart of judicial independence and must be addressed if the majesty and legitimacy of the judiciary are to be preserved.*

The trend toward searching for disqualifying
factors means that we have become less interested in how well a nominee for cabinet or
Court will do the job than in whether the individual deserves it, as though the vital question is whether the candidate should get the
chance to add the post to her resume, which
simply reinforces public cynicism about motives for entering public life. We have come
to treat public service as a reward rather than
a calling, which takes us down a rather dangerous road, for it becomes impossible to
bring any sense of proportionality to bear on
the evaluation of potential officials.

Further, the search for disqualifying factors
potentially leads to a rather freewheeling investigation into the backgrounds of nominees. The possibility of keeping one's private
life private becomes virtually nil, as only the
tissue-thin wall of news judgment stands between the nominee and the disclosure (and
condemnation) of whatever the candidate
might least wish to discuss....

In the case of Supreme Court nominees,
the disqualification problem is particularly
acute: in addition to the personal detritus
through which all nominees must wade, the
potential Justice also risks defeat if she has
written or said things that will anger powerful constituencies who are wary of the way in
which she will exercise her commission. In

principle, there is nothing wrong with trying
to get a full picture of nominees for the
Court, especially given the awesome authority that the Justices wield in contemporary society; indeed, neither the President nor the
Senate would be acting in accordance with
the constitutional design were no weight
given to the nominee's outlook. In practice,
however, the effort too often deteriorates into
a public relations campaign in which the
would-be Justice is praised or excoriated for
her likely votes in actual cases. At that point
... we are well on the way to electing our Justices, raising a serious question about why we
do not just go ahead and do it explicitly. Indeed ... if we are not prepared to change the
way we think about the Court, we probably
should consider electing its members, as is
done in most of the states, where the voters
know what they want from their judges and
how to get it.

I would prefer not to go that far; I would
prefer that we make important changes in
our national mood rather than tinker around
with the Constitution. If, however, we are too
set in our ways of envisioning the judicial role
to rethink such matters as whether it really is
wise to campaign for or against nominees according to their likely votes, then constitutional change might be our only way of
avoiding the considerable blood that is too

frequently spilled in our confirmation fights....

"[T]he appointment of a Supreme Court justice," Dean Harry Wellington has written, "and the confirmation process before the Senate must take account of the following truth: the nature of constitutional interpretation in the process of adjudication inevitably means that constitutional law is shaped, influenced, indeed made by those authorized to interpret." Further, in the words of Laurence Tribe, the interpretation of the Constitution should reflect "our values" but will do so "only if we peer closely enough, and probe deeply enough into the outlooks of those whom our Presidents name to sit on the Supreme Court." The trick is to accept this proposition while avoiding a process that rejects the point of judicial review: frustrating the popular will is precisely what the courts are often *for*.

Consider the views of Chief Justice William Rehnquist in his useful 1987 book, *The Supreme Court:* "[A] president who sets out to pack the Court does nothing more than seek to appoint people to the Court who are sympathetic to his political and philosophical principles." Franklin D. Roosevelt, in other words—and, later, Ronald Reagan—were only doing what presidents are supposed to do. Having won the popular election, they were trying to control the courts, much in the manner of, albeit less directly than, the Stuart kings, who in the years before the English Civil War often discussed pending cases with potential judges before deciding on appointments. Rehnquist's evaluation of court-packing is succinct: "There is no reason in the world why a president should not do this."

No reason? The legal scholar Mark Tushnet has put his finger on a potential problem:

[R]elying on the appointment process to check the courts simply reintroduces the problem of legislative tyranny. All that it can accomplish is the creation of repeated oscillation between a regime in which judges defer to legislative will and allow the legislature to tyrannize over those who lack sufficient political power and a regime in which judges do not defer and themselves tyrannize on behalf of parties defeated in the legislature.

Once pointed out, the objection seems an obvious one. Why in the world should anyone who believes in the Constitution believe that elected officials should try to check the Court? The institution of judicial review exists precisely to thwart, not to further, the self-interested programs of temporary majorities.

Rehnquist's answer is that the President and the Senate—he mentions both—should possess a degree of influence over the philosophy of appointees because "the manifold provisions of the Constitution with which judges must deal are by no means crystal clear in their import, and reasonable minds may differ as to which interpretation is proper."...

Because each side of the argument contains a grain of truth, a worrisome paradox emerges. On the one hand, the courts exist at least in part to limit majority sway. On the other, the courts are to be peopled with judges selected at least in part because their constitutional judgments are consistent with those of the very majority whose authority they supposedly limit....

However, the worrisome paradox may be more apparent than real, because once one moves away from the academy, it seems unlikely that many of the pundits and politicians who talk about a Court reflecting the values of the American people seriously want that. Usually, what they want instead is a Court reflecting *their own* values—that is, they want Justices who can be trusted to vote the right way. Indeed, the views of the American people tend to be the last thing that activists want the Court to heed. Perhaps this explains the phenomenon, which students of the confirmation process have long noted, of senators struggling to find grounds other than ideology on which to place their opposition that everyone understands is really ideological....

On the other hand, perhaps what seems to be confusion actually reflects something fundamental in the American character. Perhaps most Americans do not draw a distinction between personal moral belief and constitutional interpretation because they do not believe it is real—that is, if you support a woman's right to choose abortion, then, ipso facto, you believe that the Constitution should be read to protect it. After all, the mere fact that a handful of scholars who ruminate on these matters in the old fashion believe that the distinction is real does not mean that anybody else is obliged to think so....

Reforming our understanding of what disqualifies a nominee from public service will not eliminate the bloodbaths that are all too frequent when the contest involves a seat on the Supreme Court. Given the vast power that the Justices will continue to exercise in American society, one can hardly avoid the bitter battles that have characterised some 40 percent of the nominations since *Brown v. Board of Education* was decided in 1954. After all, when a seat falls vacant, there is much at stake—especially as one's most hated or loved decisions slip from a majority of 7 to 2 to one of 6 to 3 to the tantalizing 5 to 4.

The most obvious way to avoid leaving blood on the floor is to name individuals of the highest caliber and experience, with much less attention paid to their likely votes. The proper model might be the one followed by Gerald Ford, in uncovering the gem of John Paul Stevens. Ford, insisting that "ideological grounds" are not proper in judicial selection, was evidently quite serious when he instructed his attorney general—the formidable, non-political Edward Levi—to make recommendations without regard to the political views of the nominee, for the list of finalists was remarkably diverse. The Stevens nomination had opponents at the ideological extremes—Bella Abzug and Pat Buchanan were both sharply critical—but the great middle, which includes the moderate right and the moderate left, found little problem with Stevens, who was confirmed by a vote of 98–0.

President Clinton plainly had something similar in mind when he selected Ruth Bader Ginsburg in 1993, choosing, so news reports had it, between her and one other finalist, Judge Stephen Breyer. Both are judges of considerable ability who, like Stevens, are re-spected across the political spectrum. By limiting his choice to such individuals, he successfully resisted the pressure to select someone who could be counted on more reliably to vote into constitutional law his party's platform—which is approximately what Democrats accused Republicans of doing in the decade between 1981 and 1991. And although there was some conservative carping, Ginsburg was confirmed by a vote of 96–3.

Perhaps unsurprisingly, critics of recent confirmation fights seem unwilling to contemplate the possibility that the selection of nominees was an important part of the problem. They have focused instead on what has happened after the announcement of a nomination and have set forth a number of proposals that would, they believe, reduce the amount of blood on the floor.... Although we try mightily to resist the temptation, we continue to view the Court as a servant, charged with handing down decisions that most people want; when it fails to do so, we grow furious, and promise to remake it, which is, we insist, our prerogative. We demand a degree of judicial accountability, which is another way of saying that we are unhappy with genuine judicial independence. If we are unable or unwilling to alter those attitudes, then we ought to consider a quite different and more radical shift in how we think about choosing our justices. I say this without any enthusiasm for tampering with the Constitution, least of all with the delicate balance involved in the appointment process; yet in the way we think, talk, and act on the selection of Supreme Court justices, we the people have, in effect, already altered the original constitutional arrangements. All we have failed to do is codify our new understanding....

One obvious solution would be to raise the threshold vote necessary for confirmation from a simple majority of the Senate to two-thirds. This change, it is said, would force the President to find a potential Justice not strongly identified with an ideological movement, because the nominee would be unable to squeak by. By this standard, note its supporters, Robert Bork (defeated by 42 to 58) and Clarence Thomas (confirmed by 52 to 48) would never have been nominated, because each of them certainly began with one-third of the Senate in opposition, and although William Rehnquist might still have been nominated for Chief Justice in 1986, he would have been rejected, because the vote in favor was 65 to 33–1 vote short of two-thirds....

Still, the bottom line is this: had the required vote for Supreme Court confirmations been two-thirds of the Senate, Ronald Reagan would never have dared nominate Robert Bork. This would have denied the nation his services, but those services were denied in any case, and even if the Reagan Administration was unable to predict that Bork's hearings would be quite so testy, it might have been somewhat easier to predict that he would not gain a two-thirds majority. Faced with a super-majority requirement ... and already having obtained easy confirmations for Sandra Day O'Connor and Antonin Scalia, Reagan might have done initially what he did in the end: nominated a thoughtful, conservative-leaning centrist like Anthony Kennedy. When you add in other admired Justices—John Paul Stevens, for example, was confirmed by 98–0—it is plain that although the supermajority requirement would screen out nominees who were perceived, rightly or wrongly, as narrow-minded, it would not screen out quality. On the contrary: it might well screen out mediocrity. Surely if Richard Nixon in 1971 had been faced with the two-thirds hurdle, he would not have nominated Carswell, who generated Senator Roman Hruska's famous epigram: "Even if he is mediocre there are a lot of mediocre judges and people and lawyers. They are entitled to a little representation, aren't they...?" Were the nominee required to gain the affirmative votes of two-thirds of the senators (the same plurality required for treaties), the answer to Hruska's question would be an easy no.

So the two-thirds standard *could* work, as long as it encouraged the President to seek a nominee respected on all sides, able to garner votes even from those who disagree sharply on philosophy—a nominee, for example, like Ruth Bader Ginsburg (confirmed 96 to 3) or Antonin Scalia (confirmed 98 to 0). Requiring a supermajority for confirmation, in other words, would encourage consensus candidates rather than predictable ideologues. Certainly we *could* nevertheless have a bitter battle over confirmation, but a confrontation would not be likely unless the President tried to pack the Court as part of an ideological crusade. But must we go on picking Justices the way that we do? Maybe not. If we really want a democratic check—if we really think the Court should reflect the fundamental values of the American people—why not let the people choose? Again, I remind the reader that I think popular choice of Justices a terrible idea—but I think it just as bad to encourage the President and the senators to talk, nominate, and vote as though public opinion should rule constitutional law. Most voters—and certainly most politicians—seem to accept the contrary view, that their opinions on constitutional interpretation should carry some weight. It is that reality that the notion of popular choice would reflect. Let us now travel down that road briefly and see how the scenery looks....

One might object that all this talk of election constitutes a threat to judicial independence. In principle, I certainly agree; and yet the election systems that I have described are less different from what we do now than they may seem. Right now, when controversy erupts over a Supreme Court nomination, we ask the voters what they think. We fight for their opinions with television commentaries, newspaper columns, planted stories of scandal or defense, even paid advertisements. Of course, under the current system, much of the work, and all of the voting, is concentrated inside the Beltway. Were we to elect the Justices directly, rather than by proxy, the principal change would be that this game of democratic checkers, of having the chance to enshrine the values of a passing political majority as fundamental constitutional law, would be opened up to the entire voting public, to all of us—all of "we, the people"—rather than limited to the liberal and conservative Beltway activists who speak with perfect sincerity in the people's name....

One who rejects these modest proposals then, either (1) believes that potential Justices should be screened for their fidelity to "our" values, but that the people in whose name it is done are not competent to take part in it, or (2) rejects the conventional wisdom holding that the screening is appropriate to begin with. The first option reduces the screening to an elite phenomenon—in effect, an "undemocratic" check, in which small interest groups work to gain seats on the Court in order to work their will on the nation. The second option is more sensible. Indeed, the true solution to the Supreme Court confirmation mess lies in our ability to develop a public rhetoric about the Constitution that does not treat the Court as though the results it reaches are all that matters. And that change would require that we rethink our attitude about the Court and its place in our society.

What is wrong with our attitude about the Court? Three things, all of them staples of polemics from the left or the right. First, as many commentators have argued, we rely too heavily on the Justices to correct what we often view as the errors of the other branches of government, including the state and local entities where most lawmaking takes place. Second, and perhaps as a consequence of the first, we have become so bound up in the rhetorical habit of referring to constitutional rights that we have virtually lost the ability to engage in public dialogue about tough moral questions. Third, we have developed so much political machinery designed to control or influence the Justices that we have lost sight of the principal means through which change must come in a democracy, if the change is to have lasting effect: the persuasion of our fellow citizens.

75 The Political Court
Randall Kennedy

In response to Stephen Carter, Randall Kennedy defends the confirmation upheaval. Presidents will want to shape the Court, for to do so is to shape the future, says Kennedy. The nomination process, moreover, represents the only chance the public ever has to consider life-appointed judges. Zealous advocacy from all quarters is not only to be expected but also to be championed.

President Clinton will likely have the opportunity to fill several vacancies on the Supreme court. How should he go about doing it? Although the president should look to a variety of considerations, by far the most important is a prospect's substantive political commitments. By substantive political commitments, I mean a prospect's stance towards the central, inescapable, politically significant controversies of our time. In the 1850s, a president should definitely have wanted to know where a prospect stood on the slavery question; in the 1930s, where a prospect stood on the New Deal; in the 1960s, where a prospect stood with respect to the civil rights revolution. Today President Clinton should acquire knowledge that will let him know in detail and with confidence where a prospective nominee stands on all of the most vexing issues that trouble our society including reproductive freedom, race relations, freedom of expression, and the status of religion in a secular society. To acquire this information, the president (and the Senate) should directly ask prospects about their political beliefs. If a person declines to answer, the president should probably draw a negative inference, strike that prospect from the list of candidates, and move on to consider others who will allow the president access to his or her thinking.

One thing the president should not do is place a powerful branch of government in the hands of individuals whose political commitments are unknown to him. That would be folly. Yet, remarkably, that is what some observers urge.

Consider, for instance, the argument of Professor Stephen Carter of the Yale Law School. In an op-ed piece in the *New York Times*, Carter claims that the Reagan and Bush administrations "systematically eroded federal courts' independence" by applying "litmus tests to insure that those who became judges—particularly Supreme Court Justices—could be relied on to vote the way the conservatives preferred." He portrays "quizzing nominees about their views on controversial cases" as a politically depraved exercise of power heretofore practiced mainly by discredited politicos on the right.

According to Carter, "When William Brennan was badgered by Senator Joseph McCarthy about loyalty-security cases and Thurgood Marshall was interrogated by several segregationist senators about civil rights and criminal procedure cases, liberals were properly outraged that a nominee would be asked, even indirectly, about his likely votes." Carter rails against searching for information that will allow the president to predict confidently how a nominee will vote as a justice. "Certainly it is true," he concedes, "that information is usually available from which it is possible to make educated guesses about how potential justices might vote. But to emphasize those predispositions as a prerequisite for appointment politicizes the Court." The president, Carter concludes, "should forgo litmus tests and turn to one of the many experienced federal or state appellate judges whose skills are respected across the political spectrum." Otherwise, Carter warns darkly, the cycle of judicial politicization will never end and "[t]here will be less and less reason to treat the 'opinions' of the courts as authoritative and no reason at all to grant the judges—and justices—life tenure."

Carter's argument reflects much of the confusion, mysticism, and sentimentality that commonly stymies realistic understandings of the judiciary. He objects that the course I advocate would "politicize" the Court. It would be helpful if he would point to a moment in our history in which the selection process was unpoliticized—a point at which a president was blithely indifferent to the political associations and ideological predispositions of a prospective nominee and considered only "skill." He will be unable to make such a showing because, unsurprisingly, this moment has never existed. How could it? Members of the Supreme Court occupy seats with life tenure within a bureaucracy that wields considerable power. A president would be a fool or, worse, politically amoral to elevate to such an office anyone whose politics suggested a proclivity toward policies with which the president strongly disagreed. Carter's references to the Reagan and Bush administrations' ideological screening of potential nominees and his allusions to the difficulties that William Brennan and Thurgood Marshall received as nominees at the hands of McCarthyists and segregationists should scare no one. There was, and is, nothing wrong with politicians of any ideological stripe demanding to know where prospective justices stand on political issues that are likely to be implicated in cases arising before the Court. What was wrong in the instances to which Carter alludes was not the questioning but an environment in which straightforward progressive responses to the inquiries posed a danger to candidates. Instead of seeking to insulate nominees from questions, liberals and the left should seek to persuade the public of the attractiveness of progressive answers.

Carter claims that insisting upon knowing the political predispositions of nominees—or, in his lingo, imposing a litmus test—erodes the independence of the judiciary. But how so? Judicial independence means placing individuals beyond the usual means of political discipline after that person has been elevated to judicial office. That insulation is attended to by constitutional provisions that explicitly mention two mechanisms that afford ample protection to the judiciary against interference from the other branches of government. One is life tenure: once appointed and confirmed, judges can be removed only pursuant to impeachment by the House of Representatives and conviction by the Senate—a costly, cumbersome process that has never been successfully invoked to oust a recalcitrant justice.

The second is income protection: the Constitution forbids Congress from decreasing the salaries paid to members of the federal judiciary. Neither Carter nor anyone else has set forth a convincing or even plausible explanation of why judicial independence—the autonomy of sitting justices—is eroded by subjecting a person to inquiries designed to inform a president of the political virtues of one candidate as opposed to another. After all, once a person is seated as a justice, the mechanisms protecting judicial independence ensure that person can change his or her mind without fear of losing office.

Moreover, contrary to what Carter suggests, it is precisely because justices are so fully insulated from the normal rigors of political discipline (that is, periodically standing for election) that it is especially important and appropriate for those responsible for elevating them to determine as fully as possible their political character. If the electorate makes a political mistake in selecting a president or a member of the House or Senate, the electorate must wait only two, four, or six years before rectifying that mistake. If the president makes a political mistake in the selection of a justice, only the indefinite and often painfully slow process of aging can remedy it.

Why is it important to know the political character of justices? Because their interpretation of statutes and determinations of the constitutionality of laws is inevitably influenced by that character. Expertise alone is an insufficient guide by which to determine who, from the point of view of a president, would best give meaning to the ambiguous, open-ended clauses that comprise the most important and controversial parts of our written constitution: due process, equal protection of the laws, freedom of speech. "Skill" of various sorts is important. A president should certainly insist on choosing someone who will be sufficiently adept, knowledgeable, and confident to persuade colleagues, isolate adversaries, and educate the public. But juristic skill is merely a tool; it does not guarantee that a justice will reach good results. For that to happen, expertise must be guided by a good political vision. It stands to reason that the president and the Senate should avail themselves of means by which to determine a prospect's political vision. Doing so shows no disrespect for the Court. Rather, it reflects a laudable determination to avoid putting the future of the federal judiciary into the hands of persons whose political commitments are unknown.

Carter and others claim that seeking to know in detail the political views of nominees or potential nominees is bad because it suggests a desire to select persons who are close-minded. "[A]ppointing justices who make up their minds before, not after, hearing arguments threatens judicial integrity," Carter writes, "and interferes with the Court's proper functioning. It was wrong for the Republicans to do it; it would be wrong if the Democrats do it." The specter Carter invokes is a straw man. Those with whom he argues do not advocate appointing justices who are closed to argument. Rather, they maintain that any person worthy of serious consideration has already considered arguments, that such a person has likely reached conclusions (that are possibly changeable in light of additional consideration), and that whatever conclusions he or she has reached should be accessible to a president. The idea that knowing a prospect's current views somehow taints the integrity of the selection process is hard to fathom, given that many of the best people any president is likely to consider for a justiceship are people with public careers whose stances on heated topics are already known.

Pleas to de-politicize the selection and confirmation process, to cherish unpredictability in the future course of nominees, to purposefully keep ourselves ignorant about the beliefs of people we empower represent a quasi-religious yearning to make the Court into a shrine above the messiness of politics. But what the process of selection and confirmation needs is more rather than less "politics"—more widely available knowledge about nominees, more debate, more participation by the governed, more presidential accountability for nominees, and more common sense. Neither the president nor the public should be asked to accept a pig in a poke. To know fully the political character of those he is considering selecting, the president must ask pointed questions—and demand clear answers.

CHAPTER TWELVE

Civil Rights and Liberties

OVERVIEW AND SUMMARY

The Bill of Rights is America's sacred scripture, the citizens' "thou shalt nots" against intrusive government. The readings in this chapter are about the past, present, and future of civil rights and liberties.

Note that the Supreme Court cases referred to here (as well as in the other areas of the book) can be found in Appendix V. These cases presented some of the thorniest issues in the Court's docket since the 1930s and show the Court struggling to draw lines between individual rights and liberties on one side and important communal values on the other. The paradox of democracy that emerges in this chapter is that citizens have turned to the most obvious elite institution of the government to protect these most cherished aspects of democratic government.

The first readings and Court cases deal with the First Amendment. Often referred to as the First Freedom, the First Amendment guarantees freedom of speech, press, religious conscience, assembly, and association. **John Stuart Mill**, who presents what is still the best argument for the rights guaranteed by the First Amendment, claims that free speech serves at least two purposes. First, it is the indispensable requirement for the exercise of political freedom and the exchange of ideas. Second, no society can afford to be deprived of the opinions of anyone, for at some future time even the least of minority opinions may become accepted truth.

Freedom of speech occupies a hallowed station in constitutional law. But even the most ardent civil libertarian recognizes that individual rights need to be tempered by other important interests. If the freedom to swing one's arms ends at the nose of another, it must also be true that liberty at some point can be akin to license.

Can unfettered free speech apply absolutely while a nation is at war or when the country faces a serious threat of internal subversion? Does free expression also apply to obscene depiction? Is the First Amendment a pathway to ruin, and must the Court light this disastrous path? *Schenck v. U.S.* (1919) considers whether the First Amendment protects antidraft agitators in time of war. This is the case in which Justice Holmes outlined the famous "clear and present danger" exception to the free speech clause. A more recent, though no less controversial, representation of First Amendment problems is shown by *Texas v. Johnson* (1989). Here the issue is whether the beloved symbol of the patriots, the American flag, can be protected against incineration.

Next, several religion cases answer the question of whether the no-establishment clause of the First Amendment should be interpreted to ban widespread public practices that are akin to religious ceremonies. **Thomas Jefferson**'s Virginia Statute of Religious Freedom provides a principled justification for the establishment clause. Then, read *Engel v. Vitale* (1962), in which the Court banned the practice of prayer in public schools. Finally, see *Lynch v. Donnelly* (1984), which considers whether the placement of a nativity scene in a public square constitutes government sponsorship of religion.

As much as First Amendment freedoms, crime is a great concern of the public and a perennial part of the Court's docket as well. Criticism of the Court's role in criminal law has mounted ever since the Warren Court (1953–1969) decided that the Fourth Amendment (protection against unreasonable searches and seizures), Fifth Amendment (protections against self-incrimination and double jeopardy), and Sixth Amendment (right to counsel and to trial by jury) were sufficiently "implicit in a scheme of ordered liberty" to be applied to every small town and every cop on the beat. Two cases that demonstrate the Court's role in criminal law and procedure are *Gideon v. Wainwright* (1963), the "right-to-an-attorney" case, and *Miranda v. Arizona* (1966), which considered police practices in eliciting confessions.

In contrast to these cases, capital punishment offers an example of policy-making from the bottom up (see Appendix VI). In the late 1960s, public opinion began to move toward abolishing the death penalty. At the same time, states began to observe informal capital punishment moratoriums, awaiting a ruling from the Supreme Court about whether the death penalty was "cruel and unusual punishment" under the strictures of the Eighth Amendment. In *Furman v. Georgia* (1972), the Court struck down the death statutes of all fifty states on the procedural grounds of arbitrary or "freakish" administration. In reaction to the *Furman* decision, most states reinstituted their death-penalty laws, and public opinion in support of the ultimate sanction grew overwhelming. The Court upheld these laws, as long as procedural safeguards existed to check the discretion of judges and juries.

We may have come full circle in this area of the law. As evidence of freakish administration mounts and, more important, as dozens of death row inmates have proved their innocence through the use of DNA and other scientific technology, a new abolitionist movement is germinating.

Of all the issues that come before the Court, race most constitutes an American dilemma. If ever there was a story of a nation struggling to come to terms with a past it cannot quite comprehend, race relations in America is that story. The twin legacies of slavery and segregation represent, for America, the stain that will not disappear. To read the eloquent rage of **Frederick Douglass** is to know that this legacy could not and never can be quickly or easily erased. Indeed, with the end of slavery came Jim Crow laws, mandating racial segregation in all aspects of Southern society—laws that were upheld by the Court in *Plessy v. Ferguson* (1896).

On the other hand, the racial dilemma also provides one of the few examples of the Court's lead in a movement for social justice. The decision in *Brown v. Board of Education* (1954) pronounced the end of America's official segregation (see Appendix VII). It also ushered in white consciousness of the civil rights movement.

The early years of the movement culminated in the Civil Rights Act of 1964, the Voting Rights Act of 1965, and other legislation at both the state and federal levels to remove the last vestiges of Jim Crow laws. Perhaps the most important contribution of the movement was the development of a societal consensus that America did indeed have a racist stain to eradicate. However, this consensus broke down over such issues as busing to integrate public schools and affirmative action in hiring practices. The question—and conflict—was whether the country's racist past required color-conscious remedies or whether America could have a color-blind society, one where any racial classifications and preferences were abhorrent. In the signature case of affirmative action, *Regents v. Bakke* (1978), the Court, perhaps reflecting the nation's confusion, decided it both ways. The controlling opinion suggested that race can be considered as a plus (at least in university admissions) but not as the sole determining factor.

Reflecting on the history of affirmation action, **Charles Fried** sees a paradox in which the desire for a color-blind society and the use of affirmative action become the obstacle that prevents true integration. Whereas some argued that only directed, "benign" color-conscious policies could ameliorate the effects of centuries of racism, the solicitor general in the second Reagan administration argued against affirmative action. The crux of his argument then, as now, is that temporary remedies for racism are not temporary: The remedies themselves make society, if not racist, then "racialist," and in either case cannot lead to the promised land of a color-blind society. If nothing else, Fried reminds us that the American dilemma of race remains with us.

The struggle for American women is no less paradoxical and may be no less profound. Gender-based classifications are generally justified by tradition or as necessary for the "protection" of women, and thus the standards for gender-based classifications are somewhat less stringent than those for race. Nevertheless, the Court subjects gender classifications to close scrutiny and frequently strikes down these statues, as it did in *Craig v. Boren* (1978).

The struggle continues for women—and many others—in that unwritten portion of the Bill of Rights known as the unenumerated rights. Most Americans would agree that certain rights do exist even if they are not listed in the Bill of Rights. Indeed, the Ninth Amendment says as much. The right to marry, the right to travel, and freedom from intrusion by the state in matters of family are just a few of those rights recognized, but not enumerated. But where in the Constitution do such rights exist and how are they to be bounded? In *Roe v. Wade* (1973) the Court applied the right of privacy to a woman's choice to carry or not to carry a fetus to term (see Appendix VIII). **Susan Estrich** and **Kathleen Sullivan** present abortion as a classic area for judicial intervention. They claim that leaving the right of choice to the fifty states leaves this fundamental right in the hands of activist minorities armed only with the tools of organization and persuasion. It could create a situation in which the right to choose abortion is limited to urban dwellers or those with the resources to procure the procedure. It almost certainly would create a situation in which a legal medical procedure in one state would be something akin to criminal homicide in another. They conclude that if the right of reproductive freedom is fundamental, as the *Roe* case proclaimed, it is up to the judiciary to vindicate it.

Do such privacy rights extend to alternative lifestyles? The case law in this area again reflects the ambiguities of society. Whereas direct or invidious discrimination against groups such as homosexuals is almost universally struck down, the Court has been reluctant to use the equal protection clause of the Fourteenth Amendment to announce new rights in the face of state antisodomy statutes or long-standing societal practices. The dimensions of this controversy are well captured by *Dale v. Boy Scouts of America* (2000) and by **Larry P. Arrn**.

Cloning? The right to die? The disposition of frozen embryos? Assisted suicide? Genetic mapping and DNA fingerprinting? Internet snooping? High-tech surveillance of people in both public and private places? These are privacy issues at the frontiers of civil liberties in the twenty-first century. Thus, the chapter closes with a discussion of the new frontier issue of surveillance where it meets an issue from the old frontier—guns.

On the old frontier is crime and guns. Some states are again allowing licensed citizens to carry concealed weapons. Representative **Clifford Stearns** (R-FL) claims that the passage of concealed weapons laws has correlated with a significant decrease in violent crime rates. He wants to federalize right-to-carry laws and thereby extend the protection one state allows its citizens to those same citizens while traveling across state borders.

On the new frontier is high-tech surveillance. As our capacity to track individual behavior increases, some find surveillance an ideal crime-prevention technique. Law enforcement agencies, corporations, and private citizens alike show an appetite for high-tech gadgetry that allows them to keep a better watch on their property and the people who move through it. But **Thomas C. Weisert** weighs the pros and cons of a surveillance society.

The new surveillance calls into question the boundaries of the right of privacy, painfully built up over many decades. What is a "reasonable" search when video cameras are constantly turned on, when the movements of automobiles are subject to electronic tracking, or when security officers have gadgetry that can see through a person's clothing? After all, "if a man's privacy can be invaded at will, who can say he is free?" To resolve these issues, we will no doubt turn again to the most obvious elite institution of government—the Court—to protect the most cherished aspects of civil liberties. Will the Court have either the inclination or the competence to serve as our protector?

76 | *On Liberty*
John Stuart Mill

The nineteenth-century British philosopher John Stuart Mill offers his justification of free speech. To Mill, free speech does not only broaden the public discourse but also frees the human spirit.

Let us suppose, that the government is entirely at one with the people, and never thinks of exerting any power of coercion unless in agreement with what it conceives to be their voice. But I deny the right of the people to exercise such coercion, either by themselves or by their government. The power itself is illegitimate. The best government has no more title to it than the worst. It is as noxious, or more noxious, when exerted in accordance with public opinion, than when in opposition to it. If all mankind minus one, were of one opinion, and only one person were of the contrary opinion, mankind would be no more justified in silencing that one person, than he, if he had the power, would be justified in silencing mankind. Were an opinion a personal possession of no value except to the owner; if to be obstructed in the enjoyment of it were simply a private injury, it would make some difference whether the injury was inflicted only on a few persons or on many. But the peculiar evil of silencing the expression of an opinion is that it is robbing the human race; posterity as well as the existing generation; those who dissent from the opinion, still more than those who hold it. If the opinion is right, they are deprived of the opportunity of exchanging error for truth: if wrong, they lose, what is almost as great a benefit, the clearer perception and livelier impression of truth, produced by its collision with error.

It is necessary to consider separately these two hypotheses, each of which has a distinct branch of the argument corresponding to it. We can never be sure that the opinion we are endeavoring to stifle is a false opinion; and if we were sure, stifling it would be an evil still.

First: the opinion which it is attempted to suppress by authority may possibly be true. Those who desire to suppress it, of course deny its truth; but they are not infallible. They have no authority to decide the question for all mankind, and exclude every other person from the means of judging. To refuse a hearing to an opinion, because they are sure that it is false, is to assume that *their* certainty is the same thing as *absolute* certainty. All silencing of discussion is an assumption of infallibility. Its condemnation may be allowed to rest on this common argument, not the worse for being common.

Unfortunately for the good sense of mankind, the fact of their fallibility is far from carrying the weight in their practical judgment, which is always allowed to it in theory; for while every one well knows himself to be fallible, few think it necessary to take any precautions against their own fallibility, or admit the supposition that any opinion, of which they feel very certain, may be one of the examples of the error to which they acknowledge themselves to be liable. Absolute princes, or others who are accustomed to unlimited deference, usually feel this complete confidence in their own opinions on nearly all subjects. People more happily situated, who sometimes hear their opinions disputed, and are not wholly unused to be set right when they are wrong, place the same unbounded reliance only on such of their opinions as are shared by all who surround them, or to whom they habitually defer: for in proportion to a man's want of confidence in his own solitary judgment, does he usually repose, with implicit trust, on the infallibility of "the world" in general. And the world, to each individual, means the part of it with which he comes in contact; his party, his sect, his church, his class of society: the man may be called, by comparison, almost liberal and largeminded to whom it means anything so comprehensive as his own country or his own age.... Yet it is as evident in itself, as any amount of argument can make it, that ages are no more infallible than individuals; every age having held many opinions which subsequent ages have deemed not only false but absurd; and it is as certain that many opinions, now general, will be rejected by future ages, as it is that many, once general, are rejected by the present.

The objection likely to be made to this argument, would probably take some such form as the following. There is no greater assumption of infallibility in forbidding the propagation of error, than in any other thing which is done by public authority on its own judgment and responsibility. Judgment is given to men that they may use it. Because it may be used erroneously, are men to be told that they ought not to use it at all? To prohibit what they think pernicious, is not claiming exemption from error, but fulfilling the duty incumbent on them, although fallible, of acting on their conscientious conviction. If we were never to act on our opinions, because those opinions may be wrong, we should leave all our interests uncared for, and all our duties unperformed. An objection which applies to all conduct, can be no valid objection to any conduct in particular. It is the duty of governments, and of individuals, to form the truest opinions they can; to form them carefully, and never impose them upon others unless they are quite sure of being right. But when they are sure (such reasoners may say), it is not conscientiousness but cowardice to shrink from acting on their opinions, and allow doctrines which they honestly think dangerous to the welfare of mankind, either in this life or in another, to be scattered abroad without restraint, because other people, in less enlightened times, have persecuted opinions now believed to be true. Let us take care, it may be said, not to make the same mistake: but governments and nations have made mistakes in other things, which are not denied to be fit subjects for the exercise of authority: they have laid on bad taxes, made unjust wars. Ought we therefore to lay on no taxes, and, under whatever provocation, make no wars? Men, and governments, must act to the best of their ability. There is no such thing as absolute certainty, but there is assurance sufficient for the purposes of human life. We may, and must, assume our opinion to be true for the guidance of our own conduct: and it is assuming no more when we forbid bad men to pervert society by the propagation of opinions which we regard as false and pernicious.

I answer that it is assuming very much more. There is the greatest difference between presuming an opinion to be true, because, with every opportunity for contesting it, it had not been refuted, and assuming its truth for the purpose of not permitting its refutation. Complete liberty of contradicting and disproving our opinion, is the very condition which justifies us in assuming its truth for purposes of action; and on no other terms can a being with human faculties have any rational assurance of being right....

... Wrong opinions and practices gradually yield to fact and argument: but facts and arguments, to produce any effect on the mind, must be brought before it. Very few facts are able to tell their own story, without comments to bring out their meaning. The whole strength and value, then, of human judgment, depending on the one property, that it can be set right when it is wrong, reliance can be placed on it only when the means of setting it right are kept constantly at hand. In the case of any person whose judgment is really deserving of confidence, how has it become so? Because he has kept his mind open to criticism of his opinions and conduct. Because it has been his practice to listen to all that could be said against him; to profit by as much of it as was just, and expound to himself, and upon occasion to others, the fallacy of what was fallacious. Because he has felt, that the only way in which a human being can make some approach to knowing the whole of a subject, is by hearing what can be said about it by persons of every variety of opinion, and studying all modes in which it can be looked at by every character of mind. No wise man ever acquired his wisdom in any mode but this; nor is it in the nature of human intellect to become wise in any other manner. The steady habit of correcting and completing his own opinion by collating it with those of others, so far from causing doubt and hesitation in carrying it into practice, is the only stable foundation for a just reliance on it: for, being cognizant of all that can, at least obviously, be said against him, and having taken up his position against all gainsayers—knowing that he has sought for objections and difficulties, instead of avoiding them, and has shut out no light which can be thrown upon the subject from any quarter—he has a right to think his judgment better than that of any person, or any multitude, who have not gone through a similar process....

We have now recognized the necessity to the mental well-being of mankind (on which all their other well-being depends) of freedom of opinion, and freedom of the expression of opinion, on four distinct grounds; which we will now briefly recapitulate.

First, if any opinion is compelled to silence, that opinion may, for aught we can certainly know, be true. To deny this is to assume our own infallibility.

Secondly, though the silenced opinion be an error, it may, and very commonly does, contain a portion of truth; and since the general or prevailing opinion on any subject is rarely or never the whole truth, it is only by the collision of adverse opinions that the remainder of the truth has any chance of being supplied.

Thirdly, even if the received opinion be not only true, but the whole truth; unless it is suffered to be, and actually is, vigorously and earnestly contested, it will, by most of those who receive it, be held in the manner of a prejudice, with little comprehension of feeling of its rational grounds. And not only this, but fourthly, the meaning of the doctrine itself will be in danger of being lost, or enfeebled, and deprived of its vital effect on the character and conduct: the dogma becoming a mere formal profession, inefficacious for good, but cumbering the ground, and preventing the growth of any real and heartfelt conviction from reason or personal experience.

77 | *The Virginia Statute of Religious Freedom*
Thomas Jefferson

One of the three accomplishments listed on Thomas Jefferson's tombstone (the others are the writing of the Declaration of Independence and the founding of the University of Virginia) is his statement of the principles underlying the no-establishment and the free exercise clauses of the First Amendment.

I. *Whereas* Almighty God has created the mind free, so that all attempts to influence it by temporal punishments or burdens, or by civil incapacitations, tend only to beget habits of hypocrisy and meanness, and are a departure from the plan of the Holy Author of our religion, who, being Lord both of body and mind, yet chose not to propagate it by coercions on either, as was in His almighty power to do; that the impious presumption of legislators and rulers, civil as well as ecclesiastical, who, being themselves but fallible and uninspired men, have assumed dominion over the faith of others, setting up their own opinions and modes of thinking as the only true and infallible, and as such endeavoring to impose them on others, has established and maintained false religions over the greatest part of the world, and through all time; that to compel a man to furnish contributions of money for the propagation of opinions which he disbelieves is sinful and tyrannical; that even forcing him to support this or that teacher of his own religious persuasion is depriving him of the comfortable liberty of giving his contributions to the particular pastor whose morals he would make his pattern and whose powers he feels most persuasive to righteousness, and is withdrawing from the ministry those temporary rewards which, proceeding from an approbation of their personal conduct, are an additional incitement to earnest and unremitting labors for the instruction of mankind; that our civil rights have no dependence on our religious opinions, any more than our opinions in physics or geometry; that, therefore, the proscribing [of] any citizen as unworthy [of] the public confidence by laying upon him an incapacity of being called to offices of trust and emolument unless he profess or renounce this or that religious opinion is depriving him injuriously of those privileges and advantages to which in common with his fellow citizens he has a natural right; that it tends only to corrupt the principles of that ... religion it is meant to encourage, by bribing with a monopoly of worldly honors and emoluments those who will externally profess and conform to it; that though indeed these are criminal who do not withstand such temptation, yet neither are those innocent who lay the bait in their way; that to suffer the civil magistrate to intrude his powers into the field of opinion, and to restrain the profusion or propagation of principles on supposition of their ill tendency, is a dangerous fallacy which at once destroys all religious liberty, because he, being of course judge of that tendency, will make his opinions the rule of judgment, and approve or condemn the sentiments of others only as they shall square with or differ from his own; that it is time enough for the rightful purposes of civil government for its officers to interfere when principles break out into overt acts against peace and good order; and finally, that truth is great and will prevail if left to herself, that she is the proper and sufficient antagonist to error, and has nothing to fear from the conflict, unless by human interposition disarmed of her natural weapons, free argument and debate, errors ceasing to be dangerous when it is permitted freely to contradict them.

II. *Be it ... enacted by the General Assembly* that no man shall be compelled to frequent or support any religious worship, place, or ministry whatsoever, nor shall be enforced, restrained, molested, or burdened in his body or goods, nor shall otherwise suffer on account of his religious opinions or belief; but that all men shall be free to profess, and by argument to maintain, their opinion in matters of religion, and that the same shall in no wise diminish, enlarge, or affect their civil capacities.

III. And though we well know that this Assembly, elected by the people for the ordinary purposes of legislation only, have no power to restrain the acts of succeeding assemblies, constituted with powers equal to our own, and that therefore to declare this act to be irrevocable would be of no effect in law; yet as we are free to declare, and do declare, that the rights hereby asserted are of the natural rights of mankind, and that if any act shall hereafter be passed to repeal the present, or to narrow its operation, such act will be an infringement of natural right.

78 | *What to the Slave Is the Fourth of July?*
Frederick Douglass

Famous ex-slave and tribune of the antislavery movement, Frederick Douglass delivered this paean to the promise of America from the standpoint of the downtrodden. It was delivered at Rochester, New York, July 5, 1852.

Fellow-citizens—Pardon me, and allow me to ask, why am I called upon to speak here today? What have I, or those I represent, to do with your national independence? Are the great principles of political freedom and of natural justice, embodied in that Declaration of Independence, extended to us? and am I, therefore, called upon to bring our humble offering to the national altar, and to confess the benefits, and express devout gratitude for the blessings, resulting from your independence to us?

Would to God, both for your sakes and ours, that an affirmative answer could be truthfully returned to these questions? Then would my task be light and my burden easy and delightful. For who is there so cold that a nation's sympathy could not warm him? Who so obdurate and dead to the charms of gratitude, that would not thankfully acknowledge such priceless benefits? Who so stolid and

selfish, that would not give his voice to swell the hallelujahs of a nation's jubilee, when the chains of servitude had been torn from his limbs? I am not that man. In a case like that, the dumb might eloquently speak, and the "lame man leap as an hart."

But, such is not the state of the case. I say it with a sad sense of the disparity between us! I am not included within the pale of this glorious anniversary! Your high independence only reveals the immeasurable distance between us. The blessings in which you this day rejoice, are not enjoyed in common. The rich inheritance of justice, liberty, prosperity, and independence, bequeathed by your fathers, is shared by you, not by me. The sunlight that brought life and healing to you, has brought stripes and death to me. This Fourth of July is *yours,* not *mine. You* may rejoice, *I* must mourn. To drag a man in fetters into the grand illuminated temple of liberty, and call upon him to join you in joyous anthems, were inhuman mockery and sacrilegious irony. Do you mean, citizens, to mock me, by asking me to speak today? If so, there is a parallel to your conduct. And let me warn you that it is dangerous to copy the example of a nation whose crimes, towering up to heaven, were thrown down by the breath of the Almighty, burying that nation in irrecoverable ruin! ...

Fellow-citizens, above your national, tumultuous joy, I hear the mournful wail of millions, whose chains, heavy and grievous yesterday, are today rendered more intolerable by the jubilant shouts that reach them. If I do forget, if I not faithfully remember those bleeding children of sorrow this day, "may my right hand forget her cunning, and may my tongue cleave to the roof of my mouth!" To forget them, to pass lightly over their wrongs, and to chime in with the popular theme, would be treason most scandalous and shocking, and would make me a reproach before God and the world. My subject, then, fellow-citizens, is AMERICAN SLAVERY. I shall see this day and its popular characteristics from the slave's point of view. Standing there, identified with the American bondman, making his wrongs mine, I do not hesitate to declare, with all my soul, that the character and conduct of this nation never looked blacker to me than on this Fourth of July. Whether we turn to the declarations of the past, or to the professions of the present, the conduct of the nation seems equally hideous and revolting. America is false to the past, false to the present, and solemnly binds herself to be false to the future. Standing with God and the crushed and bleeding slave on this occasion, I will, in the name of humanity which is outraged, in the name of liberty which is fettered, in the name of the constitution and the bible, which are disregarded and trampled upon, dare to call in question and to denounce, with all the emphasis I can command, everything that serves to perpetuate slavery—the great sin and shame of America! "I will not equivocate: I will not excuse"; I will use the severest language I can command; and yet not one word shall escape me that any man, whose judgment is not blinded by prejudice, or who is not at heart a slaveholder, shall not confess to be right and just.

But I fancy I hear some one of my audience say, it is just in this circumstance that you and your brother abolitionists fail to make a favorable impression on the public mind. Would you argue more, and denounce less, would you persuade more and rebuke less, your cause would be much more likely to succeed. But, I submit, where all is plain there is nothing to be argued. What point in the anti-slavery creed would you have me argue? On what branch of the subject do the people of this country need light? Must I undertake to prove that the slave is a man? That point is conceded already. Nobody doubts it. The slaveholders themselves acknowledge it in the enactment of laws for their government. They acknowledge it when they punish disobedience on the part of the slave. There are seventy-two crimes in the state of Virginia, which if committed by a black man, (no matter how ignorant he be,) subject him to the punishment of death; while only two of these same crimes will subject a white man to the like punishment. What is this but the acknowledgment that the slave is a moral, intellectual, and responsible being. The manhood of the slave is conceded. It is admitted in the fact that southern statute books are covered with enactments forbidding, under severe fines and penalties, the teaching of the slave to read or write. When you can point to any such laws, in reference to the beasts of the field, then I may consent to argue the manhood of the slave. When the dogs in your streets, when the fowls of the air, when the cattle on your hills, when the fish of the sea, and the reptiles that crawl, shall be unable to distinguish the slave from a brute, then will I argue with you that the slave is a man!

For the present, it is enough to affirm the equal manhood of the negro race. It is not astonishing that, while we are plowing, planting, and reaping, using all kinds of mechanical tools, erecting houses, constructing bridges, building ships, working in metals of brass, iron, copper, silver, and gold; that, while we are reading, writing, and cyphering, acting as clerks, merchants, and secretaries, having among us lawyers, doctors, ministers, poets, authors, editors, orators, and teachers; that, while we are engaged in all manner of enterprises common to other men—digging gold—in California, capturing the whale in the Pacific, feeding sheep and cattle on the hillside, living, moving, acting, thinking, planning, living in families as husbands, wives, and children, and, above all, confessing and worshiping the Christian's God, and looking hopefully for life and immortality beyond the grave,—we are called upon to prove that we are men!

Would you have me argue that man is entitled to liberty? that he is the rightful owner of his own body? You have already declared it. Must I argue the wrongfulness of slavery? is that a question for republicans? Is it to be settled by the rules of logic and argumentation, as a matter beset with great difficulty involving a doubtful application of the principle of justice, hard to be understood? How should I look today in the presence of Americans, dividing and subdividing a discourse, to show that men have a natural right to freedom, speaking of it relatively and positively, negatively and affirmatively? To do so, would be to make myself ridiculous, and to offer an insult to your understanding. There is not a man beneath the canopy of heaven that does not know that slavery is wrong for him.

What! am I to argue that it is wrong to make men brutes, to rob them of their liberty, to work them without wages, to keep them ignorant of their relations to their fellowmen, to beat them with sticks, to flay their flesh with the lash, to load their limbs with irons, to hunt them with dogs, to sell them at auction, to sunder their families, to knock out their teeth, to burn their flesh, to starve them into obedience and submission to their masters? Must I argue that a system, thus marked with blood and stained with pollution, is wrong? No; I will not. I have better employment for my time and strength than such arguments would imply.

What, then, remains to be argued? Is it that slavery is not divine; that God did not establish it; that our doctors of divinity are mistaken? There is blasphemy in the thought. That which is inhuman cannot be divine. Who can reason on such a proposition! They that can, may; I cannot. The time for such argument is past.

At a time like this, scorching irony, not convincing argument, is needed. Oh! had I the ability, and could I reach the nation's ear, I would to-day pour out a fiery stream of biting ridicule, blasting reproach, withering sarcasm, and stern rebuke. For it is not light that is needed, but fire: it is not the gentle shower, but thunder. We need the storm, the whirlwind, and the earthquake. The feeling of the nation must be quickened; the conscience of the nation must be roused; the propriety of the nation must be startled; the hypocrisy of the nation must be exposed; and its crimes against God and man must be proclaimed and denounced.

What to the American slave is your Fourth of July? I answer, a day that reveals to him, more than all other days in the year, the gross injustice and cruelty to which he is the constant victim. To him, your celebration is a sham; your boasted liberty, an unholy license: your national greatness, swelling vanity; your sounds of rejoicing are empty and heartless, your denunciations of tyrants, brass-fronted impudence; your shouts of liberty and equality, hollow mockery: your prayers, and hymns, your sermons and thanksgivings, with all your religious parade and solemnity, are to him mere bombast, fraud, deception, impiety, and hypocrisy—a thin veil to cover up crimes which would disgrace a nation of savages. There is not a nation on the earth guilty of practices more shocking and bloody, than are the people of these United States, at this very hour.

Go where you may, search where you will, roam through all the monarchies and despotisms of the old world, travel through South America, search out every abuse, and when you have found the last, lay your facts by the side of the everyday practices of this nation, and you will say with me, that, for revolting barbarity and shameless hypocrisy, America reigns without a rival.

79 | Uneasy Preferences: Affirmative Action, in Retrospect

Charles Fried

In his capacity as soliticor-general during President Reagan's second term, Charles Fried argued against the use of racial preferences—affirmative action—by the federal government. Here he offers, first, a thumbnail history of affirmative action; then, a summary of the rationale for race-based preferences; and, finally, his own conclusion. The thorny question, according to Fried, is whether affirmative action mitigates racial discrimination or, in the long run, reinforces it.

... Racial preferences have been a source of contest ever since they became an important tool of social policy in every part of our national life—jobs, admissions to colleges and graduate schools, government contracting, and grants of licenses and political appointments at every level and in every department of government. All of this began in earnest shortly after the passage of the Civil Rights Act of 1964, a monument of legislation that was accompanied by the most explicit promise that it would never, ever be used to impose preferences, but only to ensure in private employment the same norm of nondiscrimination that the Supreme Court had in the years before proclaimed as the rule in all governmental action.

Since that time there have been waves of support for and objection to the use of racial preferences. In recent years we have seen the passage of Proposition 209 in California—a popular referendum that banned discrimination and preferences based on race or gender in state contracting, employment, and education-and the passage of Proposition 200 in Washington State, which did the same thing. Then there were the decisions of the Fifth Circuit Court of Appeals in *Hopwood v. Texas,* which made it illegal for Texas's public universities to use race as a factor when considering applicants, and the decision of the First Circuit Court in *Wessmann v. Gittens,* which ruled that the racial preferences in the Boston Latin School's admissions policy were unconstitutional.

But even as the courts have been rolling back affirmative action, powerful voices once articulately raised against the practice—I think of Nathan Glazer and Glenn Loury—have turned around entirely. And others, such as Colin Powell, President Neil Rudenstine of Harvard and former university presidents William Bowen (of Princeton) and Derek Bok (of Harvard), continue to speak eloquently in defense of preferential programs. Perhaps most significant is the fact that an attack on preferences was no part of the Contract with America, no part of Bob Dole's campaign in 1996, and is no part of Republican rhetoric today. This suggests that smart politicians sense there would be a significant reaction against the peremptory abolition of preferential policies.

What is the energy behind the resistance to affirmative action? Why has that energy waxed and waned, and what forces tug at us at this particular moment? Because I myself am perplexed and want to find a way out of my perplexity, this essay is my examination of conscience.

Affirmative Action as Pump-Priming

In a series of decisions in the 1950s and 1960s, the Supreme Court made clear that state-sponsored Jim Crow was dead. The Civil Rights Act of 1964 and subsequent legislation extended that determination to private employment, much private housing, places of public accommodation, activities receiving federal financial assistance, and voting. But while racial inequality had diminished significantly since the end of World War II, there were still very few African Americans in skilled trades, the professions, university faculty positions, or the student bodies of selective universities. And while the decisions of the Supreme Court through the 1950s and 1960s, along with the passage of the Civil Rights Act, did much to reduce institutional racial discrimination, we were still a society segmented by race, with African Americans at the lower level of this segmentation.

In those years, the hope was that integration would rapidly follow the death of Jim Crow. But it soon became apparent that this would not happen—at least not right away—merely with outreach and the extension of a warm welcome. The deficits—in education levels, in job skills, in horizons of expectation—that had accumulated through years of systematic discrimination and government neglect was too great for blacks to make up without some sort of extra assistance. Thus the grades and board scores of African-American students accepted by elite universities under affirmative action programs were on average well below those of other students, as were the average qualifications of police officers, firefighters, and teachers hired and promoted under affirmative action programs. These lower admission standards for blacks were thought to be a temporary expedient necessary to get to a critical mass, a kind of pump-priming that after a few cycles would establish itself as a natural and sustainable flow of African Americans into the upper strata of American educational and professional life.

As the next decade ended, however, many had come to the conclusion that something had gone wrong, that affirmative action programs had somehow moved out of control, that the administration of Jimmy Carter had been captured by extreme elements that were pushing the use of racial preferences too far. Part of candidate Ronald Reagan's appeal was his resistance to this trend.

Perhaps the reaction was evidence that there finally had been progress toward equality of opportunity—and that white people faced with new competitors for jobs and admissions slots didn't like it. Perhaps whites were discomfited by the presence of a significant number of African Americans as colleagues, fellow students, coworkers—or bosses. Perhaps these were the reactions of "counter revolutionaries [whose] real goal is to protect the current distribution of privilege and opportunity that has produced white-male elites in almost every sector," as Christopher Edley has put it. But that cannot have been the whole of it. Where did the rest of the energy come from?

People were also reacting to the sense that a new set of bureaucracies had sprung up with the power to order citizens about in new and intrusive ways. There was the ominous feeling—I know, because I shared it—that in enforcing racial preferences in private hiring practices, the proper distinction between public and private was being elided. Justice Brennan, though not usually a fan of that distinction, captured some of the force of that ominous feeling in his opinion for the Court in *United Steelworkers v. Weber*. The plaintiffs in the *Weber* case were white workers seeking admission to a training program jointly sponsored by the United Steelworkers and the Kaiser Steel Company in Birmingham, Alabama. Both plant and union had a terrible racial history. The white plaintiffs claimed that by setting aside a certain percentage of places for African-American candidates, the program violated the Civil Rights Act, which forbade discrimination in employment on grounds of race. Justice Brennan responded that before the Civil Rights Act private employers were—as far as the Constitution was concerned—entirely free to discriminate on the basis of race or religion or national origin or gender. That was because the Constitution's guarantees of equal protection extended only to discrimination by government. In other words, before 1964, a private employer was in theory free to discriminate not only against African-American workers, but also for them, hiring them over more-qualified whites if he chose. In fact, prior to 1964, a private employer was free under the Constitution to employ whomever he wanted: he could employ exclusively white people or exclusively black people. While the Civil Rights Act changed that, in order to provide equal opportunity to African-American people, the statute—argued Justice Brennan—sought to interfere as little as possible with the usual prerogatives of private employers. Surely, then, it should be construed to forbid only the very evil at which Congress was aiming: the denial of opportunity to African-American workers. It should not take away a prerogative private employers had always enjoyed to use their own property, and the jobs they had to offer, in order to address a social problem they saw in the way that seemed best to them, including the use of racial preferences or favoring the previously disfavored in order to integrate their workforces.

In Brennan's reading of the law, allowing affirmative action in the private sector retained, rather than diminished, the prerogatives of private employers. Brennan, sensitive in this case to the line between public and private, meant to appease those who saw in affirmative action programs a dangerous step towards the nationalization of the country's employment market and therefore of private institutions themselves. If government says who is hired and who is fired, then what makes private institutions private? The line between public and private begins to fade.

And of course when Reagan was running for president, the Cold War was at its height, providing a clear foil against which to define American private-sector hiring practices. In the East Bloc, managers of enterprises would be constrained by party politics in their hiring decisions—jobs were a form of political patronage and an instrument of party discipline. At the time, certainly, it was not hard to imagine bureaucrats in affirmative action bureaucracies beginning to do the same thing here by imposing cumbersome restrictions on private institutions. Indeed the growth of affirmative action bureaucracies within large

non-governmental institutions offered a ready channel for this. Cronyism, nepotism, and the like have always existed, working to limit the freedom to hire—but having the force of government behind hiring constraints, people feared, would make them universal and inescapable.

But what moved the Reagan voters in 1980 was not primarily concern about the takeover of the prerogatives of managers, owners, and institutions. Nor were they moved so much by the sense that racial preferences cheated whites out of a fair chance at scarce jobs, contracts, or a slot at a top university. To be sure, for whites who felt they had lost jobs or admissions slots to less-qualified blacks, affirmative action practices must have had an acute sting. But these complaints have a declining resonance in today's tight labor market. And indeed the complaint about being displaced by a less-qualified minority has always struck me as a bit lame. Even during harder economic times there simply were never that many whites actually displaced by preferential programs. And in higher education … only a few colleges have ever been in a position to exercise much selectivity, so the competitive concern may have rung truest among students who did not make it into elite programs—hardly a complaint with a broad popular appeal.

The Color-Blind Ideal

No, the real moral and emotional energy driving the resistance to preferences is captured by the slogan of color-blindness, as in the famous phrase in the dissent in *Plessy v. Ferguson*: "Our Constitution is color-blind, and neither knows nor tolerates classes among citizens." This states an ideal, a principle, and a rallying cry. And that is what I emphasized in my briefs to the Supreme Court. Here is what I said in one brief:

> In this case, petitioners were laid off from their jobs as school teachers for the sole reason that they are white.… All there is by way of justifica-

tion for the racially based misfortune visited upon petitioners are references ... to a history of "societal discrimination," "underrepresentation" of minority teachers, and the need to supply "role-models" for minority students. So casual a waving aside of the fundamental Fourteenth Amendment principle of equal treatment for all persons regardless of race and of our republic's basic moral vision of the unity of all mankind cannot be countenanced.

And that is the theme the Court took up as, in case after case, it shifted towards a strong presumption against race-conscious government action. A particularly biting statement was made by Justice Kennedy in his dissent in *Metro Broadcasting v. FCC*, a case soon to be overruled, upholding preferences in the granting of broadcasting licenses to minority-owned broadcasters. "The FCC policy seems based on the demeaning notion that members of the defined racial groups subscribe to certain 'minority views' that must be different from those of other citizens," a notion he found chillingly reminiscent of justifications offered by the apartheid government of South Africa, and one open to "exploitation by opportunists who seek to take advantage of monetary rewards" available in such programs.

If I am right, Justice Kennedy's is the sentiment that has motivated not just recent Supreme Court decisions, but also the *Hopwood* and *Boston Latin* decisions, the passage of Proposition 209 in California and Proposition 200 in Washington, and the accumulation of resistance to racial preferences that has been building since the early 1970s. But does this logic make a compelling or even a coherent moral and constitutional argument? If so, why is it that just as the anti–affirmative action arguments of deep thinkers like Nathan Glazer and Glenn Loury came to be accepted, they—along with many others—drew back from their conclusion?

I believed—and continue to believe—that at the most basic level most Americans look to what Martin Luther King looked to: a society where race does not loom large, where it does not determine life chances, where it

does not restrict life choices, where it does not determine with whom a person associates, who his friends are, or whom he loves. King's vision represents a conception of what it is to be a person, a conception that is affirmed in different ways by the Judeo-Christian tradition, by Islam, and by the Enlightenment. For these religious traditions every human being is beloved of God, and there is no more important thing about a person than that relation to God. The Enlightenment conception is most profoundly stated by Immanuel Kant, for whom the capacity to choose and to reason are the source both of each person's moral sense and of each person's moral worth. Whatever differences there are between people (and peoples) are literally of no consequence as measured against this fundamental equality.

Both the religious and the humanistic conceptions of personhood insist on an individual's essential freedom to choose—to choose his relationship to God or to his fellow man. Both conceptions reject the idea that we are made by our circumstances—by our nationality, by our biology, by our race. There is but one race and that is the human race. All the differences between us are contingent, morally irrelevant. And that is why any doctrine that would divide us into groups or castes from which we cannot escape by the exercise of our reason and our moral sense is an offense against humanity—to some, an offense against God. And this is not only an Enlightenment and religious ideal, it is the ideal which defines our nation. We are not—our history of slavery and racism notwithstanding—a nation of blood, of contingency and biology. Our conception is of ourselves as a nation of persons who choose to be Americans.

It is this conception that explains what has seemed an intellectual puzzle: why "separate but equal" (even truly equal) did not accord with what our Constitution meant by equality. This explains why *Plessy v. Ferguson* was wrong and why *Brown v. Board of Education* in this respect was an insufficiently fundamental response to our own version of apartheid. It also explains the logic of an equally important case, *Loving v. Virginia*, which struck down anti-miscegenation laws even though such laws could have been taken to bear equally on all races. The equality of which the Constitution speaks is not an equality of result or even of resources, but the equality implicit in the religious and Enlightenment conception of the unity of mankind. And that is why it is troublesome for government to govern in terms of race, to make or impose distinctions based on race. That is why the cases from *Regents of the University of California v. Bakke* (1978) onward are right in subjecting the so-called benign use of race (as in affirmative action) and its invidious use (as in segregation) to the same standard of constitutional scrutiny.

We need to understand that there is a difference between racial preferences and other preferences, some of which are exercised quite regularly by colleges and universities. Proponents of racial preferences in higher education regularly point to the ongoing and accepted use of geographical preferences and preferences for alumni, athletes, and musicians. But these are false analogies. A preference for musicians or athletes is a preference for what the person will bring in skills and interests—and the only quarrel available is whether athletic ability, for instance, should count as a desirable capacity in an undergraduate program. (Alumni and geographical preferences are another matter.) But whatever may be said to justify or attack such preferences—and there is something on both sides—they are quite different from racial preferences because they do not work to create or perpetuate a serious and historical divide in our nation. They do not segment us in the way that racial discrimination did and still does and the way that racial preferences now threaten to.

Fear of Resegregation

How to account, then, for the response of Glazer and Loury and Bowen and Bok—men of the Enlightenment—to Proposition 209 and to Hopwood and to the Supreme Court's present jurisprudence? The answer is simple and has in recent months been boldly stated by Glazer and minutely documented by Bowen and Bok in *The Shape of the River:* without preferences the elite institutions of this country might rapidly be stripped of much of their African-American presence.

But if you embrace the universalistic, non-racialist moral imperative, as I do, then why should this specter of resegregation be so troubling as to lead to an abandonment of the principle of color-blindness? The reason is obvious: a society that is segmented by race, with all the best jobs, places, honors, and titles going to whites (and Asian Americans) is simply not an integrated society, whatever the reason for the segmentation. It is two societies, separated by race. So it will appear and so it will feel to everyone in it, even if (especially if?) everyone understands that there is perfect equality of opportunity, that no exclusionary practices obtain or would be tolerated. African Americans and whites share a common humanity, but if African Americans almost invariably appear in subordinate roles, then this commonality will seem a very abstract thing indeed. It is all very well to say that color is irrelevant and that in a free and open society some will always be worse off than others. But if disadvantage is so strongly correlated with color, then color must retain its saliency.

This, I believe, is an argument for preferences that seems more effective than the elusive and sometimes contrived "diversity" argument. It is not "diversity" that is at stake here, but the exact opposite. African Americans and whites need to interact in every way and at every level, not so that they may learn to "value their differences," as it is fashionable to argue, but for precisely the opposite reason, that they may come to see that they are very much the same.

The ultimate sign of our seeing our common humanity, of seeing past superficial and irrelevant differences, is love. Intermarriage and interracial adoption are our ultimate salvation. Our classrooms, faculties, boardrooms, workplaces, or presidents' cabinets may all come to "look like America" and we still may not have been saved. But when our families look like America—then we will have been saved! But how are whites and African Americans to meet and fall in love, if they never see each other in situations of equality?

That is the horror. But is what we have now so great? It is time to admit what everyone knows: we are now deliberately segmenting ourselves on the basis of race, even as we reassemble more or less successfully in our preferentially constructed classrooms, boardrooms, workplaces. Is that better than letting the chips fall where they may? It is claimed that it is better, because it is only for a while, a kind of strenuous pump-priming until the force of gravity gets things going on their own. I am afraid that will not do either. John Jeffries's biography of Justice Lewis Powell, the author of the majority opinion in *Bakke*, tells this story:

> In the course of the discussion [of *Bakke* in the conference of the justices] Justice Stevens said that preferences might be acceptable as a temporary measure but not a permanent solution. Powell agreed. The problem was one of transition to a color-blind society. Perhaps, Stevens added, blacks would not need these programs much longer, but at this point Justice Marshall broke in to say that it would be another hundred years. This remark left Powell speechless.... [H]e recoiled from the prospect of generation upon generation of racial quotas.

And there is the dilemma. Justice Powell recoiled from generation upon generation of racial quotas because any practice that goes on for so long must become the norm and not a transition to something else. One hundred years or 25 years of government administering and counting and differentiating between us because of race—with the ultimate aim, to be sure, of uniting us—makes race a firm and official and permanent marker. If this is what is being promised in the name of transition, it must be rejected, just as Justice Powell rejected it. And it is because so many people sense that what is offered as a transition is well on its way to becoming permanent—as permanent as anything can be—that we have Proposition 209 and Hopwood, not to mention the Supreme Court decisions firmly rejecting a permanent regime of racial divide, even if justified on the ground that the dividing line is benign.

As we look at the future of affirmative action we are not talking about shutting down a regime that is unjust, that inflicts harm on innocent persons. Segregation was such a regime, and "all deliberate speed" was not too speedy to shut it down. We are considering here an approach adopted for the best of motives with many fine results, but one that was always a compromise and partial abandonment of principle. If it was ever right—and I think that at some time in the past it was—then its continuation for another year, another day, another hour cannot be wicked. It is wrong only because it threatens to become permanent. The arguments of those who seek to reassure us that they agree with that proposition in principle only make that threat more vivid. President Clinton's "mend it, don't end it" pronouncement was a certain promise of racial preferences and racial politics as far as the eye could see. But if "all deliberate speed" was fast enough for desegregation, then surely nothing speedier is required for phasing out reverse discrimination. The measures to be taken need not be immediate; they must only promise a certain end to government-supported racial preferences within the imaginative horizon of ordinary people....

Time is running out for another reason. Although ours has always been a country of immigration, in recent decades immigration from non-European countries is changing— quite literally—the complexion of the country. And it is clear that for political reasons, if for no others, the claims of these new immigrants to enjoy some version of the preferences accorded African Americans is proving irresistible. Remember that the standard predicate for claiming a minority business set-aside is being "Black, Spanish-speaking, Oriental, Indian, Eskimo or Aleut." If total preferences are limited to 10 or perhaps 20 percent, it is inevitable that these groups will jostle each other for what are after all major political, social, and economic payoffs. The adjudication of any such competition cannot help but be ugly. It would inevitably be racialist if not racist. And if the percentage enjoying preference rises much above 20 percent, then the specter of government sway over the employment market and many other domains would be upon us. And given the happy fact that many of these immigrant groups have sig-

nificant rates of exogamy, the very determination of ethnic identity promises a definitional nightmare from which we might awaken to find ourselves in a situation eerily reminiscent of the Nuremberg Laws. With that prospect in sight, would it not be best to say—in the words of the song—"let's call the whole thing off"?

80 | *Abortion Politics*
Susan Estrich and Kathleen Sullivan

The Bill of Rights was established "to withdraw certain subjects from the vicissitudes of political controversy" and thus to protect cherished liberties against the oppressions of transient, local majorities. Law professors Susan Estrich and Kathleen Sullivan argue here that the rights to privacy and to choose abortion or motherhood are some of those certain subjects.

Notwithstanding the abortion controversy, the Supreme Court has long acknowledged an unenumerated right to privacy as a species of "liberty" that the due process clauses protect. The principle is as ancient as *Meyer v. Nebraska* and *Pierce v. Society of Sisters,* which protected parents' freedom to educate their children free of the state's controlling hand. In its modern elaboration, this right continues to protect child rearing and family life from the overly intrusive reach of government. The modern privacy cases have also plainly established that decisions whether to bear children are no less fundamental than decisions about how to raise them. The Court has consistently held since *Griswold v. Connecticut* that the Constitution accords special protection to "matters so fundamentally affecting a person as the decision whether to bear or beget a child," and has therefore strictly scrutinized laws restricting contraception. *Roe* held that these principles extend no less to abortion than to contraception.

The privacy cases rest, as Justice Stevens recognized in *Thornburgh,* centrally on "the

moral fact that a person belongs to himself [or herself] and not others nor to society as a whole." Extending this principle to the abortion decision follows from the fact that "[f]ew decisions are … more basic to individual dignity and autonomy" or more appropriate to the "private sphere of individual liberty" than the uniquely personal, intimate, and self-defining decision whether or not to continue a pregnancy.

In two senses, abortion restrictions keep a woman from "belonging to herself." First and most obviously, they deprive her of bodily self-possession. As Chief Justice Rehnquist observed in another context, pregnancy entails "profound physical, emotional, and psychological consequences." To name a few, pregnancy increases a woman's uterine size 500—1000 times, her pulse rate by ten to fifteen beats a minute, and her body weight by 25 pounds or more….In addition, labor and delivery impose extraordinary physical demands, whether over the six-to-twelve-hour or longer course of vaginal delivery, or during the highly invasive surgery involved in a cesarean section, which accounts for one out of four deliveries.

By compelling pregnancy to term and delivery even where they are unwanted, abortion restrictions thus exert far more profound intrusions into bodily integrity than the stomach-pumping the Court invalidated in *Rochin v. California,* or the surgical removal of a bullet from a shoulder that the Court invalidated in *Winston v. Lee.* "The integrity of an individual's person is a cherished value of our society" because it is so essential to identity; as former Solicitor General Charles Fried, who argued for the United States in *Webster,* recognized in another context: "[to say] that my body can be used is [to say] that I can be used."

These points would be too obvious to require restatement if the state attempted to compel abortions rather than to restrict them. Indeed, in colloquy with Justice O'Connor during the *Webster* oral argument, former Solicitor General Fried conceded that in such a case, liberty principles, although unenumerated, would compel the strictest review....

Apart from this impact on bodily integrity, abortion restrictions infringe a woman's autonomy in a second sense as well; they invade the autonomy in family affairs that the Supreme Court has long deemed central to the right of privacy. Liberty requires independence in making the most important decisions in life. "The decision whether or not to beget or bear a child" lies at "the very heart of this cluster of constitutionally protected choices," because few decisions can more importantly alter the course of one's life than the decision to bring a child into the world. Bearing a child dramatically affects "what a person is, what [s]he wants, the determination of [her] life plan, of [her] concept of the good" and every other aspect of the "self-determination ...[that] give[s] substance to the concept of liberty." Becoming a parent dramatically alters a woman's educational prospects, employment opportunities, and sense of self. In light of these elemental facts, it is no surprise that the freedom to choose one's own family formation is "deeply rooted in this Nation's history and tradition."

Today virtually no one disputes that these principles require heightened scrutiny of laws restricting access to contraception. But critics of *Roe* sometimes argue that abortion is "different in kind from the decision not to conceive in the first place." Justice White, for example, has asserted that, while the liberty interest is fundamental in the contraception context, that interest falls to minimal after conception.

Such a distinction cannot stand, however, because no bright line can be drawn between contraception and abortion in light of modern scientific and medical advances. Contraception and abortion are points on a continuum. Even "conception" itself is a complex process of which fertilization is simply the first stage. According to contemporary medical authorities, conception begins not with fertilization, but rather six to seven days later when the fertilized egg becomes implanted in the uterine wall, itself a complex process.... Moreover, the most significant new developments in contraceptive technology, such as RU486, act by foiling implantation. All such contraceptives blur the line between contraception and abortion.

In the absence of a bright physiological line, there can be no bright constitutional line between the moments before and after conception. A woman's fundamental liberty does not simply evaporate when sperm meets ovum. Indeed, as Justice Stevens has recognized, "if one decision is more 'fundamental' to the individual's freedom than the other, surely it is the postconception decision that is the more serious." Saying this much does not deny that profound evolutionary changes occur between fertilization and birth. Clearly, there is some difference between "the freshly fertilized egg and ... the 9-month-gestated ... fetus on the eve of birth." But as *Roe v. Wade* fully recognized, such differences go at most to the weight of the state's justification for interfering with a pregnancy; they do not extinguish the underlying fundamental liberty.

Thus *Roe* is not a mere "thread" that the Court could pull without "unravel[ing]" the now elaborately woven fabric of the privacy decisions. Rather, *Roe* is integral to the principle that childbearing decisions come to "th[e] Court with a momentum for respect that is lacking when appeal is made to liberties which derive merely from shifting economic arrangement." The decision to become a mother is too fundamental to be equated with the decision to buy a car, choose optometry over opthalmology, take early retirement, or any other merely economic decision that the government may regulate by showing only a minimally rational basis.

Even if there were any disagreement about the degree of bodily or decisional autonomy that is essential to personhood, there is a separate alternative rationale for the privacy cases: keeping the state out of the business of reproductive decision-making. Regimentation of reproduction is a hallmark of the totalitarian state from Plato's Republic to Hitler's Germany, from Huxley's *Brave New World* to Atwood's *Handmaiden's Tale.* Whether the state compels reproduction or prevents it, "totalitarian limitation of family size … is at complete variance with our constitutional concepts." The state's monopoly of force cautions against any official reproductive orthodoxy.

For these reasons, the Supreme Court has long recognized that the privacy right protects not only the individual but also our society. As early as *Meyer* and *Pierce,* the Court acknowledged that "[t]he fundamental theory of liberty" on which a free society rests "excludes any general power of the State to standardize" its citizens. As Justice Powell likewise recognized for the *Moore* plurality, "a free society" is one that avoids the homogenization of family life.…

Those who would relegate all control over abortion to the state legislatures ignore these fundamental, systematic values. It is a red herring to focus on the question of judicial versus legislative control of reproductive decisions, as so many of *Roe's* critics do. The real distinction is that between private and public control of the decision: the private control that the courts protect through *Griswald* and *Roe,* and the public control that the popular branches could well usurp in a world without those decisions.

Precisely because of the importance of a private sphere for family, spirit, and conscience, the framers never intended to commit all moral disagreements to the political arena. Quite the contrary:

> The very purpose of a Bill of Rights was to withdraw certain subjects from the vicissitudes of political controversy, to place them beyond the reach of majorities and officials and to establish them as legal principles to be applied by the courts. One's right to life, liberty, and property, to free speech, a free press, freedom of worship and assembly, and other fundamental rights may not be submitted to vote; they depend on the outcome of no elections.

Such "withdrawal" of fundamental liberties from the political arena is basic to constitutional democracy as opposed to rank majoritarianism, and nowhere is such "withdrawal" more important than in controversies where moral convictions and passions run deepest. The inclusion of the free exercise clause attests to this point.

The framers also never intended that toleration on matters of family, conscience, and spirit would vary from state to state. The value of the states and localities as "laborator[ies for] … social and economic experiments" has never extended to "experiments at the expense of the dignity and personality of the individual." Rather as Madison once warned, "it is proper to take alarm at the first experiment on our liberties. We hold this prudent jealousy to be the first duty of citizens, and one of [the] noblest characteristics of the late Revolution."

Roe v. Wade thus properly withdrew the abortion decision, like other decisions on matters of conscience, "from the vicissitudes of political controversy." It did not withdraw that decision from the vicissitudes of moral argument or social suasion by persuasive rather than coercive means. In withdrawing the abortion decision from the hot lights of politics, *Roe* protected not only persons but the processes of constitutional democracy.

81 | Dishonoring the Boy Scouts
Larry P. Arnn

When a New Jersey scout council dismissed one of its local leaders, the leader sued. The New Jersey Supreme Court ruled that the Boy Scouts had been discriminatory and that he had to be reinstated. The U.S. Supreme Court later overturned the New Jersey court. Is this a case about discrimination? Or is it a case of First Amendment freedoms?

On August 4 [1999] the New Jersey Supreme Court ruled that the Boy Scouts of America is a "public accommodation" that must admit homosexuals as adult Scout leaders. Here is legal force used to attack one of the oldest and finest youth charities in our country....

This is the first time that a state's top court has held Scouting to be a public accommodation. The line of reasoning in the case traduces both the Boy Scouts and its principles.... The Jersey justices pretend that they do little at all, while they work a revolution. The case arose over the situation of one James Dale. Dale grew up to be an Eagle Scout. Then he became a volunteer Scout leader. Then he went to Rutgers and became leader of the gay student group. His picture and a story about his homosexual activism appeared in the Rutgers newspaper. The Monmouth, New Jersey, Scout council dismissed him from service as a volunteer leader. This being America, litigation began, which has made its way through trial, appeal, and ... the state Supreme Court....

The New Jersey court ruled that Dale must be readmitted as a Scout leader under the state's law against discrimination. It offered two grounds for the finding that Scouting is a "public accommodation." First, it is large, advertises widely for members, celebrates openness and inclusion, and has influence. Second, nothing in its creed or practice carries any particular moral meaning, or is devoted to anything that can really be called religion. Never mind that Scouting thinks, and has always thought, differently. Their Honors know better.

The chief justice wrote the opinion of the court. The core of it transforms Scouting's devotion to "moral fitness" into simple relativism: "Although one of BSA's stated purposes is to encourage members' ethical development, BSA does not endorse any specific set of moral beliefs. Instead, 'moral fitness' is deemed an individual choice." Her Honor extracts this sunbeam, not from a cucumber as in Swift, but from a fine passage in the *Boy Scout Handbook* that speaks of a Scout's duty to follow his conscience. When the Scouts encourage a boy to follow his conscience, the justices interpret this to mean that whatever the boy thinks is right is indeed right. They seem not to know that conscience cannot speak on both sides of a moral question, there being good conscience and bad conscience. Acts can be "unconscionable." Scouting is built upon this distinction. The Jersey justices do not seem to know it, which is a commentary on our time.

The absurdities of this opinion justify, these justices think, the conclusion that the Boy Scouts stand for nothing in particular. This in turn prepares the way for the conclusion that Scouting is a public accommodation. In fact, the Scouts have never held out a sign to say that the public may enter. First of all, only boys may enter. Second, only those boys may enter who will take the Scouts' Oath and follow the Scouts' Law. Other boys are excluded on the ground that they cannot pursue the central good that Scouting has to impart. The justices note that few boys are in fact ever excluded. That is true because everyone knows what Scouting is for, and those who do not like it do not apply or soon drop out. Until recently, both manners and good sense prevented people from joining Scouting merely for the purpose of changing it.

The moral teaching of Scouting is illustrated in James Dale's own experience, if the justices would but look there. His rise through Scouting was guided by the ninth edition of the *Official Boy Scout Handbook*, issued in 1979 (the 11th edition was issued this year). Dale has every reason to know the contents of this handbook because Scouts are required to carry it with them on most Scouting events. The introduction calls the handbook a Scout's "dog-eared companion" through life. It also contains the passage: "When you live up to the trust of fatherhood your sex life will fit into God's wonderful plan of creation. Fuller understanding of wholesome sex behavior can bring you lifelong happiness. A moment of so-called sexual freedom can turn into a lifetime of regrets" (p. 526; the following page begins with the heading "Once a Scout, Always a Scout"). Whatever the New Jersey judges may think of Scouting, Dale says today that Scouting was good for him and he admires it. He has every reason to know every moral teaching important to Scouting. His attack upon Scouting is therefore a breach of faith.

But getting back to the potentially good news in this New Jersey decision, it is of two kinds. The more immediate concerns Scouting itself. It has been subjected to more than a decade of legal expense and strife from defending itself against lawsuits from atheists, women's groups, and homosexuals. The national Scouting organization has approached these suits with discipline and patience. It has done whatever it could to keep them from affecting its work of helping boys (that work is thriving).... Scouting works rather as American government is supposed to work under the Constitution: Most activity is local, but there is effective guidance from principles set forth in writing that are national and from a small but significant national governing body....

The second good that could stem from this decision concerns the popular branches of government. Congress has direct power, under section 5 of the Fourteenth Amendment, to repair injuries against rights that are worked by state governments. Scouting and each person involved in it are deprived by this decision of fundamental liberties. Congressman Canady of the Constitution Subcommittee of the House Judiciary Committee has been ready to invoke Congress's power when the time is right. There can be a "Defense of the Boy Scouts Act."

As for the executive branch, the presidential campaign will drag it into the Scouting controversy.... Al Gore no less than George Bush, and George Bush no less than Elizabeth Dole and Gary Bauer, seek to establish credentials in the area of "values." In his announcement speech, Gore said: "Seven years ago, we needed to put America back to work and we did. Now we must build on that foundation. We must make family life work in America." If for Clinton it was the economy, for Gore it is the family, stupid.

It is not, of course, the job of the federal government to make the family work. And yet at the same time, the nature of the family is connected to the nature of man, and therefore to the nature of rights. To reach in politics the fundamental issue of family, one must connect it to things that are inherently political. The New Jersey case, in its errant reasoning, attempts and fails at this. Al Gore, when he endorses the platform of political homosexuality, attempts and fails at this. Given the variability of human circumstances, the family may indeed take many forms; but each form must be judged by the standard of the family in nature, and none that contradicts that standard will lead to the larger happiness of children or society. Nor can any that contradicts that standard provide the basis of a right.

George Bush, Steve Forbes, Elizabeth Dole, and Gary Bauer... can do their country no better service than to answer these attempts to divorce family and sex from their larger purpose in fatherhood and motherhood. If they complete this task, politics can then be about something both fundamental and political. If our rights are grounded in the nature of man, then those rights can be fixed and definite, and government can be limited and just. And the Boy Scouts can be free to assist the family in its natural and essential work.

CURRENT CONTROVERSY

How Far Shall We Go to Deter Crime?

82 | *For the Right to Carry*
Clifford Stearns

A Representative from Florida, Clifford Stearns argued on the floor of the House that the Fifth Amendment right to be secure in one's person includes the right to protect oneself from harm. He asserted that states that allow citizens to carry concealed weapons have drastically reduced crime rates. Thus, he concluded, the right to carry a concealed weapon ought to be extended: Citizens protected in one state by right-to-carry laws should be allowed the same protection in other states.

Mr. Speaker… I think it is useful to perhaps tone down the rhetoric and bring some statistics and some information from Dr. John Lott, a distinguished scholar at the Yale University Law School, and talk about experts on crime and what they have to say.

Mr. Speaker, I have an article from the *Washington Times* that is dated April 26… wherein Dr. Lott highlights a number of cases… detailing how anti-gun advocates routinely refuse to admit facts, figures, and they change statistics to generally develop a misinterpretation of gun ownership in America.

Along with Dr. Lott, a Professor Bill Landes from the University of Chicago has done extensive research on waiting periods, sentencing laws, background checks, and other current gun control laws and they compare those with the effect on deterring so-called "rampage killings." As to their conclusions, Mr. Speaker, I will quote directly from their article:

> While higher arrests and conviction rates, longer prison sentences and the death penalty reduce murders generally, neither these measures nor restrictive gun laws had a discernible impact on mass public shootings. We found only one policy that effectively reduces these attacks: The passage of right-to-carry laws.

Both these professors confirm that law-abiding citizens, possessing a legal right to carry concealed handguns, had a dramatic impact on multiple victim shootings. Indeed, these laws, on average, decreased multiple-victim shootings by one-fifth.

Now, in my home State of Florida, they recognized this fact. In 1987, they passed a law to allow law-abiding citizens to carry a licensed, concealed weapon.

What were the results? Florida's homicide rate dropped from 37 percent above the national average to 3 percent below the national average. The decrease in violent offenses involving firearms in Florida continues to decline.

Now, according to the Florida Department of Law Enforcement Uniform Crime Report, in 1989, firearms accounted for 30 percent of all violent offenses. Last year, firearms only accounted for 20 percent of all violent offenses. Mr. Speaker, 31 States today now have right-to-carry laws and have experienced similar results like Florida.

Dr. Lott's article further highlights the need for individual Americans to be able to defend themselves outside their home.

To address this issue, I developed and introduced legislation, H.R. 492, which is identical to my bill in the 105th Congress which was debated in the House Committee on the Judiciary. My bill establishes a national standard providing for reciprocity in regard to the manner in which nonresidents of a State may carry certain concealed firearms into the State.

Now, in order to carry a concealed firearm across State lines, a person would have to be properly licensed for carrying a concealed weapon in his home State and would have to obey the concealed weapon laws of that State they are entering.

If the State they are entering does not have a concealed weapons law, the national standard provision in this legislation would dictate the rules in which a concealed weapon would have to be maintained. For instance, the national standard would disallow the carrying of a concealed weapon in a school, police station, or a bar serving alcoholic beverages.

My bill also exempts qualified former and current law enforcement officers from State laws prohibiting the carrying of concealed handguns. Now, this language was adopted during debate on the juvenile justice bill last year.

Mr. Speaker, right-to-carry laws are an effective deterrent to these mass killings and random murders. States which have adopted such laws, on the average, have 24 percent less violent crime, 19 percent less homicides, and 39 percent less robberies. These are precisely the type of statistics which gun control supporters refuse to acknowledge.

Yesterday, the President stated that he is "subdued, frustrated, and very saddened" as he reflected on the lack of pending gun control legislation in Congress.

Mr. President, we, too, are frustrated, frustrated that those who seek to curb gun violence refuse to acknowledge the one effective deterrent, the right to carry.

So, as I stated earlier, the right-to-carry defense should not be confined to State boundaries. A law-abiding citizen legally carrying a concealed firearm in his or her State should be entitled to the same protection in any State.

I urge my colleagues to support my bill.

83 | Privacy and Surveillance Technology: Do We Really Want the Police Seeing Through Our Clothing?

Thomas C. Weisert

As more weapons become available to the public and as more states allow citizens to carry concealed weapons, Thomas Weisert points out that society is also more eager to detect illegal weapons and other contraband. The technology is here. Surveillance of private citizens is becoming ubiquitous—and more and more invasive. Is this the price of crime? Or of progress?

You are being watched. As you walk down the city streets, video cameras pervasively posted on assorted corners capture your every movement as you pass before their lenses. You arrive at your office, but the secret surveillance continues. Look into the clock on the wall, or into the smoke detector, computer speakers, or pencil sharpener. Someone is spying on you. A miniaturized video camera located in these seemingly inconsequential places incessantly keeps tabs on your actions for your employer. That same employer monitors your business phone calls, voice mail, e-mail, and computer files. And, you don't even know it. When you work on your computer, your transactions leave electronic footprints that semipermanently disclose your actions. On the way home, you stop at the ATM machine, and data are recorded. You stop at the grocery store and use a scanner swipe card, and data are recorded. As you travel down the highway, your windshield-mounted E-Z Pass, designed for efficiency and convenience, allows you to pay the tolls without stopping. Two weeks later, however, you receive in the mail a speeding ticket because police are able to use the stored E-Z Pass data to detect your rate of speed between toll booths. You are a monitored member of the Surveillance Society.

The high-tech gadgetry that allows Keanu Reeves to escape the Matrix or that makes possible the Mission Impossible of Tom Cruise is not quite with us yet. The Surveillance Society that is built on technology, however, is here and now. Thousands of government-owned video cameras populate Manhattan alone. Towns have cameras monitoring sidewalks, streets, and alleys around the clock. Nearly two-thirds of employers record employee phone calls, e-mail, or voice mail, videotape workers, or review computer files. A quarter of the spying companies never reveal the surveillance to their employees. But, isn't such governmental and private surveillance invasive of your privacy?

You bet it is, but that fact does not necessarily make it illegal. Indeed, almost invariably, such surveillance is perfectly legal. Existing state and federal law provides relatively ineffective legal recourse for the intruded-upon person. The common law or judge-made law of invasion of privacy is naturally limited and of little utility in surveillance cases. Statutory law passed by legislatures inadequately addresses the ability of emerging technology to intrude on a person's interest in privacy. Statutory law tends to operate at the margins, such as when Congress passed the Video Privacy Protection Act of 1994, which is known as the Bork Bill.

During the 1987 Supreme Court nomination fight for Judge Robert Bork, a Washington, D.C. newspaper obtained a list of the 146 videotapes the Bork family had rented from their video store. Statutes also leave legal loopholes through which you eventually can drive a virtual technological truck, such as with the Electronic Communications Privacy Act of 1986. This Act, designed to protect the transmission of oral, wire, and electronic communications, does not apply to a cordless phone transmitting via radio waves. A final example is the Federal Wiretapping Act of 1968, which prevents private individuals and organizations such as employers from intercepting certain telephone conversations, but does not apply to silent video surveillance.

Moreover, the inexorable march of technology continues to push the privacy envelope and thus holds ominous implications for civil liberties. The burgeoning Surveillance Society, by definition, invokes privacy concerns because surveillance is the intentional attempt to observe that which the targeted individual believes to be private. These concerns are compounded by the merging of physical-based surveillance with data surveillance in an information-based world. As the world grows more dependent on electronic record keeping and databases, the amount of daily activity generating personal information that is collected, recorded, processed, and disseminated for an unlimited time increases exponentially. Our capacity to control access to our personal information, therefore, grows more tenuous by the day.

Government now seeks to extend the electronic arm of the law even farther. In the mid-1990s political scientist James Q. Wilson published an essay in which he advocated that police officers take strong steps to combat violence by getting guns out of the hands of those people on the street most likely to kill. Wilson suggested that highly skilled, but unemployed, workers of the defense industry should be put to work designing "weapons" that would protect us not from a foreign enemy, but against the internal enemy of the criminal element. Wilson mused that perhaps some sort of gun detector technology, similar to an airport metal detector, could be developed that would pinpoint illegal concealed weapons at a distance without any physical search by the police. The musings reached an influential audience—President Clinton. The President circled the mention of the gun detector in the essay, wrote approving words in the margins, and passed it on with notations to At-

torney General Janet Reno. Not long after, the Department of Justice doled out separate grants totaling $2.15 million to three companies for the development of hand-held, high-technology gun detectors that would allow police to spot people carrying concealed weapons on the street; the Concealed Weapons Detection Initiative was born.

Gun detectors would provide police a superhuman power akin to Superman's x-ray vision, permitting police to "see" through clothing to detect whether the target is carrying a concealed weapon. One prototype, "Millivision," renders clothing virtually transparent by measuring the natural radiation emitted from the human body. While the detectors may not reveal a target's exact anatomical details, they could reveal a virtual 3-D image of the anatomical contours of breasts, buttocks, and genitals to the detector operator from a distance of up to ninety feet. Terming it a "gun detector" or "concealed weapons detector" is a misnomer of sorts because at least one prototype can reveal a host of additional items on a person, such as powder, plastics, ceramics, and liquids. Weapons and these other items are detectable regardless of the number of layers of clothing a target is wearing. A gun detector could even penetrate building materials used in home construction, such as wood and plaster.

Police use of a fully functioning and mass-produced gun detector has an immediate attraction given the perceived need for sophisticated technology to combat violent crime. The United States is a culture increasingly shaped for the worse by ubiquitous gun violence. People such as James Q. Wilson are correctly concerned with the prevention of crime and rightfully suggest that government through its police forces affirmatively should seek strong methods to combat violence. A concealed weapons detector certainly could serve a number of crime-related policy goals.

First, policing is a most difficult profession, and police officers are entitled to return home safely to their families at the end of a shift. A detector could improve police personal safety by allowing an officer to "electronically frisk" an individual for weapons from a distance and without physical contact. The officer would not have to approach the potentially dangerous individual, nor lay hands on the target. A hypodermic syringe, for example, would not prick an officer using a hand-held detector, while the officer conducting a physical patdown always is vulnerable to that hidden and highly contaminated needle.

A detector could also serve a second policy of improving relations between police and the communities in which they work. Physical frisks of individuals on the street, though perhaps legitimate and necessary, can poison police/community relations already infused with fear and distrust on both sides. Remote electronic frisks via gun detectors remove the need for hands-on patdowns that produce humiliation and anger for innocent individuals and heighten community disaffection with law enforcement. Finally, gun detectors ostensibly promote the most basic policy goal of getting guns off the street and thus reducing violent crime. Stemming the flow of illegal guns, of course, indirectly could further improve police/citizen peace given that gun violence consistently creates a mutual free-floating fear by putting police and the community on ever-present edge. Concealed weapons detectors, therefore, come with compelling policy reasons for their development and would seem to be welcome innovations. But, are these reasons good enough?

The great Supreme Court Justice Louis Brandeis, whose wise words are worthy of repeated invocation, reminded us in 1928 of an historical lesson even more significant today: "Experience should teach us to be most on guard to protect liberty when the Government's purposes are beneficent."

The maintenance of order is the oldest and original objective of government. We all want to live in a safe society and expect government to do something about assuring that safety. Government's provision of order through the control of human behavior, however, inherently comes at the expense of freedom. Societal order exacts costs on individual liberty, and individual liberty exacts costs on societal order. The enduring issue, again invoked by the development of gun detectors, is where the proper balance is struck between these conflictive, competing values. The Fourth Amendment to the United States Constitution embraces a similar balance. The Fourth Amendment protects against unreasonable searches and seizures. This constitutional provision seeks to constrain governmental overreaching, embodying an implicit balance between society's interests in controlling crime and public protection against the individual's liberty interest in a reasonable expectation of privacy. The constitutional Framers created this guarantee over two centuries ago when the possibility of police using sophisticated technology to see through clothing and walls was simply beyond comprehension. Nonetheless, whether raised in the context of British soldiers randomly ransacking a colonist's home or of the police pointing a super-sophisticated gun detector at people on the street, the underlying goal of the Fourth Amendment protection against unreasonable searches and seizures remains the same: to set a minimum threshold for police intrusion into the privacy of citizens.

The protection against unreasonable searches and seizures is not a wide-ranging safe harbor, however, because most privacy-intrusive activity is simply beyond the reach of the Fourth Amendment. First, the Fourth Amendment generally protects only against governmental conduct and not against searches conducted by private persons. The need for governmental conduct explains why surveillance conducted by private employers, no matter how egregious, does not implicate the Fourth Amendment. Second, the common-sense understanding of the concept of "search" is different from the legal meaning of "search"—and it is this legal meaning that counts for Fourth Amendment purposes. A "search" for constitutional purposes, the United States Supreme Court has told us, is a governmental intrusion into a place or thing in which an individual has a reasonable and justifiable expectation of privacy. Many types of privacy intrusions are not "searches" at all, meaning that the intruded-upon person cannot challenge the action under the Fourth Amendment. The crucial inquiry, therefore, is whether the governmental intrusion, through the use of surveillance technology, infringes upon an individual's legitimate privacy interest.

The Supreme Court has deemed many different types of police activities are *not* searches in a constitutional sense, even though the police conduct seems quite intrusive. An individual generally does not have a reasonable expectation of privacy in objects held out or voluntarily conveyed to the public. So, for example, drug sniffs by narcotics dogs of a passenger's luggage in an airport are not searches because individuals do not have a privacy interest in the smell of their luggage. When driving in a car, a person conveys information about the car's movement and arrival at a residence. Police do not conduct a search when they place an electronic beeper on the car to detect such movement. Police are not searching when they take aerial photographs of a particular site or when they take and look through a person's disposed items left curbside in garbage bags. Federal courts (though not yet the Supreme Court) have held that law enforcement officers are not searching even when they are using thermal imagers, which are infrared thermal detection devices. Thermal imagers detect variations in the surface temperature of targeted objects. Police point their thermal imagers at homes, acquiring evidence of indoor marijuana cultivation by capturing the degrees of waste heat emitted from the residence. (Thermal imagers nicely indicate that a gun detector hardly is a farfetched concept.) Such a use of thermal detection devices is not a search, even though thermal imagers essentially permit police to gather important information about activities inside the privacy of a home. Thermal images could be used to decipher the location of dividers, walls, and even inhabitants within a particular structure.

Courts have told us that you are being searched in a legally significant sense, however, when you pass through an airport security checkpoint. When you walk through an airport magnetometer without being physically touched or probed, you are still searched within the meaning of the Fourth Amendment because the purpose of the device is to disclose metal objects in intimate areas where there is a normal expectation of privacy. But, the inquiry is not over because the Fourth Amendment does not guard against searches, but only against *unreasonable* searches. Although magnetometer measurements are searches, the Fourth Amendment is not violated because such searches are eminently reasonable in light of the substantial need for security at airports.

When it comes to a prospective case involving a Fourth Amendment challenge to police use of a gun detector, therefore, electronic frisks may not be searches at all. Court decisions would turn significantly on which line of case law seems to hold the most apt analogy for search-and-seizure analysis. Is a gun detector more like a thermal imager, for example, and thus not a search when used? In the alternative, is a gun detector more like a magnetometer, and thus a search that is either reasonable or unreasonable? The need for such analogizing is nothing new; technological change always has challenged the scope of established legal standards. When wiretapping was the technological novelty in 1928, Justice Brandeis articulated what remains the perennial challenge: "Subtler and more far-reaching means of invading privacy have become available to the Government. Discovery and invention have made it possible for the Government, by means far more effective than stretching upon the rack, to obtain disclosure in court of what is whispered in the closet." Nearly forty years after the Justice's admonition, the Supreme Court finally forged the controlling Fourth Amendment standard for searches in an electronic-eavesdropping case. Even in the midst of technological change, Justice Brandeis suggested, what should endure are fundamental civil liberties principles: The citizen should be protected from the raw power of the state. Government should be prevented from engaging in arbitrary action and overreaching. As the development of gun detectors highlights boldly, Justice Brandeis was prescient in his prediction: "The progress of science in furnishing the Government with means of espionage is not likely to stop with wire-tapping."

But, why should you care? You are not engaged in criminal activity, after all. You don't have anything to hide, at least in terms of contraband. If police, through use of a thermal imager, catch a narcotics peddler cultivating marijuana, or if police randomly employ a gun detector and happen to discover an armed and dangerous individual, isn't that the criminal's problem alone? No, relatively unregulated government surveillance should disturb even those with absolutely nothing incriminating to hide. We allow not-very-nice people to object to the introduction of evidence seized in violation of certain legal standards, for example, not because we want to coddle criminals (I certainly don't), but for a much more selfish reason: The treatment under law that we sanction for criminals becomes the prevailing norm for the treatment of the rest of us. The innocent are the prime beneficiaries, and wrongdoers just incidental beneficiaries, when we demand that government not be allowed to train its arbitrary eye on anyone and everyone through use of a gun detector. Even if raised in the case of a gun-toting, unsympathetic defendant, the real interest at stake is the expectation of the ordinary citizen that he may carry on his daily life openly and without the corrosive and constant need to measure his every word and action against the potential that he is being watched. Laws that prevent invasions of privacy, whether common law, legislative, or constitutional, are designed not to shield wrongdoers, but ultimately to secure a measure of personal security for the rest of us. Justice Brandeis got to the bottom line when he said that the makers of the Constitution "conferred, as against the Government, the right to be let alone—the most comprehensive of

rights and the right most valued by civilized men."

This is not to say that we should be civil libertarian Chicken Littles, screaming out warnings that the constitutional sky is falling with every governmental effort to control crime. The horribles always are easy to parade out and tend only to desensitize us to meaningful civil liberties concerns. But these enduring principles should be an ongoing context in which to take issue with the incremental, nearly imperceptible governmental encroachments that threaten to erode personal privacy. Every new governmental intrusion comes with a cost, and the ever-more subtle but effective intrusions are the most insidious. As Louis Brandeis again told us in 1928, "Men born to freedom are naturally alert to repel invasion to their liberty by evil-minded rulers. The greatest dangers to liberty lurk in insidious encroachment by men of zeal, well-meaning but without understanding." Police, zealous and well-meaning, must be permitted to keep pace with technologically sophisticated criminals, but in so doing, law enforcement must not overtake the law technologically. Gun detectors are mass-producible, portable, versatile, and efficient, and thus are highly valuable for law enforcement—and therefore make personal privacy that much more vulnerable precisely for the same reasons.

In this context, think again about these gun detectors. You are walking down the street toward school, the local shopping mall, or work. Without your knowledge and without any basis for suspecting you of criminal activity or of being armed, a police officer points a hand-held gun detector at you from his patrol car positioned sixty feet away. Despite the three layers of clothing you are wearing, the video monitor on the device reveals an outline of your body and items stored inside pockets, bags, and purses. Also revealed are the sanitary napkin, the back brace, the medication, the colostomy bag, the prosthetic limb, or other such personal objects. If these objects are not personal enough for you, consider that researchers are refining technology that could scan someone standing on the street and determine whether a man has been circumcised or the diameter of a woman's nipples. You have lost your capacity to shield your body and personal items from government view. This is troublesome even in this increasingly immodest world. Going indoors to escape the spying eye of government does not necessarily help as police already use technology that can penetrate construction materials. All of this, of course, is before any private institutions, such as employers or shopping centers, get a hold of you with their own surveillance. Video cameras incessantly monitoring streets, gun detectors peering beneath clothing, thermal imagers penetrating walls of homes, miniature cameras in pencil sharpeners—your expectations of privacy are diminished gradually as you can never be assured at any point or at any place that government and others are not surveilling you.

Perhaps the concept of privacy needs a reassessment given this potential for persistent prying into nearly every personal realm. Privacy should come to incorporate the notion that a person can go about his daily life without the ever-present unease that every move is observed or that the police may be looking electronically under his or her shorts. And, the law must manifest this regard for privacy. Sometimes, however, the law moves in curious directions. Just as government is devising gun detectors to ferret out concealed weapons, more and more states are developing what may be termed "concealed-weapons" or "right-to-carry" laws. That is, a majority of the fifty states now have laws on the books that legally permit citizens to carry concealed weapons. The theory in simplest form is that armed, law-abiding citizens walking the streets with hidden handguns will fight crime (or at least allow a self-defending citizen to exact some instantaneous, OK Corral, frontier justice). Whether good public policy or not, the laws come with unintended consequences. Although both are aimed at controlling crime, concealed weapons laws ironically collide with the development of concealed weapons detectors: Concealed weapons *detec-*

tors are employed to get guns *off* the streets; concealed weapons *laws* are designed to get guns *on* the streets. This perverse convergence would be less significant if gun detectors were technologically capable of discriminating between legally-carried guns and illegally-carried guns. With gun detectors, however, a gun is a gun is a gun. A police officer using a concealed weapons detector in one of the many states with concealed weapons laws would have no way of knowing whether the detected gun is contraband or not. Presumably, a police officer could approach an individual to make further inquiries regarding a detected gun, but this means that police would accost a fair number of law-abiding citizens. Ultimately, the true value of concealed weapons detectors—the detection of illegal guns at a safe distance—is undermined. The gun detectors and gun-carry laws are bad ideas that seem to deserve each other.

In contrast, the American Bar Association (ABA) has a good idea whose time has come. Recently, the ABA approved Technologically Assisted Physical Surveillance Standards, which serve as guidelines that policymakers could use to regulate the use of surveillance tools and methods. The ABA has suggested, for instance, that law-enforcement agencies adopt written guidelines and instructions that govern officer use of technologically assisted surveillance. Other Standards include that notice of the surveillance, when appropriate, should be given; that the scope of the surveillance should be severely constrained to authorized objectives, with surveillance ending when the specified objectives are met; and that law enforcement should not select the subject of the surveillance in a discriminatory or arbitrary manner. ABA suggestions reach to detection devices, such as the concealed weapons detectors. There should be, for example, a documentation requirement that would identify the officer responsible for using the device and specify the reasons for the surveillance. Police should not be allowed to use the gun detectors randomly against any target individual, but at least should have to adhere to a "reasonably likely" standard, meaning that police must have a founded belief that they will locate contraband.

These Standards represent only one set of suggestions for securing privacy. Their greatest value is that the Standards invite us to consider anew how large a sphere of personal privacy we are entitled to expect in our Surveillance Society. Supreme Court Justice William Douglas in the 1960s framed the still-relevant issue for our watching world: "If a man's privacy can be invaded at will, who can say he is free?"

CHAPTER THIRTEEN

Government and the Economy

OVERVIEW AND SUMMARY

Few other topics of political discourse are so ubiquitous and so revealing as the economy. The topic is ubiquitous because most people harbor some concern about their economic welfare and hope that the government can make things easier. The topic is revealing because the attempt to gauge who wins and who loses when the government intervenes or declines to intervene implies who is in control; who runs the government; whose interests the government really supports; or, if you like, who are the good guys and who are the bad.

In the realm of political economy, there are, as with all political topics, several competing theories that purport to explain how national economic decisions are made or to describe how such decisions should be made. In what we have termed the civics book theory, voters are linked to the decision makers through the mechanism of elections, and the decision makers follow the will of the people or risk being thrown out of office. Such a theory would explain why Herbert Hoover (see Chapter Ten) was defeated by Franklin D. Roosevelt, why President Carter lost to Ronald Reagan, and why President Bush was defeated by William Clinton.

What the civics book model does not tend to explain or even describe is the enormous power held in those private hands that control corporations, capital, or both. Because this theory is concerned only with public officeholders, the effects of private power are largely ignored.

Pluralism does better as a theory to explain economic decision making because the interaction of interest groups is not limited to public institutions and to elected officials. The political battlegrounds include corporate headquarters, shareholder meetings, union halls, and arbitration and mediation arrangements. Thus, pluralist theorists can contend that economic decision making—whether public or private—is the result of interest group interaction: negotiating, bargaining, compromise, and accommodation. Of course, for critics of pluralist theory, that is exactly the problem: A theory that explains so much can hardly explain, much less predict, anything reliably. Every result, no matter what, is said to be the result of the clash of organized groups of various strengths. Who wins and who loses just goes to show whose alliance of groups was stronger at the moment.

Elite theories are their most appealing when describing the economy. People are pretty quick to equate an economic elite with the political elite, and economic power with political power. (Everyone seems to have heard the cliché about the golden rule: He who has the gold, rules.) For elite theorists who are also neo-Marxists (see Parenti, Chapter One), economic policy is the result of struggle among different classes of people with different interests. For elite theorists who are also democratic (see Dye and Zeigler, Chapter One), economic policy is made within the boundaries of an elite consensus, but only those elites who hold public office are subjected to evaluation by the voters and, even then, only after the fact. For yet other elite theorists, real wealth is not controlled by individuals but by institutions whose directors may or may not act in the general interest of the population.

The authors in this chapter differ greatly on the question of who has economic power as well as on who *should* have power. First, a famous capitalist from the end of the nineteenth century, **John D. Rockefeller, Jr.**, explains the problem of disparate economic stations in life and extols the virtues of private partnerships between workers and investors—partnerships free from the interfering and deadening hand of government intervention. "This is better than charity or philanthropy," he writes; "it helps men to help themselves and widens the horizons of life. Through such a process the laborer is constantly becoming the capitalist, and the accumulated fruits of present industry are made on the basis of further progress."

However persuasive Rockefeller might have been in 1916, his arguments carried little weight in the presidential election of 1932, following the collapse of the stock market and the onset of a huge economic depression. **Franklin D. Roosevelt** was elected in a landslide with the promise of a New Deal for the American worker: "Every man has a right to life; and this means that he also has a right to make a comfortable living." Roosevelt intended to use the government to intervene in the economy. He intended to "restrict the operations of the speculator, the manipulator, even the financier." Roosevelt expected that the government could do what private actors—especially the industrial elite—could not do: maintain a "balance, within which every individual may have a place ... every individual may find safety ... every individual may attain such power as his ability permits...." The government's role was to step in where private interests had failed.

The government, of course, did step in under Roosevelt's presidency, as the economy had tumbled into the Great Depression. But decades later many economists would suggest that the worst of the Depression could have been avoided by faster and more prudent reactions from the Federal Reserve Board of Governors. This still obscure body of bank regulators (the Fed), established in 1913, has enormous influence over the economy because it has enormous influence over interest rates—the price of credit. The Fed makes what is known as *monetary policy*: decisions essentially about how much money should be in circulation. Whereas today every economist understands the role of the Federal Reserve Board, the Fed's governors are not publicly elected, serve long terms, and still escape the attention of the general public. Nonetheless, our elected representatives scrutinize the Fed very carefully and are ever on the lookout for signs that the governors are or are not acting in the public interest. They know, even if the public does not, that the Fed has far more influence on the economy than does any other institution.

William Greider offers a sketch of the Fed and how much power it exercises, provoking the classic questions about elite power: Does the Fed act in its own interest or for the general good? Is the Fed insulated from public scrutiny so that it can more easily act in the public interest, or is it insulated because its interest is not the public interest? Does the Fed have too much power, or is it sufficiently balanced with the other institutions?

But whereas Greider exposes the "Secrets of the Temple" and looks at the high priests of monetary policy, most of the public still focuses on the traditional branches of the federal government. However powerful a tool the Fed and its monetary policy may be, it is nonetheless true that the actions of Congress and the president have enormous influence over the fortunes of both individuals and corporations. Congress and the executive regulate or decline to regulate private businesses. Congress and the president decide tax policy. The federal budget makers also spend money in certain sectors of the economy or fund certain social programs or don't—that is, they decide *fiscal policy*. Interest groups of every kind are, of course, keenly aware of the powers of Congress, the president, and the bureaucracy, and that is why interest groups focus their time and efforts on watching and waiting, begging and bullying, the myriad policymakers in the several branches of government. The public, too, not just interest groups, understands this and expects its public officials to intervene in the economy or, in many cases, not to interfere in the private economic lives of individuals and corporations.

Offering three very different views of government intervention in economic matters are a member of Congress from Texas, a former secretary of labor and friend of President Clinton, and a professor of political science. Representative **Pete Sessions** (R-TX) is a strong advocate of a constitutional amendment that would limit the government's ability to raise taxes by requiring a two-thirds majority in both the House and Senate for any tax bill to pass. Sessions asserts that the ability to tax is the ability to limit individual liberty. The political elite, he says, too frequently resort to raising taxes and can too easily do so. Thus, over years of bad behavior, the federal government has become "oppressive, intrusive," and "overbearing."

In contrast, **Robert B. Reich**, as secretary of labor, claimed that, despite unusually good economic times, the government is not doing enough to help the average worker. The liberty of ordinary individuals, he says, is overshadowed by private corporate power, as well as by inequalities in income and in access to education, health care, and child care. Mergers and acquisitions, he says, may be good for macroeconomic statistics, better for Wall Streeters, and perfect for the economic elite, but average workers lose their jobs while a very small number of people make huge profits. The government, then, has an obligation to try to level the playing field, to bring a bit of social justice into the marketplace, and to protect ordinary families.

Steering a middle course and proposing a "modest government," political scientist **Philip A. Mundo** disagrees with both Sessions and Reich. According to Mundo, government intervention can make things worse, as Sessions would agree, and government intervention can make things better, as Reich would agree. The lesson is not that government should or should not intervene in the private marketplace. The key, Mundo says, is to know what kinds of things the government can effectively accomplish when it does intervene: "The national government ... has accomplished much that is good. It has also failed in ways that have been well documented. Thus, goals should be chosen that fall within government's ability to act." In this modest way, at least the government will accomplish a modest amount of good.

84 | *Labor and Capital-Partners*
John D. Rockefeller, Jr.

Industrial tycoon, captain of industry, and philanthropist, John D. Rockefeller, Jr., found that public opinion had turned against him after strikers at his Colorado Fuel and Iron Company were gunned down by members of the state militia in 1914. He argues in this article from the Atlantic Monthly *that labor and capital must work together; neither should neglect the interests of the other; and economic progress, general prosperity, and indeed civilization itself depend on their harmony.*

Labor and *Capital* are rather abstract words with which to describe those vital forces, which working together become productively useful to mankind. Reduced to their simplest terms Labor and Capital are men with muscle and men with money—human beings, imbued with the same weaknesses and virtues, the same cravings and aspirations.

It follows, therefore, that the relationship of men engaged in industry are human relations. Men do not live merely to toil; they also live to play, to mingle with their fellows, to love, to worship. The test of the success of our social organization is the extent to which every man is free to realize his highest and best self; and in considering any economic or political problem, that fundamental fact should be recognized. If in the conduct of industry, therefore, the manager ever keeps in mind that in dealing with employees he is dealing with human beings with flesh and blood, with hearts and souls; and if, likewise, the workmen realize that managers and investors are themselves also human beings, how much bitterness will be avoided!

Are the interests of these human beings with labor to sell and with capital to employ necessarily antagonistic or necessarily mutual? Must the advance of one retard the progress of the other? Should their attitude toward each other be that of enemies or of partners? The answer one makes to these fundamental questions must constitute the basis for any consideration of the relationship of Labor and Capital.

Our difficulty in dealing with the industrial problem is due too often to a failure to understand the true interests of Labor and Capital. And I suspect this lack of understanding is just as prevalent among representatives of Capital as among representatives of Labor. In any event the conception one has of the fundamental nature of these interests will naturally determine one's attitude toward every phase of their relationship.

Much of the reasoning on this subject proceeds upon the theory that the wealth of the world is absolutely limited, and that if one man gets more, another necessarily gets less. Hence there are those who hold that if Labor's wages are increased or its working conditions improved, Capital suffers because it must deprive itself of the money needed to pay the bill. Some employers go so far as to justify themselves in appropriating from the product of industry all that remains after Labor has received the smallest amount which it can be induced or forced to accept; while on the other hand there are men who hold that Labor is the producer of all wealth, hence is entitled to the entire product, and that whatever is taken by Capital is stolen from Labor.

If this theory is sound, it might be maintained that the relation between Labor and Capital is fundamentally one of antagonism, and that each should consolidate and arm its forces, dividing the products of industry between them in proportion as their selfishness is enforced by their power.

But all such counsel loses sight of the fact that the riches available to man are practically without limit; that the world's wealth is constantly being developed and undergoing mutation, and that to promote this process both Labor and Capital are indispensable. If these great forces cooperate, the products of industry are steadily increased; whereas, if they fight, the production of wealth is certain to be either retarded or stopped altogether, and the well-springs of material progress choked. The problem of promoting the co-operation of Labor and Capital may well be regarded, therefore, as the most vital problem of modern civilization. Peace may be established among the nations of the world; but if the underlying factors of material growth within each nation are themselves at war, the foundations of all progress are undermined.

Capital cannot move a wheel without Labor, nor Labor advance beyond a mere primitive existence without Capital. But with Labor and Capital as partners, wealth is created and ever greater productivity made possible. In the development of this partnership, the greatest social service is rendered by that man who so cooperates in the organization of industry as to afford to the largest number of men the greatest opportunity for self-development, and the enjoyment by every man of those benefits which his own work adds to the wealth of civilization. This is better than charity or philanthropy; it helps men to help themselves and widens the horizon of life. Through such a process the laborer is constantly becoming the capitalist, and the accumulated fruits of present industry are made the basis of further progress. The world puts its richest prizes at the feet of great organizing ability, enterprise, and foresight, because such qualities are rare and yet indispensable to the development of the vast natural resources which otherwise would lie useless on the earth's surface or in its hidden depths. It is one of the noteworthy facts of industrial history that the most successful enterprises have been those which have been so well organized and so efficient in eliminating waste, that the laborers were paid high wages, the consuming public—upon whose patronage the success of every enterprise depends—enjoyed declining prices, and the owners realized large profits.

The development of industry on a large scale brought the corporation into being, a natural outgrowth of which has been the further development of organized Labor in its various forms. The right of men to associate together for their mutual advancement is incontestable; and under our modern conditions, the organization of Labor is necessary just as is the organization of Capital; both should make their contribution toward the creation of wealth and the promotion of human welfare. The labor union, among its other achievements, has undoubtedly forced public attention upon wrongs which employers of to-day would blush to practice. But employers as well as workers are more and more appreciating the human equation, and realizing that mutual respect and fairness produce larger and better results than suspicion and selfishness. We are all coming to see that there should be no stifling of Labor by Capital, or of Capital by Labor; and also that there should be no stifling of Labor by Labor, or of Capital by Capital.

While it is true that the organization of Labor has quite as important a function to perform as the organization of Capital, it cannot be gainsaid that evils are liable to develop in either of these forms of association. Combinations of Capital are sometimes conducted in an unworthy manner, contrary to law and in disregard of the interests of both Labor and the public. Such combinations cannot be too strongly condemned or too vigorously dealt with. Although combinations of this kind are the exception, such publicity is generally given to their unsocial acts that all combinations of Capital, however rightly managed or broadly beneficent, are thereby brought under suspicion. Likewise, it sometimes happens that combinations of Labor are conducted without just regard for the rights of the employer or the public, and methods and practices adopted which, because unworthy and unlawful, are deserving of public censure. Such organizations of labor bring discredit and suspicion upon other organizations which are legitimate and useful, just as is the case with improper combinations of Capital, and they should be similarly dealt with. But the occasional failure in the working of the principle of the organization of Labor or of Capital should not prejudice any one against the principle itself, for the principle is absolutely sound.

Because evils have developed and may develop as a result of these increasing complexities in industrial conditions, shall we deny ourselves the maximum benefit which may be derived from using the new devices of progress? We cannot give up the corporation and industry on a large scale; no more can we give up the organization of labor; human progress depends too much upon them. Surely there must be some avenue of approach to the solution of a problem on the ultimate working out of which depends the very existence of industrial society. To say that there is no way out except through constant warfare between Labor and Capital is an unthinkable counsel of despair; to say that progress lies in eventual surrender of everything by one factor or the other, is contrary, not only to the teachings of economic history, but also to our knowledge of human structure.

Most of the misunderstanding between men is due to a lack of knowledge of each other. When men get together and talk over their differences candidly, much of the ground for dispute vanishes. In the days when industry was on a small scale, the employer came into direct contact with his employees, and the personal sympathy and understanding which grew out of that contact made the rough places smooth. However, the use of steam and electricity, resulting in the development of large-scale industry with its attendant economies and benefits, has of necessity erected barriers to personal contact between employers and men, thus making it more difficult for them to understand each other.

In spite of the modern development of Big Business, human nature has remained the same, with all its cravings, and all its tendencies toward sympathy when it has knowledge and toward prejudice when it does not understand. The fact is that the growth of the organization of industry has proceeded faster than the adjustment of the interrelations of men engaged in industry. Must it not be, then, that an age which can bridge the Atlantic with the wireless telephone, can devise some sort of social X-ray which shall enable the vision of men to penetrate the barriers which have grown up between men in our machine-burdened civilization?

Assuming that Labor and Capital are partners, and that the fruits of industry are their joint product, to be divided fairly, there remains the question: What is a fair division? The answer is not simple—the division can never be absolutely just; and if it were just today, changed conditions would make it unjust tomorrow; but certain it is that the injustice of that division will always be greater in proportion as it is made in a spirit of selfishness and shortsightedness. Indeed, because of the kaleidoscopic changes which the factors entering into the production of wealth are always undergoing, it is unlikely that any final solution of the problem of the fair distribution of wealth will ever be reached. But the effort to devise a continually more perfect medium of approach toward an ever-fairer distribution, must be no less energetic and unceasing....

The interests of Capital can no more be neglected than those of Labor. At the same time I feel that a prime consideration in the carrying on of industry should be the well-being of the men and women engaged in it, and that the soundest industrial policy is that which has constantly in mind the welfare of the employees as well as the making of profits, and which, when the necessity arises, subordinates profits to welfare. In order to live, the wage earner must sell his labor from day to day. Unless he can do this, the earnings of that day's labor are gone forever. Capital can defer its return temporarily in the expectation of future profits, but Labor cannot. If, therefore, fair wages and reasonable living conditions cannot otherwise be provided, dividends must be deferred or the industry abandoned. On the other hand, a business, to be successful, must not only provide to Labor remunerative employment under proper working conditions but it must also render useful service to the community and earn a fair return on the money invested. The adoption of any policy toward Labor, however favorable it may seem, which results in the bankruptcy of the corporation and the discontinuance of its work, is as injurious to Labor, which is thrown out of employment, as it is to the public, which loses the services of the enterprise, and to the stockholders whose capital is impaired.

The problem of the equitable division of the fruits of industry will always be with us. The nature of the problem changes and will continue to change with the development of transportation, of invention, and the organization of commerce. The ultimate test of the rightness of any particular method of division must be the extent to which it stimulates initiative, encourages the further production of wealth, and promotes the spiritual development of men.

85 | *Redefining the Contract*
Franklin D. Roosevelt

Campaigning for the presidency in 1932, Franklin D. Roosevelt benefited from a backlash against the incumbent President Hoover and the desperation of voters caught in a severe economic depression. The following speech was given before a relatively sophisticated audience at the Commonwealth Club of San Francisco and explains and defines the need for government intervention in the economic sphere of life. New conditions, Roosevelt claimed, required a new interpretation of the social contract.

The issue of government has always been whether individual men and women will have to serve some system of government or economics, or whether a system of government and economics exists to serve individual men and women. This question has persistently dominated the discussions of government for many generations. On questions relating to these things, men have differed, and for time immemorial it is probable that honest men will continue to differ.

The final word belongs to no man; yet we can still believe in change and in progress. Democracy, as a dear old friend of mine in Indiana, Meredith Nicholson, has called it, is a quest, a never-ending seeking for better things, and in the seeking for these things and the striving for them, there are many roads to follow. But, if we map the course of these roads, we find that there are only two general directions.

When we look about us, we are likely to forget how hard people have worked to win the privilege of government. The growth of the national governments of Europe was a struggle for the development of a centralized force in the nation, strong enough to impose peace upon ruling barons. In many instances the victory of the central government, the creation of a strong central government, was a haven of refuge to the individual. The people preferred the master far away to the exploitation and cruelty of the smaller master near at hand.

But the creators of national government were perforce ruthless men. They were often cruel in their methods, but they did strive steadily toward something that society needed and very much wanted, a strong central state able to keep the peace, to stamp out civil war, to put the unruly nobleman in his place, and to permit the bulk of individuals to live safely. The man of ruthless force had his place in developing a pioneer country, just as he did in fixing the power of the central government in the development of the nations. Society paid him well for his services and its development. When the development among the nations of Europe, however, had been completed, ambition and ruthlessness, having served their term, tended to overstep their mark.

There came a growing feeling that government was conducted for the benefit of a few who thrived unduly at the expense of all. The people sought a balancing—a limiting force. There came gradually, through town councils, trade guilds, national parliaments, by constitution and by popular participation and control, limitations on arbitrary power. Another factor that tended to limit the power of those who ruled was the rise of the ethical conception that a ruler bore a responsibility for the welfare of his subjects.

The American colonies were born in this struggle. The American Revolution was a turning point in it. After the Revolution the struggle continued and shaped itself in the public life of the country. There were those who, because they had seen the confusion which attended the years of war for American independence, surrendered to the belief that popular government was essentially dangerous and essentially unworkable. They were honest people, my friends, and we cannot deny that their experience had warranted some measure of fear. The most brilliant, honest, and able exponent of this point of view was Hamilton. He was too impatient of slow-moving methods. Fundamentally he believed that the safety of the republic lay in the autocratic strength of its government, that

the destiny of individuals was to serve that government, and that fundamentally a great and strong group of central institutions, guided by a small group of able and public spirited citizens, could best direct all government.

But Mr. Jefferson, in the summer of 1776, after drafting the Declaration of Independence, turned his mind to the same problem and took a different view. He did not deceive himself with outward forms. Government to him was a means to an end, not an end in itself; it might be either a refuge and a help or a threat and a danger, depending on the circumstances. We find him carefully analyzing the society for which he was to organize a government.

> We have no paupers. The great mass of our population is of laborers, our rich who cannot live without labor, either manual or professional, being few and of moderate wealth. Most of the laboring class possess property, cultivate their own lands, have families, and from the demand for their labor are enabled to exact from the rich and the competent such prices as enable them to feed abundantly, clothe above mere decency, to labor moderately, and raise their families.

These people, he considered, had two sets of rights, those of "personal competency" and those involved in acquiring and possessing property. By "personal competency" he meant the right of free thinking, freedom of forming and expressing opinions, and freedom of personal living, each man according to his own lights. To insure the first set of rights, a government must so order its functions as not to interfere with the individual. But even Jefferson realized that the exercise of the property rights might so interfere with the rights of the individual that the government, without whose assistance the property rights could not exist, must intervene, not to destroy individualism but to protect it.

You are familiar with the great political duel which followed; and how Hamilton and his friends, building toward a dominant centralized power, were at length defeated in the great election of 1800 by Mr. Jefferson's party.

Out of that duel came the two parties, Republican and Democratic, as we know them today.

So began, in American political life, the new day, the day of the individual against the system, the day in which individualism was made the great watchword of American life. The happiest of economic conditions made that day long and splendid. On the Western frontier, land was substantially free. No one, who did not shirk the task of earning a living, was entirely without opportunity to do so. Depressions could, and did, come and go; but they could not alter the fundamental fact that most of the people lived partly by selling their labor and partly by extracting their livelihood from the soil, so that starvation and dislocation were practically impossible. At the very worst there was always the possibility of climbing into a covered wagon and moving West, where the untilled prairies afforded a haven for men to whom the East did not provide a place. So great were our natural resources that we could offer this relief, not only to our own people but to the distressed of all the world; we could invite immigration from Europe and welcome it with open arms. Traditionally, when a depression came, a new section of land was opened in the West; and even our temporary misfortune served our manifest destiny.

It was in the middle of the 19th century that a new force was released and a new dream created. The force was what is called the Industrial Revolution, the advance of steam and machinery and the rise of the forerunners of the modern industrial plant. The dream was the dream of an economic machine, able to raise the standard of living for everyone; to bring luxury within the reach of the humblest; to annihilate distance by steam power and later by electricity, and to release everyone from the drudgery of the heaviest manual toil. It was to be expected that this would necessarily affect government. Heretofore, government had merely been called upon to produce conditions within which people could live happily, labor peacefully, and rest secure. Now it was called upon to aid in the consummation of this new dream.

There was, however, a shadow over the dream. To be made real, it required use of the talents of men of tremendous will and tremendous ambition, since by no other force could the problems of financing and engineering and new developments be brought to a consummation.

So manifest were the advantages of the machine age, however, that the United States fearlessly, cheerfully, and, I think, rightly, accepted the bitter with the sweet. It was thought that no price was too high to pay for the advantages which we could draw from a finished industrial system. The history of the last half century is accordingly in large measure a history of a group of financial Titans, whose methods were not scrutinized with too much care and who were honored in proportion as they produced the results, irrespective of the means they used.

The financiers who pushed the railroads to the Pacific were always ruthless, often wasteful, and frequently corrupt; but they did build railroads, and we have them today. It has been estimated that the American investor paid for the American railway system more than three times over in the process; but, despite this fact, the net advantage was to the United States. As long as we had free land; as long as population was growing by leaps and bounds; as long as our industrial plants were insufficient to supply our own needs, society chose to give the ambitious man free play and unlimited reward provided only that he produced the economic plant so much desired.

During this period of expansion, there was equal opportunity for all and the business of government was not to interfere but to assist in the development of industry. This was done at the request of businessmen themselves. The tariff was originally imposed for the purpose of "fostering our infant industry," a phrase I think the older among you will remember as a political issue not so long ago. The railroads were subsidized, sometimes by grants of money, oftener by grants of land; some of the most valuable oil lands in the United States were granted to assist the financing of the railroad which pushed through the Southwest. A nascent merchant marine was assisted by grants of money, or by mail subsidies, so that our steamshipping might ply the seven seas.

Some of my friends tell me that they do not want the government in business. With this I agree; but I wonder whether they realize the implications of the past. For while it has been American doctrine that the government must not go into business in competition with private enterprises, still it has been traditional, particularly in Republican administrations, for business urgently to ask the government to put at private disposal all kinds of government assistance. The same man who tells you that he does not want to see the government interfere in business—and he means it, and has plenty of good reasons for saying so—is the first to go to Washington and ask the government for a prohibitory tariff on his product. When things get just bad enough, as they did two years ago, he will go with equal speed to the United States government and ask for a loan; and the Reconstruction Finance Corporation is the outcome of it. Each group has sought protection from the government for its own special interests, without realizing that the function of government must be to favor no small group at the expense of its duty to protect the rights of personal freedom and of private property of all its citizens.

In retrospect we can now see that the turn of the tide came with the turn of the century. We were reaching our last frontier; there was no more free land and our industrial combinations had become great uncontrolled and irresponsible units of power within the state. Clear-sighted men saw with fear the danger that opportunity would no longer be equal; that the growing corporation, like the feudal baron of old, might threaten the economic freedom of individuals to earn a living. In that hour, our antitrust laws were born. The cry was raised against the great corporations.

Theodore Roosevelt, the first great Republican Progressive, fought a presidential campaign on the issue of "trust busting" and talked freely about malefactors of great wealth. If the government had a policy it was rather to turn the clock back, to destroy the large combinations and to return to the time

when every man owned his individual small business. This was impossible; Theodore Roosevelt, abandoning the idea of "trust busting," was forced to work out a difference between "good" trusts and "bad" trusts. The Supreme Court set forth the famous "rule of reason" by which it seems to have meant that a concentration of industrial power was permissible if the method by which it got its power, and the use it made of that power, was reasonable.

Woodrow Wilson, elected in 1912, saw the situation more clearly. Where Jefferson had feared the encroachment of political power on the lives of individuals, Wilson knew that the new power was financial. He saw, in the highly centralized economic system, the despot of the 20th century, on whom great masses of individuals relied for their safety and their livelihood, and whose irresponsibility and greed (if it were not controlled) would reduce them to starvation and penury. The concentration of financial power had not proceeded as far in 1912 as it has today; but it had grown far enough for Mr. Wilson to realize fully its implications.

It is interesting, now, to read his speeches. What is called "radical" today (and I have reason to know whereof I speak) is mild compared to the campaign of Mr. Wilson. "No man can deny," he said,

> that the lines of endeavor have more and more narrowed and stiffened, no man who knows anything about the development of industry in this country can have failed to observe that the larger kinds of credit are more and more difficult to obtain unless you obtain them upon terms of uniting your efforts with those who already control the industry of the country, and nobody can fail to observe that every man who tries to set himself up in competition with any process of manufacture which has taken place under the control of large combinations of capital will presently find himself either squeezed out or obliged to sell and allow himself to be absorbed.

Had there been no World War—had Mr. Wilson been able to devote eight years to domestic instead of to international affair—we might have had a wholly different situation at the present time. However, the then distant roar of European cannon, growing ever louder, forced him to abandon the study of this issue. The problem he saw so clearly is left with us as a legacy; and no one of us on either side of the political controversy can deny that it is a matter of grave concern to the government.

A glance at the situation today only too clearly indicates that equality of opportunity as we have known it no longer exists. Our industrial plant is built; the problem just now is whether under existing conditions it is not overbuilt. Our last frontier has long since been reached, and there is practically no more free land. More than half of our people do not live on the farms or on lands and cannot derive a living by cultivating their own property. There is no safety valve in the form of a Western prairie to which those thrown out of work by the Eastern economic machines can go for a new start. We are not able to invite the immigration from Europe to share our endless plenty. We are now providing a drab living for our own people....

Recently, a careful study was made of the concentration of business in the United States. It showed that our economic life was dominated by some 600-odd corporations who controlled two-thirds of American industry. Ten million small businessmen divided the other third. More striking still, it appeared that if the process of concentration goes on at the same rate, at the end of another century we shall have all American industry controlled by a dozen corporations, and run by perhaps 100 men. But plainly, we are steering a steady course toward economic oligarchy, if we are not there already....

As I see it, the task of government in its relation to business is to assist the development of an economic declaration of rights, an economic constitutional order. This is the common task of statesman and businessman. It is the minimum requirement of a more permanently safe order of things....

The Declaration of Independence discusses the problem of government in terms of a contract. Government is a relation of give and take, a contract, perforce, if we would follow the thinking out of which it grew. Under such a contract, rulers were accorded power, and the people consented to that power on consideration that they be accorded certain rights. The task of statesmanship has always been the redefinition of these rights in terms of a changing and growing social order. New conditions impose new requirements upon government and those who conduct government....

Every man has a right to life; and this means that he has also a right to make a comfortable living. He may by sloth or crime decline to exercise that right; but it may not be denied him. We have no actual famine or dearth; our industrial and agricultural mechanism can produce enough and to spare. Our government, formal and informal, political and economic, owes to everyone an avenue to possess himself of a portion of that plenty sufficient for his needs, through his own work.

Every man has a right to his own property; which means a right to be assured, to the fullest extent attainable, in the safety of his savings. By no other means can men carry the burdens of those parts of life which, in the nature of things, afford no chance of labor: childhood, sickness, old age. In all thought of property, this right is paramount; all other property rights must yield to it. If, in accord with this principle, we must restrict the operations of the speculator, the manipulator, even the financier, I believe we must accept the restriction as needful, not to hamper individualism but to protect it.

These two requirements must be satisfied, in the main, by the individuals who claim and hold control of the great industrial and financial combinations which dominate so large a part of our industrial life. They have undertaken to be, not businessmen but princes—princes of property. I am not prepared to say that the system which produces them is wrong. I am very clear that they must fearlessly and competently assume the responsibility which goes with the power.

So many enlightened businessmen know this that the statement would be little more than a platitude, were it not for an added implication. This implication is, briefly, that the responsible heads of finance and industry, instead of acting each for himself, must work together to achieve the common end. They must, where necessary, sacrifice this or that private advantage; and in reciprocal self-denial must seek a general advantage. It is here that formal government—political government, if you choose—comes in.

Whenever in the pursuit of this objective the lone wolf, the unethical competitor, the reckless promoter, the Ishmael or Insull whose hand is against every man's, declines to join in achieving an end recognized as being for the public welfare and threatens to drag the industry back to a state of anarchy, the government may properly be asked to apply restraint. Likewise, should the group ever use its collective power contrary to the public welfare, the government must be swift to enter and protect the public interest.

The government should assume the function of economic regulation only as a last resort, to be tried only when private initiative, inspired by high responsibility, with such assistance and balance as government can give, has finally failed. As yet there has been no final failure, because there has been no attempt; and I decline to assume that this nation is unable to meet the situation.

The final term of the high contract was for liberty and the pursuit of happiness. We have learned a great deal of both in the past century. We know that individual liberty and individual happiness mean nothing unless both are ordered in the sense that one man's meat is not another man's poison. We know that the old "rights of personal competency," the right to read, to think, to speak, to choose, and live a mode of life must be respected at all hazards. We know that liberty to do anything which deprives others of those elemental rights is outside the protection of any compact; and that government in this regard is the maintenance of a balance, within which every individual may have a place if he will take it; in which every individual may find safety if he wishes it; in which every individual may attain such power as his ability permits, consistent with his assuming the accompanying responsibility....

Faith in America, faith in our tradition of personal responsibility, faith in our institutions, faith in ourselves demand that we recognize the new terms of the old social contract. We shall fulfill them, as we fulfilled the obligation of the apparent utopia which Jefferson imagined for us in 1776, and which Jefferson, Roosevelt, and Wilson sought to bring to realization. We must do so, lest a rising tide of misery, engendered by our common failure, engulf us all. But failure is not an American habit; and in the strength of great hope we must all shoulder our common load.

86 | *Secrets of the Temple*
William Greider

The system of regulating the economy described by William Greider is clearly an elite one. But is it pernicious or public-minded? Are the priests of the economic temple a privileged few who protect the narrow interests of their class? Or is this institution responsive to the public interest and elected officials even while they are insulated from direct public scrutiny?

In the American system, citizens were taught that the transfer of political power accompanied elections, formal events when citizens made orderly choices about who shall govern. Very few Americans, therefore, understood that the transfer of power might also occur, more subtly, without elections. Even the President did not seem to grasp this possibility, until too late. He would remain in office, surrounded still by the aura of presidential authority, but he was no longer fully in control of his government.

The American system depended upon deeper transactions than elections. It provided another mechanism of government, beyond the reach of the popular vote, one that managed the continuing conflicts of democratic capitalism, the natural tension between those two words, "democracy" and "capitalism." It was part of the national government, yet deliberately set outside the electoral process, insulated from the control of mere politicians. Indeed, it had the power to resist the random passions of popular will and even to discipline the society at large. This other structure of American governance coexisted with the elected one, shared power with Congress and the President, and collaborated with them. In some circumstances, it opposed them and thwarted them.

Citizens were taught that its activities were mechanical and nonpolitical, unaffected by the self-interested pressures of competing economic groups, and its pervasive influence over American life was largely ignored by the continuing political debate. Its decisions and internal disputes and the large consequences that flowed from them remained remote and indistinct, submerged beneath the visible politics of the nation. The details of its actions were presumed to be too esoteric for ordinary citizens to understand.

The Federal Reserve System was the crucial anomaly at the very core of representative democracy, an uncomfortable contradiction with the civic mythology of self-government. Yet the American system accepted the inconsistency. The community of elected politicians acquiesced to its power. The private economy responded to its direction. Private capital depended on it for protection. The governors of the Federal Reserve decided the largest questions of the political economy, including who shall prosper and who shall fail, yet their role remained opaque and mysterious. The Federal Reserve was shielded from scrutiny partly by its own official secrecy, but also by the curious ignorance of the American public....

...The Federal Reserve System was an odd arrangement, a unique marriage of public supervision and private interests, deliberately set apart from the elected government, though still part of it. The Fed enjoyed privileges extended to no other agency in Washington—it raised its own revenue, drafted its own operating budget and submitted neither to Congress for approval. At the top were the seven governors of the Federal Reserve Board, appointed by the President to fourteen-year terms and confirmed by the Senate. But the seven governors shared power with the presidents of the twelve Reserve Banks, each serving the private banks in its region, from Boston to Atlanta, Dallas to San Francisco. The Reserve Bank presidents were not appointed in Washington, but were elected by each district's board of directors. Six of the nine directors in each case were, in turn, elected themselves by the commercial banks, the "member banks " of the Federal Reserve System. When the Fed decided the core questions of regulating money supply, its debate and votes were conducted in a hybrid committee that combined the two levels, known as the Federal Open Market Committee. In FOMC decisions, the governors had seven votes and Reserve Bank presidents had five votes, rotated annually among the districts. Only the president of the New York Fed, more important than all the others, did not have to share; he voted at all meetings. Thus, critics complained, the nation's money regulation was decided in part by representatives of private interests—the banks.

To further complicate and darken the picture, the commercial banks held stock shares in each of the twelve Federal Reserve Banks, which misled many into assuming that the Federal Reserve System was "privately owned." In fact, the stock shares were a vestigial feature of System membership that confused and excited Populist critics, but had virtually no practical meaning. The Federal Reserve System was government, including the twelve Federal Reserve Banks, not a private entity. Commercial bankers did enjoy preferred access and influence at the Fed, but the internal power relationship gave the Board of Governors, appointed by Washington, more authority than the presidents of the twelve Federal Reserve Banks. When a regional board of directors selected its new president, the chairman at the Fed's home office could veto the choice.

The American arrangement was quite different from those of the central banks in most other industrial nations, where the appendage of regional reserve banks did not exist. The crucial difference, however, was that other central banks, even the prototypical Bank of England, were democratized in a way the Fed was not. They all operated on the same basic principles of finance, but other central bankers took their orders directly from elected politicians. When the Bank of

England wished to raise interest rates, it could not move without approval from the Prime Minister's Cabinet. The same subservient relationship applied in Japan, France and Italy. The one exception was the Bundesbank in West Germany, whose political independence resembled the Federal Reserve's and for good reason. In the reconstruction following World War II, Germany's new central bank was patterned on the American model....

The institution's official secrecy naturally enhanced the mystique. The Federal Open Market Committee met to deliberate on the money supply eight to ten times a year, but its decisions were made in secrecy. Only six or eight weeks later, after the FOMC had held its next meeting, would the Fed release a brief report on what the previous meeting had decided. Internal reports and memos, the economic analysis that supported the decisions, were kept confidential for five years. A full transcript of the committee deliberations was never available because it was no longer kept. The FOMC used to make a transcript of its deliberations available to the public after the five-year waiting period, but even that historical record was discontinued in the mid-1970s. When Congress was enacting the Freedom of Information Act, Federal Reserve Chairman Arthur Burns decided to abolish the full transcript lest litigation force it into public view prematurely and embarass Fed officials. No other agency of government, not even the Central Intelligence Agency, enjoyed such privacy.

The Fed would explain itself, but only up to a point and long after the fact. Ostensibly, this was meant to avoid market manipulations and "insider trading" on the Fed's own decisions, but it also provided political cover. The secrecy spawned an infantile anger among the Fed's critics, even from some distinguished scholars whose commentaries on Fed performance frequently seemed harsh and petulant. Not knowing was a form of impotence, and the critics' anger often sounded like the frustrated tantrums of a small child who has been excluded from the family secrets. What is going on behind the closed door? Father does not answer. It must be something important. Mother will not tell. The secret behind the bronze doors was not, of course, sex, but nearly as mysterious.

The anti-Fed polemics liked to quote Henry Ford, Sr., on the mysteries of money and the Federal Reserve: "It is well enough that the people of the nation do not understand our banking and monetary system for, if they did, I believe there would be a revolution before tomorrow morning."

The American public, not unlike its political leaders, depended on familiar cliches for its limited understanding of money. The Federal reserve controls the money supply. The Fed sets interest rates. When the government spends too much money, the Fed turns on the printing press and then we have inflation. All these crude generalities were either mistaken or too simplistic to describe the reality, and unless one was willing to move beyond them, it was impossible to understand the awesome powers of the Federal Reserve or its frailties....

... The ultimate purpose of the central bank was to control the society's overall expansion of debt—to decide, in effect, what level of hopes and promises the future could reasonably fulfill. If new credit expanded recklessly, beyond the realistic capacity of the economy to expand its output, then the future would deliver failure and disorder. If the new lending was restrained too severely, then feasible ventures would languish and the future could not realize its actual potential. The Federal Reserve's estimates of the future were calculated by scientific reasoning, of course, but the function closely resembled the prophetic role of the ancient temple priests who were given divine license to look into the future and foretell whether lean or abundant years lay ahead. The Federal Reserve governors also make prophecy but they had the ability to make their own predictions come true.

The Fed's leverage for controlling the banks' expansion of credit was a mechanism inherited from centuries of banking history, the requirement that each bank hold a portion of its total deposits in reserve, a guarantee that it would always have sufficient funds for normal banking business. The reserves must be deposited at one of the twelve Federal Reserve Banks or held as cash in the bank's vault. Reserves were like earnest money against the possibility of bad surprises, a rash of failed loans or a rush of withdrawals by depositors. The Fed's reserve requirements varied according to the size of the banks and the types of accounts, but the basic requirement set for member banks in 1979 was 16.25 percent. For every $600 a bank held in checking accounts, it must park approximately $100 at the local branch of the Fed—money, collecting no interest. Thus, the total reserves held in the Reserve Banks was about $41 billion, backing about $258 billion in demand deposits. When all the currency held by the public was added, the total came to about $362 billion. That was the nation's basic money supply, the monetary aggregate called M-1.

To expand the money supply or contract it, the Federal Reserve created more reserves for the banking system or withdrew reserves—using its two small valves, the Discount lending directly to banks or the open-market purchase and sale of U.S. government securities. When the Fed bought Treasury bills or bonds, it simply credited the newly created money to the reserve account of whichever financial institution sold it the securities. It didn't much matter which bank was the seller, because once the money was in the banking system, it was free to flow to wherever it was needed. If the Fed bought from a brokerage firm instead of a bank, it had the same effect. The Fed credited the reserve account of the broker's bank, which in turn credited the broker's individual account.

Either way, the Fed's action increased the total reserves of the banking system—and thus allowed the total money supply to grow too. The Fed injections, whether they came through the Discount window at the Reserve Banks or the Open Market Desk at the New York Federal Reserve Bank, were called "high-powered money" because of this unique property: whatever new money the Federal Reserve added would be multiplied many times through the money-creation powers of the commercial banks....

Yet as a political arrangement, the American money system was profoundly conservative. Control was concentrated in a relatively few hands—the banking system and the Federal Reserve—and was shielded from any interference by other interests. The national government, the democratic equivalent of a sovereign, possessed the unique power to create credit and money, yet it delegated the power to others, a select group of private corporations that were licensed as commercial banks, without any specifications as to how the banks should allocate the credit. Who would qualify for loans and who would be denied? Which projects in the future were worthy gambles and which were speculative or redundant? The choices made by bankers had profound political consequences: which economic sectors would flourish, which cities and neighborhoods and regions of the country would thrive, and which ones would struggle or even perish. The Federal Reserve remained silent on those questions, adhering to a laissez-faire ideology. Those priorities, it maintained, were better settled in the free-market auctions....

The chairmanship, in addition to technical expertise, required an adroit political operator, someone who could coexist peacefully with the other power centers of government and thus preserve the Federal Reserve's most cherished legacy—its own independence.

Like most bureaucracies, the Federal Reserve regarded its own survival as a preeminent political goal, not solely as a matter of self-interest, but because its officials sincerely believed (not unlike other bureaucrats in other agencies) that their functions were vital to the nation's well-being. Fed officials were constantly, sometimes obsessively, sensitive to the fact that, in theory, Congress and the President could at any time abolish their privileged sanctuary. If the Fed went too far, if the elected politicians were sufficiently angered, they could simply rewrite the laws and make the Federal Reserve directly subservient to Congress or the executive branch. A wise chairman would know how far was too far....

If the authors of anti-Fed polemics looked more closely at the personal backgrounds of Federal Reserve governors, they would not find much to corroborate their theories of global conspiracy. They might conclude, instead, that the "Powers" were located not in the eastern Establishment banks of Wall Street but somewhere in the Middle West. The National Association of Home Builders, in fact, undertook such an investigation when its members were particularly outraged about high interest rates. The study was abandoned because the only pattern of connections it found led to small towns and state universities in Indiana, Ohio and Illinois.

How Much Should the Government Intervene in the Economy?

87 | *For Limiting the Ability to Tax*
Pete Sessions

Pete Sessions, a representative from Texas (R, Fifth District), led the debate for an amendment that would require a two-thirds majority in the Senate and House to raise federal taxes. By requiring elaborate tax reporting, the Internal Revenue Service, he argues, interferes severely with the lives of every individual and limits everyone's liberty. Sessions compares the American tax burden to that of Medieval serfs, Egyptian peasants, and the ancient Israelites.

The Clerk read the title of the joint resolution....

"The text of House Joint Resolution 471 is as follows: H.J. Res. 94 Resolved by the Senate and House of Representatives of the United States of America in Congress assembled, (two-thirds of each House concurring therein), That the following article is proposed as an amendment to the Constitution of the United States, which shall be valid to all intents and purposes as part of the Constitution when ratified by the legislatures of three-fourths of the several States within seven years after the date of its submission for ratification:

"Section 1. Any bill, resolution, or other legislative measure changing the internal revenue laws shall require for final adoption in each House the concurrence of two-thirds of the Members of that House voting and present....

"Section 2. The Congress may waive the requirements of this article when a declaration of war is in effect...."

The SPEAKER pro tempore (Mr. LaTourette): The gentleman from Texas (Mr. Sessions) is recognized...."

Mr. SESSIONS.

Mr. Speaker, with tax day arriving at the end of this week, there is certainly no better time for the House to consider this important constitutional amendment. The tax limitation amendment starts from this very simple premise that it should be harder, not easier, for government to raise taxes. The average American pays more in taxes than it does in food, clothing, shelter, and transportation combined. For too long, the tax burden imposed by the Government has been going up, not going down. I am very, very proud to sponsor this constitutional amendment.

Mr. Speaker, passage of this rule will allow the House to begin debate on one of the most serious matters to be considered by this House, an amendment to the Constitution of the United States. When our Founding Fathers met more than 200 years ago to draft what became the Constitution of the United States, there was agreement on what problems our Nation faced and our Constitution was drafted to address these problems.

In many instances, they wrote specific language protecting people from what at times could be an oppressive, intrusive, or overbearing Federal Government. They protected bedrock foundations to our liberty and freedom, such as life, the pursuit of happiness, freedom of speech and freedom of religion. Just as importantly, the Founding Fathers required certain actions and laws passed by Congress to obtain a supermajority vote, not just a simple majority, because they foresaw that the people must overwhelmingly support some action.

Our Founding Fathers were so insightful and ingenious in their preparation of the Constitution that they enlisted within our system of checks and balances a Constitution which would clearly enumerate occasions where a supermajority would be appropriate as a guardian of the people. A vote of two-thirds of both houses, for example, is required to override a presidential veto. A two-thirds vote of the Senate is required to approve treaties or to convict an impeached Federal official.

But a two-thirds vote in Congress is not yet required for raising taxes. In my view, our Founding Fathers would recognize that under the current system there is an inherent bias towards raising taxes and might have supported this constitutional amendment.

There has long been a bias towards raising taxes under the current system. Spending benefits are targeted at specific groups. These special interests successfully lobby Congress and the President for more and more spending. Taxes, on the other hand, are spread among millions of people. Taxpayers usually cannot come together as efficiently as a special interest group with a specific appropriation in mind.

As Congress seeks to keep the budget in balance, yet spending has still remained high, the easiest answer always for Congress is simply to raise taxes.

The Federal budget is currently in balance, in part due to spending constraints by Congress, as well as hard work and global-leading productivity of American workers, but short economic downturns can be expected. Future Congresses may not be as fiscally responsible and return to the ways of deficit spending.

The easy answer then is to raise taxes.

Making it more difficult to raise taxes balances the options available to Congress and makes decisions on the size of government. It is critical that this balance be achieved. By requiring a supermajority to raise taxes, an incentive for government agencies would be created to eliminate waste, fraud and abuse and to create efficiency rather than simply

turning to more deficit spending or to increase taxes.

It is important to remember that there was no Federal income tax when our Founding Fathers drafted the Constitution. Not until 1913 was the 16th amendment of the Constitution passed to allow Congress to tax the American people. The first tax ranged from 1 to 7 percent and only applied to the wealthiest Americans. Today, some taxes are collected by the Federal Government at a 50 percent rate.

Medieval serfs gave 30 percent of their output to the lord of the manor. Egyptian peasants gave 20 percent of their toils in their fields to the Pharaoh. God only required 10 percent from the people of Israel. Yet in America, Federal, State and local taxes eat up many times in excess of 40 percent of the average American's income.

The burden of tax rates is not only too high, but that is only half the story. As tax rates have increased, the heavy hand of the tax-collecting branch of our government has been strengthened. It has been determined by our majority leader, the gentleman from Texas (Mr. Armey), that our Federal income tax collection agency, the Internal Revenue Service, sends out more than 8 billion pages of forms and instructions each year. Our Federal income tax collection agency is twice as big as the CIA and five times bigger than the Federal Bureau of Investigation.

No other institution poses such a threat to liberty than the Internal Revenue Service and our Tax Code, and this is all as a consequence that tax rates are too high and the Tax Code is too complex.

A constitutional amendment requiring a two-thirds vote to raise taxes would help alleviate some of this misfortune. Thomas Jefferson once wrote, "The God who gave us life gave us liberty."

I imagine that Thomas Jefferson never envisioned such an intrusive agency as the IRS. Today, unfortunately, the reality is the IRS is a prevalent part of our daily lives, particularly this week with the April 15 tax deadline fast approaching.

Every year, Americans are taxed for billions and billions of dollars. Sometimes these taxes that are passed are retroactively done so. Sometimes they are passed from generation to generation and sometimes they are forced upon us even after death by the Federal Government.

So today, Mr. Speaker, I stand before my colleagues with a bipartisan coalition to put forth to the States a question of liberty. Will we make it harder for Congress to raise taxes on its citizens? Will we require a two-thirds vote of both Houses of Congress to pass a tax increase on to working Americans and children? Will we pass this amendment to the Constitution and require a supermajority, not just a simple majority to raise taxes?

This amendment will apply to all tax increases from the Federal Government, not just tax hikes. A two-thirds vote requirement would allow Congress to raise taxes in time of war or national emergency, but would simultaneously prevent the intrusive and penalizing tax increases that have been enacted with recklessness to fund government expansion over the last decades.

As we speak, several States of this great Union, including Arizona, California, Florida and Missouri, have adopted measures requiring that any tax increase by their legislature pass by a two-thirds majority. It is time that the Federal Government joins these States in listening to the voice of the American people. It should be harder to raise taxes. Had this amendment been adopted sooner, the four largest tax increases since 1980, in 1982, 1983, 1990 and 1993 all would have failed. That tax increase in 1993 was the largest tax increase in American history and it passed just by one vote. These tax increases totaled $666 billion to the American taxpayer.

The bottom line of this debate, Mr. Speaker, is that we should make it more difficult to raise taxes on the American people. Those that oppose it will do so because they want to make it easier to raise taxes on the American people.

Mr. Speaker, this is the defining issue. Those Members who support this amendment are here to support the taxpayers of America. Those Members who oppose it

today are here to defend the tax collectors of America. It is really that simple.

We hear rhetoric from opponents of this legislation citing jurisdiction, procedure, and a slew of other glossary terms but nothing can hide the reality that America and all taxpayers support a two-thirds tax limitation because they want to make it more difficult to raise taxes.

Mr. Speaker, like many Members of this body I not only oppose raising taxes, I support making our Tax Code fairer, simpler, and flatter. The tax limitation amendment allows for tax reform and it provides that any tax reform is revenue neutral or provides a net tax cut. Also, any fundamental tax reform which would have the overall effect of lowering taxes could also still pass with a simple majority.

The tax limitation amendment also allows for a simple majority vote to eliminate tax loopholes. The *de minimis* exemption would allow nearly all loopholes to be closed without the supermajority requirement.

We may hear from opponents today, those who will be saying to make it more difficult to raise taxes that the Government would be unable to function if a supermajority is required. Well, Mr. Speaker, I would encourage Members to look back at their States. Fourteen States require a supermajority to raise taxes. Millions of Americans living in these States have enjoyed slower growth in taxes, slower growth in government spending, faster growing economies, and lower unemployment rates. Tax limitation can bring to all Americans those things that are benefits that are enjoyed by those living in tax limitation States.

This amendment protects the American people. It makes it harder for the Federal Government to raise taxes on its citizens and that is why I am here today.

Today we can take one step closer to regaining liberty and ensuring future generations the freedom of our Founding Fathers intended for all Americans to enjoy. This debate is about liberty. This debate is about requiring a two-thirds vote to raise taxes on America.

88 | *Frayed-Collar Workers in Gold-Plated Times*
Robert B. Reich

This former secretary of labor, Robert Reich, argues that prosperity is not all it is supposed to be. Ordinary people don't measure their success by macroeconomic theories and Wall Street profits. What is often good enough for business in general is harmful to individual wage earners. Thus, according to Reich, the government has an obligation to intervene in the economy to protect the average citizen from "white gloved Wall Street," to guarantee a reasonable minimum wage, provide good education, and soften the repeated blows of mergers and acquisitions.

What's happened to the American economy since last Labor Day?

A year ago the unemployment rate was 6.1 percent. We won't have August's unemployment rate until tomorrow, but July marked the eleventh consecutive month below 6 percent. A year ago, the American economy hummed with 114 million jobs. Today, it brims with well more than 116 million. A year ago, the stock market was strong. Today, it's reached dizzying heights. Corporate profits are surging. Figures released yesterday show that profits in the past year rose 5.2 percent. On Labor Day 1995, by almost every traditional measure, the economy has had a solid year.

But as I travel the country listening to American workers and their families, I hear voices that respectfully dissent from that conclusion. The business page economy might be doing fine, these voices say, but from the perspective of my home, the economy isn't doing so great. At my home, we're still living from paycheck to paycheck. We still can't save for retirement. If I want to earn enough to pay the bills, I can't spend enough time with my kids to raise them right. My job—and our health insurance—is none too secure. And how are we going to pay for college? Whose economy, they ask me, are you talking about?

The economy has caught fire. But the gains to most workers have gone up in smoke. Last year at this time, the median worker in this country—the person who'd be smack in the middle if we lined up Americans by their earnings—was taking home $479 a week. This year, factoring in inflation, the median wage is $475 a week—four dollars less in every weekly paycheck. And both this year's and last year's figures are lower (again adjusted for inflation) than the $498 median weekly wage in 1979.

On Labor Day, 1995, the earnings of most American workers are either stuck in the mud or sinking. Millions of white-collar supervisors and mid-level managers are joining blue-collar production workers in a common category, frayed-collar workers—frayed-collar workers in gold-plated times.

In macroeconomic terms, the nation is prospering. But Americans do not live by macroeconomics. They live by home economics. They don't live by official statistics. They live by the number that matters most: the figure on their family paycheck.

The state of the American work force this Labor Day is not bad—but not nearly as good, paradoxically, as the state of the economy. Profits are UP. Paychecks are not.

We should celebrate the good fortunes of Americans who are becoming wealthier—the highly-skilled and well-educated portion of the workforce. But there is something terribly wrong, terribly un-American, about the fact that the economy's prosperity is bypassing so many working people. I am not referring to some unfortunate sliver of the population. I am talking about most full-time workers.

Closing the gap between paychecks and profits is our great remaining challenge. The steady decline in the median wage and the widening gulf between the rich and the rest threatens the stability and prosperity of our nation. There are many indicators of this trend, and I direct your attention to the appendix of facts that economists in my office have compiled and that accompanies this speech.

Instead of reciting numbers, I'd like to tell a story—only the most recent tale of frayed-collar workers in gold-plated times. This week, we learned about 12,000 more American jobs that will disappear. For most of us, 12,000 jobs going away—12,000 families being affected—is bad news. But this news was greeted quite happily.

When two giant banks—Chemical and Chase Manhattan—decided to merge this week, white gloved Wall Street high-fived the market's invisible hand. The announcement sent the stock prices of each bank climbing, and shareholders stand to reap a total of $2.5 billion in gains. The corporate CEOs who hammered out the deal were praised for their vision and their toughness. So was the fund manager who helped force the deal. The lawyers and the investment bankers who hashed out the details also made out well. Almost lost in the celebration were the people who would lose these 12,000 jobs.

There are understandable reasons why banks decide to merge—economies of scale, more efficient use of new technologies. After all, none of us will prosper if we attempt to hold back technological progress or withdraw from the global economy. Chase and Chemical are not the villains of this story.

But this episode is yet another symptom of the disconnect between the paycheck economy and the paper economy. Jobs disappear and the markets cheer. There's something wrong with this picture.

Now, the men and women who lose those 12,000 jobs will likely find new ones—though perhaps not right away, perhaps not as good. But their experience, witnessed nation-wide, intensifies the pervasive sense among average

workers today that they're lucky to hold on to the jobs they have. American workers have been silenced by this, and by a thousand other such demonstrations of their easy replaceability. They won't complain if they don't get a raise, even if their company is making bundles of money. Many will even accept cuts in pay or benefits. When you feel your choices boil down to take it or leave it, there's not much to say.

So let us this weekend celebrate this silent majority of American workers. And let us not forget that this coming Tuesday, when Labor Day weekend ends, tens of millions of these hard-working Americans will rise at dawn, dress the kids, make the breakfast, drive to child care or school, put in a long day's work, pick up the kids, scrape together dinner, put the kids to bed, clean the house, and yet still find the energy to listen to their children, talk to them about their problems and their fears, and read them a story before tucking them into bed.

These are the real heroes of the American economy. These Americans need the wind at their back if they are ever to cross the gulf of prosperity.

What does this mean specifically?

It means, first, a high minimum wage. The current minimum wage of $4.25 an hour is heading toward a 40-year low. Someone who works full-time at that wage brings home $8,500 for a year's work—not enough to support a family. And some 40 percent of these people are their family's sole breadwinner.

Giving American workers a fair break also means an expanded Earned Income Tax Credit that makes work pay by putting money back in the pockets of 15 million tax-paying working families with modest incomes.

It means good schools—schools that give our kids a good start in life. We can't expect children to learn in classes of 30 or more, managed by teachers who must spend their time and energies maintaining simple order, during a school day lasting barely five hours

It means low-interest direct college loans for any student who seeks higher education—

and a family tax break for college tuition, the most important investment a family can make.

It means youth apprenticeships for kids who may not go directly on to college, so they can learn on the job. And skill vouchers for people who lose their jobs and need to get new skills at a local community college.

It means affordable and safe child care. And time off from work to take care of a sick child or parent.

It means enforcing the nation's labor laws, coming down hard on employers who cheat and abuse their workers, and shutting down sweatshops that have no place in a civilized country.

It means a robust labor union movement, so workers can boost their bargaining power in order to earn a family wage.

And it means companies that treat their workers as assets to be developed rather than as costs to be cut. Companies that don't pass out pink slips while piling up profits. Companies that give workers a share of the wealth their hard work has created. Companies that invest in their workers' skills—not just in machines to replace them.

That's what it means. And that is the agenda we are pursuing. It is an agenda centered on home economics—an agenda for the blue-collar and pink-collar and white-collar workers who are struggling to build a decent life for their families. Some of this agenda is already accomplished. But there is far, far more to do. The long-term decline in the median wage, and the widening gap between the well-off and ordinary working families, cannot be reversed easily or quickly. *We* are on our way, but it will be a long road.

And yet, there are some who want to reverse this direction. Often, they stride under the banner of "family values," but they lead a parade that's marching backwards.

They refuse to raise the minimum wage. They want to cut child care, Head Start, and the Earned Income Tax Credit for the working poor. They want to cut college loans, reduce opportunities for young people to make the transition from school to work, and slash other funds for education and job training.

They claim budget-balancing as their goal. But the details of their plan betray the values they claim to cherish.

For the fiscal year beginning October 11 they aim to spend an extra $7 billion on national defense—$7 billion more than even the Pentagon says it needs or can use—$7 billion that they want to cut from education, job training, Head Start, and other investments in the economic security of our families.

Meanwhile, they refuse to touch tens of billions of dollars of special tax loopholes and subsidies for particular industries and companies—benefits that well-heeled corporate lobbyists have written into the law—handouts which keep corporations in a perpetual state of welfare dependence. When the chairman of the House Budget Committee presented his Republican colleagues with a loophole-closing plan earlier this year, they blinked. Despite their call for austerity for working people, this Congress is open for business.

They want billions of dollars in additional tax breaks for companies that buy new machines, but not one penny of new tax breaks for investments in the skills of working men and women.

They want to chop the Earned Income Tax Credit for working families, and plan to award the proceeds to well-off Americans on the other side of the gulf of prosperity in the form of a capital gains tax break.

There's an Alice-in-Wonderland quality to their logic. Liberate the economy with deregulation and tax breaks for companies and the rich, they say, and all Americans will prosper. But the economy is already liberated enough to sprint merrily away from a majority of Americans. The problem is that wages are stagnant while profits surge—so how can higher profits be the whole solution?

Many of these politicians speak fervently of family values, but they leave out home economics. They talk passionately about the breakdown of American homes, but they neglect to mention the breakdown of family incomes.

They do recognize the frustrations of working families. But they direct these frustrations against fake targets: against immigrants, against welfare mothers, against affirmative action policies, against our own government.

The politics of resentment—of blame and intolerance—presents a distorted mirror image of the values most families try to transmit to their children. This technique pits working families against working families, or against the very poor, in a fight over a smaller and smaller slice of national income.

The true test of a society is its willingness to face up to its core problems—not to deny them, not to project them on to scapegoats, not to be diverted by issues of the moment nor become easily discouraged when the problems are not quickly solved—but to work at them with steadfast commitment and a fair sharing of whatever sacrifice is entailed.

For example, next week the Senate will debate welfare reform. There will be much pounding of fists and pious pronouncements about the decline of family values. But does anyone really doubt that the best anti-poverty, pro-family policy ever invented is a good job? That poor teenagers with the prospect of jobs and careers when they finish school are more likely to finish, and far less likely to get into trouble? Welfare must be reformed, but the claim that most welfare recipients prefer a welfare check to a job is a cynical lie.

Self-righteous talk is easy and it's cheap. Securing people good jobs is neither easy nor cheap.

Or take the issue that will likely dominate Washington's conversation in the coming months—the impending "train wreck" on the federal budget. To the pundits, this is high drama—a trillion-dollar game of "chicken,"

in which one side must blink or government must shut down. But to many people outside Washington, this is drama that could have far more personal consequences. Because out in America, where workers do the jobs that make the country go, a train wreck is already occurring—a terrifying collision between the job they need and the families they love.

The Congress can avert a budgetary disaster by addressing the real economic problem in this country—home economics.

But if it refuses, if it ignores the country's core problem, the President has vowed to give modern meaning to the ancient adage that the pen is mightier than the sword. If Congress wields its family-slashing sword, the President will respond with his family-saving pen. If the Senate cuts pro-family initiatives as the House already has, he will veto their plan and send them back to try again.

Not too long ago, another President said, "Today, the economic issues are the primary social issue. The economic disaster confronting the United States hurts family values, destroys family savings, and eats away the very heart of family hopes and dreams."

What better moment than the Labor Day weekend to heed these words of a man named Ronald Reagan? What better moment than Labor Day weekend to reaffirm our national commitment to families who are working desperately hard and trying to do right by their children? What better moment to sanctify family values by doing everything in our power to value families? What better moment to pledge to lift the lives of the silent majority of the American workforce?

89 | *A Modest Suggestion for Modest Government*
Philip A. Mundo

A professor of political science, Philip Mundo argues for the middle ground: Individuals need to be protected both from a sometimes overbearing and heavy-handed federal government and from selfish and anticompetitive corporations. Modest government, he concludes, will achieve modest but at least realizable and useful social goals.

In recent years, the time-honored question of how much government should intervene in the economy has reemerged in public discourse throughout the industrialized world. As countries that have provided "cradle-to-grave" benefits consider ways to cut back, other less-generous states struggle to reduce already below average services. The allure of markets—efficiency, growth, wealth—along with the immanent fiscal crises that would surely be caused by continued provision of benefits has forced public officials to try to find ways to take government out of society, letting the market work its magic.

The question for policy makers in all industrialized democracies then is how much government intervention in the economy is appropriate. More generally, how much of a nation's GDP [Gross Domestic Product] should go to government spending of any kind. Each nation has a different answer determined by some mix of history, culture, institutions, wealth, and demographics. This essay considers this question in the U.S.

Context

The 1980 presidential election marked a change in American thinking about the role of government in the economy. Set in motion during the Carter administration with deregulation of the American airline industry, the trend toward deregulation gained an additional boost when Ronald Reagan moved into the White House. Although the extent to which deregulation shrank the regulatory burden of the federal government is doubt-

ful, the idea that government should leave more decisions to the market became entrenched in national policy making. Thus, government agencies at the national and particularly the state level contracted out public tasks to corporations. The logic behind privatization is that business firms, which are governed by the tough competition of the market, can perform various functions more efficiently than government, which suffers from excessive bureaucratic pathologies. Politicians sought to lower taxes and in general to take government out of business as much as possible. The Interstate Commerce Commission, originally established to regulate railroads and later trucking, disappeared. A decade later, after years of negotiation, Congress, with the enthusiastic approval of a Democratic president, deregulated the financial industry.

Public officials also tried to reduce the role of the national government in redistributing wealth from richer to poorer Americans. Tax cuts in part accomplished this objective, but the more significant development was the passage of welfare reform in 1996. Largely a conservative bill, Democratic President Bill Clinton signed it in the spirit of making welfare work better, getting people off welfare roles, and accomplishing both goals by turning over more responsibility to state governments.

One should not be too exuberant about the pace and desirability of a shrinking federal government. The main reason is that it is not shrinking. The federal government continues to regulate industry, and agencies of various stripes relentlessly pile on one regulation after the other, all of which are available in the *Federal Register*. However, in the U.S., the national government has never been as involved in the economic and social aspects of society as much as governments in other industrialized democracies. The impulse to cut back government involvement in the U.S. in the last two decades is a function of the perceived excesses of New Deal–Great Society programs. The perception makes sense within the American context, not in some absolute sense or even in comparison with other rich nations.

Scholars typically call the gap between the U.S. and other nations "American exceptionalism." Although the term's meaning is inexact, it essentially refers to the U.S.'s unique history, place in the world, ethnic mix, and natural abundance. These factors cause American government to be different from other governments—e.g., decentralized, porous, untidy—and cause public policy to be different from its rich-nation counterparts—e.g., more reliant on the individual, distrustful of government, and having unusual faith in markets. This American exceptionalism does not necessarily explain, but certainly characterizes, the difference between the U.S. and other rich nations with respect to government intervention.

In the current international discussion of the changing role of the relationship between government and the economy, some find the U.S. to be an outlier. While Germany, France, and Sweden struggle with the fundamental question of whether to end the cradle-to-grave guarantee to its citizens, the U.S. has never been encumbered by such a promise. American public officials therefore are freer to explore the use of the market for the allocation of resources than their counterparts elsewhere. Americans appear to thrive on greater levels of uncertainty, opportunity, success, and failure. From abroad, this enthusiasm for the market is sometimes referred to as cowboy capitalism, an approach to the role of government in the economy that leaders of other nations decidedly wish to avoid.

If we accept for the moment that the U.S. is different—i.e., that there is meaning in the term American exceptionalism—then what should U.S. economic goals be? How much intervention should the national government engage in?

If one imagines the arguments along a continuum, at one extreme are those who believe government should do as little as possible. Libertarians advance the purest form of this position, contending that government has few legitimate responsibilities—national defense, domestic police—and everything else should be left to the market or to social organization. Less-strident versions of this perspective more realistically acknowledge a central role for the national government, but advocate limiting it wherever possible—e.g., by drastically cutting taxes.

At the other end of the continuum, proponents of extensive government intervention in society argue that government is the sole expression of the collective will in society, and it is the only institution in position to achieve certain crucial societal objectives. On the social side, government is necessary to achieve justice, say, through the redistribution of resources by means of taxes and social welfare programs. With respect to the economy, the market is replete with failures; government is necessary to allocate resources in ways that foster economic growth and promote justice. In short, markets cannot accomplish these objectives; governments can and must.

The familiar views of the political left and right set the boundaries of the debate about the proper role of government in society. Supporters of one view or the other tend to be consciously ideological; they operate from a set of premises describing a good society and seek to turn that into practice in the real world. Separating these ideological poles is a considerable middle ground that allows for a blend of government and market in determining the allocation of resources. In this space of messy compromise, untidy arguments, and marked discomfort with ideological purity lie opportunities for pragmatic solutions to concrete problems. Here, prescriptions for the role of government in society focus on the question of how government can establish an environment that fosters economic growth while at the same time ameliorating problems created by it—e.g., pollution and social inequity.

A vibrant economy energized largely by the market can create an impressive record with respect to growth and productivity. But it can also create problems that the market does not correct—i.e., so-called market failures. Government has a complex role to play here. First, it must provide a suitable context for a market economy. Second, assuming the first is successful, it must address the problems created by the successes of the market. The remainder of this essay fills in some of the details of government's complex charge in order to answer more completely the question of what government ought to do. The discussion will also consider the matter of whether government can accomplish its tasks, assuming that there is some agreement on what those tasks are.

What Government Has Done

Like it or not, in the U.S. as elsewhere, government has always been involved to some extent in the economy. In the early years of the republic, the national government engaged in an aggressive policy of improving infrastructure—e.g., canals, roads, postal service. Without these basic improvements, a capitalist economy would not have been able to take root in American soil. Along with building roads and acquiring great chunks of land, the national government protected U.S. manufacturers through a system of tariffs lasting throughout the nineteenth century. As the nation embarked upon its inevitable global significance in the twentieth century, the national government became more involved in the economy with the development of an elaborate tax structure and ever increasing regulation.

The point is that there is a tradition of government involvement in the economy in the U.S. Those who hark back to a Jeffersonian ideal of limited government in support of arguments to eliminate this program or that

agency forget that as president, Jefferson negotiated the Louisiana Purchase, the largest peaceful acquisition of territory in American history. At the same time, there has been strong sentiment in favor of limiting government because of the potential bad that big government can do. That strain of thought reappeared on the political scene in the 1980s, mainly through the voice of President Ronald Reagan. It helped put such things as deregulation and privatization on the political agenda, and it is central to the current debate over the proper role of government.

What Government Can Do

Regardless of the conclusions society might draw about the proper role of government, whether or not government can actually accomplish those objectives is another question. There are two sets of factors embedded in this question. First, can government create programs that solve specific problems? Second, does government have the capacity to implement programs effectively?

Can government create programs that solve specific problems? This question is at the root of the vast and still growing area of public policy. As social problems become more complex, they demand more complex solutions. The challenge of coming up with programs that effectively address social problems can be overwhelming. It should come as no surprise that failed policies easily outnumber successful ones. Able professionals motivated by the best of intentions may simply not have the wherewithal to understand the diverse facets of social problems sufficiently to design programs to solve them. The root of this type of failure may be that experts do not know enough to come up with programs that work. It is also unsurprising that there is disagreement over whether a program is a success or failure. Evaluating programs is difficult in itself because of such problems as vague or unspecified goals, inadequate methodology and data, and ideological bias. Thus, the first part of the answer to the question of whether government can address problems effectively is that in many instances the right program may be beyond policy experts' grasp. More knowledge is necessary to creating a good solution.

The second part of the question has to do with government's capacity to implement programs once they have been designed. Another way to put the question is: Can government make programs work?

Bureaucracy is at the center of the question of whether government can make programs work. Much maligned and hardly ever praised, bureaucracy is an ideological and political lightning rod. Conservatives never tire of haranguing the federal bureaucracy and bureaucrats, its employees, for inefficiency, ineffectiveness, and incompetence. Typically characterized as bloated and overpaid, bureaucracy is the problem, not the solution.

Bureaucracy has its defenders, however. Specialists in administration—both academics and practitioners—take a more balanced view of bureaucracy. There is no shortage of problems, of course; bureaucracy can be poorly designed, resulting in a structure of public organizations that may be ill suited for the tasks they are supposed to carry out. For example, as programs get more complex, the agencies that administer them must become more flexible. Bureaucrats need a measure of discretion in order to adjust programs to constantly changing circumstances. To the extent that the federal bureaucracy is rigid, it is poorly equipped to administer effectively appropriate programs. On the other hand, bureaucracy is not a total loss. Many agencies accomplish their tasks quite well—e.g., the Social Security Administration—and bureaucrats have proved to be innovative in devising ways to administer programs more efficiently and effectively.

The question of whether government can effectively intervene in society is enormously complex. Observers of American politics frequently make several errors in evaluating the role of government in society, one of which is failing to separate the capacity to achieve objectives from whether government *ought* to

achieve those objectives. But the question of government capacity involves two equally difficult problems: devising effective programs to address public policy problems and implementing them effectively. Any debate about the proper level of government intervention in the economy must take account of these questions. With a general understanding of government capacity in mind, we can turn to a more specific consideration of what government can and cannot do with respect to the economy.

Limits to Government Action

The U.S. government has gone through periods of intense activity intended at somehow directing the nation's economy. Policy has been at times quite ambitious with the goal of having sweeping effects on the economy. The scorecard is mixed, of course, and there is considerable disagreement on these matters among scholars and other observers of the relationship between government and the economy in the U.S.

In the late 1970s, President Jimmy Carter sought to create a comprehensive energy policy for the U.S. Covering everything from conservation of resources to the development of new technologies, the Carter administration's plan was nothing if not ambitious. Among the specific goals were efforts to develop synthetic fuels and technologies designed to extract energy from wind. In the short term, neither effort met with much success. Synthetic fuels have not taken hold in the U.S., and only in the late 1990s has wind technology begun to make some headway into the energy market.

This case illustrates the problems government encountered when trying to create a market for new energy sources. Government support for such new technologies did not result in their getting a foothold in the market. The shortcomings to this approach lie mainly in the conceptualization of the program. It was simply not possible to devise a way to turn these technologies into viable alternatives to fossil fuels; the program did not effectively ameliorate the problem.

In the 1980s, Congress and the president sought to address a rapidly worsening economic problem: the ballooning federal budget deficit. The federal government had been getting deeper in debt since 1969, with a dramatic increase in deficits in the 1980s. Congress developed a plan—usually known as Gramm-Rudman-Hollings, or GRH—to force it and the president to bring the annual budget deficit down to zero within five years. The plan did not work. It took another eight years to realize a zero-deficit budget, which was the result of a healthy economy and finally a sensible policy of deficit reduction.

In this instance, public officials eventually came up with an effective program, but it took years to reach it. The episode in budget deficit reduction is a lesson in the need to build up support for a policy over a long period of time before it can actually work. The reason for this is in part the difficulty of devising an effective program; it takes time to learn what works and what does not. It also suggests the importance of a problem's becoming so visible and significant in the public's eye that elected officials have no choice but to address it, even at their own political risk.

One of the most important economic policies carried out by the national government is taxation. Tax policy is intended to do more than secure a source of revenue for government. Through tax policy, the federal government affects the economy as a whole and specific aspects of it with targeted tax breaks. This latter form of taxation is most interesting for our purposes here, as it illustrates the government's effort to encourage quite specific activities while discouraging others. Thus, the research and development tax credit is an inducement to firms to engage in more R&D [Reasearch and Design]; whether it does this or whether it is needed are questions that corporations prefer to answer in the affirmative, while other more disinterested observers may have more doubts. Tax breaks that are really nothing more than

another form of pork are clearly not in the nation's interest and are serious flaws in U.S. tax policy.

Casting the net a bit more broadly, government has had difficulties dealing with important social problems that are related to the health of the national economy as well as to the economic conditions of individuals. Programs intended to address poverty and economic inequality have drawn a great deal of attention and criticism in recent years. It is reasonably safe to say that such programs have enjoyed both success and failure. While Social Security has relieved acute poverty among the elderly, Aid to Families with Dependent Children, the primary federal welfare program since the New Deal, presents a murkier picture. Although the program alleviated the pain of poverty for many through much of its history, agreement on the flaws of the program was widespread enough in 1996 to cause Congress and the president to eliminate it altogether, replacing it with a program that gives more authority to state officials over administering welfare benefits. If the goal was to eliminate poverty, this federal program, and others, failed. If the goal was to relieve it to some extent, or to prevent it from getting worse, then there is room for disagreement about the success or failure of AFDC and other social welfare programs. What is evident from this experience, however, is that the federal government cannot eliminate poverty and certainly cannot create anything resembling economic equality. One of capitalism's major shortcomings is that it is replete with cracks through which people, for whatever reason, fall. The U.S. national government has not yet been able to seal those cracks or rescue all who have fallen through them.

The preceding paragraphs illustrate the limits of government action in the U.S. While it is difficult to find cases of complete failure, partial failure or limited success is common. Clearly, there are things government cannot do, and trying to do them results in waste and unintended consequences, which frequently means more problems. A more ideological response to these problems would have government withdraw from as many activities as possible (the political right) or have government try to do much more (the political left), assuming that committing more resources to act in the public's interest could result in success at dealing with otherwise nettlesome problems.

Markets

The market is an alternative to government for allocating resources in society. Innumerable transactions conducted constantly throughout the economy determine who gets what, when, where, and how. Conservatives credit markets for fostering efficiency, and the more markets are allowed to operate without government interference, the better off everyone is. Less government regulation, lower taxes, and freer trade, according to market advocates, all lead to economic growth and greater welfare. Even Democrats now concede that the market is a good way to allocate resources in many instances, and government intervention should be reduced. Thus, in the 1970s, Jimmy Carter began the wave of deregulation that was continued by Ronald Reagan starting with the phasing out of the Civil Aeronautics Board, which regulated airline fares and routes. President Bill Clinton, while more supportive of government action than his Republican predecessors in the White House, prefers to place more authority for domestic policy in the states, perhaps resulting from his experience as Governor of Arkansas.

Although markets inspire awe in the hearts of conservatives and have attracted new followers among moderates, it is still clear that markets cannot do everything. Market failures open the door to government action. For example, on their own, markets do not get rid of pollution. Government action of some sort is required. This need not be in the form of command and control regulation, where government sets limits and firms abide by them or pay fines. Government has also attempted

to use market mechanisms to achieve environmental goals more efficiently. Markets also do little about poverty or the growing gap between rich people and poor people in the U.S. Indeed, a thriving capitalist economy may exacerbate the latter problem. Thus, markets can do a great deal toward improving the human condition, but they can't do everything. There is a role for government, but exactly how much government intervention in the economy and in what form remains open to debate.

...

Relying solely on either the market to allocate resources or turning to government to dominate these choices will produce good results. Government has an important role to play, and if properly designed and limited, government has the capacity to undertake significant programs effectively. Americans are known for their pragmatism. A "can-do" nation, government should be able to carry out some programs effectively. I will first discuss which problems government ought to solve, followed by a discussion of whether government has the capacity to do so.

Pragmatic Approach

A pragmatic approach to public policy and the proper role of government in the economy is likely to lie somewhere between the two ideological extremes discussed earlier in the essay. It is premised on the idea that there is considerable agreement that government ought to do something about certain problems. Pragmatic policies are not necessarily the results of compromise of the two extremes; they may also be what's left after public officials and the public itself tire of ideological wars. The programs that fall from these policies avoid ideological prescriptions; instead, they approach a problem based on what works. Determining that may be nothing more than an approximation of trial and error. Programs that work may rely on government bureaucrats, markets, private contractors, operating at the national, state, or local levels. The only test that counts is whether the program accomplishes its objectives. Designing programs of this sort is no mean task, but the guiding principle should always be workability and not ideological adherence.

What Government Should Do

Government has several large, legitimate tasks related to regulating the economy. Fiscal policy—making budgets and taxation—for example, is a central activity for any modern government. The federal government should strive for a balanced budget under normal conditions, but be flexible enough to borrow when circumstances call for it—e.g., emergencies, and economic "pump priming." The federal government can use taxes for economic as well as social ends. Targeting certain activities for tax breaks is an instrument many public officials find useful in achieving their policy objectives. Making taxes more progressive in effect redistributes wealth in society, which is a desirable end. Cutting taxes—say, instituting a flat tax—may achieve the economic end of more rapid growth, but possibly at the expense of equity. As it is apparent from these examples, practical usage of budget deficits and taxes can serve the purposes of either ideological perspective. The instruments should be used with caution, so as to minimize the risk of policy disaster.

The federal government also has responsibility for monetary policy—regulating the supply of money. To carry out this task, most industrial democracies have resorted to central banks that enjoy a measure of political independence. This is true for the U.S.; the Federal Reserve System operates in an environment that is at least insulated from direct political pressure.

Public officials ought also to use government to secure some resemblance of equity with respect to wealth. Redistributive policies can blunt the sharp differences in wealth, serving perhaps the social purpose of reducing tension among different groups in society. Doing so also serves justice, at least as it has been defined by the mainstream in the U.S. in the twentieth century. And it makes economic sense, as more people have the wherewithal to participate in the economy.

Government should regulate economic activity to address market failures and to keep the capitalist economic system on an even keel. Antitrust policy does the latter; environmental policy is an example of the former. Both types of endeavors are legitimate uses of government authority, and there is considerable room within each category for ideological differences.

This list of government activities that directly or indirectly affect the economy is hardly novel. National governments, including the U.S., have engaged in these sorts of endeavors for years. The common theme throughout is moderation. Government accomplishes objectives on which there is considerable agreement. For example, while people disagree about government's legitimate role in dealing with poverty, most agree that government should do something. Similarly, while there has been considerable disagreement regarding the budget and how to balance it, most participants agree that a balanced budget, or at least clear fiscal discipline, is a desirable end.

We should not ask government to be responsible for economic success completely, nor can we ask government to address all forms of inequality. Even if a consensus could be achieved on this goal, how it could be accomplished is unknown. Economic activity is far too uncertain to allow for government control. Nor can we ask government to solve the problem of economic inequality; one of the premises of capitalism is that everyone strives to become unequal. If one accepts capitalism as the economic system for the nation, then one must accept a measure of economic inequality. (This is nothing more than saying that some people will earn more money than others.) As much as perfect equality is an unreachable goal, equity is a desirable one. Government can do things to reduce poverty, shrink the gap between rich people and poor people, and in general insure that everyone benefits from economic growth. Finally, we should be wary of programs that purport to result in sweeping benefits for everyone. The world is a complicated place, and no one can know all the consequences of any policy, never mind large, sweeping change.

So where does this leave us? I argue for government in moderation. Modest government can accomplish modest ends for society. I subscribe neither to the idea that government that governs least governs best, nor that government is the solution to all problems. Government should pursue objectives on which there is an obvious long-term consensus in society, not on specifics, but on the broad objectives. Programs should fit within government's capacity to act. The national government, contrary to what ideologues on the right might claim, has accomplished much that is good. It has also failed in ways that have been well documented. Thus, goals should be chosen that fall within government's ability to act. Health care for everyone is one such goal, as is regulation of economic activity. Economic equality for all and government management of the economy are not.

CHAPTER FOURTEEN

International Relations

OVERVIEW AND SUMMARY

Foreign policy is often studied separately in courses on American politics, as if it were necessarily different from other kinds of policy. Not a few people have the impression that there is a clear dividing line between domestic policy and the policies that govern relations with other countries. But, if nothing else, a number of clichés has been employed to convince us that foreign policy matters: The world is called a "global village," for example, and international borders have become "transnational." Some writers are predicting the end of the nation-state and its replacement by the "virtual state." Others insist that national independence has been replaced by "interdependence" and even phrases such as *foreign policy* or *foreign news* have been replaced by *international policy* and *international news*. At the same time, others decry what they see as a new and frightful era of foreign influence over American politics, and they advocate returning to a time when the United States strongly stood apart from the rest of the world. But despite the commonly held myths on all sides of the conversation, there never was an era of splendid isolation for the United States.

From the beginning, America was entangled in one kind of alliance or another with foreign nations and empires. International commerce, for example, has always been a central concern of farmers who produce large surpluses of crops, as well as some manufacturers. Tariffs on imported goods and immigration policy have always been near the center of congressional politics. The protection of trade on the high seas and of American business personnel stationed abroad has long consumed the attention of some department of government. Hostilities between foreign nations have often enough impinged on the interests of Americans, as have some revolutions, coups d'état, and other disorders suffered by governments abroad. In the end, the American government makes scores of foreign policy decisions daily that are somehow the result of the domestic political process. But how are these decisions made? And on what principles should they be made?

George Washington thought foreign affairs to be so vexing and dangerous that in his Farewell Address he felt compelled to warn the nation away from the "mischiefs of foreign intrigue" and the "impostures of pretended patriotism." His primary concern, reflective of James Madison's view of "the people," was that the public might fall prey to its own vices. The democratic vice in foreign policy would be to place emotional attachments to, or unreasoned hatred of, some countries ahead of a coolly calculated policy that furthered interests of the United States. In a sense, whereas Washington might have thought the Constitution to be sufficient protection in most affairs against the selfish ambition of factions, he was not so sure it carried over to the making of foreign policy.

What most people remember of Washington's warnings are less his misgivings about the capacity of the people to steer clear of trouble in foreign affairs than his wish to avoid entangling alliances and his advocacy of neutrality. Such views still resonate among the American public, and Washington's address is often quoted.

Washington's memory had little faded, however, before **James Monroe**, the fifth president, found it necessary to define, on principle, what might constitute an enemy of the United States. Specifically, Monroe warned against European monarchies that might meddle in Latin America. His warning became known, after some decades, as the Monroe Doctrine and was widely interpreted as a claim by the United States to a prerogative interest in the Western Hemisphere. Monroe had indeed asserted the keen interest of the United States in the rest of the hemisphere. But the ground on which he made this claim was more important— that of defending democracy. Monroe said that the United States would oppose any country that might attempt to spread on the two continents of the New World a political system hostile to the American form of democracy.

The Monroe Doctrine was successful in building U.S. influence in the Western Hemisphere in part because, as Tocqueville had observed, the United States had the great fortune of being insulated by large oceans from the turbulence of the Asian and European continents. The United States in the remainder of the nineteenth century spent its energies in conquering its geographical frontiers and in fighting the Civil War. But the new century and the closing of the frontier seemed to turn America's attention back to Europe and Asia.

The Europeans, as well as the Japanese, competed for colonies and coaling stations at the turn of the century and later became embroiled in the Great European War, or World War I (1914–1918). President **Woodrow Wilson** campaigned for reelection in 1916 by appealing to Americans' distaste for European power politics with the slogan "he kept us out of war." Nonetheless, only a few months after his reelection, Wilson petitioned Congress for a declaration of war against Germany and its allies. Wilson, after pointing out Germany's many offenses against the neutrality of the United States, concluded that "the world must be made safe for democracy. Its peace must be planted upon the tested foundations of political liberty." The United States, he said, as a free society could not stand idly by while antidemocratic powers made war. Then, as now, not everyone agreed what America's mission or obligations were.

Senator **Robert M. La Follette** argued, two days after the president's war message, that Wilson's course of action and that of the allies were dishonorable. La Follette pointed out the allies against Germany were little better than Germany itself in the quality of their government or their conduct of the war. The United States, he contended, was doing little to protect itself or advance the cause of democracy by borrowing money from the great financiers to pay for the war, sending the poor to fight in Europe, and allying itself with governments whose commitment to democracy was limited. Moreover, he objected to the modern practice of waging war, not just on governments or armies, but also on the civilian population of the declared enemy, "starving to death the old men and women, the children, the sick and the maimed of Germany."

Generations later, upon his inauguration as president, **John F. Kennedy**, like many presidents before him, called on Americans to protect themselves and, more, to protect their ideals by assisting friends abroad in any struggle against antidemocratic forces. The United States, he declared, was "unwilling to witness or permit the slow undoing of those human rights to which this Nation has always been committed, and to which we are committed today at home and around the world." That commitment in part led to a prolonged struggle in South Vietnam, which involved hundreds of thousands of American soldiers.

The brother of the slain president later became an outspoken critic of the war and a candidate for president on an antiwar platform. **Robert F. Kennedy** argued, not unlike Robert La Follette generations before, that the country the United States fought to protect was so corrupt and so far from being a democracy that saving it was not worth expending the lives of American soldiers. Likewise, he argued, the intolerable casualties of the war were the millions of Vietnamese civilians who had lost their lives or had become refugees. He concluded that the United States had tragically misstepped and should not continue to wage war. Such is the debate that ever returns to the Congress and the American public.

As recently as March 1999, this familiar debate was rekindled when President Clinton decided to bomb Serbia to force it to relent in its persecution of the Kosovar minority. Subsequently, a senator from Texas, **Kay Bailey Hutchison**, protested that the United States was intervening in a civil war in which Americans had no evident interest. Furthermore, by using NATO (North Atlantic Treaty Organization) for this intervention, the president was effectively transforming a longstanding and successful defensive alliance into an offensive one. The senator also noted that in the civil war, Kosovars, like Serbians, had committed atrocities and were no more democratic or respectful of human rights than the Serbian government.

A Senator from Louisiana, **Mary L. Landrieu,** argued that the United States had an obligation to intervene nonetheless. As others before her, Landrieu asserted that the United States had an obligation both to protect its own liberal principles and to apply those principles to others, forcefully if necessary, when there were flagrant and atrocious attacks on basic human rights. For Landrieu, that Serbia was a European nation, bordering on both old and nascent democracies, made the case for intervention even stronger. She asked her Senate colleagues, "Will we have another rogue nation, this time in the heart of Europe, with little else motivating them besides age-old desires for revenge and an interest in interfering with the stability and prosperity of the United States and the entire European continent?"

90 The Mischiefs of Foreign Intrigue— and the Impostures of Pretended Patriotism

George Washington

Commentators on American foreign policy seem never to tire of citing the opinions of the retiring first president. Isolationists in particular are fond of echoing the famous warning against "entangling alliances." President Washington did by no means suggest that the United States should stand completely apart from the world. He did emphasize that its interests should be honored first and that passionate attachments for or against other nations should be eschewed. He advocated "liberal intercourse with all nations" but with an "equal and impartial hand." This excerpt from Washington's Farewell Address *was not orated publicly but rather published in a Philadelphia newspaper toward the end of his second term.*

Observe good faith and justice toward all nations. Cultivate peace and harmony with all. Religion and morality enjoin this conduct; and can it be that good policy does not equally enjoin it? It will be worthy of a free, enlightened, and, at no distant period, a great nation to give to mankind the magnanimous and too novel example of a people always guided by an exalted justice and benevolence. Who can doubt that in the course of time and things the fruits of such a plan would richly repay any temporary advantages which might be lost by a steady adherence to it? Can it be that Providence has not connected the permanent felicity of a nation with its virtue? The experiment, at least, is recommended by every sentiment which ennobles human nature. Alas! is it rendered impossible by its vices?

In the execution of a plan nothing is more essential than that permanent, inveterate antipathies against particular nations and passionate attachments for others should be excluded and that in place of them just and amicable feeling toward all should be cultivated. The nation which indulges toward another an habitual hatred or an habitual fondness is in some degree a slave. It is a slave to its animosity or to its affection, either of which is sufficient to lead it astray from its duty and its interest.

The great rule of foreign conduct for us, in regard to foreign nations, is in extending our commercial relations to have with them as little political connection as possible. So far as we have already formed engagements, let them be fulfilled with perfect good faith. Here let us stop.

Europe has a set of primary interests which to us have none, or a very remote relation. Hence she must be engaged in frequent controversies, the causes of which are essentially foreign to our concerns. Hence, therefore, it must be unwise in us to implicate ourselves, by artificial ties, in the ordinary vicissitudes of her politics or the ordinary combinations and collisions of her friendships or enmities.

Our detached and distant situation invites and enables us to pursue a different course. If we remain one people, under an efficient government, the period is not far off when we may defy material injury from external annoyance; when we may take such an attitude as will cause the neutrality we may at any time resolve upon to be scrupulously respected; when belligerent nations, under the impossibility of making acquisitions upon us, will not lightly hazard the giving us provocation; when we may choose peace or war as our interest guided by our justice shall counsel.

Why forgo the advantages of so peculiar a situation? Why quit our own to stand upon foreign ground? Why, by interweaving our destiny with that of any part of Europe, entangle our peace and prosperity in the toils of European ambition, rivalship, interest, humor, or caprice?

It is our true policy to steer clear of permanent alliances with any portion of the foreign world. So far, I mean, as we are now at liberty to do it, for let me not be understood as capable of patronizing infidelity to existing engagements (I hold the maxim no less applicable to public than to private affairs that honesty is always the best policy). I repeat it, therefore: let those engagements be observed in their genuine sense. But, in my opinion, it is unnecessary and would be unwise to extend them.

Taking care always to keep ourselves, by suitable establishments, on a respectably defensive posture, we may safely trust to temporary alliances for extraordinary emergencies.

Harmony, liberal intercourse with all nations are recommended by policy, humanity, and interest. But even our commercial policy should hold an equal and impartial hand, neither seeking nor granting exclusive favors or preferences; consulting the natural course of things; diffusing and diversifying by gentle means the streams of commerce but forcing nothing; establishing with powers so disposed, in order to give to trade a stable course, to define the rights of our merchants, and to enable the government to support them, conventional rules of intercourse, the best that present circumstances and mutual opinion will permit, but temporary and liable to be from time to time abandoned or varied, as experience and circumstances shall dictate; constantly keeping in view that it is folly in one nation to look for disinterested favors from another; that it must pay with a portion of its independence for whatever it may accept under that character; that, by such acceptance, it may place itself in the condition of having given equivalents for nominal favors and yet of being reproached with ingratitude for not giving more. There can be no greater error than to expect, or calculate, upon real favors from nation to nation. It is an illusion which experience must cure, which a just pride ought to discard.

In offering to you, my countrymen, these counsels of an old and affectionate friend, I dare not hope they will make the strong and lasting impression I could wish; that they will control the usual current of the passions or prevent our nation from running the course which has hitherto marked the destiny of nations. But if I may even flatter myself that they may be productive of some partial benefit, some occasional good; that they may now and then recur to moderate the fury of party-spirit, to warn against the mischiefs of foreign intrigue, to guard against the impostures of pretended patriotism, this hope will be a full recompense for the solicitude for your welfare by which they have been dictated.

91 | *The Monroe Doctrine*
James Monroe

In his message to Congress in 1823, President Monroe found it necessary to explain some foreign affairs in which the United States could not remain neutral. After decades of war and political turmoil on the European continent, Spain and Portugal were attempting to reassert control over former colonies in the Americas. Monroe decided that the United States must support the continuing independence of Latin American states, explaining that the meddling European powers (Spain and Portugal) were antidemocratic and therefore, by their nature, a threat to the United States.

Fellow-Citizens of the Senate and House of Representatives:

... [T]he occasion has been judged proper for asserting, as a principle in which the rights and interests of the United States are involved, that the American continents, by the free and independent condition which they have assumed and maintain, are henceforth not to be considered as subjects for future colonization by any European Power....

... The citizens of the United States cherish sentiments the most friendly in favor of the liberty and happiness of their fellow-men on that side of the Atlantic. In the wars of the European powers in matters relating to themselves we have never taken any part, nor does it comport with our policy so to do. It is only when our rights are invaded or seriously menaced that we resent injuries or make preparation for our defense. With the movements in this hemisphere we are of necessity more immediately connected, and by causes which must be obvious to all enlightened and impartial observers. The political system of the allied powers is essentially different in this respect from that of America. This difference proceeds from that which exists in their respective Governments; and to the defense of our own, which has been achieved by the loss of so much blood and treasure, and matured by the wisdom of their most enlightened citizens, and under which we have enjoyed unexampled felicity, this whole nation is devoted. We owe it, therefore, to candor and to the amicable relations existing between the United States and those powers to declare that we should consider any attempt on their part to extend their system to any portion of this hemisphere as dangerous to our peace and safety. With the existing colonies or dependencies of any European power we have not interfered and shall not interfere. But with the Governments who have declared their independence and maintained it, and whose independence we have, on great consideration and on just principles, acknowledged, we could not view any interposition for the purpose of oppressing them, or controlling in any other manner their destiny, by any European power in any other light than as the manifestation of an unfriendly disposition toward the United States....

The late events in Spain and Portugal shew that Europe is still unsettled. Of this important fact no stronger proof can be adduced than that the allied powers should have thought it proper, on any principle satisfactory to themselves, to have interposed by force in the internal concerns of Spain. To what extent such interposition may be carried, on the same principle, is a question in which all independent powers whose governments differ from theirs are interested, even those most remote, and surely none more so than the United States. Our policy in regard to Europe, which was adopted at an early stage of the wars which have so long agitated that quarter of the globe, nevertheless remains the same, which is, not to interfere in the internal concerns of any of its powers; to consider the government de facto as the legitimate government for us; to cultivate friendly relations with it, and to preserve those relations by a frank, firm, and manly policy, meeting in all instances the just claims of every power, submitting to injuries from none. But in regard to those continents circumstances are eminently and conspicuously different. It is impossible that the allied powers should extend their political system to any portion of either continent without endangering our peace and happiness; nor can anyone believe that our southern brethren, if [left] to themselves, would adopt it of their own accord. It is equally impossible, therefore, that we should behold such interposition in any form with indifference.

92 | *War Message: To Vindicate the Principles of Peace*
Woodrow Wilson

Though President Wilson campaigned for reelection in 1916 on the slogan "he kept us out of war," he asked for a declaration of war only months after his victory. In his view Germany's unrestricted submarine warfare finally showed the barbarity of an autocratic regime, as well as the obligation of the United States to protect itself by protecting all democracies and opposing antidemocratic nations. Thus the United States would intervene in the European war to protect universal rights of people everywhere and would "spend her blood and her might for the principles that gave her birth...."

I have called the Congress into extraordinary session because there are serious, very serious, choices of policy to be made, and made immediately, which it was neither right nor constitutionally permissible that I should assume the responsibility of making.

On the 3rd of February last, I officially laid before you the extraordinary announcement of the Imperial German government that on and after the 1st day of February it was its purpose to put aside all restraints of law or of humanity and use its submarines to sink every vessel that sought to approach either the ports of Great Britain and Ireland or the western coasts of Europe or any of the ports controlled by the enemies of Germany within the Mediterranean.

That had seemed to be the object of the German submarine warfare earlier in the war, but since April of last year the Imperial government had somewhat restrained the commanders of its undersea craft in conformity with its promise then given to us that passenger boats should not be sunk and that due warning would be given to all other vessels which its submarines might seek to destroy, when no resistance was offered or escape attempted, and care taken that their crews were given at least a fair chance to save their lives in their open boats. The precautions taken were meager and haphazard enough, as was proved in distressing instance after instance in the progress of the cruel and unmanly business, but a certain degree of restraint was observed.

The new policy has swept every restriction aside. Vessels of every kind, whatever their flag, their character, their cargo, their destination, their errand, have been ruthlessly sent to the bottom without warning and without thought of help or mercy for those on board, the vessels of friendly neutrals along with those of belligerents. Even hospital ships and ships carrying relief to the sorely bereaved and stricken people of Belgium, though the latter were provided with safe conduct through the proscribed areas by the German government itself and were distinguished by unmistakable marks of identity, have been sunk with the same reckless lack of compassion or of principle....

The present German submarine warfare against commerce is a warfare against mankind. It is a war against all nations. American ships have been sunk, American lives taken in ways which it has stirred us very deeply to learn of; but the ships and people of other neutral and friendly nations have been sunk and overwhelmed in the waters in the same way. There has been no discrimination. The challenge is to all mankind.

Each nation must decide for itself how it will meet it. The choice we make for ourselves must be made with a moderation of counsel and a temperateness of judgment befitting our character and our motives as a nation. We must put excited feeling away. Our motive will not be revenge or the victorious assertion of the physical might of the nation, but only the vindication of right, of human right, of which we are only a single champion....

...There is one choice we cannot make, we are incapable of making: we will not choose the path of submission and suffer the most sacred rights of our nation and our people to be ignored or violated. The wrongs against which we now array ourselves are no common wrongs; they cut to the very roots of human life.

With a profound sense of the solemn and even tragical character of the step I am taking and of the grave responsibilities which it involves, but in unhesitating obedience to what I deem my constitutional duty, I advise that the Congress declare the recent course of the Imperial German government to be in fact nothing less than war against the government and people of the United States; that it formally accept the status of belligerent which has thus been thrust upon it; and that it take immediate steps, not only to put the country in a more thorough state of defense but also to exert all its power and employ all its resources to bring the government of the German Empire to terms and end the war.

What this will involve is clear. It will involve the utmost practicable cooperation in counsel and action with the governments now at war with Germany and, as incident to that, the extension to those governments of the most liberal financial credits, in order that our resources may so far as possible be added to theirs. It will involve the organization and mobilization of all the material resources of the country to supply the materials of war and serve the incidental needs of the nation in the most abundant and yet the most economical and efficient way possible. It will involve the immediate full equipment of the Navy in all respects but particularly in supplying it with the best means of dealing with the enemy's submarines. It will involve the immediate addition to the armed forces of the United States already provided for by law in case of war at least 500,000 men, who should, in my opinion, be chosen upon the principle of universal liability to service, and also the authorization of subsequent additional increments of equal force so soon as they may be needed and can be handled in training.

It will involve also, of course, the granting of adequate credits to the government, sustained, I hope, so far as they can equitably be sustained by the present generation, by well-conceived taxation. I say sustained so far as may be equitable by taxation because it seems to me that it would be most unwise to base the credits which will now be necessary entirely on money borrowed. It is our duty, I most respectfully urge, to protect our people so far as we may against the very serious hardships and evils which would be likely to arise out of the inflation which would be produced by vast loans.

... While we do these things, these deeply momentous things, let us be very clear, and make very clear to all the world, what our motives and our objects are. My own thought has not been driven from its habitual and normal course by the unhappy events of the last two months, and I do not believe that the thought of the nation has been altered or clouded by them. I have exactly the same things in mind now that I had in mind when I addressed the Senate on the 22nd of January last; the same that I had in mind when I addressed the Congress on the 3rd of February and on the 26th of February.

Our object now, as then, is to vindicate the principles of peace and justice in the life of the world as against selfish and autocratic power and to set up among the really free and self-governed peoples of the world such a concert of purpose and of action as will henceforth ensure the observance of those principles. Neutrality is no longer feasible or desirable where the peace of the world is involved and the freedom of its peoples, and the menace to that peace and freedom lies in the existence of autocratic governments backed by organized force which is controlled wholly by their will, not by the will of their people. We have seen the last of neutrality in such circumstances. We are at the beginning of an age in which it will be insisted that the same standards of conduct and of responsibility for wrong done shall be observed among nations and their governments that are observed among the individual citizens of civilized states.

We have no quarrel with the German people. We have no feeling toward them but one of sympathy and friendship. It was not upon their impulse that their government acted in entering this war. It was not with their previous knowledge or approval. It was a war determined upon as wars used to be determined upon in the old, unhappy days when peoples were nowhere consulted by their rulers and wars were provoked and waged in the interest of dynasties or of little groups of ambitious men who were accustomed to use their fellowmen as pawns and tools.

Self-governed nations do not fill their neighbor states with spies or set the course of intrigue to bring about some critical posture of affairs which will give them an opportunity to strike and make conquest. Such designs can be successfully worked out only under cover and where no one has the right to ask questions. Cunningly contrived plans of deception or aggression, carried, it may be, from generation to generation, can be worked out and kept from the light only within the privacy of courts or behind the carefully guarded confidences of a narrow and privileged class. They are happily impossible where public opinion commands and insists upon full information concerning all the nation's affairs.

A steadfast concert for peace can never be maintained except by a partnership of democratic nations. No autocratic government could be trusted to keep faith within it or observe its covenants. It must be a league of honor, a partnership of opinion. Intrigue would eat its vitals away; the plottings of inner circles who could plan what they would and render account to no one would be a corruption seated at its very heart. Only free peoples can hold their purpose and their honor steady to a common end and prefer the interests of mankind to any narrow interest of their own.

Does not every American feel that assurance has been added to our hope for the future peace of the world by the wonderful and heartening things that have been happening within the last few weeks in Russia? Russia was known by those who knew it best to have been always in fact democratic at heart, in all the vital habits of her thought, in all the intimate relationships of her people that spoke their natural instinct, their habitual attitude toward life. The autocracy that crowned the summit of her political structure, long as it had stood and terrible as was the reality of its power, was not in fact Russian in origin, character, or purpose; and now it has been shaken off and the great, generous Russian people have been added in all their naive majesty and might to the forces that are fighting for freedom in the world, for justice, and for peace. Here is a fit partner for a League of Honor.

One of the things that has served to convince us that the Prussian autocracy was not and could never be our friend is that from the very outset of the present war it has filled our unsuspecting communities and even our offices of government with spies and set criminal intrigues everywhere afoot against our national unity of counsel, our peace within and without, our industries and our commerce. Indeed, it is now evident that its spies were here even before the war began; and it is unhappily not a matter of conjecture but a fact proved in our courts of justice that the intrigues which have more than once come perilously near to disturbing the peace and dislocating the industries of the country have been carried on at the instigation, with the support, and even under the personal direction of official agents of the Imperial government accredited to the government of the United States.

Even in checking these things and trying to extirpate them, we have sought to put the most generous interpretation possible upon them because we knew that their source lay, not in any hostile feeling or purpose of the German people toward us (who were no doubt as ignorant of them as we ourselves were) but only in the selfish designs of a government that did what it pleased and told its people nothing. But they have played their part in serving to convince us at last that that government entertains no real friendship for us and means to act against our peace and security at its convenience. That it means to stir up enemies against us at our very doors the intercepted note to the German minister at Mexico City is eloquent evidence.

We are accepting this challenge of hostile purpose because we know that in such a government, following such methods, we can never have a friend; and that in the presence of its organized power, always lying in wait to accomplish we know not what purpose, there can be no assured security for the democratic governments of the world. We are now about to accept gage of battle with this natural foe to liberty and shall, if necessary, spend the whole force of the nation to check and nulli-

fy its pretensions and its power. We are glad, now that we see the facts with no veil of false pretense about them, to fight thus for the ultimate peace of the world and for the liberation of its peoples, the German peoples included: for the rights of nations great and small and the privilege of men everywhere to choose their way of life and of obedience.

The world must be made safe for democracy. Its peace must be planted upon the tested foundations of political liberty. We have no selfish ends to serve. We desire no conquest, no dominion. We seek no indemnities for ourselves, no material compensation for the sacrifices we shall freely make. We are but one of the champions of the rights of mankind. We shall be satisfied when those rights have been made as secure as the faith and the freedom of nations can make them.

Just because we fight without rancor and without selfish object, seeking nothing for ourselves but what we shall wish to share with all free peoples, we shall, I feel confident, conduct our operations as belligerents without passion and ourselves observe with proud punctilio the principles of right and of fair play we profess to be fighting for.

I have said nothing of the governments allied with the Imperial government of Germany because they have not made war upon us or challenged us to defend our right and our honor. The Austro-Hungarian government has, indeed, avowed its unqualified endorsement and acceptance of the reckless and lawless submarine warfare adopted now without disguise by the Imperial German government, and it has therefore not been possible for this government to receive Count Tarnowski, the ambassador recently accredited to this government by the Imperial and Royal government of Austria-Hungary; but that government has not actually engaged in warfare against citizens of the United States on the seas, and I take the liberty, for the present at least, of postponing a discussion of our relations with the authorities at Vienna. We enter this war only where we are clearly forced into it because there are no other means of defending our rights.

It will be all the easier for us to conduct ourselves as belligerents in a high spirit of right and fairness because we act without animus, not in enmity toward a people or with the desire to bring any injury or disadvantage upon them, but only in armed opposition to an irresponsible government which has thrown aside all considerations of humanity and of right and is running amuck. We are, let me say again, the sincere friends of the German people, and shall desire nothing so much as the early reestablishment of intimate relations of mutual advantage between us— however hard it may be for them, for the time being, to believe that this is spoken from our hearts.

We have borne with their present government through all these bitter months because of that friendship—exercising a patience and forbearance which would otherwise have been impossible. We shall, happily, still have an opportunity to prove that friendship in our daily attitude and actions toward the millions of men and women of German birth and native sympathy who live among us and share our life, and we shall be proud to prove it toward all who are in fact loyal to their neighbors and to the government in the hour of test. They are, most of them, as true and loyal Americans as if they had never known any other fealty or allegiance. They will be prompt to stand with us in rebuking and restraining the few who may be of a different mind and purpose. If there should be disloyalty, it will be dealt with a firm hand of stern repression; but, if it lifts its head at all, it will lift it only here and there and without countenance except from a lawless and malignant few.

It is a distressing and oppressive duty, gentlemen of the Congress, which I have performed in thus addressing you. There are, it may be, many months of fiery trial and sacrifice ahead of us. It is a fearful thing to lead this great peaceful people into war, into the most terrible and disastrous of all wars, civilization itself seeming to be in the balance. But the right is more precious than peace, and we shall fight for the things which we have always carried nearest our hearts—for democracy, for the right of those who submit to authority to have a voice in their own governments, for the rights and liberties of small nations, for a universal dominion of right by such a concert of free peoples as shall bring peace and safety to all nations and make the world itself at last free.

To such a task we can dedicate our lives and our fortunes, everything that we are and everything that we have, with the pride of those who know that the day has come when America is privileged to spend her blood and her might for the principles that gave her birth and happiness and the peace which she has treasured. God helping her, she can do no other.

93 | *Half-Truths into the Frenzy of War*
Robert M. LaFollette

Two days after President Wilson's petition for a declaration of war against Germany, Senator Robert La Follette of Wisconsin made his protest. La Follette was an isolationist, as well as a leader of a reform movement, the National Progressive League. He argued that (1) the burden of war fell on the poor, (2) war expenditures enriched the already rich, (3) this was by design a war against civilian populations and therefore dishonorable, and (4) the governments of America's allies were little different from Germany's.

… The poor, sir, who are the ones called upon to rot in the trenches, have no organized power, have no press to voice their will upon this question of peace or war; but, oh, Mr. President, at some time they will be heard. I hope and I believe they will be heard in an orderly and a peaceful way. I think they may be heard from before long. I think, sir, if we take this step, when the people today who are staggering under the burden of supporting families at the present prices of the necessaries of life find those prices multiplied, when they are raised 100 percent, or 200 percent, as they will be quickly, aye, sir, when beyond that those who pay taxes come to have their taxes doubled and again doubled to pay the interest on the nontaxable bonds held by Morgan and his combinations, which have been issued to meet this war, there will come an awakening; they will have their day and they will be heard. It will be as certain and as inevitable as the return of the tides, and as resistless, too.…

In his message of April 2, the President said: "We have no quarrel with the German people—it was not upon their impulse that their government acted in entering this war; it was not with their previous knowledge or approval." Again he says: "We are, let me say again, sincere friends of the German people and shall desire nothing so much as the early reestablishment of intimate relations of mutual advantage between us." At least, the German people, then, are not outlaws.

What is the thing the President asks us to do to these German people of whom he speaks so highly and whose sincere friend he declares us to be? Here is what he declares we shall do in this war. We shall undertake, he says, "The utmost practicable cooperation in council and action with the governments now at war with Germany, and as an incident to that, the extension to those governments of the most liberal financial credits in order that our resources may, so far as possible, be added to theirs."

"Practicable cooperation!" Practicable cooperation with England and her allies in starving to death the old men and women, the children, the sick and maimed of Germany.…

Sir, if we are to enter upon this war in the manner the President demands, let us throw pretense to the winds, let us be honest, let us admit that this is a ruthless war against not only Germany's Army and her Navy but against her civilian population as well, and frankly state that the purpose of Germany's hereditary European enemies has become our purpose.

Again, the President says "we are about to accept the gage of battle with this natural foe of liberty and shall, if necessary, spend the whole force of the nation to check and nullify its pretensions and its power." That much, at least, is clear; that program is definite. The whole force and power of this nation, if necessary, is to be used to bring victory to the Entente Allies, and to us as their ally in this war. Remember, that not yet has the "whole force" of one of the warring nations been used.

Countless millions are suffering from want and privation; countless other millions are dead and rotting on foreign battlefields; countless other millions are crippled and maimed, blinded, and dismembered; upon all and upon their children's children for generations to come has been laid a burden of debt which must be worked out in poverty and suffering, but the "whole force" of no one of the warring nations has yet been expended; but our "whole force" shall be expended, so says the President. We are pledged by the President, so far as he can pledge us, to make this fair, free, and happy land of ours the same shambles and bottomless pit of horror that we see in Europe today.

Just a word of comment more upon one of the points in the President's address. He says that this is a war "for the things which we have always carried nearest to our hearts—for democracy, for the right of those who submit to authority to have a voice in their own government." In many places throughout the address is this exalted sentiment given expression....

But the President proposes alliance with Great Britain, which, however liberty loving its people, is a hereditary monarchy, with hereditary rules, with a hereditary landed system, with a limited and restricted suffrage for one class and a multiplied suffrage power for another, and with grinding industrial conditions for all the wageworkers. The President has not suggested that we make our support of Great Britain conditional to her granting home rule to Ireland, or Egypt, or India. We rejoice in the establishment of a democracy in Russia, but it will hardly be contended that if Russia was still an autocratic government, we would not be asked to enter this alliance with her just the same.

Italy and the lesser powers of Europe, Japan in the Orient; in fact, all the countries with whom we are to enter into alliance, except France and newly revolutionized Russia, are still of the old order—and it will be generally conceded that no one of them has done as much for its people in the solution of municipal problems, and in securing social and industrial reforms as Germany....

Now, I want to repeat. It was our absolute right as a neutral to ship food to the people of Germany. That is a position that we have fought for through all of our history. The correspondence of every secretary of state in the history of our government who has been called upon to deal with the rights of our neutral commerce as to foodstuffs is the position stated by Lord Salisbury....

In the first days of the war with Germany, Great Britain set aside, so far as her own conduct was concerned, all these rules of civilized naval warfare....

I am talking now about principles. You cannot distinguish between the principles which allowed England to mine a large area of the Atlantic Ocean and the North Sea in order to shut in Germany, and the principle on which Germany by her submarines seeks to destroy all shipping which enters the war zone which she has laid out around the British Isles.

The English mines are intended to destroy without warning every ship that enters the war zone she has proscribed, killing or drowning every passenger that cannot find some means of escape. It is neither more nor less than that which Germany tries to do with her submarines in her war zone. We acquiesced in England's action without protest. It is proposed that we now go to war with Germany for identically the same action upon her part....

I say again that when two nations are at war any neutral nation, in order to preserve its character as a neutral nation, must exact the same conduct from both warring nations; both must equally obey the principles of international law. If a neutral nation fails in that, then its rights upon the high seas—to adopt the President's phrase—are relative and not absolute. There can be no greater violation of our neutrality than the requirement that one of two belligerents shall adhere to the settled principles of law and that the other shall have the advantage of not doing so. The respect that German naval authorities were required to pay to the rights of our people upon the high seas would depend upon the question whether we had exacted the same rights from Germany's enemies. If we had not done so, we lost our character as a neutral nation and our people unfortunately had lost the protection that belongs to neutrals. Our responsibility was joint in the sense that we must exact the same conduct from both belligerents....

The failure to treat the belligerent nations of Europe alike, the failure to reject the unlawful "war zones" of both Germany and Great Britain is wholly accountable for our present dilemma. We should not seek to hide our blunder behind the smoke of battle, to inflame the mind of our people by half-truths into the frenzy of war in order that they may never appreciate the real cause of it until it is too late. I do not believe that our national honor is served by such a course. The right way is the honorable way....

94 | *Support Any Friend, Oppose Any Foe*
John F. Kennedy

The inaugural address of John F. Kennedy was replete with memorable phrases. In the throes of the Cold War, Kennedy called on Americans to persevere in the struggle. And more than that, he called on America to support those nations struggling against communist encroachments around the globe. America would "pay any price, bear any burden, meet any hardship, support any friend, oppose any foe, in order to assure the survival and the success of liberty."

Vice President Johnson, Mr. Speaker, Mr. Chief Justice, President Eisenhower, Vice President Nixon, President Truman, reverend clergy, fellow citizens, we observe today not a victory of party, but a celebration of freedom—symbolizing an end, as well as a beginning—signifying renewal, as well as change. For I have sworn before you and Almighty God the same solemn oath our forebears prescribed nearly a century and three quarters ago.

The world is very different now. For man holds in his mortal hands the power to abolish all forms of human poverty and all forms of human life. And yet the same revolutionary beliefs for which our forebears fought are still at issue around the globe—the belief that the rights of man come not from the generosity of the state, but from the hand of God.

We dare not forget today that we are the heirs of that first revolution. Let the word go forth from this time and place, to friend and foe alike, that the torch has been passed to a new generation of Americans—born in this century, tempered by war, disciplined by a hard and bitter peace, proud of our ancient heritage—and unwilling to witness or permit the slow undoing of those human rights to which this Nation has always been committed, and to which we are committed today at home and around the world.

Let every nation know, whether it wishes us well or ill, that we shall pay any price, bear any burden, meet any hardship, support any friend, oppose any foe, in order to assure the survival and the success of liberty.

This much we pledge—and more.

To those old allies whose cultural and spiritual origins we share, we pledge the loyalty of faithful friends. United, there is little we cannot do in a host of cooperative ventures. Divided, there is little we can do—for we dare not meet a powerful challenge at odds and split asunder.

To those new States whom we welcome to the ranks of the free, we pledge our word that one form of colonial control shall not have passed away merely to be replaced by a far more iron tyranny. We shall not always expect to find them supporting our view. But we shall always hope to find them strongly supporting their own freedom—and to remember that, in the past, those who foolishly sought power by riding the back of the tiger ended up inside.

To those peoples in the huts and villages across the globe struggling to break the bonds of mass misery, we pledge our best efforts to help them help themselves, for whatever period is required—not because the Communists may be doing it, not because we seek their votes, but because it is right. If a free society cannot help the many who are poor, it cannot save the few who are rich.

To our sister republics south of our border, we offer a special pledge—to convert our good words into good deeds—in a new alliance for progress—to assist free men and free governments in casting off the chains of poverty. But this peaceful revolution of hope cannot become the prey of hostile powers. Let all our neighbors know that we shall join with them to oppose aggression or subversion anywhere in the Americas. And let every other power know that this Hemisphere intends to remain the master of its own house.

To that world assembly of sovereign states, the United Nations, our last best hope in an age where the instruments of war have far outpaced the instruments of peace, we renew our pledge of support—to prevent it from becoming merely a forum for invective—to strengthen its shield of the new and the weak—and to enlarge the area in which its writ may run.

Finally, to those nations who would make themselves our adversary, we offer not a pledge but a request: that both sides begin anew the quest for peace, before the dark powers of destruction unleashed by science engulf all humanity in planned or accidental self-destruction.

We dare not tempt them with weakness. For only when our arms are sufficient beyond doubt can we be certain beyond doubt that they will never be employed.

But neither can two great and powerful groups of nations take comfort from our present course—both sides overburdened by the cost of modern weapons, both rightly alarmed by the steady spread of the deadly atom, yet both racing to alter that uncertain balance of terror that stays the hand of mankind's final war.

So let us begin anew—remembering on both sides that civility is not a sign of weakness, and sincerity is always subject to proof. Let us never negotiate out of fear. But let us never fear to negotiate.

Let both sides explore what problems unite us instead of belaboring those problems which divide us.

Let both sides, for the first time, formulate serious and precise proposals for the inspection and control of arms—and bring the absolute power to destroy other nations under the absolute control of all nations.

Let both sides seek to invoke the wonders of science instead of its terrors. Together let us explore the stars, conquer the deserts, eradicate disease, tap the ocean depths, and encourage the arts and commerce.

Let both sides unite to heed in all corners of the earth the command of Isaiah—to "undo the heavy burdens ... and to let the oppressed go free."

And if a beachhead of cooperation may push back the jungle of suspicion, let both sides join in creating a new endeavor, not a new balance of power, but a new world of law, where the strong are just and the weak secure and the peace preserved.

All this will not be finished in the first 100 days. Nor will it be finished in the first 1,000 days, nor in the life of this Administration, nor even perhaps in our lifetime on this planet. But let us begin.

In your hands, my fellow citizens, more than in mine, will rest the final success or failure of our course. Since this country was founded, each generation of Americans has been summoned to give testimony to its national loyalty. The graves of young Americans who answered the call to service surround the globe.

Now the trumpet summons us again—not as a call to bear arms, though arms we need; not as a call to battle, though embattled we are—but a call to bear the burden of a long twilight struggle, year in and year out, "rejoicing in hope, patient in tribulation"—a struggle against the common enemies of man: tyranny, poverty, disease, and war itself.

Can we forge against these enemies a grand and global alliance, North and South, East and West, that can assure a more fruitful life for all mankind? Will you join in that historic effort?

In the long history of the world, only a few generations have been granted the role of defending freedom in its hour of maximum danger. I do not shrink from this responsibility—I welcome it. I do not believe that any of us would exchange places with any other people or any other generation. The energy, the faith, the devotion which we bring to this endeavor will light our country and all who serve it—and the glow from that fire can truly light the world.

And so, my fellow Americans: ask not what your country can do for you—ask what you can do for your country.

My fellow citizens of the world: ask not what America will do for you, but what together we can do for the freedom of man.

Finally, whether you are citizens of America or citizens of the world, ask of us the same high standards of strength and sacrifice which we ask of you. With a good conscience our only sure reward, with history the final judge of our deeds, let us go forth to lead the land we love, asking His blessing and His help, but knowing that here on earth God's work must truly be our own.

95 | *False Hopes and Alluring Promises*
Robert F. Kennedy

Seven years after his brother's inauguration as president and four years after his brother's assassination, Senator Robert Kennedy of New York became an outspoken critic of the war into which his brother had introduced U.S. combat troops. This speech followed North Vietnam's surprise Tet offensive, which had inflicted terrible casualties, had failed, and was yet disheartening. Americans now had some 500,000 troops committed to this small Southeast Asian country, and it seemed as if no end to the war was in sight. What burden the United States should bear and what price it should pay was (and is) the question of the day.

... For years we have been told that the measure of our success and progress in Vietnam was increasing security and control for the population. Now we have seen that none of the population is secure and no area is under sure control. Four years ago, when we only had about 30,000 troops in Vietnam, the Viet Cong were unable to mount the assaults on cities they have now conducted against our enormous forces. At one time a suggestion that we protect enclaves was derided. Now there are no protected enclaves.

This has not happened because our men are not brave or effective, because they are. It is because we have not conceived our mission in this war. It is because we have misconceived the nature of the war. It is because we have sought to resolve by military might a conflict whose issue depends upon the will and conviction of the South Vietnamese people. It is like sending a lion to halt an epidemic of jungle rot.

This misconception rests on a second illusion, the illusion that we can win a war which the South Vietnamese cannot win for themselves.

Two Presidents and countless officials have told us for seven years that although we can help the South Vietnamese, it is their war and they must win it; as Secretary of Defense McNamara told us last month, "We cannot provide the South Vietnamese with the will to survive as an independent nation...or with the ability and self-discipline a people must have to govern themselves. These qualities and attributes are essential contributions to the struggle only the South Vietnamese can supply." Yet this wise and certain counsel has gradually become an empty slogan, as mounting frustration has led us to transform the war into an American military effort....

You cannot expect people to risk their lives and endure hardship unless they have a stake in their own society. They must have a clear sense of identification with their own government, a belief they are participating in a cause worth fighting and dying for. Political and economic reform are not simply idealistic slogans or noble goals to be postponed until the end of the fighting. They are the principal weapons of battle. People will not fight—they will simply not fight—to line the pockets of generals or swell the bank accounts of the wealthy. They are far more likely to close their eyes and shut their doors in the face of their government—even as they did last week.

More than any election, more than any proud boasts, that simple fact reveals the truth. We have an ally in name only. We support a government without supporters. Without the effort of American arms the government would not last a day.

The third illusion is that the unswerving pursuit of military victory, whatever its cost, is in the interest of either ourselves or the people of Vietnam. For the people of Vietnam, the last three years have meant little but terrible, terrible horror. Their tiny land has been devastated by a weight of bombs and shells greater than Nazi Germany knew in the whole of the Second World War. We have dropped twelve tons of bombs for every square mile in North and South Vietnam.

Whole provinces have been substantially destroyed. More than 2 million South Vietnamese are now homeless refugees. Imagine the impact in our country if an equivalent number—over 25 million Americans—were wandering homeless or interned in refugee camps, and millions more refugees were being created as New York and Chicago, Washington and Boston were being destroyed by a war raging in their streets. Whatever the outcome of these battles, it is the people we seek to defend who are the greatest losers....

The fourth illusion is that the American national interest is identical with—or should be subordinated to—the selfish interest of an incompetent military regime.

We are told, of course, that the battle for South Vietnam is in reality a struggle for 250 million Asians—the beginning of a Great Society for all of Asia. But this is a pretension. We can and should offer reasonable assistance to Asia; but we cannot build a Great Society there if we cannot build one in our own country. We cannot speak extravagantly of a struggle for 250 million Asians when a struggle for 15 million in an Asian country so strains our forces....

There is an American interest in South Vietnam. We have an interest in maintaining the strength of our commitments—and surely we have demonstrated that. With all the lives and resources we have poured into Vietnam, is there anyone to argue that a government with any support from its people, with any competence to rule, with any determination to defend itself, would not long ago have been victorious over any insurgent movement, however assisted from outside its borders?

And we have another, more immediate interest: to protect the lives of our gallant young men and to conserve American resources. But we do not have an interest in the survival of a

privileged class, growing ever more wealthy from the corruption of war, which after all our sacrifices on their behalf can ask why Vietnamese boys have to fight for Americans.

The fifth illusion is that this war can be settled in our own way and in our own time on our own terms. Such a settlement is the privilege of the triumphant, of those who crush their enemies in battle or wear away their will to fight. We simply have not done this, nor is there any prospect we will achieve such a victory.

For twenty years, first the French and then the United States have been predicting victory in Vietnam. In 1961 and in 1962, as well as 1966 and 1967, we have been told that "the tide is turning"; "there is 'light at the end of the tunnel'"; "we can soon bring home the troops—victory is near—the enemy is tiring." Once, in 1962, I participated in such predictions myself. But for twenty years we have been wrong.

The history of conflict among nations does not record another such lengthy and consistent chronicle of error as we have shown in Vietnam. It is time to discard so proven a fallacy and face the reality that a military victory is not in sight and that it probably will never come....

No war has ever demanded more bravery from our people and our government—not just bravery under fire or the bravery to make sacrifices but the bravery to discard the comfort of illusion—to do away with false hopes and alluring promises. Reality is grim and painful. But it is only a remote echo of the anguish toward which a policy founded on illusion is surely taking us.

This is a great nation and a strong people. Any who seek to comfort rather than speak plainly, reassure rather than instruct, promise satisfaction rather than reveal frustration—they deny that greatness and drain that strength. For today as it was in the beginning, it is the truth that makes us free.

When, How, and for What Should the United States Intervene with Military Force?

96 | *Civil War in a Sovereign Nation*
Kay Bailey Hutchison

As President Clinton was about to authorize air strikes on targets in Serbia in March 1999, Senator Kay Hutchison found his case for intervention less than compelling. The president said that he was responding to large-scale Serbian atrocities against its Albanian-Kosovar minority, but Hutchison argued that the United States was not pursuing or protecting American interests in this aerial campaign.

Mr. President, I rise today to talk about the situation in Kosovo. We have been watching this situation unfold for days, actually months—actually, you could say thousands of years. But it is coming to a head in the very near future, perhaps in hours. As I speak today, Richard Holbrooke is talking to Slobodan Milosevic and trying to encourage him to come to the peace table. I hope he is successful, and I know every American hopes that he is successful. But what I think we must talk about today is what happens if he is not.

What happens if Mr. Milosevic says, "No, I am not going to allow foreign troops in my country," and if he says he is going to move forward with whatever he intends to do in the governance of that country? I think we have to step back and look at the situation and the dilemma which we face, because there is no question, this is not an easy decision. What comes next?

Basically, the President has committed the United States to a policy in NATO to which he really does not have the authority to commit. The consequences are that we have to make a decision that would appear to walk away from the commitment he made without coming to Congress, and that is not a good situation. I do not like having to make such a choice, because I want our word to be good.

When the United States speaks, I want our word to be good. Whether it is to our ally or to our enemy, they need to know what we say we will do.

But the problem here is, the President has gone out with a commitment before he talked to Congress about it, and now we have really changed the whole nature of NATO without congressional approval. We are saying that we are going to bomb a sovereign country because of their mistreatment of people within their country, the province of Kosovo, and we are going to take this action, basically declaring war on a country that should not be an enemy of the United States and in fact was a partner at the peace table in the Dayton accords on Bosnia.

So now we are taking sides. We are turning NATO, which was a defense alliance—is a defense alliance—into an aggressive, perhaps, declarer-of-war on a country that is not in NATO. Mr. President, I just do not think we can take a step like that without the Congress and the American people understanding what we are doing and, furthermore, approving of it.

There is no question that Mr. Milosevic is not our kind of person. We have seen atrocities that he has committed in Kosovo. But, in fact, there have been other atrocities committed by the parties with whom we are purporting to be taking sides. The Albanians have committed atrocities as well, the Kosovar Albanians. So we are now picking sides in a civil war where I think the U.S. security interest is not clear.

I think it is incumbent on the President to come to Congress, before he takes any military action in Kosovo, to lay out the case and to get congressional approval. What would he tell Congress? First of all, before we put one American in harm's way, I want to know: What is the intention here? What is the commitment? What happens in the eventuality that Mr. Milosevic does not respond to bombing, that he declares he is going to go forward without responding to an intervention in his country? What do we do then? Do we send ground troops in to force him to come to the peace table? And if we did, could we consider that is really a peace? What if NATO decides to strike and an American plane is shot down? What if there is an American POW? What then? What is our commitment then?

My concern here is that the administration has not looked at the third, fourth, and fifth steps in a plan. They have only addressed step 1, which is, we are going to bomb because they will not come to the peace table and accept the agreement that we have hammered out. I just say, before we go bombing sovereign nations, we ought to have a plan. We ought to know what steps 3, 4, and 5 are, because I believe Congress has a right to know what this commitment is. How many people from the United States of America are going to be put in harm's way? What is it going to cost and where is the money going to come from? Is it going to come from other defense accounts, so other places in the world where we have troops are put at risk? Is it going to come at the risk of our Strategic Defense Initiative? Just where is the money going to come from? Most of all, most important of all, what is the mission? How much are we going to be required to do and what is the timetable?

Mr. President, I would support a plan that would say when the two parties come to a real peace agreement, we would put our troops, along with our European allies in NATO, together in a peacekeeping mission of a short duration which would make sure that things settle down until we could have others rotate in and take our place. I would support a plan that went that far.

I would also support a plan of helping the Kosovars, but without putting American troops in harm's way. You know, the difference between the Clinton doctrine and the Reagan doctrine is that President Reagan would support freedom fighters with arms, with monetary contributions, with intelligence—many, many forms of support for freedom fighters—but he would never put a U.S. military person in the middle of a civil war. He would help, but he would not make that commitment.

Under the Reagan doctrine, therefore, we could help Afghan rebels and Nicaraguan freedom fighters. At the same time, we could also continue to remain strong in Europe and Asia because we could allocate our resources and we would not drain our resources in small civil conflicts in chosen places around the world.

What bothers me about what has been happening in the last 3 or 4 years is that we have been putting troops into civil conflicts in certain parts of the world but not all parts of the world. So every time we do it, it makes the decision not to do it somewhere else a little harder. We practically invaded Haiti and we still have 500 troops in Haiti today. We had 18 Army Rangers killed in Somalia in a mission that was ill-defined and was actually mission creep. The original mission of feeding starving people had been accomplished, but we didn't leave. We decided to capture a warlord, something our military is not trained to do and, therefore, the miscalculation cost us the lives of 18 great young Americans.

We have inserted ourselves into places like Haiti, Somalia and Bosnia, but we have not inserted ourselves into Algeria, where there are just as many atrocities as there have been in any place in the Balkans. We have not inserted ourselves into Turkey, where there is mistreatment of the Kurds. We aren't getting involved in the Basque separatist movement in Spain. We didn't step into Iran when the

Ayatollah took over from the Shah and was assassinating almost every military leader that couldn't get out of the country, plus the religious minorities that were still there and their leadership. It is very difficult, when you start choosing where you are going to involve yourselves, to extricate yourself when there is no clear policy.

That is why so many of us in Congress are concerned and why we realize the dilemma. We understand that this is not an easy black and white decision. We are talking about a commitment that the President has made. I do not like stepping in and saying that we shouldn't keep a commitment the President has made. Overriding that great concern is the consequence of not requiring the President to have a plan and a policy that will set a precedent for the future. I think we could explain it by sitting down with our European allies and saying, first of all, if we are going to change the mission of NATO, this must be fully debated and fully accepted by every member of NATO within their own constitutional framework. If we are going to turn NATO from a defense alliance into an affirmative war-making machine, I think we need to talk about it.

I will support some affirmative action on the part of NATO, if we are able to determine exactly what would trigger that and not go off on one mission without having a precedent for a different mission and, therefore, creating expectations among more and more people that we will step in to defend the autonomy of a country such as Kosovo or Bosnia. We must not allow the expectations to be such that we are drawn into every conflict, because we will not be able to survive with the strength that we must have when only the United States will be the one standing between a real attack from a ballistic missile or a nuclear warhead or an invasion of another country where we do have a strategic interest. We cannot allow there to be so many questions because there is so little policy. That is the responsibility of Congress, to work with the President.

We will work together. Congress will work with the President to hammer out a new mission for NATO. We will always do our fair share in the world. We will never walk away from that. We have to determine what is our fair share, what is our allocation. I submit that the United States will always be the leader in technology, and we will create a ballistic missile defense that will shield not only the United States and our troops wherever they may be in any theater in the world, but we also will protect our allies, if we have the strength to go forward. We will not have the strength to go forward if we continue to spend $3 and $4 billion a year on conflicts that do not rise to the level of a U.S. security interest.

We must be able to choose where we spend our defense dollars so that we will all be protected, ourselves and our allies, from a rogue nation with a ballistic missile capability that can put a chemical or biological or nuclear warhead on it and undermine the integrity of people living in our country.

Mr. President, the consequences are too great for us to sit back and let the President commit U.S. forces in a situation that I can't remember us ever having before; that is, to take an affirmative military action against a sovereign nation that has not committed a security threat to the United States. Before we would sit back and let the President do that, I cannot in good conscience say, well, he has made the commitment, even though he didn't have the right to do it, so we have got to let him go forward. Perhaps if we aren't lucky and if Milosevic does not come to the table, we would have more and more and more responsibilities because of the potential consequences that could occur if he does not come to the table.

We must know what those consequences are and what we are prepared to do in the eventuality that an American plane is shot down, that we have an American prisoner on the ground or that we bomb and bomb and bomb and bomb and he still does not do what we have asked him to do. We have to determine what we do in that eventuality. I certainly hope that we will consult with the Russians so that this war does not escalate into something that we haven't thought about. If Russia decides to step in on the side of Serbia, we could have grief beyond what anyone is saying right now. I hope the President will work with Congress to fashion a new mission for NATO that will have the full support of Congress and the American people. I believe we could do that, because I don't think we are far apart at all. We cannot do it on an ad hoc basis. We cannot all of a sudden attack another country on an ad hoc basis and call that a policy.

I hope the President will come together with Congress and have hearings. Let's hear from the American people on just what they believe is the role of the United States. Let's hear from Congress about what our commitments should be and what is a ready division of responsibility for keeping the world as safe as we can make it, given that 30 countries have ballistic missile technology, some of whom are rogue nations. Let us step back with our European allies and determine if this is the right decision to make, or are there other ways that we could be helpful to the Kosovar Albanians.

I remember hour after hour after hour, over a 2-year period, talking about letting the Muslims have a fair fight in Bosnia, because they didn't have arms when two of their adversaries did. We never took that step. Now there is a cease-fire in Bosnia, but there are also many years to go before we will know what the cost is and if it can be lasting, because today, Bosnia is still as ethnically divided as it ever was because it is not safe for the refugees to move back in.

One can say there is disagreement on just how successful was the Bosnian mission. We do not see fighting, but NATO has just toppled a duly elected president of one of the provinces. It is pretty hard to understand. I think it is tenuous that we would go in and forcibly remove an elected president while we are touting democratic ideals.

There was a way to go into Bosnia, but Kosovo is very different. Kosovo is a civil war in a sovereign nation. There are atrocities. There have been atrocities on both sides. We are picking one side, and we are doing it without a vote of Congress. I do not think we can do it. I do not think the President has the right to declare war, and under the Constitution, he certainly does not. And under the War Powers Act, it takes an emergency. This is not an emergency. We are not being attacked. United States troops are not in harm's way at this point. We can take the time to talk about it, and the consequences are so great I think it is worth the time to set a policy that allows us to have some continuity for the next 25 years, so that our enemies and our allies will know what the greatest superpower in the world is going to do and they will not have to guess.

Mr. President, it is a dilemma, and I realize it is. I do not feel comfortable with the choice. I do not feel comfortable at a time when we have gone out on a limb, through our President who made a commitment for us, even though we were not part of it. Nevertheless, I would like to give the President that support, but it is worth it to take the time and do it right and ask the President to come forward to give us his plan, to tell us what happens when American troops are prisoners of war or on the ground or shot down. We need to know what we would do in that eventuality before we send them there. That is the least that we can expect.

I hope we can debate this resolution. I hope people will give their views. I have heard great debates already on it, not on the Senate floor, though. The time has come for us to have this debate, and let's vote up or down. There will be people voting on both sides in good conscience, seeing it a different way but with the same goal. So let's have that debate. Let's do it right. Let's don't haul off bombing an independent nation before the Senate and the House of Representatives has a plan and approves it or disapproves it. That is what our Founding Fathers intended when they wrote the Constitution, and it is more appropriate today than ever.

I hope we will do that, because then the American people will know what is going on and they will support it or not support it. If we are going to have a long-term commitment, which I hope we do not, but if we do, at least it will be with the support of Congress as Desert Storm was. That was a tough debate. People spoke from the heart on both sides. They took a vote, and Congress supported the President going into Desert Storm. That is the way it should be, Mr. President. That is the way it should be under our Constitution, under our democracy. That is the way our Government works. I hope it will again as we face the crisis today that could have very long-term consequences for our country and for every one of our young men and women in the field wearing the uniform of the United States of America. Their lives are worth a debate and a policy, and that is what we are going to try to give them in the next 24 hours.

97 | *Never Again*
Mary L. Landrieu

A Senator from Louisiana, Mary Landrieu defended what had become a prolonged bombing campaign against the Serbian government in the spring of 1999. Landrieu argues, as many before her, that the United States must protect itself by protecting the principles of human rights, not just at home, but also abroad: "So, for more than three generations, Americans have been making the sacrifices necessary to change the world in which we live and to maintain democracy in Europe and, yes, indeed, to help spread it throughout the entire world."

Mr. President, on the eve of the gathering of all of NATO to celebrate the successful completion of our first 50 years, I wanted to take this opportunity to comment on the current situation in Europe.

As you know, we are blessed to live in a country which enjoys a deeply rooted democracy and a deeply rooted sense of equality. However, these same characteristics and qualities which make America a model for the world also present very real challenges in times like these. It is often said that the most difficult task for any democracy is deciding to go to war. The reasons are self-evident. When you live in a nation that believes all people are created equal, how do you ask some citizens to sacrifice so much so that others may continue to enjoy their freedom? When you live in a nation where human life is sacred, where, in fact each individual life has dignity, how do you build a consensus for the sacrifices that may be necessary to achieve the victory that we hope for?

The task is even more complex when the challenge to American freedom is more indirect, as it is in this case. We have confronted this reality since the beginning of the war in Kosovo. No one in America believes that Serbia intends to invade the United States. We will never look out of the window and see Yugoslavian tanks driving down Pennsylvania Avenue to squelch American liberties. It remains, then, for those of us in the leadership of this Nation who support NATO operations in Kosovo to explain why we are prepared to ask American troops to make the sacrifices that may be necessary, in this seemingly remote and distant land.

I believe there is one central reason that justifies our actions, and that is the price, the tremendous price, we have already paid for freedom in America and in Europe.

Our parents' generation and their parents were asked to risk their lives to fundamentally alter the way the world operates. In World War I, President Wilson asked our grandparents to fight to make the world "safe for democracy," and they did. In World War II, when fascism threatened to conquer the democracies of Europe, President Roosevelt asked America to become "the arsenal of democracy," and we were. During the Cold War, President Kennedy called on Americans to "pay any price, to bear any burden," to meet the threat of communism, and we have. Finally, President Reagan insisted that we "tear down that wall," and it was.

We emerged victorious from World Wars I and II, as well as the Cold War, but not without a price. American blood was spilled in the trenches of World War I and on the beaches of Normandy during World War II. Americans fought and died in Korea and Vietnam to contain communism during the Cold War. So, for more than three generations, Americans have been making the sacrifices necessary to change the world in which we live and to maintain democracy in Europe and, yes, indeed, to help spread it throughout the entire world.

It is important to remember that this sacrifice has not been in vain. It is easy today to be cynical about human nature and the prospects for lasting peace in Europe. After all, these feuds in Europe predated America's existence by many centuries. But to dwell on the worst instincts of Europe and Western civilization is to ignore the very real progress and the tremendous victories that have been made possible by our allied unity and American intervention.

Who would have imagined that in a little over 50 years, since the end of World War II, bitter enemies like France and Germany, England and Italy, would be joined by a common currency, a common market, and a pledge to defend one another against a common enemy? It was the sacrifice of many, including Americans, that made it possible for Europe to turn its back on a history of bloody conflict and embrace a vision for peace and democracy across its great continent.

Ironically, as NATO expands to the east and the European Union incorporates still more of Europe, we are faced with a war in Yugoslavia that threatens to undo all of this good work. It is ironic because that is how this century began, with an act of violence from Serbia which sparked a world war.

The President is fond of saying that the war in Kosovo will either be the last war of the 20th century or the first war of the 21st. What I believe he is trying to say is, that we can defeat Milosevic and give meaning to nearly 100 years of American struggle and effort to bring peace to Europe and secure the gains of our parents and grandparents, or we can turn our backs on their sacrifice, ignore the human tragedy, ignore the tremendous financial investment that has already been made. Then we will hope against our experience that the conflict in Kosovo will simply fade away.

Many have remarked that the 20th century has been the most bloody in human history. It is hard to verify such claims. Nevertheless, it is true that we live in an era where the efficiency of industry and technology has been matched, unfortunately, by our expert ability to kill one another. We must, however, stay the course and join with our NATO allies to finish our work and eliminate military aggression and ethnic cleansing as a legitimate tool of national policy.

There is a sleepy little town in Austria, near the German border called Branau am Inn. It is not one of those towns at the crossroads of Europe; it is not the home of kings and emperors. In fact, no one in Branau, if it were not for a small event, no one in the world would have ever heard of Branau. But it is the birthplace of Adolf Hitler. The sad legacy of this town is not marked with any great monument. Instead, above the home where Hitler was born, two simple words are written: Never again.

Those two words represent a solemn pledge that this country and all civilized nations made at the close of World War II: Never again would we stand idly by while innocent men, women, and children were massacred. Never again would we allow a nation to invade its neighbors without consequences.

Some of my colleagues here in the Senate consistently remind us that Kosovo is not the Holocaust. I agree. What has occurred in the last few months does not yet compare to the crimes the Nazis perpetrated. But this is a senseless justification for inaction. Should we wait for another Holocaust to occur before we act decisively? What, then, is the point of action? How many children must be traumatized? How many homes need to be destroyed? How many women need to be victims of brutality before we can act? I say the words "never again" mean that we should not wait and we will be decisive in our action. That is why I support using whatever means is necessary to accomplish the goal set out by NATO. The President and our NATO allies believe we can achieve this purpose through air attacks. I certainly hope this is correct. But I also agree with many of my colleagues, led by Senators McCain and Biden, that we cannot rule out other measures that can assure our victory and success. I am proud to join them in cosponsoring an important resolution that they introduced earlier this week, which seeks to give the President the authority and tools necessary to win this war. I urge my colleagues to consider joining with us to send this powerful and much-needed message of resolve during the conflict.

The only way that we can have peace in the Balkans is for people like Milosevic and the thugs underneath him to understand that there are real and personal consequences for their barbaric atrocities. The reports are very disturbing and it is very hard for me to repeat them. I predict, unfortunately, that more and more horror stories will appear in our papers, as more survivors escape to tell their stories. As NATO spokesman, Jamie Shea, explained,

the Serbs are engaging in a sort of "human safari" where they methodically flush out their victims from their homes using tear gas and herd them like animals out of Kosovo. There have been repeated reports of the systematic rape of girls and women. Very conservative NATO estimates indicate that over 100,000 people have simply disappeared, many of them men who have been separated from their families—probably many to their early deaths. When we pledged "never again," these were the sorts of atrocities that we were talking about.

As a result of these reports, I intend to introduce a resolution in the Senate calling on the President to ask for war crimes indictments against the Serbian leadership before the International Criminal Tribunal for the former republic of Yugoslavia. The chief prosecutor has already announced that the jurisdiction of the tribunal extends to Kosovo.

We must ask ourselves what kind of situation will we have if Milosevic and his allies go unpunished. Will we have another rogue nation, this time in the heart of Europe, with little else motivating them besides age-old desires for revenge and an interest in interfering with the stability and prosperity of the United States and the entire European continent? We simply cannot allow another Iraq in the middle of Europe. One of the central tenets of our policy must be that these individuals will be brought to justice. Only then will these hundreds of thousands of refugees have any chance of returning to their homes. Only then will we have peace and democracy in the former Republic of Yugoslavia, and only then will we have at least begun to live up to our solemn promise of "never again."

The Unanimous Declaration of the Thirteen United States of America

Adopted by the Continental Congress on July 4, 1776, the Declaration of Independence from British rule reflects all the Lockean notions of government. Although you may have been overexposed to this document, take a fresh look to find the classic liberal ideas of individual liberty, equality under the law, the right to property, and government by collective consent.

When, in the course of human events, it becomes necessary for one people to dissolve the political bonds which have connected them with another, and to assume among the powers of the earth, the separate and equal station to which the laws of nature and of nature's God entitle them, a decent respect to the opinions of mankind requires that they should declare the causes which impel them to the separation.

We hold these truths to be self-evident, that all men are created equal, that they are endowed by their Creator with certain unalienable rights, that among these are life, liberty and the pursuit of happiness. That to secure these rights, governments are instituted among men, deriving their just powers from the consent of the governed. That whenever any form of government becomes destructive to these ends, it is the right of the people to alter or to abolish it, and to institute new government, laying its foundation on such principles and organizing its powers in such form, as to them shall seem most likely to effect their safety and happiness. Prudence, indeed, will dictate that governments long established should not be changed for light and transient causes; and accordingly all experience hath shown that mankind are more disposed to suffer, while evils are sufferable, than to right themselves by abolishing the forms to which they are accustomed. But when a long train of abuses and usurpations, pursuing invariably the same object evinces a design to reduce them under absolute despotism, it is their right, it is their duty, to throw off such government, and to provide new guards for their future security.— Such has been the patient sufferance of these colonies; and such is now the necessity which constrains them to alter their former systems of government. The history of the present King of Great Britain is a history of repeated injuries and usurpations, all having in direct object the establishment of an absolute tyranny over these states. To prove this, let facts be submitted to a candid world.

He has refused his assent to laws, the most wholesome and necessary for the public good.

He has forbidden his governors to pass laws of immediate and pressing importance, unless suspended in their operation till his assent should be obtained; and when so suspended, he has utterly neglected to attend to them.

He has refused to pass other laws for the accommodation of large districts of people, unless those people would relinquish the right of representation in the legislature, a right inestimable to them and formidable to tyrants only.

He has called together legislative bodies at places unusual, uncomfortable, and distant from the depository of their public records, for the sole purpose of fatiguing them into compliance with his measures.

He has dissolved representative houses repeatedly, for opposing with manly firmness his invasions on the rights of the people.

He has refused for a long time, after such dissolutions, to cause others to be elected; whereby the legislative powers, incapable of annihilation, have returned to the people at large for their exercise; the state remaining in the meantime exposed to all the dangers of invasion from without, and convulsions within.

He has endeavored to prevent the population of these states; for that purpose obstructing the laws for naturalization of foreigners; refusing to pass others to encourage their migration hither, and raising the conditions of new appropriations of lands.

He has obstructed the administration of justice, by refusing his assent to laws for establishing judiciary powers.

He has made judges dependent on his will alone, for the tenure of their offices, and the amount and payment of their salaries.

He has erected a multitude of new offices, and sent hither swarms of officers to harass our people, and eat out their substance.

He has kept among us, in times of peace, standing armies without the consent of our legislature.

He has affected to render the military independent of and superior to civil power.

He has combined with others to subject us to a jurisdiction foreign to our constitution, and unacknowledged by our laws; giving his assent to their acts of pretended legislation:

For quartering large bodies of armed troops among us:

For protecting them, by mock trial, from punishment for any murders which they should commit on the inhabitants of these states:

For cutting off our trade with all parts of the world:

For imposing taxes on us without our consent:

For depriving us in many cases, of the benefits of trial by jury:

For transporting us beyond seas to be tried for pretended offenses:

For abolishing the free system of English laws in a neighboring province, establishing therein an arbitrary government, and enlarging its boundaries so as to render it at once an example and fit instrument for introducing the same absolute rule in these colonies:

For taking away our charters, abolishing our most valuable laws, and altering fundamentally the forms of our governments:

For suspending our own legislatures, and declaring themselves invested with power to legislate for us in all cases whatsoever.

He has abdicated government here, by declaring us out of his protection and waging war against us.

He has plundered our seas, ravaged our coasts, burned our towns, and destroyed the lives of our people.

He is at this time transporting large armies of foreign mercenaries to complete the works of death, desolation and tyranny, already begun with circumstances of cruelty and perfidy scarcely paralleled in the most barbarous ages, and totally unworthy of the head of a civilized nation.

He has constrained our fellow citizens taken captive on the high seas to bear arms against their country, to become the executioners of their friends and brethren, or to fall themselves by their hands.

He has excited domestic insurrections amongst us, and has endeavored to bring on the inhabitants of our frontiers, the merciless Indian savages, whose known rule of warfare, is undistinguished destruction of all ages, sexes and conditions.

In every stage of these oppressions we have petitioned for redress in the most humble terms: our repeated petitions have been answered only by repeated injury. A prince, whose character is thus marked by every act which may define a tyrant, is unfit to be the ruler of a free people.

Nor have we been wanting in attention to our British brethren. We have warned them from time to time of attempts by their legislature to extend an unwarrantable jurisdiction over us. We have reminded them of the circumstances of our emigration and settlement here. We have appealed to their native justice and magnanimity, and we have conjured them by the ties of our common kindred to disavow these usurpations, which, would inevitably interrupt our connections and correspondence. We must, therefore, acquiesce in the necessity, which denounces our separation, and hold them, as we hold the rest of mankind, enemies in war, in peace friends.

We, therefore, the representatives of the United States of America, in General Congress, assembled, appealing to the Supreme Judge of the world for the rectitude of our intentions, do, in the name, and by the authority of the good people of these colonies, solemnly publish and declare, that these united colonies are, and of right ought to be free and independent states; that they are absolved from all allegiance to the British Crown, and that all political connection between them and the state of Great Britain, is and ought to be totally dissolved; and that as free and independent states, they have full power to levy war, conclude peace, contract alliances, establish commerce, and to do all other acts and things which independent states may of right do. And for the support of this declaration, with a firm reliance on the protection of Divine Providence, we mutually pledge to each other our lives, our fortunes and our sacred honor.

(Signed by John Hancock and fifty-four others, representing the various colonial governments.)

The Articles of Confederation

A permanent union of the various states was agreed to by a congress on November 15, 1777, and went into force after Maryland finally ratified the arrangement on March 1, 1781. Article II is a clear example of what was understood, before the Constitution, by federalism: "Each state retains its sovereignty, freedom, and independence, and every power, jurisdiction, and right, which is not by this Confederation expressly delegated to the United States, in Congress assembled." What are the strengths and weaknesses of this union? And how might history have worked out differently had the articles not been replaced by the Constitution of 1787?

To all to whom these Presents shall come, we the undersigned Delegates of the States affixed to our Names send greeting.

Articles of Confederation and perpetual Union between the states of New Hampshire, Massachusetts-bay, Rhode Island and Providence Plantations, Connecticut, New York, New Jersey, Pennsylvania, Delaware, Maryland, Virginia, North Carolina, South Carolina and Georgia.

I. The Stile of this Confederacy shall be "The United States of America".

II. Each state retains its sovereignty, freedom, and independence, and every power, jurisdiction, and right, which is not by this Confederation expressly delegated to the United States, in Congress assembled.

III. The said States hereby severally enter into a firm league of friendship with each other, for their common defense, the security of their liberties, and their mutual and general welfare, binding themselves to assist each other, against all force offered to, or attacks made upon them, or any of them, on account of religion, sovereignty, trade, or any other pretense whatever.

IV. The better to secure and perpetuate mutual friendship and intercourse among the people of the different States in this Union, the free inhabitants of each of these States, paupers, vagabonds, and fugitives from justice excepted, shall be entitled to all privileges and immunities of free citizens in the several States; and the people of each State shall have free ingress and regress to and from any other State, and shall enjoy therein all the privileges of trade and commerce, subject to the same duties, impositions, and restrictions as the inhabitants thereof respectively, provided that such restrictions shall not extend so far as to prevent the removal of property imported into any State, to any other State, of which the owner is an inhabitant; provided also that no imposition, duties or restriction shall be laid by any State, on the property of the United States, or either of them.

If any person guilty of, or charged with, treason, felony, or other high misdemeanor in any State, shall flee from justice, and be found in any of the United States, he shall, upon demand of the Governor or executive power of the State from which he fled, be delivered up and removed to the State having jurisdiction of his offense.

Full faith and credit shall be given in each of these States to the records, acts, and judicial proceedings of the courts and magistrates of every other State.

V. For the most convenient management of the general interests of the United States, delegates shall be annually appointed in such manner as the legislatures of each State shall direct, to meet in Congress on the first Monday in November, in every year, with a power reserved to each State to recall its delegates, or any of them, at any time within the year, and to send others in their stead for the remainder of the year.

No State shall be represented in Congress by less than two, nor more than seven members; and no person shall be capable of being a delegate for more than three years in any term of six years; nor shall any person, being a delegate, be capable of holding any office under the United States, for which he, or another for his benefit, receives any salary, fees or emolument of any kind.

Each State shall maintain its own delegates in a meeting of the States, and while they act as members of the committee of the States.

In determining questions in the United States in Congress assembled, each State shall have one vote.

Freedom of speech and debate in Congress shall not be impeached or questioned in any court or place out of Congress, and the members of Congress shall be protected in their persons from arrests or imprisonments, during the time of their going to and from, and attendence on Congress, except for treason, felony, or breach of the peace.

VI. No State, without the consent of the United States in Congress assembled, shall send any embassy to, or receive any embassy from, or enter into any conference, agreement, alliance or treaty with any King, Prince or State; nor shall any person holding any office of profit or trust under the United States, or any of them, accept any present, emolument, office or title of any kind whatever from any King,

Prince or foreign State; nor shall the United States in Congress assembled, or any of them, grant any title of nobility.

No two or more States shall enter into any treaty, confederation or alliance whatever between them, without the consent of the United States in Congress assembled, specifying accurately the purposes for which the same is to be entered into, and how long it shall continue.

No State shall lay any imposts or duties, which may interfere with any stipulations in treaties, entered into by the United States in Congress assembled, with any King, Prince or State, in pursuance of any treaties already proposed by Congress, to the courts of France and Spain.

No vessel of war shall be kept up in time of peace by any State, except such number only, as shall be deemed necessary by the United States in Congress assembled, for the defense of such State, or its trade; nor shall any body of forces be kept up by any State in time of peace, except such number only, as in the judgement of the United States in Congress assembled, shall be deemed requisite to garrison the forts necessary for the defense of such State; but every State shall always keep up a well-regulated and disciplined militia, sufficiently armed and accoutered, and shall provide and constantly have ready for use, in public stores, a due number of filed pieces and tents, and a proper quantity of arms, ammunition and camp equipage.

No State shall engage in any war without the consent of the United States in Congress assembled, unless such State be actually invaded by enemies, or shall have received certain advice of a resolution being formed by some nation of Indians to invade such State, and the danger is so imminent as not to admit of a delay till the United States in Congress assembled can be consulted; nor shall any State grant commissions to any ships or vessels of war, nor letters of marque or reprisal, except it be after a declaration of war by the United States in Congress assembled, and then only against the Kingdom or State and the subjects thereof, against which war has been so declared, and under such regulations as shall be established by the United States in Congress assembled, unless such State be infested by pirates, in which case vessels of war may be fitted out for that occasion, and kept so long as the danger shall continue, or until the United States in Congress assembled shall determine otherwise.

VII. When land forces are raised by any State for the common defense, all officers of or under the rank of colonel, shall be appointed by the legislature of each State respectively, by whom such forces shall be raised, or in such manner as such State shall direct, and all vacancies shall be filled up by the State which first made the appointment.

VIII. All charges of war, and all other expenses that shall be incurred for the common defense or general welfare, and allowed by the United States in Congress assembled, shall be defrayed out of a common treasury, which shall be supplied by the several States in proportion to the value of all land within each State, granted or surveyed for any person, as such land and the buildings and improvements thereon shall be estimated according to such mode as the United States in Congress assembled, shall from time to time direct and appoint.

The taxes for paying that proportion shall be laid and levied by the authority and direction of the legislatures of the several States within the time agreed upon by the United States in Congress assembled.

IX. The United States in Congress assembled, shall have the sole and exclusive right and power of determining on peace and war, except in the cases mentioned in the sixth article—of sending and receiving ambassadors—entering into treaties and alliances, provided that no treaty of commerce shall be made whereby the legislative power of the respective States shall be restrained from imposing such imposts and duties on foreigners, as their own people are subjected to, or from prohibiting the exportation or importation of any species of goods or commodities whatsoever—of establishing rules for deciding in all cases, what captures on land or water shall be legal, and in what manner prizes taken by land or naval forces in the service of the United States shall be divided or appropriated—of granting letters of marque and reprisal in times of peace—appointing courts for the trial of piracies and felonies commited on the high seas and establishing courts for receiving and determining finally appeals in all cases of captures, provided that no member of Congress shall be appointed a judge of any of the said courts.

The United States in Congress assembled shall also be the last resort on appeal in all disputes and differences now subsisting or that hereafter may arise between two or more States concerning boundary, jurisdiction or any other causes whatever; which authority shall always be exercised in the manner following. Whenever the legislative or executive authority or lawful agent of any State in controversy with another shall present a petition to Congress stating the matter in question and praying for a hearing, notice thereof shall be given by order of Congress to the legislative or executive authority of the other State in controversy, and a day assigned for the appearance of the parties by their lawful agents, who shall then be directed to appoint by joint consent, commissioners or judges to constitute a court for hearing and determining the matter in question: but if they cannot agree, Congress shall name three persons out of each of the United States, and from the list of such persons each party shall alternately strike out one, the petitioners beginning, until the number shall be reduced to thirteen; and from that number not less than seven, nor more than nine names as Congress shall direct, shall in the presence of Congress be drawn out by lot, and the persons whose names shall be so drawn or any five of them, shall be commissioners or judges, to hear and finally determine the controversy, so always as a major part of the judges who shall hear the cause shall agree in the determination: and if either party shall neglect to attend at the day appointed, without showing reasons, which Congress shall judge sufficient, or being present shall refuse to strike, the Congress shall proceed to nominate three persons out of each State, and the secretary of Congress shall strike in behalf of such party absent or refusing; and the judgement and sentence of the court to be appointed, in the manner before prescribed, shall be final and conclusive; and if any of the parties shall refuse to submit to the authority of such court, or to appear or defend their claim or cause, the court shall nevertheless proceed to pronounce sentence, or judgement, which shall in like manner be final and decisive, the judgement or sentence and other proceedings being in either case transmitted to Congress, and lodged among the acts of Congress for the security of the parties concerned: provided that every commissioner, before he sits in judgement, shall take an oath to be administered by one of the judges of the supreme or superior court of the State, where the cause shall be tried, 'well and truly to hear and determine the matter in question, according to the best of his judgement, without favor, affection or hope of reward': provided also, that no State shall be deprived of territory for the benefit of the United States.

All controversies concerning the private right of soil claimed under different grants of two or more States, whose jurisdictions as they may respect such lands, and the States which passed such grants are adjusted, the said grants or either of them being at the same time claimed to have originated antecedent to such settlement of jurisdiction, shall on the petition of either party to the Congress of the United States, be finally determined as near as may be in the same manner as is before prescribed for deciding disputes respecting territorial jurisdiction between different States.

The United States in Congress assembled shall also have the sole and exclusive right and power of regulating the alloy and value of coin struck by their own authority, or by that of the respective States—fixing the standards of weights and measures throughout the United States—regulating the trade and managing all affairs with the Indians, not members of any of the States, provided that the legislative right of any State within its own limits be not infringed or violated—establishing or regulating post offices from one State to another, throughout all the United States, and exacting such postage on the papers passing through the same as may be requisite to defray the expenses of the said office—appointing all officers of the land forces, in the service of the United States, excepting regimental officers—appointing all the officers of the naval forces, and commissioning all officers whatever in the service of the United States—making rules for the government and regulation of the said land and naval forces, and directing their operations.

The United States in Congress assembled shall have authority to appoint a committee, to sit in the recess of Congress, to be denominated 'A Committee of the States', and to consist of one delegate from each State; and to appoint such other committees and civil officers as may be necessary for managing the general affairs of the United States under their direction—to appoint one of their members to preside, provided that no person be allowed to serve in the office of president more than one year in any term of three years; to ascertain the necessary sums of money to be raised for the service of the United States, and to appropriate and apply the same for defraying the public expenses—to borrow money, or emit bills on the credit of the United States, transmitting every half-year to the respective States an account of the sums of money so borrowed or emitted—to build and equip a navy—to agree upon the number of land forces, and to make requisitions from each State for its quota, in proportion to the number of white inhabitants in such State; which requisition shall be binding, and thereupon the legislature of each State shall appoint the regimental officers, raise the men and cloath, arm and equip them in a solid-like manner, at the expense of the United States; and the officers and men so clothed, armed and equipped shall march to the place appointed, and within the time agreed on by the United States in Congress assembled. But if the United States in Congress assembled shall, on consideration of circumstances judge proper that any State should not raise men, or should raise a smaller number of men than the quota thereof, such extra number shall be raised, officered, clothed, armed and equipped in the same manner as the quota of each State, unless the legislature of such State shall judge that such extra number cannot be safely spread out in the same, in which case they shall raise, officer, cloth, arm and equip as many of such extra number as they judge can be safely spared. And the officers and men so clothed, armed, and equipped, shall march to the place appointed, and within the time agreed on by the United States in Congress assembled.

The United States in Congress assembled shall never engage in a war, nor grant letters of marque or reprisal in time of peace, nor enter into any treaties or alliances, nor coin money, nor regulate the value thereof, nor ascertain the sums and expenses necessary for the defense and welfare of the United States, or any of them, nor emit bills, nor borrow money on the credit of the United States, nor appropriate money, nor agree upon the number of vessels of war, to be built or purchased, or the number of land or sea forces to be raised, nor appoint a commander in chief of the army or navy, unless nine States assent to the same: nor shall a question on any other point, except for adjourning from day to day be determined, unless by the votes of the majority of the United States in Congress assembled.

The Congress of the United States shall have power to adjourn to any time within the year, and to any place within the United States, so that no period of adjournment be for a longer duration than the space of six months, and shall publish the journal of their proceedings monthly, except such parts thereof relating to treaties, alliances or military operations, as in their judgement require secrecy; and the yeas and nays of the delegates of each State on any question shall be entered on the journal, when it is desired by any delegates of a State, or any of them, at his or their request shall be furnished with a transcript of the said journal, except such parts as are above excepted, to lay before the legislatures of the several States.

X. The Committee of the States, or any nine of them, shall be authorized to execute, in the recess of Congress, such of the powers of Congress as the United States in Congress assembled, by the consent of the nine States, shall from time to time think expedient to vest them with; provided that no power be delegated to the said Committee, for the exercise of which, by the Articles of Confederation, the voice of nine States in the Congress of the United States assembled be requisite.

XI. Canada acceding to this confederation, and adjoining in the measures of the United States, shall be admitted into, and entitled to all the advantages of this Union; but no other colony shall be admitted into the same, unless such admission be agreed to by nine States.

XII. All bills of credit emitted, monies borrowed, and debts contracted by, or under the authority of Congress, before the assembling of the United States, in pursuance of the present confederation, shall be deemed and considered as a charge against the United States, for payment and satisfaction whereof the said United States, and the public faith are hereby solemnly pledged.

XIII. Every State shall abide by the determination of the United States in Congress assembled, on all questions which by this confederation are submitted to them. And the Articles of this Confederation shall be inviolably observed by every State, and the Union shall be perpetual; nor shall any alteration at any time hereafter be made in any of them; unless such alteration be agreed to in a Congress of the United States, and be afterwards confirmed by the legislatures of every State.

And Whereas it hath pleased the Great Governor of the World to incline the hearts of the legislatures we respectively represent in Congress, to approve of, and to authorize us to ratify the said Articles of Confederation and perpetual Union: Know Ye that we the undersigned delegates, by virtue of the power and authority to us given for that purpose, do by these presents, in the name and in behalf of our respective constituents, fully and entirely ratify and confirm each and every of the said Articles of Confederation and perpetual Union, and all and singular the matters and things therein contained: And we do further solemnly plight and engage the faith of our respective constituents, that they shall abide by the determinations of the United States in Congress assembled, on all questions, which by the said Confederation are submitted to them. And that the Articles thereof shall be inviolably observed by the States we respectively represent, and that the Union shall be perpetual.

In Witness whereof we have hereunto set our hands in Congress. Done at Philadelphia in the State of Pennsylvania the ninth day of July in the Year of our Lord One Thousand Seven Hundred and Seventy-Eight, and in the Third Year of the independence of America.

The Constitution of the United States

We the People of the United States, in Order to form a more perfect Union, establish Justice, insure domestic Tranquility, provide for the common defence, promote the general Welfare, and secure the Blessings of Liberty to ourselves and our Posterity, do ordain and establish this Constitution for the United States of America.

Article I

Section 1 All legislative Powers herein granted shall be vested in a Congress of the United States, which shall consist of a Senate and House of Representatives.

Section 2 The House of Representatives shall be composed of Members chosen every second Year by the People of the several States, and the Electors in each State shall have the Qualifications requisite for Electors of the most numerous Branch of the State Legislature.

No Person shall be a Representative who shall not have attained to the Age of twenty five Years, and been seven Years a Citizen of the United States, and who shall not, when elected, be an Inhabitant of that State in which he shall be chosen.

Representatives and direct Taxes shall be apportioned among the several States which may be included within this Union, according to their respective Numbers, which shall be determined by adding to the whole Number of free Persons, including those bound to Service for a Term of Years, and excluding Indians not taxed, three fifths of all other Persons [Amendment XIV, 1866–1868]. The actual Enumeration shall be made within three Years after the first Meeting of the Congress of the United States, and within every subsequent Term of ten Years, in such Manner as they shall by Law direct. The Number of Representatives shall not exceed one for every thirty Thousand, but each State shall have at Least one Representative; and until such enumeration shall be made, the State of New Hampshire shall be entitled to chuse three, Massachusetts eight, Rhode-Island and Providence Plantations one, Connecticut five, New-York six, New Jersey four, Pennsylvania eight, Delaware one, Maryland six, Virginia ten, North Carolina five, South Carolina five, and Georgia three.

When vacancies happen in the Representation from any State, the Executive Authority thereof shall issue Writs of Election to fill such Vacancies.

The House of Representatives shall chuse their Speaker and other Officers; and shall have the sole Power of Impeachment.

Section 3 The Senate of the United States shall be composed of two Senators from each State, *chosen by the Legislature thereof* [Amendment XVII, 1912–1913], for six Years; and each Senator shall have one Vote.

Immediately after they shall be assembled in Consequence of the first Election, they shall be divided as equally as may be into three Classes. The Seats of the Senators of the first Class shall be vacated at the Expiration of the second Year, of the second Class at the Expiration of the fourth Year, and of the third Class at the Expiration of the sixth Year, so that one third may be chosen every second Year; *and if Vacancies happen by Resignation, or otherwise, during the Recess of the Legislature of any State, the Executive thereof may make temporary Appointments until the next Meeting of the Legislature, which shall then fill such Vacancies* [Amendment XVII, 1912–1913].

No Person shall be a Senator who shall not have attained to the Age of thirty Years, and been nine Years a Citizen of the United States, and who shall not, when elected, be an Inhabitant of that State for which he shall be chosen.

The Vice President of the United States shall be President of the Senate, but shall have no Vote, unless they be equally divided.

The Senate shall chuse their other Officers, and also a President pro tempore, in the Absence of the Vice President, or when he shall exercise the Office of President of the United States. The Senate shall have the sole Power to try all Impeachments. When sitting for that Purpose, they shall be on Oath or Affirmation. When the President of the United States is tried, the Chief Justice shall preside: And no Person shall be convicted without the Concurrence of two thirds of the Members present.

Judgment in Cases of Impeachment shall not extend further than to removal from Office, and disqualification to hold and enjoy any Office of honor, Trust or Profit under the United States: but the Party convicted shall nevertheless be liable and subject to Indictment, Trial, Judgment and Punishment, according to Law.

Section 4 The Times, Places and Manner of holding Elections for Senators and Representatives, shall be prescribed in each State by the Legislature thereof; but the Congress may at any time by Law make or alter such Regulations, except as to the Places of chusing Senators.

The Congress shall assemble at least once in every Year, *and such Meeting shall be on the first Monday in December* [Amendment XX, 1932–1933], unless they shall by Law appoint a different Day.

Section 5 Each House shall be the Judge of the Elections, Returns and Qualifications of its own Members, and a Majority of each shall constitute a Quorum to do

Business; but a smaller Number may adjourn from day to day, and may be authorized to compel the Attendance of absent Members, in such Manner, and under such Penalties as each House may provide.

Each House may determine the Rules of its Proceedings, punish its Members for disorderly Behaviour, and, with the Concurrence of two thirds, expel a member.

Each House shall keep a Journal of its Proceedings, and from time to time publish the same, excepting such Parts as may in their Judgment require Secrecy; and the Yeas and Nays of the Members of either House on any question shall, at the Desire of one fifth of those Present, be entered on the Journal.

Neither House, during the Session of Congress, shall, without the Consent of the other, adjourn for more than three days, nor to any other Place than that in which the two Houses shall be sitting.

Section 6 The Senators and Representatives shall receive a Compensation for their Services, to be ascertained by Law, and paid out of the Treasury of the United States. They shall in all Cases, except Treason, Felony and Breach of the Peace, be privileged from Arrest during their Attendance at the Session of their respective Houses, and in going to and returning from the same; and for any Speech or Debate in either House, they shall not be questioned in any other Place.

No Senator or Representative shall, during the Time for which he was elected, be appointed to any civil Office under the Authority of the United States, which shall have been created, or the Emoluments whereof shall have been encreased during such time; and no Person holding any Office under the United States, shall be a Member of either House during his Continuance in Office.

Section 7 All Bills for raising Revenue shall originate in the House of Representatives; but the Senate may propose or concur with Amendments as on other Bills.

Every Bill which shall have passed the House of Representatives and the Senate, shall, before it become a Law, be presented to the President of the United States: If he approve he shall sign it, but if not he shall return it, with his Objections to that House in which it shall have originated, who shall enter the Objections at large on their Journal, and proceed to reconsider it. If after such Reconsideration two thirds of that House shall agree to pass the Bill, it shall be sent, together with the Objections, to the other House, by which it shall likewise be reconsidered, and if approved by two thirds of that House, it shall become a Law. But in all such Cases the Votes of both Houses shall be determined by yeas and Nays, and the Names of the Persons voting for and against the Bill shall be entered on the Journal of each House respectively. If any Bill shall not be returned by the President within ten Days (Sundays excepted) after it shall have been presented to him, the Same shall be a Law, in like Manner as if he had signed it, unless the Congress by their Adjournment prevent its Return, in which Case it shall not be a Law.

Every Order, Resolution, or Vote to which the Concurrence of the Senate and House of Representatives may be necessary (except on a question of Adjournment) shall be presented to the President of the United States; and before the Same shall take Effect, shall be approved by him, or being disapproved by him, shall be repassed by two thirds of the Senate and House of Representatives, according to the Rules and Limitations prescribed in the Case of a Bill.

Section 8 The Congress shall have Power to lay and collect Taxes, Duties, Imposts and Excises, to pay the Debts and provide for the common Defence and general Welfare of the United States; but all Duties, Imposts and Excises shall be uniform throughout the United States;

To borrow Money on the credit of the United States;

To regulate Commerce with foreign Nations, and among the several States, and with the Indian Tribes;

To establish an uniform Rule of Naturalization, and uniform Laws on the subject of Bankruptcies throughout the United States;

To coin Money, regulate the Value thereof, and of foreign Coin, and fix the Standard of Weights and Measures;

To provide for the Punishment of counterfeiting the Securities and current Coin of the United States;

To establish Post Offices and post Roads;

To promote the Progress of Science and useful Arts, by securing for limited Times to Authors and Inventors the exclusive Right to their respective Writings and Discoveries;

To constitute Tribunals inferior to the supreme Court;

To define and punish Piracies and Felonies committed on the high Seas, and Offences against the Law of Nations;

To declare War, grant Letters of Marque and Reprisal, and make Rules concerning Captures on Land and Water;

To raise and support Armies, but no Appropriation of Money to that Use shall be for a longer Term than two Years;

To provide and maintain a Navy;

To make Rules for the Government and Regulation of the land and naval Forces;

To provide for calling forth the Militia to execute the Laws of the Union, suppress Insurrections and repel Invasions;

To provide for organizing, arming, and disciplining, the Militia, and for governing such Part of them as may be employed in the Service of the United States, reserving to the States respectively, the Appointment of the Officers, and the Authority of training the Militia according to the discipline prescribed by Congress;

To exercise exclusive Legislation in all Cases whatsoever, over such District (not exceeding ten Miles square) as may, by Cession of particular States, and the Acceptance of Congress, become the Seat of the Government of the United States, and to exercise like Authority over all Places purchased by the Consent of the Legislature of the State in which the Same shall be, for the Erection of Forts, Magazines, Arsenals, dock-Yards, and other needful Buildings; —And

To make all Laws which shall be necessary and proper for carrying into Execution the foregoing Powers, and all other Powers vested by this Constitution in the Government of the United States, or in any Department or Officer thereof.

Section 9 The Migration or Importation of such Persons as any of the States now existing shall think proper to admit, shall not be prohibited by the Congress prior to the Year one thousand eight hundred and eight, but a Tax or duty may be imposed on such Importation, not exceeding ten dollars for each Person.

The Privilege of the Writ of Habeas Corpus shall not be suspended, unless when in Cases of Rebellion or Invasion the public Safety may require it.

No Bill of Attainder or ex post facto Law shall be passed.

No Capitation, or other direct, Tax shall be laid, unless in Proportion to the Census or Enumeration herein before directed to be taken.

No Tax or Duty shall be laid on Articles exported from any State.

No Preference shall be given by any Regulation of Commerce or Revenue to the Ports of one State over those of another; nor shall Vessels bound to, or from, one State, be obliged to enter, clear, or pay Duties in another.

No Money shall be drawn from the Treasury, but in Consequence of Appropriations made by Law; and a regular Statement and Account of the Receipts and Expenditures of all public Money shall be published from time to time.

No Title of Nobility shall be granted by the United States: And no Person holding any Office of Profit or Trust under them, shall, without the Consent of the Congress, accept of any present, Emolument, Office, or Title, of any kind whatever, from any King, Prince, or foreign State.

Section 10 No State shall enter into any Treaty, Alliance, or Confederation; grant Letters of Marque and Reprisal; coin Money; emit Bills of Credit; make any Thing but gold and silver Coin a Tender in Payment of Debts; pass any Bill of Attainder, ex post facto Law, or Law impairing the Obligation of Contracts, or grant any Title of Nobility.

No State shall, without the Consent of the Congress, lay any Imposts or Duties on Imports or Exports, except what may be absolutely necessary for executing it's inspection Laws; and the net Produce of all Duties and Imposts, laid by any State on Imports or Exports, shall be for the Use of the Treasury of the United States; and all such Laws shall be subject to the Revision and Controul of the Congress.

No State shall, without the Consent of Congress, lay any Duty of Tonnage, keep Troops, or Ships of War in time of Peace, enter into any Agreement or Compact with another State, or with a foreign Power, or engage in War, unless actually invaded, or in such imminent Danger as will not admit of delay.

Article II

Section 1 The executive Power shall be vested in a President of the United States of America. He shall hold his Office during the Term of four Years, and, together with the Vice President, chosen for the same Term, be elected, as follows:

Each State shall appoint, in such Manner as the Legislature thereof may direct, a Number of Electors, equal to the whole Number of Senators and Representatives to which the State may be entitled in the Congress: but no Senator or Representative, or Person holding an Office of Trust or Profit under the United States, shall be appointed an Elector.

The Electors shall meet in their respective States, and vote by Ballot for two Persons, of whom one at least shall not be an Inhabitant of the same State with themselves. And they shall make a List of all the Persons voted for, and of the Number of Votes for each; which List they shall sign and certify, and transmit sealed to the Seat of the Government of the United States, directed to the President of the Senate. The President of the Senate shall, in the Presence of the Senate and House of Representatives, open all the Certificates, and the Votes shall then be counted. The Person having the greatest Number of Votes shall be the President, if such Number be a Majority of the whole Number of Electors appointed; and if there be more than one who have such Majority, and have an equal Number of Votes, then the House of Representatives shall immediately chuse by Ballot one of them for President; and if no Person have a Majority, then from the five highest on the List the said House shall in like Manner chuse the President. But in chusing the President, the Votes shall be taken by States, the Representation from each State having one Vote; a quorum for this Purpose shall consist of a Member or Members from two thirds of the States, and a Majority of all the States shall be necessary to a Choice. In every Case, after the Choice of the President, the Person having the greatest Number of Votes of the Electors shall be the Vice President. But if there should remain two or more who have equal Votes, the Senate shall chuse from them by Ballot the Vice President [Amendment XII, 1803–1804].

The Congress may determine the Time of chusing the Electors, and the Day on which they shall give their Votes; which Day shall be the same throughout the United States.

No Person except a natural born Citizen, or a Citizen of the United States, at the time of the Adoption of this Constitution, shall be eligible to the Office of President; neither shall any Person be eligible to that Office who shall not have attained to the Age of thirty five Years, and been fourteen Years a Resident within the United States.

In Case of the Removal of the President from Office, or of his Death, Resignation, or Inability to discharge the Powers and Duties of the said Office, the Same shall devolve on the Vice President, and the Congress may by Law provide for the Case of Removal, Death, Resignation or Inability, both of the President and Vice President, declaring what Officer shall then act as President, and such Officer shall act accordingly, until the Disability be removed, or a President shall be elected [Amendment XXV, 1967].

The President shall, at stated Times, receive for his Services, a Compensation, which shall neither be increased nor diminished during the Period for which he shall have been elected, and he shall not receive within that Period any other Emolument from the United States, or any of them.

Before he enter on the Execution of his Office, he shall take the following Oath or Affirmation:—"I do solemnly swear (or affirm) that I will faithfully execute the Office of President of the United States, and will to the best of my Ability, preserve, protect and defend the Constitution of the United States."

Section 2 The President shall be Commander in Chief of the Army and Navy of the United States, and of the Militia of the several States, when called into the actual Service of the United States; he may require the Opinion, in writing, of the principal Officer in each of the executive Departments, upon any Subject relating to the Duties of their respective Offices, and he shall have Power to grant Reprieves and Pardons for Offences against the United States, except in Cases of Impeachment.

He shall have Power, by and with the Advice and Consent of the Senate, to make Treaties, provided two thirds of the Senators present concur; and he shall nominate, and by and with the Advice and Consent of the Senate, shall appoint Ambassadors, other public Ministers and Consuls, Judges of the supreme Court, and all other Officers of the United States, whose Appointments are not herein otherwise provided for, and which shall be established by Law: but the Congress may by Law vest the Appointment of such inferior Officers, as they think proper, in the President alone, in the Courts of Law, or in the Heads of Departments.

The President shall have Power to fill up all Vacancies that may happen during the Recess of the Senate, by granting Commissions which shall expire at the End of their next Session.

Section 3 He shall from time to time give to the Congress Information of the State of the Union, and recommend to their Consideration such Measures as he shall judge necessary and expedient; he may, on extraordinary Occasions, convene both Houses, or either of them, and in Case of Disagreement between them, with Respect to the Time of Adjournment, he may adjourn them to such Time as he shall think proper; he shall receive Ambassadors and other public Ministers; he shall take Care that the Laws be faithfully executed, and shall Commission all the Officers of the United States.

Section 4 The President, Vice President and all civil Officers of the United States, shall be removed from Office on Impeachment for, and Conviction of, Treason, Bribery, or other high Crimes and Misdemeanors.

Article III

Section 1 The judicial Power of the United States shall be vested in one supreme Court, and in such inferior Courts as the Congress may from time to time ordain and establish. The Judges, both of the supreme and inferior Courts, shall hold their Offices during good Behaviour, and shall, at stated Times, receive for their Services a Compensation, which shall not be diminished during their Continuance in Office.

Section 2 The judicial Power shall extend to all Cases, in Law and Equity, arising under this Constitution, the Laws of the United States, and Treaties made, or which shall be made, under their Authority;—to all Cases affecting Ambassadors, other public Ministers and Consuls;—to all Cases of admiralty and maritime Jurisdiction;—to Controversies to which the United States shall be a Party; —to Controversies between two or more States;—*between a State and Citizens of another State* [Amendment XI, 1803–1804];—between Citizens of different States;—between Citizens of the same State claiming Lands under Grants of different States, and between a State, or the Citizens thereof, and foreign States, Citizens or Subjects.

In all Cases affecting Ambassadors, other public Ministers and Consuls, and those in which a State shall be Party, the supreme Court shall have original Jurisdiction. In all the other Cases before mentioned, the supreme Court shall have appellate Jurisdiction, both as to Law and Fact, with such Exceptions, and under such Regulations as the Congress shall make.

The Trial of all Crimes, except in Cases of Impeachment, shall be by Jury; and such Trial shall be held in the State where the said Crimes shall have been committed; but when not committed within any State, the Trial shall be at such Place or Places as the Congress may by Law have directed.

Section 3 Treason against the United States shall consist only in levying War against them, or in adhering to their Enemies, giving them Aid and Comfort. No Person shall be convicted of Treason unless on the Testimony of two Witnesses to the same overt Act, or on Confession in open Court.

The Congress shall have Power to declare the Punishment of Treason, but no Attainder of Treason shall work Corruption of Blood, or Forfeiture except during the Life of the Person attainted.

Article IV

Section 1 Full Faith and Credit shall be given in each State to the public Acts, Records, and judicial Proceedings of every other State. And the Congress may by general Laws prescribe the Manner in which such Acts, Records and Proceedings shall be proved, and the Effect thereof.

Section 2 The Citizens of each State shall be entitled to all Privileges and Immunities of Citizens in the several States.

A Person charged in any State with Treason, Felony, or other Crime, who shall flee from Justice, and be found in another State, shall on Demand of the executive Authority of the State from which he fled, be delivered up, to be removed to the State having Jurisdiction of the Crime.

No Person held to Service or Labour in one State, under the Laws thereof, escaping into another, shall, in Consequence of any Law or Regulation therein, be discharged from such Service or Labour, but shall be delivered up on Claim of the Party to whom such Service or Labour may be due [Amendment XIII, 1865].

Section 3 New States may be admitted by the Congress into this Union; but no new State shall be formed or erected within the Jurisdiction of any other State; nor any State be formed by the Junction of two or more States, or Parts of States, without the Consent of the Legislatures of the States concerned as well as of the Congress.

The Congress shall have Power to dispose of and make all needful Rules and Regulations respecting the Territory or other Property belonging to the United States; and nothing in this Constitution shall be so construed as to Prejudice any Claims of the United States, or of any particular State.

Section 4 The United States shall guarantee to every State in this Union a Republican Form of Government, and shall protect each of them against Invasion; and on Application of the Legislature, or of the Executive (when the Legislature cannot be convened), against domestic Violence.

Article V

The Congress, whenever two thirds of both Houses shall deem it necessary, shall propose Amendments to this Constitution, or, on the Application of the Legislatures of two thirds of the several States, shall call a Convention for proposing Amendments, which, in either Case, shall be valid to all Intents and Purposes, as Part of this Constitution, when ratified by the Legislatures of three fourths of the several States, or by Conventions in three fourths thereof, as the one or the other Mode of Ratification may be proposed by the Congress; Provided that no Amendment which may be made prior to the Year One thousand eight hundred and eight shall in any Manner affect the first and fourth Clauses in the Ninth Section of the first Article; and that no State, without its Consent, shall be deprived of its equal Suffrage in the Senate.

Article VI

All Debts contracted and Engagements entered into, before the Adoption of this Constitution, shall be as valid against the United States under this Constitution, as under the Confederation.

This Constitution, and the Laws of the United States which shall be made in Pursuance thereof; and all Treaties made, or which shall be made, under the Authority of the United States, shall be the supreme Law of the Land; and the Judges in every State shall be bound thereby, any Thing in the Constitution or Laws of any State to the Contrary notwithstanding.

The Senators and Representatives before mentioned, and the Members of the several State Legislatures, and all executive and judicial Officers, both of the United States and of the several States, shall be bound by Oath or Affirmation, to support this Constitution; but no religious Test shall ever be required as a Qualification to any Office or public Trust under the United States.

Article VII

The Ratification of the Conventions of nine States, shall be sufficient for the Establishment of this Constitution between the States so ratifying the Same.

Attest William Jackson
Secretary

Done in Convention by the Unanimous Consent of the States present the Seventeenth Day of September in the Year of our Lord one thousand seven hundred and Eighty seven and of the Independence of the United States of America the Twelfth In witness whereof We have hereunto subscribed our Names,

Go. WASHINGTON—Presidt.
And deputy from Virginia

New Hampshire

> JOHN LANGDON
> NICHOLAS GILMAN

Massachusetts

> NATHANIEL GORHAM
> RUFUS KING

Connecticut

Judicial Process and Federalism

Marbury v. Madison (1803)

The case that established the doctrine of judicial review came with a politically charged background. Losers of the election of 1800, the Federalist Party attempted to control the federal judiciary through the creation of new courts and court personnel in the so-called Midnight Justices Act. In their haste, the Federalists failed to have all the appointments properly executed. The incoming Jefferson administration naturally refused to grant any of the unexecuted appointments. Directly affected by this situation, William Marbury sued for his appointment directly to the Supreme Court under the congressionally sanctioned mandamus procedure. Chief Justice Marshall, secretary of state in the Adams administration, wanted to rule in favor of the Federalist Marbury, but he did not dare do so. Such a ruling would surely be ignored by the Jeffersonians, at great cost to the institutional prestige of the Court. Marshall ruled that Marbury was entitled to his appointment but could not be granted relief because the statute by which Congress had granted original jurisdiction to the Supreme Court in mandamus procedures (Judiciary Act of 1789) unconstitutionally added to the Court's original jurisdictions. Thus, Marshall established the Court's fundamental power in a way the Jefferson administration could not contest.

CHIEF JUSTICE MARSHALL delivered the opinion of the Court.

... In the order in which the court has viewed this subject, the following questions have been considered and decided:

1st. Has the applicant a right to the commission he demands?

2d. If he has a right, and that right has been violated, do the laws of his country afford him a remedy?

3d. If they do afford him a remedy, is it a mandamus issuing from this court?

The first object of inquiry is—1st. Has the applicant a right to the commission he demands?...

It [is] decidedly the opinion of the court, that when a commission has been signed by the president, the appointment is made; and that the commission is complete, when the seal of the United States has been affixed to it by the secretary of state.... To withhold his commissidon, therefore, is an act deemed by the court not warranted by law, but violative of a vested legal right.

This brings us to the second inquiry; which is 2dly. If he has a right, and that right has been violated, do the laws of his country afford him a remedy?

The very essence of civil liberty certainly consists in the right of every individual to claim the protection of the laws, whenever he receives an injury. One of the first duties of government is to afford that protection....

It is, then, the opinion of the Court [that Marbury has a] right to the commission; a refusal to deliver which is a plain violation of that right, for which the laws of his country afford him a remedy. It remains to be enquired whether,

3dly. He is entitled to the remedy for which he applies. This depends on—1st. The nature of the writ applied for, and,

2dly. The power of this court.

1st. The nature of the writ. . . .

This, then, is a plain case for a mandamus, either to deliver the commission, or a copy of it from the record; and it only remains to be enquired,

Whether it can issue from this court.

The act to establish the judicial courts of the United States authorizes the Supreme Court "to issue writs of mandamus in cases warranted by the principles and usages of law, to any courts appointed, or persons holding office, under the authority of the United States."

The Secretary of State, being a person holding an office under the authority of the United States, is precisely within the letter of the description; and if this court is not authorized to issue a writ of mandamus to such an officer, it must be because the law is unconstitutional, and therefore incapable of conferring the authority, and assigning the duties which its words purport to confer and assign.

The constitution vests the whole judicial power of the United States in one Supreme Court, and such inferior courts as congress shall, from time to time, ordain and establish. This power is expressly extended to all cases arising under the laws of the United States; and, consequently, in some form, may be exercised over the present case; because the right claimed is given by a law of the United States.

In the distribution of this power it is declared that "the Supreme Court shall have original jurisdiction in all cases affecting ambassadors, other public ministers and consuls, and those in which a state shall be a party. In all other cases, the Supreme Court shall have appellate jurisdiction."

It has been insisted, at the bar, that as the original grant of jurisdiction, to the supreme and inferior courts, is general, and the clause, assigning original jurisdiction to the Supreme Court, contains no negative or restrictive words, the power remains to the legislature, to assign original jurisdiction to that court in other cases than those specified in the article which has been recited; provided those cases belong to the judicial power of the United States....

Affirmative words are often, in their operation, negative of other objects than those affirmed; and in this case, a negative or exclusive sense must be given to them or they have no operation at all.

It cannot be presumed that any clause in the constitution is intended to be without effect; and, therefore, such a construction is inadmissible, unless the words require it....

To enable this court, then, to issue a mandamus, it must be shown to be an exercise of appellate jurisdiction, or to be necessary to enable them to exercise appellate jurisdiction.

It has been stated at the bar that the appellate jurisdiction may be exercised in a variety of forms, and that if it be the will of the legislature that a mandamus should be used for that purpose, that will must be obeyed. This is true, yet the jurisdiction must be appellate, not original.

It is the essential criterion of appellate jurisdiction, that it revises and corrects the proceedings in a cause already instituted, and does not create that cause. Although, therefore, a mandamus may be directed to courts, yet to issue such a writ to an officer for the delivery of a paper, is in effect the same as to sustain an original action for that paper, and, therefore, seems not to belong to appellate, but to original jurisdiction. Neither is it necessary in such a case as this, to enable the court to exercise its appellate jurisdiction....

The constitution is either a superior, paramount law, unchangeable by ordinary means, or it is on a level with ordinary legislative acts, and, like other acts, is alterable when the legislature shall please to alter it.

If the former part of the alternative be true, then a legislative act contrary to the constitution is not law: if the latter part be true, then written constitutions are absurd attempts, on the part of the people, to limit a power in its own nature illimitable.

Certainly all those who have framed written constitutions contemplate them as forming the fundamental and paramount law of the nation, and consequently, the theory of every such government must be, that an act of the legislature, repugnant to the constitution, is void.

This theory is essentially attached to a written constitution, and is, consequently, to be considered, by this court, as one of the fundamental principles of our society. It is not therefore to be lost sight of in the further consideration of this subject.

If an act of the legislature, repugnant to the constitution, is void, does it, notwithstanding its invalidity, bind the courts, and oblige them to give it effect? Or, in other words, though it be not law, does it constitute a rule as operative as if it was a law? This would be to overthrow in fact what was established in theory; and would seem, at first view, an absurdity too gross to be insisted on. It shall, however, receive a more attentive consideration.

It is emphatically the province and duty of the judicial department to say what the law is. Those who apply the rule to particular cases, must of necessity expound and interpret that rule. If two laws conflict with each other, the courts must decide on the operation of each.

So if a law be in opposition to the constitution; if both the law and the constitution apply to a particular case, so that the court must either decide that case conformably to the law, disregarding the constitution; or conformably to the constitution, disregarding the law; the court must determine which of these conflicting rules governs the case. This is of the very essence of judicial duty.

If, then, the courts are to regard the constitution, and the constitution is superior to any ordinary act of the legislature, the constitution, and not such ordinary act, must govern the case to which they both apply.

Those then who controvert the principle that the constitution is to be considered, in court, as a paramount law, are reduced to the necessity of maintaining that the courts must close their eyes on the constitution, and see only the law.

This doctrine would subvert the very foundation of all written constitutions. It would declare that an act which, according to the principles and theory of our government, is entirely void, is yet, in practice, completely obligatory. It would declare that if the legislature shall do what is expressly forbidden, such act, notwithstanding the express prohibition, is in reality effectual. It would be giving to the legislature a practical and real omnipotence, with the same breath which professes to restrict their powers within narrow limits. It is prescribing limits, and declaring that those limits may be passed at pleasure.

That it thus reduces to nothing what we have deemed the greatest improvement on political institutions—a written constitution—would of itself be sufficient, in America, where written constitutions have been viewed with so much reverence, for rejecting the construction....

McCulloch v. Maryland (1819)

This most important case for federalism turned on two questions that reflected the debate over the power of the national government versus the power of state governments: (1) May Congress under the elastic language of the necessary and proper clause incorporate a national bank? (2) May the state of Maryland impose a tax on that bank?

CHIEF JUSTICE MARSHALL delivered the opinion of the Court.

In the case now to be determined, the defendant, a sovereign State, denies the obligation of a law enacted by the legislature of the Union, and the plaintiff, on his part, contests the validity of an act which has been passed by the legislature of that State. The constitution of our country, in its most interesting and vital parts, is to be considered; the conflicting powers of the government of the Union and of its members, as marked in that constitution, are to be discussed; and an opinion given, which may essentially influence the great operations of the government. No tribunal can approach such a question without a deep sense of its importance, and of the awful responsibility involved in its decision.

The first question made in the cause is, has Congress power to incorporate a bank?

The power now contested was exercised by the first Congress elected under the present constitution. The bill for incorporating the bank of the United States did not steal upon an unsuspecting legislature, and pass unobserved. Its principle was completely understood, and was opposed with equal zeal and ability. After being resisted, first in the fair and open field of debate, and afterwards in the executive cabinet, with as much persevering talent as any measure has ever experienced, and being supported by arguments which convinced minds as pure and as intelligent as this country can boast, it became a law. The original act was permitted to expire; but a short experience of the embarrassments to which the refusal to revive it exposed the government, convinced those who were most prejudiced against the measure of its necessity, and induced the passage of the present law. It would require no ordinary share of intre-

pidity to assert that a measure adopted under these circumstances was a bold and plain usurpation, to which the constitution gave no countenance.

The Government of the Union ... is, emphatically, and truly, a government of the people. In form and in substance it emanates from them. Its powers are granted by them, and are to be exercised directly on them, and for their benefit.

This government is acknowledged by all to be one of enumerated powers. The principle, that it can exercise only the powers granted to it, [is] now universally admitted. But the question respecting the extent of the powers actually granted, is perpetually arising, and will probably continue to arise, as long as our system shall exist....

Among the enumerated powers, we do not find that of establishing a bank or creating a corporation. But there is no phrase in the instrument which, like the articles of confederation, excludes incidental or implied powers; and which requires that everything granted shall be expressly and minutely described. Even the 10th amendment, which was framed for the purpose of quieting the excessive jealousies which had been excited, omits the word "expressly," and declares only that the powers "not delegated to the United States, nor prohibited to the States, are reserved to the States or to the people"; thus leaving the question, whether the particular power which may become the subject of contest has been delegated to the one government, or prohibited to the other, to depend on a fair construction of the whole instrument....

... Its nature, therefore, requires, that only its great outlines should be marked, its important objects designated, and the minor ingredients which compose those objects be deduced from the nature of the objects themselves. That this idea was entertained by the framers of the American constitution, is not only to be inferred from the nature of the instrument, but from the language. Why else were some of the limitations, found in the ninth section of the 1st article, introduced? It is also, in some degree, warranted by their having omitted to use any restrictive term which might prevent its receiving a fair and just interpretation. In considering this question, then, we must never forget that it is a constitution we are expounding.

Although, among the enumerated powers of government, we do not find the word "bank," or "incorporation," we find the great powers to lay and collect taxes; to borrow money; to regulate commerce; to declare and conduct a war; and to raise and support armies and navies. The sword and the purse, all the external relations, and no inconsiderable portion of the industry of the nation, are entrusted to its government. It can never be pretended that these vast powers draw after them others of inferior importance, merely because they are inferior. Such an idea can never be advanced. But it may with great reason be contended, that a government, entrusted with such ample powers, on the due execution of which the happiness and prosperity of the nation so vitally depends, must also be entrusted with ample means for their execution. The power being given, it is the interest of the nation to facilitate its execution. It can never be their interest, and cannot be presumed to have been their intention, to clog and embarrass its execution by withholding the most appropriate means....

The government which has a right to do an act, and has imposed on it the duty of performing that act, must, according to the dictates of reason, be allowed to select the means; and those who contend that it may not select any appropriate means, that one particular mode of effecting the object is excepted, take upon themselves the burden of establishing that exception....

... It is, we think, impossible to compare the sentence which prohibits a State from laying "imposts, or duties on imports or exports, except what may be absolutely necessary for

executing its inspection laws," with that which authorizes Congress "to make all laws which shall be necessary and proper for carrying into execution" the powers of the general government, without feeling a conviction that the convention understood itself to change materially the meaning of the word "necessary," by prefixing the word "absolutely." This word, then, like others, is used in various senses; and, in its construction, the subject, the context, the intention of the person using them, are all to be taken into view.

Let this be done in the case under consideration. The subject is the execution of those great powers on which the welfare of a nation essentially depends. It must have been the intention of those who gave these powers, to insure, as far as human prudence could insure, their beneficial execution. This could not be done by confiding the choice of means to such narrow limits as not to leave it in the power of Congress to adopt any which might be appropriate, and which were conducive to the end. This provision is made in a constitution intended to endure for ages to come, and, consequently, to be adapted to the various crises of human affairs. To have prescribed the means by which government should, in all future time, execute its powers, would have been to change, entirely, the character of the instrument, and give it the properties of a legal code. It would have been an unwise attempt to provide, by immutable rules, for exigencies which, if foreseen at all, must have been seen dimly, and which can be best provided for as they occur....

After the most deliberate consideration, it is the unanimous and decided opinion of this Court, that the act to incorporate the Bank of the United States is a law made in pursuance of the constitution, and is a part of the supreme law of the land....

It being the opinion of the Court, that the act incorporating the bank is constitutional; and that the power of establishing a branch in the State of Maryland might be properly exercised by the bank itself, we proceed to inquire—Whether the State of Maryland may, without violating the constitution, tax that branch?...

That the power of taxing by the States may be exercised so as to destroy it, is too obvious to be denied. But taxation is said to be an absolute power, which acknowledges no other limits than those expressly prescribed in the constitution, and like sovereign power of every other description, is trusted to the discretion of those who use it....

If we apply the principle for which the State of Maryland contends, to the constitution generally, we shall find it capable of changing totally the character of that instrument. We shall find it capable of arresting all the measures of the government, and of prostrating it at the foot of the States. The American people have declared their constitution, and the laws made in pursuance thereof, to be supreme; but this principle would transfer the supremacy, in fact, to the States.

If the States may tax one instrument, employed by the government in the execution of its powers, they may tax any and every other instrument. They may tax the mail; they may tax the mint; they may tax patent rights; they may tax the papers of the custom-house; they may tax judicial process; they may tax all the means employed by the government, to an excess which would defeat all the ends of government. This was not intended by the American people. They did not design to make their government dependent on the States....

We are unanimously of opinion, that the law passed by the legislature of Maryland, imposing a tax on the Bank of the United States, is unconstitutional and void.

This opinion does not deprive the States of any resources which they originally possessed. It does not extend to a tax paid by the real property of the bank, in common with the other real property within the State, nor to a tax imposed on the interest which the citizens of Maryland may hold in this institution, in common with other property of the same description throughout the State. But this is a tax on the operations of the bank, and is, consequently, a tax on the operation of an instrument employed by the government of the Union to carry its powers into execution. Such a tax must be unconstitutional.

Youngstown Sheet & Tube Co. et al. v. Sawyer (1952)

A classic case in the separation of powers, Youngstown v. Sawyer *dealt with President Truman's seizure of private steel mills during the Korean War. In the face of strikes that could have crippled war production in a national emergency, Truman justified the seizure through the president's power as commander in chief and other inherhent powers of the office whether expressed or implied. But by 6 to 3, the Court held that the president had overreached his authority in an area where Congress had expressly denied it. Given the gravity of the case, each justice in the majority (while joining Justice Black's opinion) expressed his own view. Some justices claimed that the majority opinion was not deferential enough to presidential prerogatives. Thus, this case also is a good example of the role of separate opinions in the processes of the Supreme Court.*

MR. JUSTICE BLACK delivered the opinion of the Court....

We are asked to decide whether the President was acting within his constitutional power when he issued an order directing the Secretary of Commerce to take possession of and operate most of the Nation's steel mills. The mill owners argue that the President's order amounts to lawmaking, a legislative function which the Constitution has expressly confided to the Congress and not to the President. The Government's position is that the order was made on findings of the President that his action was necessary to avert a national catastrophe which would inevitably result from a stoppage of steel production, and that in meeting this grave emergency the President was acting within the aggregate of his constitutional powers as the Nation's Chief Executive and the Commander in Chief of the Armed Forces of the United States....

The President's power, if any, to issue the order must stem either from an act of Congress or from the Constitution itself. There is no statute that expressly authorizes the President to take possession of property as he did here. Nor is there any act of Congress to which our attention has been directed from which such a power can fairly be implied....

Moreover, the use of the seizure technique to solve labor disputes in order to prevent work stoppages was not only unauthorized by any congressional enactment; prior to this controversy, Congress had refused to adopt that method of settling labor disputes. When the Taft-Hartley Act was under consideration in 1947, Congress rejected an amendment which would have authorized such governmental seizures in cases of emergency. Apparently it was thought that the technique of seizure, like that of compulsory arbitration, would interfere with the process of collective bargaining. Consequently, the plan Congress adopted in that Act did not provide for seizure under any circumstances....

It is clear that if the President had authority to issue the order he did, it must be found in some provision of the Constitution. And it is not claimed that express constitutional language grants this power to the President. The contention is that presidential power should be implied from the aggregate of his powers under the Constitution. Particular reliance is placed on provisions in Article II which say that "The executive Power shall be vested in a President..."; that "he shall take Care that the Laws be faithfully executed"; and that he "shall be Commander in Chief of the Army and Navy of the United States."...

The order cannot properly be sustained as an exercise of the President's military power as Commander in Chief of the Armed Forces.... Even though "theater of war" be an expanding concept, we cannot with faithfulness to our constitutional system hold that the Commander in Chief of the Armed Forces has the ultimate power as such to take possession of private property in order to keep labor disputes from stopping production. This is a job for the Nation's lawmakers, not for its military authorities....

Nor can the seizure order be sustained because of the several constitutional provisions that grant executive power to the President. In the framework of our Constitution, the President's power to see that the laws are faithfully executed refutes the idea that he is to be a lawmaker. The Constitution limits his functions in the lawmaking process to the recommending of laws he thinks wise and the vetoing of laws he thinks bad. And the Constitution is neither silent nor equivocal about who shall make laws which the President is to execute....

The Founders of this Nation entrusted the lawmaking power to the Congress alone in both good and bad times. It would do no good to recall the historical events, the fears of power and the hopes for freedom that lay behind their choice. Such a review would but confirm our holding that this seizure order cannot stand.

The judgment of the District Court is Affirmed.

Mr. Justice Frankfurter, concurring.

Before the cares of the White House were his own, President Harding is reported to have said that government after all is a very simple thing. He must have said that, if he said it, as a fleeting inhabitant of fairyland. The opposite is the truth. A constitutional democracy like ours is perhaps the most difficult of man's social arrangements to manage successfully. Our scheme of society is more dependent than any other form of government on knowledge and wisdom and self-discipline for the achievement of its aims. For our democracy implies the reign of reason on the most extensive scale. The Founders of this Nation were not imbued with the modern cynicism that the only thing that history teaches is that it teaches nothing. They acted on the conviction that the experience of man sheds a good deal of light on his nature. It sheds a good deal of light not merely on the need for effective power, if a society is to be at once cohesive and civilized, but also on the need for limitations on the power of governors over the governed.

To that end they rested the structure of our central government on the system of checks and balances. For them the doctrine of separation of powers was not mere theory; it was a felt necessity....

The question before the Court comes in this setting. Congress has frequently—at least 16 times since 1916—specifically provided for executive seizure of production, transportation, communications, or storage facilities. In every case it has qualified this grant of power with limitations and safeguards.... This body of enactments ... demonstrates that Congress deemed seizure so drastic a power as to require that it be carefully circumscribed whenever the President was vested with this extraordinary authority... Its exercise has been restricted to particular circumstances such as "time of war or when war is imminent," the needs of "public safety" or of "national security or defense," or "urgent and impending need.".…

... (N)othing can be plainer than that Congress made a conscious choice of policy in a field full of perplexity and peculiarly within legislative responsibility for choice. In formulating legislation for dealing with industrial conflicts, Congress could not more clearly and emphatically have withheld authority than it did in 1947. Perhaps as much so as is true of any piece of modern legislation, Congress acted with full consciousness of what it was doing and in the light of much recent history.... Instead of giving him even limited powers, Congress in 1947 deemed it wise to require the President, upon failure of attempts to reach a voluntary settlement, to report to Congress if he deemed the power of seizure a needed shot for his locker....

It is one thing to draw an intention of Congress from general language and to say that Congress would have explicitly written what is inferred, where Congress has not addressed itself to a specific situation. It is quite impossible, however, when Congress did specifically address itself to a problem, as Congress did to that of seizure, to find secreted in the interstices of legislation the very grant of power which Congress consciously withheld. To find authority so explicitly withheld is not merely to disregard in a particular instance the clear will of Congress. It is to disrespect the whole legislative process and the constitutional division of authority between President and Congress....

A scheme of government like ours no doubt at times feels the lack of power to act with complete, all-embracing, swiftly moving authority. No doubt a government with distributed authority, subject to be challenged in the courts of law, at least long enough to consider and adjudicate the challenge, labors under restrictions from which other governments are free. It has not been our tradition to envy such governments. In any event our government was designed to have such restrictions. The price was deemed not too high in view of the safeguards which these restrictions afford. I know no more impressive words on this subject than those of Mr. Justice Brandeis:

> The doctrine of the separation of powers was adopted by the Convention of 1787, not to promote efficiency but to preclude the exercise of arbitrary power. The purpose was, not to avoid friction, but, by means of the inevitable friction incident to the distribution of the governmental powers among three departments, to save the people from autocracy.

MR. JUSTICE DOUGLAS, concurring....

The great office of President is not a weak and powerless one.... The impact of the man and the philosophy he represents may at times be thwarted by the Congress. Stalemates may occur when emergencies mount and the Nation suffers for lack of harmonious, reciprocal action between the White House and Capitol Hill. That is a risk inherent in our system of separation of powers. The tragedy of such stalemates might be avoided by allowing the President the use of some legislative authority. The Framers with memories of the tyrannies produced by a blending of executive and legislative power rejected that political arrangement.... We could not sanction the seizures and condemnations of the steel plants in this case without

reading Article II as giving the President not only the power to execute the laws but to make some. Such a step would most assuredly alter the pattern of the Constitution.

We pay a price for our system of checks and balances, for the distribution of power among the three branches of government. It is a price that today may seem exorbitant to many. Today a kindly President uses the seizure power to effect a wage increase and to keep the steel furnaces in production. Yet tomorrow another President might use the same power to prevent a wage increase, to curb trade-unionists, to regiment labor as oppressively as industry thinks it has been regimented by this seizure.

MR. JUSTICE JACKSON, concurring in the judgment and opinion of the Court.

That comprehensive and undefined presidential powers hold both practical advantages and grave dangers for the country will impress anyone who has served as legal adviser to a President in time of transition and public anxiety. While an interval of detached reflection may temper teachings of that experience, they probably are a more realistic influence on my views than the conventional materials of judicial decision which seem unduly to accentuate doctrine and legal fiction. But as we approach the question of presidential power, we half overcome mental hazards by recognizing them....

The actual art of governing under our Constitution does not and cannot conform to judicial definitions of the power of any of its branches based on isolated clauses or even single Articles torn from context. While the Constitution diffuses power the better to secure liberty, it also contemplates that practice will integrate the dispersed powers into a workable government. It enjoins upon its branches separateness but interdependence, autonomy but reciprocity. Presidential powers are not fixed but fluctuate, depending upon their disjunction or conjunction with those of Congress....

Executive power has the advantage of concentration in a single head in whose choice the whole Nation has a part, making him the focus of public hopes and expectations. In drama, magnitude and finality his decisions so far overshadow any others that almost alone he fills the public eye and ear. No other personality in public life can begin to compete with him in access to the public mind through modern methods of communications. By his prestige as head of state and his influence upon public opinion he exerts a leverage upon those who are supposed to check and balance his power which often cancels their effectiveness....

I have no illusion that any decision by this Court can keep power in the hands of Congress if it is not wise and timely in meeting its problems. A crisis that challenges the President equally, or perhaps primarily, challenges Congress. If not good law, there was worldly wisdom in the maxim attributed to Napoleon that "The tools belong to the man who can use them." We may say that power to legislate for emergencies belongs in the hands of Congress, but only Congress itself can prevent power from slipping through its fingers.

The essence of our free Government is "leave to live by no man's leave, underneath the law" —to be governed by those impersonal forces which we call law. Our Government is fashioned to fulfill this concept so far as humanly possible. The Executive, except for recommendation and veto, has no legislative power. The executive action we have here originates in the individual will of the President and represents an exercise of authority without law.... With all its defects, delays and inconveniences, men have discovered no technique for long preserving free government except that the Executive be under the law, and that the law be made by parliamentary deliberations.

Such institutions may be destined to pass away. But it is the duty of the Court to be last, not first, to give them up.

MR. JUSTICE BURTON, concurring in both the opinion and judgment of the Court.

The foregoing circumstances distinguish this emergency from one in which Congress takes no action and outlines no governmental policy. In the case before us, Congress authorized a procedure which the President declined to follow. Instead, he followed another procedure which he hoped might eliminate the need for the first. Upon its failure, he issued an executive order to seize the steel properties in the face of the reserved right of Congress to adopt or reject that course as a matter of legislative policy....

The controlling fact here is that Congress, within its constitutionally delegated power, has prescribed for the President specific procedures, exclusive of seizure, for his use in meeting the present type of emergency. Congress has reserved to itself the right to determine where and when to authorize the seizure of property in meeting such an emergency. Under these circumstances, the President's order of April 8 invaded the jurisdiction of Congress. It violated the essence of the principle of the separation of governmental powers. Accordingly, the injunction against its effectiveness should be sustained....

MR. JUSTICE CLARK, concurring in the judgment of the Court....

The limits of presidential power are obscure. However, Article II, no less than Article I, is part of "a constitution intended to endure for ages to come, and, consequently, to be adapted to the various crises of human affairs." Some of our Presidents, such as Lincoln, "felt that measures otherwise unconstitutional might become lawful by becoming indispensable to the preservation of the Constitution through the preservation of the nation." Others, such as Theodore Roosevelt, thought the President to be capable, as a "steward" of the people, of exerting all power save that which is specifically prohibited by the Constitution or the Congress.... In describing this authority I care not whether one calls it "residual," "inherent," "moral," "implied," "aggregate," "emergency," or otherwise. I am of the conviction that those who have had the gratifying experience of being the President's lawyer have used one or more of these adjectives only with the utmost of sincerity and the highest of purpose.

I conclude that where Congress has laid down specific procedures to deal with the type of crisis confronting the President, he must follow those procedures in meeting the crisis; but that in the absence of such action by Congress, the President's independent power to act depends upon the gravity of the situation confronting the nation. I cannot sustain the seizure in question because...Congress had prescribed methods to be followed by the President in meeting the emergency at hand....

MR. CHIEF JUSTICE VINSON, with whom MR. JUSTICE REED and MR. JUSTICE MINTON join, dissenting.

Those who suggest that this is a case involving extraordinary powers should be mindful that these are extraordinary times. A world not yet recovered from the devastation of World War II has been forced to face the threat of another and more terrifying global conflict.

Accepting in full measure its responsibility in the world community, the United States was instrumental in securing adoption of the United Nations Charter, approved by the Senate by a vote of 89 to 2. The first purpose of the United Nations is to "maintain international peace and security, and to that end: to take effective collective measures for the prevention and removal of threats to the peace, and for the suppression of acts of aggression or other breaches of the peace,"... In 1950, when the United Nations called upon member nations "to render every assistance" to repel aggression in Korea, the United States furnished its vigorous support. For almost two full years, our armed forces have been fighting in Korea, suffering casualties of over 108,000 men. Hostilities have not abated. The "determination of the United Nations to continue its action in Korea to meet the aggression" has been reaffirmed. Congressional support of the action in Korea has been manifested by provisions for increased military manpower and equipment and for economic stabilization....

One is not here called upon even to consider the possibility of executive seizure of a farm, a corner grocery store or even a single industrial plant. Such considerations arise only when one ignores the central fact of this case—that the Nation's entire basic steel production would have shut down completely if there had been no Government seizure....

Accordingly, if the President has any power under the Constitution to meet a critical situation in the absence of express statutory authorization, there is no basis whatever for criticizing the exercise of such power in this case....

The President reported to Congress the morning after the seizure that he acted because a work stoppage in steel production would immediately imperil the safety of the Nation by preventing execution of the legislative programs for procurement of military equipment. And, while a shutdown could be averted by granting the price concessions requested by plaintiffs, granting such concessions would disrupt the price stabilization program also enacted by Congress. Rather than fail to execute either legislative program, the President acted to execute both....

Whatever the extent of Presidential power on more tranquil occasions, and whatever the right of the President to execute legislative programs as he sees fit without reporting the mode of execution to Congress, the single Presidential purpose disclosed on this record is to faithfully execute the laws by acting in an emergency to maintain the status quo, thereby preventing collapse of the legislative programs until Congress could act.... Consequently, there is no evidence whatever of any Presidential purpose to defy Congress or act in any way inconsistent with the legislative will....

The diversity of views expressed in the six opinions of the majority, the lack of reference to authoritative precedent, the repeated reliance upon prior dissenting opinions, the complete disregard of the uncontroverted facts showing the gravity of the emergency and the temporary nature of the taking all serve to demonstrate how far afield one must go to affirm the order of the District Court.

The broad executive power granted by Article II to an officer on duty 365 days a year cannot, it is said, be invoked to avert disaster. Instead, the President must confine himself to sending a message to Congress recommending action. Under this messenger-boy concept of the Office, the President cannot even act to preserve legislative programs from destruction so that Congress will have something left to act upon. There is no judicial finding that the executive action was unwarranted because there was in fact no basis for the President's finding of the existence of an emergency for, under this view, the gravity of the emergency and the immediacy of the threatened disaster are considered irrelevant as a matter of law.

Seizure of plaintiffs' property is not a pleasant undertaking. Similarly unpleasant to a free country are the draft which disrupts the home and military procurement which causes economic dislocation and compels adoption of price controls, wage stabilization and allocation of materials.... A sturdy judiciary should not be swayed by the unpleasantness or unpopularity of necessary executive action, but must independently determine for itself whether the President was acting, as required by the Constitution, to "take Care that the Laws be faithfully executed.."...

Faced with the duty of executing the defense programs which Congress had enacted and the disastrous effects that any stoppage in steel production would have on those programs, the President acted to preserve those programs by seizing the steel mills. There is no question that the possession was other than temporary in character and subject to congressional direction—either approving, disapproving or regulating the manner in which the mills were to be administered and returned to the owners. The President immediately informed Congress of his action and clearly stated his intention to abide by the legislative will. No basis for claims of arbitrary action, unlimited powers or dictatorial usurpation of congressional power appears from the facts of this case. On the contrary, judicial, legislative and executive precedents throughout our history demonstrate that in this case the President acted in full conformity with his duties under the Constitution. Accordingly, we would reverse the order of the District Court.

First Amendment

Schenck v. U. S. (1919)

The Schenk case deals with protesters who obstructed the draft during World War I and were prosecuted for violating the Espionage Act of 1917. Justice Holmes here delivers the famous exception to the free-speech clause of the First Amendment: "in such circumstances... as to create a clear and present danger."

MR. JUSTICE HOLMES delivered the opinion of the Court:

This is an indictment in three counts. The first charges a conspiracy to violate the Espionage Act of June 15, 1917, by causing and attempting to cause insubordination, in the military and naval forces of the United States, and to obstruct the recruiting and enlistment service of the United States, when the United States was at war with the German Empire, to-wit, that the defendants wilfully conspired to have printed and circulated to men who had been called and accepted for military service under the Act of May 18, 1917, a document set forth and alleged to be calculated to cause such insubordination and obstruction. The count alleges overt acts in pursuance of the conspiracy, ending in the distribution of the document set forth. The second count alleges a conspiracy to commit an offence against the United States, to-wit, to use the mails for the transmission of the above mentioned document. The third count charges an unlawful use of the mails for the transmission of the same matter and otherwise as above. The defendants were found guilty on all the counts. They set up the First Amendment to the Constitution forbidding Congress to make any law abridging the freedom of speech, or of the press, and bringing the case here on that ground have argued some other points also of which we must dispose.... The document in question upon its first printed side recited the first section of the Thirteenth Amendment, said that the idea embodied in it was violated by the Conscription Act and that a conscript is little better than a convict. In impassioned language it intimated that conscription was despotism in its worst form and a monstrous wrong against humanity in the interest of Wall Street's chosen few. It said "Do not submit to intimidation," but in form at least confined itself to peaceful measures such as a petition for the repeal of the act. The other and later printed side of the sheet was headed "Assert Your Rights." ... [I]t denied the power to send our citizens away to foreign shores to shoot up the people of other lands, and added that words could not express the condemnation such coldblooded ruthlessness deserves, &c., &c., winding up "You must do your share to maintain. support and uphold the rights of the people of this country." Of course the document would not have been sent unless it had been intended to have some effect, and we do not see what effect it could be expected to have upon persons subject to the draft except to influence them to obstruct the carrying of it out. The defendants do not deny that the jury might find against them on this point.

But it is said, suppose that that was the tendency of this circular, it is protected by the First Amendment to the Constitution.... We admit that in many places and in ordinary times the defendants in saying all that was said in the circular would have been within their constitutional rights. But the character of every act depends upon the circumstances in which it is done. The most stringent pro-tection of free speech would not protect a man in falsely shouting fire in a theatre and causing a panic. It does not even protect a man from an injunction against uttering words that may have all the effect of force. The question in every case is whether the words used are used in such circumstances and are of such a nature as to create clear and present danger that they will bring about the substantive evils that Congress has a right to prevent. It is a question of proximity and degree. When a nation is at war many things that might be said in time of peace are such a hindrance to its effort that their utterance will not be endured so long as men fight and that no Court could regard them as protected by any constitutional right. It seems to be admitted that if an actual obstruction of the recruiting service were proved, liability for words that produced that effect might he enforced. The statute of 1917 punishes conspiracies to obstruct as well as actual obstruction. If the act, (speaking, or circulating a paper), its tendency and the intent with which it is done are the same, we perceive no ground for saying that success alone warrants making the act a crime.

Judgments affirmed.

Texas v. Johnson (1989)

Does desecrating the flag of the United States constitute an exercise in free speech? Or is flag burning a clear intent to breach the peace? The court decided by the narrow majority of 5 to 4 in favor of the respondent Gregory Johnson.

JUSTICE BRENNAN delivered the opinion of the Court.

After publicly burning an American flag as a means of political protest, Gregory Lee Johnson was convicted of desecrating a flag in violation of Texas law. This case presents the question whether his conviction is consistent with the First Amendment. We hold that it is not.

While the Republican National Convention was taking place in Dallas in 1984, respondent Johnson participated in a political demonstration dubbed the "Republican War Chest Tour." As explained in literature distributed by the demonstrators and in speeches made by them, the purpose of this event was to protest the policies of the Reagan administration and of certain Dallas-based corporations. The demonstrators marched through the Dallas streets, chanting political slogans and stopping at several corporate locations to stage "die-ins" intended to dramatize the consequences of nuclear war. On several occasions they spray-painted the walls of buildings and overturned potted plants, but Johnson himself took no part in such activities. He did, however, accept an American flag handed to him by a fellow protestor who had taken it from a flagpole outside one of the targeted buildings.

The demonstration ended in front of Dallas City Hall, where Johnson unfurled the American flag, doused it with kerosene, and set it on fire. While the flag burned, the protestors chanted: "America, the red, white, and blue, we spit on you." After the demonstrators dispersed, a witness to the flag burning collected the flag's remains and buried them in his backyard. No one was physically injured or threatened with injury, though several witnesses testified that they had been seriously offended by the flag burning.

Of the approximately 100 demonstrators, Johnson alone was charged with a crime. The only criminal offense with which he was charged was the desecration of a venerated object in violation of Tex. Penal Code Ann. 42.09(a)(3) (1989). After a trial, he was convicted, sentenced to one year in prison, and fined $2,000....

Especially pertinent to this case are our decisions recognizing the communicative nature of conduct relating to flags. Attaching a peace sign to the flag, refusing to salute the flag, and displaying a red flag, we have held, all may find shelter under the First Amendment.... That we have had little difficulty identifying an expressive element in conduct relating to flags should not be surprising. The very purpose of a national flag is to serve as a symbol of our country; it is, one might say, "the one visible manifestation of two hundred years of nationhood."...

Texas claims that its interest in preventing breaches of the peace justifies Johnson's conviction for flag desecration. However, no disturbance of the peace actually occurred or threatened to occur because of Johnson's burning of the flag.

The State's position, therefore, amounts to a claim that an audience that takes serious offense at particular expression is necessarily likely to disturb the peace and that the expression may be prohibited on this basis. Our precedents do not countenance such a presumption. On the contrary, they recognize that a principal "function of free speech under our system of government is to invite dispute. It may indeed best serve its high purpose when it induces a condition of unrest, creates dissatisfaction with conditions as they are, or even stirs people to anger."...

We thus conclude that the State's interest in maintaining order is not implicated on these facts. The State need not worry that our holding will disable it from preserving the peace. We do not suggest that the First Amendment forbids a State to prevent "imminent lawless action." And, in fact, Texas already has a statute specifically prohibiting breaches of the peace, Tex. Penal Code Ann. 42.01 (1989), which tends to confirm that Texas need not punish this flag desecration in order to keep the peace.

It remains to consider whether the State's interest in preserving the flag as a symbol of nationhood and national unity justifies Johnson's conviction....

... Johnson's political expression was restricted because of the content of the message he conveyed. We must therefore subject the State's asserted interest in preserving the special symbolic character of the flag to "the most exacting scrutiny." Texas argues that its interest in preserving the flag as a symbol of nationhood and national unity survives this close analysis. Quoting extensively from the writings of this Court chronicling the flag's historic and symbolic role in our society, the State emphasizes the "special place" reserved for the flag in our Nation.... According to Texas, if one physically treats the flag in a way that would tend to cast doubt on either the idea that nationhood and national unity are the flag's referents or that national unity actually exists, the message conveyed thereby is a harmful one and therefore may be prohibited.

If there is a bedrock principle underlying the First Amendment, it is that the government may not prohibit the expression of an idea simply because society finds the idea itself offensive or disagreeable.

We have not recognized an exception to this principle even where our flag has been involved....

... If we were to hold that a State may forbid flag burning wherever it is likely to endanger the flag's symbolic role, but allow it wherever burning a flag promotes that role—as where, for example, a person ceremoniously burns a dirty flag—we would be saying that when it comes to impairing the flag's physical integrity, the flag itself may be used as a symbol—as a substitute for the written or spoken word or a "short cut from mind to mind"—only in one direction. We would be permitting a State to "prescribe what shall be orthodox" by saying that one may burn the flag to convey one's attitude toward it and its referents only if one does not endanger the flag's representation of nationhood and national unity.

We never before have held that the Government may ensure that a symbol be used to express only one view of that symbol or its referents.

... To conclude that the government may permit designated symbols to be used to communicate only a limited set of messages would be to enter territory having no discernible or defensible boundaries. Could the government, on this theory, prohibit the burning of state flags? Of copies of the Presidential seal? Of the Constitution? In evaluating these choices under the First Amendment, how would we decide which symbols were sufficiently special to warrant this unique status? To do so, we would be forced to consult our own political preferences, and impose them on the citizenry, in the very way that the First Amendment forbids us to do....

... The way to preserve the flag's special role is not to punish those who feel differently about these matters. It is to persuade them that they are wrong. "To courageous, self-reliant men, with confidence in the power of free and fearless reasoning applied through the processes of popular government, no danger flowing from speech can be deemed clear and present, unless the incidence of the evil apprehended is so imminent that it may befall before there is opportunity for full discussion. If there be time to expose through discussion the falsehood and fallacies, to avert the evil by the processes of education, the remedy to be applied is more speech, not enforced silence." And, precisely because it is our flag that is involved, one's response to the flag burner may exploit the uniquely persuasive power of the flag itself. We can imagine no more appropriate response to burning a flag than waving one's own, no better way to counter a flag burner's message than by saluting the flag that burns, no surer means of preserving the dignity even of the flag that burned than by—as one witness here did—according its remains a respectful burial. We do not consecrate the flag by punishing its desecration, for in doing so we dilute the freedom that this cherished emblem represents....

CHIEF JUSTICE REHNQUIST, with whom JUSTICE WHITE and JUSTICE O'CONNOR join, dissenting.

In holding this Texas statute unconstitutional, the Court ignores Justice Holmes' familiar aphorism that "a page of history is worth a volume of logic." For more than 200 years, the American flag has occupied a unique position as the symbol of our Nation, a uniqueness that justifies a governmental prohibition against flag burning in the way respondent Johnson did here.

The American flag, then, throughout more than 200 years of our history, has come to be the visible symbol embodying our Nation. It does not represent the views of any particular political party, and it does not represent any particular political philosophy. The flag is not simply another "idea" or "point of view" competing for recognition in the marketplace of ideas. Millions and millions of Americans regard it with an almost mystical reverence regardless of what sort of social, political, or philosophical beliefs they may have. I cannot agree that the First Amendment invalidates the Act of Congress, and the laws of 48 of the 50 States, which make criminal the public burning of the flag....

Here it may equally well be said that the public burning of the American flag by Johnson was no essential part of any exposition of ideas, and at the same time it had a tendency to incite a breach of the peace. Johnson was free to make any verbal denunciation of the flag that he wished; indeed, he was free to burn the flag in private. He could publicly burn other symbols of the Government or effigies of political leaders. He did lead a march through the streets of Dallas, and conducted a rally in front of the Dallas City Hall. He engaged in a "die-in" to protest nuclear weapons. He shouted out various slogans during the march, including: "Reagan, Mondale which will it be? Either one means World War III"; "Ronald Reagan, killer of the hour, Perfect example of U.S. power"; and "red, white and blue, we spit on you, you stand for plunder, you will go under." For none of these acts was he arrested or prosecuted; it was only when he proceeded to burn publicly an American flag stolen from its rightful owner that he violated the Texas statute.

... As with "fighting words," so with flag burning, for purposes of the First Amendment: It is "no essential part of any exposition of ideas, and [is] of such slight social value as a step to truth that any benefit that may be derived from [it] is clearly outweighed" by the public interest in avoiding a probable breach of the peace. The highest courts of several States have upheld state statutes prohibiting the public burning of the flag on the grounds that it is so inherently inflammatory that it may cause a breach of public order.... The Texas statute deprived Johnson of only one rather inarticulate symbolic form of protest— a form of protest that was profoundly offensive to many—and left him with a full panoply of other symbols and every conceivable form of verbal expression to express his deep disapproval of national policy. Thus, in no way can it be said that Texas is punishing him because his hearers—or any other group of people—were profoundly opposed to the message that he sought to convey. Such opposition is no proper basis for restricting speech or expression under the First Amendment. It was Johnson's use of this particular symbol, and not the idea that he sought to convey by it or by his many other expressions, for which he was punished....

Engel v. Vitale (1962)

Few decisions have been as contentious as the Court's holding that the once widespread practice of prayer in public schools (and, a year later, Bible reading, in Abington School District v. Schempp) *violates the establishment clause of the Constitution. Nevertheless, the Court decided it was so by 6 to 1.*

MR. JUSTICE BLACK delivered the opinion of the Court.

The respondent Board of Education of Union Free School District No. 9, New Hyde Park, New York, acting in its official capacity under state law, directed the School District's principal to cause the following prayer to be said aloud by each class in the presence of a teacher at the beginning of each school day:

> Almighty God, we acknowledge our dependence upon Thee, and we beg Thy blessings upon us, our parents, our teachers and our Country.

This daily procedure was adopted on the recommendation of the State Board of Regents, a governmental agency created by the State Constitution to which the New York Legislature has granted broad supervisory, executive, and legislative powers over the State's public school system. These state officials composed the prayer which they recommended and published as a part of their "Statement on Moral and Spiritual Training in the Schools," saying: "We believe that this Statement will be subscribed to by all men and women of good will, and we call upon all of them to aid in giving life to our program."

Shortly after the practice of reciting the Regents' prayer was adopted by the School District, the parents of ten pupils brought this action in a New York State Court insisting that use of this official prayer in the public schools was contrary to the beliefs, religions, or religious practices of both themselves and their children. Among other things, these parents challenged the constitutionality of both the state law authorizing the School District to direct the use of prayer in public schools and

the School District's regulation ordering the recitation of this particular prayer on the ground that these actions of official governmental agencies violate that part of the First Amendment of the Federal Constitution which commands that "Congress shall make no law respecting an establishment of religion"—a command which was "made applicable to the State of New York by the Fourteenth Amendment of the said Constitution." The New York Court of Appeals, over the dissents of Judges Dye and Fuld, sustained an order of the lower state courts which had upheld the power of New York to use the Regents' prayer as a part of the daily procedures of its public schools so long as the schools did not compel any pupil to join in the prayer over his or his parents' objection. We granted certiorari to review this important decision involving rights protected by the First and Fourteenth Amendments.

We think that by using its public school system to encourage recitation of the Regents' prayer, the State of New York has adopted a practice wholly inconsistent with the Establishment Clause. There can, of course, be no doubt that New York's program of daily classroom invocation of God's blessings as prescribed in the Regents' prayer is a religious activity. It is a solemn avowal of divine faith and supplication for the blessings of the Almighty. The nature of such a prayer has always been religious, none of the respondents has denied this and the trial court expressly so found....

The petitioners contend among other things that the state laws requiring or permitting use of the Regents' prayer must be struck down as a violation of the Establishment Clause because that prayer was composed by governmental officials as a part of a governmental program to further religious beliefs. For this reason, petitioners argue, the State's use of the Regents' prayer in its public school system breaches the constitutional wall of separation between Church and State. We agree with that contention since we think that the constitutional prohibition against laws respecting an establishment of religion must at least mean that in this country it is no part of the business of government to compose official prayers for any group of the American people to recite as a part of a religious program carried on by government....

There can be no doubt that New York's state prayer program officially establishes the religious beliefs embodied in the Regents' prayer. The respondents' argument to the contrary, which is largely based upon the contention that the Regents' prayer is "non-denominational" and the fact that the program, as modified and approved by state courts, does not require all pupils to recite the prayer but permits those who wish to do so to remain silent or be excused from the room, ignores the essential nature of the program's constitutional defects. Neither the fact that the prayer may be denominationally neutral nor the fact that its observance on the part of the students is voluntary can serve to free it from the limitations of the Establishment Clause, as it might from the Free Exercise Clause, of the First Amendment, both of which are operative against the States by virtue of the Fourteenth Amendment. Although these two clauses may in certain instances overlap, they forbid two quite different kinds of governmental encroachment upon religious freedom. The Establishment Clause, unlike the Free Exercise Clause, does not depend upon any showing of direct governmental compulsion and is violated by the enactment of laws which establish an official religion whether those laws operate directly to coerce nonobserving individuals or not. This is not to say, of course, that laws officially prescribing a particular form of religious worship do not involve coercion of such individuals. When the power, prestige and financial support of government

is placed behind a particular religious belief, the indirect coercive pressure upon religious minorities to conform to the prevailing officially approved religion is plain. But the purposes underlying the Establishment Clause go much further than that. Its first and most immediate purpose rested on the belief that a union of government and religion tends to destroy government and to degrade religion. The history of governmentally established religion, both in England and in this country, showed that whenever government had allied itself with one particular form of religion, the inevitable result had been that it had incurred the hatred, disrespect and even contempt of those who held contrary beliefs. That same history showed that many people had lost their respect for any religion that had relied upon the support of government to spread its faith. The Establishment Clause thus stands as an expression of principle on the part of the Founders of our Constitution that religion is too personal, too sacred, too holy, to permit its "unhallowed perversion" by a civil magistrate. Another purpose of the Establishment Clause rested upon an awareness of the historical fact that governmentally established religions and religious persecutions go hand in hand. The Founders knew that only a few years after the Book of Common Prayer became the only accepted form of religious services in the established Church of England, an Act of Uniformity was passed to compel all Englishmen to attend those services and to make it a criminal offense to conduct or attend religious gatherings of any other kind—a law which was consistently flouted by dissenting religious groups in England and which contributed to widespread persecutions of people like John Bunyan who persisted in holding "unlawful [religious] meetings ... to the great disturbance and distraction of the good subjects of this kingdom...." And they knew that similar persecutions had received the sanction of law in several of the colonies in this country soon after the establishment of official religions in those colonies. It was in large part to get completely away from this sort of systematic religious persecution that the Founders brought into being our Nation, our Constitution, and our Bill of Rights with its prohibition against any governmental establishment of religion. The New York laws officially prescribing the Regents' prayer are inconsistent both with the purposes of the Establishment Clause and with the Establishment Clause itself.

It has been argued that to apply the Constitution in such a way as to prohibit state laws respecting an establishment of religious services in public schools is to indicate a hostility toward religion or toward prayer. Nothing, of course, could be more wrong. The history of man is inseparable from the history of religion. And perhaps it is not too much to say that since the beginning of that history many people have devoutly believed that "More things are wrought by prayer than this world dreams of." It was doubtless largely due to men who believed this that there grew up a sentiment that caused men to leave the cross-currents of officially established state religions and religious persecution in Europe and come to this country filled with the hope that they could find a place in which they could pray when they pleased to the God of their faith in the language they chose. And there were men of this same faith in the power of prayer who led the fight for adoption of our Constitution and also for our Bill of Rights with the very guarantees of religious freedom that forbid the sort of governmental activity which New York has attempted here. These men knew that the First Amendment, which tried to put an end to governmental control of religion and of prayer, was not written to destroy either. They knew rather that it was written to quiet well-justified fears which nearly all of them felt arising out of an awareness that governments of the past had shackled men's tongues to make them speak only the religious thoughts that government wanted them to speak and to pray only to the God that government wanted them to pray to. It is neither sacrilegious nor antireligious to say that each separate government in this country should stay out of the business of writing or sanctioning official prayers and leave that purely religious function to the people themselves and to those the people choose to look to for religious guidance.

It is true that New York's establishment of its Regents' prayer as an officially approved religious doctrine of that State does not amount to a total establishment of one particular religious sect to the exclusion of all others—that, indeed, the governmental endorsement of that prayer seems relatively insignificant when compared to the governmental encroachments upon religion which were commonplace 200 years ago. To those who may subscribe to the view that because the Regents' official prayer is so brief and general there can be no danger to religious freedom in its governmental establishment, however, it may be appropriate to say in the words of James Madison, the author of the First Amendment:

> [I]t is proper to take alarm at the first experiment on our liberties. . . Who does not see that the same authority which can establish Christianity, in exclusion of all other Religions, may establish with the same ease any particular sect of Christians, in exclusion of all other Sects? That the same authority which can force a citizen to contribute three pence only of his property for the support of any one establishment, may force him to conform to any other establishment in all cases whatsoever?

The judgment of the Court of Appeals of New York is reversed and the cause remanded for further proceedings not inconsistent with this opinion.

Reversed and remanded.

MR. JUSTICE STEWART, dissenting.

A local school board in New York has provided that those pupils who wish to do so may join in a brief prayer at the beginning of each school day, acknowledging their dependence upon God and asking His blessing upon them and upon their parents, their teachers, and their country. The Court today decides that in permitting this brief nondenominational prayer the school board has violated the Constitution of the United States. I think this decision is wrong.

The Court does not hold, nor could it, that New York has interfered with the free exercise of anybody's religion. For the state courts have made clear that those who object to reciting the prayer must be entirely free of any compulsion to do so, including any "embarrassments and pressures." But the Court says that in permitting school children to say this simple prayer, the New York authorities have established "an official religion."

With all respect, I think the Court has misapplied a great constitutional principle. I cannot see how an "official religion" is established by letting those who want to say a prayer say it. On the contrary, I think that to deny the wish of these school children to join in reciting this prayer is to deny them the opportunity of sharing in the spiritual heritage of our Nation....

At the opening of each day's Session of this Court we stand, while one of our officials invokes the protection of God. Since the days of John Marshall our Crier has said, "God save the United States and this Honorable Court." Both the Senate and the House of Representatives open their daily Sessions with prayer. Each of our Presidents, from George Washington to John F. Kennedy, has upon assuming his Office asked the protection and help of God....

I do not believe that this Court, or the Congress, or the President has by the actions and practices I have mentioned established an "official religion" in violation of the Constitution. And I do not believe the State of New York has done so in this case. What each has done has been to recognize and to follow the deeply entrenched and highly cherished spiritual traditions of our Nation—traditions which come down to us from those who almost two hundred years ago avowed their "firm Reliance on the Protection of divine Providence" when they proclaimed the freedom and independence of this brave new world.

I dissent.

Lynch v. Donnelly (1984)

Lynch v. Donnelly is one of a number of cases that deal with the public accommodation of religion. Here, the Court decided by a narrow 5 to 4 vote that the public display of a Christmas creche does pass muster under the First Amendment.

CHIEF JUSTICE BURGER delivered the opinion of the Court.

We granted certiorari to decide whether the Establishment Clause of the First Amendment prohibits a municipality from including a creche, or Nativity scene, in its annual Christmas display.

I

Each year, in cooperation with the downtown retail merchants' association, the city of Pawtucket, R.I., erects a Christmas display as part of its observance of the Christmas holiday season. The display is situated in a park owned by a nonprofit organization and located in the heart of the shopping district. The display is essentially like those to be found in hundreds of towns or cities across the Nation—often on public grounds—during the Christmas season. The Pawtucket display comprises many of the figures and decorations traditionally associated with Christmas, including, among other things, a Santa Claus house, reindeer pulling Santa's sleigh, candy-striped poles, a Christmas tree, carolers, cutout figures representing such characters as a clown, an elephant, and a teddy bear, hundreds of colored lights, a large banner that reads "SEASONS GREETINGS," and the creche at issue here. All components of this display are owned by the city.

The creche, which has been included in the display for 40 or more years, consists of the traditional figures, including the Infant Jesus, Mary and Joseph, angels, shepherds, kings, and animals, all ranging in height from 5" to 5'. In 1973, when the present creche was acquired, it cost the city $1,365; it now is valued at $200. The erection and dismantling of the creche costs the city about $20 per year;

nominal expenses are incurred in lighting the creche. No money has been expended on its maintenance for the past 10 years. Respondents, Pawtucket residents and individual members of the Rhode Island affiliate of the American Civil Liberties Union, and the affiliate itself, brought this action in the United States District Court for Rhode Island, challenging the city's inclusion of the creche in the annual display. The District Court held that the city's inclusion of the creche in the display violates the Establishment Clause, which is binding on the states through the Fourteenth Amendment. The District Court found that, by including the creche in the Christmas display, the city has "tried to endorse and promulgate religious beliefs," and that "erection of the creche has the real and substantial effect of affiliating the City with the Christian beliefs that the creche represents." This "appearance of official sponsorship," it believed, "confers more than a remote and incidental benefit on Christianity." Last, although the court acknowledged the absence of administrative entanglement, it found that excessive entanglement has been fostered as a result of the political divisiveness of including the creche in the celebration. The city was permanently enjoined from including the creche in the display.

A divided panel of the Court of Appeals for the First Circuit affirmed. We granted certiorari, and we reverse.

II A

This Court has explained that the purpose of the Establishment and Free Exercise Clauses of the First Amendment is "to prevent, as far as possible, the intrusion of either [the church or the state] into the precincts of the other."

At the same time, however, the Court has recognized that "total separation is not possible in an absolute sense. Some relationship between government and religious organizations is inevitable." In every Establishment Clause case, we must reconcile the inescapable tension between the objective of preventing unnecessary intrusion of either the church or the state upon the other, and the reality that, as the Court has so often noted, total separation of the two is not possible.

The Court has sometimes described the Religion Clauses as erecting a "wall" between church and state. The concept of a "wall" of separation is a useful figure of speech probably deriving from views of Thomas Jefferson. The metaphor has served as a reminder that the Establishment Clause forbids an established church or anything approaching it. But the metaphor itself is not a wholly accurate description of the practical aspects of the relationship that in fact exists between church and state....

B

...Our history is replete with official references to the value and invocation of Divine guidance in deliberations and pronouncements of the Founding Fathers and contemporary leaders. Beginning in the early colonial period long before Independence, a day of Thanksgiving was celebrated as a religious holiday to give thanks for the bounties of Nature as gifts from God. President Washington and his successors proclaimed Thanksgiving, with all its religious overtones, a day of national celebration and Congress made it a National Holiday more than a century ago. That holiday has not lost its theme of expressing thanks for Divine aid any more than has Christmas lost its religious significance.

Executive Orders and other official announcements of Presidents and of the Congress have proclaimed both Christmas and Thanksgiving National Holidays in religious terms. And, by Acts of Congress, it has long been the practice that federal employees are released from duties on these National Holidays, while being paid from the same public revenues that provide the compensation of the Chaplains of the Senate and the House and the military services. Thus, it is clear that Government has long recognized—indeed it has subsidized—holidays with religious significance.

Other examples of reference to our religious heritage are found in the statutorily prescribed national motto "In God We Trust," 36 U.S.C. 186, which Congress and the President mandated for our currency, and in the language "One nation under God," as part of the Pledge of Allegiance to the American flag. That pledge is recited by many thousands of public school children—and adults—every year.

III

This history may help explain why the Court consistently has declined to take a rigid, absolutist view of the Establishment Clause. We have refused "to construe the Religion Clauses with a literalness that would undermine the ultimate constitutional objective as illuminated by history." In our modern, complex society, whose traditions and constitutional underpinnings rest on and encourage diversity and pluralism in all areas, an absolutist approach in applying the Establishment Clause is simplistic and has been uniformly rejected by the Court....

In each case, the inquiry calls for line-drawing; no fixed, per se rule can be framed. The Establishment Clause like the Due Process Clauses is not a precise, detailed provision in a legal code capable of ready application. The purpose of the Establishment Clause "was to state an objective, not to write a statute." The line between permissible relationships and those barred by the Clause can no more be straight and unwavering than due process can be defined in a single stroke or phrase or test. The Clause erects a "blurred, indistinct, and variable barrier depending on all the circumstances of a particular relationship."

In the line-drawing process we have often found it useful to inquire whether the challenged law or conduct has a secular purpose, whether its principal or primary effect is to advance or inhibit religion, and whether it creates an excessive entanglement of government with religion. But, we have repeatedly emphasized our unwillingness to be confined to any single test or criterion in this sensitive area....

The narrow question is whether there is a secular purpose for Pawtucket's display of the creche. The display is sponsored by the city to celebrate the Holiday and to depict the origins of that Holiday. These are legitimate secular purposes. The District Court's inference, drawn from the religious nature of the creche, that the city has no secular purpose was, on this record, clearly erroneous.

The District Court found that the primary effect of including the creche is to confer a substantial and impermissible benefit on religion in general and on the Christian faith in particular. Comparisons of the relative benefits to religion of different forms of governmental support are elusive and difficult to make. But to conclude that the primary effect of including the creche is to advance religion in violation of the Establishment Clause would require that we view it as more beneficial to and more an endorsement of religion, for example, than expenditure of large sums of public money for textbooks supplied throughout the country to students attending church-sponsored schools, expenditure of public funds for transportation of students to church-sponsored schools, federal grants for college buildings of church-sponsored institutions of higher education combining secular and religious education, noncategorical grants to church-sponsored colleges and universities,and the tax exemptions for church properties....

We are unable to discern a greater aid to religion deriving from inclusion of the creche than from these benefits and endorsements previously held not violative of the Establishment Clause.... Entanglement is a question of kind and degree. In this case, however, there is no reason to disturb the District Court's finding on the absence of administrative entanglement. There is no evidence of contact with church authorities concerning the content or design of the exhibit prior to or since Pawtucket's purchase of the creche. No expenditures for maintenance of the creche have been necessary; and since the city owns the creche, now valued at $200, the tangible material it contributes is *de minimis.* In many respects the display requires far less ongoing, day-to-day interaction between church and state than religious paintings in public galleries....

The Court of Appeals correctly observed that this Court has not held that political divisiveness alone can serve to invalidate otherwise permissible conduct. And we decline to so hold today. This case does not involve a direct subsidy to church-sponsored schools or colleges, or other religious institutions, and hence no inquiry into potential political divisiveness is even called for. In any event, apart from this litigation there is no evidence of political friction or divisiveness over the creche in the 40-year history of Pawtucket's Christmas celebration. The District Court stated that the inclusion of the creche for the 40 years has been "marked by no apparent dissension" and that the display has had a "calm history."...

We are satisfied that the city has a secular purpose for including the creche, that the city has not impermissibly advanced religion, and that including the creche does not create excessive entanglement between religion and government.

IV

JUSTICE BRENNAN describes the creche as a "re-creation of an event that lies at the heart of Christian faith." The creche, like a painting, is passive; admittedly it is a reminder of the origins of Christmas. Even the traditional, purely secular displays extant at Christmas, with or without a creche, would inevitably recall the religious nature of the Holiday. The display engenders a friendly community spirit of goodwill in keeping with the season. The creche may well have special meaning to those whose faith includes the celebration of religious Masses, but none who sense the origins of the Christmas celebration would fail to be aware of its religious implications. That the display brings people into the central city, and serves commercial interests and benefits merchants and their employees, does not, as the dissent points out, determine the character of the display. That a prayer invoking Divine guidance in Congress is preceded and followed by debate and partisan conflict over taxes, budgets, national defense, and myriad mundane subjects, for example, has never been thought to demean or taint the sacredness of the invocation.

Of course the creche is identified with one religious faith but no more so than the examples we have set out from prior cases in which we found no conflict with the Establishment. It would be ironic, however, if the inclusion of a single symbol of a particular historic religious event, as part of a celebration acknowledged in the Western World for 20 centuries, and in this country by the people, by the Executive Branch, by the Congress, and the courts for 2 centuries, would so "taint" the city's exhibit as to render it violative of the Establishment Clause. To forbid the use of this one passive symbol—the creche—at the very time people are taking note of the season with Christmas hymns and carols in public schools and other public places, and while the Congress and legislatures open sessions with prayers by paid chaplains, would be a stilted overreaction contrary to our history and to our holdings. If the presence of the creche in this display violates the Establishment Clause, a host of other forms of taking official note of Christmas, and of our religious heritage, are equally offensive to the Constitution.

JUSTICE BRENNAN, with whom JUSTICE MARSHALL, JUSTICE BLACKMUN, and JUSTICE STEVENS join, dissenting....

Under our constitutional scheme, the role of safeguarding our "religious heritage" and of promoting religious beliefs is reserved as the exclusive prerogative of our Nation's churches, religious institutions, and spiritual leaders. Because the Framers of the Establishment Clause understood that "religion is too personal, too sacred, too holy to permit its 'unhallowed perversion' by civil [authorities]," the Clause demands that government play no role in this effort. The Court today brushes aside these concerns by insisting that Pawtucket has done nothing more than include a "traditional" symbol of Christmas in its celebration of this national holiday, thereby muting the religious content of the creche. But the city's action should be recognized for what it is: a coercive, though perhaps small, step toward establishing the sectarian preferences of the majority at the expense of the minority, accomplished by placing public facilities and funds in support of the religious symbolism and theological tidings that the creche conveys. As Justice Frankfurter, writing in *McGowan v. Maryland*, observed, the Establishment Clause "withdr[aws] from the sphere of legitimate legislative concern and competence a specific, but comprehensive, area of human conduct: man's belief or disbelief in the verity of some transcendental idea and man's expression in action of that belief or disbelief." That the Constitution sets this realm of thought and feeling apart from the pressures and antagonisms of government is one of its supreme achievements. Regrettably, the Court today tarnishes that achievement.

I dissent.

Criminal Justice

Gideon v. Wainwright (1963)

Gideon is the celebrated right-to-counsel case. Note the discussion of the incorporation doctrine—the principle that the Fourteenth Amendment makes most of the Bill of Rights binding on state governments.

MR. JUSTICE BLACK delivered the opinion of the Court.

Petitioner was charged in a Florida state court with having broken and entered a poolroom with intent to commit a misdemeanor. This offense is a felony under Florida law. Appearing in court without funds and without a lawyer, petitioner asked the court to appoint counsel for him, whereupon the following colloquy took place:

The COURT: Mr. Gideon, I am sorry, but I cannot appoint Counsel to represent you in this case. Under the laws of the State of Florida, the only time the Court can appoint Counsel to represent a Defendant is when that person is charged with a capital offense. I am sorry, but I will have to deny your request to appoint Counsel to defend you in this case.

The DEFENDANT: The United States Supreme Court says I am entitled to be represented by Counsel.

Put to trial before a jury, Gideon conducted his defense about as well as could be expected from a layman. He made an opening statement to the jury, cross-examined the State's witnesses, presented witnesses in his own defense, declined to testify himself, and made a short argument "emphasizing his innocence to the charge contained in the Information filed in this case." The jury returned a verdict of guilty, and petitioner was sentenced to serve five years in the state prison. Later, petitioner filed in the Florida Supreme Court this habeas corpus petition attacking his conviction and sentence on the ground that the trial court's refusal to appoint counsel for him denied him rights "guaranteed by the Constitution and the Bill of Rights by the United States Government." Treating the petition for habeas corpus as properly before it, the State Supreme Court, "upon consideration thereof" but without an opinion, denied all relief. Since 1942, when *Betts v. Brady* was decided by a divided Court, the problem of a defendant's federal constitutional right to counsel in a state court has been a continuing source of controversy and litigation in both state and federal courts. To give this problem another review here, we granted certiorari. Since Gideon was proceeding *in forma pauperis*, we appointed counsel to represent him and requested both sides to discuss in their briefs and oral arguments the following: "Should this Court's holding in *Betts v. Brady* be reconsidered?"...

Treating due process as "a concept less rigid and more fluid than those envisaged in other specific and particular provisions of the Bill of Rights," the Court held that refusal to appoint counsel under the particular facts and circumstances in the *Betts* case was not so "offensive to the common and fundamental ideas of fairness" as to amount to a denial of due process. Since the facts and circumstances of the two cases are so nearly indistinguishable, we think the *Betts v. Brady* holding if left standing would require us to reject Gideon's claim that the Constitution guarantees him the assistance of counsel. Upon full reconsideration we conclude that *Betts v. Brady* should be overruled.

The Sixth Amendment provides, "In all criminal prosecutions, the accused shall enjoy the right ... to have the Assistance of Counsel for his defence." We have construed this to mean that in federal courts counsel must be provided for defendants unable to employ counsel unless the right is competently and intelligently waived. *Betts* argued that this right is extended to indigent defendants in state courts by the Fourteenth Amendment. In response the Court stated that, while the Sixth Amendment laid down "no rule for the conduct of the States, the question recurs whether the constraint laid by the Amendment upon the national courts expresses a rule so fundamental and essential to a fair trial, and so, to due process of law, that it is made obligatory upon the States by the Fourteenth Amendment."...

We think the Court in *Betts* had ample precedent for acknowledging that those guarantees of the Bill of Rights which are fundamental safeguards of liberty immune from federal abridgment are equally protected against state invasion by the Due Process Clause of the Fourteenth Amendment. This same principle was recognized, explained, and applied in *Powell v. Alabama*, a case upholding the right of counsel, where the Court held that... the Fourteenth Amendment "embraced" those "'fundamental principles of liberty and justice which lie at the base of all our civil and political institutions,'" even though they had been "specifically dealt with in another part of the federal Constitution." In many cases other than *Powell* and *Betts*, this Court has looked to the fundamental nature of original Bill of Rights guarantees to decide whether the Fourteenth Amendment makes them obligatory on the States. Explicitly recognized to be of this "fundamental nature" and therefore made immune from state invasion by the Fourteenth, or some part of it, are the First Amendment's freedoms of speech, press, religion, assembly, association, and petition for redress of grievances. For the same reason, though not always in precisely the same terminology, the Court has made obligatory on the States the Fifth Amendment's command that private property shall not be taken for public use without just compensation, the Fourth Amendment's prohibition of unreasonable searches and seizures, and the Eighth's ban on cruel and unusual punishment. On the other hand, this Court in *Palko v. Connecticut* refused to hold that the Fourteenth Amendment made the double jeopardy provision of the Fifth Amendment obligatory on the States. In so refusing, however, the Court, speaking through Mr. Justice Cardozo, was careful to emphasize that "immunities that are valid as against the federal government by force of the specific pledges of particular amendments have been found to be implicit in the concept of ordered liberty, and thus, through the Fourteenth Amendment, become valid as against the states" and that guarantees "in their origin ... effective against the federal government alone" had by prior cases "been taken over from the earlier articles of the federal bill of rights and brought within the Fourteenth Amendment by a process of absorption."

We accept *Betts v. Brady*'s assumption, based as it was on our prior cases, that a provision of the Bill of Rights which is "fundamental and essential to a fair trial" is made obligatory upon the States by the Fourteenth Amendment. We think the Court in *Betts* was wrong, however, in concluding that the Sixth Amendment's guarantee of counsel is not one of these fundamental rights. Ten years before *Betts v. Brady*, this Court, after full consideration of all the historical data examined in *Betts*, had unequivocally declared that "the right to the aid of counsel is of this fundamental character."

... The fact is that in deciding as it did— that "appointment of counsel is not a fundamental right, essential to a fair trial" —the Court in *Betts v. Brady* made an abrupt break with its own well-considered precedents. In returning to these old precedents, sounder we believe than the new, we but restore constitutional principles established to achieve a fair system of justice. Not only these precedents but also reason and reflection require us to recognize that in our adversary system of criminal justice, any person haled into court, who is too poor to hire a lawyer, cannot be assured a fair trial unless counsel is provided for him. This seems to us to be an obvious truth. Governments, both state and federal, quite properly spend vast sums of money to establish machinery to try defendants accused of crime. Lawyers to prosecute are everywhere deemed essential to protect the public's interest in an orderly society. Similarly, there are few defendants charged with crime, few indeed, who fail to hire the best lawyers they can get to prepare and present their defenses. That government hires lawyers to prosecute and defendants who have the money hire lawyers to defend are the strongest indications of the widespread belief that lawyers in criminal courts are necessities, not luxuries. The right of one charged with crime to counsel may not be deemed fundamental and essential to fair trials in some countries, but it is in ours. From the very beginning, our state and national constitutions and laws have laid great emphasis on procedural and substantive safeguards designed to assure fair trials before impartial tribunals in which every defendant stands equal before the law. This noble ideal cannot be realized if the poor man charged with crime has to face his accusers without a lawyer to assist him....

Miranda v. Arizona (1966)

In a highly contentious 5 to 4 decision, the Court decided that the Fifth Amendment's guarantee against self-incrimination applies even to the "custodial interrogation of the accused." The Court's majority required police at all levels to inform those in custody of their right to remain silent and their right to have a lawyer present prior to any questioning. The decision seems not to have impeded local law enforcement, and indeed, some have argued that Miranda v. Arizona *hastened the professionalisation of local police forces. Although more conservative Courts have trimmed away some of the original holdings of the case, the basic policy still stands.*

MR. CHIEF JUSTICE WARREN delivered the opinion of the Court.

The cases before us raise questions which go to the roots of our concepts of American criminal jurisprudence: the restraints society must observe consistent with the Federal Constitution in prosecuting individuals for crime. More specifically, we deal with the admissibility of statements obtained from an individual who is subjected to custodial police interrogation and the necessity for procedures which assure that the individual is accorded his privilege under the Fifth Amendment to the Constitution not to be compelled to incriminate himself.

We dealt with certain phases of this problem recently in *Escobedo v. Illinois*.... There, as in the four cases before us, law enforcement officials took the defendant into custody and interrogated him in a police station for the purpose of obtaining a confession. The police did not effectively advise him of his right to remain silent or of his right to consult with his attorney. Rather, they confronted him with an alleged accomplice who accused him of having perpetrated a murder. When the defendant denied the accusation and said "I didn't shoot Manuel, you did it," they handcuffed him and took him to an interrogation room. There, while handcuffed and standing, he was questioned for four hours until he confessed. During this interrogation, the police denied his request to speak to his attorney, and they prevented his retained attorney, who had come to the police station, from consulting with him. At his

trial, the State, over his objection, introduced the confession against him. We held that the statements thus made were constitutionally inadmissible....

We start here, as we did in *Escobedo*, with the premise that our holding is not an innovation in our jurisprudence, but is an application of principles long recognized and applied in other settings. We have undertaken a thorough re-examination of the Escobedo decision and the principles it announced, and we reaffirm it. That case was but an explication of basic rights that are enshrined in our Constitution—that "No person ... shall be compelled in any criminal case to be a witness against himself," and that "the accused shall ... have the Assistance of Counsel"—rights which were put in jeopardy in that case through official overbearing. These precious rights were fixed in our Constitution only after centuries of persecution and struggle. And in the words of Chief Justice Marshall, they were secured "for ages to come, and... designed to approach immortality as nearly as human institutions can approach it."...

Our holding will be spelled out with some specificity in the pages which follow but briefly stated it is this: the prosecution may not use statements, whether exculpatory or inculpatory, stemming from custodial interrogation of the defendant unless it demonstrates the use of procedural safeguards effective to secure the privilege against self-incrimination. By custodial interrogation, we mean questioning initiated by law enforcement officers after a person has been taken into custody or otherwise deprived of his freedom of action in any significant way. As for the procedural safeguards to be employed, unless other fully effective means are devised to inform accused persons of their right of silence and to assure a continuous opportunity to exercise it, the following measures are required. Prior to any questioning, the person must be warned that he has a right to remain silent, that any statement he does make may be used as evidence against him, and that he has a right to the presence of an attorney, either retained or appointed. The defendant may waive effectuation of these rights, provided the waiver is made voluntarily, knowingly and intelligently. If, however, he indicates in any manner and at any stage of the process that he wishes to consult with an attorney before speaking there can be no questioning. Likewise, if the individual is alone and indicates in any manner that he does not wish to be interrogated, the police may not question him. The mere fact that he may have answered some questions or volunteered some statements on his own does not deprive him of the right to refrain from answering any further inquiries until he has consulted with an attorney and thereafter consents to be questioned....

The question in these cases is whether the privilege is fully applicable during a period of custodial interrogation. In this Court, the privilege has consistently been accorded a liberal construction. We are satisfied that all the principles embodied in the privilege apply to informal compulsion exerted by law-enforcement officers during in-custody questioning. An individual swept from familiar surroundings into police custody, surrounded by antagonistic forces, and subjected to the techniques of persuasion described above cannot be otherwise than under compulsion to speak. As a practical matter, the compulsion to speak in the isolated setting of the police station may well be greater than in courts or other official investigations, where there are often impartial observers to guard against intimidation or trickery....

Today... there can be no doubt that the Fifth Amendment privilege is available outside of criminal court proceedings and serves to protect persons in all settings in which their freedom of action is curtailed in any significant way from being compelled to incriminate themselves. We have concluded that without proper safeguards the process of in-custody interrogation of persons suspected or accused of crime contains inherently compelling pressures which work to undermine the individual's will to resist and to compel him to speak where he would not otherwise do so freely. In order to combat these pressures and to permit a full opportunity to exercise the privilege against self-incrimination, the accused must be adequately and effectively apprised of his rights and the exercise of those rights must be fully honored....

... [W]e are not unmindful of the burdens which law enforcement officials must bear, often under trying circumstances. We also fully recognize the obligation of all citizens to aid in enforcing the criminal laws. This Court, while protecting individual rights, has always given ample latitude to law enforcement agencies in the legitimate exercise of their duties. The limits we have placed on the interrogation process should not constitute an undue interference with a proper system of law enforcement. As we have noted, our decision does not in any way preclude police from carrying out their traditional investigatory functions. Although confessions may play an important role in some convictions, the cases before us present graphic examples of the overstatement of the "need" for confessions. In each case authorities conducted interrogations ranging up to five days in duration despite the presence, through standard investigating practices, of considerable evidence against each defendant....

Over the years the Federal Bureau of Investigation has compiled an exemplary record of effective law enforcement while advising any suspect or arrested person, at the outset of an interview, that he is not required to make a statement, that any statement may be used against him in court, that the individual may obtain the services of an attorney of his own choice and, more recently, that he has a right to free counsel if he is unable to pay....

The practice of the FBI can readily be emulated by state and local enforcement agencies. The argument that the FBI deals with different crimes than are dealt with by state authorities does not mitigate the significance of the FBI experience....

... In any event, however, the issues presented are of constitutional dimensions and must be determined by the courts. The admissibility of a statement in the face of a claim that it was obtained in violation of the defendant's constitutional rights is an issue the resolution of which has long since been undertaken by this Court. Judicial solutions to problems of constitutional dimension have evolved decade by decade. As courts have been presented with the need to enforce constitutional rights, they have found means of doing so. That was our responsibility when *Escobedo* was before us and it is our responsibility today. Where rights secured by the Constitution are involved, there can be no rule making or legislation which would abrogate them.

Mr. Justice White, with whom Mr. Justice Harlan and Mr. Justice Stewart join, dissenting.

The proposition that the privilege against self-incrimination forbids in-custody interrogation without the warnings specified in the majority opinion and without a clear waiver of counsel has no significant support in the history of the privilege or in the language of the Fifth Amendment....

Only a tiny minority of our judges who have dealt with the question, including today's majority, have considered in-custody interrogation, without more, to be a violation of the Fifth Amendment. And this Court, as every member knows, has left standing literally thousands of criminal convictions that rested at least in part on confessions taken in the course of interrogation by the police after arrest.

That the Court's holding today is neither compelled nor even strongly suggested by the language of the Fifth Amendment, is at odds with American and English legal history, and involves a departure from a long line of precedent does not prove either that the Court has exceeded its powers or that the Court is wrong or unwise in its present reinterpretation of the Fifth Amendment. It does, however, underscore the obvious—that the Court has not discovered or found the law in making today's decision, nor has it derived it from some irrefutable sources; what it has done is to make new law and new public policy in much the same way that it has in the course of interpreting other great clauses of the Constitution....

The obvious underpinning of the Court's decision is a deep-seated distrust of all confessions. As the Court declares that the accused may not be interrogated without counsel present, absent a waiver of the right to counsel, and as the Court all but admonishes the lawyer to advise the accused to remain silent, the result adds up to a judicial judgment that evidence from the accused should not be used against him in any way, whether compelled or not. This is the not so subtle overtone of the opinion—that it is inherently wrong for the police to gather evidence from the accused himself. And this is precisely the nub of this dissent. I see nothing wrong or immoral, and certainly nothing unconstitutional, in the police's asking a suspect whom they have reasonable cause to arrest whether or not he killed his wife or in confronting him with the evidence on which the arrest was based, at least where he has been plainly advised that he may remain completely silent. Until today, "the admissions or confessions of the prisoner, when voluntarily and freely made, have always ranked high in the scale of incriminating evidence." Particularly when corroborated, as where the police have confirmed the accused's disclosure of the hiding place of implements or fruits of the crime, such confessions have the highest reliability and significantly contribute to the certitude with which we may believe the accused is guilty. Moreover, it is by no means certain that the process of confessing is injurious to the accused. To the contrary it may provide psychological relief and enhance the prospects for rehabilitation....

The most basic function of any government is to provide for the security of the individual and of his property. These ends of society are served by the criminal laws which for the most part are aimed at the prevention of crime. Without the reasonably effective performance of the task of preventing private violence and retaliation, it is idle to talk about human dignity and civilized values....

The rule announced today will measurably weaken the ability of the criminal law to perform these tasks. It is a deliberate calculus to prevent interrogations, to reduce the incidence of confessions and pleas of guilty and to increase the number of trials. Criminal trials, no matter how efficient the police are, are not sure bets for the prosecution, nor should they be if the evidence is not forthcoming. Under the present law, the prosecution fails to prove its case in about 30% of the criminal cases actually tried in the federal courts. But it is something else again to remove from the ordinary criminal case all those confessions which heretofore have been held to be free and voluntary acts of the accused and to thus establish a new constitutional barrier to the ascertainment of truth by the judicial process. There is, in my view, every reason to believe that a good many criminal defendants who otherwise would have been convicted on what this Court has previously thought to be the most satisfactory kind of evidence will now, under this new version of the Fifth Amendment, either not be tried at all or will be acquitted if the State's evidence, minus the confession, is put to the test of litigation.

I have no desire whatsoever to share the responsibility for any such impact on the present criminal process. In some unknown number of cases the Court's rule will return a killer, a rapist or other criminal to the streets and to the environment which produced him, to repeat his crime whenever it pleases him. As a consequence, there will not be a gain, but a loss, in human dignity....

Furman v. Georgia (1972)

Beginning in 1967 the nation had observed an informal moratorium on capitol punishment, awaiting the Court's decision of whether the death penalty constituted "cruel and unusual punishment" under the Eighth Amendment. In the two controlling opinions here, Justices Stewart and White struck down the death penalty on procedural grounds. The decision had a galvanizing effect on public opinion, for in short order the legislatures of several states reinstituted the penalty. Only four years later, in Gregg v. Georgia *the Court ruled that given adequate procedural safeguards, the death penalty is permissible under the Eighth Amendment.*

MR. JUSTICE STEWART concurring.

The penalty of death differs from all other forms of criminal punishment, not in degree but in kind. It is unique in its total irrevocability. It is unique in its rejection of rehabilitation of the convict as a basic purpose of criminal justice. And it is unique, finally, in its absolute renunciation of all that is embodied in our concept of humanity....

... I cannot agree that retribution is a constitutionally impermissible ingredient in the imposition of punishment. The instinct for retribution is part of the nature of man, and channeling that instinct in the administration of criminal justice serves an important purpose in promoting the stability of a society governed by law....

... [T]he death sentences now before us are the product of a legal system that brings them, I believe, within the very core of the Eighth Amendment's guarantee against cruel and unusual punishments, a guarantee applicable against the States through the Fourteenth Amendment....In the first place, it is clear that these sentences are "cruel" in the sense that they excessively go beyond, not in degree but in kind, the punishments that the state legislatures have determined to be necessary.... In the second place, it is equally clear that these sentences are "unusual" in the sense that the penalty of death is infrequently imposed for murder, and that its imposition for rape is extraordinarily rare. But I do not rest my conclusion upon these two propositions alone. These death sentences are cruel and unusual in the same way that being struck by lightning is cruel and unusual. For, of all the people convicted of rapes and murders in 1967 and 1968, many just as reprehensible as these, the petitioners are among a capriciously selected random handful upon whom the sentence of death has in fact been imposed. My concurring Brothers have demonstrated that, if any basis can be discerned for the selection of these few to be sentenced to die, it is the constitutionally impermissible basis of race....But racial discrimination has not been proved, and I put it to one side. I simply conclude that the Eighth and Fourteenth Amendments cannot tolerate the infliction of a sentence of death under legal systems that permit this unique penalty to be so wantonly and so freakishly imposed.

For these reasons I concur in the judgments of the Court.

MR. JUSTICE WHITE concurring.

... I do not at all intimate that the death penalty is unconstitutional *per se* or that there is no system of capital punishment that would comport with the Eighth Amendment. That question, ably argued by several of my Brethren, is not presented by these cases and need not be decided.

The narrower question to which I address myself concerns the constitutionality of capital punishment statutes under which (1) the legislature authorizes the imposition of the death penalty for murder or rape; (2) the legislature does not itself mandate the penalty in any particular class or kind of case (that is, legislative will is not frustrated if the penalty is never imposed) but delegates to judges or juries the decisions as to those cases, if any, in which the penalty will be utilized; and (3) judges and juries have ordered the death penalty with such infrequency that the odds are now very much against imposition and execution of the penalty with respect to any convicted murderer or rapist. It is in this context that we must consider whether the execution of these petitioners violates the Eighth Amendment.

I begin with what I consider a near truism: that the death penalty could so seldom be imposed that it would cease to be a credible deterrent or measurable to contribute to any other end of punishment in the criminal justice system. It is perhaps true that no matter how infrequently those convicted of rape or murder are executed, the penalty so imposed is not disproportionate to the crime and those executed may deserve exactly what they received. It would also be clear that executed defendants are finally and completely incapacitated from again committing rape or murder or any other crime. But when imposition of the penalty reaches a certain degree of infrequency, it would be very doubtful that any existing general need for retribution would be measurably satisfied. Nor could it be said with confidence that society's need for specific deterrence justifies death for so few when for so many in like circumstances life

imprisonment or shorter prison terms are indeed sufficient, or that community values are measurably reinforced by authorizing a penalty so rarely invoked.

Most important, a major goal of the criminal law—to deter others by punishing the convicted criminal—would not be substantially served where the penalty is so seldom invoked that it ceases to be the credible threat essential to influence the conduct of others. For present purposes I accept the morality and utility of punishing one person to influence another. I accept also the effectiveness of punishment generally and need not reject the death penalty as a more effective deterrent than a lesser punishment. But common sense and experience tell us that seldom-enforced laws become ineffective measures for controlling human conduct and that the death penalty, unless imposed with sufficient frequency, will make little contribution to deterring those crimes for which is may be exacted.

...The short of it is that the policy of vesting sentencing authority primarily in juries—a decision largely motivated by the desire to mitigate the harshness of the law and to bring community judgment to bear on the sentence as well as guilt or innocence—has so effectively achieved its aims that capital punishment within the confines of the statues now before us has for all practical purposes run its course.

Civil Rights

Brown v. Board of Education (1954)

To many, the Court's finest accomplishment was the decision that overturned its own ruling in Plessy v. Ferguson *(1896) and a long legacy of racial segregation. The Chief Justice spoke for a unanimous Court.*

MR. CHIEF JUSTICE WARREN delivered the opinion of the Court....

In each of the cases, minors of the Negro race, through their legal representatives, seek the aid of the courts in obtaining admission to the public schools of their community on a nonsegregated basis. In each instance, they had been denied admission to schools attended by white children under laws requiring or permitting segregation according to race. This segregation was alleged to deprive the plaintiffs of the equal protection of the laws under the Fourteenth Amendment. In each of the cases other than the Delaware case, a three-judge federal district court denied relief to the plaintiffs on the so-called "separate but equal" doctrine announced by this Court in *Plessy* v. *Ferguson.* Under that doctrine, equality of treatment is accorded when the races are provided substantially equal facilities, even though these facilities be separate. In the Delaware case, the Supreme Court of Delaware adhered

to that doctrine, but ordered that the plaintiffs be admitted to the white schools because of their superiority to the Negro schools.

The plaintiffs contend that segregated public schools are not "equal" and cannot be made "equal," and that hence they are deprived of the equal protection of the laws. Because of the obvious importance of the question presented, the Court took jurisdiction. Argument was heard in the 1952 Term, and reargument was heard this Term on certain questions propounded by the Court.

Reargument was largely devoted to the circumstances surrounding the adoption of the Fourteenth Amendment in 1868. It covered exhaustively consideration of the Amendment in Congress, ratification by the states, then existing practices in racial segregation, and the views of proponents and opponents of the Amendment. This discussion and our own investigation convince us that, although these sources cast some light, it is not enough to resolve the problem with which we are faced. At best, they are inconclusive. The most avid proponents of the post-War Amendments undoubtedly intended them to remove all legal distinctions among "all persons born or naturalized in the United States." Their opponents, just as certainly, were antagonistic to both the letter and the spirit of the Amendments and wished them to have the most limited effect. What others in Congress and the state legislatures had in mind cannot be determined with any degree of certainty.

An additional reason for the inconclusive nature of the Amendment's history, with respect to segregated schools, is the status of public education at that time. In the South, the movement toward free common schools, supported by general taxation, had not yet taken hold. Education of white children was largely in the hands of private groups. Education of Negroes was almost nonexistent, and practically all of the race were illiterate. In fact, any education of Negroes was forbidden by law in some states. Today, in contrast, many Negroes have achieved outstanding success in the arts and sciences as well as in the business and professional world. It is true that public school education at the time of the Amendment had advanced further in the North, but the effect of the Amendment on Northern States was generally ignored in the congressional debates. Even in the North, the conditions of public education did not approximate those existing today. The curriculum was usually rudimentary; ungraded schools were common in rural areas; the school term was but three months a year in many states; and compulsory school attendance was virtually unknown. As a consequence, it is not surprising that there should be so little in the history of the Fourteenth Amendment relating to its intended effect on public education.

In the first cases in this Court construing the Fourteenth Amendment, decided shortly after its adoption, the Court interpreted it as proscribing all state-imposed discriminations against the Negro race. The doctrine of "separate but equal" did not make its appearance in this Court until 1896 in the case of *Plessy v. Ferguson* ... the Court expressly reserved decision on the question whether *Plessy v. Ferguson* should be held inapplicable to public education.

In the instant cases, that question is directly presented. Here, unlike *Sweatt v. Painter*, there are findings below that the Negro and white schools involved have been equalized, or are being equalized, with respect to buildings, curricula, qualifications and salaries of teachers, and other "tangible" factors. Our decision, therefore, cannot turn on merely a comparison of these tangible factors in the Negro and white schools involved in each of the cases. We must look instead to the effect of segregation itself on public education....

Today, education is perhaps the most important function of state and local governments. Compulsory school attendance laws and the great expenditures for education both demonstrate our recognition of the importance of education to our democratic society. It is required in the performance of our most basic public responsibilities, even service in the armed forces. It is the very foundation of good citizenship. Today it is a principal instrument in awakening the child to cultural values, in preparing him for later professional training, and in helping him to adjust normally to his environment. In these days, it is doubtful that any child may reasonably be expected to succeed in life if he is denied the opportunity of an education. Such an opportunity, where the state has undertaken to provide it, is a right which must be made available to all on equal terms.

We come then to the question presented: Does segregation of children in public schools solely on the basis of race, even though the physical facilities and other "tangible" factors may be equal, deprive the children of the minority group of equal educational opportunities? We believe that it does.

In *Sweatt v. Painter* ... in finding that a segregated law school for Negroes could not provide them equal educational opportunities, this Court relied in large part on "those qualities which are incapable of objective measurement but which make for greatness in a law school." In *McLaurin v. Oklahoma State Regents* ... the Court, in requiring that a Negro admitted to a white graduate school be treated like all other students, again resorted to intangible considerations: "... his ability to study, to engage in discussions and exchange views with other students, and, in general, to learn his profession." Such considerations apply with added force to children in grade and high schools. To separate them from others of similar age and qualifications solely because of their race generates a feeling of inferiority as to their status in the community that may affect their hearts and minds in a way unlikely ever to be undone. The effect of this separation on their educational opportunities was well stated by a finding in the Kansas case by a court which nevertheless felt compelled to rule against the Negro plaintiffs:

> Segregation of white and colored children in public schools has a detrimental effect upon the colored children. The impact is greater when it has the sanction of the law; for the policy of separating the races is usually interpreted as denoting the inferiority of the negro group. A sense of inferiority affects the motivation of a child to learn. Segregation with the sanction of law, therefore, has a tendency to [retard] the educational and mental development of negro children and to deprive them of some of the benefits they would receive in a racial[ly] integrated school system.

Whatever may have been the extent of psychological knowledge at the time of *Plessy v. Ferguson*, this finding is amply supported by modern authority. Any language in *Plessy v. Ferguson* contrary to this finding is rejected.

We conclude that in the field of public education the doctrine of "separate but equal" has no place. Separate educational facilities are inherently unequal. Therefore, we hold that the plaintiffs and others similarly situated for whom the actions have been brought are, by reason of the segregation complained of, deprived of the equal protection of the laws guaranteed by the Fourteenth Amendment. This disposition makes unnecessary any discussion whether such segregation also violates the Due Process Clause of the Fourteenth Amendment....

Craig v. Boren (1976)

The statute at issue is one from Oklahoma that allowed eighteen-year-old women to be served 3.2 percent beer but prohibited such sales to men under twenty-one. By 7 to 2 the Court struck down this sex-based classification and set the standard for sex discrimination cases. For these cases, the Court eschewed both the argument of "compelling state interest" (see Brown*) and the "rational basis" test. Instead, the Court offered an "intermediate-scrutiny standard," asking whether sex classifications (1) serve an important governmental objective and (2) are substantially related to that objective.*

MR. JUSTICE BRENNAN delivered the opinion of the Court....

Analysis may appropriately begin with the reminder that *Reed* emphasized that statutory classifications that distinguish between males and females are "subject to scrutiny under the Equal Protection Clause." To withstand constitutional challenge, previous cases establish that classifications by gender must serve important governmental objectives and must be substantially related to achievement of those objectives. Thus, in *Reed*, the objectives of "reducing the workload on probate courts," and "avoiding intrafamily controversy," were deemed of insufficient importance to sustain use of an overt gender criterion in the appointment of administrators of intestate decedents' estates. Decisions following *Reed* similarly have rejected administrative ease and convenience as sufficiently important objectives to justify gender-based classifications....

We accept for purposes of discussion the District Court's identification of the objective underlying 241 and 245 as the enhancement of traffic safety. Clearly, the protection of public health and safety represents an important function of state and local governments. However, appellees' statistics in our view cannot support the conclusion that the gender-based distinction closely serves to achieve that objective and therefore the distinction cannot under *Reed* withstand equal protection challenge. The appellees introduced a variety of statistical surveys. First, an analysis of arrest statistics for 1973 demonstrated that 18-20-year-old male arrests for "driving under the influence" and "drunkenness" substantially exceeded female arrests for that same age pe-

riod. Similarly, youths aged 17-21 were found to be overrepresented among those killed or injured in traffic accidents, with males again numerically exceeding females in this regard. Third, a random roadside survey in Oklahoma City revealed that young males were more inclined to drive and drink beer than were their female counterparts. Fourth, Federal Bureau of Investigation nationwide statistics exhibited a notable increase in arrests for "driving under the influence." Finally, statistical evidence gathered in other jurisdictions, particularly Minnesota and Michigan, was offered to corroborate Oklahoma's experience by indicating the pervasiveness of youthful participation in motor vehicle accidents following the imbibing of alcohol.... The most focused and relevant of the statistical surveys, arrests of 18-20-year-olds for alcohol-related driving offenses, exemplifies the ultimate unpersuasiveness of this evidentiary record. Viewed in terms of the correlation between sex and the actual activity that Oklahoma seeks to regulate—driving while under the influence of alcohol—the statistics broadly establish that 18% of females and 2% of males in that age group were arrested for that offense. While such a disparity is not trivial in a statistical sense, it hardly can form the basis for employment of a gender line as a classifying device....

Certainly if maleness is to serve as a proxy for drinking and driving, a correlation of 2% must be considered an unduly tenuous "fit." Indeed, prior cases have consistently rejected the use of sex as a decisionmaking factor even though the statutes in question certainly rested on far more predictive empirical relationships than this.

There is no reason to belabor this line of analysis. It is unrealistic to expect either members of the judiciary or state officials to be well versed in the rigors of experimental or statistical technique. But this merely illustrates that proving broad sociological propositions by statistics is a dubious business, and one that inevitably is in tension with the normative philosophy that underlies the Equal Protection Clause. Suffice to say that the showing offered by the appellees does not satisfy us that sex represents a legitimate, accurate proxy for the regulation of drinking and driving. In fact, when it is further recognized that Oklahoma's statute prohibits only the selling of 3.2% beer to young males and not their drinking the beverage once acquired (even after purchase by their 18-20-year-old female companions), the relationship between gender and traffic safety becomes far too tenuous to satisfy *Reed's* requirement that the gender-based difference be substantially related to achievement of the statutory objective.

We hold, therefore, that under *Reed*, Oklahoma's 3.2% beer statute invidiously discriminates against males 18-20 years of age.

Justice Rehnquist dissented.

The Court's disposition of this case is objectionable on two grounds. First is its conclusion that men challenging a gender-based statute which treats them less favorably than women may invoke a more stringent standard of judicial review than pertains to most other types of classifications. Second is the Court's enunciation of this standard, without citation to any source, as being that "classifications by gender must serve important governmental objectives and must be substantially related to achievement of those objectives." The only redeeming feature of the Court's opinion, to my mind, is that it apparently signals a retreat by those who joined the plurality opinion in *Frontiero v. Richardson,* from their view that sex is a "suspect" classification for purposes of equal protection analysis. I think the Oklahoma statute challenged here need pass only the "rational basis" equal protection analysis... and I believe that it is constitutional under that analysis.

In *Frontiero v. Richardson* the opinion for the plurality sets forth the reasons of four Justices for concluding that sex should be regarded as a suspect classification for purposes of equal protection analysis. These reasons center on our Nation's "long and unfortunate history of sex discrimination," which has been reflected in a whole range of restrictions on the legal rights of women, not the least of which have concerned the ownership of property and participation in the electoral process....

... However, the Court's application here of an elevated or "intermediate" level scrutiny, like that invoked in cases dealing with discrimination against females, raises the question of why the statute here should be treated any differently from countless legislative classifications unrelated to sex which have been upheld under a minimum rationality standard....

The Court's conclusion that a law which treats males less favorably than females "must serve important governmental objectives and must be substantially related to achievement of those objectives" apparently comes out of thin air. The Equal Protection Clause contains no such language, and none of our previous cases adopt that standard. I would think we have had enough difficulty with the two standards of review which our cases have recognized—the norm of "rational basis," and the "compelling state interest" required where a "suspect classification" is involved—so as to counsel weightily against the insertion of still another "standard" between those two....

Regents of the University of California v. Bakke (1978)

The University of California Davis Medical School set aside a certain number of seats for members of minority groups. Thus, Alan Bakke was denied admission even though his qualifications were better than those of some of the students who were admitted. Being a newly opened medical school, there were no issues of past discrimination to muddy the waters at Davis. The question was whether Davis could institute a special admissions program to promote diversity at the school, as well as in the profession, and thus to address societal discrimination. Four justices (the Stevens group—opinion omitted) argued that the "color blind" thrust of Brown v. Board of Education *implied that all racial classifications should be struck down. Four others (the Brennan group—opinion omitted) argued that such classifications address a long legacy of racism and are "benign." Meanwhile, by writing only for himself and agreeing in part with each of the two groups, Justice Powell anchored two 5 to 4 majorities. The effect of the Court's decision was to admit Bakke to the medical school and to disallow the quota system, but also to hold that race can be considered as one criterion for admissions. Subsequent cases have gone in both directions, often turning on fine distinctions.*

MR. JUSTICE POWELL announced the judgment of the Court.

This case presents a challenge to the special admissions program of the petitioner, the Medical School of the University of California at Davis, which is designed to assure the admission of a specified number of students from certain minority groups....

... The special admissions program is undeniably a classification based on race and ethnic background. To the extent that there existed a pool of at least minimally qualified minority applicants to fill the 16 special admissions seats, white applicants could compete only for 84 seats in the entering class, rather than the 100 open to minority applicants. Whether this limitation is described as a quota or a goal, it is a line drawn on the basis of race and ethnic status.

The guarantees of the Fourteenth Amendment extend to all persons. Its language is explicit: "No State shall ... deny to any person within its jurisdiction the equal protection of the laws." It is settled beyond question that the "rights created by the first section of the Fourteenth Amendment are, by its terms, guaranteed to the individual. The rights established are personal rights." The guarantee of equal protection cannot mean one thing when applied to one individual and something else when applied to a person of another color. If both are not accorded the same protection, then it is not equal.

Nevertheless, petitioner argues that the court below erred in applying strict scrutiny to the special admissions program because white males, such as respondent, are not a "discrete and insular minority" requiring extraordinary protection from the majoritarian political process. This rationale, however, has never been invoked in our decisions as a prerequisite to subjecting racial or ethnic distinctions to strict scrutiny. Nor has this Court held that discreteness and insularity constitute necessary preconditions to a holding that a particular classification is invidious. These characteristics may be relevant in deciding whether or not to add new types of classifications to the list of "suspect" categories or whether a particular classification survives close examination....

Over the past 30 years, this Court has embarked upon the crucial mission of interpreting the Equal Protection Clause with the view of assuring to all persons "the protection of equal laws," in a Nation confronting a legacy of slavery and racial discrimination. Because the landmark decisions in this area arose in response to the continued exclusion of Negroes from the mainstream of American society, they could be characterized as involving discrimination by the "majority" white race against the Negro minority....

Petitioner urges us to adopt for the first time a more restrictive view of the Equal Protection Clause and hold that discrimination against members of the white "majority" cannot be suspect if its purpose can be characterized as "benign." The clock of our liberties, however, cannot be turned back to 1868. It is far too late to argue that the guarantee of equal protection to all persons permits the recognition of special wards entitled to a degree of protection greater than that accorded others. "The Fourteenth Amendment is not directed solely against discrimination due to a 'two-class theory'—that is, based upon differences between 'white' and Negro."...

Moreover, there are serious problems of justice connected with the idea of preference itself. First, it may not always be clear that a so-called preference is in fact benign.

Courts may be asked to validate burdens imposed upon individual members of a particular group in order to advance the group's general interest.... Second, preferential programs may only reinforce common stereotypes holding that certain groups are unable to achieve success without special protection based on a factor having no relationship to individual worth. Third, there is a measure of inequity in forcing innocent persons in respondent's position to bear the burdens of redressing grievances not of their making. By hitching the meaning of the Equal Protection Clause to these transitory considerations, we would be holding, as a constitutional principle, that judicial scrutiny of classifications touching on racial and ethnic background may vary with the ebb and flow of political forces. Disparate constitutional tolerance of such classifications well may serve to exacerbate racial and ethnic antagonisms rather than alleviate them.... In expounding the Constitution, the Court's role is to discern "principles sufficiently absolute to give them roots throughout the community and continuity over significant periods of time, and to

lift them above the level of the pragmatic political judgments of a particular time and place.".…

A

If petitioner's purpose is to assure within its student body some specified percentage of a particular group merely because of its race or ethnic origin, such a preferential purpose must be rejected not as insubstantial but as facially invalid. Preferring members of any one group for no reason other than race or ethnic origin is discrimination for its own sake. This the Constitution forbids.

B

The State certainly has a legitimate and substantial interest in ameliorating, or eliminating where feasible, the disabling effects of identified discrimination.... [But] the purpose of helping certain groups whom the faculty of the Davis Medical School perceived as victims of "societal discrimination" does not justify a classification that imposes disadvantages upon persons like respondent, who bear no responsibility for whatever harm the beneficiaries of the special admissions program are thought to have suffered. To hold otherwise would be to convert a remedy heretofore reserved for violations of legal rights into a privilege that all institutions throughout the Nation could grant at their pleasure to whatever groups are perceived as victims of societal discrimination. That is a step we have never approved.

C

Petitioner identifies, as another purpose of its program, improving the delivery of health-care services to communities currently underserved. It may be assumed that in some situations a State's interest in facilitating the health care of its citizens is sufficiently compelling to support the use of a suspect classification. But there is virtually no evidence in the record indicating that petitioner's special admissions program is either needed or geared to promote that goal....

D

The fourth goal asserted by petitioner is the attainment of a diverse student body. This clearly is a constitutionally permissible goal for an institution of higher education. Academic freedom, though not a specifically enumerated constitutional right, long has been viewed as a special concern of the First Amendment. The freedom of a university to make its own judgments as to education includes the selection of its student body....

As the interest of diversity is compelling in the context of a university's admissions program, the question remains whether the program's racial classification is necessary to promote this interest.

It may be assumed that the reservation of a specified number of seats in each class for individuals from the preferred ethnic groups would contribute to the attainment of considerable ethnic diversity in the student body. But petitioner's argument that this is the only effective means of serving the interest of diversity is seriously flawed.... Petitioner's special admissions program, focused solely on ethnic diversity, would hinder rather than further attainment of genuine diversity....

The experience of other university admissions programs, which take race into account in achieving the educational diversity valued by the First Amendment, demonstrates that the assignment of a fixed number of places to a minority group is not a necessary means toward that end....

In summary, it is evident that the Davis special admissions program involves the use of an explicit racial classification never before countenanced by this Court. It tells applicants who are not Negro, Asian, or Chicano that they are totally excluded from a specific percentage of the seats in an entering class. No matter how strong their qualifications, quantitative and extracurricular, including their own potential for contribution to educational diversity, they are never afforded the chance to compete with applicants from the preferred groups for the special admissions seats. At the same time, the preferred applicants have the opportunity to compete for every seat in the class.

The fatal flaw in petitioner's preferential program is its disregard of individual rights as guaranteed by the Fourteenth Amendment. Such rights are not absolute. But when a State's distribution of benefits or imposition of burdens hinges on ancestry or the color of a person's skin, that individual is entitled to a demonstration that the challenged classification is necessary to promote a substantial state interest. Petitioner has failed to carry this burden. For this reason, that portion of the California court's judgment holding petitioner's special admissions program invalid under the Fourteenth Amendment must be affirmed.

In enjoining petitioner from ever considering the race of any applicant, however, the courts below failed to recognize that the State has a substantial interest that legitimately may be served by a properly devised admissions program involving the competitive consideration of race and ethnic origin. For this reason, so much of the California court's judgment as enjoins petitioner from any consideration of the race of any applicant must be reversed....

Privacy

Griswold v. Connecticut (1965)

This case is presented with two purposes. First, it is important as the case that first found a constitutional right to privacy, which has since been used to undergird the right to have an abortion. Second, it is also offered as a teaching tool. Whereas Douglas's opinion garnered the necessary five votes, four separate opinions show different approaches to invalidating the Connecticut law, which had banned the use or suggesting the use of birth-control devices. Meanwhile, in separate dissenting opinions, Justices Black and Stewart refused to find this unenumerated right to privacy.

MR. JUSTICE DOUGLAS delivered the opinion of the Court.

Appellant Griswold is Executive Director of the Planned Parenthood League of Connecticut. Appellant Buxton is a licensed physician and a professor at the Yale Medical School who served as Medical Director for the League at its Center in New Haven—a center open ... when the appellants were arrested.

They gave information, instruction, and medical advice to married persons as to the means of preventing conception. They examined the wife and prescribed the best contraceptive device or material for her use. Fees were usually charged, although some couples were serviced free.

The statutes whose constitutionality is involved in this appeal are 53-32 and 54-196 of the General Statutes for Connecticut. The former provides:

> Any person who uses any drug, medicinal article or instrument for the purpose of preventing conception shall be fined not less than fifty dollars or imprisoned not less than sixty days nor more than one year or be both fined and imprisoned.

Section 54-196 provides:

> Any person who assists, abets counsels, causes, hires or commands another to commit any offense may be prosecuted and punished as if he were the principal offender.

465

The appellants were found guilty as accessories and fined $100 dollars each, against the claim that the accessory statute as so applied violated the Fourteenth Amendment. The Appellate Division of the Circuit Court affirmed. The Supreme Court of Errors affirmed that judgment....

Coming to the merits, we are met with a wide range of questions that implicate the Due Process Clause of the Fourteenth Amendment. Overtones of some arguments suggest that *Lochner v. New York* should be our guide.

But we decline that invitation.... We do not sit as a super-legislature to determine the wisdom, need, and propriety of laws that touch economic problems, business affairs, or social conditions. This law, however, operates directly on an intimate relation of husband and wife and their physician's role in one aspect of that relation.

The association of people is not mentioned in the Constitution nor in the Bill of Rights. The right to educate a child in a school of the parents' choice—whether public or private or parochial—is also not mentioned. Nor is the right to study any particular subject or any foreign language. Yet the First Amendment has been construed to include certain of those rights.

... Those cases involve more than the "right of assembly"—a right that extends to all irrespective of their race or ideology.... The right of "association," like the right of belief, is more than the right to attend a meeting; it includes the right to express one's attitudes or philosophies by membership in a group or by affiliation with it or by other lawful means. Association in that context is a form of expression of opinion; and while it is not expressly included in the First Amendment its existence is necessary in making the express guarantees fully meaningful.

...[Those] cases suggest that specific guarantees in the Bill of Rights have penumbras, formed by emanations from those guarantees that help give them life and substance.... Various guarantees create zones of privacy. The right of association contained in the penumbra of the First Amendment is one, as we have seen. The Third Amendment in its prohibition against the quartering of soldiers "in any house" in time of peace without the consent of the owner is another facet of that privacy. The Fourth Amendment explicitly affirms the "right of the people to be secure in their persons, houses, papers, and effects, against unreasonable searches and seizures." The Fifth Amendment in its Self-Incrimination Clause enables the citizen to create a zone of privacy which government may not force him to surrender to his detriment. The Ninth Amendment provides: "The enumeration in the Constitution, of certain rights, shall not be construed to deny or disparage others retained by the people." ...

We have had many controversies over these penumbral rights of "privacy and repose." These cases bear witness that the right of privacy which presses for recognition here is a legitimate one.

The present case, then, concerns a relationship lying within the zone of privacy created by several fundamental constitutional guarantees. And it concerns a law which, in forbidding the *use* of contraceptives rather than regulating their manufacture or sale, seeks to achieve its goals by means having a maximum destructive impact upon that relationship. Such a law cannot stand in light of the familiar principle, so often applied by this Court, that a "governmental purpose to control or prevent activities constitutionally subject to state regulation may not be achieved by means which sweep unnecessarily broadly and thereby invade the area of protected freedoms." ... Would we allow the police to search the sacred precincts of marital bedrooms for telltale signs of the use of contraceptives? The very idea is repulsive to the notions of privacy surrounding the marriage relationship.

We deal with a right of privacy older than the Bill of Rights—older than our political parties, older than our school system. Marriage is a coming together for better or for worse, hopefully enduring, and intimate to the degree of being sacred. It is an association that promotes a way of life, not causes; a harmony in living, not political faiths; a bilateral loyalty, not commercial or social projects. Yet it is an association for as noble a purpose as any involved in our prior decisions.

Reversed.

JUSTICE GOLDBERG, whom CHIEF JUSTICE WARREN and JUSTICE BRENNAN joined, concurred.

I agree with the Court that Connecticut's birth-control law unconstitutionally intrudes upon the right of marital privacy, and I join in its opinion and judgment....

While this Court has had little occasion to interpret the Ninth Amendment, "[i]t cannot be presumed that any clause in the constitution is intended to be without effect." ... In interpreting the Constitution, "real effect should be given to all the words it uses."... The Ninth Amendment to the Constitution may be regarded by some as a recent discovery and may be forgotten by others, but since 1791 it has been a basic part of the Constitution which we are sworn to uphold. To hold that a right so basic and fundamental and so deep-rooted in our society as the right of privacy in marriage may be infringed because that right is not guaranteed in so many words by the first eight amendments to the Constitution is to ignore the Ninth Amendment and to give it no effect whatsoever. Moreover, a judicial construction that this fundamental right is not protected by the Constitution because it is not mentioned in explicit terms by one of the first eight amendments or elsewhere in the Constitution would violate the Ninth Amendment, which specifically states that "[t]he enumeration in the Constitution, of certain rights, shall not be *construed* to deny or disparage others retained by the people." (Emphasis added.)

... The entire fabric of the Constitution and the purposes that clearly underlie its specific guarantees demonstrate that the rights to marital privacy and to marry and raise a family are of similar order and magnitude as the fundamental rights specifically protected.

Although the Constitution does not speak in so many words of the right of privacy in marriage, I cannot believe that it offers these fundamental rights no protection. The fact that no particular provision of the Constitution explicitly forbids the State from disrupting the traditional relation of the family—a relation as old and as fundamental as our entire civilization—surely does not show that the Government was meant to have the power to do so. Rather, as the Ninth Amendment expressly recognises, there are fundamental personal rights such as this one, which are protected from abridgement by the Government though not specifically mentioned in the Constitution....

In sum, I believe that the right of privacy in the marital relation is fundamental and basic—a personal right "retained by the people," within the meaning of the Ninth Amendment. Connecticut cannot constitutionally abridge this fundamental right, which is protected by the Fourteenth Amendment from infringement by the States. I agree with the Court that petitioners' convictions must therefore be reversed.

JUSTICE HARLAN concurring in the judgment.

I fully agree with the judgment of reversal, but find myself unable to join the Court's opinion. The reason is that it seems to me to evince an approach to this case very much like that taken by my Brothers Black and Stewart in dissent, namely: the Due Process Clause of the Fourteenth Amendment does not touch this Connecticut statute unless the enactment is found to violate some right assured by the letter or penumbra of the Bill of Rights.

In other words, what I find implicit in the Court's opinion is that the "incorporation" doctrine may be used to *restrict* the reach of Fourteenth Amendment Due Process. For me this is just as unacceptable constitutional doctrine as is the use of the "incorporation" approach to *impose* upon the States all the requirements of the Bill of Rights as found in the provisions of the first eight amendments and in the decisions of this Court interpreting them....

In my view, the proper constitutional inquiry in this case is whether this Connecticut statute infringes the Due Process Clause of the Fourteenth Amendment because the enactment violates basic values "implicit in the concept of ordered liberty." ... For reasons stated at length in my dissenting opinion in *Poe v. Ullman,* ... I believe that it does. While the relevant inquiry may be aided by resort to one or more of the provisions of the Bill of Rights, it is not dependent on them or any of their radiations. The Due Process Clause of the Fourteenth Amendment stands, in my opinion, on its own bottom.

JUSTICE STEWART, with whom JUSTICE BLACK joined, dissented.

Since 1897 Connecticut has had on its book a law which forbids the use of contraceptives by anyone. I think this is an uncommonly silly law. As a practical matter, the law is obviously unenforceable, except in the oblique context of the present case. As a philosophical matter, I believe the use of contraceptives in the relationship of marriage should be left to personal and private choice, based upon each individual's moral, ethical , and religious beliefs. As a matter of social policy, I think professional counsel about methods of birth control should be available to all, so that each individual's choice can be meaningfully made. But we are not asked in this case to say whether we think this law is unwise, or even asinine. We are asked to hold that it violates the United States Constitution. And that I cannot do.

Roe v. Wade (1973)

Roe v. Wade, the famous abortion rights decision, is still very much under contention.

MR. JUSTICE BLACKMUN delivered the opinion of the Court....

Jane Roe, a single woman who was residing in Dallas County, Texas, instituted this federal action in March 1970 against the District Attorney of the county. She sought a declaratory judgment that the Texas criminal abortion statutes were unconstitutional on their face, and an injunction restraining the defendant from enforcing the statutes.

Roe alleged that she was unmarried and pregnant; that she wished to terminate her pregnancy by an abortion "performed by a competent, licensed physician, under safe clinical conditions"; that she was unable to get a "legal" abortion in Texas because her life did not appear to be threatened by the continuation of her pregnancy; and that she could not afford to travel to another jurisdiction in order to secure a legal abortion under safe conditions. She claimed that the Texas statutes were unconstitutionally vague and that they abridged her right of personal privacy, protected by the First, Fourth, Fifth, Ninth, and Fourteenth Amendments. By an amendment to her complaint Roe purported to sue "on behalf of herself and all other women" similarly situated....

The principal thrust of appellant's attack on the Texas statutes is that they improperly invade a right, said to be possessed by the pregnant woman, to choose to terminate her pregnancy. Appellant would discover this right in the concept of personal "liberty" embodied in the Fourteenth Amendment's Due Process Clause; or in personal, marital, familial, and sexual privacy said to be protected by the Bill of Rights or its penumbras, or among those rights reserved to the people by the Ninth Amendment....

This right of privacy, whether it be founded in the Fourteenth Amendment's concept of personal liberty and restrictions upon state action, as we feel it is, or, as the District Court determined, in the Ninth Amendment's reservation of rights to the people, is broad enough to encompass a woman's decision whether or not to terminate her pregnancy. The detriment that the State would impose upon the pregnant woman by denying this choice altogether is apparent....

... Where certain "fundamental rights" are involved, the Court has held that regulation limiting these rights may be justified only by a "compelling state interest," and that legislative enactments must be narrowly drawn to express only the legitimate state interests at stake.

The appellee and certain amici argue that the fetus is a "person" within the language and meaning of the Fourteenth Amendment. In support of this, they outline at length and in detail the well-known facts of fetal development. If this suggestion of personhood is established, the appellant's case, of course, collapses, for the fetus' right to life would then be guaranteed specifically by the Amendment. The appellant conceded as much on reargument. On the other hand, the appellee conceded on reargument that no case could be cited that holds that a fetus is a person within the meaning of the Fourteenth Amendment.

The Constitution does not define "person" in so many words. Section 1 of the Fourteenth Amendment contains three references to "person." The first, in defining "citizens," speaks of "persons born or naturalized in the United States."...

But in nearly all these instances, the use of the word is such that it has application only postnatally. None indicates, with any assurance, that it has any possible pre-natal application. All this, together with our observation, supra, that throughout the major portion of the 19th century prevailing legal abortion practices were far freer than they are today, persuades us that the word "person," as used in the Fourteenth Amendment, does not include the unborn.

The pregnant woman cannot be isolated in her privacy. She carries an embryo and, later, a fetus, if one accepts the medical definitions of the developing young in the human uterus. The situation therefore is inherently different from marital intimacy, or bedroom possession of obscene material, or marriage, or procreation, or education.... As we have intimated above, it is reasonable and appropriate for a State to decide that at some point in time another interest, that of health of the mother or that of potential human life, becomes significantly involved. The woman's privacy is no longer sole and any right of privacy she possesses must be measured accordingly.

Texas urges that, apart from the Fourteenth Amendment, life begins at conception and is present throughout pregnancy, and that, therefore, the State has a compelling interest in protecting that life from and after conception. We need not resolve the difficult question of when life begins. When those trained in the respective disciplines of medicine, philosophy, and theology are unable to arrive at any consensus, the judiciary, at this point in the development of man's knowledge, is not in a position to speculate as to the answer.

In view of all this, we do not agree that, by adopting one theory of life, Texas may override the rights of the pregnant woman that are at stake. We repeat, however, that the State does have an important and legitimate interest in preserving and protecting the health of the pregnant woman, whether she be a resident of the State or a nonresident who seeks medical consultation and treatment there, and that it has still another important and legitimate interest in protecting the potentiality of human life. These interests are separate and distinct. Each grows in substantiality as the woman approaches term and, at a point during pregnancy, each becomes "compelling."

With respect to the State's important and legitimate interest in the health of the mother, the "compelling" point, in the light of present medical knowledge, is at approximately the end of the first trimester. This is so because of the now-established medical fact, referred to above at 149, that until the end of the first trimester mortality in abortion may be less than mortality in normal childbirth. It follows that, from and after this point, a State may regulate the abortion procedure to the extent that the regulation reasonably relates to the preservation and protection of maternal health. Examples of permissible state regulation in this area are requirements as to the qualifications of the person who is to perform the abortion; as to the licensure of that person; as to the facility in which the procedure is to be performed, that is, whether it must be a hospital or may be a clinic or some other place of less-than-hospital status; as to the licensing of the facility; and the like.

This means, on the other hand, that, for the period of pregnancy prior to this "compelling" point, the attending physician, in consultation with his patient, is free to determine, without regulation by the State, that, in his medical judgment, the patient's pregnancy should be terminated. If that decision is reached, the judgment may be effectuated by an abortion free of interference by the State.

With respect to the State's important and legitimate interest in potential life, the "compelling" point is at viability. This is so because the fetus then presumably has the capability of meaningful life outside the mother's womb. State regulation protective of fetal life after viability thus has both logical and biological justifications. If the State is interested in protecting fetal life after viability, it may go so far as to proscribe abortion during that period, except when it is necessary to preserve the life or health of the mother....

To summarize and to repeat:

1. A state criminal abortion statute of the current Texas type, that excepts from criminality only a life-saving procedure on behalf of the mother, without regard to pregnancy stage and without recognition of the other interests involved, is violative of the Due Process Clause of the Fourteenth Amendment.

(a) For the stage prior to approximately the end of the first trimester, the abortion decision and its effectuation must be left to the medical judgment of the pregnant woman's attending physician.

(b) For the stage subsequent to approximately the end of the first trimester, the State, in promoting its interest in the health of the mother, may, if it chooses, regulate the abortion procedure in ways that are reasonably related to maternal health.

(c) For the stage subsequent to viability, the State in promoting its interest in the potentiality of human life may, if it chooses, regulate, and even proscribe, abortion except where it is necessary, in appropriate medical judgment, for the preservation of the life or health of the mother.

This holding, we feel, is consistent with the relative weights of the respective interests involved, with the lessons and examples of medical and legal history,with the lenity of the common law, and with the demands of the profound problems of the present day. The decision leaves the State free to place increasing restrictions on abortion as the period of pregnancy lengthens, so long as those restrictions are tailored to the recognized state interests. The decision vindicates the right of the physician to administer medical treatment according to his professional judgment up to the points where important state interests provide compelling justifications for intervention. Up to those points, the abortion decision in all its aspects is inherently, and primarily, a medical decision, and

basic responsibility for it must rest with the physician....

MR. JUSTICE REHNQUIST, dissenting.

... While the Court's opinion quotes from the dissent of Mr. Justice Holmes in *Lochner v. New York*, the result it reaches is more closely attuned to the majority opinion of Mr. Justice Peckham in that case. As in *Lochner* and similar cases applying substantive due process standards to economic and social welfare legislation, the adoption of the compelling state interest standard will inevitably require this Court to examine the legislative policies and pass on the wisdom of these policies in the very process of deciding whether a particular state interest put forward may or may not be "compelling." The decision here to break pregnancy into three distinct terms and to outline the permissible restrictions the State may impose in each one, for example, partakes more of judicial legislation than it does of a determination of the intent of the drafters of the Fourteenth Amendment.

The fact that a majority of the States reflecting, after all, the majority sentiment in those States, have had restrictions on abortions for at least a century is a strong indication, it seems to me, that the asserted right to an abortion is not "so rooted in the traditions and conscience of our people as to be ranked as fundamental." Even today, when society's views on abortion are changing, the very existence of the debate is evidence that the "right" to an abortion is not so universally accepted as the appellant would have us believe....

Boy Scouts of America et al. v. Dale (2000)

The Court held by 5 to 4 that the New Jersey Supreme Court decision prohibiting the Boy Scouts from dismissing a gay scoutmaster violated the associational rights of the organization.

MR. CHIEF JUSTICE REHNQUIST delivered the opinion of the Court.

Petitioners are the Boy Scouts of America and the Monmouth Council, a division of the Boy Scouts of America (collectively, Boy Scouts). The Boy Scouts is a private, not-for-profit organization engaged in instilling its system of values in young people. The Boy Scouts asserts that homosexual conduct is inconsistent with the values it seeks to instill. Respondent is James Dale, a former Eagle Scout whose adult membership in the Boy Scouts was revoked when the Boy Scouts learned that he is an avowed homosexual and gay rights activist. The New Jersey Supreme Court held that New Jersey's public accommodations law requires that the Boy Scouts admit Dale. This case presents the question whether applying New Jersey's public accommodations law in this way violates the Boy Scouts' First Amendment right of expressive association. We hold that it does....

In *Roberts v. United States Jaycees,* (1984), we observed that "implicit in the right to engage in activities protected by the First Amendment" is "a corresponding right to associate with others in pursuit of a wide variety of political, social, economic, educational, religious, and cultural ends." This right is crucial in preventing the majority from imposing its views on groups that would rather express other, perhaps unpopular, ideas.... Forcing a group to accept certain members may impair the ability of the group to express those views, and only those views, that it intends to express. Thus, "[f]reedom of association.... plainly presupposes a freedom not to associate."

The forced inclusion of an unwanted person in a group infringes the group's freedom of expressive association if the presence of that person affects in a significant way the group's ability to advocate public or private viewpoints.... But the freedom of expressive association, like many freedoms, is not absolute. We have held that the freedom could be overridden "by regulations adopted to serve compelling state interests, unrelated to the suppression of ideas, that cannot be achieved through means significantly less restrictive of associational freedoms."

To determine whether a group is protected by the First Amendment's expressive associational right, we must determine whether the group engages in "expressive association." The First Amendment's protection of expressive association is not reserved for advocacy groups. But to come within its ambit, a group must engage in some form of expression, whether it be public or private....

... (T)he general mission of the Boy Scouts is clear: "[T]o instill values in young people." The Boy Scouts seeks to instill these values by having its adult leaders spend time with the youth members, instructing and engaging them in activities like camping, archery, and fishing. During the time spent with the youth members, the scoutmasters and assistant scoutmasters inculcate them with the Boy Scouts' values—both expressly and by example. It seems indisputable that an association that seeks to transmit such a system of values engages in expressive activity....

Given that the Boy Scouts engages in expressive activity, we must determine whether the forced inclusion of Dale as an assistant scoutmaster would significantly affect the Boy Scouts' ability to advocate public or private viewpoints. This inquiry necessarily requires us first to explore, to a limited extent, the nature of the Boy Scouts' view of homosexuality.

The values the Boy Scouts seeks to instill are "based on" those listed in the Scout Oath and Law. The Boy Scouts explains that the Scout Oath and Law provide "a positive moral code for living; they are a list of 'do's' rather than 'don'ts.'" The Boy Scouts asserts that homosexual conduct is inconsistent with the values embodied in the Scout Oath and Law, particularly with the values represented by the terms "morally straight" and "clean."

Obviously, the Scout Oath and Law do not expressly mention sexuality or sexual orientation. And the terms "morally straight" and "clean" are by no means self-defining. Different people would attribute to those terms very different meanings. For example, some people may believe that engaging in homosexual conduct is not at odds with being "morally straight" and "clean." And others may believe that engaging in homosexual conduct is contrary to being "morally straight" and "clean." The Boy Scouts says it falls within the latter category....

The Boy Scouts asserts that it "teach[es] that homosexual conduct is not morally straight," and that it does "not want to promote homosexual conduct as a legitimate form of behavior," ... We accept the Boy Scouts' assertion. We need not inquire further to determine the nature of the Boy Scouts' expression with respect to homosexuality....

We must then determine whether Dale's presence as an assistant scoutmaster would significantly burden the Boy Scouts' desire to not "promote homosexual conduct as a legitimate form of behavior." As we give deference to an association's assertions regarding the nature of its expression, we must also give deference to an association's view of what would impair its expression.... That is not to say that an expressive association can erect a shield against antidiscrimination laws simply by asserting that mere acceptance of a member from a particular group would impair its message. But here Dale, by his own admission, is one of a group of gay Scouts who have "become leaders in their community and are open and honest about their sexual orientation."...

The New Jersey Supreme Court determined that the Boy Scouts' ability to disseminate its message was not significantly affected by the forced inclusion of Dale as an assistant scoutmaster because of the following findings:

> Boy Scout members do not associate for the purpose of disseminating the belief that homosexuality is immoral; Boy Scouts discourages its leaders from disseminating *any* views on sexual issues; and Boy Scouts includes sponsors and members who subscribe to different views in respect of homosexuality.

We disagree with the New Jersey Supreme Court's conclusion drawn from these findings.

First, associations do not have to associate for the "purpose" of disseminating a certain message in order to be entitled to the protections of the First Amendment. An association must merely engage in expressive activity that could be impaired in order to be entitled to protection....

Second, even if the Boy Scouts discourages Scout leaders from disseminating views on sexual issues—a fact that the Boy Scouts disputes with contrary evidence—the First Amendment protects the Boy Scouts' method of expression. If the Boy Scouts wishes Scout leaders to avoid questions of sexuality and teach only by example, this fact does not negate the sincerity of its belief discussed above.

Third, the First Amendment simply does not require that every member of a group agree on every issue in order for the group's policy to be "expressive association." The Boy Scouts takes an official position with respect to homosexual conduct, and that is sufficient for First Amendment purposes. In this same vein, Dale makes much of the claim that the Boy Scouts does not revoke the membership of heterosexual Scout leaders that openly disagree with the Boy Scouts' policy on sexual orientation. But if this is true, it is irrelevant. The presence of an avowed homosexual and gay rights activist in an assistant scoutmaster's uniform sends a distinctly different message from the presence of a heterosexual assistant scoutmaster who is on record as disagreeing with Boy Scouts policy. The Boy Scouts has a First Amendment right to choose to send one message but not the other. The fact that the organization does not trumpet its views from the housetops, or that it tolerates dissent within its ranks, does not mean that its views receive no First Amendment protection....

We have already concluded that a state requirement that the Boy Scouts retain Dale as an assistant scoutmaster would significantly burden the organization's right to oppose or disfavor homosexual conduct. The state interests embodied in New Jersey's public accommodations law do not justify such a severe intrusion on the Boy Scouts' rights to freedom of expressive association. That being the case, we hold that the First Amendment prohibits the State from imposing such a requirement through the application of its public accommodations law....

We are not, as we must not be, guided by our views of whether the Boy Scouts' teachings with respect to homosexual conduct are right or wrong; public or judicial disapproval of a tenet of an organization's expression does not justify the State's effort to compel the organization to accept members where such acceptance would derogate from the organization's expressive message. "While the law is free to promote all sorts of conduct in place of harmful behavior, it is not free to interfere with speech for no better reason than promoting an approved message or discouraging a disfavored one, however enlightened either purpose may strike the government."

The judgment of the New Jersey Supreme Court is reversed, and the cause remanded for further proceedings not inconsistent with this opinion.

JUSTICE STEVENS, with whom JUSTICE SOUTER, JUSTICE GINSBURG and JUSTICE BREYER join, dissenting.

New Jersey "prides itself on judging each individual by his or her merits" and on being "in the vanguard in the fight to eradicate the cancer of unlawful discrimination of all types from our society."... The New Jersey Supreme Court's construction of the statutory definition of a "place of public accommodation" has given its statute a more expansive cover-

age than most similar state statutes. And as amended in 1991, the law prohibits discrimination on the basis of nine different traits including an individual's "sexual orientation." The question in this case is whether that expansive construction trenches on the federal constitutional rights of the Boy Scouts of America (BSA)....

In this case, Boy Scouts of America contends that it teaches the young boys who are Scouts that homosexuality is immoral. Consequently, it argues, it would violate its right to associate to force it to admit homosexuals as members, as doing so would be at odds with its own shared goals and values. This contention, quite plainly, requires us to look at what, exactly, are the values that BSA actually teaches....

It is clear... that nothing in (their) policy statements supports BSA's claim. The only policy written before the revocation of Dale's membership was an equivocal, undisclosed statement that evidences no connection between the group's discriminatory intentions and its expressive interests. The later policies demonstrate a brief—though ultimately abandoned—attempt to tie BSA's exclusion to its expression, but other than a single sentence, BSA fails to show that it ever taught Scouts that homosexuality is not "morally straight" or "clean," or that such a view was part of the group's collective efforts to foster a belief. Furthermore, BSA's policy statements fail to establish any clear, consistent, and unequivocal position on homosexuality. Nor did BSA have any reason to think Dale's sexual *conduct*, as opposed to his orientation, was contrary to the group's values.

Several principles are made perfectly clear by *Jaycees* and *Rotary Club*. First, to prevail on a claim of expressive association in the face of a State's antidiscrimination law, it is not enough simply to engage in *some kind* of expressive activity. Both the Jaycees and the Rotary Club engaged in expressive activity protected by the First Amendment, yet that fact was not dispositive. Second, it is not enough to adopt an openly avowed exclusionary membership policy. Both the Jaycees and the Rotary Club did that as well. Third, it is not sufficient merely to articulate *some* connection between the group's expressive activities and its exclusionary policy. The Rotary Club, for example, justified its male-only membership policy by pointing to the "'aspect of fellowship … that is enjoyed by the [exclusively] male membership'" and by claiming that only with an exclusively male membership could it "operate effectively" in foreign countries.…

The relevant question is whether the mere inclusion of the person at issue would "impose any serious burden," "affect in any significant way," or be "a substantial restraint upon" the organization's "shared goals," "basic goals," or "collective effort to foster beliefs." Accordingly, it is necessary to examine what, exactly, are BSA's shared goals and the degree to which its expressive activities would be burdened, affected, or restrained by including homosexuals.

The evidence before this Court makes it exceptionally clear that BSA has, at most, simply adopted an exclusionary membership policy and has no shared goal of disapproving of homosexuality. BSA's mission statement and federal charter say nothing on the matter; its official membership policy is silent; its Scout Oath and Law—and accompanying definitions—are devoid of any view on the topic; its guidance for Scouts and Scoutmasters on sexuality declare that such matters are "not construed to be Scouting's proper area," but are the province of a Scout's parents and pastor; and BSA's posture respecting religion tolerates a wide variety of views on the issue of homosexuality. Moreover, there is simply no evidence that BSA otherwise teaches anything in this area, or that it instructs Scouts on matters involving homosexuality in ways not conveyed in the Boy Scout or Scoutmaster Handbooks. In short, Boy Scouts of America is simply silent on homosexuality. There is no shared goal or collective effort to foster a belief about homosexuality at all—let alone one that is significantly burdened by admitting homosexuals.…

As noted earlier, nothing in our cases suggests that a group can prevail on a right to expressive association if it, effectively, speaks out of both sides of its mouth. A State's antidiscrimination law does not impose a "serious burden" or a "substantial restraint" upon the group's "shared goals" if the group itself is unable to identify its own stance with any clarity.

The majority pretermits this entire analysis. It finds that BSA in fact "'teach[es] that homosexual conduct is not morally straight.'" This conclusion, remarkably, rests entirely on statements in BSA's briefs.…

This is an astounding view of the law. I am unaware of any previous instance in which our analysis of the scope of a constitutional right was determined by looking at what a litigant asserts in his or her brief and inquiring no further. It is even more astonishing in the First Amendment area, because, as the majority itself acknowledges, "we are obligated to independently review the factual record.".… It is an odd form of independent review that consists of deferring entirely to whatever a litigant claims. But the majority insists that our inquiry must be "limited," because "it is not the role of the courts to reject a group's expressed values because they disagree with those values or find them internally inconsistent.".…

BSA has not contended, nor does the record support, that Dale had ever advocated a view on homosexuality to his troop before his membership was revoked. Accordingly, BSA's revocation could only have been based on an assumption that he would do so in the future.…

The majority, though, does not rest its conclusion on the claim that Dale will use his position as a bully pulpit. Rather, it contends that Dale's mere presence among the Boy Scouts will itself force the group to convey a message about homosexuality—even if Dale has no intention of doing so. The majority holds that "[t]he presence of an avowed homosexual and gay rights activist in an assistant scoutmaster's uniform sends a distinc[t] … message," and, accordingly, BSA is entitled to exclude that message. In particular, "Dale's presence in the Boy Scouts would, at the very least, force the organization to send a message, both to the youth members and the world, that the Boy

Scouts accepts homosexual conduct as a legitimate form of behavior."...

Dale's inclusion in the Boy Scouts... sends no cognizable message to the Scouts or to the world.... Dale did not carry a banner or a sign; he did not distribute any fact sheet; and he expressed no intent to send any message. If there is any kind of message being sent, then, it is by the mere act of joining the Boy Scouts....

The only apparent explanation for the majority's holding, then, is that homosexuals are simply so different from the rest of society that their presence alone—unlike any other individual's—should be singled out for special First Amendment treatment. Under the majority's reasoning, an openly gay male is irreversibly affixed with the label "homosexual." That label, even though unseen, communicates a message that permits his exclusion wherever he goes. His openness is the sole and sufficient justification for his ostracism. Though unintended, reliance on such a justification is tantamount to a constitutionally prescribed symbol of inferiority....

That such prejudices are still prevalent and that they have caused serious and tangible harm to countless members of the class New Jersey seeks to protect are established matters of fact that neither the Boy Scouts nor the Court disputes. That harm can only be aggravated by the creation of a constitutional shield for a policy that is itself the product of a habitual way of thinking about strangers. As Justice Brandeis so wisely advised, "we must be ever on our guard, lest we erect our prejudices into legal principles."

If we would guide by the light of reason, we must let our minds be bold. I respectfully dissent.

Competing Theories of American Government

	Traditional Democratic Theories		Pluralist Theories		Elite Theories		
	Direct Democracy	Civics Book Democracy	According to Pluralists	As Interest Group Liberalism	E.g., Neo-Marxists	E.g., C. Wright Mills	E.g., Dye & Zeigler
Fundamental Unit of Political Action or Value	Individual		Interest Groups		Elites		
Link between Government and People?	Voting		Group Leaders		None		
Significant Competition Among Elite?	Yes		Yes	No	No		
Prescriptive (Ought or Ought not.)?	Yes		No	Yes	Yes	No	Yes
Descriptive (Explains how things are.)?	No	Yes	Yes	Yes	Yes	Yes	Yes
Equality of Resources?	Yes		Yes	No	No		
Government Acts in Interest of Public?	Yes	Yes	Yes	No	No	NA	Yes